NICHOLSON

The London Guide

THE MOST COMPREHENSIVE GUIDE TO LONDON

KT-488-453

CONTENTS

Nicholson

An Imprint of Bartholomew
A Division of HarperCollinsPublishers

A Nicholson Guide

© Nicholson 1993

First published 1967
Thirteenth edition 1993

Illustrations by Claire Littlejohn
River Maps by Dominic Beddow, Draughtsman Maps
Design by Bob Vickers

London Maps
© Nicholson, generated from the
Bartholomew London Digital Database

London Underground Map by kind
permission of London Regional Transport
LRT Registered User No 93/1496

All other maps
© Nicholson

Nicholson
HarperCollins*Publishers*
77-85 Fulham Palace Road
Hammersmith
London W6 8JB

Great care has been taken throughout this book to be accurate,
but the publishers cannot accept responsibility for any errors or
their consequences.

Printed in Great Britain by Scotprint Ltd, Musselburgh

ISBN 0 7028 2237 X

67/13/2525

SYMBOLS AND ABBREVIATIONS

A	Access/Mastercard/Eurocard
Ax	American Express
Dc	Diners Club
V	Visa/Barclaycard

Average prices for a three-course meal for one without wine but including
VAT (these prices are for guidance only):

£	£10.00 or under
££	£10.00-£20.00
£££	£20.00-£30.00
£££+	£30.00 and over

Reserve – advisable to reserve

L	lunch
D	dinner
B	bar food
☕	open all day 11.00-23.00 Mon-Sat, 12.00-14.30 & 19.00-22.30 Sun
(M)	membership required

Opening times

Many places are closed on Xmas Day, New Year's Day and Good Friday,
and general opening times are subject to change, so it is always advisable
to check first.

Sightseeing

Tourist information

British Travel Centre 4 **D3**
12 Lower Regent St SW1. Personal callers only. British Tourist Authority Information Centre, incorporating the American Express Travel Service Office, British Rail ticket office and a bureau de change. Details on where to go throughout the UK. Book a room, coach trip or theatre ticket; buy plane or train tickets, hire a car; all under one roof. Also regular exhibitions, videos, travel bookshop and gift shop. *OPEN 09.00-18.30 Mon-Fri, 10.00-16.00 Sat & Sun (09.00-17.30 Sat in Jun-Sep only).*

City of London Information 5 **D2**
Centre
St Paul's Churchyard EC4. 071-260 1456. Information and advice with specific reference to the 'Square Mile'. Free literature. Essential to get monthly Diary of Events which lists a big choice of free entertainment in the City. *OPEN May-Sep 09.30-17.00 Mon-Sun; Oct-Apr 09.30-17.00 Mon-Fri, 09.30-12.30 Sat.*

Guildhall Library 5 **D2**
Aldermanbury EC2. 071-260 1868. Will be able to provide historical information about London. *OPEN 09.30-17.00 Mon-Fri. Limited sections OPEN 09.30-17.00 Sat.*

London Transport Travel
Information Centres
London Transport information 071-222 1234 (24 hrs). London Transport offices for enquiries on travel (underground and buses). Free maps of the underground and bus routes, plus information leaflets in French, German and English. *OPENING times vary. Phone for details.*

Euston Underground Station 1 **F4**
Heathrow Central Underground Station
King's Cross Underground Station 1 **G3**
Oxford Circus Underground Station 4 **D2**
Piccadilly Circus Underground 4 **E3**
Station
Victoria British Rail Station 7 **B1**
West Croydon Bus Station
London Tourist Board 7 **B1**
Information Centre
Victoria Station Forecourt SW1. (0839) 123456. Travel and tourist information for London and England. Most languages spoken. Also instant hotel reservations, theatre and tour bookings, sales of guide books, maps and gifts. *OPEN Apr-Oct*

08.00-19.00 Mon-Sun; Nov-Mar 08.00-19.00 Mon-Sat, 08.00-16.00 Sun.
Other tourist information centres at:
Heathrow Central Underground Station
Liverpool Street Station EC2 5 **F1**
Selfridges, 400 Oxford St W1 4 **B2**
Scottish Tourist Board 4 **E4**
19 Cockspur St SW1. 071-930 8661. Tourist leaflets and information on mainland Scotland and the islands. *OPEN for leaflets and information May-Sep 09.00-18.00 Mon-Fri (to 18.30 Thur), 10.00-16.00 Sat (Jun-Aug only); Oct-Apr 09.30-17.30 Mon-Fri (to 18.30 Thur). OPEN 09.30-17.00 Mon-Fri all year for bookings.*

Wales Tourist Board 4 **D3**
12 Lower Regent St W1. 071-409 0969. Leaflets and information for the visitor to Wales. *OPEN 09.00-18.30 Mon-Fri, 10.00-16.00 Sat & Sun (09.00-17.30 Sat in Jun-Sep only).*

Telephone services

London numbers are prefixed with 071- or 081- depending on area; central London numbers are 071- and Greater London 081-. Codes can be checked with the operator (dial 100) or Directory Enquiries (dial 142/192); telephone directories and The Code Book also have full details. If dialling from London to an exchange elsewhere, you must find the code of the exchange. The codes are listed in The Code Book or the operator (dial 100) will tell you. If you are using a public telephone in London it will almost certainly be a push-button one. You will need 10p, 20p, 50p or £1 coins. The coins must be inserted before you can dial but if you do not get through the money will be refunded when you replace the receiver. It is best to use smaller denominations as percentages of larger ones will not be refunded. More and more public telephones take phonecards as a form of payment. British Telecom phonecards can be bought in denominations from 20 units (£2.00) to 200 units (£20.00). Mercury phones accept only Mercury phonecards or credit cards (A.Ax.Dc.V.). Phonecards are obtainable from newsagents, chemists and post offices.

Emergency calls Dial 999 and ask for police, fire or ambulance service.

Directory enquiries 142 for London postal addresses, 192 for other British addresses.

Transfer charge (collect) calls or difficulty in getting through to a number – 100 for the operator.

International calls You can dial direct to many countries. Codes are listed in *The Code Book* or ask the operator.

Viewpoints

Get a fresh perspective on London by looking down on it from a tall building or a natural high point. There are many places which command a view of almost the entire metropolis, and from them you can appreciate its sheer magnitude.

Alexandra Palace
On Muswell Hill N22. About 250ft (76.3m). View from the terrace over north London, Kent, Surrey, Essex and Hertfordshire.

Eltham Park SE9
View of central London. Best view from the ornamental pond.

Hampstead Heath NW3
Constable's famous view of London. Good vantage points are Whitestone Pond and Parliament Hill.

Highgate Archway N6
From the top you see the whole of London laid out before you.

Jack Straw's Castle
North End Way NW3. 071-435 8885. Lunch and dinner in the restaurant 450ft (137m) with long views across London to the distant Kentish hills. *LD Reserve. Last orders 22.00 Mon-Sun.*

Heathrow Airport
Roof of Queen's Building, Heathrow, Middx. 081-745 5259. A favourite for children. Aircraft continuously landing and taking off. *OPEN 09.00-½ hr before dusk. Charge.*

Kenwood House
Hampstead La NW3. 081-348 1286. Panorama of almost the whole of London. View from the gazebo by the coach house. *OPEN summer 10.00-18.00, winter 10.00-1600.*

London Hilton   **4 B4**
22 Park La W1. 071-493 8000. 'Windows Bar' at 320ft (97.6m). Lift. Fine views over Hyde Park, Buckingham Palace and Mayfair.

Monument   **5 E3**
Monument St EC3. 071-626 2717. Magnificent view from the top, but it is 202ft (61.6m) high and there are 311 stairs to climb! *OPEN Apr-Sep 09.00-*

17.40 Mon-Fri, 14.00-17.40 Sat & Sun; Oct-Mar 09.00-15.40 Mon-Sat. Charge. Due to close in 1993 for renovations. Phone for details before making your visit.

Point Hill
Blackheath SE10. Commanding view of a wide arc from the docks in the east to Alexandra Palace in the north and the City and Westminster in the west.

Pole Hill
Chingford E4. The high point of Epping Forest. View towards the river and of Shooters Hill south of the river.

Primrose Hill NW8   **1 B2**
A simple grassy hill 206ft (61.7m) high giving a fine view over London. A helpful table identifies some of London's most prominent landmarks.

Queen's Tower   **3 E6**
Imperial College, off Exhibition Rd SW7. 071-589 5111. 287ft (87.5m) high tower in the middle of Imperial College campus offers a unique and uninterrupted view of London. *OPEN May-Sep 10.00-17.30 Mon-Sun. Charge.*

St Paul's Cathedral   **5 D2**
Ludgate Hill EC4. 071-248 2705. Magnificent view from the Golden Gallery of the City, the Wren churches, the Tower and London Pool. 335ft (102.2m), 530 steps. *OPEN 09.45-16.15 Mon-Sat. Charge.*

Shrewsbury Park SE18
View of the river, the docks to the north and east along the river towards Tilbury.

Tower Bridge SE1   **5 G4**
071-407 0922. Breathtaking views of London and the Thames from high walkways. *OPEN Apr-Oct 10.00-18.30 Mon-Sun; Nov-Mar 10.00-16.45 Mon-Sun. Last admission 45 mins before closing time. CLOSED B. hols. Charge.*

Westminster Cathedral   **7 C1**
Ashley Pl, off Victoria St SW1. 071-834 7452. View over Westminster and the Thames from the top of 273ft (83.3m) campanile. Lift usually *OPEN Apr-Sep 09.00-17.00 Mon-Sun. Charge.*

Daily ceremonies and events

Pageantry

These are the main ceremonies which occur throughout the year. Phone the London Tourist Board on (0839) 123456 for details of events on the day you want to go.

Ceremony of the Keys   **5 G3**
Tower of London, Tower Hill EC3. 071-709 0765. The Chief Warder of the

Yeomen Warders, with an escort of the Brigade of Guards, locks the West Gates, the Middle Tower and Byward Tower. One of the oldest continuous military ceremonies in the world. *21.40 Mon-Sun, by written application to the Governor of the Tower well in advance, enclosing sae.*

Changing of the Guard   **4 D5**
Buckingham Palace SW1. Takes place inside the palace railings (*in summer the crowd makes it impossible to see much*). An alternative is to see the Guards on their way from Chelsea or Wellington Barracks; phone the London Tourist Board to find out which they are leaving from on the day you are going. *Mon-Sun in summer, alternate days in winter.* Leave Chelsea Barracks at *10.45* or Wellington Barracks at *11.00.* Palace ceremony *11.30.*

St James's Palace SW1   **4 D4**
A detachment of the Buckingham Palace Guard changes here. Guards change *11.15 (days as above).*

Whitehall SW1   **4 F4**
Horse Guards Pde SW1. Changing of the Queen's Life Guard mounted on splendid horses. Guards leave Hyde Park Barracks *10.38 Mon-Sat, 09.39 Sun.* Ceremony *11.00 Mon-Sat, 10.00 Sun.*

Windsor Castle
Windsor, Berks. (0753) 868286. The Queen's out of town and favoured residence. Changing of the Guard at *11.00-11.30 Mon-Sun summer, alternate days winter.* A military band enlivens the pageant.

Other events

Speakers' Corner: A remaining vestige of the British tradition of free speech is this institution of impromptu discourses by unknown orators, usually on religion or politics. At Speakers' Corner (Marble Arch corner of Hyde Park (**4 A3**), usually on *Sun*). Also Lincoln's Inn Fields (**4 G2**) and Tower Hill (**5 G3**) *Mon-Fri lunchtime.*
Feeding the pigeons: In Trafalgar Square (**4 F4**) – a famous tradition. You will soon be accosted by touts who want to sell you bird-seed and photographs of yourself covered in pigeons.

Annual events

The following list presents not only the most important annual events but also some of the more obscure London customs in order to cover as wide a field as possible. For exact days, times and *places, where not given, and to find out whether or not there is a charge, contact one of the centres given under 'Tourist information'.*

January

Chinese New Year   **4 E3**
Gerrard St W1. Papier-mâché dragons, the lion dance and firecrackers bring Chinatown to life. *Jan or Feb.*

International Boat Show   **6 A3**
Earl's Court Exhibition Centre, Warwick Rd SW5. 071-385 1200. The latest pleasure craft, yachts and equipment. The largest boat show in Europe. *Early Jan.*

January sales
Most of the London stores have stock-clearing sales after the Xmas shopping spree. Some fantastic bargains, especially at Harrods, but these go quickly – the real fanatics camp outside the store the night before the sale starts to be first in the queue – and there are always big crowds. Start *early Jan.*

Lord Mayor of Westminster's New Year's Day Parade
One of the largest parades in Europe with some 5000 performers, from marching bands to colourful floats. Starts at *12.30* on Piccadilly (**4 D4**) and ends at Hyde Park (**4 A4**).

Model Engineer Exhibition
Olympia Exhibition Centre, Hammersmith Rd W14. 071-603 3344. Model cars, trains, planes, boats. *Early Jan.*

Royal Epiphany Gifts   **4 D4**
Chapel Royal, St James's Pl, Marlborough Rd SW1. Picturesque ceremony, when two 'Gentlemen Ushers' offer gold, frankincense and myrrh on behalf of the Queen. *6 Jan 11.30. Admission by ticket only.*

February

Cruft's Dog Show   **6 A3**
Earl's Court Exhibition Centre, Warwick Rd SW5. 071-385 1200. *Early Feb.*

Daily Express Motor Racing Show   **6 A3**
Earl's Court Exhibition Centre, Warwick Rd SW5. 071-385 1200. A must for motor racing enthusiasts. *Mid Feb.*

Holiday on Ice
Wembley Arena, Wembley, Middx. 081-900 1234. Pantomime on ice.

Road Racing & Superbike Show
Alexandra Pavilion, Alexandra Palace & Park N22. 081-365 2121. *Early Feb.*

Soho Pancake Day Race   **4 D3**
Carnaby St W1. 071-287 0907. Watch

various teams running with frying pans, tossing their pancakes as they go.

March

Chelsea Spring Antiques Fair 6 E3
Chelsea Old Town Hall, King's Rd SW3. 071-352 3619. *Mid Mar.*

Classic Car Show
Alexandra Palace, Alexandra Park N22. 081-365 2121. Classic car display and auction, car parts jumble stall. *Late Mar.*

Daily Mail Ideal Home Exhibition 6 A3
Earl's Court Exhibition Centre, Warwick Rd SW5. 071-385 1200. Full of new and interesting gadgets. Very popular and always crowded. *Mid Mar.*

John Stow Memorial Service 5 F2
Church of St Andrew Undershaft, St Mary Axe EC3. The Lord Mayor attends this commemoration of London's first historian and places a new quill pen in the hand of Stow's statue. *Sun in Mar or Apr, 11.30.*

Oranges & Lemons Service 5 A2
St Clement Danes, Strand WC2. 071-242 8282. After a special service, oranges and lemons are distributed to children while the traditional tune is played on handbells. *No fixed date.*

Oxford v Cambridge Boat Race
River Thames, Putney to Mortlake. University boat race over four miles. View from the banks of the river or one of the bridges. Get there early for a good view. *Sat afternoon in Mar or Apr.*

Royal Film Performance
A selected film gets royal patronage in aid of charity. Celebrities and glitter at one of the big cinemas. *No fixed date.*

Sailboat
Crystal Palace National Sports Centre SE19. 081-778 0131. Britain's largest exhibition of dinghies and small sailing craft. *No fixed date.*

St David's Day
Windsor, Berks. Leeks given to the Welsh Guards. Generally attended by the Duke of Edinburgh. *1 Mar.*

St Patrick's Day
Pirbright, Surrey. Shamrocks given to the Irish Guards by Her Majesty the Queen Mother. *17 Mar.*

Spring Stampex 7 D2
Royal Horticultural Society Halls, 80 Vincent Sq SW1. 071-834 4333. National stamp exhibition. Contact the British Philatelic Centre 071-490 1005 for details. *Early Mar. Also hold Autumn Stampex late Sep-early Oct.*

April

Annual Spital Sermon 5 D2
St Lawrence Jewry, Gresham St EC2. 071-600 9478. Governors of the two great hospitals, Christ's and Bridewell, attend with the Lord Mayor, sheriffs and aldermen. *Coincides with the first meeting of the aldermen and Court of Common Council.*

Butterworth Charity 5 C1
St Bartholomew-the-Great, Smithfield EC1. 071-606 5171. Presentation of hot-cross buns, traditionally to 'poor widows', now to children. *Good Fri following 11.00 service.*

Easter Procession & Carols 4 F6
Westminster Abbey SW1. 071-222 5152. *Easter Sun.*

Easter Show 6 F5
Battersea Park SW11. Colourful carnival – fairground, side stalls, various stage acts. *Easter Sun.*

International Spring Gardening Fair
Wembley Conference and Exhibition Centre, Wembley, Middx. Contact 071-782 6871 for information. *Early Apr.*

London Harness Horse Parade 1 C4
Regent's Park NW1. Fine horses and carts; brewers' vans and drays on parade. Judging *starts at* 09.45 followed by a procession twice round the Inner Circle *at about 12.00. Easter Mon.*

The London Marathon
The famous 26-mile race starting 09.30 at Greenwich Park SE10 and Blackheath SE3 and finishing at Westminster Bridge SW1 (4 **F5**). For information ring 081-948 7935. *Late Apr.*

Tower of London Church Parade 5 G3
Tower of London, Tower Hill EC3. 071-709 0765. The Yeomen Warders in state dress are inspected, and parade before and after morning service on *Easter Sun, 11.00. Also Whit Sun & Sun before Xmas.*

May

Beating the Bounds 5 F3
071-488 4772. From All-Hallows-by-the-Tower to St Dunstan's, Idol Lane EC3. The boundaries of the parishes of London were once proclaimed by a special ceremony. Now the pupils of St Dunstan's School march from All-Hallows, carrying sticks to beat the boundary marks around the Tower of London, one of which is in the Thames! The Lord Mayor usually attends the service at *17.00* at All-Hallows. Every third year the Tower of London yeomen meet the beaters at

about 19.00 for some good-natured jeering! *Ascension Day.*

Chelsea Flower Show 6 F3
Royal Hospital Grounds, Chelsea SW3. 071-834 4333 (24-hr information line 071-828 1744). Superb flower displays. *For 3 days late May.*

FA Cup Final
Wembley Stadium, Wembley, Middx. 081-900 1234. The climax of the English football season. *Late Apr/early May.*

Festival for Mind, Body & Spirit 7 D1
The New Hall, Royal Horticultural Society Halls, Greycoat St SW1. Development of human consciousness and natural health. Includes astrology, alternative medicine, healing, animal welfare, ecology, spiritual development, personal growth and the psychic arts. Demonstrations, consultations and lectures. Contact 071-938 3788 for information. *Late May.*

Glyndebourne Festival Opera Season
Glyndebourne, nr Lewes, E. Sussex. (0273) 541111. Opera lovers don evening dress and flock from town to hear superlative singing, and sup on the lawn if the summer air is clement. *Late May-mid Aug.*

Open Air Art Exhibitions
Victoria Embankment Gardens WC2 (4 **F4**) (next to Embankment underground station). Artists and their work on exhibition. *2-14 May; Aug, Mon-Sat.* The Terrace, Richmond Hill, Richmond, Surrey. Run by Richmond Art Group. Fine views from terrace. *May or Jun 10.00-20.00 Sat & Sun.* Royal Av, King's Rd SW3 (6 **F3**). *May-Oct 11.00-18.00 Sat.* The Green Park side of Piccadilly (4 **C4**), where a multitude of street artists set up their pictures against the railings. And along Bayswater Rd, outside Kensington Gardens and Hyde Park (3**D3**). *Every Sun morning.*

Putney & Hammersmith Amateur Regattas
Rowing regattas make exciting watching from the banks of the Thames. Contact the Amateur Rowing Assn (ARA) for information 081-748 3632. *Late Apr/early May.*

Rugby League Challenge Cup Final
Wembley Stadium, Wembley, Middx. Contact Rugby Football League. (0532) 624637. *Late Apr/early May.*

Rugby Union Cup Final
Twickenham Rugby Football Ground, Whitton Rd, Twickenham, Middx. 081-892 8161. *Early May.*

Samuel Pepys Commemoration Service 5 F3
St Olave's, Hart St EC3. 071-488 4318.

The Lord Mayor lays a wreath on Pepys' monument. *Late May or early Jun.*

June

Antiquarian Book Fair 4 C4
Park Lane Hotel, Piccadilly W1. 071-499 6321. International fair with books, documents, musical scores. *Late Jun.*

Beating the Retreat 4 F4
Horse Guards Parade SW1. 071-839 6815. Military display of marching and drilling bands. Trumpeters, massed bands and pipe and drums. Some floodlit performances. Phone 071-839 6815 for tickets. *Jun.*

The Derby
Epsom Racecourse, Surrey. (03727) 26311. World-famous flat horserace. *Early Jun.*

Election of Sheriffs of the City of London 5 D2
Guildhall EC2. 071-606 3030. Lord Mayor and Aldermen in a colourful ceremony. Posies are carried traditionally to ward off 'the plague'. *Midsummer's Day (unless it falls on a Sat or Sun).*

Founder's Day 7 A3
Royal Hospital, Chelsea SW3. 071-730 0161. Chelsea pensioners parade in their colourful uniforms for inspection, sometimes by royalty. *Early Jun.*

The Garter Ceremony
Service attended by the Queen at St George's Chapel, Windsor, preceded by a colourful procession with the Household Cavalry and Yeomen of the Guard. Ceremony dates from 14th*C. Mon afternoon of Ascot week (usually 3rd week in Jun).*

Kenwood Lakeside Concerts
Kenwood House, Hampstead La NW3. 071-973 3427. Bookings: 071-379 4444. Classical concerts beside Kenwood Lake on Hampstead Heath performed by some of the most famous orchestras in the world. Often end with spectacular firework displays. *Sat evenings Jun-Aug. Charge.*

Lord's Test Match
Lord's Cricket Ground, St John's Wood Rd NW8. Ring 071-289 1615 for tickets, 071-289 8011 for information on state of play. *Jun or Jul.*

Royal Ascot Races
(0344) 22211. A fashionable society event where the hats often attract more attention than the horses. The Queen and other members of the royal party travel the course in open carriages before the race. *Jun.*

Summer Art Exhibition 4 D3
Royal Academy, Burlington House, Piccadilly W1. 071-439 7438. Aspiring

Cézannes and Hockneys enter their works to be admired and hopefully bought! *Jun–mid Aug.*

Trooping the Colour

The route is from Buckingham Palace SW1 (**4 D5**) along the Mall (**4 D5**) to Horse Guards Parade (**4 F4**), then to Whitehall (**4 F4**) and back again. Pageantry at its best for the Queen's official birthday. *11.00, Sat nearest 11 Jun.*

Wimbledon Lawn Tennis Championships

All England Lawn Tennis & Croquet Club, Church Rd SW19. 081-946 2244. 'Wimbledon Fortnight', the world's most famous championship. Matches from *14.00 Mon-Sat. Last week Jun & 1st week Jul.*

July

Annual London International Festival of Street Entertainers 4 D3

A competition taking place around Carnaby Street and Golden Square W1. Acts change about *every 20 minutes* with plenty of variety – juggling, clowning, dance, theatre and mime. Contact 071-287 0907 (Alternative Arts) for further details. *Third weekend Jul.*

City of London Festival

071-377 0540. Held in the Barbican, the Tower of London, Mansion House, the City's livery halls, St Paul's Cathedral, many fine churches and the City's open spaces. Concerts, opera, exhibitions, poetry, drama, dance, jazz, street events and full supporting fringe. *Three weeks in Jul.*

Doggetts Coat & Badge Race

The Thames, Tower Pier (**5 F4**) to Chelsea (**7 B4**). 071-626 3531. Rowing race for Thames Watermen, originated in 1715. Sometimes called the 'Watermen's Derby'. *Late Jul.*

Henley Royal Regatta

Henley-on-Thames, Oxon. (0491) 572153. Steeped in tradition; rowing and socialising side by side. *Early Jul.*

Proms (Henry Wood Promenade Concerts) 3 E5

Royal Albert Hall, Kensington Gore SW7. 071-589 8212. Concerts of classical music. Ticket qualification system for famous 'Last Night' celebrations. *Late Jul until Sep. No fixed date.*

Richmond Festival

Amateur and professional performing and visual arts. Venues include Richmond Theatre, Orange Tree Theatre, Richmond Green, the Thames. 081-332 0534. *Mid Jul.*

Royal Tournament 4 F4

Earl's Court Exhibition Centre, Warwick Rd SW5. 071-373 8141. Impressive military spectacle with marching displays and massed brass bands. *Two weeks mid Jul.*

Royal Tournament March Past 4 F4

Horse Guards, Whitehall SW1. Colourful parade by all troops taking part in the Royal Tournament. *Sun before Tournament.*

Swan Upping 5 E3

Starts: London Bridge (Temple Stairs) *09.00-09.30.* Ownership of the swans on the Thames is divided between the Dyers Company, the Vintners Company and the Sovereign. Each *Jul* a census of the swans on the reaches up to Henley is taken, and the cygnets are branded by nicking their beaks. *No fixed date.* Phone 071-236 1863 to find out exactly where the fleet is at any one time.

August

Notting Hill Carnival 3 B4

Ladbroke Grove and Notting Hill W11. West Indian carnival with colourful floats, steel bands and dancing in the streets. *B.hol Sun & Mon.*

September

Battle of Britain Week 4 F6

Thanksgiving service at Westminster Abbey SW1. 071-222 5152. Also Biggin Hill Flying Display. *Early Sep.*

Chelsea Autumn Antiques Fair 6 E3

Chelsea Old Town Hall, King's Rd SW3. 071-352 3619. *For ten days mid Sep.*

Christ's Hospital March

Founded by Edward VI as a hospital for orphans. 'Bluecoats' (the distinctive long coats which the boys wear date from this time) march through the City. *St Matthew's Day; on or near 21 Sep.*

Election of Lord Mayor of London 5 D2

Procession from the church of St Lawrence Jewry, Gresham St EC2, to the Guildhall EC2. 071-606 3030. *Michaelmas Day, 29 Sep.*

Last Night of the Proms 3 E5

Royal Albert Hall, Kensington Gore SW7. 071-589 8212. The culmination of the Proms concerts. Traditional rousing performance of *Land of Hope and Glory.* Tickets by qualification system only. *15 Sep or nearest Sat.*

London to Brighton Walk 4 F5

Starts Westminster Bridge SW1. Originated in 1903. *Early Sep, 07.00.*

October

Annual Full Tidal Closure
Thames Barrier, Unity Way, Eastmoor St SE18. 081-854 1373. The annual closing of the Thames Barrier. See the huge barriers lifting out of the water.

Costermonger's Harvest Festival　　　　　　　　**4 F3**
St Martin-in-the-Fields, Trafalgar Sq WC2. 071-930 1862. Service attended by the Pearly Kings and Queens in their colourful regalia. *15.30, second Sun in Oct.*

Daily Mail International Ski Show　　　　　　　　**6 A3**
Olympia Exhibition Centre, Hammersmith Rd W14. 071-603 3344. Holiday kit for the keen skier. *Late Oct.*

Her Majesty's Judges & Queen's Counsels Annual Breakfast　　　　　　　　**4 F6**
After a special service at Westminster Abbey there is a procession to the House of Lords for the opening of the Law term. *1 Oct.*

Quit-Rent Ceremony　　　　　　　　**5 B2**
The Queen's Remembrancer receives the Quit-rent of a bill-hook, a hatchet, six horseshoes and 61 nails for two holdings from the Comptroller and the City Solicitor: an annual ceremony since 1234. *Tickets from the Chief Clerk to the Queen's Remembrancer, Room 118, Royal Courts of Justice, Strand WC2.*

Trafalgar Day Service & Parade　　　　　　　　**4 F4**
Trafalgar Sq WC2. 071-540 8222. Organised by the Navy League. *Sun nearest Trafalgar Day 21 Oct.*

Horse of the Year Show
Wembley Arena, Wembley, Middx. 081-902 8833. Fine show jumping. *Early Oct.*

November

Admission of the Lord Mayor Elect　　　　　　　　**5 D2**
Guildhall, Gresham St EC2. 071-606 3030. The Lord Mayor takes office. Colourful ceremony including handing over of insignia by former Lord Mayor. *Fri before Lord Mayor's show (second Fri in Nov).*

Christmas Lights　　　　　　　　**4 D2**
Regent St and Oxford St W1. Festive illuminations to attract Christmas shoppers. Best seen *from 16.00 onwards. Late Nov-6 Jan (12th Night).*

Guy Fawkes Night
Anniversary of the Gunpowder Plot of 1605. Private and public firework displays throughout London. *Evening, 5 Nov.*

London to Brighton Veteran Car Run　　　　　　　　**4 B5**
Hyde Park Corner W1. Cars leave here for Brighton. Colourful event with contestants in period costume. Commemorates the anniversary of Emancipation Day. *08.00, 1st Sun in Nov.*

Lord Mayor's Procession & Show
The newly elected Lord Mayor is driven in his state coach from the Guildhall (**5 D2**) to the Law Courts (**5 A2**) to be received by the Lord Chief Justice. The biggest ceremonial event in the City. *2nd Sat in Nov.*

Remembrance Sunday　　　　　　　　**4 F5**
Poppies sold in the streets to raise money for ex-servicemen. Service at the Cenotaph, Whitehall SW1 with a salute of guns. *11.00, 2nd Sun in Nov.*

State Opening of Parliament
The Queen, in the Irish state coach, is driven from Buckingham Palace (**4 D5**) to the House of Lords (**4 F5**). A royal salute is fired from St James's Park. *Early Nov.*

December

Carol Services　　　　　　　　**4 F6**
Westminster Abbey, Broad Sanctuary SW1. 071-222 7110. Carol services on *26, 27 & 28 Dec.*

Carol Singing　　　　　　　　**4 E4**
Trafalgar Sq WC2. Recorded on tape. *Early evening from about 14 Dec.*

Christmas Tree　　　　　　　　**4 E4**
Trafalgar Sq WC2. Norwegian spruce donated each year by the citizens of Oslo. Brightly lit *from 16.00.* Carol singing round the tree. *Mid Dec-6 Jan (12th Night).*

New Year's Eve　　　　　　　　**4 E4**
Trafalgar Sq WC2. Singing of 'Auld Lang Syne' by massed crowds – also dancing around the fountains (now usually protected behind screens).

Royal Smithfield Show　　　　　　　　**6 A3**
Earl's Court Exhibition Centre, Warwick Rd SW5. 071-385 1200. Exhibition of agricultural machinery, supplies and services. Also livestock. *Early Dec.*

Tower of London Church Parades　　　　　　　　**5 G3**
Tower Hill EC3. 071-709 0765. The Yeomen Warders in state dress are inspected and parade before and after morning service on the *Sun before Xmas, 11.00. Also Easter Sun & Whit Sun.*

Watchnight Service　　　　　　　　**5 D2**
St Paul's Cathedral, Ludgate Hill EC4. 071-248 2705. *22.00-24.00, 31 Dec.*

London tours

London tours: by coach

Sightseeing tours, usually on double-decker buses or coaches. Some take several hours and the passengers stay on the bus listening to a commentary which is often translated into a number of different languages. Others take the whole day, and include guided tours of various sights, plus lunch. The London Tourist Board Information Centre, Victoria Station Forecourt SW1 (7 B1) sells tickets for a selection of sightseeing tours; alternatively you can telephone the organisations direct to reserve seats.

Cityrama
Silverthorne Rd SW8. 071-720 6663. 20-mile sightseeing tour of all the main London sights. Coaches leave *every 30 mins* and tours take *1-1½ hrs*. Coaches leave from Coventry St W1 (4 **E3**) and Grosvenor Gdns SW1 (4 **C6**). Also tours to Bath, Stonehenge, Stratford-upon-Avon and Windsor.

Docklands Tours
London Docklands Visitor Centre, 3 Limeharbour, Isle of Dogs E14. 071-512 1111. *2-hr* tours of Docklands accompanied by guides from the London Docklands Development Corporation. See restored wharves and warehouses, conservation areas, historic buildings, magnificent waterside views. Audio-visual presentation in Visitor Centre *45 mins* prior to departure. Tours at 14.00 Tue; 10.30 Thur & Sun. Book in advance.

Evan Evans   4 **E4**
26 Cockspur St SW1. 071-930 2377. Operates a variety of tours; full day, morning, afternoon, plus a *2½-hr* general drive around the capital and *30-min* cruise on the Thames. Also extended tours out of London.

Frames Rickards   1 **G5**
11 Herbrand St WC1. 071-837 3111. *Morning* and *afternoon* tours of the City and the West End, evening cruises on the Thames. Tours to Windsor, Stratford-upon-Avon and many other tourist destinations.

Harrods   6 **F1**
Sightseeing Tours Dept, Harrods, Knightsbridge SW1. 071-730 1234. The Mercedes Benz B10 undoubtedly provides the most luxurious coach tour of London. The tour takes *2 hrs*. Taped commentary in eight languages, plus refreshments served by multi-lingual stewardesses. Harrods also operate tours to Stratford-upon-Avon and Blenheim Palace. Ticket reservations and information: 071-581 3603.

Original London Sightseeing Tours
London Coaches, Jew's Row SW18. Information: 081-877 1722. Round London tours in traditional double-decker buses, some of which are open-topped.

Star Safari
Full day and *afternoon* tours taking in the lives and lifestyles of the rich and famous with commentary by guides who will give you an insight into London and its glitterati. Tours depart from the Forum Hotel SW7 (6 **C2**), Bressenden Place SW1 (7 **C1**) and Trafalgar Square WC2 (4 **E4**). Details and bookings on (0932) 854721.

London tours: by helicopter

Cabair
Elstree Aerodrome, Borehamwood, Herts. 081-953 4411. *1-hr* sightseeing trips over London. *Sun by appointment only.*

CB
Westland Heliport, Lombard Rd SW11. 071-228 3232. Helicopter flights over London. Minimum 16 passengers. *By appointment only.*

London tours: by horse & carriage

London Carriages   1 **G1**
071-609 9462. Sightseeing tours of the capital by horse and carriage. Experienced handlers. Open and closed carriages. *15-40-min* tours. Extended tours can be arranged. Look out for them departing Leicester Square (4 **E3**) during summer. *Phone above number to book in advance.*

London tours: by private guide

The Guild of Guide Lecturers   4 **F5**
2 Bridge St SW1. 071-839 7438. This is the professional association for Tourist Board Registered Guides, with over 1000 trained members, all specialists in their subjects and speaking more than 35 languages between them. The Guild compiles an annual list of Registered Guides.

The London Tourist Board   7 **B1**
(Guides Dept)
26 Grosvenor Gdns SW1. 071-730 3450. Can provide assistance in finding registered guides.

The following companies all use registered guides:

British Tours   4 **C2**
6 South Molton St W1. 071-629 5267.

Wide variety of individual tours throughout London and surrounding areas with qualified driver/guides.

Go-By-Guides Ltd
17 Woodfield, Parkhill Rd NW3. 071-722 7506. Sightseeing tours by private car accompanied by trained driver/guides. *Half, full and multi-day* tours covering the entire UK.

London Docklands Development Corporation
Group and individual tours organised in the London Docklands area. For details and prices phone 071-512 1111.

Tour Guides Ltd   **4 F5**
2 Bridge St SW1. 071-839 2498. Tourist Board registered guides will escort individuals or groups on car, coach or walking tours. *24 hr service.*

London tours: walking

Canal Walks
Inland Waterways Association, 114 Regent's Park Rd NW1. 071-586 2556. Two walks along the Regent's Canal starting from Camden Town tube station, then either west to Little Venice or east to the City Road Basin. Other walks. *Phone for details.*

Citisights of London
213 Brooke Rd E5. 081-806 4325. Archaeologists and historians working in association with the Museum of London provide a series of walks and tours concerning the history and archaeology of London.

City Walks   **2 B1**
147 Offord Rd N1. 071-700 6931. Wide variety of walks from *Rock and Roll Soho* to *Ghosts, Ghouls and Graveyards*. *Mon-Sun.*

Historical Walks of London
3 Florence Rd, South Croydon, Surrey. 081-668 4019. Wide variety of walks from *A City in the Blitz* to *Jack the Ripper Murder Trail.* Last about *2 hrs* and take place regardless of weather or numbers. *Mon-Sun.*

The Londoners
3 Springfield Av N10. 081-883 2656. Discover some of the links with London's past with visits to four or five of her famous pubs. Different route *each week.* From Temple tube station *19.30 Fri.*

London Wall Walk   **5 D1**
Museum of London, London Wall EC2. 071-600 3699. Devised by the Museum of London, this is the best way to see the Roman and medieval city walls. The route takes about *1-2 hours* to complete and in

that time you'll cover about 2 miles (3.2km) of London's streets. Buy the booklet *Roman Wall Walk* from the museum shop to set you on the right trail.

London Walks
PO Box 1708 NW6. 071-624 3978. Meet at various tube stations for stimulating walks through London lasting *1½ to 2 hrs.* A choice of more than 40 walks including *Dickens' London, Ghosts of the City* and *Jack the Ripper haunts.* Also pub walks. *Phone for details.*

Silver Jubilee Walkway
Buy a booklet from the London Tourist Board Information Centre (**7 B1**) or follow the paving stones marked with Jubilee crowns. This pedestrian trail takes you across London from Leicester Square (**4 E3**) to Tower Hill (**5 G3**).

Streets of London
16 The Grove N3. 081-346 9255. Guided walking tours with regular programme of scheduled tours, regardless of weather. Themes include *Dickens' London* and *History of London.* Also private tours for clubs, societies, schools etc.

River trips

The Thames is a fascinatingly beautiful river, never more so than as it passes through London. One of the best ways of appreciating the city is to take a boat trip. The buildings which line the banks range from decrepit warehouses to palaces, conjuring up a whole host of historic, artistic and literary associations. Daily services run from the piers listed below, but travellers may board at any of the other piers en route. It is important to note that times vary according to the tides and the weather and it's always advisable to telephone for details first. The London Tourist Board provides an excellent recorded River Trips Information Service on (0839) 123432.
NB: always check times of return boats at the pier on arrival.

Downriver services

Charing Cross Pier   **4 F4**
Victoria Embankment WC2. 071-839 3572. Trips to the Tower *(20-min journey)* and Greenwich *(45-min journey)* every 30 mins between 10.30-16.00 Apr-Oct; every 45 mins between 10.30-15.00 Nov-Mar. 2-hr luncheon cruise 12.45 Sun only; all year.

THE RIVER THAMES

BRENTFORD

KEW

MORTLAKE

ISLEWORTH

RICHMOND

STRAWBERRY HILL

HAM

HAMPTON WICK

KINGSTON

NORTH BANK
2 Hampton Court Palace is bordered by **3 Hampton Court Park**. Embarking at Barge Walk, by **1 Hampton Court Bridge**, you can get a good idea of what travelling to London was like for royal residents. **4 Bushy Park** used to be enclosed as part of the Hampton Court estate; it was opened to the public by Queen Victoria in 1838. Hampton Wick, to the left, is a residential area. Around the bend lies **8 Teddington Lock**. From here towards London the Thames is tidal.

Twickenham, past Strawberry Hill, offers beautiful riverside settings. The path of the river is dotted with several willow-covered islands, among them **9 Eel Pie Island**. The Twickenham ferry **11** runs from the Boat House to Ham House. **12 Marble Hill House**, an 18thC Palladian villa, looms gracefully from its spacious riverside park. Through Richmond (see south bank) is **16 Richmond Lock and Footbridge**, with good riverside walks. Isleworth, by **17 Isleworth Eyot**, became a fashionable place to live in the 18thC. Vincent Van Gogh taught here and used the Thames as the subject for his first attempts at painting. **18** The **London Apprentice** pub, built around 1741, is part of a charming setting with the 15thC tower of All Saint's Church and several Georgian houses. **20 Syon House** is set in Syon Park behind wooded banks to the north and the Royal Botanic Gardens to the south. Heading towards **25 Kew Bridge** is Brentford. **22** The **Grand Union Canal**, a direct link to Birmingham, still joins the Thames here, although it is no longer busy with commercial traffic. Past Kew Bridge, the residential area of Chiswick is fronted by **26 Strand-on-the-Green**, a riverside path with pubs and several notable 18thC houses, home to many famous residents including Nancy Mitford, William Morris and Dylan Thomas. Flooding was common here at high tide until the construction of the Thames Barrier.

Boats moored at the riverside gardens of grand 18thC houses on **31 Chiswick Mall** are a continuing reminder of the wealthy riverside village it once was. Similar houses line the banks along **32 Upper Mall** and **33 Lower Mall**, where there are several popular historic pubs – the Blue Anchor, the Dove (whose past imbibers include Nell Gwynne,

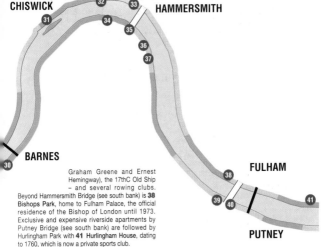

CHISWICK

HAMMERSMITH

BARNES

FULHAM

PUTNEY

Graham Greene and Ernest Hemingway), the 17thC Old Ship – and several rowing clubs. Beyond Hammersmith Bridge (see south bank) is **38 Bishops Park**, home to Fulham Palace, the official residence of the Bishop of London until 1973. Exclusive and expensive riverside apartments by Putney Bridge (see south bank) are followed by Hurlingham Park with **41 Hurlingham House**, dating to 1760, which is now a private sports club.

SOUTH BANK

Behind **5 Kingston Bridge** lies Kingston, an early fishing village, market town and royal borough with a wide range of shops and a good river frontage. Passing **6 Stevens Eyot** and **7 Trowlock Island**, all around is rural greenery. **8 Teddington Lock** marks the beginning of the tidal Thames. To the east is Ham, a largely residential area with parkland bordering the river. Within the parkland is **10 Ham House**, built in 1610 by Sir Thomas Vavasour for the Earls of Dysart. Owned by the National Trust, it has been restored to its full baroque splendour.

9 Eel Pie Island, now a luxury housing development accessible only by boat, once housed a noisy nightclub which played host to many famous groups, including the Rolling Stones. From here the Thames enters Richmond, the only London borough with land on both sides of the Thames. Just under **13** the 18thC **Richmond Bridge** is **14** a delightful towpath with several drinking and eating spots, among them the White Cross Hotel. Behind is Richmond, whose focal point is the river. Full of royal, historic and theatrical associations, it was named by Henry VII when he rebuilt Richmond Palace (now destroyed) in 1497. Passing **15 Twickenham Bridge**, **16 Richmond Lock** and **17 Isleworth Eyot** you will see stretches of **21 Old Deer Park**, the former garden and park of Richmond Palace. **19 Kew Observatory**, within the park, was built by Sir William Chambers for George III and was the Meteorological Office until 1981. The river now passes between Syon Park and **23** the **Royal Botanic Gardens**. Started in 1759 with a small area devoted to botanic collections, the gardens today are among the greatest in the world with over 25,000 plant specimens. They also contain **24 Kew Palace**, the favourite home of Georges II and III. Kew, behind **25 Kew Bridge**, is a mainly

residential area with a long history due to its easy access by river. The name is derived from a word meaning 'neck of land by a landing place'. Past **27 Kew Railway Bridge** is Mortlake, where in 1619 Flemish weavers made tapestries; today local trade continues at Watney's Brewery. Along the waterfront are The Limes, several 18thC houses with gardens leading to the river. By **28 Chiswick Bridge**, along **29 Thames Bank**, is a cluster of attractive houses, among them Leyden House, a 15thC timber-framed building behind an 18thC façade. It is here the annual Oxford v. Cambridge Boat Race ends.

On the edge of the loop is **30 Barnes Terrace**, behind whose attractive ironwork façades lies delightful Barnes village. The terrace was and is a fashionable place to live, with former residents including Sheridan and Gustav Holst. At the tip of Barnes is **34 St Paul's School**, an exclusive public school founded originally in 1509 by the Dean of St Paul's Cathedral. Famous pupils include John Milton, Samuel Pepys, Judge Jeffreys and Edmond Halley, the astronomer. **35 Hammersmith Bridge** was the first suspension bridge in London. The original, built 1824 by William T. Clarke, was replaced in 1883 by the present construction by Sir Joseph Bazalgette. Beyond the bridge is **36 Harrods Repository**, a storage depot for the great shop. **37 Barn Elms Reservoir** is host to a variety of watersports, plus fishing and birdwatching. Along Putney Embankment are several rowing clubs – the Oxford v. Cambridge Boat Race starts from here. By **39 Putney Pier** are some good pubs, among them the Duke's Head and the Star & Garter. **40 Putney Bridge** originally linked old Fulham to the once farming and fishing community at Putney. First completed in 1727, the original arch spans were of such differing sizes that they presented serious difficulties for navigators and were reduced in 1870. The bridge was entirely replaced in 1882.

NORTH BANK

Under **43** Wandsworth Bridge and past Battersea Reach is **44** Chelsea Harbour with its smart shops, apartments, restaurants and marina. **46** Chelsea Wharf has been transformed from old warehouses into modern business units. Beyond Battersea Bridge (see south bank) is fashionable **48** Cheyne Walk; still a smart address, grand houses here were occupied by such famous former residents as Isambard Kingdom Brunel, Hilaire Belloc and James Whistler. Chelsea Old Church, the last resting place of Sir Thomas More, lies on its western point. **49** Albert Bridge is a three-span bridge built 1871 by R.M. Ordish. The bridge was strengthened in 1971 to increase traffic loads. It is particularly beautiful at night when illuminated. Beyond the bridge is **50** Chelsea Royal Hospital, established by Charles II for veteran soldiers. It opened in 1689, admitting 476 army pensioners. The Chelsea Flower Show is held in the grounds annually in May. Beyond Chelsea Bridge (see south bank) and behind the wharves of Pimlico and **55** Pimlico Gardens lies genteel residential charm. Past **57** Vauxhall Bridge, the first iron bridge to span the Thames, is **59** the Tate Gallery, housing the national collection of modern and British art. It stands on the site of the Millbank Penitentiary, where criminals awaited boats to carry them downriver to be deported to Australia. Next door is **60** Vickers Tower, one of London's earliest glass-walled office skyscrapers (1960–63). Beyond Lambeth Bridge (see south bank) **64** the Houses of Parliament by Augustus Pugin and Charles Barry come into view. In 1856 the 'Great Stink' from untreated sewage in the river became so bad that canvases soaked in chloride of lime were hung at the windows to counteract the smell. Nowadays, in summer, you can see MPs on the terraces taking refreshment and entertaining their guests. **65** Westminster Bridge opened in 1750. The watermen of the Thames were paid £25,000 in compensation when it was built. Present structure is cast iron and was built in 1854 to a design by Thomas Page. **67** Victoria Embankment was created by Sir Joseph Bazalgette in 1868 by reclaiming 37 acres (15.4ha) of mud. This made the river narrower and the water flow faster, so ending the skating era on the once-frozen waters. Halfway along the Embankment are **68** Whitehall Stairs, once part of Whitehall Palace (destroyed by fire in 1698). Cardinal Wolsey descended these steps to be rowed to Henry VIII at

Greenwich, and in 1688 James II escaped by them from William of Orange. There are several ships along this stretch; **69** PS *Tattershall Castle*, once a paddle-steamer, now converted into a restaurant and bar, **73** RS *Hispaniola*, once a ferry on the Firth of Clyde in Scotland and now a restaurant, and **74** TS *Queen Mary*, a pub and functions venue. **71** Embankment Place is a new development above Charing Cross Station; the vaults below the station have also been revitalised and now house retail outlets and restaurants. The imposing gateway on the north side of Victoria Embankment Gardens is **75** York Watergate, built in 1626 by Nicholas Stone as the riverside entrance to York House which once had gardens sweeping down to the Thames. It marks the position of the north bank of the Thames before the construction of the Victoria Embankment. The rooftops of **77** the Savoy Hotel are clearly discernible from the river. The famous and the wealthy stay here to enjoy some of the best views of the Thames. It was from one of the hotel's balconies that Claude Monet painted 18 canvases of **78** Waterloo Bridge. Originally built in 1811 by Rennie, the bridge was opened on the anniversary of the Battle of Waterloo. Present bridge was designed by Sir Giles Gilbert Scott and was constructed in 1937–42. Just by the Savoy is **76** Cleopatra's Needle, a 60ft (18m)-high ancient Egyptian granite obelisk brought to London by sea in 1878. When it was erected various articles were buried beneath it for posterity – the morning's newspapers, a razor, coins, four Bibles in different languages and photographs of '12 of the best-looking Englishwomen of the day'. The bronze sphinxes were added (facing the wrong way!) in 1882. **80** Thames Sailing Barge Wilfred at Temple Stairs, is now a wine bar and restaurant. **81** Somerset House stands on the site of an unfinished Renaissance palace. Best seen from the river, its long, elegant façade is a magnificent landmark. The river once lapped against its terraces and through river entrances, but is now separated from it by Embankment. After a long history of royal inhabitants, it houses offices of the Inland Revenue, and the Courtauld Institute Galleries. **82** HMS

CHELSEA

SOUTH BANK

The once rural village of Wandsworth, named after the tributary, the River Wandle, now presents an industrial, somewhat drab scene. Past residents include Defoe, Thackeray and Voltaire. There's a good pub, **42** the Ship, just by Wandsworth Bridge. Several wharves and jetties along this part of the river are testament to the days of thriving trade – Huguenot refugees settled here making hats and dying cloth in the 18thC. In the vestry of **45** the riverside Church of St Mary, J.M.W. Turner sat and watched the sunsets across the river. **47** Battersea Bridge replaced the ferry between Chelsea and Battersea, transforming Chelsea from a village to a thriving small town. Original bridge (1771) was replaced in 1886–90 by the present one, designed by Sir Joseph Bazalgette. Past pretty Albert Bridge

FULHAM

WANDSWORTH

President was once used by the Royal Naval Reserve; it now houses an educational charity. **83 Blackfriars Bridge** was built in 1760. It cost £230,000 and was mainly paid for by fines which had accumulated from men refusing the post of Sheriff. Replaced by the present structure in 1860.

As you round the corner, you can see the dome and spire of St Paul's Cathedral and the NatWest Tower rising above the rooftops of the City. You pass under Southwark Bridge (see south bank) and then **82 London Bridge**, with the towering monoliths of the City behind. Originally a wooden construction built by the Romans, it was replaced with a stone one in the 12thC which carried houses, shops and the heads of traitors on spikes. Has been replaced many times and in 1971 the granite construction by Rennie (1832) was shipped off to Lake Havasu City, Arizona. Present bridge dates to 1973. **91 Fishmongers' Hall** is dedicated to the Worshipful Company of Fishmongers, one of the 96 City Livery companies. On the other side of London Bridge is **93 Monument**, a Doric column 202ft (61.5m) high commemorating the Great Fire of London. Along this stretch and set back from the river is **94 Watermen's Hall**, founded for the watermen of the city of London, who once operated all water transport. They had the monopoly on passenger carriage until the arrival of hackney coaches, sedan chairs and more bridges, which obviated the need for ferries. The company is still active.

CITY

WESTMINSTER

LAMBETH

PIMLICO

VAUXHALL

London residence of the Archbishop of Canterbury since 1197. **63 St Thomas's Hospital**, named after Thomas à Becket, originally had strict rules; patients were only fed if they went daily to chapel and no person could be admitted for the same disease twice! Florence Nightingale established her nursing school here. On the other side of Westminster Bridge (see north bank) is **66 County Hall**, a massive edifice designed in 1911 for the Greater London Council (abolished in 1986). With its 2100ft (640m) river frontage and 2390 rooms, there are plans for it to become a hotel and leisure complex. **70 Hungerford Railway Bridge** has excellent views from its footbridge and next to it is **72 the South Bank Centre** with the Royal Festival Hall, National Film Theatre, Queen Elizabeth Hall, Purcell Room and, nestling behind, the Hayward Gallery, complete with colourful neon sculpture. Past Waterloo Bridge (see north bank) is **79 the National Theatre** with the Museum of the Moving Image beside it. **84 Gabriel's Wharf** is a lively market, the south bank's answer to Covent Garden. **85 The art deco 'OXO' Tower**, decorated thus because advertising was forbidden on buildings, was once the dominant building in this part of the city.

From **87 Bankside** are fine views of St Paul's Cathedral and the City. No.49 while his cathedral and city were being built after the Great Fire of 1666. Dominated by **88** the now disused **Bankside Power Station**, there are riverside walks here and **86 the Anchor**, an historic pub with strong smuggling connections, built in 1770. It is also the site of one of Shakespeare's theatres, the Globe, which is being rebuilt to the original plans. **89 Southwark Bridge** was built in 1814 and is the largest bridge ever built of cast iron. Replaced 1912–21 by the present steel structure. Just before London Bridge (see north bank) is **90** the schooner **Kathleen & May**, moored in St Mary Overy Dock. It is the last surviving three-masted, topsail, trading schooner and now a floating museum. In the Pool of London is the vast **95 HMS Belfast**, the last survivor of the Royal Navy's Second World War cruisers. Behind it is **96 the London Bridge City** development, incorporating Hay's Galleria, an elegant shopping and leisure complex.

(see north bank) lies **52 Battersea Park**, with **51** the striking **London Peace Pagoda**, dedicated to world peace. **53 Chelsea Bridge** was built in 1858 by Thomas Page. It was entirely replaced in 1934 by another suspension bridge (Rendel, Palmer and Tritton). **54 Battersea Power Station** is now disused; although somewhat ugly, it is a remarkable landmark. Industrial areas now loom on the banks with busy Nine Elms Lane, on which stands **56 New Covent Garden Market**, moved in 1974 from its central London site. On the other side of Vauxhall Bridge (see north bank) is **58 Vauxhall Cross**, a ten-storey glass office block rising in layers from the bank of the Thames, built to house government offices. **61 Lambeth Bridge** (1861) was originally the only place where it was possible to cross the river with a coach and horses. Replaced by present bridge 1929. Beyond the bridge you can see **62** the Tudor gatehouse of impressive Gothic **Lambeth Palace**, the official

NORTH BANK

97 The Tower of London lies solid and forbidding; it is easy to imagine the terror of the criminals as they were brought silently downriver through Traitors' Gate to await their fate. Elizabeth I would have had a particularly distressing arrival seeing the head of her mother, Anne Boleyn, on a spike at the gate. Today it is a lot safer to disembark and explore London's oldest medieval fortress. **98** **Tower Bridge** was completed in 1894. Designed by Sir Horace Jones and John Wolfe-Barry, this dramatic Victorian-Gothic structure opens to allow tall ships to pass. Each section of the double-bascule drawbridge weighs over 1000 tonnes but can be raised in under two minutes. Stretching from Tower Pier to Beckton (off map) is London's Docklands. The area has undergone massive change from a thriving, commercial port through closure to regeneration. The London Docklands Development Corporation (LDDC) was set up in 1981 to create a 'new city for the 21stC' with riverside apartments, shops, restaurants and offices. **99** St Katharine's Dock was the first of the docks to be rejuvenated. Built on 23 acres (9.5ha), the original docks were closed down in 1968. Five years later an £80 million building scheme was begun which included **100** the **Tower Thistle Hotel** and the **World Trade Centre**. The magnificent warehouses have been restored and now house shops, apartments, offices, restaurants, a yacht club and marina. Visiting cruisers nestle alongside resident yachts and barges. The Dickens Inn is a particularly popular drinking spot. Wapping is a mainly residential area with a good selection of pubs including **104** the **Prospect of Whitby**, dating to the reign of Henry VIII and once known as the Devil's Tavern, such were its associations with thieves and smugglers. Next door is **106** the **Town of Ramsgate** with an equally grisly past, where convicts were chained in cellars at the inn before deportation to Australia. By the pub is **105** **Wapping Old Stairs**, where Colonel Blood was

WAPPING

ROTHERHITHE

SOUTHWARK

BERMONDSEY

DEPTFORD

MILLW

SOUTH BANK

Past Tower Bridge (see north bank) is **101** Butler's Wharf, transformed from narrow alleys, where Oliver Twist's Bill Sikes met his end, into a smart restaurant, Le Pont de la Tour, and offices. **102** The **Design Museum**, charting designs past and present, is further along. There are few docks on the south bank, although the transformation of **103** St Saviour's Dock won an award. Bermondsey (inland, behind St Saviour's Dock) has retained a good deal of its old dockland atmosphere, as has Rotherhithe, which is named from two Saxon words: 'redhra' – mariner, and 'hyth' – haven, and started life as a small maritime settlement along the river. By **107** Cherry Garden Pier, where a ship sounds her horn if she needs Tower Bridge opened, and from where J.M.W. Turner painted The Fighting Téméraire, is **108** the historic **Angel** pub. It dates from the 15thC with part of the inn built on piles over the river. Trapdoors in the floor were once used by smugglers, and 'Hanging' Judge Jeffreys reportedly sat here watching pirates being hanged at Execution Dock opposite (now moved downstream to Blackwall). **109** The **Mayflower** pub, a 17thC inn, was renamed to commemorate the sailing of the Pilgrim Fathers' boat, the Mayflower, carrying pilgrims to America in 1620. It is still the only inn licensed to sell stamps to British and foreign sailors. **110** the Rotherhithe Tunnel, built 1904–8 by Sir Maurice Fitzmarice, is still used as a thoroughfare. The top of the tunnel is 48ft (14.5m) below the high-water mark to allow for large ships passing above. Old warehouses and former shipbuilding yards line the banks as far as **114** Deptford Creek, where the Royal Dock was built in 1513 for Henry VIII's navy. It was here Elizabeth I visited Sir Francis Drake's ship the Golden Hind and from here Captain Cook's Discovery set sail. Deptford is still used by some big cargo ships. Greenwich is rich in nautical history. Here, in dry dock, are the Cutty Sark, the only surviving tea-caught trying to escape with the Crown Jewels. Shadwell, behind Wapping, was once densely populated with watermen, lightermen and sailors. Captain James Cook stayed here in between his three Pacific explorations. Limehouse, named after its lime kilns, was originally a ship-building centre and was where the first Chinese sailors set up their community. Later, hounded out by British seamen, they moved away and are now only remembered by a few street names (Pekin, Nankin, Canton) and restaurants. The Isle of Dogs, so called because it was once the royal kennel, was uninhabited until **111 the West India Docks** were built in 1800. At the northernmost strip of these waters is **112 Canary Wharf**, an 80-acre (35ha) 'new district' with shops, offices, apartments, restaurants, gardens and waterfront promenades. It is also home to the tallest building in the United Kingdom, One Canada Square, which stands 50 storeys high, at 800ft (244m), and dominates the skyline for miles around. The West India Docks are also now the site of **113**

Billingsgate Fish Market, which was moved here from its old site near London Bridge. Millwall provides good opportunities to see smart, colourful riverside apartments next to old housing. Wherever you go, the high tracks of the Docklands Light Railway rise unexpectedly behind houses and between streets. At the tip of the Isle of Dogs at **115 Island Gardens** is **116 the Greenwich Foot Tunnel**, built 1902, for pedestrians only. From the Island Gardens side are excellent views of Wren's Royal Naval College set off by Greenwich Park. From Greenwich you can take a river trip to the Thames Barrier (see south bank) via the vast docks (off map) Royal Victoria, Royal Albert and King George V, the last to be built (1921). With immense resources for cargo and passengers, the docks enjoyed prime importance until closure in the early 1970s. They were later transformed into an airstrip (London City Airport) and a centre for watersports. The river here is peppered with wharves and jetties, a reminder of the days of merchants and constant cargo deliveries.

stainless steel barrage to stem periodically dangerous high tides. Each gate weighs 3000 tonnes and is the equivalent of a five-storey building in height. The structures housing the machines which operate the gates seem to have been inspired by the 'sails' of Sydney Opera House. Blackwall Reach, on the way to the Flood Barrier, was where, in 1606, Captain John Smith and the Virginia Settlers left on their journey to found the first permanent colony in America. Here also the Cutty Sark unloaded her valuable cargoes. **120 Execution Dock** is at the entrance to Blackwall Tunnel. This is where, until the late 19thC, the bodies of convicted pirates were hung in iron cages until three tides had washed over them. A warning to all passing sailors! **121 the Blackwall Tunnel** was built in 1897 by Sir Alexander Binnie. There are now two tunnels; the second opened in 1967. One is for northbound traffic, the other for southbound. Queen Elizabeth II Bridge (off map) was opened in 1991 to ease the traffic through Dartford Tunnel; it is used by southbound vehicles. It is the largest bridge of its type in Europe with twin towers rising nearly 450ft (130m) above the Thames and a total length of nearly two miles.

clipper, and Sir Francis Chichester's tiny ketch Gipsy Moth IV. Right by Greenwich Pier is Sir Christopher Wren's beautiful baroque building, **117 the Royal Naval College**. Behind it are **118 the National Maritime Museum** and on a hilltop setting within Greenwich Park, **119 the Old Royal Observatory**, home of the Greenwich Meridian. From here it is a short boat ride to **122 the Thames Flood Barrier**, best seen from the river. Rounding the bend, the steel fins rise up from the water. Completed in 1982, it is the world's largest movable flood barrier and is designed to swing up from the river bed and create a

Greenwich Pier
Return services to Charing Cross Pier (45-min journey), Tower Pier (30-min journey) and Westminster Pier (45-min journey). *Phone the individual piers for details.*

Tower Pier   5 F4
071-488 0344. Trips to Greenwich (30-min journey) every 30 mins 11.00-17.00 in summer (departures at 10.15, 12.30 and 14.45 Nov-Mar). Ferry to HMS Belfast (5 mins) every 15 mins in summer only.

Westminster Pier   4 F5
Victoria Embankment SW1. 071-930 4097. Trips to the Tower (30-min journey) every 20 mins 10.30-16.00 and to Greenwich (50 mins) every half hour 10.30-16.00; all year. Special trips to the Thames Flood Barrier (1¼ hrs each way) 10.00, 11.15, 12.45, 13.45 and 15.15 Mar-Nov. Disco cruises 19.00 Fri & 20.00 Sat; all year.

Upriver services

Run from Westminster Pier only, all services call at Putney Embankment.

Westminster Pier   4 F5
Victoria Embankment SW1. Westminster Passenger Services operate boat trips during *summer only* to Putney (30-min journey), Kew (1½-hr journey), Richmond (2-hr journey) and Hampton Court (3-4-hr journey). Phone 071-930 2062 for departure times.
There are local services to Hampton Court from Richmond and Kingston (Easter-Sep). Phone 081-546 2434 for details.

Upper Thames

Salter Bros
Follybridge, Oxford. (0865) 243421. Salter's steamers run from Oxford-Abingdon, Reading-Henley, Maidenhead-Windsor and Windsor-Staines; *May-Sep Mon-Sun.* Private hire available. *Phone for details.*

Canal trips

Canal Water Bus   1 D1
London Waterbus Co, Camden Lock Pl NW1. 071-482 2550. Boat leaves from Little Venice stopping at the zoo and continuing to Camden Lock. *Apr-Sep 10.00-17.00 Mon-Sun; Oct 10.30-15.45 Mon-Sun; Nov-Mar 10.30-15.45 Sat & Sun.*

Also run Limehouse/River Lea trips which explore the architecture and industrial history of London's quiet canalways; *May-Oct 09.30-18.00 Sat.*

Jason's Trip   3 C1
Opposite 60 Blomfield Rd W9. 071-286 3428. The traditional narrowboat *Jason* leaves Little Venice for 1½-hr return trip, with commentary, through Regent's Park and zoo to Camden Lock. Disembark to look round the craft shops if you like, or the market at weekends. Refreshments. Depart *Apr, May & Sep 10.30, 12.30 & 14.30; Jun-Aug 10.30, 12.30, 14.30 & 16.30. Evening cruise Tue.* Private parties of all kinds can be booked. *Phone for details.*

Jenny Wren Cruises   1 D1
250 Camden High St NW1. 071-485 4433. 1½-hr round trips along Regent's Canal passing the zoo and Little Venice. Up to four tours a day *Feb-Nov Mon-Sun.* Also longer and evening trips. Also runs *My Fair Lady*, a cruising restaurant, for dinner cruise evenings *20.00-23.00 Tue-Sat, & Sun lunch 13.00-15.30.*

Charter boats

Boat Enquiries
43 Botley Rd, Oxford. (0865) 727288. Will arrange cruiser and narrowboat hire in England.

Catamaran Cruisers   4 F4
Charing Cross Pier, Victoria Embankment WC2. 071-987 1185. Can be hired for private parties or business functions. Disco, dinner dance and cabaret cruises. *Phone for details.*

Thames Pleasure Craft
PO Box 15, Blackheath SE3. 071-709 9697/071-488 1939. *Daytime* and *evening* cruises. Fully licensed launches with dancing space. Embark at various piers *by arrangement.*

Inland Waterways Association   1 B2
114 Regent's Park Rd NW1. 071-586 2556. Publish the *Inland Waterways Guide* with general details of hire companies nationwide.

Woods River Services
PO Box 177 SE3. 071-481 2711. Modern all-weather passenger launches. *Silver Barracuda* – 280-passenger. *Silver Dolphin* – 140-passenger. Fully-fitted dancefloor, film projector and licensed bar. Guided tours arranged. Private charter only. Luncheon club – *2nd & 4th Fri of the month.*

Day trips from London

Every era, from prehistoric times, has altered, and left its mark on, the English landscape. Ancient heath and moorland contrast with stately gardens and manor houses. Centuries mingle in the architecture along village streets. The ruins of a Norman or Tudor castle are not far from a Victorian cathedral or 14thC parish church. The 19thC pleasure-dome in Brighton is a short drive away from thatched cottages in Sussex and hop fields in Kent. The English countryside is a constantly changing, often magical landscape – well worth exploring. All the places listed below are easily accessible on a day trip from London.

For information about train, coach and bus services out of London see 'Tourist information' and 'Transport in London'.

Ashdown Forest, E. Sussex
Excellent walking. High sandy country of heather and bracken with wind-blown pine trees, silver birch and beech in the valleys – each with its stream. 'Winnie-the-Pooh' country. Start from Crowborough, Hartfield, Forest Row or Three Bridges. London 30 miles (A22).

Bath, Avon
A delightful Georgian town rich in architectural detail such as the dramatic sweeping curve of Ionic columns which forms the Royal Crescent. Lots of museums including the Roman Baths and Pump Room. Natural hot springs bubbling out of the ground and the bathing complex built when it was the Roman town of Aquae Sulis are still very visible. Good shopping and lots of charming cafés and restaurants. Train 1½ hrs. London 107 miles (M4).

Bath

Battle, E. Sussex
Site of the famous battle of 1066. An abbey, which William the Conqueror had vowed to build should he win the battle, is now in ruins but the Gateway still stands on Battle Hill. Opposite this is the 12thC church of St Mary. London 56 miles (A21).

Brighton, E. Sussex
Known as 'Little London by the Sea', this once poor fishing village has been a lively, bustling seaside resort ever since the Prince Regent set up his court in the fabulous Oriental-domed Pavilion. Fashionable shops, splendid Regency terraces, good pubs and restaurants, cockle stalls, fairs and sport of all kinds. Five miles of beach and a magical Victorian pier. Train 1 hr. London 48 miles (A23).

Cambridge, Cambs
A great university city of spires, mellow colleges and riverside meadows, bordering the Cam. The famous 'Backs' and the lovely bridges are best seen by hiring a punt. The 20 or so colleges date from the 13thC onwards including Trinity by Wren, King's by James Gibbs and the modern Queen's by Basil Spence. The city contains the superb Fitzwilliam Museum, the notable Botanic Garden and some fine churches. Train 1½ hrs. London 55 miles (M11).

Canterbury, Kent
Pleasant, old, walled city on the river Stour, dominated by the magnificent Gothic cathedral, containing the shrine of Thomas à Becket (murdered 1170) and the tomb of the Black Prince. Good local museum in West Gate. Train 1½ hrs. London 56 miles (M2).

Canterbury Cathedral

Chichester, W. Sussex
An old Roman city walled by the Saxons and graced by its beautiful 12thC cathedral. Now mostly Georgian in character. Fine 16thC Butter Cross, a medieval Guildhall and modern Festival Theatre, built 1962. Excellent harbour for sailing. Train 1½ hrs. London 63 miles (A3, A286).

The Chilterns
A 40-mile-long ridge of chalk hills with fine views. Open downs, wheat fields, magnificent beech woods and charming villages. Start from Henley, Great Missenden, Stokenchurch, Wendover or Whipsnade. London 20-30 miles (M1 or M40).

Colchester, Essex

England's first Roman city, with many visible remains: the city wall, a Mithraic temple, and arches, windows and doorways built from Roman bricks. Norman relics include Colchester Castle (now housing a museum) and the ruins of the church of St Botolph. There is a small harbour and an oyster fishery. The famous 'Colchester Oyster Feast' takes place every year, *about 20 Oct*. Train *1 hr*. London 52 miles (A12).

Cotswolds

A beautiful area west of London with buildings constructed from Cotswold stone and towns and villages full of Tudor and Jacobean architecture. Stow-on-the-Wold has a fine market place and Bourton-on-the-Water holds many delights. There's also the Wildlife Park at Burford, Blenheim Palace and Sudeley Castle. Gloucester and Cheltenham are two cities on the edge of the Cotswolds which are worth a visit. London 50-100 miles (M4).

Devil's Punchbowl, Surrey

A vast and impressive bowl scooped out of the high open hills. Good views. Start from Haslemere or Hindhead. Train *1 hr*. London 30 miles (A3).

Henley-on-Thames, Oxon

Situated on a very pretty part of the Thames and most famous for the Regatta, held in *early Jul*. The arched bridge was built in 1786. In St Mary's churchyard are 16thC almshouses and a rare unspoilt 15thC timber-framed building – the Chantry House. The Regatta is held on the straight mile of the river downstream from the bridge. Train *1 hr*. London 36 miles (A4).

The North Downs

An outcrop of high chalk hills with magnificent views over the Weald of Kent. The Pilgrim's Way runs along the south face of the hills. Farming country with open beech and oak woods, pleasant villages and pubs. Start from Dorking, Box Hill, Woldingham or Otford. London 15-20 miles (A24, A23 or A21).

Oxford, Oxon

A university city of spires and fine college buildings on the Thames and the Cherwell and dating from the 13thC. The Sheldonian Theatre by Wren, the Radcliffe Camera by Gibbs and the 15thC Bodleian Library are particularly notable. Visit also the famous old Botanic Garden and the Ashmolean Museum. Train *1½ hrs*. London 65 miles (A40).

Portsmouth

Old, historic battleships and new, modern warships lie side by side at Portsmouth's Naval Base, which has been the home of the Royal Navy since Henry VII first founded the Royal Dockyard. The Royal Naval Museum is also here. Train *1½ hrs*. London 77 miles (A3).

Salisbury & Stonehenge, Wiltshire

Salisbury is famous for its 13thC cathedral, apparently built where a random arrow was fired. Its spire is the highest in England. The town is rich in medieval architecture. Cathedral Close boasts the most interesting buildings such as the Bishop's Palace and the King's House. The market square is dominated by 600-year-old Poultry Cross. Stonehenge is 10 miles away and the best British example of groups of ancient stone circles known as Druid's Circles. Estimated that it took 30 million years to come about, but what it was originally erected for is still a mystery. Ringed by perimeter fence but still good views. London 90 miles (A30, A303). *Charge*.

Stonehenge

The South Downs

Grassy slopes and ridges which follow the Sussex coast ending in high chalk cliffs by the sea. The steep escarpments face the North Downs across the Weald. The South Downs Way follows 80 miles of ancient paths where Stone Age man grazed sheep 5000 years ago. The section from Bramber to Washington (6½ miles) is particularly pleasant. London 45 miles (A24).

Southend-on-Sea, Essex

Traditionally the Cockney's weekend seaside resort. Fun-fairs and every sort of entertainment and attraction. Visit Westcliff-on-Sea nearby and Shoeburyness for cockle-beds, boats and paddling. Train *1 hr*. London 40 miles (A127).

Stratford-upon-Avon, Warks

The birthplace of William Shakespeare (1564-1616). The town is still Elizabethan in atmosphere with overhanging gables and timbered inns. Visit the playwright's birthplace in Henley Street, his house at New Place, Anne Hathaway's cottage and the museum and picture gallery. The Shakespeare Memorial Theatre in Waterside is thriving and progressive. Train *2½ hrs*. London 90 miles (A40, A34).

Thames Estuary

Unusual and sometimes tough walking along the tidal sea wall. Not everyone's cup of tea; it can be cold, windy or foggy. Take binoculars and wrap up well. Thousands of sea birds, a constant traffic

Arundel Castle

of ships and the lonely marshes. Romantic and isolated but you have to be able to absorb the odd oil refinery or factory and accept that commerce is part of it all. Start from Cliffe, Higham or Gravesend in Kent, Tilbury or Mucking in Essex. London 20-25 miles (A2 or A13).

Winchester, Hants

The ancient Saxon capital of England set among lovely rolling chalk downland. The massive, square-towered Norman cathedral, with its superb vaulted Gothic nave, contains the graves of King Canute, Izaac Walton and Jane Austen. The 'round table of King Arthur' is in the remains of the Norman castle. Train 1½ hrs. London 65 miles (A30).

Great houses, castles and gardens near London

England's country houses and their gardens have been loved and written about for nearly 400 years; even the socialist reformer H. G. Wells said of them: 'It is the country house that has opened the way to human equality.' The country house represents a blending of many strands in English history: rural life, great architecture, landscaping, collecting, pride and patronage. Not that they, any more than other buildings, are unaffected by social and economic change; less than half of the 5000 stately homes reckoned to have been standing in 1920 have survived to the present day. Fortunately, however, not only have many of the most splendid examples been preserved but, thanks to organisations such as the National Trust and English Heritage, a number of these are open to the public. These are some of the great country houses within a 70-mile radius of London, dating from the 11th to the 19thC. Each property has been selected as being characteristic of its period; many were designed by such famous architects as Inigo Jones, Christopher Wren and Robert Adam. The gardens and parks were laid out by various inspired landscape gardeners including Sir John Vanbrugh, William Kent, Capability Brown and Humphry Repton. Almost without exception they contain great richness of interior decoration and ornament, and often famous collections or works of art.

Arundel Castle

Arundel, W. Sussex. (0903) 883136. An imposing feudal stronghold set among the beech woods of the South Downs, overlooking the tidal river Arun. Built at the time of Edward the Confessor, it has been the home of the Dukes of Norfolk for the last 700 years. Completely restored in 1890 by the 15th Duke. Paintings by Van Dyck, Holbein and Gainsborough; important collection of portraits of the Howard family. London 58 miles (A29). *OPEN Apr-Oct 11.00-17.00 Mon-Fri & Sun (CLOSED Sat). Last admission 1 hr before closing. Charge.*

Audley End

Saffron Walden, Essex. (0799) 522399. A great Jacobean mansion standing mellow and serene in its park near the road to Cambridge. Imposing as it now is, Audley End was once three times its present size. Built 1605-14, it served for a while as a royal country palace. In 1721 Vanbrugh demolished two thirds of the building. Fine state rooms – some decorated by Robert Adam, others 19thC neo-Jacobean. London 40 miles (A11). House *OPEN Easter-Sep 13.00-17.00 Tue-Sun & B.hol Mon in Aug 13.00-17.00.* Grounds *OPEN Easter-Oct 12.00-18.30 Tue-Sun & B.hol Mon in Aug 12.00-18.30. Charge.*

Blenheim Palace

Woodstock, Oxon. (0993) 811325. A

Blenheim Palace

DAY TRIPS FROM LONDON

Worcester

Warwick Castle
▲ Warwick

Northampton

Stratford-upon-Avon

M1

Banbury

Milton Keynes

Sudeley Castle ▲

Buckingham

M50

Cheltenham

Woburn Abbey ▲

Gloucester

A41

COTSWOLDS

Blenheim Palace ▲

CHILTERN HILLS

Cotswold Wildlife Park

Oxford

Severn

M5

M40

A40

M4

Swindon

Henley

Windsor Castle ▲

Bristol

A4

Reading

Bath

Windsor

A30

Basingstoke

Guildford

A3

Stonehenge ▲

M3

A303

A30

Winchester

Salisbury

Haslemere

Petworth House ▲

Southampton

Goodwood House ▲

NEW FOREST

M27

Chichester

A31

Portsmouth

Arundel Castle ▲

Poole

Bournemouth

Dorchester
Weymouth

ISLE OF WIGHT

© Nicholson

great classical-style ducal palace built 1705-22 by Sir John Vanbrugh. The estate was given by Queen Anne to John Churchill, Duke of Marlborough for his victory over Louis XIV at Blenheim in 1704. Winston Churchill was born here. Fine paintings, tapestries and furniture. The park was landscaped first by Henry Wise and later by Capability Brown in 1760, who dammed the small stream to create two great lakes, keeping Vanbrugh's original bridge. London 60 miles (A34). OPEN Mar-Oct 10.30-17.30 Mon-Sun. Charge.

Bodiam Castle

Robertsbridge, E. Sussex. (0580) 830436. A romantic and lovely medieval castle completely surrounded by a wide moat. A mighty fortress built 1385 as a defence against the French. London 45 miles (A21). OPEN Apr-Oct 10.00-17.30 Mon-Sun; Nov-Mar 10.00-½ hr before sunset Mon-Sat. Charge.

Boston Manor House

Boston Manor Rd, Brentford, Middx. 081-570 7728 ex5798. Jacobean mansion with park and gardens. London 8 miles. House OPEN May-Sep 14.00-16.30 Sun only. Free. Gardens OPEN dawn-dusk Mon-Sun. Free.

Buscot Park

Faringdon, Oxon. (0367) 20786. A charming late 18thC house in the Adam style. Notable for its splendid painted panels by the pre-Raphaelite painter Burne-Jones in the 'Sleeping Beauty' room. Also paintings by Reynolds, Murillo and Rembrandt. Pleasant park and lake. London 70 miles (A417). OPEN Apr-Sep 14.00-18.00 Wed-Fri, 2nd & 4th weekends. Charge.

Clandon Park

West Clandon, Surrey. (0483) 222482. Superb Palladian house built c1733 by the Venetian architect Leoni. Magnificent marble halls. Original wallpapers uncovered in restoration. Furniture, porcelain and needlework collections. London 25 miles (A247. Close to M25). OPEN Apr-end Oct 13.30-17.00 Sat-Wed. CLOSED Thur & Fri. Charge.

Claydon House

Middle Claydon, nr Buckingham. (0296) 730252. Built in 1752-68 as an ambitious effort to outdo the splendours of the 2nd Earl Verney to outdo the splendours of the Grenvilles' rival seat at Stowe. Never completed, this remaining wing contains marvellous rococo state rooms decorated by the inspired carvings of a relatively unknown craftsman called Lightfoot. The Chinese Room is notable. Family museum which includes Florence Nightingale memorabilia. Tea rooms. London 45 miles (off A413 & A41). OPEN Apr-Oct 13.00-17.00 Mon-Wed & Sat-Sun. Charge.

Cliveden

Nr Maidenhead, Bucks. (0628) 605069. Superbly sited in wooded grounds overlooking the Thames. An imposing and famous country house built for the Duke of Sutherland in 1850 by Sir Charles Barry, in Italian palazzo style, replacing the two previous buildings destroyed by fire. Formal gardens with fine sculpture from the Villa Borghese and temples by Giacomo Leoni. The house is now a hotel. London 25 miles (M4). House (3 rooms) OPEN Apr-Oct 15.00-18.00 Thur & Sun. Gardens OPEN Mar-Dec 11.00-18.00 (or sunset) Mon-Sun. Charge.

Goodwood House

Nr Chichester, W. Sussex. (0243) 774107. An 18thC house planned by James Wyatt to have eight sides, of which only three were completed. Stables by Sir William Chambers. A fine example of building in Sussex flint. Excellent paintings; some of Canaletto's London views and portraits by Van Dyck, Romney, Kneller and Reynolds. Also a particularly interesting collection of early Stubbs. Magnificent Sèvres porcelain, considered to be as fine as any in France; Gobelin tapestries; Louis XV and XVI furniture. Afternoon teas. London 60 miles (off A285 & A286). OPEN May-Oct 14.00-17.00 Sun & Mon (& Easter Sun & Mon). Also Tue-Thur in Aug. Charge.

Hall Place

Bexley, Kent. (0322) 526574. Tudor mansion, 1540, in a park with rose garden, conservatories and fine water garden. Mansion OPEN Apr-Oct 10.00-17.00 Mon-Sat, 14.00-18.00 Sun; Nov-Mar 10.00-16.00 Mon-Sat only. Free. Park OPEN every day during daylight. Free.

Ham House

Petersham, Surrey. 081-940 1950. Superb 17thC country house built on an 'H' plan. Lavish Restoration interior. Important collection of Stuart furniture. OPEN Tue-Sun 11.00-17.00 throughout the year. Charge.

Hampton Court Palace

Hampton Court, East Molesey, Surrey. 081-781 9500. Royal riverside palace built 1514 for Cardinal Wolsey with later additions by Henry VIII and Wren. Sumptuous state rooms painted by Vanbrugh, Verrio and Thornhill. Famous picture gallery of Italian masterpieces. Orangery, mellow courtyards, the 'great vine' and the maze. The formal gardens are probably among the greatest in the world. A Tudor character is preserved in

Hampton Court Palace

some of the plants. *OPEN Apr-Sep 09.30-18.00 Mon-Sun; Oct-Mar 10.15-16.30 Mon, 09.30-16.30 Tue-Sun. Charge.*

Hatfield House
Hatfield, Herts. (0707) 262823. A mellow and completely preserved Jacobean mansion with magnificent interior built in 1607-11 by Robert Cecil, 1st Earl of Salisbury and still the home of the Cecil family. The Tudor Old Royal Palace nearby was the home of Queen Elizabeth I. Collection of 16th, 17th and 18thC portraits, manuscripts and relics. London 20 miles (A1). For Elizabethan banquets phone (0707) 262055, *all year. House OPEN end Mar-mid Oct 12.00-17.00 Tue-Sat, 13.00-17.00 Sun, 11.00-17.00 B.hols. Charge.*

Hever Castle
Nr Edenbridge, Kent. (0732) 865224. 13th and 15thC moated castle once the home of Anne Boleyn who was courted here by Henry VIII. Excellent furnished rooms of the period and many fine portraits. A delightful garden and lake, landscaped by the first Viscount Astor in 1905 and containing a walled Italianate garden with statues, topiary and fountains. London 25 miles (A21). *OPEN end Mar-end Oct 12.00-18.00 Mon-Sun* (grounds and gardens *from 11.00). Charge.*

Hughenden Manor
High Wycombe, Bucks. (0494) 528051. Benjamin Disraeli's country seat from 1847 until his death in 1881, altered from its original Georgian to typical mid-Victorian. Museum of Disraeli relics. Terraced garden. London 30 miles (A40). *OPEN Apr-Oct 14.00-18.00 Wed-Sun &*

B.hols. Mar 14.00-18.00 Sat & Sun. Charge.

Knebworth House
Knebworth, Herts. (0438) 812661. A successful and imaginative re-creation from the original Tudor built by the 1st Lord Lytton, the Victorian novelist, in 1844. Pleasant garden with adventure playground for children. Barns Restaurant, (0438) 813825. London 30 miles (A1). *OPEN Apr & Jun-Aug, Tue-Sun; May & Sep Sat & Sun;* park *OPEN 11.00-17.30,* house and garden *OPEN 12.00-16.30. CLOSED Oct-Mar. Parties by arrangement. Charge.*

Knole
Sevenoaks, Kent. (0732) 450608. A great Jacobean country house with a splendid park. The family home of the Sackvilles since 1566. The house and its interior survive intact. It is a treasure house of robust gilded decoration and ornament, fine furniture, tapestries and paintings of 16th-18thC. Many ancient trees in the large park with a fine herd of deer (not to be fed). London 25 miles (A21). *OPEN Apr-Oct 11.00-17.00 Wed, Fri, Sat, Sun & B.hols; 14.00-17.00 Thur (guided tours 10.00-13.00 Thur only). Charge.* Gardens *OPEN 1st Wed of month May-Sep. Charge.*

Leeds Castle
Maidstone, Kent. (0622) 765400. A beautiful castle which was traditionally a gift from the Kings of England to their Queens. The moat is in fact a lake fed by the River Len. 200 hectares of parkland include a cottage garden, the Wood Garden, greenhouses, aviaries, the Duckery and the Vineyard. Inside is a wine cellar dating to the 12thC, the

Hatfield House

Leeds Castle

Queen's Gallery, Banqueting Hall, Chapel and Seminar Room. Shop, restaurant, golf course. London 40 miles (M20). *OPEN Mar-Oct 11.00-17.00 Mon-Sun; Nov-Feb 10.00-15.00 Mon-Sun. Charge.*

Leonardslee Gardens
Lower Beeding, Horsham, W. Sussex. (0403) 891212. Overlooking the South Downs and containing ancient 'hammer ponds' from the time when the Weald was a great iron-producing area. Famous for magnolias, azaleas, rhododendrons and camellias. Lovely views and woodland walks. Wallabies and deer. No dogs allowed. Plants for sale. Restaurant and café. London 35 miles (M23). *OPEN Apr-Oct 10.00-18.00 Mon-Sun. Charge.*

Luton Hoo
Luton, Beds. (0582) 22955. Imposing front of original house designed by Robert Adam 1767. Altered in 1903 and interior decorated in French 18thC style. Park designed by Capability Brown. Particularly notable for the Wernher Collection, several large gardens, and important private collection of paintings, tapestries, English porcelain, Fabergé jewels and an unusual collection of mementoes and portraits of the Russian imperial family. London 30 miles (M1, Exit 10). *OPEN Apr-Oct 13.30-17.00 Tue-Sun & B.hols. Charge.*

Marble Hill House
Richmond Rd, Twickenham, Middx. 081-892 5115. Perfect Palladian villa by the Thames. Built 1724-9 for Henrietta Howard, mistress of George II, with interior and furnishings in period. London 11 miles. *OPEN Sep-Apr 10.00-18.00 Mon-Sun. Free.*

Nymans Garden
Handcross, W. Sussex. (0444) 400321. One of the great gardens of the Sussex Weald, originally designed by Colonel Messel. Consists of a heather garden, a sunken garden, a walled garden with herbaceous borders and a rose garden. The rhododendrons are features of great beauty and around the lawns are plants from foreign countries, many of which are rarely seen in England. London 40 miles (M23). *OPEN Apr-Oct 11.00-19.00 (or*

sunset) Tue-Thur, Sat, Sun & B.hols. Charge.

Osterley Park House
Thornbury Rd, Osterley, Middx. 081-560 3918. Remodelled by Robert Adam 1761-78 on an already fine Elizabethan building built round a courtyard. The magnificent interiors with furniture, mirrors, carpets and tapestry all show the elegance and richness of Adam's genius. London 11 miles. *OPEN Apr-Oct 13.00-17.00 Wed-Sat, 11.00-17.00 Sun & B.hols. Charge. Park OPEN all year 09.00-dusk. Free.*

Osterley Park House

Parham
Pulborough, W. Sussex. (0903) 742021. Fine Elizabethan house in a great deer park facing the South Downs, with a superb Great Hall and Long Gallery, and a good collection of portraits. Parham Church is in the grounds. London 50 miles (A24). *OPEN Easter Sun-1st Sun in Oct 14.00-18.00 Sun, Wed, Thur & B.hols. Charge. Gardens OPEN 13.00-18.00. Charge.*

Penshurst Place
Penshurst, Tonbridge, Kent. (0892) 870307. A serene medieval house set amidst flat lawns. Built 1340 and enlarged during Elizabeth I's reign. Magnificent Great Hall with carved timber roof, fine portraits of the Sidney family, early Georgian and Chippendale furniture, and a delightful formal walled garden with ponds and ancient apple trees. London 30 miles (off A21). *OPEN end Mar-Oct 12.00-17.30 (last admission 17.00) Mon-Sun (grounds 11.00-18.00). Guided tours by arrangement; mornings only. Charge.*

Petworth House
Petworth, W. Sussex. (0798) 42207. An impressive 320ft-long (97.6m) house, rebuilt late 17thC and containing a range

of magnificent state rooms. Famous for its splendid 'Carved Room' by the greatest carver in wood, Grinling Gibbons, and a most important collection of paintings including Van Dycks, Reynolds, many Dutch pictures and some particularly superb Turners. Fine deer park. London 50 miles (A283). *OPEN Apr-Oct 13.00-17.00 Tue-Thur, Sat, Sun & B.hols. CLOSED Tue after B.hols. Extra rooms shown Tue, Wed & Thur (except Tue following B.hols). Charge.*

Rousham
Steeple Aston, Oxon. (0869) 47110. One of the best remaining examples of the work of William Kent, carried out 1738-40. Original interior decoration, painted ceilings and furniture within the Jacobean house. Kent's delightful classic garden beside the Cherwell, with statues (by Van Nost), glades and cascades, remains unaltered. London 65 miles (A423). *OPEN Apr-Sep 14.00-16.30 Wed, Sun & B.hols. Guided tours. Garden OPEN all year 10.00-16.30 (last admission). Charge.*

Royal Pavilion, Brighton
Old Steine, Brighton, E. Sussex. (0273) 603005. A fantastic Oriental seaside 'villa', complete with onion domes, and minarets, built for the Prince Regent (later George IV), when John Nash in 1815-22. The lavish Chinese-style state rooms are breathtaking, the original furniture has been returned from Buckingham Palace and the exemplary restorations, after years of neglect, were completed in 1991. London 45 miles (A23). *OPEN Jun-Sep 10.00-18.00 Mon-Sun; Oct-May 10.00-17.00 Mon-Sun. Charge.*

Sheffield Park Garden
Nr Uckfield, E. Sussex. (0825) 790655. Magnificent garden by Capability Brown 1775. London 43 miles (A22). *OPEN Apr-beg Nov 11.00-18.00 (or sunset) Tue-Sat, 14.00 (13.00 Oct & Nov)-18.00 (or sunset) Sun & B.hol Mons. CLOSED Mon & Tue following B.hol Mon. Last admission 1 hr before closing. Charge.*

Royal Pavilion

Sissinghurst Castle
Sissinghurst, Kent. (0580) 712850. The soft red-brick remains of the walls and buildings of a once extensive Tudor manor, enchantingly transformed by the late Victoria Sackville-West and Sir Harold Nicolson into numerous enclosed walled gardens. Each is different in character and outstandingly beautiful in its richness of flowers and shrubs. No dogs. London 40 miles (A21). *OPEN Apr-Oct 13.00-18.30 Tue-Fri, 10.00-18.30 Sat, Sun & Good Friday. CLOSED Mon (inc B.hols). Charge.*

Stowe School
Stowe, nr Buckingham, Bucks. (0280) 822850. Chiefly famous for its succession of notable landscape gardeners and garden architects: Bridgeman, Vanbrugh, James Gibbs, William Kent and Capability Brown. They produced the fine gardens, park, lake and Palladian bridges, temples and garden pavilions. London 55 miles (A413). *Garden. OPEN in school holidays 10.00-18.00 Mon-Sun. Phone for details of opening times during term-time. Charge.*

Strawberry Hill
Waldegrave Rd, Twickenham, Middx. 081-892 0051. One of the earliest examples of the Gothic Revival, this romantic, rococo building was converted from 'a little plaything house' (1750-76) by Horace Walpole. It now stands in the grounds of a college. *Appt only.*

Syon House
Park Rd, Brentford, Middx. 081-560 0881. The exterior is the original convent building of the 15thC, but the interior 1762-9 is by Robert Adam. The imaginative elegance and variety in each room is unsurpassed. Garden by Capability Brown. Additional attractions include the London Butterfly House and an excellent garden centre. *House OPEN Apr-Oct 11.00-17.00 Wed-Sun & B.hol Mon. Charge. Gardens OPEN Apr-Oct 10.00-18.00 Mon-Sun; Nov-Mar 10.00-17.00 Mon-Sun. Butterfly House OPEN Mar-Nov 10.00-17.00 Mon-Sun; Dec-Feb*

10.00-15.30. *Charge.* Garden centre
OPEN all year 09.30-17.30 Mon-Sun.

Uppark House

Petersfield, Hants. (0730) 825317.
Beautifully simple 17thC house on the
ridge of the South Downs, by William
Talman 1690. Home of Emma Hamilton
and H. G. Wells' mother. Faultless 18thC
interiors with fine plasterwork and ceilings.
(Due to fire damage only reconstruction
work is on view, although the grounds are
open.) London 50 miles (A3). No dogs.
*Phone for opening times. CLOSED Oct-
Mar. Charge.*

The Vyne

Sherborne St John, Basingstoke, Hants.
(0256) 881337. Early 16thC mansion with
private chapel containing original glass. A
classic-style portico was added in 1654.
Fine Long Gallery with 'linenfold' carving
on the panels throughout its length.
18thC staircase by John Chute. London
45 miles (M3). Tea-room and shop. *OPEN
Apr-Oct 13.30 (grounds from 12.30)-
17.30 Tue-Thur, Sat & Sun, 11.00-17.30
B.hols (CLOSED following Tue). Last
admission 17.00. Charge.*

Waddesdon Manor

Nr Aylesbury, Bucks. (0296) 651211. An
extraordinary house built 1874-89 for
Baron Ferdinand de Rothschild by the
French architect Gabriel-Hippolyte
Destailleur, in the style of a great château
in Touraine. The garden, fountains and
large aviary of rare birds are enchanting.
The house contains a superb collection of
works of art, mostly of the 17th and
18thC. Fine French furniture, Savonnerie
carpets, 18thC terracotta figures, and
remarkable collections of Sèvres and
Meissen porcelain. The paintings include
Rubens' *Garden of Love*, eight views of
Venice by Guardi, many portraits by
Gainsborough and Reynolds, including
the latter's *Pink Boy*, and paintings by
Watteau and Boucher. London 45 miles
(A41). Grounds, tea room and aviary
*OPEN 11.00-17.00 Wed-Sun. House
closed for restoration at time of
publication.*

Warwick Castle

Warwick, Warks. (0926) 495421. One of
the finest medieval castles in the country,
famed for its dungeons and peacocks.
The views from the ramparts are breathtaking. Inside the castle, in private royal
apartments, is a re-creation of a Royal
Weekend Party which gives an insight
into the former glory of the castle and its
occupants. Grounds landscaped by
Capability Brown. Victorian Rose Garden
laid out to the original designs. Café,
restaurant. London 85 miles (A41). *OPEN
Mar-Oct 10.00-17.30 Mon-Sun; Nov-Feb
10.00-16.30 Mon-Sun.* Victorian Rose
Garden *OPEN all year.*

West Wycombe Park

High Wycombe, Bucks. (0494) 524411.
Georgian house rebuilt 1745-71, by Sir
Francis Dashwood. Still the home of the
Dashwood family, it has good furniture,
painted ceilings and frescoed walls. The
landscaped grounds are dotted with
garden buildings, including Roman and
Greek temples, a flint mausoleum and, on
the opposite hill, the cave where the
notorious 18thC drinking club, the Hell
Fire Club, is reputed to have met. London
30 miles (A40). House and grounds
*OPEN Jun-Aug 14.00-17.00 Sun-Thur.
Charge. Caves OPEN Apr-Sep 11.00-
18.00 Mon-Sun; Oct-Mar 13.00-17.00
Mon-Sun. Charge.*

Windsor Castle

Windsor, Berks. (0753) 868286. An
imposing 800-year-old medieval fortress.
12thC Round Tower built by Henry II.
St George's chapel is fine 16thC perpen-
dicular. Magnificent state apartments.
London 20 miles (M4). Castle precinct
*OPEN Apr-Oct 10.00-18.00 Mon-Sun;
Nov-Mar 10.00-16.00 Mon-Sun.
CLOSED Garter Day (2nd or 3rd Mon in
Jun) and any State Visit arrival day.
Charge.* State Apartments *OPEN Apr-Oct
10.30-17.00 Mon-Sun; Oct-Mar 10.30-
16.00 Mon-Sun. CLOSED when Queen is
in residence – usually 6 weeks at Easter,
3 weeks in Jun and 3 weeks at Xmas.
Charge.*

Woburn Abbey

Woburn, Beds. (0525) 290666. The Duke
of Bedford's 18thC mansion, set in a fine
3000-acre (1215ha) park landscaped by

Warwick Castle

Woburn
Abbey

Humphry Repton (part of which has been converted into a safari park). The house retains the quadrangular plan of the medieval monastery from which it also derived its site and name. Remodelling has occurred at different periods; the west front and the magnificent state apartments were done in 1747-60 by Henry Flitcroft; the south side, the lovely Chinese dairy and the orangery in 1802 by Henry Holland. Incomparable collec-tion of pictures by Rembrandt, Van Dyck, Reynolds, Gainsborough, Holbein, and a famous group of fine Canalettos. English and French furniture, porcelain and silver. London 40 miles (M1). Abbey OPEN Apr-Oct 11.00-17.00 Mon-Sat, 11.00-17.30 Sun & B.hols; Nov-Feb 11.00-17.30 Sat & Sun. Charge. Safari Park OPEN Mar-Oct 10.00-17.00 Mon-Sun. Charge. Deer Park OPEN Apr-Oct 10.00-16.45 Mon-Sat, 10.00-17.45 Sun.

Historic London

London's history begins in AD43 when invading Romans bridged the Thames. Around AD200 they built the London Wall (traces of which are still visible today, see entry in this chapter). This was to determine the shape of what we still call the City of London for some 1300 years. The Normans incorporated the Wall into their defences and, despite the extensive devastation and damage caused by the Great Fire of 1666, no radical replanning took place within the 'Square Mile'.

However, post-Fire London was to expand well beyond the historic City and its neighbour Westminster – originally a Saxon religious settlement and a seat of government in Norman times – absorbing in the process numerous surrounding villages which have now given their names to districts of the capital.

London's growth resulted from rising commercial importance (the City is still one of the world's major financial centres), the industrial revolution and, more recently, developing public transport which pushed new suburbs well out into the countryside. Cities change; London has changed more than many. But despite the Blitz and decades of redevelopment, every stage of London's history, including the present, can be traced in her buildings, monuments, churches and famous houses.

Looking at history

The following entries are of important places, buildings, characteristic areas and also some of those elements that make London unique in its people and its history.

Abbey Mills Pumping Station

Abbey La E15. 081-534 6717. An unusu-al building of cupolas and domes built in 1865 to pump the 83 miles of main sewers draining the 100 sq miles of London. This remarkable piece of drainage engineering was the work of the engineer Joseph Bazalgette and still survives intact and perfect after well over 100 years of use. Visits by arrangement. Maximum 15 people.

Admiralty Arch   4 **E4**

Entrance to the Mall SW1. Massive Edwardian triple arch by Sir Aston Webb 1910. A memorial to Queen Victoria.

Admiralty Arch

Albany 4 D4

Piccadilly W1. Patrician Georgian mansion 1770-4 by Sir William Chambers. Now privately-owned residences with quiet public forecourt.

Albert Memorial 3 E5

Kensington Gore SW7. Gothic memorial to Prince Albert, consort of Queen Victoria, by Sir George Gilbert Scott 1872. *Due to extensive restoration work, the memorial is currently covered.*

Albert Memorial

Annesley Lodge

Platts La NW3. A fine example of an Art Nouveau house by C.F.A. Voysey, built 1895.

Apsley House 4 B5

149 Piccadilly W1. 071-499 5676. Robert Adam 1771-8 but altered in 1828 by Wyatt. Home of the Duke of Wellington from 1817-52, it now houses the Wellington Museum containing paintings, silver plate, porcelain and personal and military relics. Near-naked statue of Napoleon stands a startling 11ft (3.4m) high in the staircase well. *OPEN 11.00-17.00 Tue-Sun. Charge. Closed for restoration at time of publication.*

Apsley House

Atlas House 5 D2

3 King St EC2. One of London's earliest surviving purpose-designed office buildings completed in 1836 by Thomas Hopper for the Atlas Insurance Company.

Ball Court 5 E2

Next to 39 Cornhill EC3. Straight out of Dickens. Simpson's chop house built in 1757.

Bank of England 5 E2

Threadneedle St EC2. 071-601 5545. The vaults hold the nation's gold

Bank of England

reserves. Outer walls are still the original design by Sir John Soane, architect to the Bank 1788-1833. Rebuilt by Sir Herbert Baker 1925-39. Museum *OPEN Easter-Sep 10.00-17.00 Mon-Fri, 11.00-17.00 Sat & Sun; Oct-Easter 10.00-17.00 Mon-Fri, CLOSED Sat & Sun. Special presentations by appt only. Free.*

Bankside 5 D3

Southwark SE1. Thames-side walk with the finest views of St Paul's and the City across the river and 'The Anchor', historic riverside inn rebuilt c1750. Here were Shakespeare's theatres; his Globe is marked by a plaque in Park St and a working reconstruction of it, following the original designs of 1599, is being constructed in Emerson St, now renamed New Globe Walk. Number 49 Bankside is reputed to be the house in which Wren lodged while St Paul's was being built.

Bedford Park W4

Just north of Turnham Green station, the earliest planned suburb, laid out 1875-81 by Norman Shaw, who designed a number of the houses.

Belgravia SW1 7 A1

Thomas Cubitt converted a swamp almost level with the Thames and intersected by mud banks into the posh village of Belgravia. Draining the site, he turned its clay into bricks, built up its substrata of gravel and, in 1827, started on streets, mansions and houses from designs by George Basevi, Disraeli's uncle. Cubitt died in 1856, but his firm then completed Cubitt Town in Poplar, one of the great industrial parishes on the Thames.

Blackheath SE3

High, open and grassy. Bordered by 18thC houses including 'The Paragon', and the pleasant village of Blackheath.

The Blitz

Although the Docks and the City were

prime targets during World War II, bombs rained all over London. The Blitz (prolonged intensive attacks by German bombers) lasted for nine months beginning Sep 1940. In June 1944 a renewed assault with V1s ('Doodlebugs') began and lasted nearly a year. Later, V2 rockets arrived with such speed (3600 mph) that they were virtually invisible; the first fell at Chiswick but was heard at Westminster; another hit a New Cross Woolworth's and killed 160 people. Many Londoners spent their nights in air-raid shelters or bedded down in the tube stations. Ten thousand people could fit into Liverpool Street tube station. Over 1.5 million homes were damaged by bombing and 100,000 houses were destroyed. In the City alone, 164 out of 460 acres (66.4 out of 186.3ha) were wiped out. Historic buildings, including churches, were destroyed and damaged.

Bloomsbury Squares WC1　　1 G6
Elegant Regency-style houses and squares: Bedford Sq, Russell Sq, Tavistock Sq etc. Many by Thomas Cubitt, mid 19thC.

Bond Street W1　　4 C3
Fashionable high street. Originally laid out in the 1680s, it no longer has any architectural distinction but is noted for its art dealers' galleries, fashion and quality shops.

Bridges
The tidal Thames has 17 bridges. Noteworthy ones in central London are:

Albert Bridge　　6 E4
Unusual rigid chain suspension. Built by Ordish 1871-3.

Chelsea Bridge　　7 B4
Original 1858. Rebuilt as suspension bridge by Rendel, Palmer & Tritton 1935-7.

London Bridge　　5 E4
The site of many replacements. Wooden construction until 12thC; the famous stone bridge that followed carried houses and shops. Granite bridge built in 1832 by

Tower Bridge

Rennie was shipped off to Lake Havasu City, Arizona in 1971. Latest construction completed 1973.

Tower Bridge　　5 G4
071-407 0922. Victorian-Gothic towers with hydraulic twin drawbridge. Jones and Wolfe-Barry 1894. Enter by the tower closest to the Tower of London and take lift to high walkways for breathtaking views of London and the Thames. 1994 is Tower Bridge's centenary year and a new permanent museum exhibition, 'The Celebration Story', will bring to life the history, human endeavour and engineering achievement which created this famous landmark. *OPEN Apr-Oct 10.00-18.30 Mon-Sun; Nov-Mar 10.00-17.15 Mon-Sun. Charge. The museum will be closed during 1993 while the new exhibition is being built. Phone for details.*

Waterloo Bridge　　4 G3
Concrete. Fine design by Sir Giles Gilbert Scott 1937-42.

Westminster Bridge　　4 F5
Graceful cast iron. Thomas Page 1862.

Brixton Windmill
Blenheim Gdns SW2. Elegant windmill of the tower type, built 1816. Now restored.

Buckingham Palace　　4 D5
St James's Park SW1. The official London residence of the Sovereign. Originally built 1705, remodelled by Nash 1825 and Edward Blore 1830-47; refaced 1913 by Sir Aston Webb. Open to the public for the first time; visitors can see most of the state apartments and the

Albert Bridge

Buckingham Palace

Queen's Picture Gallery. *OPEN Aug & Sep. Phone 071-930 5526 for tickets.*

Burlington Arcade   **4 D3**
Piccadilly W1. 1819 Regency shopping promenade with original shop windows. Still employs a beadle to preserve the gracious atmosphere.

Burlington House   **4 D3**
Piccadilly W1. Victorian-Renaissance facade on one of the great 18thC palaces. Houses the Royal Academy and various Royal Societies.

Cadogan Square SW1   **6 F1**
A typical 19thC Chelsea square of red-brick houses.

Canals
Many years before railways were built canals carried goods in and out of London. The Grand Union Canal (opened in 1800) provided a link from Brentford to the Midlands; in 1820 a direct link to the Thames dockland was completed. The Regent's Canal, once London's main artery, is still in good condition although its working days are over. At Camden, where the lock starts a 90ft (27.5m) drop to the Thames, you can see houseboats bobbing stem to stern and, occasionally, a cruising pleasure boat. Towpaths there, at Little Venice in Paddington, and a tree-lined cutting that goes through the zoo in Regent's Park, afford close-up views of the canal.

Cemeteries
Cemeteries didn't exist until the 19thC. Before that churchyards sufficed but the pressing burial needs of a rapidly expanding population caused problems of over-crowding (and sometimes cholera). Thus large non-denominational cemeteries were started. They were privately owned and designed by architects and land-scape gardeners, though nowadays they are mostly overgrown. The following are notable:

Brompton   **6 B4**
Old Brompton Rd SW10. Classical architecture; circular central colonnade beneath which lie the catacombs.

City of London
Aldersbrook Rd E12. 200 acres (81ha) of avenues, rhododendrons and Gothic chapels and catacombs. The largest municipal cemetery in Europe.

Highgate
Swains La N6. 081-340 1834. Designed by Stephen Geary. The Friends of Highgate Cemetery guide visitors round the beautiful older western section: tours *Apr-Oct at 12.00, 14.00 & 16.00 Mon-Fri, on the hour 11.00-16.00 Sat & Sun; Nov-Mar at 12.00, 14.00 & 15.00 Tue-Fri, on the hour 11.00-15.00 Sat & Sun.* Thanks to their efforts much of the aggressive sycamore has been removed to allow native woodland to flourish, and wild flowers and birds abound. The eclectic assembly of 19thC society buried here includes bare-fisted prizefighter Tom Sayers, whose grave is guarded by a mastiff who attended his master's funeral in a carriage of his own; and menagerist George Wombwell, lying beneath a colossal, slumbering lion. Other funerary sculpture highlighting the Victorian way of death includes hovering angels, ivy-clad mourners making ephemeral appearances beside winding paths, and the celebrated female figure of *Religion* by Joseph Edwards, lost beneath wreathing ivy for many years. The grand Egyptian gateway leads to the Cedar of Lebanon Circle. Look out for the towering classical mausoleum to financier Julius Beer and for the occasional Gothic shrine. The eastern cemetery, resting place of George Eliot, George Holyoake (pioneer organiser of workers' co-operatives), Herbert Spencer (sociologist and philosopher), Sir Ralph Richardson and, of course, Karl Marx is *OPEN Apr-Oct 10.00-17.00 Mon-Sun; Nov-Mar 10.00-16.00 Mon-Sun. CLOSED during funerals. Charge.*

Kensal Green
Harrow Rd W10. In its splendid 56 acres (22.7ha) of stone and marble tombs there can be traced the decline of the 'classic' and the use of the Gothic. Wilkie Collins, the two Brunels, Princess Sophia, the Duke of Sussex, Thackeray and Trollope lie here.

Tower Hamlets
Southern Gro E3. Privately built in 1841 to provide burial space for wealthy Londoners, this Victorian cemetery has provided a superb natural habitat for a variety of wildlife since it ceased being used for burials in 1966. Gothic architecture. Cemetery tree trail.

The Cenotaph   4 F5
Whitehall SW1. Designed 1920 by Sir Edwin Lutyens to honour the dead of World War I. The annual service of remembrance takes place here.

Chandos House   4 C1
Chandos St W1. Fine Robert Adam house built 1869-70.

Charing Cross WC2   4 F4
The Charing Cross was the last of the stone crosses set up by Edward I to mark the funeral resting places of Queen Eleanor's body on its way to Westminster Abbey. Originally placed where Trafalgar Sq now is, it was demolished in 1647 and the statue of Charles I now stands in its place. The stone cross in the station courtyard is an 1865 replica.

Charlton House
See under Greenwich.

Charterhouse   2 D6
Charterhouse Sq EC1. 071-253 9503. 14thC Carthusian monastery then a private house 1545-1611 which was converted into an almshouse and school. Now a house for 'gentlemen pensioners'. Cloister and Cell with 16thC Great Hall. *OPEN Apr-Jul. Guided tour at 14.15. Charge.*

Chelsea Royal Hospital   6 F3
Royal Hospital Rd SW3. 071-730 0161. Fine, austere building. 1682 by Wren. Stables 1814-17 by Sir John Soane. Museum. *OPEN 10.00-12.00 & 14.00-16.00 Mon-Sat, 14.00-16.00 Sun. CLOSED Sun Oct-Mar. Free.*

Chiswick House
Burlington La W4. 081-995 0508. Lovely Palladian villa built in the grand manner by 3rd Earl of Burlington 1725-30. Fine interiors and gardens by William Kent. *OPEN Apr-Sep 10.00-13.00 & 14.00-18.00 Mon-Sun; Oct-Mar 10.00-13.00 & 14.00-16.00 Mon-Sun. Charge.*

Chiswick House

Chiswick Mall W4
17th-18thC riverside houses.

The Citadel   4 E4
The Mall SW1. Creeper-covered concrete. Built as a bomb proof unit by the Admiralty 1940.

Clarence House   4 D5
Stable Yard Gate SW1. Mansion by Nash 1825. Now the home of the Queen Mother.

Cleopatra's Needle   5 A3
Victoria Embankment SW1. From Heliopolis. 1500BC. Presented by Egypt and set up next to the Thames 1878.

41-42 Cloth Fair EC1   5 C1
A rare domestic survivor of the Great Fire, with its two-storey bay windows of timber (forbidden in post-Fire reconstruction) much restored. Peep round the corner in Cloth Ct at the dummy window painted with a faded Victorian parlour scene.

Cock Lane   5 C1
Scene of the notorious 'ghost' hoax of the 18thC and once the only walk licensed for prostitutes within the City.

Cockney or rhyming slang
A particular accent and form of language still exists today which was once the common language of the people of the slums of London, particularly of the East End. To an acute ear a mere sentence at one time would reveal where in London you were born, which school your parents could afford and what your father did for a living. In addition to this very characteristic accent, the petty criminals of the City and the East End developed their own way of communicating by obscuring a dangerous word in a form of 'rhyming slang'. This in turn developed into a general misuse of most words – to the utter mystification of strangers. Instances are: 'apples and pears' for stairs, 'Lady Godiva' for fiver (£5 note); 'Cain and Abel' for table; 'Dickie dirt' for shirt – there are countless others.

College of Arms   5 D3
Queen Victoria St EC4. 071-248 2762. Handsome late 17thC building which houses the official records of English, Welsh and Irish heraldry and genealogy. *OPEN 10.00-16.00 Mon-Fri. Free.*

Covent Garden Market WC2   4 F3
Originally designed by Inigo Jones (with his St Paul's church) as a residential square in the 1630s. Market buildings dating from 1830 by Fowler. Floral Hall added in 1860 by E.M. Barry, architect of the Royal Opera House (1858). In 1974 the market moved to Nine Elms, but the area survived to become a flourishing new community, with eclectic, though

expensive, shopping centre, restaurants, London Transport Museum and Theatre Museum.

Crewe House   4 **C4**

15 Curzon St W1. Georgian town house, 1735 by Edward Shepherd, who gave his name to Shepherd Market nearby. It was for many years the home of the Marquess of Crewe.

Croydon Palace

Old Palace Rd, Croydon, Surrey. 081-680 5877. A 'standing house' of the Archbishops of Canterbury for over 1000 years, Croydon Palace is now a girls' school. Magnificent 15thC banqueting hall and Tudor chapel. Tours *14.00-14.30 Mon-Sat during certain school hols, Apr, May & Jul. Charge.*

Custom House   5 **F3**

Lower Thames St EC3. Rebuilt many times. Admired for its classical river front by Robert Smirke.

Downing Street SW1   4 **F5**

17thC street; houses built by Sir George Downing. No. 10 is the official residence of the Prime Minister; No. 11 that of the Chancellor of the Exchequer.

Drapers Company Hall   5 **E2**

Throgmorton Av EC2. City Livery Hall dating from 1667 but largely rebuilt in 1870. Fine staircase and collection of plate. For information on tours of all Livery Company Halls contact the City Information Centre, St Paul's Churchyard EC4 (5 **D2**). 071-606 3030 ex1456.

Eltham Palace

Off Court Yd, Eltham SE9. 081-859 2112. 15thC royal palace until Henry VIII. Also remains of earlier royal residences. Great Hall with hammer beam roof and a very fine 15thC bridge over the moat. *OPEN summer 10.00-18.00 Thur & Sun; winter 10.00-16.00. Free.*

Fitzroy Square W1   1 **E5**

The south and east sides 1790-4 by Robert Adam. Now pedestrianised with a landscaped garden.

Flamsteed House

See Greenwich: Old Royal Observatory.

Fleet Street EC4   5 **B2**

London's 'Street of Ink' associated with printing since Caxton. Most newspapers have moved to new hi-tech offices and only a few remain but the association continues.

Fulham Gasometer   6 **C6**

Fulham Gasworks SW6. The oldest gasholder in the world; built in 1830 by Winsor & Mindock. Diameter 100ft (30.5m), capacity 250,000 ft³ (7075m³). An extraordinary piece of early industrial engineering.

Fulham Palace

Fulham Palace Rd SW6. 071-736 5821. Ex-residence of the Bishop of London. 16thC building with riverside park. Grounds *OPEN daily.* **Museum of Fulham Palace** 071-736 3233. *OPEN Mar-Oct 14.00-17.00 Wed-Sun; Nov-Feb 13.00-16.00 Wed-Sun. Charge.*

George Inn   5 **E4**

77 Borough High St SE1. 071-407 2056. Built 1677. London's only surviving galleried inn of the kind which inspired early English theatre design.

Goldsmiths' Hall   5 **D2**

Foster La EC2. 071-606 7010. Pre-Victorian classical-style palazzo built in 1835 by Hardwick. Occasional exhibitions. For information on tours of all Livery Company Halls contact the City Information Centre, St Paul's Churchyard EC4 (5 **D2**). 071-606 3030 ex1456.

Goodwin's Court   4 **F3**

St Martin's La WC2. A completely intact row of bow-windowed 17thC houses.

Gray's Inn   5 **B1**

High Holborn WC1. 071-405 8164. Entrance from passage next to Cittie of York pub, 22 High Holborn. An Inn of Court since 14thC. The Hall (16thC) and 'Buildings' restored after bomb damage. Gardens were laid out by Francis Bacon. Hall *OPEN by written application to the Under Treasurer.* Gardens *OPEN 12.00-14.30 Mon-Fri. Free.*

Greenwich

Six miles downriver and associated with England's former sea power. The following are notable:

Charlton House

Charlton Rd SE7. 081-856 3951. Perfect small red-brick Jacobean manor house on an 'H' plan, built 1607-12. Fine ceilings, staircase and some bizarre chimney-pieces. A very active community centre. Staff happy to show visitors round when circumstances permit. Lunchtime is easiest. *Phone manager for appt. Free.*

The Cutty Sark

King William Wlk SE10. 081-858 3445. Stands in dry-dock. One of the great sailing tea-clippers, built 1869. *Gipsy Moth IV*, the boat in which Sir Francis Chichester sailed the world in 1966, stands in dry-dock next to the *Cutty Sark*. Both ships *OPEN Apr-Sep 10.00-17.30 Mon-Sat, 12.00-17.30 Sun; Oct-Mar 10.00-16.30 Mon-Sat, 12.00-16.30 Sun. Charge.*

National Maritime Museum

Romney Rd SE10. 081-858 4422. Finest maritime collection of paintings, navigational instruments, costumes and

National Maritime Museum

weapons. *'Twentieth Century Seapower'* is a permanent gallery illustrating seapower on a global scale with paintings, watercolours, ship models, photographs and medals. *OPEN Apr-Oct 10.00-18.00 Mon-Sat, 14.00-18.00 Sun; Nov-Mar 10.00-17.00 Mon-Sat, 14.00-17.00 Sun. Charge.*

The Queen's House
Romney Rd SE10. 081-858 4422. Now part of the National Maritime Museum. Built by Inigo Jones, 1619-40, for the Queen of Denmark. Recently renovated. *OPEN summer 10.00-18.00 Mon-Sat, 12.00-18.00 Sun; winter 10.00-17.00 Sat, 14.00-17.00 Sun. Charge.*

The Queen's House

Old Royal Observatory
Greenwich Park SE10. 081-858 1167. Formerly the Greenwich Observatory. Part of the National Maritime Museum and includes Flamsteed House. Designed by Wren and founded by Charles II in 1675. Time and astronomical instruments; the Meridian Line; largest refracting telescope in the UK. Most of the pioneer work in the development of astronomy and nautical navigation was done here. *OPEN Apr-Oct 10.00-18.00 Mon-Sat, 14.00-18.00 Sun; Nov-Mar 10.00-17.00 Mon-Sat, 14.00-17.00 Sun. Charge.*

Ranger's House
Chesterfield Wlk SE10. 081-853 0035. 18thC red-brick villa, once home to the 4th Earl of Charterfield. Suffolk Collection

Royal Naval College

of paintings. *OPEN Easter-Sep 10.00-13.00 & 14.00-18.00 Mon-Sun; Oct-Mar 10.00-13.00 & 14.00-16.00 Mon-Sun. Free.*

Royal Naval College
Greenwich SE10. 081-858 2154. The site of the former royal palace of the Tudor sovereigns. A fine and interesting group of classical buildings by Webb 1664, Wren 1694 and Vanbrugh 1728. Chapel by James 'Athenian' Stuart 1789 and Painted Hall by Thornhill 1708. *OPEN 14.30-16.45. CLOSED Thur. Free.*

Rotunda Museum
Woolwich Common SE18. 081-854 2242 ex3127. Pavilion by Nash 1814. Renowned museum displaying a highly impressive array of artillery starting with the 1346 Crécy bombard. *OPEN Apr-Oct 12.00-17.00 Mon-Fri, 13.00-17.00 Sat & Sun; Nov-Mar 12.00-16.00 Mon-Fri, 13.00-16.00 Sat & Sun. Free.*

Vanbrugh Castle
3 Westcombe Park Rd, Maze Hill SE3. Sir John Vanbrugh's own house 1717-26. Outside of the house can be seen – best view from east side of the park.

Guildhall

Guildhall   5 D2
Off Gresham St EC2. 071-606 3030. 15thC with alterations to the facade by George Dance, 1789, and later restorations by Sir Giles Gilbert Scott. The Great Hall is used for ceremonial occasions. Medieval groined vaulting in crypts. Roman amphitheatre recently excavated in the courtyard *(viewing only by special arrangement)*. Great Hall *OPEN 09.00-17.00 Mon-Sat. Free.* Library *OPEN 09.30-17.00 Mon-Sat. Free.* The Museum of the Clockmakers Company is contained within the library and is *OPEN 09.30-16.45 Mon-Fri. Free.*

Houses of Parliament

Gunnersbury Park W3
081-992 1612. Regency house of the Rothschilds. Museum of local history, including transport. Park. *OPEN Mar-Oct 13.00-17.00 Mon-Fri, 13.00-18.00 Sat & Sun; Nov-Feb 13.00-16.00 Mon-Sun. Free.*

Hammersmith Mall
Upper & Lower Mall W6. Boathouses, riverside pubs and terraces of Georgian houses, including Kelmscott House, 1780, where William Morris lived and founded his printing press.

Hampstead Garden Suburb
Good pioneering suburban planning. Laid out by Sir Raymond Unwin and Barry Parker, 1907.

Hampstead Village NW3
Still very much a village of Georgian houses and alleyways. Church Row, Holly Mount and Regency houses on Downshire Hill, including Keats' House, are notable.

Highgate N6
Here you stand level with the cross of St Paul's. A village full of 18thC surprises.

Highgate Archway N6
Carries Hornsey La across Archway Rd. London's first 'flyover'. Originally built in 1813 and replaced by present structure in 1897. From the top you see the whole of London laid out before you.

Holborn Viaduct EC1   5 C2
William Heyward, 1869. Fine example of Victorian cast iron, and a pioneer traffic improvement scheme.

Holland House   3 A5
Holland Park W8. Jacobean house restored after extensive war damage and now used partly as a youth hostel and open-air theatre.

Honourable Artillery   2 F5
Company
Armoury House, City Rd EC1. 071-606 4644. Victorian castellated fortress (1857) hides the Georgian (1735) headquarters of the oldest regiment in the British Army. Supplies Guard of Honour for Lord

Mayor's Shows and for Royalty visiting the City. *OPEN by arrangement only. Write in advance to the Chief Executive at the above address.*

House of St Barnabas   4 E2
1 Greek St W1. 071-437 1894. Early Georgian town house in Soho Sq with mock-Gothic chapel, fine carvings and rococo plasterwork. Connections with Dickens and Gladstone. Now a temporary refuge for distressed women. *OPEN 14.30-16.15 Wed, 11.00-12.30 Thur. Free.*

Houses of Parliament   4 F5
St Margaret St SW1. 071-219 3000. Victorian-Gothic building 1840-68 by Sir Charles Barry and A.W.N. Pugin. Westminster Hall was built in 1099 as the Great Hall of William Rufus' new palace; the roof dates from the late 14thC. *Admission to the House of Commons during debates by application to your MP (or embassy for foreigners) or by queueing. Tours of Westminster Hall and the Palace of Westminster by application to your MP. Free.*

Hyde Park Corner SW1   4 B5
Consists of Constitution Arch at the top of Constitution Hill, and the Ionic screen of three classical-style triumphal arches at the entry to Hyde Park, by Decimus Burton, 1825. Admire too the Duke of Wellington's former home Apsley House, once known as 'Number One, London'.

Constitution Arch

Inns of Chancery   5 B1
Before the 18thC, a student of law had first to go through one of the nine Inns of

Chancery then existing. They have now mostly disappeared. Staple Inn, High Holborn remains a fine Elizabethan building. Others survive only as names: Clifford Inn, Thavies Inn and Furnival's Inn.

Jewel Tower   4 F6
Old Palace Yd SW1. 071-222 2219. 14thC fragment of the old palace of Westminster. *OPEN Easter-Sep 10.00-18.00 Mon-Sun; Oct-Easter 10.00-16.00 Tue-Sun. CLOSED 13.00-14.00. Charge.*

Kensington Palace   3 C4
Kensington Gdns W8. 071-937 9561. Bought in 1689 by William III and altered by Wren, Hawksmoor and William Kent; attribution of the Orangery, of exceptionally fine brick, is uncertain. Queen Victoria and Queen Mary born here. State apartments and Costume Museum. *OPEN 09.00-17.00 Mon-Sat, 11.00-17.00 Sun (last admission 16.15). Charge.*

Kensington Palace Gardens W8   3 C4
A street of prosperous town mansions in the grand Italianate style, laid out by Pennethorne in 1843, but continued by other famous architects. No. 8a is by Owen Jones and Decimus Burton; No. 12a James Murray; Nos. 18 & 20 by Banks and Barry; No. 13 by C.J. Richardson.

Kenwood House (Iveagh Bequest)
Hampstead La NW3. 081-348 1286. Robert Adam house and interior 1767-9. English 18thC paintings and furniture. Also fine paintings by Rembrandt, Van Dyck and Vermeer. Gardens and wooded estate of 200 acres (81ha). *OPEN Mon-Sun, Easter-Sep 10.00-18.00; Oct-Easter 10.00-16.00. Free.* Refreshments in the coach house.

Kew Palace
Kew, Surrey. 081-332 5216. Small red-brick house in Dutch style. Built 1631. Souvenirs of George III and Queen Charlotte. *OPEN Apr-Sep 10.00-17.30 Mon-Sun. Kew Gardens OPEN 09.30 to dusk Mon-Sun. Charge.*

Kew Palace

Lambeth Palace

Lambeth Palace   7 F1
Lambeth Palace Rd SE1. 071-928 8282. The London residence of the Archbishop of Canterbury since 1197. Remarkable Tudor gatehouse, fine medieval crypt. 14thC Hall with a splendid roof and portraits of archbishops on its walls. The Guard Room, which houses the library, was rebuilt in medieval style in 1633; prominent pendants and blackamoors' heads decorate its elaborate timber roof; the gloves worn by Charles I when he went to the scaffold are on display. Look out for the famous spreading fig tree, planted during Mary Tudor's reign by the last Catholic archbishop, Cardinal Pole; for the brass plate commemorating the negligence of a gardener who put his fork through Archbishop Laud's tortoise, and for the picture of the original Nosy Parker – archbishop under Elizabeth I and the first to have no allegiance to Rome – so called because he had a big nose. *Tours (very restricted) on a Wed or Thur by written application to the Booking Secretary. Charge.*

Lancaster Gate W2   3 E3
Area of fine stucco houses 1865, in and around Lancaster Gate. (Queen's Gdns, Cleveland Sq and Cleveland Gdns.)

Lancaster House   4 D5
Stable Yd, St James's SW1. Early Victorian London town house. Lavish state apartments and painted ceilings. Used for official functions.

Lancaster House

Law Courts   5 B2
Strand WC2. 071-936 6000. Massive Victorian-Gothic building housing the Royal Courts of Justice. *OPEN to public 09.00-17.00 Mon-Fri. Over 16s only. Courts not in session Aug and Sep but open to public. Free.*

Leadenhall Market 5 F2
Gracechurch St EC3. Impressive Victorian glass and iron hall 1881 by Horace Jones preserving the old street pattern; on the site of the Roman basilica.

Lincoln's Inn 5 A2
Lincoln's Inn WC2. 071-405 1393. An Inn of Court 17thC. New Sq, gardens, barristers' chambers and solicitors' offices. A chapel by Inigo Jones (1623), the New Hall and the 15thC Old Hall. Great Hall was built in 1845. The 'Stone Buildings' are by Sir Robert Taylor and were begun in 1774. Still has Dickensian atmosphere. *OPEN 10.00-16.00 Mon-Fri (gardens 12.00-14.30 only). CLOSED Sat & Sun. Admission to the Chapel outside these hours, and to the Hall and Library, by written application to the Treasury Office, Whitehall SW1. Free.*

Lincoln's Inn Fields WC2 5 A2
Seven acres (2.8ha) of gardens laid out by Inigo Jones 1618. Once a famous duelling ground. Criminals were occasionally hanged from its plane trees. Nos. 13 & 14 built 1792 by Sir John Soane. Nos. 57 & 58 built 1730 by Henry Joynes. Nos. 59 & 60 built 1640 attributed to Inigo Jones.

Little Venice 3 D1
W2. Artists, writers, converted barges and the Grand Union Canal.

Lloyds of London 5 F2
Lime St EC3. 071-327 6210. World-famous international insurance market. Huge dealing room in a 240ft (75m) high atrium housing the famous Lutine Bell. Viewing gallery *OPEN to pre-booked groups only.*

London Stone 5 E3
Cannon St EC4. Set into the wall of the Bank of China opposite Cannon Street station. Possibly the Roman Millarium from which all road distances were measured.

London Wall 5 D1
Surviving parts of the Roman and medieval wall around the old city of London can still be seen at St Alphage on the north side of London Wall EC2; St Giles Churchyard, Cripplegate EC1; Jewry St EC3 (5 **G2**); off Trinity Sq EC3 (5 **G3**); and in the Tower of London EC3 (5 **G3**).

Mansion House 5 E2
Walbrook EC4. 071-626 2500. Opposite the Bank of England. Official residence of the Lord Mayor. Palladian building by George Dance 1739. Completed 1752. Sumptuous Egyptian Hall. *OPEN (to parties of 15-40 people only) Tue-Thur by written application. Free Closed for renovation at time of publication.*

Mansion House

Marble Arch W1 3 G3
Designed by John Nash, 1827, based on the Arch of Constantine in Rome. Intended to be a grand new entrance for Buckingham Palace, it wasn't until it was finished that it was discovered that the arch was too narrow for the state coach to pass through so it had to be moved to its present site. From the 14thC to 1783 this was the spot for the Tyburn Gallows, the main execution site where hangings took place watched by excited crowds.

Melbury Road W14 3 A6
Near Holland Park. Contains several notable houses; No. 29 William Burges' Tower House 1875-80; Nos. 8 & 31 are by Norman Shaw 1876 & 1877, and No. 14 Holland Park Rd nearby is by Philip Webb.

Metropolitan Police
In the 18thC, highway robbery on new bridges across the Thames and on roads leading from the Angel and Islington across the fields into the city, necessitated armed patrols for convoys of pedestrians. Nevertheless, the idea of a permanent police force was considered an infringement of freedom by many Londoners. The Metropolitan Police Act, 1829, was pressed into being by Home Secretary Robert Peel; thus the first policemen were known as 'Peelers' and 'Bobbies'. They carried rattles in their coat-tail pockets and police batons. In 1860 a whistle replaced the rattle. In the 20thC women were recruited. The London Bobby, relatively the most benign cop in the world, still doesn't carry a gun on his normal duties. Riot shields have, however, been used in recent disturbances.

Monument 5 E3
Monument St EC3. 071-626 2717. A

Monument

17thC hollow fluted column by Wren to commemorate the Great Fire of London; stands at 202ft (61.5m), a foot in height for every foot in distance from where the fire started in Pudding Lane. Magnificent view. *OPEN Apr-Sep 09.00-17.40 Mon-Fri, 14.00-17.40 Sat & Sun; Oct-Mar 09.00-15.40 Mon-Sat. Charge. Due to close in 1993 for renovation.*

Morden College
19 St Germain's Pl, Morden Rd SE3. 081-858 3365. Characteristic domestic architecture in 18thC landscaped grounds. *Specialist groups only, by written application. Free.*

Nelson's Column   4 E4
Trafalgar Sq WC2. 145ft (44m) high column by William Railton 1839-42. Weighs 16 tons. At the top a statue of Nelson by Baily 1843, minus his eye and arm, both lost in battle.

Nelson's Column

Old Bailey   5 C2
Old Bailey EC4. 071-248 3277. The Central Criminal Court. On the site of old Newgate Prison. Trials open to the public. Gallery *OPEN 10.30-13.00 & 14.00-16.00 Mon-Fri. Minimum age 14 (must be accompanied by an adult until 16). Free.*

Old Operating Theatre   5 E4
Museum & Herb Garrit
9a St Thomas's St, London Bridge SE1. 071-955 4791. A well-preserved early 19thC operating theatre, located in the ex-parish church and old chapel of St Thomas's Hospital (now the Chapter House of Southwark Cathedral). Owned by the Diocese of Southwark. *OPEN 12.30-16.00 Mon, Wed & Fri, and the first Sun of every month. Charge.*

Old Swan House   6 F4
17 Chelsea Embankment SW3. Late 19thC house by R. Norman Shaw.

Pall Mall SW1   4 D4
Early 19thC opulence. This fine street and its surroundings express the confidence and wealth of the London of this period. Pall Mall itself contains two fine buildings by Sir Charles Barry, the Travellers' Club, 1829-32 (Italian-Renaissance revival), and his more mature Reform Club, 1837-41.

Piccadilly Circus W1   4 E3
The confluence of five major thoroughfares. Fountains and statue of Eros 6ft (1.8m) by Gilbert 1893, commemorating Victorian philanthropist Lord Shaftesbury. Its fame is largely sentimental.

Eros

Pimlico SW1   7 C3
Laid out by Cubitt in the 1840s as a less grand neighbour to Belgravia.

Pitshanger Manor
Mattock La W5. 081-567 1227. 18thC country house rebuilt by Soane 1800-10 to create a Regency villa. Recently restored, it has a collection of Martinware pottery and is surrounded by Walpole Park. *OPEN 10.00-17.00 Tue-Sat. Free.*

Postman's Park   5 D2
Churchyard of St Botolph, Aldersgate EC1. Under an alcove are some remarkable tiles recording Victorian deeds of bravery (1880).

Prince Henry's Room   5 B2
17 Fleet St EC4. 071-936 2710. From 1610; oldest domestic building in London. Named after the elder son of James I. Fine plaster ceiling and carved oak panelling. *OPEN 11.00-14.00 Mon-Sat. CLOSED Xmas, New Year, B.hols. Free.*

Prisons
Prisons were not used for punishment until the 19thC. Before that time they were used only for debtors and for those awaiting trial. In those days the principal punishment was death or transportation to Australia and America. The industrial revolution introduced the 'hulks', prison ships moored in the Thames. In the early 19thC the government built prisons in which the most abominable conditions existed. Things gradually changed after many middle-class suffragettes and conscientious objectors were imprisoned around the time of the First World War. Prison improvement has been badly neglected in recent years so that most are now seriously overcrowded. Many of London's prisons (from the outside) are formidable and important buildings architecturally – including Brixton, Holloway, Pentonville, Wandsworth and Wormwood Scrubs – a chilling list.

Queen Anne's Gate SW1   4 E5
Quiet, completely preserved 18thC street in its original state. Close to St James's Park. Statue of Queen Anne near No. 13.

Regent's Canal   3 E1
Paddington Bridge W2 to Regent's Canal Dock E14. The canal was built by James Morgan in 1820 to connect Paddington with the Thames, thus allowing goods to be shipped direct from Birmingham to the Thames by the canal network. The best way to see the canal is to take a boat trip (see 'Canal trips').

Regent's Park environs   1 C4
The park and the surrounding Regency architecture were planned almost entirely by John Nash, 1812-26. Particularly notable are Park Cres, Park Sq, Cambridge Ter, York Ter and Chester Ter. Decimus Burton designed the facades of Cornwall Ter and Clarence Ter.

Regent Street   4 D3
John Nash, asked by George IV (then Prince of Wales) to construct an artery from Carlton House to the royal country home near Regent's Park, not only designed the route for Regent Street but also most of the houses. This took many years since it was pieced together to conform with the various architectural styles along the way. Initially acclaimed, its imminent destruction was celebrated in 1927 when King George V and his Queen drove down its flower-decked length; it was then rebuilt from end to end.

Roman Bath   5 A3
5 Strand La WC2. Disputed origin, restored in the 17thC. Not open but visible from the pathway.

Royal Exchange

Royal Exchange   5 E2
Corner of Threadneedle St and Cornhill EC3. Built in 1884 by Tite. The third building on this site. Originally founded as a market for merchants and craftsmen in 1564, and destroyed in the Great Fire. The second building was also burnt down, in 1838.

Royal Mews   4 C6
Buckingham Palace Rd SW1. 071-930 4832 ex634. The Queen's horses and carriages including the Coronation coach. *OPEN Jan-Mar & Oct-Dec 12.00-16.00 Wed; Apr-Sep 12.00-16.00 Tue-Thur. Last admission 15.30. CLOSED on royal occasions. Charge.*

Royal Opera Arcade   4 E4
Between Pall Mall and Charles II St SW1. John Nash 1816. London's earliest arcade. Pure Regency; bow-fronted shops, glass-domed vaults and elegant lamps.

Royal Society of Arts   4 F3
6-8 John Adam St WC2. 071-930 5115. Built 1774 after the Society was founded in 1754. Fine surviving example of Adam architecture, from the original Adelphi area (now almost entirely demolished).

St James's Palace   4 D4
Pall Mall SW1. Built by Henry VIII with many later additions. Still officially a royal residence. Ceiling of Chapel Royal possibly by Holbein. *No admission to palace. Entry to courtyards only. Free.*

St James's Palace

St James's Street SW1   4 D4
Celebrated for its fine shops and gentlemen's clubs since the early 18thC. Two shops still survive; Berry Bros & Rudd, wine merchants, (No.3), and Lock's the hatters (No.6). Amongst the surviving clubs are Boodle's (No.28) 1775 by J. Crunden and Brooks's (No.60) 1788 by Henry Holland.

St John's Gate   2 D5
St John's La EC1. Once a gateway to the Priory of the Knights Hospitallers of St John of Jerusalem. Built in 1504, it is the only monastic gateway left in London. **Museum of the Order of St John**. 071-253 6644. *OPEN 10.00-17.00 Mon-Fri, to 16.00 Sat; tours at 11.00 & 14.30 Tue, Fri & Sat. Donations welcome.*

Skinners Hall   5 E3
8 Dowgate Hill EC4. 071-236 5629. 17th-18thC buildings and quiet arcaded courtyard. Open days; occasional visits by

arrangement with City Information Centre, St Paul's Churchyard EC4 (**5 D2**). 071-606 3030 ex1456.

Smithfield EC1   **5 C1**

Once 'Smooth Field'. Historical site of the murder of Wat Tyler, tournaments, public executions, cattle market and the famous Bartholomew Fair. In north-east corner original Tudor gatehouse built over 13thC archway leading to Church of St Bartholomew-the-Great (*see 'Churches'*). South-east side occupied by St Bartholomew's Hospital, London's oldest hospital, founded in 1123. Gateway (1702) bears London's only statue of Henry VIII. Smithfield Market is the largest meat market in the world (10 acres – 4ha). The Italianate-style market buildings with some ornamental ironwork were designed by Horace Jones and erected between 1868 and 1899.

Soho   **4 E2**

An area bounded by Regent St, Oxford St, Shaftesbury Av and Charing Cross Rd. Lively and notorious but perfectly safe, except for touts for peep show, nude encounter and strip joint customers. Narrow 18thC streets full of fascinating foreign food shops, restaurants, street markets, flashing neon and nightlife of all sorts. Visit London's 'Chinatown' around Gerrard St.

Somerset House   **4 G3**

Strand WC2. 071-438 6622. On the site of an unfinished 16thC palace. By Sir W. Chambers, 1776. Used to house the register of births, marriages and deaths in England and Wales, now holds the register of divorce, wills and probate, the Inland Revenue and the Courtauld Collection. Admission only to Courtauld Institute Galleries. *OPEN 10.00-18.00 Mon-Sat, 14.00-18.00 Sun. Charge. No admission to Somerset House.*

Spitalfields E1   **5 G1**

This centre of silk-weaving in England was established by the influx of Flemish and French weavers in the 16th and 17thC. The industry reached its height at the end of the 18th and early 19thC when about 17,000 looms were in use and a large area of East London was dependent on these family concerns. Fournier Street is a good example of typical Dutch-style houses of the time. The industry collapsed some 100 years ago.

Stations

Some good examples of 19thC 'railway architecture':

King's Cross   **1 G3**

Euston Rd NW1. Functional. 1851, by Lewis Cubitt.

St Pancras   **1 G4**

Euston Rd NW1. Impressive glass and iron roof by Barlow & Ordish 1863-7. Victorian Gothic facade and former Midland Grand Hotel by Sir George Gilbert Scott 1868-72.

Paddington   **3 E2**

Praed St W2. 1850-2. 'Railway cathedral' engineering at its best by Brunel; the Gothic ornament by Wyatt and Owen Jones; the Renaissance-style hotel by Hardwick.

Stock Exchange   **5 E2**

Old Broad St EC2. 071-588 2355. The home of trading in stocks and shares, where fortunes are made and lost. The public gallery is now closed as a result of a bombing attack in 1990. At present there are no plans to re-open it.

Strand WC2   **4 F3**

Once a 'Strand' – a walk along the river – bordered in Stuart times with mansions and gardens down to the Thames. Their names still survive in the streets: Bedford, Buckingham, Villiers. A major commercial thoroughfare.

The Temple   **5 B3**

Inner Temple, Crown Office Row EC4. 071-797 8217. Middle Temple, Middle Temple La EC4. 071-353 4355. Both are Inns of Court. Enter by the gatehouse, 1685, in Middle Temple La. An extensive area of courtyards, alleys, gardens and warm brick buildings. Step back into the 19thC on misty winter afternoons when the lamplighter lights the gas lamps. Middle Temple Hall 1570. The restored Temple Church is one of only four remaining early Gothic round churches built by the Templars in England. 12th-13thC. Inner Temple *OPEN 10.00-16.00 Mon-Fri by arrangement. CLOSED Sat & Sun, B.hols & legal vacations.* Middle Temple Hall *OPEN 10.00-12.00 & 15.00-16.00 Mon-Fri by arrangement. CLOSED Sat & Sun, B.hols, Aug & during examinations. Free.*

Temple of Mithras,   **5 E2**
Bucklersbury House

3 Queen Victoria St EC4. Originally discovered 18ft (5.5m) underground in Walbrook and moved here with other Roman relics.

Thames Tunnels
Rotherhithe to Wapping

The first tunnel under the Thames built by Sir Marc Isambard Brunel (the elder), and completed in 1843 after many deaths by accident and illness. Now used by underground trains and still a perfect feat of engineering – withstanding over 100 years of train vibration. Original tunnel can be seen at Wapping station – also stairs and handrails. **The Engine House**, Railway Ave SE16, 081-318 2489 houses the sole surviving example of a compound horizontal V steam pumping engine and a permanent exhibition.

Rotherhithe
1908. For vehicles and pedestrians.

Blackwall
1897 by Binnie. Now incorporated in a two-way system with the new tunnel, completed in 1967. For vehicles and pedestrians.

Greenwich and Woolwich
1902 and 1912. Pedestrians only.

Tower of London   5 G3
Tower Hill EC3. 071-709 0765. A keep, a prison and still a fortress. Famous for the Bloody Tower, Traitors' Gate, the ravens, Crown Jewels, the Armouries and the Yeomen Warders. Edward I's Medieval Palace has been restored and is now open to the public. *OPEN Mar-Oct 09.00-18.00 Mon-Sat, 10.00-18.00 Sun; Nov-Feb 09.30-17.00 Mon-Sat, 10.00-18.00 Sun. Charge.*

Tower of London

Trafalgar Square WC2   4 F4
Laid out by Sir Charles Barry 1830-40. Nelson's column (granite) by William Railton 1839-42. Statue by Baily. Bronze lions by Landseer 1868. Fountains by Lutyens. Famous for political rallies, pigeons and the excesses of New Year's Eve revellers.

The Underground
Although overground railways existed in the mid-19thC, a need for more transport in a rapidly expanding London resulted in the 'underground'. The world's first was the Metropolitan Line with 30,000 passengers taking an opening day ride (in March 1863) from Bishops Rd, Paddington to Farringdon St. The original carriages were open trucks drawn by steam trains. The line was cut out by the 'trench' system, usually under a road, lined with brick and the street relaid on top. The Tower subway, opened in 1870, was the world's first iron-lined tube railway. A small cable-hauled car carried 12 passengers at a time from the Tower to Bermondsey. (Today, the 'tube' houses water mains.) Early underground passengers endured dimly lit carriages and windows closed against smoke. To this day two dummy housefronts in Leinster Gardens W2 puzzle passers-by. They conceal part of the street which had to be demolished for the underground and were built at the insistence of the irate local residents. Twenty-one years after the Metropolitan Line opened, the Circle Line was completed. The underground system has steadily expanded since then – there are now 11 lines (including the Docklands Light Railway).

Watermen's Hall   5 F3
18 St Mary at Hill EC3. Adam-style front surviving from 1780. Unexpectedly beautiful amid drab surroundings. Visits arranged in *summer* through City Information Centre, St Paul's Churchyard EC4 (**5 D2**). 071-606 3030 ex1456.

Whitefriars Crypt   5 B2
30 Bouverie St EC4. 071-353 3030. 14thC crypt belonging to a House of Carmelites. Discovered in 1895 and restored by the proprietors of the *News of the World* and *The Sun* when they occupied the offices above.

Whitehall SW1   4 F4
Wide thoroughfare used for ceremonial and State processions; contains the Cenotaph and several notable statues. Lined with Government offices.

Old Admiralty
1725-8 by T. Ripley. Fine Robert Adam columnar screen 1760. The New Admiralty 1887 lies behind.

Old Scotland Yard
1888. An asymmetrical building by Shaw.

War Office
1898-1907 by William Young. Victorian-baroque.

Horse Guards Parade
1750-60 by William Kent. Changing of the Guard in the forecourt daily – *see 'Daily ceremonies'*.

Horse Guards

Banqueting House
071-930 4179. 17thC Palladian-style by Inigo Jones. 1619-25. Rubens ceilings

Banqueting House

1630. *OPEN 10.00-17.00 Mon-Sat. Charge.*

Dover House
1755-8 by Paine. Entrance screen and rotunda 1787 by Henry Holland.

Treasury
1846 by Sir C. Barry. Victorian columned facade on Whitehall. Earlier facade overlooking Horse Guards Parade 1733-6 by William Kent.

Foreign Office
Mid-Victorian palazzo-style by Gilbert Scott. Completed by Ministry of Housing 1920.

Whittington Stone
Highgate Hill N6, near junction with Dartmouth Park Hill. Milestone marking the spot where tradition says young Dick Whittington rested on his way home from London and heard Bow Bells ring out 'Turn again Whittington, thrice Lord Mayor of London', and returned to become London's most famous Mayor.

Woolwich Arsenal
Woolwich SE18. Fine example of early 18thC ordnance architecture. Sir John Vanbrugh, 1716-19. *OPEN by appt only. Free.*

York Watergate   4 F4
Watergate Wlk, off Villiers St WC2. Built in 1626 by Nicholas Stone as the watergate to York House, it marks the position of the north bank of the Thames before the construction of the Victoria Embankment in 1862. The arms and motto are those of the Villiers family.

Houses of famous people

Visiting the homes of the famous has had its attractions since long before the days of tourism and mass travel. As early as the 17thC, for example, the birthplace of John Milton was one of London's most important sights; while in the next century Boswell anticipated the tourist guides and gazetteers of today by conscientiously listing all the London houses where Dr Johnson had ever lived. Only in rare cases, of course, is the house of someone famous retained as a shrine and opened to the public. Most such houses are simply houses, and they have carried on being lived in as private homes, marked perhaps with a commemorative plaque (see next section). Below, however, is a selection of the most interesting and worthwhile of those houses that are open to the public.

Carlyle's House   6 E4
24 Cheyne Row SW3. 071-352 7087. A modest early 18thC terraced house where Carlyle lived for 42 years until his death in 1881. *OPEN 11.00-17.00 (last admission 16.30) Wed-Sun and B.hols except Good Friday. CLOSED Nov-Mar. Charge.*

Churchill's House
Chartwell, nr Westerham, Kent. (0732) 866368. A famous house full of recent political history. The water gardens, grounds and views of the Weald of Kent are memorable. Gardens *OPEN Apr-Oct 12.00-17.00 Tue-Thur, 11.00-17.00 Sat & Sun, 11.00-17.00 B.hols. CLOSED Tue following B.hol.* House *OPEN Mar & Nov 11.00-16.00 Wed, Sat & Sun. Charge.*

Darwin's House
Down House, Downe, Kent. (0689) 859119. Charles Darwin lived and worked here. Two rooms are as they were in his day and others contain exhibitions illuminating his work. Investigate the Sand Walk where Darwin pondered his theory of evolution. *OPEN 13.00-18.00 Wed-Sun. CLOSED Mon (except B.hols), & Tue. Charge.*

Dickens' House   2 B5
48 Doughty St WC1. 071-405 2127. Regency terrace house. Relics of Dickens' life and writings. He lived here from 1837 to 1839. Be sure to see the reconstructed drawing room. *OPEN 10.00-17.00 (last admission 16.30). CLOSED Sun & B.hols. Charge.*

Disraeli's House
Hughenden Manor, High Wycombe, Bucks. (0494) 532580. Disraeli lived here from 1847 until his death in 1881. Contains much of his furniture, pictures, books and other relics. *OPEN Apr-Oct 14.00-18.00 Wed-Sat, 12.00-18.00 Sun & B.hols; Mar 14.00-18.00 (or sunset) Sat & Sun. Charge.*

Freud Museum
20 Maresfield Gdns NW3. 071-435 2002. This was Freud's last home from 1938-9. The museum contains a major collection of Freud's personal effects: library, correspondence, antiquities, carpets and furniture including the famous couch on which psychoanalysis was pioneered. *OPEN 12.00-17.00 Wed-Sun. Charge.*

Hogarth's House

Hogarth La, Great West Rd W4. 081-994 6757. The 17thC country villa of William Hogarth; relics and late impressions of his engravings. *OPEN Apr-Sep 11.00-18.00 Mon & Wed-Sat; 14.00-18.00 Sun. Oct-Mar 11.00-16.00 Mon & Wed-Sat; 14.00-16.00 Sun. CLOSED Tue and first 2 weeks of Sep & last 3 weeks of Dec. Free.*

Dr Johnson's House   5 B2

17 Gough Sq, Fleet St EC4. 071-353 3745. 17thC house. Relics and contemporary portraits. He lived here from 1748 to 1759. *OPEN May-Sep 11.00-17.30 Mon-Sat; Oct-Apr 11.00-17.00 Mon-Sat. CLOSED Sun & B.hols. Small charge.*

Keats' House

Wentworth Pl, Keats Gro NW3. 071-435 2062. The poet John Keats lived here during his prolific period 1818-20. *OPEN May-Oct 10.00-13.00 & 14.00-18.00 Mon-Fri, 10.00-13.00 & 14.00-17.00 Sat, 14.00-17.00 Sun; Nov-Apr 13.00-17.00 Mon-Fri, 10.00-13.00 & 14.00-17.00 Sat, 14.00-17.00 Sun. Charge.*

Kipling's House

Bateman's, Burwash, E. Sussex. (0435) 882302. The house, built in 1634, contains Kipling's furniture and a Kipling exhibition. The surroundings are described in *Puck of Pooks Hill* and *Rewards and Fairies*. *OPEN Apr-Oct 11.00-17.30 Sat-Wed. CLOSED Thur & Fri. Charge.*

Leighton House   3 A6

12 Holland Park Rd W14. 071-602 3316. Centre for Victorian studies and special exhibitions. Arab hall with decorations of 14th-16thC Oriental tiles. Paintings by Leighton and Burne-Jones. Watts and De Morgan pottery. *OPEN 11.00-17.00 Mon-Sat. CLOSED Sun & B.hols. Free.*

William Morris Gallery

Water House, Lloyd Park, Forest Rd E17. 081-527 3782. 18thC house. Textiles, wallpapers, carpets, woodwork and designs by Morris, pre-Raphaelites and contemporaries, housed in Morris's boyhood home. *OPEN all year 10.00-13.00 & 14.00-17.00 Tue-Sat, 10.00-12.00 & 14.00-17.00 1st Sun in month. CLOSED Mon & B.hols. Free.*

Linley Sambourne House   3 B5

18 Stafford Ter W8. Home of Linley Sambourne, leading *Punch* cartoonist of the late Victorian and Edwardian eras. Unique interior reflecting artistic taste of the period. Contact the Victorian Society, 081-994 1019. *OPEN Wed 10.00-16.00 & Sun 14.00-17.00 Mar-Oct. Parties at other times by appt. Charge.*

Shaw's Corner

Ayot St Lawrence, Welwyn, Herts. (0438) 820307. George Bernard Shaw lived here from 1906 until his death in 1950. *OPEN Apr-Oct 14.00-18.00 Wed-Sat, 12.00-18.00 Sun & B.hols. CLOSED Nov-Mar except by appt. Charge.*

Wellington Museum   4 B5

Apsley House, 149 Piccadilly W1. 071-499 5676. Originally known as 'Number One London'. Duke of Wellington's house. Built 1771-8 from designs by Robert Adam and altered 1828 by B. D. Wyatt. Contains Wellington relics, fine Spanish (Velázquez) and Dutch paintings, silver plate and porcelain. *OPEN 11.00-16.30 Tue-Sun. Charge. Closed for essential works until Spring 1994.*

Wesley's House & chapel   2 F5

47 City Rd EC1. 071-253 2262. John Wesley's possessions and personal relics. His tomb is in the chapel grounds. The chapel crypt houses a museum which tells the story of Methodism and displays Wesleyan memorabilia. *OPEN 10.00-16.00 Mon-Sat, 12.00-15.00 Sun.* (There is also a service at 11.00 on Sun, followed by lunch and a guided tour). *Small charge.*

Wolfe's House

Quebec House, Westerham, Kent. (0959) 562206. Mainly 17thC house where General Wolfe spent his early years. Contains a collection of 'Wolfiana'. *OPEN Apr-Oct 14.00-18.00 Sun-Wed & Fri. CLOSED Thur & Sat. Charge.*

Commemorative plaques

Marking houses and other buildings associated with famous people or events with the now familiar blue plaques has been a feature of London's street scene since 1866. Originally on the private initiative of the Royal Society of Arts in 1901, they came under the aegis of the London County Council, later the Greater London Council. Since 1 April 1986 the plaques have been the responsibility of English Heritage. There are now nearly 400 of them, commemorating important events in the lives of architects, artists, composers, politicians, scientists, soldiers and writers. The following are some of the best known:

Adam, Robert

Lived at 1-3 Robert St, Adelphi WC2. **4 F3**

Arnold, Matthew

Lived at 2 Chester Sq SW1.   **7 B1**

Asquith, Herbert Henry
Lived at 20 Cavendish Sq W1.   **4 C2**

Baden-Powell, Robert
Lived at 9 Hyde Park Gate SW7.   **3 D5**

Baird, John Logie
First demonstrated television at
22 Frith St W1.   **4 E2**

Baldwin, Stanley
Lived at 93 Eaton Sq SW1.   **7 A1**

Barrie, Sir James M.
Lived at 100 Bayswater Rd W2   **3 D3**
and at 1-3 Robert St, Adelphi WC2. **4 F3**

Beardsley, Aubrey
Lived at 114 Cambridge St SW1.   **7 B3**

Bennett, Arnold
Lived at 75 Cadogan Sq SW1.   **6 F1**

Berlioz, Hector
Stayed at 58 Queen Anne St W1.   **4 C1**

Bligh, William
Commander of the *Bounty* lived at
100 Lambeth Rd SE1.   **7 G1**

Boswell, James
Lived and died on the site of
122 Great Portland St W1.   **4 C1**

Browning, Elizabeth Barrett
Lived on site of 50 Wimpole St   **4 C2**
and at 99 Gloucester Pl W1.   **4 A1**

Brunel, Isambard Kingdom
Lived at 98 Cheyne Walk SW3.   **6 E4**

Burne-Jones, Sir Edward
Lived at 17 Red Lion Sq WC1.   **4 G1**

Canaletto, Antonio
Lived at 41 Beak St W1.   **4 D3**

Carlyle, Thomas
Lived at 24 Cheyne Row SW3.   **6 E4**

Chamberlain, Neville
Lived at 37 Eaton Sq SW1.   **7 A1**

Chaplin, Charlie
Lived at 287 Kennington Rd SE11. **7 G2**

Chesterton, Gilbert Keith
Lived at 11 Warwick Gdns W14.   **3 A6**

Chippendale, Thomas
and his son had their workshop near
61 St Martin's La WC2.   **4 F3**

Churchill, Sir Winston
Lived at 34 Eccleston Sq SW1.   **7 B2**

Clive of India, Lord
Lived at 45 Berkeley Sq W1.   **4 C3**

Conan Doyle, Sir Arthur
Lived not as you might imagine at 221b
Baker St, but at 12 Tennison Rd SE25.

Constable, John
Lived at 40 Well Wlk NW3.

Cook, Captain James
Lived on the site of 88 Mile End Rd E1.

Darwin, Charles
Lived on the site of 110 Gower St
WC1.   **1 F5**

Defoe, Daniel
Lived on the site of 95 Stoke Newington
Church St N16.

Dickens, Charles
Lived at 48 Doughty St WC1.   **2 B5**

Disraeli, Benjamin
Born at 22 Theobalds Rd WC1   **2 B6**
and died at 19 Curzon St W1.   **4 C4**

Eliot, George (Mary Ann Evans)
Lived at Holly Lodge, 31 Wimbledon
Park Rd SW18 and
died at 4 Cheyne Wlk SW3.   **6 E4**

Engels, Friedrich
Lived at 121 Regent's Park Rd
NW1.   **1 B2**

Faraday, Michael
Apprenticed at 48 Blandford St W1. **4 B1**

Fielding, Henry
Lived at 19-20 Bow St WC2   **4 F2**
and at Milbourne House, Station Rd
SW13.

Ford, Ford Madox
Lived at 80 Campden Hill Rd W8.   **3 B4**

Franklin, Benjamin
Lived at 36 Craven St WC2.   **4 F4**

Freud, Sigmund
Lived at 20 Maresfield Gdns NW3.

Fry, Elizabeth
Lived at St Mildred's Ct, Poultry
EC2.   **5 E2**

Gainsborough, Thomas
Lived at 82 Pall Mall SW1.   **4 E4**

Galsworthy, John
Lived at Grove Lodge, Hampstead Gro
NW3
and at 1-3 Robert St, Adelphi WC2. **4 F3**

Garrett Anderson, Elizabeth
Lived at 20 Upper Berkeley St W1.   **4 A2**

Gibbon, Edward
Lived on the site of 7 Bentinck St
W1.   **4 B2**

Gibbons, Grinling
Lived at 19-20 Bow St WC2.   **4 F2**

Gladstone, William Ewart
Lived at 11 Carlton House Ter SW1 **4 E4**
at 10 St James's Sq SW1   **4 E4**
and at 73 Harley St W1.   **4 C1**

Handel, George Frideric
Lived and died at 25 Brook St W1.   **4 C3**

Hardy, Thomas
Lived at 172 Trinity Rd SW17
and at Adelphi Ter WC2.   **4 F3**

Hazlitt, William
Lived on the site of 6 Bouverie St
EC4   **5 B2**
and died at 6 Frith St W1.   **4 E2**

Holman-Hunt, William
Lived and died at 18 Melbury Rd
W14.   **3 A6**

Housman, A. E.
Lived at 17 North Rd N6.

Irving, Sir Henry
Lived at 15a Grafton St W1.   **4 C3**

James, Henry
Lived at 34 De Vere Gdns W8.   **3 D5**

Johnson, Dr Samuel
Lived at 17 Gough Sq EC4.   **5 B2**
and at Johnson's Ct, Fleet St EC4.   **5 B2**
Keats, John
Lived at Wentworth Pl, Keats Gro NW3
and was born on the site of the
Swan & Hoop public house, 86
Moorgate EC2.   **5 E1**
Keynes, John Maynard
Lived at 46 Gordon Sq WC1.   **1 F5**
Kingsley, Charles
Lived at 56 Old Church St SW3.   **6 E4**
Kipling, Rudyard
Lived at 43 Villiers St WC2.   **4 F4**
Kitchener of Khartoum
Lived at 2 Carlton Gdns SW1.   **4 E4**
Lamb, Charles
Lived at Colebrook Cottage, 64 Duncan
Ter N1.   **2 D3**
Lawrence, David Herbert
Lived at 1 Byron Villas, Vale of Health
NW3.
**Lawrence, T. E. ('Lawrence of
Arabia')**
Lived at 14 Barton St SW1.   **7 E1**
Lear, Edward
Lived at 30 Seymour St W1.   **4 A2**
Lind, Jenny
Lived at 189 Old Brompton Rd SW5. **6 B3**
Lloyd George, David
Lived at 3 Routh Rd SW18.
Lutyens, Sir Edwin Landseer
Lived at 13 Mansfield St W1.   **4 C1**
MacDonald, Ramsay
Lived at 9 Howitt Rd NW3.
Mansfield, Katherine
Lived at 17 East Heath Rd NW3.
Marconi, Guglielmo
Lived at 71 Hereford Rd W2.   **3 B2**
Marx, Karl
Lived at 28 Dean St W1.   **4 E2**
Maugham, W. Somerset
Lived at 6 Chesterfield St W1.   **4 C4**
Millais, Sir John Everett
Lived and died at 2 Palace Gate
W8.   **3 D5**
Morris, William
Lived at 17 Red Lion Sq WC1   **2 B6**
and at Kelmscott House, 26 Upper
Mall W6.
Mozart, Wolfgang Amadeus
Composed his first symphony at 180
Ebury St SW1.   **7 A2**
Napoleon III
Lived at 1c King St SW1.   **4 D4**
Nelson, Lord (Horatio)
Lived on the site of 147 New Bond
St W1   **4 C3**
and at 103 New Bond St W1.   **4 C2**
Newton, Sir Isaac
Lived on the site of 87 Jermyn St
SW1.   **4 D4**

Nightingale, Florence
Lived and died on the site of 10 South
St W1.   **4 B4**
**Palmerston, Lord (Henry John
Temple)**
Born at 20 Queen Anne's Gate
SW1.   **4 E5**
Lived at 4 Carlton Gdns SW1   **4 E4**
and at Naval and Military Club,
94 Piccadilly W1.   **4 D4**
Pepys, Samuel
Lived on the site of 12 & 14 Buckingham
St WC2.   **4 F3**
Pitt, William
Lived at 10 St James's Sq SW1.   **4 E4**
Pitt, William (The Younger)
Lived at 120 Baker St W1.   **1 B6**
Reynolds, Sir Joshua
Lived and died on the site of Fanum
House,
47 Leicester Sq WC2.   **4 E3**
Rossetti, Dante Gabriel
Born on the site of 110 Hallam St
W1.   **1 D6**
Lived at 17 Red Lion Sq WC1   **2 B6**
and at 16 Cheyne Wlk SW3.   **6 E4**
Ruskin, John
Lived on the site of 26 Herne Hill SE24.
Scott, Captain Robert Falcon
Lived at 56 Oakley St SW3.   **6 E4**
Shackleton, Sir Ernest
Lived at 12 Westwood Hill SE26.
Shaw, George Bernard
Lived at 29 Fitzroy Sq W1.   **2 E5**
Shelley, Percy Bysshe
Lived at 15 Poland St W1.   **4 D2**
Sheraton, Thomas
Lived at 163 Wardour St W1.   **4 E2**
Sheridan, Richard Brinsley
Lived at 14 Savile Row W1   **4 D3**
and at 10 Hertford St W1.   **4 C4**
Stephenson, Robert
Died on the site of 35 Gloucester
Sq W2.   **3 E2**
Swinburne, Algernon Charles
Lived at 16 Cheyne Wlk SW3   **6 E4**
and died at 11 Putney Hill SW15.
Thackeray, William Makepeace
Lived at 16 Young St W8   **3 C5**
at 2 Palace Grn W8   **3 C5**
and at 36 Onslow Sq SW7.   **6 D2**
Trollope, Anthony
Lived at 39 Montagu Sq W1.   **4 A2**
Turner, Joseph Mallord William
Lived at 23 Queen Anne St W1   **4 C1**
and at 119 Cheyne Wlk SW3   **6 E4**
Twain, Mark (Samuel L. Clemens)
Lived at 23 Tedworth Sq SW3.   **4 F3**
Vaughan Williams, Ralph
Lived at 10 Hanover Ter NW1.   **1 B4**
Wallace, Edgar
Lived at 6 Tressillian Cres SE4.

Walpole, Sir Robert
Lived at 5 Arlington St SW1.   **4 D4**

Wells, H. G.
Lived and died at 13 Hanover Ter
NW1.   **1 B4**

Wesley, John
Lived at 47 City Rd EC1.   **2 F5**

Whistler, James Abbott McNeil
Lived at 96 Cheyne Wlk SW3.   **6 E4**

Whittington, Richard ('Dick')
House of Whittington stood at 20 College
Hill EC4.   **5 D3**
'Dick' died in 1423 and was buried in
the church of St Michael Royal, College
Hill EC4.   **5 D3**

Wilberforce, William
Lived at 111 Broomwood Rd SW11
and at 44 Cadogan Pl SW1.   **6 F1**

Wilde, Oscar
Lived at 34 Tite St SW3.   **6 F4**

Wolfe, General James
Lived at Macartney House, Greenwich
Park SE10.

Wood, Sir Henry
Lived at 4 Elsworthy Rd NW3.

Woolf, Virginia
Lived at 29 Fitzroy Sq W1.   **1 E5**

Wren, Sir Christopher
Lived at 49 Bankside SE1.   **5 D3**

Wyndham, Sir Charles
Lived at 43 York Ter NW1.   **1 C5**

Yeats, William Butler
Lived at 23 Fitzroy Rd NW1.   **1 C2**

Statues

*London has some 1700 outdoor statues,
memorials and pieces of historic sculpture. Their subjects range from classical
mythology to modern statesmen. From
such a number it is only possible to sug-
gest a selection of some of the best and
most interesting, which are listed below.*

Achilles   **4 B4**
Hyde Park W1. Westmacott, 1822.
Erected to honour Wellington. London's
first nude statue.

Alfred the Great   **5 D6**
Trinity Church Sq SE1. Origin unknown
but it possibly came from Westminster
Hall, in which case it dates from 1395 and
is by far the oldest statue in London.

Queen Anne   **5 D2**
In front of St Paul's Cathedral EC4. After
Bird, 1712. This is a copy (1886) of the
original. Surrounding the Queen are fig-
ures representing England, France,
Ireland and North America.

Queen Anne   **4 E5**
Queen Anne's Gate SW1. Origin uncertain but probably by Francis Bird early

18thC; believed to have stood originally
over the portico of the church of St Mary-
le-Strand.

Boadicea (Boudicca)   **4 F5**
Westminster Bridge SW1. Thornycroft,
unveiled 1902. Famous group showing
the ancient British Queen with her daugh-
ters in her war chariot.

George Canning   **4 F5**
Parliament Sq SW1. Westmacott, 1832.
Fell over while in the sculptor's studio and
killed a man.

Nurse Cavell   **4 F3**
St Martin's Pl WC2. Frampton, 1920.
Simple and impressive memorial to the
nurse who was shot for assisting prison-
ers to escape during World War I.

Charles I   **4 E4**
Trafalgar Sq SW1. Le Sueur, 1633. The
oldest equestrian statue in London, and
one of the finest. Ordered to be destroyed
during the Civil War and buried until the
Restoration. It was erected on its present
site between 1675 and 1677.

Charles II   **6 G3**
Royal Hospital, Royal Hospital Rd SW3.
Bronze. Grinling Gibbons, 1676. King in
Roman costume. The statue is wreathed
in oak leaves on Oak Apple Day, 29 May.

Sir Charles Chaplin   **4 E3**
Leicester Sq WC2. John Doubleday,
1981. Bronze. Appropriately surrounded
by the cinemas of Leicester Sq. Charlie
Chaplin with his characteristic cane and
bowler hat is probably still the cinema's
greatest comedian.

Sir Winston Churchill   **4 F5**
Parliament Sq SW1. Ivor Roberts-Jones,
1973. Large bronze statue of one of
Britain's greatest statesmen, half-facing
the House of Commons.

Crimea Memorial   **4 E4**
Waterloo Pl SW1. Bell, 1859. Figures of
Guards cast from melted down cannon
taken in battle. A pile of actual cannons
decorates the back. Memorial includes a
statue of:

Florence Nightingale   **4 E4**
Waterloo Pl SW1. Waller, 1915. She is
shown holding an oil lamp, whereas the
famous lamp which gave her the name
'The lady with the lamp' was actually a
candle lantern.

Oliver Cromwell   **4 F5**
Old Palace Yd SW1. Thornycroft, 1899.
Significantly with his back turned on
Parliament.

Edward VII   **4 E4**
Waterloo Pl SW1. Sir Bertram Mackennal,
1921. Memorial statue showing the King
in military uniform. Bronze and Portland
stone.

Queen Elizabeth I 5 B2
St Dunstan-in-the-West, Fleet St EC4. Originally stood over Lud Gate. Made during the queen's lifetime in 1586 by William Kerwin, it is one of London's oldest statues.

Eros 4 E3
Piccadilly Circus W1. Gilbert, 1893. Officially the Angel of Christian Charity. It is part of the memorial to the Victorian philanthropist Lord Shaftesbury. Made in aluminium. Fully restored in 1984 and returned in 1986 to a site just south of its original position.

George III 4 E4
Cockspur St SW1. Wyatt, 1836. The best statue of this king, on a fine spirited horse.

George IV 4 E4
Trafalgar Sq WC2. Chantrey, 1834. Rides without boots on a horse without saddle or stirrups. Originally intended for the top of Marble Arch.

George V 4 F6
Old Palace Yd SW1. Reid Dick, 1947.

Sir Henry Irving 4 F3
By the side of the National Portrait Gallery, St Martin's Pl WC2. Brock, 1910.

James II 4 E3
Outside National Gallery, Trafalgar Sq WC2. Grinling Gibbons, 1686. One of London's finest statues.

Dr Samuel Johnson 5 A2
St Clement Danes churchyard, Strand WC2. Fitzgerald, 1910.

Abraham Lincoln 4 F5
Parliament Sq SW1. Saint-Gaudens, 1920. Replica of the one in Chicago.

Sir Thomas More 6 E4
Cheyne Wlk SW3. Outside parish church. Bronze of the Tudor statesman and martyr by L. Cubitt Bevis unveiled in 1969.

Lord Nelson 4 F4
On column in Trafalgar Sq WC2. Baily, 1843. The statue is 17ft (5.2m) high; weighs 16 tons. Made of stone, it was hoisted into position in three pieces.

Peter Pan 3 E4
Kensington Gardens W2. Frampton, 1912. Charming fairy figure. Erected overnight as a surprise for the children.

Sir Joshua Reynolds 4 D3
Forecourt of Burlington House, Piccadilly W1. Drury, 1931.

Richard I 4 F6
Old Palace Yd SW1. Marochetti, 1860.

Franklin D. Roosevelt 4 B3
Grosvenor Sq W1. Reid Dick, 1948.

Royal Artillery Memorial 4 B5
Hyde Park Corner SW1. Jagger, 1925. London's best war memorial, with its great stone howitzer aimed at the Somme where the men it commemorates lost their lives. The bronze figures of soldiers are possibly the finest sculptures to be seen in London.

Captain Scott 4 E4
Waterloo Pl SW1. Lady Scott, 1915. 'Scott of the Antarctic' modelled by his widow.

William Shakespeare 4 E3
Leicester Sq WC2. Fontana after Scheemakers, 1740. Copy (1874) of the memorial in Westminster Abbey for which David Garrick is said to have posed.

Victoria Memorial 4 D5
In front of Buckingham Palace SW1. Brock, 1911. Impressive memorial to Queen Victoria which includes a fine dignified figure of the queen, the best of the many statues of her.

George Washington 4 E3
Outside National Gallery, Trafalgar Sq WC2. Replica of the statue by Houdon in the Capitol at Richmond, Virginia, and presented by that state in 1921.

Duke of Wellington 5 E2
Outside Royal Exchange EC3. Chantrey, 1844. Like the same sculptor's statue of George IV, his horse has no saddle or stirrups and he wears no boots.

Duke of Wellington 4 B5
Hyde Park Corner SW1. Boehm, 1888. Equestrian statue of the Duke. The memorial is distinguished by four well-modelled figures of soldiers in full kit. The Duke rides his favourite horse, Copenhagen, and he looks towards Apsley House, in which he lived.

William III 4 E4
St James's Sq SW1. Bacon, 1807. First proposed in 1697 but not erected until 1808. Beneath one of the horse's hooves is the molehill over which the horse stumbled, killing the king.

Duke of York 4 E4
On column, Waterloo Pl SW1. Westmacott, 1834. Cost £30,000 and was paid for by deducting a day's pay from every officer and man in the British Army.

Modern outdoor sculpture

Good modern sculpture on open view is still rather rare in London – a reflection of a lack of both private and public commissions – although the royal parks are regularly used for major displays and there is a permanent exhibition (with changing exhibits) in Regent's Park (south-east corner near Chester Gate NW1, 1 D4). Among the best permanently-sited pieces are:

Michael Ayrton (1921-1974)
Postman's Park, Aldersgate EC2.
'Minotaur' expressing energy.   **5 D2**

Geoffrey Clark (b. 1924)
Thorn Bldg, Upper St Martin's La WC2.Bronze relief.   **4 F3**

Sir Jacob Epstein (1880-1959)
Heythrop College, 11 Cavendish Sq W1.
Bronze 'Madonna and Child', 1952. **4 C2**
St James's Park underground station.
Fine sculpture of 'Day and Night'.   **4 E6**
South of Nursery Enclosure, Hyde Park.
'Rima'.   **3 F4**
Edinburgh Gate, Hyde Park. 'Return of Spring'.   **3 G5**

Elizabeth Frink (b. 1930)
Carlton Tower Hotel, Cadogan Sq SW1.
Beaten copper relief on facade.   **6 F1**

Dame Barbara Hepworth (1903-1975)
John Lewis Store, Oxford St W1. Bronze relief.   **4 C2**
State House, High Holborn WC1. Fine abstract 'Meridian'.   **5 A1**
Hyde Park. 'Family of Man' (on indefinite loan).   **3 F4**

Karin Jonzen (b. 1914)
Bassishaw Highwalk, south of London Wall EC2.
'Beyond Tomorrow', male and female figures.   **5 D1**

David Kemp (b. 1945)
Hay's Galleria, Tooley St SE1. 'The Navigators', a kinetic sculpture in bronze with moving parts.   **5 F4**

Bernard Meadows (b. 1915)
TUC Building, Great Russell St WC1.
Bronze group.   **4 E2**

Henry Moore (1898-1986)
Abingdon St Gdns SW1. 'Knife Edge Two-Piece' bronze, 1967.   **4 F6**
Kensington Gardens SW7. 'The Arch' overlooking the Long Water. Marble, 1980.   **3 E4**
Riverside House, Millbank SW1. 'Locking Pieces' bronze in garden close to Vauxhall Bridge.   **7 E3**
Time & Life Bldg, New Bond St W1.
Fine stone relief; open sculpture court yard.   **4 C3**

Michael Sandle (b. 1936)
Dorset Rise EC4. 'St George and The Dragon'. Powerful bronze horse and rider.   **5 C2**

Walenty Pytel (b. 1941)
Parliament Sq SW1. 'Silver Jubilee Fountain', a highly elaborate and impressive steel sculpture.   **4 F5**

Places of worship

In their buildings, ruins, sites and associations, London's churches and cathedrals represent nearly 1400 years of Christianity in Britain (the first St Paul's Cathedral is ascribed to the beginning of the 7thC). Norman work survives in St Helen's Bishopsgate and Westminster Abbey and at the time of the Great Fire of 1666 there were over 100 churches in the present area of the City of London, a density peculiar to English cities.

The Fire set the scene for Wren's great rebuilding programme, including St Paul's Cathedral and 50 churches, most of which have survived later demolitions and war damage. Hawksmoor and Inigo Jones were other 17th and early 18thC church designers whose work we can still admire.

The Victorians too were great church builders and the 19thC produced a wealth of new churches, many of them in the triumphant Gothic style, for Anglican and other denominations. The neo-Byzantine Westminster RC Cathedral of 1903 is outstanding.

Non-Christian religions also have their part in London's history, with synagogues as at Bevis Marks and, most recently, the Regent's Park Mosque for London's growing Islamic community. London's most important religious buildings are listed below.

Abbeys & cathedrals

St George's RC Cathedral, Southwark   **5 B6**
Lambeth Rd (opp Imperial War Museum) SE1. 071-928 5256. By A.W. Pugin, 1848. Spire never completed. Burnt out in last war and interior restored in 1958.
St Paul's Cathedral   **5 D2**
Ludgate Hill EC4. 071-248 4619/2705.
Wren's greatest work; built 1675-1710

St Paul's Cathedral

replacing the previous church destroyed by the Great Fire. Superb dome, porches and funerary monuments. Contains magnificent stalls by Grinling Gibbons. Ironwork by Tijou, paintings by Thornhill and mosaics by Salviati and Sir William Richmond. *OPEN 07.15-18.00 Mon-Sun except during special services. Crypt & Ambulatory OPEN 09.00-16.15 Mon-Sat. Galleries OPEN 09.45-16.15 Mon-Sat. Charge.*

Southwark Cathedral 5 E4
Borough High St SE1. 071-407 2939. Much restored. Built by Augustinian Canons but destroyed by fire in 1206. Beautiful early English choir and retro-choir. Tower built c1520, nave by Blomfield 1894-7. Work by Comper includes the altar screen. Chapter House developed in 1988 with restaurant. *OPEN 08.30-18.00 Mon-Fri.*

Southwark Cathedral

Westminster Abbey 4 F6
(The Collegiate Church of St Peter in Westminster) Broad Sanctuary SW1. 071-222 5152. Original church by Edward the Confessor 1065. Rebuilding commenced in 1245 by Henry III who was largely influenced by the new French cathedrals. Completed by Henry Yevele and others 1376-1506 (towers incomplete and finished by Hawksmoor 1734). Henry VII Chapel added 1503; fine perpendicular with wonderful fan vaulting. The Abbey contains the Coronation Chair, and many tombs and memorials of the Kings and Queens of England and their subjects. Starting place for pilgrimage to

Westminster Abbey

Canterbury Cathedral. Nave and Cloisters *OPEN 08.00-18.00 Mon-Sun. Free. Royal Chapels OPEN 09.00-16.45 Mon-Fri, 09.00-14.45 & 16.00-17.45 Sat. Charge. OPEN 18.00-19.45 Wed (photography permitted). Free. Services only Sun. Museum OPEN 10.30-16.00 daily. Charge.*

Westminster RC Cathedral 4 D6
Ashley Pl SW1. 071-834 7452. Early Christian Byzantine-style church by J.F. Bentley, 1903. The most important Roman Catholic church in England. Fine marbled interior.

Churches & other places of worship

All Hallows-by-the-Tower 5 F3
Byward St EC3. 071-481 2928. Foundations date from AD675. Audaciously restored by Lord Mottistone after bombing. Fine copper steeple. Crypt museum with Roman pavement. Brass rubbing. Organ recitals every *Thur lunchtime. Church OPEN 10.00-18.00 Mon-Sat, 12.30-17.00 Sun. Free. Crypt OPEN by appt only. Charge.*

All Hallows London Wall 5 F2
83 London Wall EC2. 071-588 3388. Rebuilt 1765-7 by George Dance jun. Restored 1962 by David Nye as centre for church art. Charming interior.

All Saints Margaret St 4 D2
Margaret St W1. 071-636 9961. Gothic Revival masterpiece. William Butterfield, 1859. Paintings by Ninian Comper. Fine musical tradition. *OPEN 07.00-19.00 Mon-Sun. Free.*

All Souls Langham Place 4 C1
Langham Pl W1. 071-580 4357. John Nash, 1822-4; Nash's only church. Corinthian columns with needle spire. Restored after bomb damage. Interior refitted 1976. Exterior restored 1987-8.

Bevis Marks Synagogue 5 F2
Heneage La (off Bevis Marks) EC3. 071-626 1274. Avis, 1700. Fine windows. Brass chandeliers from Amsterdam.

Brompton Oratory 6 E1
Brompton Rd SW7. 071-589 4811. Large Italian Mannerist-style church designed by H. Gribble, 1884. Fine marbled interior and original statues from the Cathedral of Siena. Noted choral tradition. *OPEN 06.30-20.30.*

Capel Bedyddwyr Cymreig 4 D2
30 Eastcastle St W1. Highly imaginative Welsh Baptist chapel.

Central Hall 4 E5
Storey's Gate SW1. 071-222 8010. 'Cathedral of Methodism' 1912 by

Lanchester & Rickards, the greatest exponents of the Baroque style in Edwardian London. Listed building.

Chapel Royal of St John   **5 G3**
White Tower, Tower of London EC3. 071-709 0765. The oldest Norman church in London, c1085, still retains its original pillars.

Chelsea Old Church, All Saints   **6 E4**
Chelsea Embankment SW3. 071-352 5627. Rebuilt after severe bombing. 13thC chapels, one restored by Sir Thomas More, 1528. Jacobean altar table, many historic monuments and capitals attributed to Holbein.

Christ Church Newgate St   **5 D2**
Newgate St EC1. Wren, 1691. Only the tower, dating to 1704, and four walls remain.

Christ Church Spitalfields   **5 G1**
Commercial St E1. 071-247 7202. Fine church by Hawksmoor, 1714-29, partly restored. Notable tower and spire, and lofty interior. Crypt a rehabilitation centre for alcoholics. Annual international music festival in *Jun*.

Christ the King   **1 F5**
Gordon Sq WC1. 071-387 0670. The University church and the Catholic Apostolic church. Cruciform, cathedral-like building by Raphael Brandon, 1853. West front and tower unfinished.

City Temple   **5 C2**
Holborn Viaduct EC1. 071-583 5532. City's Free Church, 1874, by Lockwood, restored after bombing.

Cole Abbey Presbyterian Church   **5 D3**
Queen Victoria St EC4. 071-248 5213. Affiliated to the Free Church of Scotland. Originally by Wren, 1671-81, and restored with similar spire after bombing. Rich stained glass by Keith New.

Crown Court Church of Scotland, Covent Garden   **4 F2**
Russell St WC2. 071-836 5643. Longest-established Presbyterian church south of the border, dating from 1719. It was rebuilt in 1909 and is situated in the heart of London's theatreland.

Dutch Church   **5 E2**
7 Austin Friars EC2. 071-588 1684. 13thC origin, given to Dutch Protestants after the Reformation. Rebuilt 1950-3 after 1940 destruction. Part of the present structure dates from 1550. *OPEN 11.00-15.00 Mon-Thur.*

French Protestant Church   **4 E2**
9 Soho Sq W1. 071-437 5311. By Aston Webb in 1893, exterior surprisingly like an office building.

Grosvenor Chapel   **4 B3**
South Audley St W1. 071-499 1684. 'Colonial'-looking chapel built 1730. Decorations by Comper added in 1912.

The Guards Chapel   **4 E5**
Wellington Barracks, Birdcage Wlk SW1. 071-414 3228. Original chapel, built 1838 was destroyed in 1944 with the loss of 121 lives. New chapel, finished 1963, is austere but complements the original surviving apse.

Holy Trinity   **6 G2**
Sloane St SW1. 071-730 7270. By Sedding in 1890. London's most elaborate church of the 'Arts and Crafts' movement.

Immaculate Conception   **4 B3**
114 Mount St W1. 071-493 7811. 1849 by J.J. Scoles. Headquarters of the Jesuit Order in Britain.

London Central Mosque   **1 A4**
Hanover Gate NW1. 071-724 3363. A graceful building on the edge of Regent's Park, it was completed in 1978 and is the religious centre for London's Muslims.

Notre Dame de France   **4 E3**
5 Leicester Pl WC2. 071-437 9363. First church 1865, rebuilt 1955 after bombing. Circular. Large Aubusson tapestry, mural by Jean Cocteau and statue of Our Lady by Georges Sanpique.

Queen's Chapel of the Savoy   **4 G3**
Savoy Hill, Strand WC2. 071-836 7221. Late perpendicular style, built 1508. Some 13th and 15thC glass.

The Queen's Chapel, St James's Palace   **4 D4**
Marlborough Rd SW1. 071-930 3007. Built by Inigo Jones, 1623. Fine restored woodwork and coffered ceiling. *OPEN (for services only) Easter-end Jul 08.30 & 11.15 Sun.*

St Alban Holborn   **5 B1**
Brooke St EC1. 071-405 1831. Originally by Butterfield, 1859. Rebuilt by Adrian Scott after bomb damage. Soaring arches. Sculpture and huge mural by Hans Feibusch.

St Alban Wood St   **5 D1**
Wood St EC2. Wren. Only the tower remains 1697-8 (modern pinnacles).

St Andrew Holborn   **5 B2**
Holborn Circus EC4. 071-353 3544. Largest of Wren's parish churches. 1686. Restored 1961 after bombing. Pulpit, font, organ and tomb of Thomas Coram, from the chapel of the 18thC Foundling Hospital.

St Andrew-by-the-Wardrobe   **5 C3**
Queen Victoria St EC4. 071-248 7546. Fine City church by Wren, 1685-95. Restored 1959-61, after bomb damage.

St Andrew Undershaft 5 F2
St Mary Axe EC3. 071-283 7382. Rebuilt 1532. Altar rails by Tijou, font by Nicholas Stone. Monument to John Stow, London's first historian.

St Anne Limehouse
Commercial Rd E14. 071-987 1502. Hawksmoor, built 1712-24. Highest public clock (added 1839) after Big Ben. Organ, built for 1851 Great Exhibition, is one of finest unaltered Victorian examples in the country.

St Anne Soho 4 E3
57 Dean St W1. 071-437 6727. Steeple only, by Cockerell, 1802-6. The church, by Wren, was destroyed by bombing.

St Anne & St Agnes (Lutheran) 5 D2
Gresham St EC2. 071-373 5566. Wren, 1676-87. Attractive church restored after bomb damage. Regular lunchtime concerts.

St Augustine Watling St 5 D2
Watling St EC4. Wren, 1687. Only tower remains after bombing, with new spire after the original design. Now part of cathedral choir school.

St Bartholomew-the-Great 5 C1
West Smithfield EC1. 071-606 1575. The oldest church in London. Norman choir of Augustinian Priory 1123 with later Lady Chapel; unusual oriel window and the only pre-Reformation font in City. Tomb of founder, who also founded St Bartholomew's Hospital, and other fine monuments. Hogarth was christened here 1697.

St Bartholomew-the-Less 5 C1
West Smithfield EC1. 071-601 8888. Inside 'Barts' hospital (serves as its parish church). Tower and west end medieval, rest rebuilt 1789 and 1823. Octagonal interior.

St Benet Church 5 D3
Queen Victoria St EC4. 071-723 3104. Attractive church by Wren, 1683, on foundations dating from 1098. Brick with stone dressings. A Guild Church. Also known as the Metropolitan Welsh Church. The Chapel of the College of Arms. Burial place of Inigo Jones.

St Botolph Aldersgate 5 D2
Aldersgate EC1. 071-623 6970. Nathaniel Wright, 1788, with additions in 1831. Charming interior.

St Botolph Aldgate 5 G2
Aldgate High St EC3. 071-283 1670. Rebuilt 1741-4 by Dance senior. Restored by Bentley, 1880s, and again 1966. Fine monuments. Lies north and south. Renatus Harris organ (1674). Peal of eight bells (1744). Recent large addition to the crypt, which is a centre for homeless single people.

St Botolph without Bishopsgate 5 F2
Bishopsgate EC2. 071-588 1053. First recorded 1212, rebuilt 1571-2, demolished 1724. Rebuilt 1725-9 by James Gould. Baroque steeple at east end. Large churchyard. Irreplaceable stained glass was destroyed in a bomb attack in April 1993.

St Bride's Church 5 B2
Fleet St EC4. 071-353 1301. Wren, 1670-84. Famous spire 1701-4. Restored after bomb damage. Fine City church.

St Clement Danes 5 A2
Strand WC2. 071-242 8282. First built by the Danes, 9thC. Spire by Gibbs. Rebuilt by Wren, 1681. Destroyed in air raids 1941 and restored and rededicated in 1958 as the central church of the RAF. Bells ring 'Oranges and Lemons' occasionally. Fine moulded plaster ceiling.

St Clement nr Eastcheap 5 E3
Clements La, King William St EC4. 071-283 8154. Wren, 1687. Restored by Butterfield, 1872, and by Comper, 1933. Notable 17thC woodwork and fine organ (1695).

St Columba 6 F1
Pont St SW1. 071-584 2321. Church of Scotland, new building by Maufe, 1950-5, replacing destroyed Victorian one.

St Cyprian 1 B5
Glentworth St, Clarence Gate NW1. 071-402 6979. Outstanding example of a complete church by Comper, in his early style. 1903. Renowned interior.

St Dunstan-in-the-East 5 F3
St Dunstan's Hill EC3. Only the delicately poised spire by Wren remains. 1696-1701.

St Dunstan-in-the-West 5 B2
Fleet St EC4. 071-242 6027. Octagonal church by John Shaw, 1831-3. Early example of Gothic Revival restored in 1950. Fine lantern-steeple clock with 'striking jacks' from old church. Early statue of Elizabeth I from Ludgate. Orthodox chapel with icon screen brought from Antim Monastery in Bucharest. Monuments to an honest solicitor, and to a swordsman. Also Lord Mayor's sword from Battle of Culloden 1745.

St Dunstan All Saints, Stepney
White Horse Rd E1. 071-790 4194. Mother church of East London, late

15thC. Mostly rebuilt. Fine interior. Notable Saxon crucifix.

St Edmund the King   **5 E2**
Lombard St EC3. 071-623 6970. Rebuilt by Wren, 1670-90, and lies north and south, like the pre-Fire church. Restored after slight damage in both world wars. Fine woodwork, distinctive 90ft (27.5m) steeple.

St Ethelburga-the-Virgin   **5 F2**
70 Bishopsgate EC2. 071-588 3596. Site of one of London's oldest churches (15thC) which was destroyed in a bomb attack in April 1993.

St Etheldreda   **5 B1**
Ely Pl EC1. 071-405 1061. Former bishop's chapel built c1300 with possibly Roman walls in the crypt, restored in the 19thC to Catholic use. Some fine postwar glass.

St George Bloomsbury   **4 F1**
Bloomsbury Way WC1. 071-405 3044. Hawksmoor, 1730. Unusual tower modelled on the Mausoleum at Halicarnassus. Statue of George I on top of steeple, posing as St George. Six-column Corinthian portico. Classical interior.

St George Hanover Sq   **4 C2**
St George St W1. 071-629 0874. Classical church by John James, 1721-4 with 16thC Flemish glass in the east windows. Restored by Blomfield in 1894. Altarpiece of 'Last Supper' by Kent.

St George-in-the-East
Cannon Street Rd E1. 071-709 9074. Remarkable church by Hawksmoor, 1715-23. Modern rebuilding (1964) within the bomb-ruined walls.

St George the Martyr Southwark   **5 D5**
Borough High St SE1. 071-407 2796. A Georgian building with fine ornamental plaster ceiling. 'Little Dorrit's' church. Rebuilt 1734-6 by J. Price.

St Giles Cripplegate
Fore St EC2. 071-606 3630. 12thC church rebuilt 16thC then restored 1952 after bombing. Where Cromwell was married and contains Milton's grave. Remains of London Wall in churchyard.

St Giles in the Fields   **4 E2**
St Giles High St WC2. 071-240 2532. Flitcroft, 1731-3. Well restored 1952. Wesley's pulpit from West St Chapel is here.

St Helen Bishopsgate   **5 F2**
Great St Helen's EC3. 071-283 2231. Built 1150. Has two naves, northern originally a nunnery, southern parochial. Contains fine monuments of many City worthies, some excellent brasses and a notable organ case (Victorian). Original nun's squint.

St James   **3 E3**
Sussex Gdns W2. 071-723 8119. Rebuilt to the designs of Street, 1881. Contains an unusual stained glass memorial to Alexander Fleming showing him at work in his laboratory. The discovery of penicillin was made nearby at St Mary's Hospital.

St James Bermondsey
Jamaica Rd SE1. 071-232 2329. A Waterloo church built by James Savage in 1825-9 in the style of a Greek temple with four columned porticos. Has a purpose-built Bishop organ with rare manual keyboard for pedal organ. Original peal of ten bells. Golden dragon weathervane.

St James Clerkenwell   **2 D5**
Clerkenwell Grn EC1. 071-833 8947. Rebuilt 1788-92 by James Carr. Fine Wren-like steeple. Good interior. Some monuments from old church.

St James Garlickhythe   **5 D3**
Garlick Hill EC4. 071-236 1719. Fine City church by Wren, 1673-83, well-restored steeple 1717. Good ironwork and woodwork.

St James Piccadilly   **4 D3**
Piccadilly W1. 071-734 4511. Wren, 1684. Restored by Sir Albert Richardson in 1954 after serious bomb damage. Reredos and organ casing by Grinling Gibbons. Famous 'Father Smith' organ presented by Queen Mary in 1691 and brought from Whitehall Palace. Healing ministry. Major programme of concerts and lectures. Lunchtime recitals every *Thur & Fri at 13.10.* Restaurant *OPEN 08.00-19.00 Mon-Sat, 10.00-17.00 Sun. Donation.*

St James the Less Westminster   **7 D2**
Thorndike St, Vauxhall Bridge Rd SW1. 071-821 9865. G.E. Street, 1860; largely unaltered, its furnishings are complete. Notice the patterned brick walls.

St John Clerkenwell   **2 D5**
St John's Sq EC1. 071-253 6644. Originally a round church. Became a parish church in 1723. 15thC nave, 16thC gate, well-preserved crypt dating from 1140.

St John Smith Sq   **7 E1**
Smith Sq SW1. 071-222 2168. Nicknamed 'Queen Anne's Footstool'. Built by Archer, 1721-8. Gutted by fire 1742; interior re-designed. Blitzed 1941; restored to Archer's original design by

charitable trust. Opened as a concert hall in 1969. Footstool Gallery has monthly exhibitions. Restaurant & gallery *OPEN 10.00-17.00 Mon-Fri*. Also *OPEN* eves if there is a concert. *Free*.

St John's Wood Church
St John's Wood High St NW8. 071-722 4378. Thomas Hardwick, 1813. White and gold interior with carved ceilings supported by impressive Doric and Etruscan columns.

St John Waterloo Rd   5 B4
Waterloo Rd SE1. 071-633 9819. Bedford, 1824. Four walls, steeple and portico remained after bombing. Restored by Ford in 1951 as part of the Festival of Britain. There was a fine reredos which has now been replaced by Hans Feibusch murals.

St Katherine Cree   5 F2
Leadenhall St EC3. 071-283 5733. Rebuilt under Bishop Laud 1631 in hybrid Gothic and classical style, restored 1962. 17thC organ once played by Handel.

St Lawrence Jewry   5 D2
Gresham St EC2. 071-600 9478. Wren, 1671-7. Tower and four walls remained after bombing. Restored in 1957. Replicas of steeple and original Wren ceiling. Official church of City Corporation.

St Leonard Shoreditch
119 High St E1. 071-739 2063. Rebuilt 1736-40 by Dance senior. Fine steeple and woodwork, including the beautiful clock surround. *OPEN Mon-Fri 12.00-14.00*. *Free*.

St Luke Chelsea   6 E3
Sydney St SW3. 071-351 7365/6. Savage, 1824. First church to be built in sumptuous style of early Gothic revival. Dickens married here.

St Magnus the Martyr   5 E3
Lower Thames St EC3. 071-626 4481. Wren, 1671-87. One of Wren's finest steeples, 185ft (55.9m) high, added 1705-6. Anglo-Catholic baroque interior. Fine pulpit and furnishings.

St Margaret Lothbury   5 E2
Lothbury EC2. 071-606 8330. Wren, 1686-93. Steeple 1698-1700. Fine fittings, including a 17thC open-work screen. Bust of Ann Simpson by Nollekens. Grinling Gibbons font and communion rail.

St Margaret Pattens   5 F3
Rood La, Eastcheap EC3. 071-623 6630. Church by Wren, 1684-9. Fine spire 1698-1702. Unusual canopied pews.

St Margaret Westminster   4 F6
Parliament Sq SW1. 071-222 6382. Rebuilt 1486-1523 and again after repeated war damage. Splendid early

St Margaret Westminster

16thC east window and an excellent series of stained-glass windows by John Piper. The parish church of the House of Commons. Many distinguished marriages and burials.

St Martin-in-the-Fields   4 F3
Trafalgar Sq WC2. 071-930 1862. James Gibbs, 1722-4. Famous spire and portico. Fine Venetian east window and white and gold moulded plaster ceiling. Handsome pulpit. The open space of Trafalgar Square creates a pleasing prominence for the church. Lunchtime music *13.05-14.00 Mon, Tue & Fri*. *Free*. Crypt *OPEN 10.00-20.00 Mon-Sat, 12.00-18.00 Sun*; bookshop *OPEN 11.30-19.30 Mon-Sat, 12.00-18.00 Sun*; brass rubbing centre *OPEN 10.00-18.00 Mon-Sat, 12.00-18.00 Sun (Charge)*; craft market and gallery *OPEN 10.00-18.00 Mon-Sun*.

St Martin-in-the-Fields

St Martin Ludgate   5 C2
Ludgate Hill EC4. 071-248 6054. Wren, 1677-84, now restored. Elegant spire, fine interior, notable woodwork, *Ascension* by Benjamin West.

St Mary Abbots Kensington   3 C5
Kensington Church St W8. 071-937 5136. Scott, 1872. Transitional between early-English and decorated style.

St Mary Abchurch 5 E3
Abchurch Yd EC4. 071-626 0306. Wren, 1681-7. Fine ceiling by William Snow. Reredos by Grinling Gibbons.

St Mary Aldermary 5 D2
Watling St EC4. 071-248 4906. Late Gothic rebuilt by Wren. Fine fan vaulting with saucer domes. Pulpit, west door and wooden sword rest by Grinling Gibbons, 1682.

St Mary-at-Hill 5 F3
Lovat La EC3. 071-626 4184. Wren, 1676, tower, 1788. The interior which featured box pews and magnificent fittings has recently been destroyed by fire.

St Mary-at-Lambeth 7 F1
Beside Lambeth Palace, Lambeth Rd SE1. 071-261 1891. Rebuilt (except tower) by P. Hardwick, 1850. The tomb of Captain Bligh (Mutiny on the *Bounty*) has been restored. Now houses the Museum of Garden History.

St Mary Islington 2 D2
Upper St N1. 071-226 3400. Launcelot Dowbiggin, 1750. Restored 1956, after bomb damage. Fine baroque steeple.

St Marylebone Parish Church 1 C5
Marylebone Rd NW1. 071-935 7315. Thomas Hardwick, 1813-17. Thomas Harris added the chancel in 1884. Imposing white and gold interior.

St Mary-le-Bow 5 D2
Cheapside EC2. 071-248 5139. The church of 'Bow Bells' fame by Wren, 1670-83. Crypt dates from 1087. Restored by Laurence King after bomb damage. Superb steeple.

St Mary-le-Strand 4 G3
Strand WC2. 071-836 3205. James Gibbs, 1714-17. A perfect small baroque church in the middle of the Strand, sadly encircled by heavy traffic. The official church of the WRNS.

St Mary-le-Strand

St Mary Magdalen Bermondsey 5 F6
Bermondsey St SE1. 071-232 2329. Rebuilt 1680. Charming classical interior. Gothic west end, 1830.

St Mary Somerset 5 D3
Upper Thames St EC4. Wren, 1694. Only the imposing eight-pinnacled tower remains.

St Mary Woolnoth 5 E2
Lombard St EC3. 071-626 9701. Remarkable Baroque Guild Church by Hawksmoor. Church of England services on *weekdays*. Lunchtime relaxation sessions.

St Michael Chester Square 7 A2
Chester Sq SW1. 071-730 8889. Cundy, 1846. War memorial chapel added in 1920. Fine coloured alabaster.

St Michael Paternoster Royal 5 D3
College Hill EC4. 071-248 5202. Wren, 1694, steeple 1713. Recently restored. Dick Whittington buried here (commemorative stained-glass window). Tower used as office by The Missions to Seamen.

St Michael-upon-Cornhill 5 E2
Cornhill EC3. 071-626 8841. Wren, 1677, much restored by Scott. Handsome Gothic tower added 1722. Twelve magnificent bells which are always rung on *Sundays*. First rate choir and organ.

St Olave Hart St 5 F3
8 Hart St EC3. 071-488 4318. Originally early 13thC, on the site of a wooden church of 1080, it was enlarged in 1450. Samuel Pepys' church. Restored by Glanfield after bomb damage. Fine vestry and crypt.

St Pancras New Church 1 F4
Euston Rd NW1. 071-387 8250. W. and H. Inwood, 1822. One of the finest Neoclassical churches in Britain, it is a copy of the Erechtheion in Athens complete with caryatids and Ionic columns. The largest unsupported ceiling in England. Noted for its choir and organ recitals.

St Pancras Old Church 1 F3
Pancras Rd NW1. 071-387 7301. Church with country atmosphere. Added to and transformed 1848. 4thC foundations. Saxon altar stone (AD600). Third oldest Christian site in Europe. A monument to Sir John Soane, which he designed himself, in the churchyard.

St Paul Covent Garden 4 F3
Covent Garden WC2. 071-836 5221. Fine 'ecclesiastical barn' by Inigo Jones affectionately known as the 'Actors' Church'. Rebuilt by Thomas Hardwick after fire of 1795. Pleasant gardens at Bedford St entrance.

St Paul Knightsbridge 4 B5
32a Wilton Pl SW1. 071-235 3460.

Victorian church by Cundy, 1843. Chancel by Bodley. Rich, colourful interior.

St Peter-ad-Vincula 5 G3
Tower of London, Tower Hill EC3. 071-709 0765. Much restored church built about 1512. Many historic monuments. *Admission by guided tour only. Frequent tours (except in bad weather) from 09.45 Mon-Sat & Sun afternoons. Charge (included in entrance charge to Tower of London). Sun services at 09.15 & 11.00.*

St Peter-upon-Cornhill 5 E2
Cornhill EC3. 071-626 9483. Very fine church by Wren, 1677-87. Oldest church site in City, reputedly AD179. Organ built by Schmidt. Fine carved screen. 14th and 15thC plays performed at *Xmas*.

St Sepulchre Without Newgate 5 C2
Holborn Viaduct EC1. 071-248 1660. Rebuilt in 15thC, 1667 and again in the 18th and 19thC. Tombs of Sir Henry Wood and Captain John Smith. Execution bell and the Bells of Old Bailey from the nursery rhyme.

St Stephen Walbrook 5 D2
Walbrook EC4. 071-283 4444. Masterpiece by Wren, 1672-9; steeple 1714-17. Dome, with eight arches, supported by Corinthian pillars, all beautifully restored. Directly under the dome is an intricately carved cylindrical altar in Roman travertine marble sculpted by Henry Moore. Fine fittings. Lord Mayor of London's church and the home since 1953 of 'The Samaritans' who help the suicidal and desperate.

The Temple Church 5 B3
Inner Temple La EC4. 071-353 1736. Completely restored. 12thC round nave and 13thC choir. Fine effigies. Reredos designed by Wren.

Modern architecture

'Modern' architecture came relatively late to England as compared with the USA or Continental Europe. The 1920s and 1930s provide isolated examples, but the 1950s really set the scene, following the 1951 Festival of Britain, with post-war reconstruction needs (both from the intensive bombing and the growth of London itself) creating the impetus for massive housebuilding and town centre redevelopment programmes. Town planning became a major new profession, intended originally to guide development in the public interest but, with the property boom of the 1960s, often acting as the willing ally of the new commercial developers with their vast schemes. Too much in too short a time was the result. The Barbican, London Wall, Victoria Street South West and Commercial Union/P & O, all described in the following pages, show what could be done, as do some of the schools, hospitals, new towns and universities for which British designers have become internationally renowned. But much of London, as of other cities and towns, suffered from the uncontrolled impact of scale, height, form, materials and building technology. With the collapse of the property boom, however, and the growth of conservationist pressure, both phenomena of the 1970s, more balanced policies prevailed and there was growing interest in the saving and re-use of worthwhile buildings. In the 1980s a series of proposals for major new office blocks raised controversy, and the proponents of hi-tech and postmodern architecture began to make their contributions to the city. Docklands was transformed by a massive building boom and is a showplace for 1980s architecture; gleaming office blocks and waterfront apartments replaced disused warehouses and derelict wharves. (These can best be seen from the river.) The most recent building designs in London reflect the varied contemporary scene and different ways of approaching architecture. Some of London's most interesting and innovative buildings are listed below.

Architectural Dialogue
West Hill House, 6 Swains La N6. 081-341 1371. Organise architectural tours of London. *Phone or write for details.*

Alexandra Road Housing
Abbey Rd NW8. London Borough of Camden Architects Dept, Neave Brown 1977. Huge new housing development in which dwellings are stacked in stepped terraces, like the curving contours of artificial hills, enclosing the pedestrian access road in the valley. Dazzling white concrete finish, the detailing of which is of a very high standard.

Alton West Estate (Roehampton)
Roehampton La SW15. London County Council Architects Dept, 1956-61. One of the earliest and most dramatic of post-war housing schemes, mixing high and low-rise blocks in a parkland setting in what should have been a blueprint for future developments.

Apollo Victoria 7 C1
17 Wilton Rd SW1. E. Walmsley-Lewis, 1928-9. London's first cinema built for the 'talkies', its modernistic exterior, in the

contemporary Continental horizontal style, concealing a 'fairy palace' of an interior. Now a theatre.

The Ark
Talgarth Rd W6. Ralph Erskine, 1989-92. A remarkable and ambitious purpose-built office building, the shape of which stems from the shape of the site, bound on one side by the Hammersmith flyover, and on the other by tube tracks. Striking feature is the inclined facade; the cladding comprises alternate bands of clear and tinted triple glazing with copper panels between floors. Internal open terraces overlook a dramatic central atrium; this is the first building in Europe to be treated as one room. A glass-sided wall-climber lift travels through the roof of the atrium to the Summit Room which is 220ft (67m) above London; the view sweeps from Docklands to Heathrow. In spite of winning several architectural awards, the building has been empty since construction.

Barbican   5 D1
London Wall EC2. Chamberlin, Powell & Bon, 1955. A competition-winning city within a city, with over 2000 flats, some in 40-storey towers, a water garden, the restored St Giles' Church, a girls' school, pubs, shops and an arts centre all linked by pedestrian decks to the office towers of London Wall (see below).

British Telecom Tower   4 D1
Howland St W1. Ministry of Public Building & Works, 1966. A dramatic landmark: 580ft (176.9m) tower housing telecommunications equipment and offices. Formerly the Post Office Tower. Marked the start of a trend to high-rise buildings.

Brunswick Centre   2 A5
Brunswick Sq WC1. Patrick Hodgkinson, 1973. A scaled-down version of the megastructure concept. Housing, stepped upwards in the form of a ziggurat, overlooks a pleasant raised shopping plaza. Car parking out of sight below.

Bush Lane House   5 E3
80 Cannon St EC4. Arup Associates, 1976. An inside-out building in which the structural skeleton of stainless steel tubes is exposed, and the transparent skin suspended within a metal cage. This was a solution to the structural constraints imposed by the need to have open floor-plans, unimpeded by columns, and restrictions on foundation depth due to the presence of Cannon Street station.

Canary Wharf Tower
One Canada Sq, Canary Wharf E14.

Cesar Pelli, 1988-90. At 800ft (244m) this is the tallest building in the UK. Clad in stainless steel and topped with a pyramid, the 50-storey building boasts a magnificent lobby finished in Italian and Guatemalan marble. 32 passenger lifts operate from the lobby and are the fastest in the country. Canary Wharf itself is full of elegant architecture, stately streets, well-planted squares and outdoor spaces. Intended as office space, a large proportion of the complex has remained unoccupied, although several international companies have now taken up residence.

Clore Gallery   7 E2
Millbank SW1. James Stirling, Michael Wilford & Assoc, 1986. Housing the Turner Museum, the gallery forms a striking visual link between its two neighbours, the Tate Gallery and the Edwardian military hospital. It adopts characteristics from each – classical stonework on one side, brickwork on the other.

Commercial Union and   5 F2
P & O Buildings
Leadenhall St EC3. GMW Ptnrs, 1987. These buildings represent a unique occurrence in City redevelopment. The two companies, finding that they both needed rehousing, merged to jointly hire the Gollins, Melvin, Ward Partnership to design two separate but complementary buildings. Deliberately contrasted, the tall, sheer CU building stands in an open piazza next to the smaller horizontally-emphasised P & O building and creates a striking effect.

Economist Building   4 D4
25 St James's St SW1. Alison & Peter Smithson, 1964-6. A very beautiful and harmonious group of buildings with its own raised piazza. The design was intended to demonstrate a general principle for the redevelopment of dense commercial areas and is a rare example of new building in an area with a traditional street pattern.

Embankment Place   4 F4
Charing Cross WC2. Terry Farrell, 1987-90. This massive redevelopment of Charing Cross provides 625,000 sq ft of office space, retail outlets and restaurants, as well as the conversion and revitalisation of the vaults below the station. The nine-storey building is suspended from steel arches supported by diameter concrete columns and steel sections. Within the barrel-vault roof are dormer windows, doors and a huge atrium.

Foster Olsen Building

Millwall Dock, Isle of Dogs. Norman Foster, 1970. First building in Britain to make use of special heat and light-reflecting mirror glass. Houses London Docklands Development Corporation.

Hoover Building

Perivale on the A40 just outside Central London. Wallis, Gilbert & Ptnrs, 1932. Blend of Art Deco and Modern Movement. Hoover factory until 1987; restored by Lyons, Sleeman & Hoare; now a superstore.

Lillington Gardens   **7 C2**

Vauxhall Bridge Rd SW1. Darbourne & Darke, 1968-72. Award-winning example of the low-rise, high-density public sector housing which followed the over-exploitation of the tower block. Some tenants have their own gardens.

Lloyds Building   **5 F2**

Lime St EC3. Richard Rogers Ptnrs, 1986. A new hi-tech monument in the City from the architect jointly responsible for the Pompidou Centre in Paris. This multi-faceted, 12-storey, 6-towered structure is the headquarters for the international insurance market. The huge dealing room is housed in a 246ft (75m)-high atrium.

Lloyds

London Bridge City   **5 F4**

Tooley St SE1. St Martin's Property Corporation, 1987. Includes Hay's Galleria, an elegant and lofty shopping and restaurant arcade with a barrel-vaulted glass roof, reminiscent of Victorian railway architecture or perhaps the Crystal Palace. Also includes No.1 London Bridge, an office building of pink granite, comprised of two towers – one of 12 storeys, in the form of an arch, and the other of nine storeys.

London Central Mosque   **1 A4**

Regent's Park, entrance by Hanover Gate NW1. Sir Frederick Gibberd & Ptnrs, 1978. Islam's aesthetic and functional needs blend with the constraints of a small and sensitive site adjacent to Nash terraces in a dramatic focus for London's Muslim community.

London Pavilion   **4 E3**

Piccadilly Circus W1. Chapman Taylor Ptnrs, 1988. Listed building redeveloped as a shopping and leisure complex. The elegant Neo-classical exterior remains as it was originally but two extra storeys have been added and topped with sculptures of classical maidens.

London Wall office development   **5 D1**

London Wall EC2. Early post-1945 comprehensive planning in a badly blitzed area. Six 18-storey office towers (interspersed with smaller blocks) laid out on the City planners' grid and among the first in Britain with all-glass curtain walling. At the north-west end of London Wall, the most recent tower stands on top of the Museum of London.

Minster Court   **5 F3**

Mincing La EC3. GMW Ptnrs, 1988-91. Group of three Gothic buildings surrounding a glass-roofed court. Clad in granite with pannelised curtain walling, the buildings contribute to the patchwork of forms and colours which now make up the City. Built to provide high quality office space, 85% of which is occupied.

Museum of London   **5 D1**

London Wall EC2. Powell & Moya, 1978. Highly ingenious planning. The Museum (combining the Guildhall and London Museum collections) serves as the podium for an office block and bridges London Wall to descend into a garden restaurant inside a traffic roundabout.

National Westminster Tower   **5 F2**

25 Old Broad St EC2. Richard Seifert, 1978-81. Extraordinarily slender, shining structure, the closeness of its vertical lines giving a pin-striped effect. Higher than Telecom Tower. Believed to be the tallest cantilevered building in the world at 600ft (183m), it gracefully dominates London's skyline. Houses the National Westminster Bank's International Division.

New Zealand House   **4 E4**

Haymarket SW1. Robert Matthew, Johnson-Marshall & Ptnrs, 1963. A finely modelled 15-storey glass tower on a 4-storey podium. Good material and detailing and an exciting entrance hall. A particularly interesting foil to its flamboyant Victorian neighbour – 'Her Majesty's Theatre'.

Regent's Park Zoo 1 C3

North side of Regent's Park NW1. Contains a number of interesting buildings: Gorilla House by Lubetkin & Tecton 1935; Penguin Pool by Tecton 1935; Aviary by Viscount Snowdon, Cedric Price & Frank Newby 1965-6; Elephant House by Casson, Conder & Ptnrs 1965-6; Small Mammal House by Design Research Unit 1967; Sobell Apes & Monkeys Pavilion 1972; New Lion Terraces 1976; Amphitheatre by John Toovey 1982-5; African Aviary remodelled by John S. Bonnington Ptnrs 1989-90 (previously Eastern Aviary 1863).

St Paul's Cathedral Choir School 5 D2

New Change EC4. Architects' Co-Partnership, 1967. Incorporates the surviving tower of Wren's war-destroyed St Augustine's, a good example of old blended with new and a better neighbour to the Cathedral than the office plaza to its west.

St Katharine's Dock development 5 G4

St Katharine-by-the-Tower E1. The first major bid to regenerate London's former dockland, an £80 million scheme by Taylor Woodrow following a competition in 1969. The World Trade Centre and the Tower Hotel are modern buildings by Renton Howard Wood Levin; the restored Ivory House, a 19thC warehouse, is now apartments, shops, offices, a yacht club and a restaurant.

South Bank Arts Centre 5 A4

Waterloo SE1. First came the Royal Festival Hall (Robert Matthew and Leslie Martin, London County Council Architects Dept), musical focus of the 1951 Festival of Britain which spurred the redevelopment of this run-down area. Most recent is the Museum of the Moving Image (Avery Assoc) opened in 1988. In between came the National Theatre (Denys Lasdun) completed in 1977 with its three auditoria; the Hayward Art Gallery and the Queen Elizabeth Hall and Purcell Room, by the Greater London Council Architects Dept. Concrete dominates.

Sudbury Town underground station

Bridgewater Rd, Wembley, Middx. Charles Holden, 1932. First in a series of modern underground stations.

Thames Flood Barrier

Unity Way, Eastmoor St SE18. This visually and technologically exciting structure is one of the most impressive examples of modern engineering in Europe. Completed in 1982, its gates swing up through 90 degrees from the river bed and create a stainless steel barrage to stem dangerously high tides which periodically threaten London. The Thames Barrier Visitor Centre houses an exhibition and presentation, illuminating the engineering feats involved in the barrier's construction. *Charge.*

Tobacco Dock

Pennington St E1. Terry Farrell, 1989. 19thC former warehouse converted into a shopping and leisure complex. Impressive brick undervaults; roof pierced by clock and gazebo. Development work carried out using original suppliers of materials wherever possible.

Trocadero 4 E3

Coventry St W1. Originally a dance hall, gutted and rebuilt by Robinson and Arun in 1985, the old Victorian facade hides a modern shopping, restaurant and leisure complex.

Vauxhall Cross 7 E3

85 Albert Embankment SE1. Terry Farrell, 1990-2. 10-storey glass construction built to house the headquarters of a government department. Rises in layers from the bank of the River Thames to form a group of three blocks linked by glazed courtyards and atria. 25 different make-ups of glass exist throughout the building.

Vickers' Tower 7 E2

Millbank SW1. Ronald Ward & Ptnrs, 1960-3. One of London's earliest glass-walled office skyscrapers, and still one of the most elegant.

Victoria Street South West redevelopment 7 C1

Victoria St SW1. Elsom Pack & Roberts, 1975. Broken by a piazza giving for the first time a front view of Westminster Cathedral, this is modern commercial development of the highest quality – a notable improvement on the rest of Victoria Street.

Museums and galleries

London's national museums and galleries contain some of the richest collections in the world; and are full of surprising treasures and oddities. They range from the vast British Museum to more recent and specialist additions, many of which incorporate interactive displays and exhibits Access to special items or collections not on show is willingly given. In addition they offer a service of advice and scholarly reference unequalled anywhere in the world. Note that their reference libraries and print collections are further described under 'Reference libraries'.

The British Museum, the V & A and other national galleries give expert opinions on the age or identity of objects or paintings – they will not however give you a valuation. Apart from the national art collections in the Tate Gallery, the National Gallery and the National Portrait Gallery, London is further enriched by other, once private, collections, now open to the public.

It has long been a tradition that national museums and galleries are free, but some have now found it necessary to introduce either voluntary contributions or a fixed admission fee. Special exhibitions usually have an entrance fee.

Artillery Museum
The Rotunda, Repository Rd, Woolwich Common SE18. 081-316 5402. The Rotunda was an architectural 'tent' once erected in Carlton House (1814). Notable collection of guns, muskets, ammunition and cannons. Usually *OPEN 12.00-17.00 Mon-Fri, 13.00-17.00 (16.00 Nov-Mar) Sat & Sun. Please phone to check. Free.*

Bank of England Museum   5 E2
Threadneedle St EC2. 071-601 5545. History of the 'Old Lady of Threadneedle Street' recreated through reconstructions of Soane's original designs, displays and an interactive video game. Also see the history of the banknote and real gold bars. Exhibits include Bank's first strong-box and the reproduction of the original Banking Hall. Audio cassette tour for visually-handicapped visitors. *OPEN 10.00-17.00 Mon-Fri, 11.00-17.00 Sat. Free.*

Barbican Art Gallery   2 E6
Barbican Centre EC2. Recorded information: 071-588 9023. Large temporary exhibition gallery with a varied programme of international, contemporary and histori-

cal shows. *OPEN 10.00-18.45 Mon-Sat, 12.00-17.45 Sun & B.hols. Charge.*

HMS *Belfast*   5 F4
Morgan's La, Tooley St SE1. 071-407 6434. The last survivor of the Royal Navy's World War II war cruisers. Seven decks to explore bringing to life a sailor's experiences of war at sea. *OPEN 10.00-18.00 Mon-Sun (to 16.30 Nov-Mar). Charge.*

HMS *Belfast*

Bramah Tea & Coffee Museum 5 G5
The Clore Buildings, Maguire St SE1. 071-378 0222. Charts the development of tea and coffee, from the 17th and 18thC coffee houses frequented by Pepys, Boswell and Dr Johnson, to the Boston Tea Party and the 19thC tea clipper races, up to the arrival of instant coffee and tea bags. Café where tea and coffee can be sampled; special Bramah house blends are available. *OPEN 10.00-17.30 Mon-Sun. Charge.*

British Museum   1 G6
Great Russell St WC1. 071-636 1555. One of the largest and greatest museums in the world. The Egyptian sculpture gallery dramatically highlights colossi of pharaohs, sphinxes, sarcophagi, priests, chantresses, architectural elements and the Rosetta Stone. Upstairs mummies preside, striking a chill and thrill to the heart. Other rooms contain tomb paintings and papyri, including editions of the Book of the Dead, and domestic utensils which were used by the living.

Cycladic, Bronze Age and Archaic remains are part of an extensive Greek and Roman collection. The Elgin marbles, sculptures from the Parthenon in Athens, and Roman pavements, are impressively displayed and still generate a sense of awe. Personified breezes in the Nereid room convey a similar sense of movement and life. The Portland Vase and the bronze head of Augustus with staring glass eyes are remarkable among the Roman exhibits. The Wolfson galleries in the basement also house an immense collection of classical sculpture.

Be sure to see the colossal winged lion and bull with human heads in the Assyrian Transept, the sculptures from the throne-room of the palace at Nimrud and harps and lyres in the Babylonian Room. Europe 1500-1800 is a new exhibition, opening in late 1993, which brings together European collections from the Renaissance to the Neo-classical period. Coins and Medals, Medieval and Later Antiquities, Oriental Antiquities, Korean Art, Amaravati Buddhist Sculptures, Japanese Antiquities, Prehistoric and Romano-British Antiquities, Prints and Drawings, are some other collections on view. All are outstanding. Building 1823-47 by Sir Robert Smirke; the domed reading room 1857 is by Sidney Smirke. Museum *OPEN 10.00-17.00 Mon-Sat, 14.30-18.00 Sun.* Films *Tue-Fri*, lectures *Tue-Sat*, gallery talks. *Free.* Reading room *OPEN to members only.*

Cabinet War Rooms 4 E5
Clive Steps, King Charles St SW1. 071-930 6961. Fascinating reconstruction of the underground emergency accommodation, comprising a suite of 21 rooms, used by Winston Churchill, his War Cabinet and the Chiefs of Staff of Britain's armed forces during World War II. *OPEN 10.00-17.15 Mon-Sun. Charge.*

Chelsea Royal Hospital 6 G3
Royal Hospital Rd SW3. 071-730 0161. Small museum housed in a part of the hospital built in 1819 by Sir John Soane. Prints, drawings, manuscripts, uniforms, medals and other items related to the history of the hospital. *OPEN 10.00-12.00 & 14.00-16.00 Mon-Sat, 14.00-16.00 Sun. CLOSED Sun Oct-Mar & B.hols. Free.*

Church Farm House Museum
Greyhound Hill NW4. 081-203 0130. A 17thC gabled farmhouse, whose stone-floored kitchen with its huge fireplace is equipped with Victorian cooking utensils. Parlour and bedrooms are used for small, changing exhibitions. *OPEN 10.00-13.00 & 14.00-17.30 Mon & Wed-Sat, 10.00-13.00 Tue, 14.00-17.30 Sun. CLOSED Fri. Free.*

Commonwealth Institute 3 B6
Kensington High St W8. 071-603 4535. Centre for Commonwealth education and culture. Promotes the Commonwealth countries through a programme of permanent and special exhibitions reflecting Commonwealth peoples and issues. Scenery, natural resources, way of life and industrial development of Commonwealth countries. Reference library of current Commonwealth literature. Cinema, theatre, art exhibitions, craft shop, book-

shop. *OPEN 10.00-17.00 Mon-Sat, 14.00-17.00 Sun. CLOSED B.hols. Free (charge for special exhibitions).*

Courtauld Institute Galleries 4 G3
Somerset House, Strand WC2. 071-873 2526. The Courtauld Collection of French Impressionists (including fine paintings by Cézanne, Van Gogh, Gauguin) and the Lee, Gambier-Parry and Fry, Hunter & Brouse Collections. The Princes Gate collection of Flemish and Italian Old Masters is on permanent exhibition. *OPEN 10.00-18.00 Mon-Sat, 14.00-18.00 Sun. Charge.*

Crafts Council Gallery 2 C3
44a Pentonville Rd, N1. 071-278 7700. Six main exhibitions a year of contemporary craft; also an information service on where to learn about or buy crafts; picture library which surveys the best of crafts in Britain. Shop. Café. *OPEN 11.00-18.00 Tue-Sat, 14.00-18.00 Sun. CLOSED Mon & B.hols. Free.*

Cricket Museum
Lord's Cricket Ground NW8. 071-266 3825. Tours of the whole ground including museum run daily throughout the year. Collection includes the 'Ashes', Wisden Trophy and cricket memorabilia. Modern displays include a 'talking head' of W.G. Grace and videos of great performances. Donations. *OPEN matchdays 10.00-17.00. Charge (reduced if you buy a match ticket).*

Cuming Museum
Newington District Library, Walworth Rd SE17. 071-703 3324. The archaeology and history of Southwark from earliest times to the present. Also houses the Lovett collection of London superstitions. *OPEN 10.00-17.00 Tue-Fri (to 19.00 Thur, to 17.00 Sat). CLOSED Sun, Mon & B.hols. Free.*

Design Museum
Butler's Wharf, Shad Thames SE1. 071-403 6933. A fascinating introduction to 20thC design, technology and consumer culture. Examines the role of design in everyday life through a changing programme of exhibitions and displays – which includes cars, furniture, domestic appliances, graphics and ceramics. Also has a library, bookshop and riverside café/bar. *OPEN 10.30-18.30 Mon-Sun (to 17.00 Sat). Charge.*

Dulwich Picture Gallery
College Rd SE21. 081-693 5254. English, Italian, Spanish, Dutch and French paintings exhibited in one of the oldest and most beautiful art galleries in England. Notable works by Rembrandt, Rubens, Canaletto and Gainsborough. Building

1811-14 by Sir John Soane. *OPEN 10.00-13.00 & 14.00-17.00 Tue-Fri, 11.00-17.00 Sat, 14.00-17.00 Sun. CLOSED Mon & B.hols. Small charge.*

Fenton House
Hampstead Gro NW3. 071-435 3471. Built in 1693. The Benton Fletcher collection of early keyboard instruments and the Binning collection of porcelain and furniture. *OPEN Apr-Oct 11.00-18.00 Sat-Wed; Mar 14.00-17.00 Sat & Sun only. CLOSED Nov-Feb. Charge.*

Florence Nightingale Museum   4 G5
St Thomas' Hospital, 2 Lambeth Palace Rd SE1. 071-620 0374. Mementoes of the 'Lady with the lamp' together with the re-creation of a ward during the Crimean War. Films and lectures. *OPEN 10.00-16.00 Tue-Sun. CLOSED Mon. Charge.*

Geffrye Museum
Kingsland Rd E2. 071-739 9893. Housed in former 18thC almshouses. Period rooms and furniture from 1600 to the 1950s. *OPEN 10.00-17.00 Tue-Sat, 14.00-17.00 Sun. CLOSED Mon except B.hols. Free.*

Goldsmiths' Hall   5 D2
Foster La EC2. 071-606 7010. Fine collection of antique plate. The largest collection of modern silver and jewellery in the country. *Special public open days: phone for details.*

Guildhall Gallery   5 D2
Aldermanbury EC2. 071-606 3030. Selections from the Guildhall's permanent collection, loan exhibitions and shows of art societies. New gallery in planning stage. *Viewing by special arrangement only. Free.*

Gunnersbury Park Museum
Gunnersbury Park W3. 081-992 1612. Items illustrating the local history of Ealing and Hounslow, including archaeology, costume, transport, domestic life, trades, crafts and industries. Housed in former Rothschild Regency country mansion in large park. *OPEN Mar-Oct 13.00-17.00 Mon-Fri, 14.00-18.00 Sat & Sun; Nov-Feb 13.00-16.00 Mon-Sun. Free.*

Hayward Gallery   5 A4
Belvedere Rd, South Bank Centre SE1. 071-928 3144. Changing exhibitions of major works of art arranged by the Arts Council. Fine modern building and river setting. *OPEN 10.00-20.00 Tue & Wed, 10.00-18.00 Thur-Mon. Charge.*

Heinz Gallery   4 B2
Royal Institute of British Architects Drawings Collection, 21 Portman Sq W1. 071-580 5533. Regular exhibitions of architectural drawings. *OPEN 11.00-17.00 Mon-Fri, 10.00-13.00 Sat. Free.*

Horniman Museum & Gardens
100 London Rd SE23. 081-699 2339. Varied collections of ethnography, musical instruments and natural history. Started by Frederick J. Horniman who was a tea magnate and an instinctive collector. In the new Music Room (opening in September 1993) computer displays will allow visitors to explore an instrument's evolution, while sampling its sound through headphones. 'Living Waters' aquarium helps visitors discover the complex ecology of waterlife. Education centre and reference library. Café. Gardens. *OPEN 10.30-17.30 Mon-Sat, 14.00-17.30 Sun. CLOSED B.hols. Free.*

Imperial War Museum   5 B6
Lambeth Rd SE1. 071-416 5000. This popular national museum tells the story of wartime from Flanders to the Gulf War. Weapons, aircraft, submarines, sound and film exhibits, art galleries. The 'Blitz and Trench Experience', multi-sensory displays, and operation 'Jericho', where visitors can experience at first hand what it was like to fly with the RAF on their daring 1944 raid over France, are not to be missed. Education and research programmes. Guided tours *(by arrangement – phone 071-416 5350)*. Shop and café. *OPEN 10.00-18.00 Mon-Sun. Charge (free after 16.30).*

Imperial War Museum

Institute of Contemporary Arts (ICA)   4 E4
Nash House, The Mall SW1. 071-930 3647. Three galleries in which changing exhibitions explore new themes and media in contemporary art. Also two cinemas, theatre, lunchtime and evening talks; bar, restaurant and bookshop. *OPEN 12.00-23.00 (Galleries to 20.00) Mon-Sun. Charge.*

Iveagh Bequest, Kenwood
Kenwood House, Hampstead La NW3. 081-348 1286. Fine house by Robert Adam. Paintings by Rembrandt, Vermeer, Reynolds and Gainsborough. Also sculpture and 18thC English furniture. Music

and poetry recitals. *OPEN Apr-Sep 10.00-18.00 Mon-Sun; Oct-Mar 10.00-16.00 Mon-Sun. Free.*

Jewish Museum   1 **F5**
Woburn House, Tavistock Sq WC1. 071-388 4525. Jewish festivals and history illustrated by ceremonial objects. Two audio-visual programmes. Shop. *OPEN 10.00-16.00 Tue-Fri (to 12.45 only Fri, Oct-Mar); 10.00-16.00 Sun. CLOSED Sat, Mon, Jewish & B.hols. Charge.*

London Canal Museum
12-13 New Wharf Rd N1. 071-713 0836. Housed in an 1850s ice house on Battlebridge Basin; blocks of ice imported from Norway were carried here on the Regent's Canal to vast ice wells, one of which has been partly excavated and is on show. Museum tells the story of the development of London's canals, from the early days as an important trade route, to today's more leisurely pursuits. Exhibitions, special events, shop. *OPEN 10.00-16.30 Tue-Sun. Charge.*

London Planetarium   1 **C5**
Marylebone Rd NW1. 071-486 1121. A study of planets, stars and the universe. Tickets include entry to the 'Space Trail', where you go on an exciting voyage of discovery into space before taking your seats for the star show. Shows *every 40 mins Mon-Sun. First show 10.20; last show 17.00. Charge.*

London Transport Museum   4 **F3**
The Piazza, Covent Garden WC2. 071-379 6344. Story of London's transport. Historic road and rail vehicles, working exhibits and audio-visual displays. Shop. *OPEN 10.00-18.00 (last admission 17.15) Mon-Sun. Charge.*

Madame Tussaud's   1 **C5**
Marylebone Rd NW1. 071-935 6861. Among waxwork effigies of the famous and notorious, meet the Royal Family, Pavarotti, Nelson Mandela and Cher. Murderers lurk in the Chamber of Horrors. Mingle with celebrities at 'The Garden Party'. Experience some of the greatest events that have shaped London's heritage at 'The Spirit of London' where you journey through 400 years of London's history in a replica of a black taxi cab. *OPEN 10.00-17.30 Mon-Fri, 09.30-17.30 Sat & Sun. Charge.*

Martinware Pottery Collection
Public Library, 9-11 Osterley Park Rd, Southall, Middx. 081-574 3412. Collection of Martinware, including birds, face mugs and grotesques. *OPEN 09.00-19.45 Tue, Thur & Fri, 09.00-17.00 Wed & Sat. CLOSED B.hols. Free.*

Museum of Garden History   7 **F1**
St Mary-at-Lambeth, Lambeth Rd SE1. 071-261 1891. The church beside Lambeth Palace was rescued from demolition in the 1970s, and exhibits the discoveries and travels of the two John Tradescants, father and son, buried in the churchyard beside Captain Bligh of the *Bounty*. Successively gardeners to Charles I and Henrietta Maria, they introduced plants from abroad, some of which feature in the churchyard garden. Café. *OPEN mid Mar-mid Dec 11.00-15.00 Mon-Fri, 10.30-17.00 Sun. CLOSED Sat. Free.*

Museum of London   5 **D1**
150 London Wall EC2. 071-600 3699. A three-dimensional history of the City and London area, with models, reconstructions and even the Lord Mayor's Coach of 1756. A new permanent display, 'Tudor and Stuart Theatres' shows a model of the Rose Theatre based on evidence excavated by museum archaeologists. Lectures, films, shop and restaurant. *OPEN 10.00-18.00 Tue-Sat, 12.00-17.50 Sun. CLOSED Mon. Free.*

Museum of Mankind   4 **D3**
6 Burlington Gdns W1. 071-437 2224. Exciting collection of primitive artefacts and clothing. Changing exhibitions illustrate a variety of non-Western societies and cultures. Film shows *13.30, 15.00 Tue-Fri. Café. OPEN 10.00-17.00 Mon-Sat, 14.30-18.00 Sun. Free.*

Museum of the Moving   5 **A4**
Image (MOMI)
Under Waterloo Bridge, South Bank SE1. 071-928 3535. Part of the South Bank complex, this bright, exciting museum charts the history of moving images from Chinese shadow puppets to film, television, video, satellite and hologram technology. Forty main exhibit areas plus changing exhibitions. Plenty of opportunity for taking part. Lectures, films, Victorian magic lantern shows. *OPEN 10.00-18.00 Mon-Sun. Charge.*

Musical Museum
368 High St, Brentford, Middx. 081-560 8108. The only musical museum in Europe that has ten reproducing pianos and three reproducing pipe organs all under one roof. In all around 200 instruments, some of which will be played during the 1½-hr tour. *OPEN Jul & Aug 14.00-17.00 Wed-Sat; Sep-Jun 14.00-17.00 Sat & Sun. Charge. No small children. Parties by arrangement.* Send sae for list of concerts.

National Army Museum   6 **F4**
Royal Hospital Rd SW3. 071-730 0717.

National Gallery

The story of the Army from 1480 to present day, its triumphs and disasters, its professional and social life all over the world. Uniforms, pictures, weapons and personal relics. *OPEN 10.00-17.30 Mon-Sun. Free.*

National Gallery   **4 E3**
Trafalgar Sq WC2. 071-839 3321. Houses the national collection of Western European painting, comprising over 2000 pictures dating from the 13thC to the early 20thC. Galleries are divided, by period, into four areas comprising paintings of various schools, hung to emphasise the links existing between painters of different nationalities. Rich in early Italian (Leonardo da Vinci, Raphael, Botticelli and Titian), Dutch and Flemish (Rembrandt, Rubens, Frans Hals, Van Dyck), Spanish 15-18thC (Velázquez and El Greco), British 18th and 19thC (Constable, Turner, Gainsborough and Reynolds), Impressionists (Monet, Cézanne and Van Gogh). A booklet, *20 Great Paintings*, on sale in the shop in several languages, leads the time-pressed to 20 masterpieces. Daily guided tours (except *Sun*) highlight selected pictures. Brasserie and café. Films and lectures. Building 1838 by W. Wilkins. Sainsbury Wing, R. Venturi 1991. *OPEN 10.00-18.00 Mon-Sat (to 20.00 Wed, Jun-Aug), 14.00-18.00 Sun. Free (charge for special exhibitions).*

National Maritime Museum
See under Greenwich in *'Historic London'.*

National Portrait Gallery   **4 E3**
2 St Martin's Pl WC2. 071-306 0055. Founded in 1856, an historic collection of contemporary portraits of famous British men and women, forming a fascinating study of human personality. There are now over 9000 portraits in the primary collection, from Henry VIII to Churchill, Shakespeare to the Princess of Wales, and Lawrence of Arabia to Mick Jagger. The importance of the sitter is the main criterion for inclusion. The collection includes paintings, miniatures, sculptures, drawings, caricatures and photographs, and is arranged chronologically, from the medieval period to the present day; the new Galleries of Modern British History and a special gallery devoted to photography are due to open in late 1993. The gallery has constantly changing displays and a programme of special temporary exhibitions; the annual competition for young portrait painters produces exciting developments in modern portraiture. Education centre, resource centre, library, bookshop. *OPEN 10.00-17.00 Mon-Fri, 10.00-18.00 Sat, 14.00-18.00 Sun. CLOSED some B.hols. Free (charge for some special exhibitions).*

National Postal Museum   **5 D2**
King Edward Bldg, King Edward St EC1. 071-239 5420. Superb displays of stamps including the Phillips collection and the 'Berne' collection. Reference library. Tours by *prior arrangement. OPEN 09.30-16.30 Mon-Thur, 09.30-16.00 Fri. CLOSED Sat, Sun & B.hols. Free.*

Natural History Museum   **6 D1**
& Geological Museum
Cromwell Rd SW7. 071-938 9123. Made up of the Life Galleries and Earth Galleries where advanced and innovative methods of display involve, interest and entertain visitors of all ages. In the Life Galleries walk among huge skeletons and watch moving dinosaurs come to life. Exhibits on human biology, marine invertabrates and meteorites. Don't miss 'Creepy Crawlies', the world of anthropods revealed using audio-visual aids, or the lifesize model of a 90ft (27.5m) blue whale. In the Earth Galleries learn about the Earth's resources, Britain's fossils and minerals, and see brilliant gems on view. Discovery Centre, shops, café, picnic area. *OPEN 10.00-18.00 Mon-Sat, 11.00-18.00 Sun. Charge (free 16.30-*

Natural History Museum

18.00 Mon-Fri except B.hols and for educational groups booking in advance).

North Woolwich Old Station Museum

Pier Rd E16. 071-474 7244. Housed in what was North Woolwich station are three exhibition galleries telling the story of the Great Eastern Railway in photographs, plans, models, documents and relics. Houses GER steam locomotive built in 1876 and a restored Victorian station booking office. *OPEN 10.00-17.00 Mon-Wed & Sat, 14.00-17.00 Sun & B.hols. CLOSED Thur & Fri. Free.*

Old Royal Observatory

See under Greenwich in 'Historic London'.

Passmore Edwards Museum

Romford Rd E15. 081-534 2274. Collections of Essex archaeology, local history, geology and biology. Good collection of Bow porcelain. *OPEN 11.00-17.00 Wed-Fri, 13.00-17.00 Sat, 14.00-17.00 Sun. CLOSED Mon & Tue. Free.*

Percival David Foundation of   **1 F5** Chinese Art

53 Gordon Sq WC1. 071-387 3909. Chinese ceramics from Sung to Ch'ing dynasty. Reference library. *OPEN 10.30-17.00 Mon-Fri. CLOSED Sat, Sun & B.hols. Free.*

Photographers' Gallery   **4 E3**

5 & 8 Great Newport St WC2. 071-831 1772. Frequent exhibitions, often with new British work. Print room, coffee bar, bookshop. *OPEN 11.00-19.00 Tue-Sat. CLOSED Sun & Mon. Free.*

Pollock's Toy Museum   **4 D1**

1 Scala St W1. 071-636 3452. Three rickety floors packed with a magical mix of bygone toys. Look out for the oldest teddy in the world. *OPEN 10.00-17.00 Mon-Sat. CLOSED Sun & B.hols. Charge.*

Public Record Office   **5 B2**

Chancery La WC2. 071-831 7065. Permanent display of records on major events in the history of England. Houses the Domesday Book of 1086 and one of the four existing Magna Cartas. *OPEN 09.30-17.00 Mon-Fri. CLOSED Sat, Sun & B.hols. Free.*

Queen's Gallery   **4 C5**

Buckingham Palace, Buckingham Palace Rd SW1. 071-930 4832. Pictures and works of art from all parts of the Royal collection. Exhibitions changed at intervals. *OPEN 10.30-17.00 Tue-Sat, 14.00-17.00 Sun. CLOSED Mon except B.hols. Charge.*

Rock Circus   **4 E3**

London Pavilion, Piccadilly W1. 071-734

8025. The skills and artistry of Madame Tussaud's combined with the latest audio techniques bring to life the great rock stars. See the Beatles, Buddy Holly, Stevie Wonder, Madonna. *OPEN 11.00-22.00 Mon-Sun. Charge.*

Royal Academy of Arts   **4 D3**

Burlington House, Piccadilly W1. 071-439 7438. Presents Britain's major exhibitions of visual arts and holds a series of major special-loan exhibitions throughout the year. Probably most famous for its annual Summer Exhibition *May-Aug*, in which the work of living artists is displayed, and in most cases is for sale. Some works from its permanent collection, including paintings by Constable and Reynolds, have been copied in relief 'thermoforms' for the blind and visually impaired. Restaurant. *OPEN 10.00-18.00 Mon-Sun. Charge.*

Royal Air Force Museum

Grahame Park Way NW9. 081-205 2266. (10-min walk from Colindale station on the Northern Line.) The first national museum of aviation telling the fascinating story of flight through the display of over 65 historic aircraft. Situated on the site of a former wartime airfield, see the legendary Sopwith Camel, the mighty Vulcan, the Spitfire, Hurricane, Lancaster, Wellington, Flying Fortress plus others. One hall commemorates the 50th anniversary of the Battle of Britain and uses the latest display techniques. Also a new flight simulator which allows visitors to experience the thrill of flying in an RAF Tornado and a replica of the No.11 Group Operations Room at RAF Uxbridge. A *20-minute* video gives the complete story of this important period. Cinema, shop. The Bomber Command Hall is also incorporated into the museum. *OPEN 10.00-17.30 Mon-Sun. CLOSED B.hols. Charge.*

Royal Mews   **4 C6**

Buckingham Palace Rd SW1. 071-930 4832. The Queen's horses are on view here plus the royal and state carriages including the gold coach and the glass coach. The gold state coach has been used for every coronation since George IV. It is 24ft (8m) long, weighs four tonnes and when in use is drawn by eight horses. The glass coach is used for royal weddings. *Open Jan-Mar 12.00-16.00 Wed; Apr-Sep 12.00-16.00 Tue-Thur; Oct-Dec 12.00-16.00 Wed; except on state occasions. Last admission 15.30. Charge.*

St Bride's Crypt Museum   **5 C2**

St Bride's Church, Fleet St EC4. 071-353 1301. Interesting relics found during excavations. A unique continuity of remains from Roman London to the present day. *OPEN 09.00-17.00 Mon-Fri, occasionally Sat & Sun. Free.*

Science Museum 3 E6

Exhibition Rd SW7. 071-938 8123/8111. The history of science and its application to industry. A large collection of very fine engineering models, steam engines, early motor cars, aeroplanes and all aspects of applied physics and chemistry. Explore the history of printing, textiles, and many other industries through working models. Special features include space exploration, with the actual Apollo 10 space capsule. The Wellcome galleries examine the history of medicine with a reconstruction of a 1980s operating theatre. The 'Launch Pad' is a popular interactive hands-on gallery of large working models which demonstrate scientific principles and present challenging activities. *OPEN 10.00-18.00 Mon-Sat, 14.30-18.00 Sun. CLOSED B.hols. Charge. Free lectures & films, or write for brochure.*

Serpentine Gallery 3 E4

Kensington Gardens W2. 071-402 6075. Changing monthly exhibitions of contemporary art, sculpture, paintings, drawings and prints. *OPEN 10.00-18.00 Mon-Sun. Free.*

Shakespeare Globe Museum 5 D4

1 Bear Gdns, Bankside SE1. 071-928 6342. Converted 18thC warehouse on site of 16thC bear-baiting ring and the Hope Playhouse. Permanent exhibition of Shakespearian theatre. The theatre is being reconstructed to the design of 1599 and can be viewed. Scheduled for completion in Spring 1994. *OPEN 10.00-17.00 Mon-Sat, 13.30-17.30 Sun. Charge.*

Sherlock Holmes Museum 1 B5

221b Baker St NW1. 071-935 8866. In a Grade II listed building, a collection of Victorian memorabilia relating to Sherlock Holmes and his friend Dr Watson, the world-famous characters created by Sir Arthur Conan Doyle. Personal exhibits on display. *OPEN 10.00-18.00 summer, 09.30-17.30 winter. Charge.*

Sir John Soane's Museum 4 G2

13 Lincoln's Inn Fields WC2. 071-405 2107. Soane's personal collection of antiquities, paintings and drawings, including Hogarth's Election and the Rake's Progress, original Piranesi drawings and most of the architectural drawings of the Adam brothers. Building designed by Soane, 1810-13. *OPEN 10.00-17.00 Tue-Sat. Free lecture tour 14.30 Sat (limited to 25 people, no parties. Parties welcome at other times by arrangement). CLOSED B.hols. Free. Library, appt only.*

South London Art Gallery

65 Peckham Rd SE5. 071-703 6120. Holds varied exhibitions each year with a policy to explore new developments in the visual arts. Founded in 1891, it was the first gallery to open on a Sun. *OPEN during exhibitions 10.00-18.00 Tue-Sat, 15.00-18.00 Sun. CLOSED Mon & B.hols. Free.*

Tate Gallery 7 E2

Millbank SW1. 071-821 1313. Recorded information: 071-821 7128. Representative collections of British painting from the 16thC to the present day. Fine examples of Blake, Turner, Hogarth, the pre-Raphaelites, Ben Nicolson, Spencer and Francis Bacon; sculpture by Moore and Hepworth. Also a particularly rich collection of foreign paintings and sculpture from 1880 to the present day, including paintings by Picasso, Chagall, Mondrian, Pollock, Lichtenstein, Rothko, Degas, Marini and Giacometti. Sculpture tours for the visually handicapped (by appointment). Policy of annual rotation. Designed 1897 by Sidney H.J. Smith. The Clore Gallery was built to house the Turner bequest. *OPEN 10.00-17.50 Mon-Sat, 14.00-17.50 Sun. Lectures and films at various times. Restaurant. Shop. Free (charge for some special exhibitions).*

Tate Gallery

Theatre Museum   4 **F3**
1e Tavistock St WC2. 071-831 1227.
Branch of the V & A. Devoted to theatre,
ballet, opera, circus and music hall.
Costumes, playbills, scenery, props.
Café. *OPEN 11.00-19.00 Tue-Sun.
Charge.*

Tower of London, the   5 **G3**
Armouries
Tower Hill EC3. 071-709 0765. The
Crown Jewels (heavily guarded).
London's oldest museum with the largest
collection of armour and arms in Britain:
10-20thC. *OPEN 09.30-17.45 Mon-Sat
(to 16.30 winter), 10.00-17.30 Sun.
Charge.*

Victoria and Albert Museum   6 **D1**
Cromwell Rd SW7. 071-938 8500. The
V & A is Britain's National Museum of Art
and Design and has some of the world's
finest collections of furniture, ceramics
and glass, metalwork and jewellery,
textiles and dress from the Middle Ages
to the 20thC, as well as paintings, prints
and drawings, posters and photographs,
and sculpture. It also has superb collections from China, Japan, India and the
Middle East. More than 300 paintings
hang the length of the restored Great
Staircase in the Henry Cole wing. There is
a full programme of courses, events and
introductory tours. Restaurant (Jazz
Brunch on *Sun*) and café. *OPEN 10.00-
17.50 Mon-Sat, 14.30-17.50 Sun.
Admission by voluntary donation.*

Wallace Collection   4 **B2**
Hertford House, Manchester Sq W1.
071-935 0687. A private collection of outstanding works of art which was
bequeathed to the nation by Lady

Wallace in 1897. Splendid representation
of the French 17th and 18thC artists,
including paintings by Boucher, Watteau
and Fragonard. Home to the 'Laughing
Cavalier' by Frans Hals and also several
Rembrandts, a Titian, some Rubens, and
paintings by Canaletto and Guardi.
Important collections of French furniture,
Sèvres porcelain, Majolica, Limoges
enamel and armour. *OPEN 10.00-17.00
Mon-Sat, 14.00-17.00 Sun. CLOSED
some B.hols. Free.*

Westminster Abbey   4 **F6**
Treasures
The Cloisters, Westminster Abbey SW1.
071-222 5152. The Cloisters contain the
famous wax effigies of British monarchs
including Elizabeth I and Charles II, and
Admiral Lord Nelson. Also plans, paintings, prints and documents. Forms part of
a new complex with the Chapter House
and the Chapter of Pyx. *OPEN 10.30-
16.00 Mon-Sun. Charge.*

Whitechapel Art Gallery
80 Whitechapel High St E1. 071-377
0107. Frequent public exhibitions of great
interest. The Whitechapel has successfully introduced new ideas on modern British
art into London. *OPEN 11.00-17.00 Tue
& Thur-Sun, 11.00-20.00 Wed. CLOSED
Mon & B.hols. Free.*

Wimbledon Lawn Tennis Museum
Church Rd SW19. 081-946 6131. Display
of tennis through the ages including
equipment, clothing, photographs and
videos offering the viewer any pre-record-
ed tournament match. Also a library of
tennis literature. *OPEN 11.00-17.00 Tue-
Sat, 14.00-17.00 Sun. CLOSED Mon &
B.hols. Charge.*

Outdoor London

Parks and gardens

*London is particularly rich in parks,
gardens, commons, forests and heath-
land with over 80 parks within ten miles of
the centre of London. They are all that
remain of early London's natural surrounding countryside and range from the
vast open spaces of Richmond Park to
the manicured gardens of Regent's Park.
Left by accident, gift, or longsighted
social intention, they provide a welcome
breathing space. The ten royal parks are
still the property of the Crown and were
originally the grounds of royal homes or
palaces. All parks are free, but there may
be charges for some facilities. (See under
'Children's London' for Playparks and
One o'clock clubs.)*

Garden Day Tours
62 Redington Rd NW3. 071-431 2758.
Guided tours of private London gardens,
and visits to gardens and houses in the

surrounding countryside. *Phone for details.*

Alexandra Park & Palace N22
081-365 2121. Home to the Victorian Palace, at one time the BBC headquarters. Set in 196 acres (79.4ha) of parkland with a superb view of the London skyline, the Palace is now an exhibition, entertainments and leisure venue. Attractions include a boating lake, pitch & putt, ice rink, animal enclosure, children's playground, conservation area and arboretum. *OPEN 24 hrs.*

Battersea Park SW1   6 F5
081-871 7530. An interesting riverside park of 200 acres (81ha) which was a favourite dueling spot in the early 19thC. Redesigned in the 1950s for the Festival of Britain. Boating lake, deer park and children's zoo. The London Peace Pagoda which stands close to the river was built by monks and nuns of the Japanese Buddhist order Nipponzan Myohoji and completed in 1985. Based on ancient Indian and Japanese designs, it stands at 110 ft (33.5m) and has a double roof. The park also contains an Alpine showhouse, herb garden and greenhouse. All-weather sports surface. Floodlit football pitch. Easter Show. *OPEN dawn-dusk.* Greenhouse *OPEN 09.30-dusk.* Playing fields, athletics track, tennis courts *OPEN 08.00-dusk.*

Blackheath SE3
081-305 1807 (for the area north of the A2, Shooters Hill). 081-852 1762 (for the area to the south). 275 acres (111.4ha) of open grassland jointly administered by the boroughs of Lewisham and Greenwich and used for general recreation. Ideal for kite-flying and watching the sunset. Good views in all directions especially from Point Hill in the north-west. Play soccer and cricket, sail model boats on Prince of Wales pond. Bowling green and tennis courts. Migratory birds in winter, particularly seagulls. Occasional circuses, festivals and funfairs. Some of the advanced runners competing in the London Marathon, held *every* spring, start from here. *OPEN 24 hrs.*

Bostall Heath SE2
081-311 1674. Woods and heath. Fine views of London and the Thames Estuary. Orienteering courses and cricket practice nets. Bowling green. *OPEN Apr-Sep 13.30-20.30 Mon-Sat, 10.30-20.30 Sun.* Heath *OPEN 24 hrs.*

Brockwell Park SE24
Dulwich Rd SE24. 071-926 0105. Fine old English garden with an attractive chain of ornamental lakes, a walled gar-

den and a yew arch. Tennis courts. *OPEN 09.00-dusk.*

Clissold Park N16
081-800 1021. Originally a private estate, the mansion surrounded by gardens still survives. 54 acres (21.9ha) including a fishing lake, bowling green, playpark for children, croquet lawn, flower garden, rose garden and many chestnut trees which are splendid in spring. Also an aviary of tropical birds; fallow deer graze here. *OPEN 07.00-dusk.*

Crystal Palace Park SE20
081-778 7148. Named after Paxton's 1851 Great Exhibition building which was moved here from Hyde Park and unfortunately burnt to the ground in 1936; the vast, impressive ruins still remain. Now a National Youth & Sports Centre with an Olympic swimming pool and fine modern sports stadium in an open park of 70 acres (28.4ha). Has boating lake with pedalos (in *summer*). Fishing lake; four islands in the lake are 'colonised' by 20 life-sized replicas of primeval animals. Playpark, farmyard, shire horse cart rides, ranger-guided walks, circular maze. *OPEN 08.00-½ hr before dusk.*

Danson Park
Bexleyheath, Kent. 081-303 7777. Pleasant 200-acre (81ha) park with large lake. 'Old English' garden, rock garden, aviary. Landscaped about 1760 by Capability Brown, Palladian mansion by Sir Robert Taylor, 1756. Wide variety of recreational facilities, including boating and windsurfing. *OPEN 07.30-sunset Mon-Fri, 09.00-sunset Sat & Sun.*

Dulwich Park SE21
081-693 5737. Famous for its rhododendrons and azaleas. A favourite garden of Queen Mary, wife of George V. Boating lake and tennis courts. Good for kite-flying. Tree trail. 'Touch maps' for the blind. *OPEN 08.00-21.00 (to 16.30 winter).*

Eltham Park SE9
081-850 2031. Split by a railway line into two sections, the south is recreational open space but the north is woodland: oaks, chestnuts, birches, bluebells, anemones. The ornamental pond complete with ducks commands a view right across to central London. *OPEN 24 hrs.*

Epping Forest, Essex
6000 acres (2430ha) of natural woodland, six miles long and two miles wide stretching from Chingford to Epping. It was 'dedicated to the delectation of the public forever' in 1878. Many hornbeam, oak, ash, maple, beech and birch trees; it also offers a superb variety of all kinds of natural life – so many grey squirrels that

Royal Naval College

they have become a problem. High Beech is a popular spot and there are large areas to ramble through where you can get thoroughly lost, or even stumble upon the remains of two ancient British camps at least 2000 years old – Loughton Camp and Ambersbury Banks. *OPEN 24 hrs.*

Finsbury Park N4
071-263 5001. 115 acres (46.6ha) opened in 1869. Many sporting activities – soccer, American and Gaelic football, cricket, fishing, bowling, tennis, boating. Also floodlit athletics track, two children's playgrounds, nursery and tea-room. Plane trees predominate. The oldest aqueduct in London runs through the park and there is a reservoir underground. *OPEN 06.30-½ hr after sunset.*

Greenwich Park SE10
081-858 2608. A royal park of 200 acres (81ha) with pleasant avenues lined with chestnut trees, sloping down to the Thames. Impressive views of the river and two classical buildings: the Queen's House by Inigo Jones and the Royal Naval College (once a Tudor royal palace). Contains the National Maritime Museum and the Old Royal Observatory. 13 acres (5.3ha) of wooded deer park, a bird sanctuary and Bronze age tumuli. Children's boating lake; entertainment in *summer*. The London Marathon, held *every spring*, starts from here. Bandstand used in *summer*. *OPEN 07.00 (for traffic, 05.00 for pedestrians)-22.00 summer, 07.00-18.00 (or dusk) winter.*

Hainault Forest, Essex
081-500 3106. Formerly part of the great forest of Essex, or Waltham Forest. Now a Country Park of 1100 acres (445.5ha) of extensive woodland, with a lake, two 18-hole golf courses, a playing field and facilities for angling, riding, picnicking, cross-country running and orienteering. Country farm with rare species. *OPEN 24 hrs.*

Hampstead Heath NW3
071-485 4491/081-455 5183. Open, hilly 800 acres (324ha) of park and woods. Fine views of London. Foxes can sometimes be seen. Crowded on *Bank holidays* with visitors to the famous fair and the equally famous pubs – the Bull & Bush, Spaniard's Inn and Jack Straw's Castle. Includes Parliament Hill (*the* place for kite-flyers), Golders Hill (containing a fine English town garden) and Kenwood. Ponds, open-air concerts in *summer*, tennis courts. Olympic track, orienteering, cricket, football, rugby, rounders, horse-riding (for permit holders). Also swimming in Hampstead Ponds, a children's zoo and bandstand at Golders Hill, and much of interest to the ornithologist (over 100 species). *OPEN 24 hrs.* Kenwood and Golders Hill *OPEN dawn-dusk.*

Hampton Court & Bushy Park, Surrey
081-781 9500. 2000 acres (810ha) of royal park bounded on two sides by the Thames. Hampton is the formal park of the great Tudor palace with ancient courts, superb flower gardens, gracious lawns, formal Dutch-style ponds and roses, the famous maze and the 'great vine' planted in 1768 during the reign of George III. Bushy Park is natural parkland with an artificial plantation, aquatic plants and ponds. Two herds of deer, red and fallow, run in the park. Both parks have many fine avenues including the mile-long Chestnut Avenue with 'Diana' fountain in Bushy Park. Hampton Court itself is described in *'Sightseeing'. OPEN 07.00-dusk.*

Holland Park W8   3 A5
071-602 2226. Behind the bustle of Kensington High St. 55 acres (22.3ha) of calm and secluded lawns and gardens with peacocks. Once the private garden of Holland House (partially restored after bombing during the war). Dutch garden dating from 1812 with fine tulip displays.

Hampton Court Palace

Also iris and rose gardens, yucca lawn, Japanese garden and the Orangery, where craft fairs, art exhibitions and other events are held during *May–Sep*. On the north side is a remarkable woodland of 28 acres (11.3ha) containing 3000 species of rare British trees and plants. Full of birds – exotic species including Muscovy ducks and Polish bantams, distinguished by feathers on their feet. Open-air theatre in *summer*. Restaurant, OPEN *to 24.00*, looks out onto Flower Garden which is illuminated at night. *OPEN 07.30-sunset summer; 07.30-dusk winter.*

Hyde Park W1   3 F4
071-262 5484. A royal park since 1536, it was once part of the forest reserved by Henry VIII for hunting wild boar and bulls. Queen Elizabeth I held military reviews here (still held on special occasions). It was the haunt of highwaymen until 1750 and even today is patrolled at night by police. The Great Exhibition of 1851 was held opposite Prince of Wales Gate. Hyde Park now has 360 acres (137.7ha) of parkland, walks, Rotten Row for horse-riders, and the Serpentine – a fine lake for boating and swimming. The Serpentine Bridge is by George Rennie, 1826. The famous Speakers' Corner, a tribute to British democracy, is near Marble Arch – public executions were held at Tyburn gallows nearby until 1783. Baseball and soft-ball often played. Bandstand used in *summer*. OPEN *05.00-24.00*. The Lido OPEN *May-Sep & B.hols 10.00-18.00*. Charge for swimming.

Kensington Gardens W8   3 D4
071-262 5484. A formal and elegant addition to Hyde Park; when the gardens were first opened to the public, soldiers, sailors and servants were not allowed in! 275 acres (111.4ha) of royal park containing William III's lovely Kensington Palace, Queen Anne's Orangery, the peaceful 'Sunken Garden' nearby, the Round Pond, perfect for sailing model boats, and, on the south, the magnificent Albert Memorial – the nation's monument to Queen Victoria's husband. *(Due to extensive restoration work, the memorial is currently covered.)* The famous Broad Walk, originally flanked by ancient elms, is now replanted with fragrant limes and maples, and the nearby 'Flower Walk' is the home of wild birds, woodpeckers, flycatchers and tree-creepers. 'Jubilee Walk', running down the west side of the park, was completely blown down by the storms of Oct 1987. Queen Caroline produced both the Long Water (Peter Pan's statue is here) and the Serpentine by ordering the

damming of the Westbourne river. A stone balustrade separates the Long Water from formal ponds and fountains. Good children's playground with the Elfin Oak, carved with lots of birds and animals. *OPEN dawn-dusk.*

Lee Valley Park
(0992) 717711. A huge expanse stretching 23 miles from Ware in Hertfordshire to the East End, following the course of the River Lea. The park offers sailing, angling, windsurfing, swimming, football, badminton, golf, tennis, squash, horse-riding, bowls, cycling, ice-skating. Also a rifle range, botanic gardens, open farm, bird-watching. Riverside chalets, camping and caravanning. *Telephone above number for further details.*

Lesnes Abbey Woods SE2
081-310 2777. Commemorates the former 800-year-old abbey, now excavated. Woods and open ground with good views. 20 acres (8.1ha) of wild daffodils in the *spring*. Café. OPEN *08.00-16.30 winter, 08.00-20.00 (or dusk) summer.*

Osterley Park
Isleworth, Middx. 081-560 3918. Used to be the private estate of the Earl of Jersey, part of it is still farmland. Also incorporates a bird sanctuary. An open park but some cedars and cork trees. Osterley Park House is a classic building designed by Robert Adam. OPEN *13.00-17.00 (last admission 16.30) Wed-Sat, 11.00-17.00 Sun. CLOSED Mon & Tue.* Charge. Park OPEN *10.00-sunset.* Free.

Osterley Park House

Peckham Rye Park SE15
081-693 3791. Open park with good English, Japanese and water gardens. Sporting facilities include bowling, tennis and football. OPEN *06.00-½ hr after sunset.*

Primrose Hill NW8   1 B2
081-486 7905. A minor royal park of simple grassy hill 206ft (61.7m) high giving a fine view over London. Children's play areas and a boating lake. Puppet shows in *summer*. OPEN *24 hrs.*

Regent's Park NW1   1 C4
071-486 7905. A royal park of 472 acres (191ha), was originally part of Henry VIII's great hunting forest in the 16thC. The Prince Regent in 1811 planned to connect the park (and a new palace) via

the newly built Regent Street to Carlton House. Although never fully completed, the design (1812-26) by John Nash is of great distinction. It forms two concentric circles – the Inner with gardens and Outer with Regency terraces and imposing gateways. Contains London Zoo, the Regent's Canal, a fine boating lake with 30 species of birds, a bandstand, fragrant flower gardens and the very fine Queen Mary's Rose Garden. It is also home to the golden-domed London Mosque. Open-air theatre. Restaurant and cafeterias. Sports facilities include football, baseball, softball, cricket, hockey and rugby. There are also tennis courts and an athletics track. *OPEN 05.00 (or dawn)-dusk.*

Richmond Park, Surrey
081-948 3209. The largest and wildest of London's royal parks; 2358 acres (954.2ha) first enclosed as a hunting ground by Charles I in 1637. Retains all the qualities of a great English feudal estate – a natural open park of spinneys and plantations, bracken and ancient oaks (survivors of the great oak forests of the Middle Ages) and over 600 red and fallow deer. Badgers, weasels and the occasional fox can be seen. Pen Ponds are well stocked with fish. Fine views of the Thames valley from White Lodge (early 18thC and once a royal residence) and the restaurant of Pembroke Lodge. Golf, riding, polo (for spectators), rugby, football. *OPEN 07.00-½ hr before dusk (from 07.30 in winter).*

Royal Botanic Gardens, Kew
Kew Road, Richmond, Surrey. 081-940 1171. Superb botanical gardens of 300 acres (121.5ha). Founded in 1759 by Princess Augusta. Delightful natural gardens and woods bounded by the river on one side, and stocked with thousands of flowers and trees. The lake, aquatic garden and pagoda were designed by Sir William Chambers in 1760. The magnificent curved glass Palm House and the Temperate House, 1844-8, are by Decimus Burton. Beneath the Palm House is a Marine Display with examples of flowering marine plants and coral reef. The Princess of Wales Conservatory houses orchids and cacti, and water lilies the size of mattresses. Kew's scientific aspect was developed by

Palm House

its two directors Sir William and Sir Joseph Hooker and the many famous botanists who worked here. 17thC Queen's Garden with formal rosebed. Cafeteria and gift shop in the Orangery. *1-hr* tours available from the Victoria Gate Visitor Centre. Gardens *OPEN 09.30; closing times vary according to season. Charge.*

St James's Park   **4 E5**
& Green Park SW1   **4 C5**
071-930 1793. St James's Park is the oldest royal park, acquired in 1532 by Henry VIII, laid out in imitation 'Versailles' style by Charles II and finally redesigned in the grand manner for George IV by John Nash in the 1820s. A most attractive park with fine promenades and walks, and a romantic Chinese-style lake, bridge, and weeping willows. The bird sanctuary on Duck Island has some magnificent pelicans and over 20 species of duck and goose. Good views of Buckingham Palace, the grand sweep of Carlton House Terrace, the domes and spires of Whitehall and, to the south, Westminster Abbey. The Mall and Constitution Hill are frequently part of ceremonial and royal occasions. Bandstand used in *summer*. *OPEN dawn-24.00.* Green Park is just that – a welcome green space in the heart of London with an abundance of lime, plane and hawthorn trees. *OPEN dawn-dusk.*

Shooters Hill SE18
081-856 1015. Hundreds of acres of woods and open parkland containing Oxleas Woods, Jackwood and Eltham Parks. Castlewood has a folly erected 1784 to Sir William James for his exploits in India. *OPEN 24 hrs.*

Streatham Common SW16
071-926 9331. The Rookery was formerly the garden of an 18thC mansion; rock garden, wild garden, a 'white' garden and splendid old cedars. Paddling pools. Play area. Café. Common *OPEN 24 hrs.* Rookery and café *OPEN 09.00-dusk.*

Trent Park, Enfield
081-449 8706. Formerly part of the royal hunting forest Enfield Chase. Now a country park of 413 acres (167.3ha) of woodland and grassland, with a water garden, two lakes, animal enclosure, a nature trail, horse rides and several new self-guided trails. Guided walks *throughout the year*. Picnic facilities and a trail for the blind. *OPEN 07.30-dusk.*

Victoria Embankment   **4 F3**
Gardens WC2
The joy of the lunchtime office worker on a fine summer day. Banked flowers, a

OPEN SPACES IN LONDON

band, shady trees, deckchairs and a crowded open-air café.

Victoria Park E9

081-985 1957. With 217 acres (87.9ha) and a four-mile perimeter, this park was known as 'the lung of the East End'; it is also the oldest, established in 1845 by Sir James Pennythorne (who also laid out Battersea Park). Several listed historical buildings survive; of note are two alcoves from the original London Bridge which were placed at the east end of the park in 1861, a splendid drinking fountain erected for Burdett Coutts, and two gate pillars at Bonner Bridge. The four gate lodges also date back to 1850. Of natural interest are planes, oaks, birches, hawthorns, cherries, honey locusts, gladitsia, a Kentucky coffee tree and a bitter orange. A wide variety of sports. Also fallow deer and various fowl. Children's shows 11.00 or 15.00 summer hols. OPEN 06.00-½ hr after sunset.

Waterlow Park N6

071-272 2825. Presented by Sir Sidney Waterlow to the people of London in 1889. 26 acres (10.5ha). Contains Lauderdale House where Nell Gwynne lived. OPEN 07.30-dusk.

Wimbledon Common SW19

081-788 7655. 1100 acres (445.5ha), including Putney Heath, comprising wild woodland, open heath and several ponds. Golf course, 16 miles of horse rides. Playing fields. Bronze age remains. Rare and British flora. Protected by act of 1871 as a 'wild area' for perpetuity. Said to be haunted by an 18thC highwayman who gallops across the Common by night. Famous old 19thC windmill with a museum inside. Museum OPEN Apr-Oct 14.00-17.00 Sat, Sun & B.hols. Tea room OPEN 09.30-17.30. Park OPEN 24 hrs. Cars not admitted after dusk.

Botanic gardens and arboreta

Many of the London parks have living botanical collections; Holland Park has a good arboretum, and others have bog gardens, rock gardens, and extensive rose gardens. Queen Mary's Rose Garden in Regent's Park is an outstanding example. Most of the 'great houses' have fine collections of plants, often specialising in one botanical aspect. Some of the specialist commercial nurseries are almost miniature botanical gardens; for instance Syon Park in Middlesex.

Avery Hill

Bexley Rd SE9. 081-850 2666. A Kew in miniature. Good collection of tropical and temperate Asian and Australasian plants in glasshouses, including a selection of economic crops. OPEN 13.00-16.00 Mon-Fri, 10.00-18.30 Sat & Sun. Park OPEN 07.00-½ hr before dusk (or 21.00). Free.

Bedgebury National Pinetum

Goudhurst, Kent. (0580) 212060. Situated in the lovely undulating country-side of the Weald of Kent. First planted in 1925, the forest consists of over 200 species of temperate zone cone-bearing trees laid out in genera. Of great use to foresters and botanists. OPEN 10.00-dusk. Charge.

Borde Hill Arboretum

Haywards Heath, W. Sussex. (0444) 450326. Created by Col Stephenson R. Clarke at the end of the 19thC. The garden and park now extend to nearly 400 acres (162ha). Comprehensive collections of native and exotic trees and shrubs from Eastern Asia. OPEN Apr-Oct 10.00-18.00 Tue-Thur, Sat, Sun & B.hols. Small charge.

Cambridge University Botanic Garden

Bateman St, Cambridge. (0223) 336265. The first garden was established in 1761 and moved to its present 40-acre (16.2ha) site ¾ mile (1.2km) south of the city in 1846. Extensive collection of living plants; fine specimens of trees and shrubs; glasshouses, pinetum, ecological area, chronological bed, scented garden and geographically arranged alpine garden. OPEN Mar-Sep 08.00-18.00 Mon-Sat, 10.00-18.00 Sun; Feb & Oct 08.00-17.00 Mon-Sat, 10.00-17.00 Sun; Nov-Jan 08.00-16.00 Mon-Sat, 10.00-16.00 Sun. Glasshouse OPEN all year 10.00-12.30 & 14.00-16.00 Mon-Sun. Free (charge on Sun).

Chelsea Physic Garden   6 F4

Royal Hospital Rd SW3. 071-352 5646. Founded in 1673 by the Worshipful Society of Apothecaries to study the therapeutic qualities of plants. Still used for medical teaching purposes today. Glasshouses full of plant exotica, rockery, beds of plants associated with past gardeners. OPEN Apr-Oct 14.00-17.00 Wed, Sun & other times by appt. Charge.

Oxford Botanic Garden

Rose La, by Magdalen Bridge, Oxford. (0865) 276920. Oldest botanical garden in Britain founded in 1621 by Henry, Lord Danvers. About 3 acres (1.2ha) within high stone walls, another 3 acres (1.2ha) outside pleasantly situated by the river. Glasshouses, rock garden, some notable trees. Entrance arch by Inigo Jones. *OPEN 09.00-17.00 (to 16.30 winter) Mon-Sun. Free (charge Jul & Aug).*

Royal Botanic Gardens, Kew
Kew Rd, Richmond, Surrey. 081-940 1171. One of the world's great botanical gardens. Famous for its natural collections, identification of rare plants, economic botany and scientific research. Nearly 300 acres (121.5ha) of pure aesthetic pleasure. Arboretum, alpine, water and rhododendron gardens. Magnificent tropical orchid, palm, temperate and Australasian houses including the Princess of Wales Conservatory with several different climatic zones under one roof. Herbarium contains Sir Joseph Hooker's famous *HMS Erebus* and Indian plant collections. Marine Display with examples of flowering marine plants and coral reef. Library of rare books on botany and exploration. Gardens *OPEN 09.30; closing times vary according to season. Charge.*

Savill Garden, Windsor Great Park
(0753) 860222. Approach by Englefield Green. Created by Sir Eric Savill in 1930s. Outstanding woodland garden together with large collections of roses, herbaceous plants and alpines, in 35 acres (14.2ha). There is also a lake. *OPEN 10.00-dusk daily all year. Charge.*

Sheffield Park Garden
Nr Uckfield, E. Sussex. (0825) 790655. Gardens with five lakes and house by James Wyatt. Magnificent rhododendrons and azaleas in *May* and *Jun.* Brilliant *autumn* colours with maples and other shrubs. *OPEN Apr-Nov 11.00-dusk (or 18.00) Tue-Sat, 14.00-dusk (or 18.00) Sun & B.hols. CLOSED Tue following B.hol Mon. Charge.*

Syon Park
Brentford, Middx. 081-560 0881. 55 acres (22.3ha) of gardens surrounding a 16thC mansion house designed by Robert Adam. The main gardens surround the lake, and around the lakeside are weeping willows and swamp cypresses. The Great Conservatory has an impressive central dome and elegant curving wings. Formal bedding areas and lawns. Garden centre. Butterfly House. *OPEN 10.00-17.00 Mon-Fri, 10.00-17.30 Sat & Sun. Charge.*

Wakehurst Place
Ardingly, W. Sussex. (0444) 892701. A very lovely 500-acre (202.5ha) 'satellite' garden to the Royal Botanic Gardens at Kew; chosen because of its humid climate, clear air, lakes and running streams, and its variety of soils. The open woodland and high forest contain large numbers of rare trees, shrubs and plants from all over the world, particularly from Chile, SE Asia and New Zealand. Mansion open to the public. *OPEN Apr-Sep 10.00-19.00 Mon-Sun; Oct-Mar 10.00-16.00 Mon-Sun. Charge.*

Wisley Gardens
Wisley, Surrey. (0483) 224234. A fine 240-acre (97.2ha) horticultural garden originally created by C.F. Wilson as a wild and woodland garden, acquired by the Royal Horticultural Society in 1904. Famous for its trials and improvements of new varieties. Greenhouses and pinetum. Notable collections of old-fashioned and new roses, rhododendrons, camellias, heathers, rock garden plants and bulbs from the Near East. *OPEN Mar-Oct 10.00-19.00 Mon-Sat; Nov-Feb 10.00-16.30 Mon-Sat. OPEN Sun 09.00-19.00 (to members of RHS only.) Charge.*

Zoos, aquaria and wildlife parks

All zoos ask visitors not to bring dogs.

Aquaria

Brighton Sea Life Centre
Marine Pde & Madeira Dri (opp Palace Pier), Brighton, E. Sussex. (0273) 604233. Oldest public aquarium in Britain containing 48 tanks of marine and freshwater fish. Main feature is the Shark Tunnel; watch the sharks and other fish swim above you. *OPEN summer 10.00-21.00 Mon-Sun, winter 10.00-18.00 Mon-Sun. Charge.*

London Aquarium 1 C3
Regent's Park NW1. 071-722 3333. Marine and Tropical Halls. Excellently lit and displayed. A well-stocked aquarium of both sea and freshwater fish and amphibians from European and tropical waters. Particularly notable are the free sea fish, the octopuses and stingrays. *OPEN Mar-Oct 10.00-17.30 Mon-Sun; Nov-Feb 10.00-dusk Mon-Sun. CLOSED Xmas Day. Charge (includes admittance to London Zoo).*

Underwater World
Holt Pound, Farnham, Surrey. (0420) 22140. A large, indoor aquarium full of amazing tropical fish. Next door is **Birdworld** where you will find a huge variety of birds from the tiny humming bird to the huge ostrich. Both *OPEN Apr-Aug*

09.30-18.00 Mon-Sun; Sep 09.30-17.00 Mon-Sun; Oct-Mar 09.30-16.00 Mon-Sun. Charge.

Zoos: London

London Zoo
1 C3

Regent's Park NW1. 071-722 3333. Having survived threatened closure on several occasions over the last few years, a ten-year redevelopment plan has been launched to turn this famous zoo into a centre for animal conservation and captive breeding. The zoo was originally laid out by Decimus Burton in 1827; since then many famous architects have designed special animal houses. Reptile House, Moonlight World (where day and night are reversed so that rarely seen nocturnal animals are kept awake during the day), Penguin Pool, Invertebrate House. Animal feeding. Children's zoo. *OPEN Mar-Oct 10.00-17.30 Mon-Sun; Nov-Feb 10.00-dusk Mon-Sun. CLOSED Xmas Day. Charge (includes admittance to London Aquarium).*

Zoos and wildlife parks: out of London

Chessington World of Adventures
Leatherhead Rd, Chessington, Surrey. (0372) 727227. A zoo of 65 acres (26.3ha) on the outskirts of London. A monorail travels high above the zoo animals. Also spectacular theme park – The Mystic East, Calamity Canyon, Circus World and Toytown. London 12 miles (A3). *OPEN Apr-Oct (all attractions) 10.00-17.00 Mon-Sun; Nov-Mar (zoo only) 10.00-16.00 Mon-Sun. CLOSED Xmas Day. Charge.*

Colchester Zoo
Standway Hall, Colchester, Essex. (0206) 330253. A good general collection, including an aquarium and reptile house. 40 acres (16.2ha). London 50 miles (A12). *OPEN 09.30-dusk Mon-Sun. Charge.*

Cotswold Wildlife Park
Bradwell Gro, nr Burford, Oxon. (099382) 3006. Set in 120 acres (48.6ha) of gardens and parkland. Tropical birds, rhinos, zebras and otters. Reptile house. Tropical marine aquarium. Adventure playground, farmyard. Narrow gauge railway (in *summer*). London 70 miles (M40). *OPEN 10.00-18.00 (or dusk) Mon-Sun. CLOSED Xmas Day. Charge.*

Hollanden Farm Park
Great Hollanden Farm, Mill Lane, Hildenborough, Kent. (0732) 833858. 60 rare breeds within a natural farming environment. Coffee shop, farm shop, gift shop. Group visits *by prior arrangement.* London 45 miles (A2). *OPEN Easter-Sep 10.30-17.00 Mon-Sun. Charge.*

Howletts Zoo Park
Bekesbourne, nr Canterbury, Kent. (0227) 721410. 55 acres (22.3ha) of zoo park including the largest collection of gorillas and tigers in the world. Leopards, African elephants, deer, monkeys. London 60 miles (A2). *OPEN Apr-Oct 10.00-17.00 Mon-Sun; Nov-Mar 10.00-dusk (or 16.00) Mon-Sun. Charge.*

Linton Zoo
Hadstock Rd, Linton, Cambs. (0223) 891308. A wonderful combination of beautiful gardens and wildlife from all over the world set in over ten acres (4.1ha) of grassland. Animals include lions, leopards, panthers, reptiles, tarantulas. London 55 miles (M11). *OPEN 10.00-dusk Mon-Sun. Charge.*

Longleat Lion Reserve
Warminster, Wilts. (0985) 844266. Visitors to the magnificent Renaissance house can choose to drive through the game park where lions roam at will. You can stop your car and watch in safety but it is extremely foolhardy to get out, however friendly the lions seem. Also has a chimpanzee island. No soft-topped cars allowed. London 90 miles (M4). *OPEN mid Mar-Oct 10.00-17.30 Mon-Sun. CLOSED Nov-Feb. Charge.*

Marwell Zoological Park
Colden Common, Nr Winchester, Hants. (0962) 777406. 100 acres (40.5 ha) of park with a two-mile road system. Specialise in breeding endangered wildlife species – big cats, wild horses and asses, scimitar-horned oryx. Also a semi-aquatic mammal house. London 70 miles (M3). *OPEN 10.00-18.00 (to 17.00 winter) Mon-Sun. CLOSED Xmas Day. Charge.*

Mole Hall Wildlife Park
Mole Hall, Widdington, nr Newport, Essex. (0799) 40400. In grounds of moated manor. 25 acres (10.1 ha) of grass. Animals include chimps, otters, llamas, wallabies and flamingoes. Butterfly House, pets corner, picnic and play areas, café and shop. London 35 miles (A11). *OPEN 10.30-18.00 (or dusk) Mon-Sun. Charge.*

Port Lympne Zoo Park
Port Lympne, Lympne, nr Hythe, Kent. (0303) 264646. 270 acres (109.4 ha) of spaciously laid out animal park, including 15 acres (6.1 ha) of splendid terraced gardens and Sir Philip Sassoon's historic house. Siberian and Indian tigers, black

rhinos, Indian elephants, black panthers, antelope, deer, capucin monkeys, timber wolves. London 60 miles (M20). *OPEN Apr-Oct 10.00-17.00 Mon-Sun; Nov-Mar 10.00-dusk Mon-Sun. Charge.*

Whipsnade Wild Animal Park
Dunstable, Beds. (0582) 872171. A 500-acre (202.5 ha) 'natural' zoo of woods and downland in the Chilterns. Over 3000 rare and exciting animals in large open-air enclosures. Some species roam freely throughout the park. You can travel within the park in your own car or aboard the miniature motor-coach train. There is a Discovery Centre with hands-on displays, a miniature desert and wall-to-wall rainforest. You can picnic in the grounds. Children's adventure playground. London 35 miles (M1). *OPEN Apr-Oct 10.00-dusk Mon-Sun; Nov-Mar 10.00-16.00 Mon-Sun. CLOSED Xmas Day. Charge.*

Woburn Wild Animal Kingdom
Woburn, Beds. (0525) 290407. Britain's largest drive-through wildlife park. The Safari Trail takes you past tigers, bears, wolves, rhinos and monkeys. Sealion and parrot shows. Leisure area with rides, boating lakes, cable car. London 40 miles (M1). *OPEN mid Mar-Oct 10.00-17.00 Mon-Sun; Nov-mid Mar 11.00-15.00 Sat & Sun. Charge.*

Children's London

Looking at London

London is full of fascinating things for children (and parents) to see and do – traditional ceremonies and events, historic sights and museums, festivals and fairs, shows and films, clubs, classes, junior sports and plenty of open spaces. It can also be tiring and expensive, so it's best to plan expeditions round a few places at a time; start with one of the famous sights – Changing of the Guard, St Paul's, the Tower, or a well-known museum – and combine it with a river trip, picnic in a park, a swim at one of London's many pools or a children's show. Take advantage of discounts on admission. Most attractions offer half-price tickets for children under 16. Phone Kidsline: 071-222 8070 for information on events and entertainments 09.00-16.00 Mon-Fri during holidays, 16.00-18.00 Mon-Fri during term time. Under 5s travel free on buses and tubes, and under 14s pay a reduced flat fare until 22.00, as do 14 and 15 year olds with a Child Rate Photocard. It is also advisable to avoid travelling in the rush hour (08.00-09.30 & 16.30-18.30 Mon-Fri).
For more information on what London has to offer children see Nicholson's Children's London.

Sights

HMS Belfast   **5 F4**
Morgan's La, Tooley St SE1. 071-407 6434. Last survivor of the Royal Navy's World War II cruisers moored near Tower Bridge. Explore bridge, seven decks, gun turrets, sick bay, galleys, engine rooms and punishment cells. Educational activities for children: film shows and lectures. Contact the schools' officer for further information. Cross gangplank from Symon's Wharf, or by ferry *(summer only)* from Tower Pier. *OPEN 10.00-18.00 Mon-Sun (to 16.00 Nov-Mar). Charge.*

Buckingham Palace   **4 D5**
St James's Park SW1. The official London residence of the Queen; now open to the public *(see 'Historic London')*. The royal flag flies from the roof if the Queen is at home. A popular time to visit is *11.30* for the Changing of the Guard *(every day in summer, alternate days in winter)*.

Cutty Sark & Gipsy Moth IV
King William Wlk SE10. 081-858 3445. Explore the old, romantic Cutty Sark tea-clipper. Below deck there is a fascinating collection of photographs, ship's logs and figure-heads. Gipsy Moth IV nearby, is the small boat in which Sir Francis Chichester sailed single-handed around the world in 1966. *OPEN 10.30-18.00 Mon-Sat, 12.00-18.00 Sun (17.00 winter). Charge.*

Houses of Parliament   **4 F5**
St Margaret St SW1. 071-219 3000. Site of the old Palace of Westminster. Tours of medieval, hammer-beamed Westminster Hall available by contacting local member of parliament to obtain a permit. The

appealing, small 14thC Jewel Tower with moat, opposite, is a further surviving fragment. Children's guide available on the door. Education sheets on application to the education office. *OPEN 10.00-13.00 & 14.00-18.00 Mon-Sun (to 16.00 Oct-Easter). Charge.*

London Dungeon   **5 E4**
34 Tooley St SE1. 071-403 0606. Gruesome and realistic exhibition displaying the darker side of British history – murders, executions and tortures – in an eerie, vaulted cellar under London Bridge station. Children under 10 must be accompanied by an adult. *OPEN 10.00-17.30 Mon-Sun (to 16.30 Oct-Apr). Charge.*

London Planetarium   **1 C5**
Marylebone Rd NW1. 071-486 1121. Boggle your mind with stories of stars, space and the cosmos. Programmes through the day 10.20-17.00 *Mon-Sun. Charge (combined ticket with Madame Tussaud's available).*

Madame Tussaud's   **1 C5**
Marylebone Rd NW1. 071-935 6861. Life-size wax figures of historic and contemporary, famous and notorious people. Royalty, pop stars, film stars, statesmen and astronauts. Journey through 400 years of London's history in a replica of a black taxi cab at 'The Spirit of London'. Chamber of Horrors genuinely gruesome, unsuitable for young children. *OPEN 10.00-17.30 Mon-Fri, 09.30-17.30 Sat & Sun. Charge (combined ticket with Planetarium available).*

Monument   **5 E3**
Monument St EC3. 071-626 2717. A City landmark – stone column topped by a viewing platform and shining golden urn. Commemorates the Great Fire of 1666; it stands 202ft (61m) from where it started in Pudding Lane. Steep spiral staircase (311 steps) inside column leads to a great view. *OPEN Apr-Sep 09.00-17.40 Mon-Fri, 14.00-17.40 Sat & Sun; Oct-Mar 09.00-15.40 Mon-Sat. Due to close in 1993 for renovations. Phone for details. Charge.*

Old Royal Observatory
Greenwich Park SE10. 081-858 1167. Most of the pioneer work in the development of astronomy and nautical navigation was done here. Stand astride the Meridian Line. Interactive science stations. Sound and light show in a dome which houses the largest refracting telescope in the UK. See the 17thC Astronomer Royal's rooms and the restored Octagon room by Wren. Houses a collection of old clocks and telescopes.

OPEN Apr-Oct 10.00-18.00 Mon-Sat, 12.00-18.00 Sun; Nov-Mar 10.00-17.00 Mon-Sat, 14.00-17.00 Sun. Charge.

Royal Mews   **4 C6**
Buckingham Palace Rd SW1. 071-930 4832. The Queen's horses and coaches, ready for use on state occasions, including the huge gold Coronation coach (used for every coronation since George IV) and the glass State coach (used mainly for Royal weddings). *OPEN Jan-Mar 12.00-16.00 Wed; Apr-Sep 12.00-16.00 Tue-Thur; Oct-Dec 12.00-16.00 Wed; except on state occasions. Charge.*

St Katharine's Dock   **5 G4**
St Katharine's Way, Tower Bridge E1. 071-488 2400. Home to the Nore Lightship and magnificent Thames barges. Also a yacht haven, with shops and restaurants.

St Paul's Cathedral   **5 D2**
Ludgate Hill EC4. 071-248 2705. Exciting climb to the Dome, for a terrific view over the roof-tops and river. 259 steps take you to the Whispering Gallery, inside the Dome; 120 more up a narrow stone staircase lead to the broad Stone Gallery, at the base of the Dome; then the final, and most hair-raising climb, is to the Golden Gallery, at the top of the Dome. *OPEN 09.00-16.00 Mon-Sat. Access to Golden Gallery 09.45-16.15 Mon-Sat. Charge.*

Thames Flood Barrier
Unity Way, Eastmoor St SE18. 081-854 1373. A shining, technological marvel, built as a bulwark against dangerously high tides. The Thames Barrier Visitor Centre has an exhibition, a film show on the history of the river and a video about the construction of the barrier. Shop. Café. 25-min cruise from Barrier Pier. *Charge. OPEN 10.00-17.00 Mon-Fri, 10.00-17.30 Sat, Sun & B. hols.*

Tower of London   **5 G3**
Tower Hill EC3. 071-709 0765. The best time to visit the Tower is definitely between Nov-Feb, when it's not only cheaper to get in, but much less crowded. An amazing fortress, scene of the famous executions of Anne Boleyn and Sir Thomas More – you need plenty of time to explore all the different towers, the vast collection of armour and weapons, and the Crown Jewels in their steel-lined underground strongroom. Edward I's Medieval Palace has been restored, and costumed interpreters help recreate the atmosphere of Edward's court in the 1280s. No unaccompanied children under 10. *OPEN Mar-Oct 09.30-18.00 Mon-Sat, 10.00-18.00 Sun; Nov-Feb*

09.30-17.00 Mon-Sat. 10.00-17.00 Sun. Charge.

Trafalgar Square WC2   **4 E4**
Always popular with children who like to chase and feed the pigeons, climb the lions and watch the fountains. Parents will enjoy the bustling, colourful crowd which always congregates here. On the north wall, look for the Imperial Standards of Length (in yards, feet and inches). Carol singing round a giant Christmas tree every evening for ten days before Christmas. Traditional revelry on New Year's Eve.

Trocadero   **4 E3**
Coventry Street W1. Modern shopping, restaurant and leisure complex which houses the Guinness World of Records exhibition (071-439 7331); Funland (071-734 3859), a games centre with kiddy rides, video games and virtuality simulation rides; Quasar (071-734 8151), a hi-tech version of hide and seek with laser beams. *OPEN 10.00-22.00 Mon-Sun. Charge.*

Westminster Abbey   **4 F6**
Broad Sanctuary SW1. 071-222 7110. The Abbey is easiest to explore if you think of it in three sections: the Nave and Transept (with Poets' Corner and the tomb of the Unknown Soldier); Chapel and Shrine of Edward the Confessor (with the Coronation Chair); and Henry VII's Chapel, with a wonderful fan-vaulted roof and the tombs of many kings and queens. The Abbey Museum, in the East Cloister, has a collection of death masks and funeral effigies, including Nelson in his uniform and King Charles II in his garter robes. Royal chapels *OPEN 09.30-16.00 Mon-Fri, 09.30-14.00 & 15.45-17.00 Sat. Charge. Museum OPEN 10.30-16.00 Mon-Sun. Charge.*

Westminster Cathedral   **7 C1**
Ashley Pl, off Victoria St SW1. 071-834 7452. Striking Byzantine-style building in red and white brick. See view from the top of Campanile (273ft – 83.7m) over Westminster and the Thames. Lift usually *OPEN Apr-Sep 09.00-17.00 Mon-Sun. Charge.*

Trips & tours

See also 'London tours' in 'Sightseeing'.
Citisights of London
213 Brooke Rd E5. 081-806 4325. Archaeologists and historians working in association with the Museum of London provide a series of walks and tours looking at the history and archaeology of London.

London from the top of a bus
Original London Sightseeing Tours (081-877 1722) will take you round London in traditional double-decker buses, some of which are open-topped, or, armed with a (free) LRT Bus Map, you can devise your own 'tour' by taking one of the cross-town routes through the centre. For example, the no. 6 bus goes from Marble Arch to St Paul's Cathedral via Oxford St, Regent St, Piccadilly Circus, Trafalgar Sq, Strand, Fleet St and Ludgate Hill.

London Wall Walk   **5 D1**
Follow a sequence of tile panels tracing 1¾ miles (2.8km) of the City's Roman and medieval defensive wall – parts of which survive – between the Museum of London and Tower Hill. A map of Roman London on sale in the Museum of London incorporates the route.

River trips
See 'Sightseeing'.
On the Thames you can take a trip downriver to Greenwich, or to the docks at Tilbury to see the 'big ships', or upriver to Battersea, or further up towards Hampton Court. Or take a canal trip from Little Venice to Regent's Park Zoo in one of the original painted narrowboats.

Silver Jubilee Walkway
12 mile (19km) walkway created for the Queen's Silver Jubilee in 1977. Circles the centre of London, passing close to many famous and historic buildings. Start at Leicester Square (**4 E3**) and follow the discs set in the pavement. Leaflet obtainable from the London Tourist Board Information Centre, Victoria Station Forecourt SW1 (**7 B1**).

Ceremonies

Take advantage of the splendid pageantry which still survives by watching the Changing of the Queen's Guards (daily in summer) or pick one of the seasonal celebrations: Trooping the Colour – one of the most spectacular ceremonies in England which marks the Queen's official birthday in Jun, the Lord Mayor's Procession (Nov), or the Chinese New Year celebrations (Jan/Feb). See 'Sightseeing': 'Daily ceremonies and events' and 'Annual events'.

London at work

See what goes on behind the scenes – a chance to see how things work. Some places offer organised tours or group visits.

Airports

London Gatwick
West Sussex. (0293) 503843. Busy airport with all types of aircraft, including light planes. 800 ft (244 m) viewing gallery gives close view of aircraft movements. *OPEN Apr-Oct 08.00-17.00 Mon-Sun; Nov-Mar 09.00-16.00 Mon-Sun. Charge.*

London Heathrow
Middx. 081-759 4321. Underground straight to Heathrow Central. From the viewing terrace watch the planes landing and taking off. Telescopes and refreshments. *OPEN 09.00-½ hr before dusk. Charge.*

Arts

Royal National Theatre   **5 A4**
South Bank SE1. 071-928 2252. Gives you a glimpse of the hard work and effort which goes into making the magic of the stage. A chance to see the prop stores, costume room and workshops. *Young children must be accompanied. To arrange tours phone or write to the above address. Tours last approximately 1 hour and take place at 10.15. 12.45 & 17.30 Mon-Sat. Charge.*

Royal Opera House   **4 F2**
Bow St WC2. 071-240 1200. Visit workshops, dressing rooms, rehearsal rooms and the incredible wardrobe. *Young children must be accompanied. Essential to pre-book. Groups must be a minimum of 16 and maximum of 25. To arrange tours phone or write to the above address. Charge.*

Business & finance

Bank of England   **5 E2**
Threadneedle St EC2. 071-601 4444. Museum of the Bank of England with exhibits relating to its history together with a video explaining the work of the bank today (aimed at 13 plus). *OPEN Apr-Sep 10.00-17.00 Mon-Fri, 11.00-17.00 Sun; Oct-Mar 10.00-17.00 Mon-Fri. Free.*

Lloyds of London   **5 F2**
Lime St EC3. 071-327 6210. Remarkable building with outside glass lifts. Exhibition, video and a look at the hub of Lloyds including the underwriting room with the famous Lutine Bell at the centre. Suitable for 14 plus. Maximum of 20. *Telephone in advance if visiting in a group. Viewing gallery OPEN 09.30-12.30 & 14.00-16.00 Mon-Fri (by appointment only).*

Diamonds

London Diamond Centre   **4 C2**
10 Hanover St W1. 071-629 5511. See the evolution of a diamond from rough stone to glittering gem, as well as the largest collection of diamonds in London. Two days' notice required for groups. *OPEN 10.30-17.30 Mon-Fri, 10.00-16.30 Sat. CLOSED B.hols. Charge.*

Fire stations

Be right on the spot when the siren goes. For permission to visit your local fire station (only for children of 12 years and above) write to the PR Dept, London Fire Brigade HQ, 8 Albert Embankment SE1.

Glass blowing

London Glass-blowing Workshop
109 Rotherhithe St SE16. 071-237 0394. One of the longest-established studios in Britain, famous worldwide for innovative use of swirling, iridescent colour. *No organised tours but visitors welcome 11.00-18.00 Mon-Fri and by appointment Sat & Sun.*

The Glasshouse   **4 F2**
65 Long Acre WC2. 071-836 9785. Watch glass being blown in the workshop from viewing gallery. Telephone to arrange suitable time. *OPEN 10.00-18.00 Mon-Fri, 11.00-17.00 Sat. CLOSED Sun. Free.*

Law

Old Bailey   **5 C2**
Old Bailey EC4. 071-248 3277. Trials in the Central Criminal Court can be watched from the public galleries. Worth going to see the wigs and robes worn by the judges and barristers. Minimum age 14. Under 16s must be accompanied by an adult. *OPEN 10.30-13.00 & 14.00-16.00 Mon-Fri. CLOSED B.hols. Free.*

Music

Boosey & Hawkes Musical Instrument Factory
Deansbrook Rd, Edgware, Middx. 081-952 7711. Tour shows how a flat piece of brass is transformed into a shiny, tuneful instrument. Write well in advance. Minimum age 11. *Tours at 10.00 & 14.00 Wed. Charge (includes refreshments).*

Royal Philharmonic Orchestra   **4 G 1**
34 Red Lion Sq WC1. 071-608 2381.

Rehearsal seats available to members of the RPO Club or concert ticket holders only. *Minimum age 10. To attend a rehearsal individuals should write several weeks in advance. Free.*

Politics

Houses of Parliament   **4 F5**
St Margaret St W1. 071-219 3000. To attend a debate in the House of Commons *apply to your local MP in writing, or queue at the St Stephen's entrance* (long queues in *summer). Tours of Westminster Hall and Palace of Westminster also by application to your local MP. Free.*

Postal services

Several of the large central offices offer conducted tours. At each place you can see sorting, postal machinery and the Post Office underground railway. Minimum age 12. In each case, write in advance to the Postmaster Controller. Mark envelope 'Visits'.

Mount Pleasant   **2 C5**
Rosebery Av EC1. 071-239 2191. Biggest sorting office in the country; underground railway. *Groups of 30* (children should be over 10). *Visits Jan-Nov. Book ten days in advance. Free.*

West Central District Office   **4 F2**
21-31 New Oxford St WC1. 071-239 5809. Fully-mechanised sorting office, also linked to underground railway. *Enquire for visiting details. Free.*

Sport

Lord's Cricket Ground
St John's Wood Rd NW8. 071-266 3825. A chance to learn some of the history of cricket and to look round the cricket memorial gallery. *Visits to the famous pavilion by appointment only. Minimum age 7. Young children must be accompanied. Tours 12.00 & 14.00 Mon-Sun, 10.00 on a match day. Charge.*

Wembley Stadium
Empire Way, Wembley, Middx. 081-902 8833. See behind the scenes and view the famous turf on a guided tour. Visit the dressing rooms, walk through the players' tunnel and on to the pitch, then climb to the Royal box to collect the cup! *Tours summer 10.00-15.00 Mon-Sun. Charge.*

Wimbledon Lawn Tennis Museum
All England Club, Church Rd SW19. 081-946 6131. The history of lawn tennis with an excellent video showing films of great matches. You are even allowed to peek into the famous Centre Court. *OPEN 11.00-17.00 Tue-Sat, 14.00-17.00 Sun. CLOSED Mon. Charge.*

Telephone services

Story of Telecommunications   **5 C3**
145 Queen Victoria St EC4. 071-248 7444. Displays history of telecommunications, highlighting the best of present-day design and offering a glimpse of the future. *OPEN 10.00-17.00 Mon-Fri. CLOSED B.hols. Free.*

Museums for children

For a full list see 'Museums and galleries'. Many museums have educational events or programmes, such as quizzes, trails, lectures and film shows. Ask about project sheets which have information and activities based on the displays. The following have special features of particular interest to children.

Baden-Powell House   **6 C2**
Queen's Gate SW7. 071-584 7030. Exhibition of the life of Baden-Powell, founder of the scout movement. *OPEN 09.00-17.00 Mon-Sun. Free.*

Bethnal Green Museum of Childhood
Cambridge Heath Rd E2. 081-980 2415. An enchanting collection of historic toys, dolls and dolls' houses and model theatres, including an 18thC Venetian marionette theatre. Special collection of children's costume. Regular *Sat* workshop provides facilities for drawing, puppetry and story-telling. Shop sells replicas of old-fashioned games and toys. *OPEN 10.00-17.50 Mon-Thur & Sat, 14.30-17.50 Sun. Free.*

Cabaret Mechanical Theatre   **4 F3**
Unit 33, Covent Gdn Market WC2. 071-379 7961. A unique collection of contemporary automata and mechanical sculpture; over 100 hand-carved, hand-painted moving models operated by push-button. Great fun for inquisitive children as the mechanics of the pieces are all exposed. *OPEN 12.00-18.30 Mon, 10.00-18.30 Tue-Sun. Charge.*

Guinness World of Records   **4 E3**
Trocadero, Coventry St W1. 071-439 7331. Thousands of world records recreated at the touch of a button. A three-dimensional display of all that is superlative around the globe from the

heaviest man to the tallest skyline to the largest mammal. *OPEN 10.00-22.00 Mon-Sun. Charge (under 4s free).*

Gunnersbury Park Museum
Gunnersbury Park W3. 081-992 1612. Set in a beautiful park, the Rothschild Regency family mansion, now a museum with collection of coaches, including a travelling chariot, town chariot and hansom cab. Costume gallery. Hands-on exhibitions. Shop, café in the park. *OPEN Mar-Oct 13.00-17.00 Mon-Fri, 13.00-18.00 Sat & Sun; Nov-Feb 13.00-16.00 Mon-Sun. Free.*

Horniman Museum
100 London Rd SE23. 081-699 2339. Collection includes arts, crafts and musical instruments from all over the world. African masks, American Indian and Eskimo art, stuffed animals, 'Living Waters', a live aquaria and an observation beehive. In the new Music Room (opening September 1993) instruments of all periods come alive at the touch of a computer key. Refreshments. *OPEN 10.30-17.00 Mon-Sat, 14.00-17.30 Sun. CLOSED B.hols. Free.* Children's Centre provides crafts, drawing materials etc for children over 8. Art and craft work is based on observation and drawing of the museum exhibits. *OPEN 10.30-12.30 & 13.30-15.30 Sat during termtime, Mon-Sat during school hols. CLOSED B.hols. Free.*

Kew Bridge Steam Museum
Green Dragon La, Brentford, Middx. 081-568 4757. Huge Victorian building housing six gigantic beam engines, restored to working order by volunteers. Under steam at weekends. Also a collection of old traction engines and working forge. Tearoom. *OPEN 11.00-17.00 Mon-Sun inc B.hols. Charge (under 5s free).*

London Fire Brigade Museum   5 D5
94a Southwark Bridge Rd SE1. 071-587 4273. Exhibits fire-fighting gear from the 17thC to the present. You can see the old uniforms and leather buckets that were once used. *OPEN 09.30-16.00 Mon-Fri. Free.*

London Toy & Model Museum   3 D3
21-23 Craven Hill W2. 071-262 9450. Toys, dolls and trains including collection of pre-1914 toys, in a Victorian house. Model railway in the garden. *OPEN 10.00-17.30 Tue-Sat, 11.00-17.30 Sun. CLOSED Mon & winter B.hols. Charge.*

London Transport Museum   4 G3
The Piazza, Covent Gdn WC2. 071-379 6344. History of London's public transport told on video, with working exhibits and gleamingly-preserved historic vehicles of road and rail. 'Drive' a bus or tube or work the signals. Activity sheets available. *OPEN 10.00-18.00 (last admission 17.15) Mon-Sun. Charge. Closed during 1993 for renovations. Phone for details.*

Museum of the Moving   5 B4
Image (MOMI)
Under Waterloo Bridge, South Bank SE1. 071-928 3535. Tells the history of moving images from Chinese puppet shows to hologram technology. Take part in film and television-making processes. Lectures and study rooms for groups. *OPEN 10.00-18.00 Mon-Sun. Charge.*

National Army Museum   6 F3
Royal Hospital Rd SW3. 071-730 0717. Spacious museum tells the story of the British Army from 1485 to the present day. Uniforms, armour, weapon gallery, music and soldiers' songs on push-button machines. Junior Club during *summer hols. OPEN 10.00-17.30 Mon-Sun. Free.*

Pollock's Toy Museum   4 D1
1 Scala St W1. 071-636 3452. Old toys, theatres and dolls crammed into two houses. Also toys for sale, including the colourful Victorian cut-out theatres for which Pollock's is famous. *OPEN 10.00-17.00 Mon-Sat. CLOSED Sun & B.hols. Charge.*

Ragged School Museum
46-48 Copperfield Rd E3. 081-980 6405. Photographs, documents and objects concerned with the lives of the children who attended Dr Barnardo's Free Ragged Schools which he started in the 1880s after seeing the awful living conditions of London's poor children. Attend a Victorian school lesson in the recreated classroom. Changing programme of exhibitions. *OPEN 10.00-17.00 Wed & Thur and 14.00-17.00 first Sun of the month. Free (voluntary donation).*

Royal Air Force Museum
Grahame Park Way NW9. 081-205 2266. Plane-spotters will particularly enjoy this impressive collection of aircraft which are all exhibited in former hangars, including a man-lifting kite, airship, historic planes from World Wars I and II, and modern bombers and missiles. *OPEN 10.00-18.00 Mon-Sun. CLOSED B.hols. Charge.* Also comprises the Battle of Britain Hall and Bomber Command Hall. *OPEN same hours. Charge.*

Sherlock Holmes Museum   1 B5
221b Baker St NW1. 071-935 8866. Said to be the actual house on which Conan Doyle modelled his imaginary 221b. The

great detective's domestic world has been recreated based on detailed study of the stories. See Holmes' cluttered sitting room and bedroom, full of personal touches. In Dr Watson's room you can sit by the fire and read the stories and period magazines. *OPEN 10.00-18.00 Mon-Sun. Charge.*

Tower Hill Pageant　　　**5 G3**
1 Tower Hill Terrace EC3. 071-709 0081. London's first 'darkride' museum where an automated car takes you on a journey through converted wine vaults near the Tower of London. The Pageant focuses on the riverside port area and depicts scenes from 2000 years of London's history. See Londoners fleeing in panic before the Great Fire of 1666 and get a bird's eye view of the city from a German bomber as it blitzed the docks in 1940. *OPEN Apr-Oct 09.30-17.30 Mon-Sun; Nov-Mar 09.30-16.30 Mon-Sun. Charge.*

Winston Churchill's Britain　**5 F4**
at War Theme Museum
64-66 Tooley St SE1. 071-403 3171. A hands-on theme museum where you can relive the drama of life in Britain during the Second World War. Journey to the London underground where many spent sleepless nights while the bombing raids went on overhead. Hear Hitler's declaration of war and Churchill's promise that Britain would never be defeated. Huddle inside an Anderson shelter. Wait for the 'all-clear'. Experience the sights, sounds and smells of the Blitz. *OPEN Apr-Sep 10.00-17.30 Mon-Sun; Oct-Mar 10.00-16.30 Mon-Sun. Charge.*

London's countryside

London's parks and surrounding countryside are surprisingly rich in outdoor pursuits, and there is a great variety of wildlife to be found even in the heart of the metropolis. Some of the opportunities are listed here.

Aeroplanes

The airshow season runs from Apr-Oct, and gives children a chance to see planes at close quarters.

Shuttleworth Collection
Old Warden Aerodrome, nr Biggleswade, Beds. (0767) 627288. Famous collection of vintage aircraft. Film and introductory talk for pre-booked groups. *OPEN Apr-end Oct 10.00-17.00 Mon-Sun; Nov-Mar 10.00-16.00 Mon-Sun. Special flying*

displays *first Sun of May, Jun, Aug & Sep. Charge.*

Animal & bird enclosures in parks

These are local parks with small animal and bird enclosures. They are open from dawn till dusk Mon-Sun, unless otherwise stated, and all are free. See also 'Zoos, aquaria and wildlife parks'.

Battersea Park SW11　　**6 G5**
081-871 7540. Zoo with small collection of animals. Reptile house, wide variety of primates, otter, meerkat and mongoose enclosures, flamingoes, ponies and donkeys, deer, wallabies, rheas. *OPEN Easter-Oct 11.00-18.00 Mon-Sun; Nov-Mar 10.30-dusk Sat & Sun only. CLOSED 2 weeks in Feb.*

Brockwell Park SE24
071-926 0105. Small collection of birds including doves, canaries, finches budgerigars and chickens.

Clissold Park N16
081-800 1021. Fallow deer, rabbits, guinea pigs, tropical birds including a mynah bird, a peacock and a collection of waterfowl.

Crystal Palace Park SE20
081-778 7148. Farm with shire horses, cows, pigs, rabbits, chickens, donkeys, penguins, otters, goats, sheep and ponies. Shire horse cart rides round the park for children. *OPEN 11.00-17.00 Mon-Sun.*

Golders Hill Park NW11
081-455 5183. Fallow deer, pygmy goats, wallabies and blackbuck. Birds include pheasants, cranes, flamingoes and rheas.

Hainault Forest, Essex
081-500 3106. Ponies, donkeys, cows and pigs. Also small collection of domestic and wild fowl, including peacocks and guinea fowl.

Holland Park W8　　　　**3 A5**
071-602 9483. Collection of birds, including peacocks, bantams, muscovy ducks and peafowl.

Maryon Wilson Park SE7
081-854 0446. Ponies, goats, a donkey, fallow deer and Jacob sheep, as well as rabbits and chickens.

Plashet Park E6
081-503 5994. A mini-zoo with a collection of small animals. Tropical aviary and butterfly house. *OPEN summer 10.00-18.00 Mon-Sun; winter 10.00-16.30 Mon-Sun.*

Sydenham Wells Park SE26
Wells Park Rd. 081-695 6000. Aviary

where they breed budgies; also ducks, colourful pheasants and geese. Rabbits in their warrens.

Syon Park, Brentford

London Butterfly House, Syon Park, Brentford, Middx. 081-560 7272. A greenhouse full of tropical and temperate butterflies. Gallery featuring variety of insects and bizarre invertebrates. *OPEN Apr-Oct 10.00-17.00 Mon-Sun; Nov-Mar 10.00-15.30 Mon-Sun. Charge.*

Victoria Park E2

081-985 1957. A small enclosure on the eastern side of the park with fallow deer and pygmy goats. A wide variety of wild birds can be seen on the other side of the park.

Birdwatching

See *'Natural history'* under *'Activities and Interests'*.

Cemeteries

Some children find cemeteries fascinating rather than morbid or frightening, and many of London's older cemeteries are wonderful places to explore, not only for their monumental stonework and strange epitaphs but also as the peaceful haunt of many small animals and birds. See 'Looking at history' in 'Historic London'.

Fairs

There are over 200 fairs a week held in England during the summer; the following is a selection of some in London.

Holiday Fairs

Alexandra Park, Blackheath, Hampstead Heath and Wormwood Scrubs (*Easter, spring & summer B.hols*).

Other Occasional Fairs

Clapham Common (*mid Apr*), Crystal Palace (*early May & Aug*), Tooting Bec Common (*early May*), Victoria Park (*early May*).

Farms

There are several farms in and around London which are open to visitors. In London itself, there are small city farms which welcome visits from families and school groups; it is advisable to phone in advance if you're going in a large group. Outside London you can visit large working farms which organise open days and farm trails.

College Farm

Fitzalan Rd N3. 081-349 0690. Small

children's farm with cows, goats, pigs, sheep and shire horses. Special events on *first Sun of month* – craft stalls, donkey rides, bouncy castle. *OPEN 10.00-18.00 Mon-Sun. Charge.*

Freightliners Farm

Entrance: Sheringham Rd N7. 071-609 0467. Small, busy city farm with cows and calves, sheep, goats and kids, ducks, pigs, geese, bees and chickens. Lots of opportunities to get involved with the animals. Café and farmshop. Playgroup *Wed afternoons* and *Sat mornings* for under 5s. *Phone for times of tours. Groups must phone in advance. OPEN 09.00-13.00 & 14.00-17.00 Tue-Sun. CLOSED Mon. Free (voluntary donation).*

Hackney City Farm

1a Goldsmith's Row, off Hackney Rd E2. 071-729 6381. Sheep, goats, rabbits, calves, guinea pigs, poultry, ducks and bees. Pottery, spinning and weaving classes. Ecological pond, beekeeping, butterfly tunnel. Loan scheme under which schools can borrow animals. *OPEN 10.00-16.30 Tue-Sun. CLOSED Mon. Free.*

Kentish Town City Farm

Grafton Rd NW5. 071-482 2861. Horses, pigs, chickens, sheep, goats and rabbits. Feeding twice daily. *OPEN 09.30-17.30 Tue-Sun. CLOSED MON. Free.*

Mudchute Farm

Pier St E14. 071-515 5901. Large (32-acre – 13ha) city farm run by staff and volunteers who look after the beef cattle, ponies, sheep, goats, pigs, poultry, rabbits and bees. There is also a riding school and pony club, a nature study centre and café. The Mudchute is the venue for the annual Isle of Dogs Agricultural Show. *OPEN 09.00-17.00 Mon-Sun. Free.*

Stepping Stones Farm

Stepney Way E1. 071-790 8204. Local volunteers are invited to help out on all sorts of jobs, and everyone is welcome to visit this 6-acre (2.4ha) urban farm in the East End. Activities vary with the seasons, but the livestock population usually includes pigs, goats, cows, sheep, ducks, geese, rabbits and donkeys. Wildlife pond. Picnic garden. Produce shop. *OPEN 09.30-13.00, 14.00-18.00 Tue-Sun. CLOSED Mon. Free (voluntary donation).*

Surrey Docks Farm

Rotherhithe St SE16. 071-231 1010. 2-acre (0.8ha) site with goats, pigs, donkeys, ducks, geese and hens plus small orchard, vegetable garden, duck-pond herb garden and riverside walk. Blacksmith demonstrates traditional skills. Farm shop sells fresh produce. *OPEN 10.00-13.00 & 14.00-17.00 Tue-Sun. CLOSED Mon & Fri in school hols. Free.*

Vauxhall City Farm
Tyers St SE11. 071-582 4204. Tours to visit the pigs, goats, sheep and rabbits. Pony and donkey rides. *OPEN 10.30-17.00 Tue-Thur, Sat & Sun. Charge (for tours only).*

Fish & fishing

The river Thames is now cleaner than it has been for centuries, and supports a growing number of fish including salmon and trout. Many fish are to be found in London's ponds, lakes and canals. See 'Fishing' and 'Fishing: lakes and ponds' under 'Sport'.

London Anglers' Association
Forest Road Hall, Hervey Park Rd E17. 081-520 7477. Junior membership gives information about places to fish and a London Anglers' Licence for coarse fishing on the Grand Union/Regent's Canal and River Lea. *Annual charge.*

Kite-flying

Flying your own kite is a great pleasure but you can meet other kite-flyers, or see the experts in action, at the following places in London: Blackheath, Clapham Common, Dulwich Park, Hampstead Heath on the top of Parliament Hill Fields, Primrose Hill, Richmond Park and near the Round Pond in Kensington Gardens. There are regular stunt kite events at Blackheath. Phone 071-275 8799 for details.

Model villages

Bekonscot
Warwick Rd, Beaconsfield, Bucks. (0494) 672919. A raised viewing platform offers a bird's eye view of the miniature land of shops, houses, cottages, pubs. Model (gauge 1) railway travels round the village. Picnic facilities and playground. *OPEN Mar-Oct 10.00-17.00 Mon-Sun. Charge.*

Nature reserves & nature trails

Nature Conservancy Council
Northminster House, Peterborough, Cambs. (0733) 340345. Will give regional office number who will supply a list of reserves and leaflets about individual reserves in Great Britain; also a children's reading list.

Camley Street Natural Park   1 G3
12 Camley St NW1. 071-833 2311. A park which has been created in a former coal drop on the Grand Union Canal to provide a wildlife refuge and a place to enjoy nature in the city. Visitor centre, classroom. *OPEN 10.00-17.00 Mon-Fri, 1.00-17.00 Sat & Sun. CLOSED B.hols. Free (voluntary donation).*

East Ham Nature Reserve
Norman Rd E6. 081-470 4525. A nature reserve in the heart of East London's largest churchyard. Follow the nature trail. See pheasants and butterflies. Special activities during *school hols. OPEN 09.00-17.00 (dusk in winter) Mon-Sun. Visitor Centre OPEN 14.00-17.00 Sat & Sun. Free.*

Horniman Gardens
London Rd SE23. 071-699 8924. Three walks: Coach trail, Dutch Barn trail and Railway trail following the track of the old Crystal Palace high level railway line. *OPEN 24hrs Mon-Sun. Free.*

Steam & traction engines

*Once common, these early engines have now become collectors' pieces. Rallies are held periodically by clubs in various parts of the country. They are colourful and unusual, and the engines themselves are superb. Contact the **National Traction Engine Trust** for a list of rallies and clubs. The junior section is called the Steam Apprentice Club and is for enthusiasts under 21. For information write to Mrs Sylvia Dudley, 12 Hillway, Woburn Sands, Bucks. A useful book is Traction Engines by Harold Bonnett (Shire Publications). Apart from the Science Museum, the following collections are worth seeing:*

Kew Bridge Steam Museum
See 'Museums for children' section.

National Motor Museum
Beaulieu, Hants. (0590) 612345. More than 250 vehicles and displays which illustrate the story of motoring, including the traction engine, 'Lord Nelson'. *OPEN May-Sep 10.00-18.00 Mon-Sun; Oct-Apr 10.00-17.00 Mon-Sun. Charge.*

Thursford Museum
Thursford, Fakenham, Norfolk. (0328) 878477. A superb collection of various engines and machines including fairground and other organs, fairground rides and steam and traction engines – all working. *OPEN Easter-Oct 13.00 (11.00 Jun, Jul & Aug)-17.00 Mon-Sun. Charge.*

Windmills

Once a prominent feature of south-east England, though most are now derelict. Discovering Windmills by J. Vince (Shire Publications) is an inexpensive introduction and guide. Two remaining in London are:

Brixton Windmill
Blenheim Gdns, Brixton Hill SW9. A reminder of Lambeth's rural past. The early 19thC tower mill was in use until 1934. OPEN to school parties by appointment only.

Wimbledon Windmill
Wimbledon Common SW19. Contact: Honorary Curator, 081-947 2825, for information. A hollow post mill, built in 1817, now housing a museum with models and photographs explaining how windmills work. *OPEN Apr-Oct 14.00-17.00 Sat, Sun & B.hols. Small charge.*

Zoos

See under 'Zoos, aquaria and wildlife parks' in 'Outdoor London'.

Activities and interests

In London you can enjoy just about every hobby you can imagine, from arts, crafts and theatre to natural history, science and sport (see 'Sport'). Scouts, guides and youth clubs are also listed here under 'Youth organisations'.

Archaeology

The best way to get experience, and maybe join in a dig, is to join the junior section of an archaeological society – for local clubs, enquire at your nearest library or contact the organisations below:

London and Middlesex   **5 D1**
Archaeological Society (LAMAS)
Contact: Young LAMAS, c/o MOLAS, Number One London Wall EC2. 081-423 5134. The junior section organises lectures and activities plus visits on Sats and school hols.

Young Archaeologists' Club
Contact: Dr Kate Perry, Homerton College, Hill's Rd, Cambridge CB2 2PH. (0223) 411141. For 9-18 year olds. The club is linked to British Archaeology and organises visits to sites, fieldwork and lectures (usually outside London). Magazine with news from around the world.

Arts & crafts

Also see 'Community arts centres', and 'Museums for children' (several have painting and crafts workshops).

Camden Arts Centre
Arkwright Rd NW3. 071-435 2643. *Sat morning and afternoon sessions* for 5-16 year-olds in painting and drawing, sculpture and ceramics. *After-school classes* plus courses *during school hols.* Local schools visit *during term time. Charge.*

Chelsea Pottery   **6 F3**
13 Radnor Walk SW3. 071-352 1366. Good, well-established studio. Children's classes *10.00-13.00 & 14.00-17.00 Sat.* Minimum age 5. Annual membership. Charge.

Susan Meyer-Michael
99 North End Rd NW11. 081-455 0817. Pottery and clay modelling. Small groups, family groups, or individuals. *Sessions by arrangement only. Charge.*

Astronomy

Greenwich Planetarium (Old Royal Observatory) and the London Planetarium show projections of the sky and stars (see 'Looking at London'). There is also an annual Astronomy Exhibition held in London each Feb. Phone 071-915 0054 for details.

Hampstead Scientific Society
The Secretary, 22 Flask Wlk NW3. 071-794 9341. Organises talks and outings, and also has its own observatory at Lower Ter NW3 (nr Whitestone Pond). *OPEN Sep-Apr 20.00-22.00 Fri & Sat, 11.00-13.00 Sun, weather permitting. Monthly meetings Sep-Jun. Annual junior subscription.*

Junior Astronomical Society
The Secretary, 36 Fairway, Keyworth, Notts. For interested beginners of any age. Meets four times a year in London. Quarterly magazine and bi-monthly newsletter sent to members. *Annual subscription.*

Boat clubs

Opportunities to learn canoeing, rowing and sailing. (You can hire rowing boats by the hour in some parks. See 'Parks and gardens' in 'Outdoor London'.)

The Sports Council
Greater London & SE Region, Crystal Palace National Sports Centre, Ledrington Rd SE19. 081-778 9600. The information 'unit' can provide you with a list of canoeing and sailing centres in and around London.

Westminster Boating Base   **7 D4**
Dinorvic Wharf, 136 Grosvenor Rd, SW1.
071-821 7389. Youth programme including canoeing and sailing.

Book clubs

Bookworm
W. Heffer & Sons, 20 Trinity St,
Cambridge. (0223) 358351. Bookworm is
for 7-12 year-olds. Early Worm for 0-7
year-olds. Both clubs are run through
schools or groups.

Puffin School Book Club   **3 C6**
c/o Penguin Books Ltd, 27 Wright's La
W8. 071-938 2200. Well-established
book club for 1-13 year-olds. Encourages
an interest in reading and books. There
are three clubs: Fledgling (0-6 years),
Flight (7-9 years) and Post (9-13 years).

Scholastic Publications
Westfield Rd, Southam, Leamington Spa,
Warks. (0926) 813910. Promotes a
variety of book clubs: Seesaw (0-6 yrs),
Lucky (7-9 yrs), Hip (9-12 yrs) and Scene
(12+ yrs). Monthly Club News. Children
join through their schools.

Brass rubbing

*You can learn how to make your
own rubbings at brass rubbing centres,
which provide replicas of many historic
monumental brasses plus everything you
need. The cost of rubbings is graded
according to the sizes of the brasses.
Once experienced, search out brasses in
old churches all over the country but ask
for permission first.*

All Hallows-by-the-Tower   **5 F3**
Byward St EC3. 071-481 2928. At the
west end of the church, an appealing
assembly of about 30 brasses, although
space allows for no more than 10 people
to make rubbings at one time. Free
instruction available. *OPEN 11.00-16.30
Mon-Sun. Book for groups. Charge.*

London Brass Rubbing Centre   **4 F3**
St-Martin-in-the-Fields WC2. 071-437
6023. Replicas on display of 70 British
and European brasses ranging from animal figures, children and wool merchants
to a crusader knight which stands 7ft
(2.1m) tall. Instruction available. *OPEN
10.00-18.00 Mon-Sat, 12.00-18.00 Sun.
Charge.*

Community arts centres

*These are centres which organise a great
variety of activities for both children and
adults. Usually a small charge.*

Battersea Arts Centre
Lavender Hill SW11. 071-223 6557.
Children's day on *Sat*, with workshops,
acting classes and puppetry, plus shows
and films. Workshops *during school hols*.

Inter-Action Social   **5 B3**
Enterprise Trust
HMS President (1918), nr Blackfriars
Bridge, Victoria Embankment EC4. 071-
583 2652. Facilities for computing,
children's workshops and a hands-on
technology centre.

Jackson's Lane Community Centre
269a Archway Rd N6. 081-340 5226.
After-school and *holiday* workshops for
children including arts and crafts, dance
and shadow puppets, plus an excellent
programme of visiting theatre and dance
groups. Also run a parent and toddlers
group.

Riverside Studios
Crisp Rd W6. 081-748 3354. Spacious
arts centre which organises some
children's educational visits and holiday
activities. Children's entertainment at
weekends.

Cricket

*Many London parks have practice nets
which can be booked through the park
authorities.*

English Schools Cricket Association
c/o Mr Lake, 38 Mill House, Woods Lane,
Cottingham, North Humberside (0482)
844446. Governing body for cricket in
schools.

MCC Indoor Cricket School
Lord's Cricket Ground, St John's Wood
Rd NW8. 071-286 3649. Coaching
from 8 years upwards, beginners and
advanced.

Cycling

British Cycling Federation
36 Rockingham Rd, Kettering, Northants.
(0536) 412211. A society for all sorts of
cyclists: racers, commuters, tourists and
general leisure riders. They offer members
comprehensive insurance, an annual
handbook with advice and tips, a coaching service and information on racing.

Cycling Proficiency Tests
Most boroughs organise their own cycling
proficiency lessons and tests for 9-13
year-olds. Certificates are issued to those
who pass tests in the theory and practice
of safe bicycling. Enquire at your local
town hall for details or contact the Royal
Society for the Prevention of Accidents
(RSPA), Cannon House, The Priory,
Queensway, Birmingham. 021-200 2461.

Eastway Cycle Circuit
Temple Mills La E15. 081-534 6085. Coaching to improve cycling ability, training ground for more experienced racing cyclists. Book through schools. Bikes for hire. BMX track. Minimum age 7. *OPEN Mar-Oct 08.00-20.00 Mon-Sun; Nov-Feb 08.00-17.00 Mon-Sun. Charge.*

Dancing

Dance Works   **4 B2**
16 Balderton St W1. 071-629 6183. Classes on Sat for 5-10 year-olds in classical ballet. *Mon evening* classes in tap and jazz for 3-5 yrs, 5-9 yrs, 9-16 yrs. *Thur evening* classes in contemporary dance for 5-10 yrs. *Charge.*

Imperial Society of Teachers 2 A4 of Dancing
Euston Hall, Birkenhead St WC1. 071-837 9967. Teachers of ballet by the Cecchetti method and other types of dance. Send sae for a list of teachers and local dance schools.

Islington Dance Factory
Vergers Cottage, 2 Parkhurst Rd N7. 071-607 0561. Community arts centre specialising in dance and music. Classes for 5-18 year-olds *after school* and on *Sat*: ballet for 5-11s, dance theatre workshop for 8-12s and 13+, contemporary elementary dance class for 15-18s, boys ballet classes, adult *evening* classes for 15-18 year-olds. *Charge.*

The Place   **1 F4**
17 Duke's Rd WC1. 071-388 8956. The Young Place offers classes in contemporary, jazz and classical ballet for ages 6-8, 8-10, 10-12 and 13-17 on *Sat mornings.* Also the home of the London Contemporary Dance Theatre. A new Youth Dance Group offers extensive and exciting dance experience for 10-16 year-olds.

Rambert School of Ballet
West London Institute of Higher Education, Gordon House, 300 St Margaret's Rd, Twickenham, Middx. 081-891 0121 (for application, auditions and interviews). Classes for children 3½-11, *after school* and on *Sat mornings. Charge.* This is the junior school of the famous Ballet Rambert Dance Company.

Royal Academy of Dancing   6 D6
36 Battersea Sq, SW11. 071-223 0091. Classes in classical ballet for children aged 5-17, leading to RAD graded examinations. Entry to all classes is by audition only. Send sae for lists of teachers, addressed to the Registration & Membership Department.

Royal Ballet School
White Lodge, Richmond Park, Surrey. 081-748 6335. This is the Lower School for children aged 11-16. Auditions are held to determine potential for classical ballet training. Accepted children receive a full-time general education in addition to being taught classical ballet.

Drama workshops

Anna Scher Children's   2 C2 Theatre
70 Barnsbury Rd N1. 071-278 2101. *After-school* classes for children from age 6 in improvisation, poetry, production, stage technique and theory of theatre. Lessons are imaginatively and thoroughly planned. Long waiting list for places. *Charge.*

Arts Junior School
West London Institute of Higher Education, 300 St Margaret's Rd, Twickenham, Middx. 081-891 0121. Drama class on *Sat mornings* for age 9 upwards – covers acting, stage management and lighting.

Greenwich and Lewisham Young People's Theatre
Burrage Rd SE18. 081-854 1316. Lively *eve* workshops *Mon-Fri during school terms* for 11-25 year-olds, ranging from drama to music and visual arts. Occasional performances by outside groups. *Charge.*

National Youth Theatre
Holloway Rd N7. 071-281 3863. Ages 14-21. Auditions are held in *Feb & Mar* (closing date to apply for audition *end Dec*) to select the casts of plays to be rehearsed and performed during the *summer hols*. Only cost is your own food and accommodation during the *summer* and sometimes a few *weekends* in between.

Polka Children's Theatre
240 The Broadway SW19. 081-543 4888. Workshops and courses for 3 year-olds upwards. Music, clowning and puppet-making may be on the agenda.

Questors Theatre
Mattock La W5. 081-567 0011. Excellent amateur theatre club with drama playgroups on *Sat mornings* for 5-9 year-olds. Emphasis on imaginative play and role-playing activities. Junior Drama Workshops are held on *weekday evenings* and *Sun mornings*. Role-playing, improvisation and acting exercises. Groups graded according to age and experience. *Charge.*

Theatre Royal Stratford East
Gerry Raffles Sq E15. 081-534 0310.
Theatre workshop for 9-14 year-olds on
Sat mornings and on *Mon evenings* for
those aged 14 upwards. Drama, games,
mime, scriptwork, maskwork. Usually
lead to performances in the theatre. *Free.*

Upstream Children's Theatre
Ilderton School, Varcoe Rd, off Old Kent
Rd SE16 (entrance in Ilderton Rd). 071-
232 2869. Educational drama and theatre
workshops for 3-12 year-olds. Workshops include improvisation, story-telling,
stage make-up, puppetry, music.

Film making

Children's Film Unit
9 Hamilton House, Upper Richmond Rd,
SW15. 081-871 2006. Organises movie
making for 8-16 year-olds. Acting, camera
skills, sound, make-up, continuity, script-
writing. Sessions on *Sat* and full length
movie made in the *summer holidays.*

Folk music & dancing

English Folk Song & Dance 1 C2
Society
Cecil Sharp House, 2 Regent's Park Rd
NW1. 071-485 2206. The Hobby Horse
Club is the children's section. Members
receive a badge, a birthday card, newslet-
ters and a list of festivals where there will
be children's events. There is a children's
day of dance held *once a month.*

Football

Football Association 3 D3
16 Lancaster Gate W2. 071-262 4542.
Each county has a youth section that the
Football Association will put you in touch
with or you can contact the English
Schools Association, 4a Eastgate St,
Stafford, Staffs. (0785) 51142. Almost all
sports centres (*see 'Sport, Health and
Fitness'*) offer five-a-side football as one of
their activities.

Go-karting

British Motor Sports Council
Motor Sports House, Riverside Park,
Colnbrook, Slough, Berks. (0753) 681736.
Organise go-karting for children from 8
years on. Supply information on fixture lists
and regulations, as well as safety details.

Gymnastics

*Most sports centres provide classes and
coaching for all ages, including under-5s.*

Amateur Gymnastics Association
The Secretary, Mrs J. Thatch, 4 Victoria
Rd E4. 081-529 1142. Organising body
for the sport; will provide advice and a list
of clubs.

Life-saving

*Your local swimming baths should
provide information about coaching and
tests.*
Royal Life-Saving Society
Mountbatten House, Studley, Warks.
(052785) 3943. They will send you information on your local branch.

Music

*There is a professional register of music
teachers which should be available in the
reference section of your library.*
London College of Music
Thames Valley University, St Mary's
Road, Ealing W5. 081-231 2304. *Sat
morning* junior music school for children
over 5. Also individual lessons for any
instrument.

National Youth Jazz Orchestra
Meets at the London Studio Centre, 42-
50 York Way, Kings Cross on *Sat.* Two
sessions – *10.30* and *14.00.* Musicians
must be of a high standard. Details from
11 Victor Rd, Harrow, Middx. 081-863
2717.

**National Youth Orchestra of Great
Britain**
Causeway House, Lodge Causeway,
Fishponds, Bristol BS16 3HD. Write for
detailed information and application
forms. Children aged 11-17 can apply for
audition to be trained, and once a member of the orchestra remain so until they
are 19 (subject to annual re-audition).

Youth Music Centre
Henrietta Barnett School, Bigwood Rd
NW11. 081-907 8018. Lively centre with
music school, orchestras and classes on
Sat mornings during term time for ages
3-16. All types of classical music. High
standard. *Charge.*

Natural history & conservation

*In urban areas, reservoirs have become
an important habitat for birds.*
Barn Elms Reservoirs SW13
Walthamstow Reservoirs N17
Walton Reservoirs, Surrey
Phone or write to: Thames Water,
Customer Services Centre, PO Box 1850,
Swindon, Wilts SN1 4TW (0734) 591159

to obtain their free leaflet *'Reservoir Leisure Guide'*.

Lifewatch Explorers Club   1 C3

London Zoo, Regent's Park NW1. 071-722 3333. For 4-15 year-olds. Membership (*charge*) gives free entry to London Zoo and Whipsnade Wild Animal Park *throughout the year*, subscription to the zoo magazine three times a year, hol lectures, films and outings.

London Natural History Society

Contact: Mr Barrett, Secretary, 21 Green Way, Frinton-on-Sea, Essex CO13 9AL. (0255) 674 678. Welcomes junior members to the regular outings and meetings in London and elsewhere. Birdwatching excursions *midweek* and most *weekends*. Covers the area within a 20-mile (32km) radius of St Paul's Cathedral. Newsletter and bulletin every two months. *Charge*.

Young Ornithologists' Club

c/o The Royal Society for the Protection of Birds (RSPB), The Lodge, Sandy, Beds. (0767) 680551. Junior membership gives a badge, a bi-monthly magazine (*Bird Life*) and a chance to take part in outings to RSPB reserves and join in special projects. They also organise holiday courses. Family, school and group membership also available. *Charge*.

Poetry

Poetry Society   4 F2

22 Betterton St, Covent Garden WC2. 071-240 4810. Occasional children's workshops and events including children's poetry competitions. Also runs the Poets in Schools scheme whereby well-known poets visit schools. Enquiries to Education Officer.

Puppetry

Puppet Centre Trust

Battersea Arts Centre, Lavender Hill SW11. 071-228 5335. National reference centre for everything to do with puppetry. Offers information and consultancy service, exhibition and shop, training courses for children. Bi-monthly magazine.

Youth organisations

Girl Guides Association   4 C6

17-19 Buckingham Palace Rd SW1. 071-834 6242. For girls aged 7-11 there are Brownie packs and at the age of 10 girls can become Guides. From 14-18 they become Rangers.

London Union of Youth Clubs

64 Camberwell Rd SE5. 071-701 6366. To put you in touch with your local clubs. If you live in Greater London you should contact youth and community departments in local boroughs. The Union is for 7-25 year-olds but mainly deals with 12-21 year-olds.

National Association of Boys' Clubs

369 Kennington Lane SE11. 071-793 0787. For information about clubs, adventure courses and activity holidays.

Scout Association   3 D5

Baden-Powell House, 65 Queen's Gate SW7. 071-584 7030. Headquarters of the movement. They will give you the address of your nearest company. Boys aged 6-8 become Beavers, those aged 8-11 become Cubs and above that age Scouts. 16-21 year-olds can become Venture Scouts. Girls can now also join the Scout movement – *phone for details.*

Playgrounds and playcentres

Most parks offer facilities for children's play – swings, roundabouts, slides etc.

Adventure playgrounds

Community-based playgrounds, run by playworkers, who organise activities indoors and out for school-age children. Children are usually free to build dens, using old timber and junk. For more information contact London Adventure Playground Association, 28 Underwood Rd E1. 071-377 0314. *OPEN after school, at weekends and during school hols.*

Conventional playgrounds

Provided by borough councils in most local parks. They usually have tarmac surfaces with swings, roundabouts, slides, seesaws, climbing frames, and iron rocking-horses. Some of this equipment is potentially dangerous for small children and newer, safer playgrounds have swings made of rubber tyres, rubber matting instead of concrete and built-up slides made of durable plastic. *OPEN 08.00-19.00 (or dusk) Mon-Sun.*

Handicapped Adventure Playground Association

Fulham Palace, Bishops Av SW6. 071-736 4443. The Association runs five playgrounds for the handicapped in London and provides information about its services as well as play ideas for handicapped children. All the playgrounds are carefully planned and landscaped with children with special needs in mind. Also advisory service which gives help to those wishing to set up their own playground.

One o'clock clubs

Enclosed area in some parks for children under 5. Each club has a building for indoor play (painting, drawing, modelling etc) and an enclosure with climbing frames, swings and sandpit for outdoor play. There are playworkers to supervise activities but a parent or guardian is expected to stay on the premises. Informal and friendly. To find your nearest club, contact the local borough council. *OPEN 13.00-16.30 Mon-Fri. Free.*

Playparks

Intended for children of 5-15 years – the aim is towards free play with structures for climbing, swinging etc and playworkers to supervise. You'll find them in Alexandra Park, Battersea Park, Crystal Palace Park, Holland Park and on Hampstead Heath (Parliament Hill Fields). Contact the local borough council for information. *OPEN summer 11.30-20.00 Mon-Sun.*

There are innumerable organisations which arrange holidays for unaccompanied children, and others which arrange family holidays.

Camp Beaumont

9 West St, Godmanchester, Huntingdon, Cambs. (0480) 456123. Residential and day camps around London – Brentwood, Mill Hill, Windsor and Wimbledon – during the summer. An incredible range of activities to get involved in – water sports, ball sports, motor sports, stage and screen. Centres vary in the activities they offer so everyone is matched to a suitable centre. From the nursery day camps for the small ones to holidays for the independent teenager.

English Tourist Board   7 B1

4 Grosvenor Gdns SW1. 071-730 3488. Their annual publication Activity and Hobby Holidays is packed with information covering a huge range of holidays in England, from walking, riding, sailing, birdwatching and painting to underwater swimming, archery or fossil hunting. Also multi-activity holidays. There is a special section on holidays for unaccompanied children, and places welcoming families are indicated.

PGL Young Adventure

Alton Court, Penyard Lane, Ross-on-Wye, Herefordshire. (0989) 764211.

Holidays for ages 3-18. Up to 40 activities including canoeing, pony trekking, sailing, camping, hobby holidays under expert guidance at 30 locations in Britain and abroad. Also family holidays. Brochures available.

Trent Park Equestrian Centre

Bramley Rd, Southgate N14. 081-363 8630/9005. 'Own-a-Pony' weeks where everyone 'adopts' a pony and visits the stable every day for a week to look after and ride it. Also 4-day holidays looking after a pony and riding it twice a day. *Phone for details.*

YHA Adventure Holidays

Youth Hostel Association, Trevelyan House, St Stephen's Hill, St Albans, Herts. (0727) 55215. Adventure holidays for 11-15 year-olds (in groups of 10-12) with experienced instructors. Large range of special interest holidays as well as multi-activity holidays. Older YHA members can also arrange their own cycling or walking holidays and make use of the YHA hostels.

Amitié Internationale des Jeunes

Beaver House, 10a Woodborough Rd SW15. 081-788 6857. Exchanges between French and British school-children, 11-18 year-olds. Escorts are provided on the journey between London and Paris.

**Central Bureau for   4 B2
Educational Visits & Exchanges**

Seymour Mews House, Seymour Mews W1. 071-486 5101. They publish several excellent guides including Volunteer Work, Working Holidays, A Year Between, Study Holidays and Home From Home covering opportunities both at home and abroad. Send an sae (no personal callers).

Venues which provide children's shows, films and concerts. See children's section in Time Out.

The following theatres put on children's shows regularly throughout the year. Phone for programme details. For drama workshops, see 'Activities and interests'.

Barbican   5 D1

Silk St EC2. 071-638 4141 ex218. Annual festival for all the family in the *summer hols* with concerts, clowns, scavenger hunts and workshops. *Phone for details.*

Little Angel Marionette Theatre　　　　　　　　　**2 D2**

14 Dagmar Passage, off Cross St N1. 071-226 1787. London's only permanent puppet theatre, which presents an excellent variety of shows by the resident company and visiting puppeteers. Essential to book in advance. Regular performances at *15.00 Sat & Sun* for older children and adults. Special show for the very young (3-6 year-olds) *11.00 Sat & Sun.* Extra shows during *half-term and school hols.*

Polka Children's Theatre

240 The Broadway, Wimbledon SW19. 081-543 4888. Extremely attractive theatre complex. 300-seat theatre with plays, puppet shows and concerts; exhibitions of toys and puppets; children's workshop, adventure room, garden playground and café catering with children in mind. Age 3 upwards. Full facilities for handicapped children including a loop system for deaf children. *OPEN Tue-Sat.*

Puppet Theatre Barge

Bookings and details from 78 Middleton Rd E8. 071-249 6876. A marionette theatre in a converted Thames barge, which has regular moorings at Little Venice *Sep-May.* Tours up the Thames to Oxford from *May-Sep* and is moored at different places on the waterways. Its position is listed in the London entertainment guides. Performances *Sat & Sun* and *daily during school holidays.*

Tricycle Theatre

269 Kilburn High Rd NW6. 071-328 1000. Fun children's shows *every Sat 11.00 & 14.00,* plus two productions per year by the Tricycle themselves, put on at *half terms.* Children under 7 yrs must be accompanied by a paying adult. *Term time and half term workshops.* Essential to book in advance. Wheelchair access and a loop system for deaf children.

Unicorn Theatre for Children　　**4 F3**

Arts Theatre, Great Newport St WC2. 071-836 3334. Well-established children's theatre which presents plays (often specially commissioned) and other entertainment for the 4-12s. Public performances *14.30 Sat & 11.00 & 14.30 Sun* (extra performances during *school hols).* Performances for schools *Tue-Fri* during termtime. Also a children's club, which organises workshop sessions.

Young Vic Theatre　　　　　　　　**5 B5**

66 The Cut SE1. 071-928 6363. Young repertory company putting on a good choice of revivals and new experimental theatre, specially written children's plays and adaptations of Shakespeare. A comprehensive education service, out-of-school workshops, touring group staging children's plays. Age approx 11 upwards.

Children's films

Remember there are age limits for certain films: U = suitable for all ages; PG = parental guidance advised and unsuitable for young children; 12 = suitable for 12 years and over; 15 = suitable for 15 years and over; 18 = suitable for 18 years and over.

Saturday morning cinema clubs show children's films at cheap prices. See children's section in Time Out.

Barbican　　　　　　　　　　　　　**5 D1**

Silk St EC2. 071-638 4141 ex 263. Children's cinema club on *Sat;* films for members *14.30.*

National Film Theatre　　　　　　**5 A4**

South Bank SE1. 071-928 3232. Junior matinees, usually *Sat & Sun afternoons.*

Children's concerts

Several organisations arrange children's concerts (mainly classical music) through the autumn and winter. Also look out for steel bands, brass bands and jazz bands at summer festivals and fairs in the parks. For details of pop concerts look in Melody Maker, New Musical Express *and* Time Out.

Arthur Davison Orchestral Concerts

Fairfield Hall, Croydon, Surrey. 081-688 9291. Orchestral concerts for children – selection of short pieces, using a wide variety of instruments. A good way of introducing children to music. Season tickets available for seven concerts *Sep-May 11.00 Sat. Charge.*

Ernest Read Concerts for Children　　　　　　　　　　　　**5 A4**

Royal Festival Hall, South Bank SE1. 071-928 3191. Orchestral concerts for children over 7, arranged by the Ernest Read Music Association. Season tickets available for six concerts, *Oct-May.* Tickets issued from May. *Phone 081-366 0777 for details. Charge.*

Morley College Family Concerts　　　　　　　　　　　　**5 B0**

61 Westminster Bridge Rd SE1. 071-928 8501. Series of informal concerts designed to introduce children and their parents to a wide variety of music, from classical to pop, ethnic to electronic. Season tickets available for eight monthly concerts, *Oct-May 10.30-12.30 Sat.*

Tickets issued in *Sep* or can be purchased at the door.

Music for Youth

4 Blade Mews, Deodar Road SW15. 081-870 9624. *Every Nov* over 1200 talented young performers chosen from the National Festival of Music for Youth on the South Bank appear in three public concerts at the Royal Albert Hall.

Radio & TV shows

See 'Radio and TV shows' in 'Theatres, cinemas, music and comedy'.

Children's restaurants

Fast food restaurants or sandwich bars are always a good idea and can be found all over London. In case you are looking for something more substantial, below are listed a selection of restaurants which welcome children.

Garfunkels　　　　　　　　**4 C2**

265 Regent St W1. 071-629 1870. Chain of family restaurants with vast American-style menu and separate menu for children. *OPEN 11.30-23.30 Mon-Sat, 12.00-23.30 Sun.*

Selfridges Food Garden Café　**4 B2**

Oxford St W1. 071-629 1234. A useful one to remember if in Oxford Street. Burgers and pasta in half portions. *OPEN 09.30-18.45 Mon-Sat (to 19.45 Thur).*

Smollensky's Balloon　　　**4 D4**

1 Dover St W1. 071-491 1199. Excellent international menu with special junior dishes. Entertainments on *Sat & Sun afternoons*; Punch & Judy, magicians, clowns and story-tellers. *OPEN 12.00-23.45 Mon-Sat, 12.00-22.30 Sun.*

Children's shopping

Books & comics

Foyles, Dillons, and Hatchards have good children's book departments. See 'Shopping'.

Children's Book Centre　　**3 B6**

237 Kensington High St W8. 071-937 7497. The largest children's bookshop in the country with some 30,000 titles. In the *school hols* there are story-telling sessions. *OPEN 09.30-18.30 Mon-Sat (to 19.00 Thur), 12.30-18.00 Sun.*

Comic Showcase　　　　　**4 F2**

76 Neal St WC2. 071-240 3664. Lots of whizzy reading for the whole family.

OPEN 10.00-18.00 Mon-Sat (to 19.00 Thur).

Puffin Bookshop　　　　　**4 F3**

1 Covent Garden Mkt WC2. 071-379 6465. Large stock of children's books, including the full Puffin range. *OPEN 10.00-18.00 Mon-Sat, 12.00-18.00 Sun.*

Carnival & party novelties

Barnum's

67 Hammersmith Rd W14. 071-602 1211. Masks, fairground novelties, balloons, flags. For hire and sale. *OPEN 09.00-18.00 Mon-Fri, 10.00-17.00 Sat.*

Escapade

150 Camden High St NW1. 071-485 7384. Get all your party kit here. Stuffed full of costumes, jokes, tricks, masks, wigs and novelties. *OPEN 10.00-19.00 Mon-Fri, 10.00-18.00 Sat.*

Theatre Zoo　　　　　　　**4 F2**

21 Earlham St WC2. 071-836 3150. Animal costumes for hire; grotesque and unusual face masks, false feet, hats, hands and moustaches, and stage make-up. *OPEN 09.00-17.30 Mon-Fri.*

Magic, jokes & tricks

Davenports Magic Shop　　**4 F4**

Charing Cross Underground Shopping Concourse WC2. 071-836 0408. Jokes, tricks, puzzles, practical jokes – some at pocket money prices. Plus elaborate tricks for the professionals. *OPEN 10.15-17.30 Mon-Fri, 09.30-16.30 Sat.*

Models

See 'Models' under 'Shops and services.'

Party entertainers

Frog Frolics　　　　　　　**4 J4**

123 Ifield Rd SW10. 071-370 4358. Provides presents, toys and paper tableware. Hires out low tables and chairs and has a list of recommended entertainers. *OPEN 10.00-17.00 Mon-Fri.*

Len Belmont

48 Morland Estate E8. 071-254 8300. Well-known and popular children's entertainer with ventriloquist, magic and balloon modelling acts. Guaranteed to get a party started.

'Prof'Alexander's Punch & Judy

59 Wilton Way E8. 071-254 0416. Traditional show lasting ½ hr or longer. Also does magic shows.

Posters

Athena   4 E3
1-4 Leicester Sq WC2. 071-437 6780. All
sorts of posters from pop idols to Disney
characters. OPEN 09.30-24.00 Mon-Fri,
10.00-24.00 Sat, 10.00-23.00 Sun.

Poster Shop   4 F3
28 James St WC2. 071-240 2526. A vast
range of colourful posters. OPEN 10.00-
20.00 Mon-Sat, 12.00-18.00 Sun.

Toys & games

*Many department stores have very good
toy departments, especially Harrods,
Selfridges and Heal's. Most of the following specialist shops will send catalogues
on request. Remember you can also
borrow toys. Contact Play Matters,
Association of Toy and Leisure Libraries,
68 Churchway NW1 (071-387 9592) for
details of your local toy library.*

Doll's House   4 F3
29 Covent Garden Mkt WC2. 071-379
7243. Wide range of hand-made
dolls' houses and miniature furniture in
attractive antique styles for children
and collectors. OPEN 10.00-20.00 Mon-
Sat.

Dolls' Hospital
16 Dawes Rd SW6. 071-385 2081.
Casualty department for broken limbs,
spare part surgery, antique restoration,
etc. Also a few toys and dolls for sale.
Phone for opening times.

Early Learning Centre   3 B6
225 Kensington High St W8. 071-937
0419. Bright, durable, educational toys for
babies upwards. Play area for under 8s.
Other branches. OPEN 09.00-18.00
Mon-Sat.

Hamleys   4 D3
188-196 Regent St W1. 071-734
3161. Largest toyshop in London.
Play area. Has nearly everything. All
ages. OPEN 10.00-18.00 Mon-Wed, to
20.00 Thur, to 18.30 Fri, 09.30-18.30
Sun.

Just Games   4 D3
71 Brewer St W1. 071-734 6124. All the
old favourites such as Scrabble and
Spillikins as well as some more unusual
new ones. OPEN 10.00-18.00 Mon-Sat
(to 19.00 Thur).

Kristin Baybars
7 Mansfield Rd NW3. 071-267 0934. Tiny
treasure chest which specialises in crafts-
man-made dolls' houses, miniatures and
unusual small toys. OPEN 11.15-18.00
Tue-Sat. CLOSED Mon.

Benjamin Pollock's Toy Shop   4 F3
44 Covent Garden Mkt WC2. 071-
379 7866. In addition to toys and
Victorian cut-out model theatres, sells
antique dolls for children and
collectors. Also specialise in christen-
ing presents. OPEN 10.30-18.00 Mon-
Sat.

Singing Tree
69 New King's Rd SW6. 071-736 4527.
Not just for children, this amazing shop
stocks new and antique dolls' houses
and everything imaginable to go in
them. Collectors' items in miniature. Mail
order service. OPEN 10.00-17.30 Mon-
Sat.

Eric Snook's Toyshop   4 F3
32 The Market, Covent Garden WC2.
071-379 7681. Smart toyshop selling
Beatrix Potter characters and hand-made
wooden toys. OPEN 10.00-18.00 Mon-
Sat, 11.00-18.00 Sun.

Toys 'R' Us
Tilling Rd, Brent Cross NW2. Huge toy
warehouse selling games and toys for
children of all ages. OPEN 09.00-20.00
Mon-Sat, 10.00-18.00 Sun.

Virgin Games Centre   4 D2
100 Oxford St W1. 071-637 7911.
Renowned for its incredible fantasy
games. Whole department devoted to
war games. Complete Trivial Pursuit
range and a whole floor of computer
games. OPEN 09.30-19.00 Mon-Sat, (to
20.00 Thur) 12.00-17.00 Sun.

Children's clothes

*For everyday wear the best buys are
in the chain stores and department
stores but you can also find stylish
designer wear for even the youngest
children.*

C & A   4 B2
501-509 Oxford St W1. 071-629 7272.
(Main branch.) Good selection of inexpensive clothes, especially sports kit, for
children up to 16. OPEN 09.30-19.00
Mon-Sat (to 20.00 Thur).

Circus Circus
176 Wandsworth Bridge Rd SW6. 071-
731 4128. Lively atmosphere. Some
inexpensive clothing. Nursery equipment.
Second-hand goods. OPEN 09.30-18.30
Mon-Sat.

The Gap   4 D3
144-146 Regent St W1. 071-287 5095.
All-American denims, sweatshirts and
cotton knits for 2-13 year-olds. Other
branches. OPEN 09.30-19.00 Mon-Sat
(to 20.00 Thur).

Hennes   **4 D2**
Oxford Circus W1. 071-493 4004. Huge selection of casual fun clothes for children (and adults). High fashion at budget prices. *OPEN 10.00-18.45 Mon-Fri (to 20.00 Thur), 09.15-18.15 Sat.*

Laura Ashley   **4 D2**
256 Regent St W1. 071-437 9760. Pastoral prints on cotton lawn, corduroys and drills, smocks, shirts and Victorian party dresses. Sailor suits. Straw boaters with lots of flowers. *OPEN 10.00-18.30 Mon & Tue, to 19.00 Wed & Fri, to 20.00 Thur, 09.30-19.00 Sat.*

Marks & Spencer   **4 B2**
458 Oxford St W1. 071-935 7954. (Largest branch, first to get the new ranges.) Excellent value for children's clothes. *OPEN 09.00-19.00 Mon, Wed & Sat, 09.00-20.00 Thur & Fri.*

Mothercare   **4 B2**
461 Oxford St W1. 071-629 6621. (Main branch.) Good quality everyday clothes at reasonable prices. Co-ordinated tops and bottoms as well as accessories for babies and children up to 11. *OPEN 09.30-19.00 Mon-Sat.*

Next   **3 C5**
54-60 Kensington High St W8. 071-938 4211. Special section full of trendy childrenswear: thick cotton tracksuits, tartan duffle coats and a small range of interesting shoes. *OPEN 10.00-19.00 Mon-Fri, 10.00-18.00 Sat.*

012   **4 C3**
22 South Molton St W1. 071-409 1599. Junior version of Benetton. Colourful Italian clothes. Other branches. *OPEN 10.00-18.00 Mon-Sat (to 19.00 Thur).*

Pollyanna
811 Fulham Rd SW6. 071-731 0673. Beautifully designed, practical but unusual clothes for boys and girls up to 12. *OPEN 09.30-18.00 Mon-Sat.*

Help for parents

Education & schools

Advisory Centre for Education (ACE)
Unit 1b, Aberdeen Studios, 22-24 Highbury Grove N5. 071-354 8321. Provides free help and advice for parents, students and teachers. Ask for their list of publications. They also publish information sheets and an excellent magazine, *ACE Bulletin*, available by annual subscription. *Manned 14.00-17.00 Mon-Fri.*

Gabbitas, Truman & Thring   **4 D3**
Educational Trust
6 Sackville St W1. 071-734 0161. Expert advice on the choice of independent schools and colleges, higher education and careers.

Independent Schools   **4 D6**
Information Service (ISIS)
50 Buckingham Gate SW1. 071-630 8793 (Head Office). Information about independent and private schools.

National Association for Gifted Children
Park Campus, Boughton Green Rd, Northampton. (0604) 792300. Advice of all kinds for parents and teachers of gifted children. Activities for the children. Newsletter *four times a year.*

Pre-school playgroups

London Pre-school   **7 C1**
Playgroups Association
314 Vauxhall Bridge Rd SW1. 071-828 2417. For information about playgroups in inner and outer London.

Pre-school Playgroups   **2 B4**
Association
Head Office, 61 King's Cross Rd WC1. 071-833 0991. For publications and advice on pre-school education.

Children in hospital

Action for Sick Children   **1 G4**
Argyle House, 29-31 Euston Rd NW1. 071-833 2041. Help and advice for parents in preparing children for hospital stays.

Babysitters & childminders

Babysitters Unlimited
2 Napoleon Rd, Twickenham, Middx. 081-892 8888. *Annual membership and fee at each booking. Hourly rates vary according to the time of day.* Covers central London.

Childminders   **1 C6**
9 Paddington St W1. 071-935 9763/2049. Covers 20-mile radius from central London. *Annual membership and fee at each booking. Hourly rates.*

Theatres, cinemas, music and comedy

Ticket agencies and theatre information

Ticket agencies will book tickets for all occasions – but remember they charge a commission. Lists of current theatre, cinema, dance, music and comedy programmes can be found in the daily papers, Time Out, and What's On & Where to Go.

Artsline   **1 E3**
5 Crowndale Rd NW1. 071-388 2227. Free advice and information for disabled people on access to arts and entertainment.

Curtain Call
(0891) 888788. 24-hr entertainment, information service giving previews and reviews of theatre, dance, musicals and opera.

Fenchurch Booking Agency   **5 C4**
94 Southwark St SE1. 071-928 8585. A.V.

First Call
071-240 7200. A.Ax.Dc.V.

Keith Prowse
071-379 9901. A.Ax.Dc.V.

Society of West End Theatre   **4 E3**
Half-Price Ticket Booth (SWET)
Leicester Sq WC2. Unsold tickets at half-price on the day of performance from the pavilion' on the south side of Leicester Square. OPEN from 12.00 (for matinées) & 14.30-18.30 (for evening performances). Maximum 4 tickets. No credit cards.

Ticketmaster UK Ltd   **4 F3**
78 St Martin's La WC2. 071-379 4444. A.Ax.V.

Theatre

The tradition of live theatre in London has flourished for more than four centuries, since the first regular playhouse – aptly named the Theatre – went up in Shoreditch in 1576. A penny bought standing room in the circular roofless building; tuppence included a stool for 'quiet standing'. Marlowe's Tamburlaine electrified audiences with its new style of 'great and thundering speech'. During a

performance of Dr Faustus the Theatre actually cracked. In 1597 bankruptcy (due to inflation) set in and the building's timber and materials were transported across the river to become the Globe, made famous by Shakespeare. In 1644 the Globe was pulled down; a working reconstruction of the theatre is now being built at Bankside, close to its original site, following the original designs of 1599. It is due for completion in April 1994. The Drury Lane, where Pepys caught cold from draughts in 1663, still stands on its original site despite fire, plague and World War II bombs. Covent Garden, built in 1732, and the Haymarket, 1721, are national monuments, while the reputation of London theatre has never been equalled due to the number and quality of theatre people and stage-names – from Garrick to Frohman, from Nell Gwynne to Bernhardt, from Sheridan to Shaw, from Chaplin to the Ballet Rambert. Government subsidies during and after World War II sustained the tradition which partly gave way in the 70s to sex, farce and formula: the West End's answer to inflation. Subsidised companies such as the National and the Royal Shakespeare continue to stage quality productions including new plays, revivals, Shakespeare and large-scale musicals. The Theatre of Comedy Company, formed in 1982, has also made a significant contribution to the nature of West End theatre with its nucleus of leading actors, actresses, writers and directors presenting limited seasons of high-quality comedies. Fringe theatre adds an alternative – and usually less expensive – source of vitality, providing opportunities for new talent and new ideas.

West End theatres

Adelphi   **4 F3**
Strand WC2. 071-836 7611. Musicals including Me and My Girl.

Albery   **4 F3**
St Martin's La WC2. 071-867 1115. Originally the New Theatre. Renamed 1973. Musicals, comedy and drama.

Aldwych   **4 G3**
Aldwych WC2. 071-836 6404. Former

Aldwych

London home of the Royal Shakespeare Company. Offers a varied programme of plays, comedies and musicals.

Ambassadors   **4 E2**
West St WC2. 071-836 6111. Small theatre. Original home of *The Mousetrap*.

Apollo   **4 E3**
Shaftesbury Av W1. 071-494 5070. Old tradition of musical comedy. Now presents musicals, comedy and drama.

Apollo Victoria   **7 C2**
17 Wilton Rd SW1. 071-494 5070. Auditorium completely transformed to accommodate the hit rollerskating railway musical *Starlight Express*.

Barbican   **2 E6**
Barbican Centre, Silk St EC2. 071-638 8891. Purpose-built for the Royal Shakespeare Company; main auditorium for large-scale productions in repertory and the Pit, a smaller studio theatre, for new works.

Cambridge   **4 F2**
Earlham St WC2. 071-494 5040. Large theatre well suited to musical productions.

Comedy   **4 E3**
Panton St SW1. 071-930 2578. Good intimate theatre showing unusual comedy and small-cast plays.

Criterion   **4 E3**
Piccadilly Circus W1. 071-930 0314. Listed building housing the only underground auditorium in London.

Criterion

Drury Lane (Theatre Royal)   **4 G2**
Catherine St WC2. 071-494 5062. Operated under Royal charter by Thomas Killigrew in 1663 and has been burnt or pulled down and rebuilt four times. Nell Gwynne was an actress here and Orange Moll sold her oranges. Garrick, Mrs Siddons, Kean and others played here. General policy now is vast musicals like *Miss Saigon*.

Duchess   **4 G3**
Catherine St WC2. 071-494 5075. Opened 1929. Plays, serious drama, light comedy and musicals.

Duke of York's   **4 F3**
St Martin's La WC2. 071-836 5122. Built by 'Mad (Violet) Melnotte' in 1892. Associated with names like Frohman, G. B. Shaw, Granville Barker, Chaplin and the Ballet Rambert. Refurbished by the present owners, Capital Radio, for major productions.

Fortune   **4 F2**
Russell St WC2. 071-836 2238. Small compared with its neighbour, Drury Lane. Intimate revues (Peter Cook and Dudley Moore shot to fame here in *Beyond the Fringe*), musicals and modern drama.

Garrick   **4 F3**
Charing Cross Rd WC2. 071-494 5085. Built 1897. Notable managers included Bourchier and Jack Buchanan. Varied bills.

Globe   **4 E3**
Shaftesbury Av W1. 071-494 5065. A wide variety of successful plays and comedies. The third theatre of this name in London.

Globe

Greenwich Theatre
Crooms Hill SE10. 081-858 7755. Stages a season of eight plays annually including new works, revivals and classics, often with famous names in the cast.

Haymarket (Theatre Royal)   **4 E3**
Haymarket SW1. 071-930 9832. Originally built in 1721 as the little Theatre in the Hay, it became Royal 50 years later. The present theatre was built by

Haymarket

Nash in 1821 and is sometimes enlivened by the ghost of Mr Buckstone, Queen Victoria's favourite actor-manager. He no doubt approves of the policy to present plays of quality.

Her Majesty's   4 E4
Haymarket SW1. 071-494 5050. A fine Victorian baroque theatre founded by Beerbohm Tree. Successes include *West Side Story, Fiddler on the Roof; Amadeus* and most recently, Lloyd Webber's *Phantom of the Opera.*

Her Majesty's

London Palladium   4 D2
8 Argyll St W1. 071-494 5038. Second in size to the Coliseum; houses top variety shows, television specials and star-studded annual pantomimes.

Lyric   4 E3
Shaftesbury Av W1. 071-437 3686. Oldest theatre in Shaftesbury Avenue (built 1888). Eleonora Duse, Sarah Bernhardt, Owen Nares and Tallulah Bankhead all had long runs here. Plays.

Lyric Hammersmith
King St W6. 081-741 2311. Rebuilt and restored to original Victorian splendour inside modern shell. Also studio theatre. Wide-ranging productions.

Mermaid   5 C3
Puddle Dock, Blackfriars EC4. 071-410 0102. Plays and musicals. Restaurant; two bars overlooking the Thames.

National Theatre   5 A4
South Bank SE1. Box office 071-928 2252. Complex of three theatres, Olivier,

Lyttelton and Cottesloe. Home of the Royal National Theatre Company. Stages a wide mixture of plays in repertory, including new works, revivals, Shakespeare and musicals. Also foyer entertainment, bookstall, and tours of the building including backstage and workshops. Restaurants, bars, exhibitions.

New London Theatre   4 F2
Drury La WC2. 071-405 0072. Can convert from a 900-seat conventional theatre to an intimate theatre-in-the-round within minutes. Opened 1972 on the site of the old Winter Gardens. The hit musical *Cats* is well-established here.

Old Vic   5 B5
Waterloo Rd SE1. 071-928 7616. Built 1818. For a long time the home of the National Theatre Company, then housed the Prospect Theatre Company. It now shows plays and musicals amid recreated Victorian decor.

Palace   4 E2
Shaftesbury Av W1. 071-434 0909. Listed building. Originally intended by D'Oyly Carte to be the Royal English Opera House but eventually became the Palace Theatre of Varieties. Staged performances by Pavlova and Nijinski. Now owned by Sir Andrew Lloyd Webber whose musical *Jesus Christ Superstar* enjoyed a record run here; *Les Misérables* is its latest success story.

Palace

Phoenix   4 E2
Charing Cross Rd WC2. 071-867 1044. A large theatre showing comedies, plays and musicals.

Piccadilly   4 E3
Denman St W1. 071-867 1118. A pre-war theatre which showed the first season of 'Talkies' in Britain. A varied post-war history of light comedy, plays and musicals. Many Royal Shakespeare Company productions staged here. Transformed into a cabaret theatre 1983.

Playhouse   4 F4
Northumberland Av WC2. 071-839 4401. Edwardian theatre used as a BBC studio

and then closed in 1975. Restored to former glory and re-opened in 1987. Stages musicals, serious drama and comedies.

Prince Edward   **4 F4**
Old Compton St W1. 071-734 8951. Started life as a cabaret spot called the London Casino in 1936 and has also been a cinema. Now a large theatre where musicals are staged, including the hit show *Evita* which ran for 2900 performances.

Prince of Wales   **4 E3**
Coventry St W1. 071-839 5987. Rebuilt 1937, this large, modern theatre has housed many musicals.

Queen's   **4 E3**
Shaftesbury Av W1. 071-494 5040. Very successful between the wars. Still presents good drama and varied productions.

Royal Court   **6 G2**
Sloane Sq SW1. 071-730 1745. Home of the English Stage Company which produces many major experimental plays.

St Martin's   **4 E2**
West St WC2. 071-836 1443. Intimate playhouse with unusual polished teak doors. *The Mousetrap* continues its record run here having transferred from the Ambassadors, its original home.

Savoy   **4 G3**
Strand WC2. 071-836 8888. Entrance is in the forecourt of the Savoy hotel. The first London theatre to be fully electrically lit and fireproofed, it was, ironically, badly damaged by fire in 1990, but has been restored to its Art Deco splendour. Produces a variety of plays, comedies and musicals.

Shaftesbury   **4 E3**
Shaftesbury Av WC2. 071-379 5399. Permanent base of the Theatre of Comedy Company.

Strand   **4 F3**
Aldwych WC2. 071-930 8800. Large theatre presenting a mixture of straight plays, comedies and musicals.

Vaudeville   **4 F3**
Strand WC2. 071-836 9987. Listed building which originally ran farce and burlesque (hence the name), then became 'straight' (which for the most part it remains).

Victoria Palace   **7 C1**
Victoria St SW1. 071-834 1317. Musicals, variety shows and plays. Once home of the Crazy Gang and the *Black and White Minstrel Show*, the musical *Buddy* is a recent success.

Whitehall   **4 F4**
14 Whitehall SW1. 071-867 1119. Restored to its full Art Deco splendour.

Now one of the Wyndham Theatres group staging varied productions.

Wyndham's   **4 F3**
Charing Cross Rd WC2. 071-867 1116. Small, pretty and successful theatre founded by Sir Charles Wyndham, the famous actor-manager. Edgar Wallace was a manager here for a while. Plays, comedy and musicals.

Young Vic   **5 B5**
66 The Cut SE1. 071-928 6363. Young people's repertoire theatre mainly showing the classics and established modern plays, but also some new plays and musicals.

Fringe, pub & experimental theatre

The best weekly listings are in Time Out. *Many fringe theatres are clubs. If membership (**M**) is necessary it can be bought before the performance.*

Almeida   **2 D1**
Almeida St N1. 071-359 4404. Best known for international contemporary dance, theatre and music work. Good off-beat productions.

Arts Theatre   **4 F3**
6 Great Newport St WC2. 071-836 2132. A 340-seat theatre showing plays for adults in the evening. Performances by the Unicorn Theatre for Children which has programmes at *10.30 & 14.00* Tue-Fri for schools, and for general public at *14.30* Sat & Sun. Lounge and vegetarian snackbar.

Baron's Court Theatre
Baron's Ale House, 28 Comeragh Rd W14. 071-602 0235. Exciting and innovative productions at this small theatre-in-the-round. (**M**)

Bloomsbury   **1 F5**
15 Gordon St WC1. 071-387 9629. Owned by University College and used by the students 12 weeks a year. International plays, dance, cabaret and opera.

Bridge Lane   **6 E6**
Bridge La SW11. 071-228 8828. Professional companies offering new or neglected plays. (**M**)

Bush Theatre
Bush Hotel, Shepherd's Bush Grn W12. 081-743 3388. Première performances of British and international plays, some of which transfer to the West End. (**M**)

Canal Café Theatre   **3 D1**
Bridge House, Delamere Ter W2. 071-289 6054. Lively, friendly upstairs theatre restaurant. Flexible programme of plays or cabaret and late-night satirical review. All-

inclusive price for complete evening or separate dinner and show.

Cochrane Theatre   **2 A6**
Southampton Row WC1. 071-242 7040. Home of the black theatre company, 'Talawa', who produce 3/4 plays per year. Visiting theatre companies.

Cockpit Theatre   **1 A5**
Gateforth St NW8. 071-402 5081. Fringe theatre venue for professional companies with a modern theatre-in-the-round which is also adaptable to other forms of staging.

Donmar Warehouse   **4 F2**
41 Earlham St WC2. 071-867 1150. Welcomes touring companies but also mounts its own productions.

The Gate   **3 B3**
Prince Albert Pub, 11 Pembridge Rd W11. 071-229 0706. British premières of foreign works and rare revivals. **(M)**

Grace Theatre   **6 F6**
The Latchmere Pub, 503 Battersea Pk Rd SW11. 071-228 2620. Quality productions of new work, contemporary drama classics, musicals. **(M)**

Hampstead Theatre
Swiss Cottage Centre, Avenue Rd NW3. 071-722 9301. Dedicated to the presentation of new plays and the encouragement of new writers. Bar and snacks. **(M)**

King's Head Theatre Club   **2 D2**
115 Upper St N1. 071-226 1916. Theatre at the back. One of London's leading fringe theatres with many West End transfers. Encourages new work but also performs revivals. Tickets available for performance only or for dinner and performance. **(M)**

Lilian Baylis   **2 C4**
Sadler's Wells Theatre, Rosebery Av EC1. 071-837 4104. Small studio theatre staging conternporary dance and high-quality productions by visiting drama companies.

Man in the Moon   **6 D4**
392 King's Rd SW3. 071-351 2876. Successful fringe theatre that performs lots of new plays or revives old plays that haven't been performed for some time. **(M)**

Old Red Lion
418 St John's St N1. 071-837 7816. Performances of a mixed bag of new plays and revivals. Pub has good food at all times.

Orange Tree
1 Clarence St, Richmond, Surrey. 081-940 3633. Highly successful established fringe theatre which started life above an early Victorian pub. Now in a new theatre offering a full range of productions – classes, revivals, new work and musicals.

Questors
Matlock La W5. 081-567 5184. Plays by well-known writers plus some off-beat productions. **(M)**

Theatre Royal Stratford East
Gerry Raffles Sq E15. 081-534 0310. Joan Littlewood's brainchild; has its own company which stages new plays and musicals. Bar and snack bar.

Theatre Upstairs   **6 G2**
Royal Court Theatre, Sloane Sq SW1. 071-730 2554. New plays and playwrights in a small studio space above the main theatre.

Tom Allen Centre
Grove Crescent Rd E15. 081-519 6818. Touring companies, workshop productions, youth theatre and world music in this community arts centre.

Tricycle Theatre
269 Kilburn High Rd NW6. 071-328 1000. Well-established fringe theatre where an excellent selection of new plays is performed. *Sat morning* children's shows. Youth theatre workshop, art gallery, restaurant and bar.

Tube Theatre
071-586 6828. A comedian poses as a clumsy commuter. You follow and see the reaction! In its 22nd year; labelled the 'longest running show under the West End'. Group bookings only; minimum 12 people.

Vanbrugh   **1 F6**
Malet St WC1. 071-580 7982. Theatre club presenting a complete range of classic and contemporary drama by RADA students. Three theatres. Members bar. **(M)**

Marionette theatre

The Little Angel   **2 D2**
14 Dagmar Pas, Cross St N1. 071-226 1787. London's only permanent puppet theatre. Excellent shows *15.00 daily during school holidays (5s and over).* Otherwise *15.00 Sat & Sun only*, and *11.00 Sat & Sun (3-5 year-olds).*

Puppet Theatre Barge
Little Venice W9. 071-249 6876. Marionette performances in a converted barge. Moored in London *Oct-May*, travels up the Thames as far as Oxford in *summer.* Shows at *15.00 Sat, Sun & B.hols; 15.00 Mon-Fri during school holidays.* Book in advance to avoid disappointment.

Open-air theatre

Holland Park Theatre   **3 A5**
Holland Park W8. 071-602 7856. 600-

seat open-air theatre (covered by canopy) which gives performances of dance, opera and theatre *Jun-Aug*. Days and times vary so check with booking office.

Regent's Park Open-air   **1 C4**
Theatre
Inner Circle, Regent's Park NW1. 071-486 2431. Lovely in good weather. Plays by Shakespeare and others. *End May-Sep 20.00 Mon-Sat* and *14.30 Wed, Thur & Sat*. Book in advance.

Wimbledon Open-air Theatre
Cannizaro Park, Westside, Wimbledon Common SW19. 081-540 0362. Enchantingly set in a walled garden with seating for 500. Plays and opera *Jul & Aug*.

Opera, ballet and dance

English ballet lagged almost two centuries behind the Danes and Russians with the founding of the Royal Academy of Dancing in 1920. By 1930, Marie Rambert's Ballet Club had landed with some éclat on to the West End stage. That same year Ninette de Valois was assembling the Sadler's Wells company up in Islington. One night in 1934 an unknown dancer stepped out of the Sadler's corps to do her first solo at the Old Vic; in 1946 that same dancer and company opened at Covent Garden to mass hysteria. Margot Fonteyn in her 40 years as a ballerina became the embodiment of British ballet history. The première of Benjamin Britten's Peter Grimes, also in 1946, marked the birth of British opera. Very shortly thereafter a permanent British opera school and orchestra were established; regular and festival seasons came into being; a string of high achievers suddenly appeared. Such composers as Walton, Tippett, Searle, Bennet and Davies provided an

Coliseum

exciting repertory that launched British opera onto a worldwide stage.

Coliseum   **4 F3**
St Martin's La WC2. 071-836 3161. Largest London theatre, seating 2400. Houses the resident English National Opera *Aug-Jun*, and visiting companies during summer months.

The Place   **1 F4**
17 Duke's Rd WC1. 071-387 0031. This 250-seat theatre is the home of the London Contemporary Dance Theatre and the London School of Contemporary Dance, an exciting and creative modern dance company. Immaculate productions with interesting choreographic ideas.

Royal Opera House, Covent   **4 F2**
Garden
Royal Opera House, Bow St WC2. 071-240 1066. Recorded information 071-836 6903. The world-famous Royal Opera and Royal Ballet companies maintain an international reputation. Summer 'Proms' performances.

Royal Opera House

Sadler's Wells   **2 C4**
Rosebery Av EC1. 071-278 8916. Recorded information 071-278 5450. Once a spa (the original well discovered by Richard Sadler is under a trap-door at the back of the stalls). Birthplace of the English National Opera and the Royal Ballet Company. Host to leading national and international ballet, dance and opera companies.

Music

Jazz, folk & rock

Britain is world-famous for its contemporary music scene and London is the hub of the industry, attracting well-known bands and soloists as well as those trying to make the charts. There is a vast number of different places to go to hear live bands from huge concert arenas to shady basement clubs. The major concert halls are listed below along with some of the more established and popular smaller venues. Consult Time Out, City Limits *or* New Musical Express *to find out who's playing when and where.*

Academy Brixton
211 Stockwell Rd SW9. 071-326 1022. Huge venue with space for about 4000. Lively atmosphere, good sound systems. 'Alternative' as well as usual rock bands.

Africa Centre   4 F3
38 King St WC2. 071-836 1973. A popular venue for African and London-based black bands.

Astoria   4 E2
157 Charing Cross Rd WC2. 071-434 0403. Large auditorium for live music – anything from hard rock to classical. Restaurant and bars.

Bass Clef   2 G4
35 Coronet St, off Hoxton Sq N1. 071-729 2476. A very popular venue to hear jazz, Latin American and African music. The atmosphere is relaxed and the restaurant offers good meals.

Bull & Gate
389 Kentish Town Rd NW5. 071-485 5358. Small, established venue staging a mixed bag of indie and rock bands.

Cecil Sharpe House   1 C2
2 Regent's Park Rd NW1. 071-485 2206. Regular live folk bands perform in the huge dance hall.

Dingwalls   1 D1
Camden Lock NW1. 071-267 1999. A good selection of live bands in this club by the Regent's Canal. R&B, jazz.

Dominion   4 E2
Tottenham Court Rd W1. 071-580 9562. Seating-only venue for well-known performers.

Earl's Court Exhibition Centre 6 A3
Warwick Rd SW5. 071-385 1200. Massive hall for top pop and rock stars.

Fairfield Hall
Croydon, Surrey. 081-688 9291. A modern concert hall with a number of large bands or soloists.

The Forum
9-17 Highgate Rd NW5. 071-284 2200. Formerly the Town & Country Club, this remains one of the best live music venues in London.

The Grand
St John's Hill SW11. 071-738 9000. Converted theatre offering indie, rock and reggae.

Hammersmith Apollo
Queen Caroline St W6. 081-741 4868. Formerly the Hammersmith Odeon, this is west London's legendary live music venue. Plays host to a wide range of musical talents.

Jazz Café   1 D2
5 Parkway NW1. 071-284 4358. All kinds of jazz at this popular Art Deco Camden venue. Restaurant and café.

Marquee   4 E2
105 Charing Cross Rd WC2. 071-437 6603. One of the original London rock clubs; a popular and lively spot.

Mean Fiddler
24-28a Harlesden High St NW10. 081-965 2487. Stages well-known indie rock bands plus folk and country & western.

National Ballroom, Kilburn
234 Kilburn High Rd NW6. 071-328 3141. Stages big rock acts.

100 Club   4 D2
100 Oxford St W1. 071-636 0933. Historically the home of trad jazz. Friendly and comfortable, it features live jazz groups (trad, modern and African) and the occasional new-wave band.

Powerhaus   2 C3
1 Liverpool Rd N1. 071-837 3218. Packed venue offering the best in new indie and rock.

Rock Garden   4 F3
6-7 The Piazza, Covent Gdn WC2. 071-240 3961. Restaurant upstairs and on street level. Live concerts downstairs in a converted vegetable warehouse. Five bands a night with focus on new, up-and-coming bands.

Ronnie Scott's   4 E2
47 Frith St W1. 071-439 0747. Reputedly the best jazz in London. On the stand a succession of big name jazz men and women. Can be typically hot, smoky and sleazy on a busy night. Advisable to book.

Royal Albert Hall   3 E5
Kensington Gore SW7. 071-589 8212. Has a varied selection of artistes throughout the year.

Venue, New Cross
21 Clifton Rise SE14. 081-692 4077. Former cinema and dance hall, now stages up to three bands per night.

Wembley Arena
Empire Way, Wembley, Middx. 081-900 1234. Enormous capacity auditorium for major concerts.

Wembley Stadium
Empire Way, Wembley, Middx. 081-900 1234. London's largest pop venue, used for the real megastars. Open-air.

Classical music

Barbican Hall   5 C1
Barbican Centre, Silk St EC2. 071-638 8891. Base of the London Symphony Orchestra. Three one-month seasons a year.

Central Hall   4 E5
Storey's Gate SW1. 071-222 8010. A

large hall offering organ recitals and orchestral concerts. Listed building – housed the first meeting of the General Assembly of the United Nations in 1946.

Conway Hall   4 **G1**
Red Lion Sq WC1. 071-242 8032. Seats 550. Two halls, one of which is famous for *Sun eve* chamber music concerts *Oct-Apr.*

Purcell Room   5 **A4**
South Bank SE1. 071-928 3002. Smallest of the three South Bank concert halls; ideal for chamber music and solo concerts.

Queen Elizabeth Hall   5 **A4**
South Bank SE1. 071-928 3002. Orchestral and choral works, chamber music and recitals. Also film shows.

Royal Albert Hall   3 **E5**
Kensington Gore SW7. 071-589 8212. Victorian domed hall named after Prince Albert, built 1871. Orchestral, choral, pop concerts, sporting events and public meetings. Famous for the 'Proms' a series of concerts by a variety of orchestras, ensembles and individuals from all over the world.

Royal Albert Hall

Royal College of Music   3 **E6**
Prince Consort Rd SW7. 071-589 3643. Chamber, orchestral and choral concerts plus operas performed by the students in their own theatre (*term time only*). High standard.

Royal Festival Hall   5 **A4**
South Bank SE1. 071-928 3002. Built in 1951 for the Festival of Britain. Seats 3000. Orchestral and choral concerts. Foyer bar and music.

St John's Smith Square   7 **E1**
Smith Sq SW1. 071-222 1061. Unique 18thC church used for solo recitals, chamber, orchestral and choral works. Seats approx 800. Restaurant. Art exhibitions held in the crypt.

Wigmore Hall   4 **C2**
36 Wigmore St W1. 071-935 2141. Seats 550. Instrumental, song, chamber music and chamber orchestral recitals. Fine acoustics for chamber music and solo recitals. Popular Coffee Concerts. Intimate atmosphere.

Church music

The following churches have above-average choirs or organists.
All Hallows-by-the-Tower, Byward St EC3; All Saints, Margaret St W1; All Souls, Langham Pl W1; Bloomsbury Central, Shaftesbury Av WC2; Brompton Oratory, Brompton Rd SW7; Central Hall, Storey's Gate SW1; St Botolph Aldgate, Aldgate High St EC3; St Bride, Fleet St EC4; St Giles Cripplegate, Fore St EC2; St James, Spanish Pl W1; St Lawrence Jewry, Gresham St EC2; St Martin-in-the-Fields, Trafalgar Sq WC2; St Mary the Virgin, Bourne St SW1; St Michael-upon-Cornhill, Cornhill EC3; St Paul's Cathedral, Ludgate Hill EC4; Southwark Cathedral, London Bridge SE1; Westminster Abbey, Broad Sanctuary SW1; Westminster Cathedral, Ashley Pl SW1.

Lunchtime concerts

Mostly held in the City churches at lunchtime Mon-Fri. Chamber music, choral music, violin, piano and organ recitals. Concerts are usually free though donations are customary.

All Hallows-by-the-Tower   5 **F3**
Byward St EC3. 071-481 2928. Mainly classical hi-fi recordings *13.00 Mon.* Organ recitals *12.15 & 13.15 Thur. Free.*

Bishopsgate Institute   5 **F2**
230 Bishopsgate EC2. 071-247 6844. Classical and chamber music. *13.05 Tue Jan-end Apr & Sep-end Dec. Free.*

St Anne & St Agnes (Lutheran) 5 **D2**
Gresham St EC2. 071-373 5566. Chamber ensembles *13.10 Mon (except B.hols)* and *13.10 Fri* (not *every Fri*). Services with voices and instruments *13.10 Wed. Free.*

St Bride   5 **B2**
Fleet St EC4. 071-353 1301. Organ recitals *13.15 Wed.* Song, piano or chamber recitals *Tue & Fri 13.15. During City of London July Festival* recitals every lunchtime at *13.05 (except Sun). Free (charge during Festival).*

St John's   7 **E1**
Smith Sq SW1. 071-222 1061. Solo recitals and chamber music in unique 18thC church. *13.00 Mon* (for BBC Radio broadcast from *Oct-Jul*) & *13.15 alt Thur in the crypt from Sep-Jul.* Concerts most eves (phone for details). Restaurant and Footstool Gallery. *OPEN 11.30-14.45 Mon-Fri & during eve concerts. Charge.*

St Lawrence Jewry   5 **D2**
Gresham St EC2. 071-600 9478. Concert pianist recitals *13.00 Mon (except B.hols).*

Organ recitals *13.00 Tue. Music every lunchtime in Aug. Free.*

St Martin-in-the-Fields   **4 F3**
Trafalgar Sq WC2. 071-839 1930. Wide variety of classical music. *13.05 Mon, Tue & Fri. Free.*

St Mary-le-Bow   **5 D2**
Cheapside EC2. 071-248 5139. Live classical music concerts. *13.05 Thur. Free.*

St Mary Woolnoth   **5 E2**
Lombard St EC3. 071-626 9701. City Singers rehearse *13.05 Mon.* There is a 'singers workshop' to rehearse church music *13.05 Fri.* Visitors welcome. *Free.*

St Michael-upon-Cornhill   **5 E2**
Cornhill EC3. 071-626 8841. Organ recitals *13.00 Mon. Free.*

St Olave   **5 F3**
Hart St EC3. 071-488 4318. Lunchtime recitals of chamber music *13.05 Wed & Thur. Free.*

St Paul's Cathedral   **5 D2**
Ludgate Hill EC4. 071-248 2705. Organ recitals *13.15 Fri (except Aug, Oct, Easter & Xmas). Free.*

St Sepulchre Without   **5 C2**
Newgate
Holborn Viaduct EC1. 071-248 1660. Live recital of vocal, instrumental and organ music *13.10 Fri.* Choral service *13.10 Tue. Free.* Occasional Memorial concerts.

Southwark Cathedral   **5 E4**
Borough High St SE1. 071-407 3708. Organ recitals *13.10 Mon.* Live music recitals *13.10 Tue.* Recorded music *13.10 Thur. Free.*

Open-air music

There is a surprising variety of summertime outdoor music in London from lunchtime brass bands in squares and gardens to evening concerts and opera in vast parks. Many are free, and any charge is usually nominal. For current programmes, see Time Out *and* What's On & Where to Go.

Alexandra Park
Wood Green N22. 081-883 7173. Very enthusiastic community music programme. International music and dancing *Jun-Aug 15.00-17.00 Sun.* Mixed performances *school summer hols 14.00-15.00 Thur. Free.*

City venues
Information from City Information Centre, St Paul's Churchyard EC4. 071-606 3030. There are often lunchtime musical events in the summer but dates and times vary so it is advisable to collect a copy of the Diary of Events, *issued monthly, for exact details.*

Broadgate   **5 F1**
EC2. Lunchtime jazz. *Free.*

Finsbury Circus Gardens   **5 E1**
Moorgate EC2. Lunchtime band concerts. *Free.*

Paternoster Square   **5 C2**
EC4. Mostly military bands. Eat lunch at an open-air café and listen to the music. *Free.*

St Paul's Steps   **5 C2**
St Paul's Cathedral, Ludgate Hill EC4. Delightful setting. Military bands. *Free.*

Crystal Palace Bowl
Crystal Palace Park SE26. 081-313 0527. Summer season only of concerts in the lakeland bowl. *Phone for details.*

Greenwich Park
SE10. 081-858 2608. Brass bands. *End May-end Aug 15.00 & 18.00-19.30 Sun & B.hols. Free.*

Holland Park   **3 A5**
W8. Varied programme in the Court Theatre in the evening. *Charge.*

Hyde Park   **4 B4**
W2. 071-262 5484. Military and brass bands. *End May-end Aug 15.00-16.30 & 18.00-19.30 Sun & B.hols. Free.*

Kenwood
Hampstead La NW3. Contact English Heritage 071-973 3000 for details. Lakeside symphony concerts by leading orchestras, opera, jazz and brass in fine park. *Jun-end Aug 19.30 Sat.* Also recitals in the Orangery of the 18thC house. *Apr-May & Aug-Oct 19.30 Sun.* Booking 071-379 4444.

Lincoln's Inn Fields   **4 G2**
WC2. Military bands entertain *some summer lunchtimes. Free.*

Marble Hill House
Richmond Rd, Twickenham, Middx. 081-892 5115. Orchestral concerts, brass bands or jazz, sometimes accompanied by fireworks. *Early Jul-early Aug 19.30 Sun. Charge.*

Regent's Park   **1 C4**
NW1. 071-486 7905. Military and brass bands. *End May-end Aug 12.30-14.00 & 17.30-19.00 Mon-Sat, 15.00-16.30 & 18.00-19.30 Sun & B.hols. (Not every day, check for times.) Free.*

St James's Park   **4 E5**
SW1. 071-930 1793. Military and concert bands. *End May-end Aug 12.30-14.00 & 17.30-19.00 Mon-Sat, 15.00-16.30 & 18.00-19.30 Sun & B.hols. Free.*

Tower Place   **5 F3**
EC3. Military bands play in a modern pedestrian square with fine views of the

Tower and the Thames. *Some summer lunchtimes. Free.*

Victoria Embankment   4 F4
Gardens
Nr Embankment Tube Station WC2. Riverside setting for military bands, massed bands and light orchestras. *Some summer lunchtimes. Free.*

Arts centres

Put on shows – theatre, music, dance – and usually have workshop facilities and classes in a variety of arts skills.

Africa Centre   4 F3
38 King St WC2. 071-836 1973. Courses in African languages, dance and politics. Library, art gallery, exhibition space, bookshop. Hall for film shows, plays, dance or music performances by travelling companies. Restaurant and bar.

Tom Allen Centre
Grove Crescent Rd E15. 081-555 7289. East End community arts centre with cinema, theatre, exhibition space and workshops. Bar.

Barbican   2 E6
Barbican Centre, Silk St EC2. 071-638 8891. A concert hall, two theatres, three cinemas, a public library, an art gallery and sculpture court. Foyer entertainment. Restaurants. Gift shops.

Battersea Arts Centre (BAC)
Old Town Hall, Lavender Hill SW11. 071-223 2223. A lively, informal community arts centre with theatre, cabaret space, gallery, café and bookshop. Fringe and alternative theatre productions.

Drill Hall Arts Centre   4 E1
16 Chenies St WC1. 071-631 1353. Extensive fringe programme of drama, cabaret, live music and opera. Drama and dance workshops; photography courses and darkrooms available. Popular with feminist companies. *Women-only night Mon, free crèche facilities Mon, Fri & Sat eves.* Bar and restaurant.

Institute of Contemporary   4 E4
Arts (ICA)
Nash House, The Mall SW1. 071-930 3647. A good range of arts entertainment. Three galleries, theatre, two cinemas, seminar-room for lectures and talks, video reference library, arts bookshop, bar and restaurant. Membership available on daily and annual basis.

Oval House
54 Kennington Oval SE11. 071-735 2786. Two theatres for fringe and experimental work. Workshops and classes in theatre, dance, music and drama. Holiday projects for children. Coffee bar and restaurant.

Riverside Studios
Crisp Rd W6. 081-748 3354. Mixture of events – theatre, dance, films, visual arts and all kinds of music. Classes in contemporary dance. Workshops, lectures, discussions. Gallery with varied exhibitions. Bar and restaurant serving excellent food.

South Bank Centre   5 A4
South Bank SE1. Consists of National Theatre (071-928 2252), the Royal Festival Hall (071-928 3002), the Queen Elizabeth Hall (071-928 3002), the Purcell Room (071-928 3191), the Hayward Gallery (071-928 3144), the National Film Theatre (071-928 3232) and the Museum of the Moving Image (071-928 3535). *See separate entries in relevant sections.*

Watermans Arts Centre
40 High St, Brentford, Middx. 081-568 1176. Broad range of arts activities and entertainment. Theatre, cinema and exhibition gallery. Studio where youth drama classes are held. Bar and self-service restaurant overlooking the river.

Comedy and cabaret

London's live cabaret circuit provides some of the capital's cheapest, liveliest grass-roots entertainment. At 'new comedy' clubs anything goes – from mime and dance to slapstick and satire. Improvisation nights – unscripted comedy from regular performers – are popular. The clubs are to be found in the back rooms of pubs, at fringe theatres or in purpose-built cabaret clubs. The major venues are listed below, but the circuit is ever-changing, with new places opening and one-nighters changing venue. Check Time Out *for details.*

Aztec Comedy Club
The Borderland, 47-49 Westow St SE19. 081-771 0885. Lively comedy club above a Mexican restaurant. Food served at your table.

Banana Cabaret
The Bedford, Bedford Hill SW12. 081-673 8904. Great venue, rated highly on the cabaret circuit. Top comedians. Also in Acton; *phone for details.*

Battersea Arts Centre (BAC)
Old Town Hall, Lavender Hill SW11. 071-223 2223. Adaptable theatre accommodates a lively mix of dance, cabaret and mime. Licensed café.

Canal Cafe Theatre   3 D1
The Bridge House, Delamere Terrace W2. 071-289 6054. Different cabaret shows.

Newsrevue is a favourite, a topical comedy based on current affairs with sketches and songs. Bar and restaurant.

Cartoon at Clapham

The Plough Inn, 196-198 Clapham High St SW4. 071-738 8763. Strong line-ups at this large, comfortable pub venue.

Chuckle Club   **2 A5**

The Marquis Cornwallis, 31 Marchmont St WC1. 071-476 1672. Top cabaret acts presented by compere Eugene Cheese. Also at The Shakespeare's Head, Carnaby St W1 (**4 D2**).

Comedy Café   **2 G4**

66 Rivington St EC2. 071-739 5706. Open spot for new acts, established acts, black comedians, Irish comedy nights. Bar. Food available.

Comedy Store   **4 E3**

28a Leicester Sq WC2. (0426) 914433. The London comedy venue where a lively array of comedians line up for a 2-3-hour show. The audience is encouraged to join in at the end. Improvisation from the famous Comedy Store Players. Food and drink available to 18s and over.

Downstairs at The King's Head

2 Crouch End Hill N8. 081-340 1028. A fine selection of acts in this club below a popular Crouch End pub. Monthly try-out nights.

East Dulwich Cabaret

The East Dulwich Tavern, 1 Lordship Lane SE22. 081-299 4138. Pub venue with quality comedy line-ups.

Gate Theatre Club   **3 B3**

Prince Albert Pub, 11 Pembridge Rd W11. 071-229 0706. Improvised comedy shows. Late shows.

Jongleurs Battersea

The Cornet, 49 Lavender Gardens SW11. (0426) 933711. Booking: 071-924 2766. Very popular venue where the show comprises at least five acts – three comedians, a compère, visual acts, music and dance. A varied high-quality bill. Good wholesome food. Essential to book.

Jongleurs Camden Lock   **1 D1**

211-216 Chalk Farm Rd NW1. (0426) 933711. Booking: 071-924 2766. Newer Jongleurs venue where the show has the same formula of comedy and audience baiting as its Battersea counterpart. Seats 500. Restaurant. Spacious bar. Essential to book.

Meccano Club   **2 D2**

The Market Tavern, 2 Essex Rd N1. 081-800 2236. Good comedy, often from big names, in this pub basement venue. Improvisation a speciality. Food available.

Oranje Boom Boom   **4 E3**

De Hems Dutch Coffee Bar, Macclesfield St W1. 081-694 1710. Stand-up comedy and variety from established and new acts. Licensed bar.

Red Rose Club

129 Seven Sisters Rd N7. 071-263 7265. One of north London's premier cabaret venues, featuring varied and consistently high-quality acts at low prices. Food available.

Up the Creek

302 Creek Rd SE10. 081-858 4581. Regular comedy, music and magic. Late bar and Indian food.

Cinemas

*Cinema came to Britain before World War I and became so popular that moralists feared for the future of church attendance and novel reading. Picture palaces sprung up everywhere in the '20s. The ornate, gilded buildings with huge chandeliers, elaborate ceilings and luxurious carpets certainly lived up to their name at first but were gradually reclassified by the audience as 'flea pits' and 'dumps'. With the advent of television after World War II it seemed there would be no need for cinemas and many did close down or become bingo halls. However, in the '70s the cinema was saved from economic collapse by the development of complexes whereby one large cinema became at least two smaller ones, each showing a different new release. These cinemas have even survived videos. There has been increasing interest in foreign, experimental and classical films and these audiences are catered for by specialist organisations like the National Film Theatre and the Institute of Contemporary Arts, but also by cinemas which present 'alternative', rather than 'blockbuster/commercial' films. For current programmes see the Evening Standard, Time Out or What's On & Where to Go. Alternatively telephone the cinemas, many of which have 24-hr answering services giving details of programmes. See local papers for suburban programmes. All cinemas show general new release films unless otherwise indicated. (**M**) = membership.*

Astral   **4 E3**

3-7 Brewer St W1. 071-734 6387. Censored sex films.

Barbican   **2 E6**

Barbican Centre, Silk St EC2. 071-638 8891. Cinema 1 shows general current releases, 2 repertory and 3 is usually used for conferences.

Camden Plaza   1 D2
211 Camden High St NW1. 071-485 2443. Quality films.

Chelsea Cinema   6 E3
King's Rd SW3. 071-351 3742. Quality films, often foreign. Spacious seating.

Clapham Picture House
Venn St SW4. 071-498 2242. Mixed programme of new releases and 'art-house' films.

Coronet Notting Hill   3 B4
Notting Hill Gate W11. 071-727 6705.

Curzon Mayfair   4 C4
Curzon St W1. 071-465 8865. Specially selected new films in very plush surroundings.

Curzon Phoenix   4 E2
Phoenix Theatre, Charing Cross Rd WC2. 071-240 9661. Under same management as Curzon Mayfair and showing a similar selection of films.

Curzon West End   4 E3
93 Shaftesbury Av W1. 071-439 4805. Formerly the Columbia; now under the same management as the Curzon Mayfair and showing a similar selection of films.

Electric   3 A2
191 Portobello Rd W11. 071-792 2020. Everything from mainstream American to obscure imports.

Empire   4 E3
Leicester Sq WC2. 071-437 1234. Three screens. Bookable first releases in cavernous 'movie palace'. Adjustable seats, perfect vision, Dolby stereo.

Everyman
Holly Bush Vale NW3. 071-435 1525. Weekly classic revivals.

Gate Cinema   3 B4
Notting Hill Gate W11. 071-727 4043. Quality art films. *Late shows Fri & Sat.*

Institute of Contemporary   4 E4
Arts (ICA)
Nash House, The Mall SW1. 071-930 3647. Two cinemas with bookable seats. Films by contemporary directors. Also seasons of foreign and unusual theme films. Day, associate or full (**M**) on-the-spot.

Lumière   4 F3
42 St Martin's La WC2. 071-836 0691. Foreign and quality films. *Late shows Fri & Sat.*

Metro   4 E3
11 Rupert St W1. 071-437 0757. Independent cinema showing foreign and quality films.

MGM Baker Street   1 B6
Station Approach, Marylebone Rd NW1.

071-935 9772. Two modern cinemas. *Late shows Fri & Sat.*

MGM Chelsea   6 D4
279 King's Rd SW3. 071-352 5096. Four screens.

MGM Fulham Road   6 C3
Fulham Rd SW10. 071-370 2636. Five screens.

MGM Hampstead
Pond St NW3. 071-794 4000. Three screens.

MGM Haymarket   4 E3
Haymarket SW1. 071-839 1527. Three screens showing long-running British and American releases and new releases. *Late shows Fri & Sat.*

MGM Oxford Street   4 E2
Oxford St W1. 071-636 0310. Five screens. *Late shows Fri & Sat.*

MGM Panton Street   4 E3
Panton St SW1. 071-930 0631. Four small cinemas under one roof showing long-running and very new releases.

MGM Piccadilly   4 E3
215-217 Piccadilly W1. 071-437 3561. Two screens. *Late shows Fri & Sat.*

MGM Shaftesbury Avenue   4 E2
135 Shaftesbury Av W1. 071-836 8861. Two screens.

MGM Swiss Centre   4 E3
Swiss Centre, Leicester Sq WC2. 071-439 4470. Four screens.

MGM Tottenham Court Road   1 F6
Tottenham Court Rd W1. 071-636 6148. Three screens.

MGM Trocadero   4 E3
Piccadilly Circus W1. 071-434 0031. Seven screens. *Late shows Fri & Sat.*

Minema   4 B5
45 Knightsbridge SW1. 071-235 4225. Intimate cinema showing modern classics.

National Film Theatre   5 A4
South Bank SE1. 071-928 3232. Shows rare foreign films, revivals of classics and seasons of notable directors' works. London Film Festival *each Nov.* (**M**)

Odeon Haymarket   4 E3
Haymarket SW1. (0426) 915353.

Odeon Kensington   3 B6
Kensington High St W8. (0426) 914666. Six screens. *Late shows Fri & Sat.*

Odeon Leicester Square   4 E3
Leicester Sq WC2. (0426) 915683. *Late shows Fri & Sat.*

Odeon Marble Arch   3 G2
10 Edgeware Rd W2. (0426) 914501. *Late shows Fri & Sat.*

Odeon Mezzanine   4 E3
Leicester Sq WC2. (0426) 915683. Five screens.

Odeon Swiss Cottage
Finchley Rd NW3. (0426) 914098. Four screens.

Odeon West End   **4 E3**
Leicester Sq WC2. (0426) 915574. Two screens. Preserved exterior with completely modernised interior. Built by Jack Buchanan – licensed bar named after him. New releases.

Phoenix
52 High Rd N2. 081-883 2233. European, American and Asian films.

Plaza   **4 E3**
Lower Regent St W1. 071-437 1234. Four screens.

Prince Charles   **4 E3**
Leicester Pl, Leicester Sq WC2. 071-437 8181. Small cinema showing films between first run and video release.

Renoir   **2 A5**
Brunswick Sq WC1. 071-837 8402. Quality and foreign films.

Rio
107 Kingsland High St E8. 071-254 6677. Everything from European films to cult American pictures. *Late show Sat.*

Riverside Studios
Crisp Rd W6. 081-748 3354. Mixed programme. Often have themes to coincide with studio theatre productions.

Scala   **1 G4**
275-277 Pentonville Rd N1. 071-278 8052. Ever-changing repertory of double bills. *All-night films.*

Screen on Baker Street   **1 B5**
96 Baker St NW1. 071-935 2772. *Late show Sat.*

Screen on the Green   **2 D2**
Islington Grn, 83 Upper St N1. 071-226 3520. *Late shows Fri & Sat.*

Screen on the Hill
203 Haverstock Hill NW3. 071-435 3366. Quality films. *Late shows Fri & Sat.*

UCI   **3 C2**
Whiteleys, Queensway W2. 071-792 3332. Huge 8-screen complex showing latest releases.

Warner West End   **4 E3**
Five screens. *Currently undergoing re-building.*

Radio and TV shows

Free tickets obtainable. Write enclosing stamped addressed envelope and preference of programme.

BBC Radio & Television   **1 D6**
Ticket Unit, Broadcasting House, Portland Pl W1.

Capital Radio   **1 E5**
Euston Tower, Euston Rd NW1.

Carlton Television
071-240 4000. Programmes are made by various production companies, but they will refer you to the relevant contact for tickets.

London Weekend Television   **5 B4**
Kent House, Upper Ground SE1.

Poetry

The societies and venues listed below are well established. There are many other poetry readings and discussions on offer every week but as the venues change, new groups are formed and others fade, it is advisable to check the weekly listings in Time Out.

Apples & Snakes
Contact: 071-639 9656. Performance poetry in cabaret style. Different programme each week. Venues listed in press.

City Lit   **4 F2**
Stukeley St WC2. 071-242 9872. Day and evening classes on the writing and appreciation of verse, contemporary poetry, verse speaking and poetry workshops.

Institute of Contemporary Arts (ICA)   **4 E4**
The Mall SW1. 071-930 3647. Occasional lectures and readings by distinguished poets followed by discussion.

Pentameters
Three Horseshoes Pub, Heath St NW3. 071-435 6757. Arranges readings by distinguished poets at regular intervals.

Poetry Library   **4 G2**
Royal Festival Hall, South Bank Centre SE1. 071-921 0943. Information on poetry competitions, workshops, day and evening classes and readings. Lists of poetry groups, magazines and bookshops are also available. Constantly expanding audio and video collection and special children's poetry information service.

Poetry Round   **6 B2**
Barkston Hotel, Barkston Gdns SW5. 071-373 7851. Weekly poetry forum. *20.00 Mon.*

Poetry Society   **4 F2**
22 Betterton St WC2. 071-240 4810. Produces a quarterly journal *Poetry Review* in which both new and established poets can appear. Holds readings and discussions.

071-

THEATRES

071-

Adelphi 836 7611
Albert 867 1115
Aldwych 836 6404
Ambassadors 836 1171
Apollo 494 5070
Apollo Victoria 828 8665
Arts 836 2132
Bloomsbury 387 9629
Cambridge 379 5299
Comedy 867 1045
Criterion 839 4488
Donmar Warehouse 240 8230
Drury Lane 494 5060
Duchess 836 7075
Duke of York's 836 5122
Fortune 836 2238
Garrick 494 5085
Globe 494 5065
Her Majesty's 494 5400
ICA 930 3647
London Coliseum 836 3161
London Palladium 494 5020
Lyric 494 5045
Mermaid 410 0000
New London 405 0072
Old Vic 928 7616
Palace 434 0909
Phoenix 867 1044

Piccadilly 867 1118
Players 839 1134
Playhouse 839 4401
Prince Edward 734 8951
Prince of Wales 839 5987
Queen's 494 5040
Royal Court 730 1745
Royal Festival Hall 928 8800
Royal National 928 2252
Royal Opera House 240 1066
Royalty 494 5090
St. Martin's 836 1443
Savoy 836 8117
Shaftesbury 379 5399
Strand 930 8800
Theatre Royal, Drury Lane 494 5000
Theatre Royal, Haymarket 930 8800
Vaudeville 836 9987
Victoria Palace 834 1317
Whitehall 867 1119
Wigmore Hall 935 2141
Wyndham's 867 1116
Young Vic 928 6363

CINEMAS

071-

Astral 734 6287
Curzon Mayfair 465 8865
Curzon Phoenix 240 9661
Curzon West End 439 4805
Empire 437 1234
ICA 930 3647
Lumière 836 0691
MGM Haymarket 839 1527
MGM Oxford St 636 0310
MGM Panton St 930 0631
MGM Piccadilly 930 6111
MGM Shaftesbury Ave 836 6279
MGM Swiss Centre 439 4470
MGM Tottenham Court Rd 636 6148
MGM Trocadero 434 0031

Metro 437 0757
Minema 235 4225
National Film Theatre 928 3232
Odeon Haymarket 839 7697
Odeon Leicester Sq 930 6111
Odeon Marble Arch 723 2011
Odeon Mezzanine (Odeon Leicester Sq) 930 6111
Odeon West End 930 5252
Plaza 437 1234
Prince Charles 437 8181
Renoir 837 8402
Warner West End
Waterloo Place
(Temporarily closed)

WEST END THEATRES & CINEMAS

♦ Theatres
♠ Cinemas
Not to scale

© Nicholson

Nightlife

After the theatres, cinemas, pubs and wine bars have locked their doors, life goes on in London. Whether you're after soulful tunes, Seventies disco classics or hard-core rave sounds, there is a club, or club night, to suit. If it's a more exclusive clientele and relaxed ambience you're after, members-only clubs provide good food, good wine and lavish entertainment. And if you're starving in the small hours a number of cafés and restaurants are only too happy to fill that gap.

As in any major city, London's nightlife on the whole tends to be expensive, but it needn't break the bank. To save money find out about night buses for your journey home (see night bus map) or join the hardened clubbers in one of the all-night cafés and get the first tube home! For more detailed information see Nicholson's London Nightlife Guide.

£ = *low priced* **££** = *medium priced* **£££** = *high priced.*

Nightclubs

The following is a selection of clubs to suit every age and taste. One-nighter clubs are inspired by the latest dance music and the DJ is the main attraction. However, trends change continually so it is worth checking Time Out for a roundup of club nights.

Strict dress codes are generally a thing of the past but check with the club beforehand if you're unsure of their door policy. Entry fees are around £5 during the week and £10 at weekends.

Annabel's   **4 C3**
44 Berkeley Sq W1. 071-629 2350. Legendary haunt of the rich and famous. Exclusive, expensive and very difficult to join. (**M**) – long waiting list. Temporary membership (3 weeks) available. *OPEN to 03.00 Mon-Sat.*

Astoria   **4 E2**
157 Charing Cross Rd WC2. 071-434 0403. Semi-converted theatre hosting various one-nighters. Also a live music venue. *OPEN to 03.00.*

Café de Paris   **4 E3**
3 Coventry St W1. 071-287 3602. Sweeping staircases, a surrounding balcony and a good-sized dancefloor. Various one-nighters. *OPEN to 03.00, to 06.00 Fri & Sat.*

Camden Palace   **1 E3**
1a Camden High St NW1. 071-387 0428. Spacious and lively disco which attracts the young and trendy. Different one-nighters with a rave crowd at weekends. *OPEN to 02.30 Tue-Sat.*

Electric Ballroom   **1 D2**
184 Camden High St NW1. 071-485 9006. Established venue with two clubs in one, offering anything from rock and glamour punk to House dance. *OPEN to 02.00, to 03.00 Fri & Sat.*

Equinox   **4 E3**
Leicester Sq WC2. 071-437 1446. Huge, luxurious venue hosting a variety of one-nighters. *OPEN to 03.30, to 04.00 Fri & Sat.*

The Fridge
Town Hall Pde SW2. 071-326 5100. Huge, perennially hip dance venue. Various club nights. *OPEN to 03.00 Mon-Sat.*

The Gardening Club   **4 F3**
4 The Piazza WC2. 071-497 3154. Small, atmospheric underground club. Good range of one-nighters. *OPEN to 03.00, to 06.00 Fri & Sat.*

Hippodrome   **4 E3**
Hippodrome Cnr WC2. 071-437 4311. One of London's landmarks, but not a club many Londoners frequent. A black cave of brass and chrome illuminated by an amazing light system. Popular with young European tourists. *OPEN to 03.30 Mon-Sat.*

Legends   **4 D3**
29 Old Burlington St W1. 071-437 9933. Sleek with lot of chrome and contrasting colours. Attracts a smart crowd. *OPEN to 02.00 Mon-Thur, to 03.00 Fri & Sat.*

Limelight   **4 E3**
136 Shaftesbury Av W1. 071-434 0572. Uniquely housed in a converted church this club is a maze of wood-panelled passages and stairs leading to three levels. One-nighters range from rock to dance and reggae. *OPEN to 03.00 Mon-Sat.*

Maximus   **4 E3**
14 Leicester Sq WC2. 071-734 4111. Mainstream disco with alcoved seating and a packed dancefloor. *OPEN to 03.00, to 06.00 Fri & Sat.*

Ministry of Sound   **5 D6**
103 Gaunt St SE1. 071-378 6528. Huge New York-style venue offering the biggest sound system in Britain, big-name DJs

and a cinema. Unlicensed. *OPEN from midnight Fri to 08.00 Sat & from midnight Sat to 10.00 Sun.*

Le Palais
242 Shepherd's Bush Rd W6. 081-748 2812. Mainstream disco with lasers, video wall, fast-food, bar and theme party nights. Regularly hosts live acts. *OPEN to 02.00 Wed & Thur, to 03.00 Fri & Sat.*

Samantha's   **4 D3**
3 New Burlington St W1. 071-734 6249. Long-established, ever-popular split-level disco with two dance floors, four bars, cocktail bar and games room. *OPEN to 03.00 Mon-Sat.*

Stringfellows   **4 F3**
16-19 Upper St Martin's La WC2. 071-240 5534. Celebrity spot. Mirrored walls create endless reflections of pulsating coloured lights in disco below. (**M**) or entrance fee. *OPEN to 03.00 Mon-Sat.*

Subterrania   **3 A1**
12 Acklam Rd W10. 081-960 4590. A trendy and friendly venue under the Westway flyoever. Stylish interior. Regularly features live bands. *OPEN to 01.30 Mon-Thur, to 02.30 Fri & Sat.*

Tokyo Joe's   **4 D3**
85 Piccadilly W1. 071-409 1832. Fashionable and exclusive basement night club. Two bars and a restaurant serving French food. Attracts a prestigious clientele. (**M**) *OPEN to 03.30 Mon-Sat.*

Wag Club   **4 E3**
35-37 Wardour St W1. 071-437 5534. Once the trendiest club in town, the Wag still attracts an exuberant, young clientele. Always busy at weekends. *OPEN to 03.30 Mon-Thur, to 06.00 Fri & Sat.*

Xenon   **4 D3**
196 Piccadilly W1. 071-734 9344. Up-market but unpretentious club with an impressive light show and cabaret acts. Cocktail bar. *OPEN to 03.00, to 06.00 Fri & Sat.*

Members-only clubs

To join an exclusive clientele in a relaxed and well-tended setting, choose one of London's traditional members-only clubs or casinos. They cater, in most cases, for expense account businessmen and employ hostesses whose job it is to boost the sales of drinks.
Membership: For most of these clubs you have to be a member, although short-term membership is usually available for visitors. You can only enter a gaming house as a member or a guest of a member. By law, when you join a gaming club, you will not be admitted until you have filled in a declaration of your intent to gamble and 48 hours have elapsed from the time you signed this declaration. Membership charges vary considerably. In some clubs visitors from overseas get reduced rates or free membership. A few clubs may insist on a potential member being proposed by an existing member.
These clubs generally close at 04.00, except on Sat when they close at 03.00. The number (48) after the club's title means that the 48 hours rule applies. (M) means that membership is usually necessary for entry.

The Clubman's Club   **4 D3**
5 Albemarle St W1. 071-493 4292. For an annual subscription fee, you can obtain free membership or benefits at several hundred clubs all over Britain and worldwide. Also discounts for car hire and hotels.

Clubs

Director's Lodge   **4 B2**
13 Mason's Yard, Duke St SW1. 071-839 6109. Wine, dine and dance to a resident band and guest singer. Hostesses. (**M**). *OPEN to 03.00 Mon-Fri.* A.Ax. Dc.V. **£££**

New Georgian Club   **4 D3**
4 Mill St W1. 071-629 2042. Club with cabaret. Lounge bar and hostesses. Gourmet restaurant. (**M**). *OPEN to 03.00 Mon-Fri.* A.Ax.Dc.V. **£££**

Pinstripe   **4 D3**
21 Beak St W1. 071-437 5143. Victorian decor and topless waitresses. Restaurant and bar. (**M**) or entrance fee. *OPEN to 03.00 Mon-Fri.* A.Ax.Dc.V. **££**

Casinos

Charlie Chester Casino (48)   **4 E3**
12 Archer St W1. 071-734 0255. Modern night club and casino. (**M**). *OPEN to 04.00.* No credit cards. **£**

Clermont Club (48)   **4 C3**
44 Berkeley Sq W1. 071-493 5587. An opulent 18thC town house. A la carte restaurant. (**M**). *OPEN to 04.00.* A.Ax.Dc.V. **£££**

Golden Horseshoe (48)   **3 C3**
79-81 Queensway W2. 071-221 8788. Casino on two floors with a bar and small restaurant. (**M**). *OPEN to 04.00.* A.Ax.Dc.V. **££**

Dinner and entertainment

Restaurants where music, dancing and cabaret complement the cuisine. Booking is advisable.

Barbarella 1   6 B5
428 Fulham Rd SW6. 071-385 9434. Stylish and sophisticated Anglo-Italian restaurant where you can dance until the early hours. OPEN to 03.00 Mon-Sat. A.Ax.Dc.V. **££**

Beefeater by the Tower   5 G4
of London
Ivory House, St Katharine's Way E1. 081-568 1616. Five-course medieval banquets are served nightly with jugglers and magicians performing between courses. Henry VIII in full costume proposes the toasts. Unlimited wine and beer. OPEN to 23.30 Mon-Sat. A.Ax.Dc.V. **£££+**

Brick Lane Music Hall   5 G1
152 Brick La E1. 071-377 8787. Music hall entertainment for the 1990s in the Old Bull and Bush style. Traditional three-course English dinner. OPEN to 23.00 Wed-Sat. A.Dc.V. **£££**

Cockney Cabaret   4 C2
161 Tottenham Court Rd W1. 081-568 1616. True London hospitality. Pearly Kings and Queens, Buskers and four-course meal. Music hall revue and cabaret while you eat. Late-night dancing. OPEN to 23.30. A.Ax.Dc.V. **£££+**

Costa Dorada   4 E2
47-55 Hanway St W1. 071-631 5117. Spanish cuisine with flamenco dancers and cabaret nightly. OPEN to 03.00 Mon-Sat, to 24.00 Sun. A.Dc.V. **£££**

Entrecôte   4 F1
124a Southampton Row WC1. 071-405 1466. Romantic candlelit restaurant with wide-ranging menu. Resident dance band 21.00-01.00 Fri & Sat. Last orders 23.45 (22.45 Sun). A.Ax.Dc.V. **££**

Flanagan's   4 B1
100 Baker St W1. 071-935 0287. Completely phoney but enjoyable Victorian dining rooms. Cockney songs and elegantly costumed waiters and serving girls. Steak 'n' kidney pudding and enormous plates of fish and chips. OPEN to 23.00. A.Ax.Dc.V. **££**

L'Hirondelle   4 D3
199 Swallow St W1. 071-734 1511. Theatre restaurant with two floor-shows nightly and a cabaret. International à la carte menu. OPEN to 03.00 Mon-Sat. Floor shows 23.00 & 01.00. A.Ax.Dc.V. **£££+**

Kerzenstüberl   4 B2
9 St Christopher's Pl W1. 071-486 3196. Dinner dancing. Plenty of 'gute Stimmung' here to warm the heart; an informal, hearty atmosphere and loads of goodwill backed up by excellent Austrian cooking. Accordion music nightly. OPEN to 23.00 Mon-Sat. Music to 01.00. A.Ax.Dc.V. **££**

Royal Roof Restaurant   3 B6
Royal Garden Hotel, 2-24 Kensington High St W8. 071-937 8000. Anglo-French restaurant with dinner dancing on Sat eve. OPEN to 22.30, to 23.00 Sat. A.Ax.Dc.V. **£££+**

Savoy Restaurant   4 G3
Savoy Hotel, Strand WC2. 071-836 4343. Elegant and formal with resident quartet. Worldwide and well-deserved reputation for classic cooking and service. OPEN to 23.30 Mon-Sat. A.Ax. Dc.V. **£££+**

Talk of London   4 F2
Drury La cnr Parker St WC2. 081-568 1616. Modern purpose-built theatre restaurant with tiered seating. 'International' menu. Features some of London's most popular cabaret acts. OPEN to 23.00 Mon-Sun. A.Ax.Dc. V. **£££+**

Terrace Restaurant   4 B4
Dorchester Hotel, Park La W1. 071-629 8888. Stately and gracious for elegant dinner dances. French cuisine. OPEN to 01.00 Mon-Sat. A.Ax.Dc.V. **£££**

Gay nightlife

London boasts an eclectic mix of gay bars and clubs but the scene changes fast and often, so keep an eye on the weekly gay listings in Time Out.
A reliable source of information on all gay clubs and meeting places is Gay *Switchboard 071-837 7324 (24-hr service).*
See also 'Gay pubs' in 'Eating and drinking'.

London Lesbian & Gay Centre   2 D6
67-69 Cowcross St EC1. 071-608 1471. The meeting place for various groups, plus discos, a café and a gym. OPEN to 23.00 Mon-Wed, to 24.00 Thur & Fri, to 03.00 Fri & Sat. Gym OPEN to 22.00.

Bang! (at Busby's)   4 E2
157 Charing Cross Rd WC2. 071-734 6963. Enormous barn-like disco with lasers and video screens. OPEN to 03.00.

The Backstreet
Wentworth Mews E3. 081-980 8557. A

popular venue for men only. Dress code strictly rubber or leather. *OPEN to 02.30 Thur-Sat, to 01.00 Sun.*

The Bell   **2 B3**
259 Pentonville Rd N1. 071-837 5617. Large, comfy pub next to the Scala cinema, with alternative discos every night. Very popular with a young, lively and varied clientele. *OPEN to 24.00 Sun-Wed, to 02.00 Thur (mainly women), to 02.00 Fri & Sat.*

Club Copa   **6 A1**
180 Earl's Court Rd SW5. 071-373 3407. Lively, atmospheric disco and bar. One of the most popular gay venues in south west London. No-smoking area. *OPEN to 02.00 Mon-Sat, to 24.00 Sun.*

Club Industria   **4 D2**
9 Hanover St W1. 071-493 0689. Funky mixed gay crowd. Various one-nighters. *OPEN to 03.30, to 06.00 Fri & Sat, to 01.00 Sun (women only). CLOSED Mon.*

Heaven   **4 F4**
The Arches, Villiers St WC2. 071-839 3852. Vast dancefloor, great sound system, three bars and a stage for the odd cabaret performance. Amazing light show. *OPEN to 03.00.*

London Apprentice   **2 G4**
333 Old St EC1. 071-739 5949. Two large bars, plus dancefloor, pool tables, videos, atmospheric lighting. Predominantly gay male crowd. *OPEN to 03.00 Mon-Thur, to 05.00 Fri & Sat, to 23.30 Sun.*

Madame Jo Jo   **4 D3**
8-10 Brewer St W1. 071-734 2473. Camp, comfortable and fun transvestite venue where everyone has a good time. Drag acts and cabaret. *OPEN to 03.00 Mon-Sat.*

Sex, sleaze and strip clubs

Soho, once the red-light area of London, now flashes its neon only at unsuspecting tourists. The number of establishments permitted to show naked flesh is severely limited and hostess bars are not even licensed, so don't be tempted by billboards promising lewd bed shows, hostess bars and peep shows.
A relatively new arrival on the West End scene are strip shows for women in the form of male dance troupes such as The Chippendales who will strip down to the tiniest G-string. Such shows are good for a laugh and are always packed. Check the theatre listings in Time Out *or the* Evening Standard *for details.*

Carnival Revue Club   **4 E2**
12 Old Compton St W1. 071-437 8337. Continuous performances *12.00-23.00 Mon-Sat.*

Raymond Revuebar   **4 D3**
Walkers Ct, off Brewer St W1. 071-734 1593. Considered the most 'respectable' of its kind. Performances at *20.00* & *22.00 Mon-Sat.*

Sunset Strip   **4 E2**
30 Dean St W1. 071-437 7229. Continuous strip shows *12.30-23.00 Mon-Sat.*

All-night bars and cafés

Some hotel coffee shops stay OPEN 24 hrs and serve light meals to non-residents.

Bar Italia   **4 E2**
22 Frith St W1. 071-437 4520. Authentic Italian café serving pizza, panettone and parma ham sandwiches. *OPEN to 04.00; 24 hrs Sat & Sun.* No credit cards. **£**

Harry's Bar   **4 D3**
19 Kingly St W1. 071-434 0309. Do people go to Harry's because they have stayed out late, or do they stay out late because they are going to Harry's? Excellent late-night cooked breakfasts at this nightclubbers' institution. *OPEN to 06.30.* No credit cards. **£**

Istanbul Iskembecisi
4 Stoke Newington Rd N16. 071-254 7291. Shish kebabs and moussaka are among the Turkish dishes served in this relaxed all-night restaurant. *OPEN to 05.00.* No credit cards. **£**

Lido   **4 E3**
41 Gerrard St W1. 071-437 4437. Wonderful Chinese restaurant open till dawn. Busy and friendly. *OPEN to 04.00.* A.Ax.Dc.V. **££**

Ridley Hot Bagel Bakery
13-15 Ridley Rd E8. 071-241 1047. Delicious fresh, hot bagels with fillings such as chopped liver, cream cheese and smoked salmon. *OPEN 24 hrs.* No credit cards. **£**

Up All Night   **6 C4**
325 Fulham Rd SW10. 071-352 1996. Steaks, burgers and spaghetti. *OPEN to 06.00. CLOSED Sun.* A.Ax.V. **£**

Yung's   **4 E3**
23 Wardour St W1. 071-437 4986. Small, comfortable Chinese restaurant. Excellent fish dishes. *OPEN to 04.30.* A.Ax.Dc. V. **££**

Eating and drinking

Restaurants

These have been chosen primarily for authentic food and good cooking. They cover a selection from classic cuisine in elegant surroundings to a late-night supper in Chinatown. For more detailed information on where and what to eat see Nicholson's London Restaurant Guide. *Restaurant Services, 081-888 8080 offers free up-to-the-minute information and advice on London's restaurants from 09.00-20.00 Mon-Sat. They will also make reservations.*

Average prices for a full meal for one including VAT but without wine:

£	*Under £10*
££	*£10-£20*
£££	*£20-£30*
£££+	*Over £30*
Reserve	*It is advisable to reserve*
OPEN	*Last orders to . . .*
A	*Access (incorporating Mastercard, Eurocard)*
Ax	*American Express*
Dc	*Diners Club*
V	*Visa (incorporating Barclaycard)*
B	*Breakfast*
L	*Lunch*
D	*Dinner*

Service charge: *many restaurants now add service on to the bill, usually at 12½%, but do not always say so – if in doubt ask. However they do usually say if service is not included. 12½% is normally the minimum; give up to 15% for above-average service.*

Cover charge: *not to be confused with the service charge. This is for napkins, bread and water, and is normally added to the bill. Most restaurants, however, have now dispensed with this charge.*

African & Caribbean

African and Caribbean cooking is influenced by Indian, Chinese and European cuisines. Great use is made of fruit, vegetables, rice and coconut, and a wide range of exotic ingredients and fiery pepper sauces liven up meat and fish stews. Food tends to be spicy and filling.

Afric-Carib
1 Stroud Green Rd N4. 071-263 7440. Restaurant and takeaway specialising in spicy Nigerian dishes. Chicken, beef or fish with plantains and yams. Palm wine and African music. Relaxed, informal atmosphere. *LD OPEN to 23.00.* A.V. **£**

Brixtonian Backayard   **4 F2**
4 Neal's Yard, off Neal St WC2. 071-240 2769. A large, bright restaurant with a menu inspired by the West Indies. Sweet potato and salmon patties, deep fried salt cod, chicken Columbo and fried snapper with red bean sauce are some of the tempting dishes. *LD OPEN to 23.00. CLOSED Sun & Mon.* A.Ax.V. **££**

The Calabash   **4 F3**
38 King St WC2. 071-836 1976. African cuisine in the basement of the Africa Centre in Covent Garden. Masks, headdresses and African textiles adorn the walls and a tasty selection of regional dishes is available. Beef with green bananas and coconut cream, couscous, chicken and groundnut stew, vegetarian dishes. African wine and beer available. Friendly service. *LD OPEN to 22.30. CLOSED L Sat & LD Sun.* A.Ax.Dc.V. **££**

Cuba   **3 B6**
11-13 Kensington High St W8. 071-938 4137. This restaurant/bar is a relaxed and friendly place to discover Cuban cuisine; dishes like Cuban meatloaf, lobster tails served with a sweet creole sauce and boniato (sweet potato filled with shredded beef). Cuban coffee and rum. *LD Reserve. OPEN to 01.00, to 23.00 Sun. CLOSED L Sun.* No credit cards. **££**

American

American restaurants now offer not only traditional burgers and pecan pie but increasingly popular Cajun and southern dishes.

Blues Brothers
50 Clapham High St SW4. 071-622 0070. Relaxed, mellow atmosphere in which to enjoy spicy jerk chicken, sizzling beef steak, Dover sole fillet. Live music *at weekends. LD OPEN to 24.00, to 22.30 Sun.* A.Ax.V. **££**

Chicago Rib Shack   **3 G5**
1 Raphael St SW7. 071-581 5595. Wood-smoked barbecued meats with salads and trimmings. Cheesecake, mud pie and ice-cream to follow. *LD OPEN to 23.30, to 23.00 Sun.* A.Ax.V. **££**

Criterion Brasserie   **4 E3**
Piccadilly Circus W1. 071-925 0909. Housed in a Victorian entertainment com-

plex, this opulent restaurant is worth visiting just for the surroundings. Cuisine is Cal-Ital, a blend of American and Italian food. Dishes include grilled chicken with bruschetta, Caesar salad and sticky toffee pudding. *LD OPEN to 23.30. CLOSED Sun & B.hol Mon.* A.Ax.Dc.V. **££**

Ed's Easy Diner 4 E2
12 Moor St W1. 071-439 1955. '50s and '60s diner with counter-top juke-boxes and stools. Burgers, cheese fries, malts, milkshakes and US beers. Other branches. *LD OPEN to 24.00 Mon-Thur, to 01.00 Fri & Sat, to 23.00 Sun.* No credit cards. **£**

Fatboy's Diner 4 F3
21-22 Maiden Lane WC2. 071-240 1902. A 1940s American dining carriage which served for many years before being transported across the Atlantic. Lively and noisy offering huge, tasty burgers, hot dogs, ice-cream floats. *LD OPEN to 24.00, to 22.30 Sun.* No credit cards. **££**

Hard Rock Café 4 C5
150 Old Park La W1. 071-629 0382. Ever-popular hamburger joint identifiable by the long queues outside. Vast room on two levels with a shorts bar. Good quality food and non-stop rock. Huge collection of American memorabilia. *LD OPEN to 00.15, to 00.45 Fri & Sat.* A.Ax.Dc. **££**

Joe Allen 4 G3
13 Exeter St WC2. 071-836 0651. In a converted Covent Garden warehouse, the London 'Joe Allen' follows the pattern of the New York and Paris restaurants. First-rate cocktail bar for diners. Steaks, burgers, delicious spinach salad, spare ribs and chilli, followed by cheesecake or brownies. *LD Reserve. OPEN to 00.45, to 24.00 Sun.* No credit cards. **£££**

Old Orleans 4 G3
29 Wellington St WC2. 071-497 2433. Huge portions of Deep South food. Seafood gumbo, blackened snapper, vast burgers, chocolate fudge brownies. Cocktail bar. Other brances. *LD OPEN to 23.00.* A.Ax.Dc.V. **££**

Planet Hollywood 4 E3
13 Coventry St W1. 071-287 1000. The biggest restaurant in Europe, packed with movie memorabilia, and a three-dimensional diorama of its celebrity backers, Arnold Schwarzenegger, Sylvester Stallone and Bruce Willis. Burgers, ribs, swordfish, pizzas and pasta, plus Mexican dishes and a wide range of desserts. Bar area. Memorabilia shop next door in Trocadero Centre *(OPEN to 24.00). LD (no reservations). OPEN to 01.00.* A.Ax.Dc.V. **££**

Rock Island Diner 4 E3
London Pavilion, Piccadilly Circus W1. 071-287 5500. '50s and '60s diner. Party atmosphere with dancing waiters and waitresses and its own radio station. Burgers, ribs, chilli, salads. *LD OPEN to 23.30.* A.Ax.Dc.V. **£**

Thank God It's Friday's 4 F3
(TGI Friday's)
6 Bedford St WC2. 071-379 0585. Large, loud and lively. Burgers are the mainstay, but there's also chicken chimichanga and blackened Cajun chicken. Over 600 cocktails! Other branches. *LD OPEN to 23.30, to 23.00 Sun.* A.Ax.V. **££**

Central European

Covering the cuisines of Austria, Germany and Switzerland. Lots of meat-based dishes, but also cheeses and vegetables. Sausages, red cabbage and sauerkraut characterise German cooking. Dumplings are widely used in Austria. Fondue is a well-known Swiss speciality which involves dipping bread into melted cheese or meat into hot oil. Hearty and filling food.

Kerzernstüberl 4 B2
9 St Christopher's Pl W1. 071-486 3196. Authentic Austrian food, accordion music, dancing and singing. Leberknödel soup, Bauernschmaus, Viennese goulash. Sachertorte to follow. *LD Reserve. OPEN to 23.00. Licensed to 01.00. CLOSED L Sat & LD Sun.* A.Ax.Dc.V. **£££**

St Moritz 4 E3
161 Wardour St W1. 071-734 3324. Two floors rigged out like a ski hut in the famous resort. Cheese and beef fondues are the house speciality. Also assiette de grison (mountain-air dried and cured beef), veal in cream and mushroom sauce. Nightclub downstairs. *LD Reserve. OPEN to 23.30. CLOSED L Sat & Sun.* A.Ax.Dc.V. **££**

Twin Brothers 3 C5
51 Kensington Church St W8. 071-937 4152. Intimate, old-style German restaurant started up by twin brothers and still run by one – a very colourful character. Bismarck herring, Schweizer onion soup, Wiener or Holsteiner schnitzel and apple cake are just some of the traditional dishes served. *D OPEN to 23.00. CLOSED Sun.* No credit cards. **££**

Chinese

Contrary to popular belief, Chinese cuisine offers a huge variety of styles and ingredients. Most of the Chinese restaurants in this country are Cantonese. Dishes are savoury and cooked simply and quickly in order to bring out the natural flavour of the food. Blends of meat and seafood and stir-fried vegetables are traditional. Steamed dim sum (lunch-time snacks) are a great way to experiment with unfamiliar flavours; they are normally served until 18.00. Pekingese food from the north is considered the highest form of Chinese cuisine. Drier and more highly seasoned than Cantonese, it shows Muslim and Mongolian influences. Great dishes are Peking duck and Mongolian hot-pot. Szechuan cooking from western China is characterised by strong flavours. Double-cooked pork and tea-smoked duck are specialities. Gerrard Street in Soho (4 E3) is the heart of London's Chinatown.

Chuen Cheng Ku   **4 E3**
17 Wardour St W1. 071-437 1398. Authentic Cantonese restaurant, popular with Chinese customers. Delicious fish dishes, dim sum and excellent value lunches. *LD Reserve D. OPEN to 23.45.* A.Ax.Dc.V. **££**

Dragon Gate   **4 E3**
7 Gerrard St W1. 071-734 5154. The first and probably the best Szechuan restaurant in London. Sliced pork with garlic and chilli, aromatic duck. Pancakes or almond curd to follow. *LD OPEN to 23.30.* A.Ax.Dc.V. **££**

Dumpling Inn   **4 E3**
15a Gerrard St W1. 071-437 2567. Small, lively restaurant with genuine Pekingese cooking. Very crowded. Prawns in chilli sauce, beef and dumplings in oyster sauce. *LD OPEN to 23.45.* A.Ax.V. **££**

Fung Shing   **4 E3**
15 Lisle St WC2. 071-437 1539. A broad cross-section of Cantonese dishes on offer. Huge choice of seafood dishes. Hotpots (chicken with clam sauce) are a speciality. Vegetarian dishes. Excellent service. *LD Reserve D. OPEN to 23.30.* A.Ax.Dc.V. **££**

Gallery Rendezvous   **4 D3**
53-55 Beak St W1. 071-734 0445. Delicious Pekingese food, many specialities. Snow prawn balls, shark fin soup, Peking duck. Banqueting suite where you can dine in splendour. *LD Reserve. OPEN to 23.00.* A.Ax.Dc.V. **££**

Good Earth   **6 E1**
233 Brompton Rd SW3. 071-584 3658. Predominantly Cantonese cuisine with a large selection of meat-free dishes such as flaked yellow fish in hot piquant sauce. An ample menu for meat-eaters too. *LD Reserve. OPEN to 23.00, to 22.30 Sun.* A.Ax.Dc.V. **££**

Good Friends
139-141 Salmon La E14. 071-987 5498. Cantonese restaurant in the original Chinatown of Limehouse, where London's first wave of Chinese immigrants arrived as seamen in the late 18thC. Excellent reputation. *LD Reserve.* OPEN to 23.00. A.Ax.Dc.V. **££**

Ken Lo's Memories of China   **7 A2**
67-69 Ebury St SW1. 071-730 7734. Ken Lo's cookery books have popularised Chinese cuisine. The windows of his restaurants are etched with Tang dynasty horses and the menu features regional specialities: Cantonese sea bass, Szechuan crispy beef. Cantonese seafood with black bean sauce. *LD OPEN to 23.00. CLOSED B.hols.* A.Ax.Dc.V. **£££+**

Kuo Yuan
217 Willesden High Rd NW10. 081-459 2297. Some of the best Pekingese food in London is served in this modest, 'local' restaurant. Try the Peking duck. *D Reserve Sat. OPEN to 23.00.* No credit cards. **££**

Lee Ho Fook   **4 E3**
15-16 Gerrard St W1. 071-734 9578. Renowned Cantonese cooking, very popular with local Chinese. Huge portions at reasonable prices. Dim sum at lunchtime. *LD OPEN to 23.30 (to 22.30 Sun).* A.Ax.Dc.V. **£**

Mr Chow   **3 F5**
151 Knightsbridge SW1. 071-589 7347. Pekingese food in surroundings of old-style opulence. Peking duck, sole in wine and Mr Chow's noodles. *LD Reserve. OPEN to 23.45.* A.Ax.Dc.V. **£££**

Mr Kai of Mayfair   **4 B4**
65 South Audley St W1. 071-493 8988. Modern, stylish restaurant with simple decor and creative cuisine. Sizzling lamb, chilli prawns in fresh pineapple, crispy Peking duck. *LD Reserve. OPEN to 23.15.* A.Ax.Dc.V. **£££+**

Now & Zen   **4 F3**
4a Upper St Martin's Lane WC2. 071-497 0376. Stylishly designed, you walk over a thick, glass gangplank to enter this restaurant, one of the Zen chain. Modern oriental menu with snack menu in the evenings; eat as many snacks as you like from a list of 50 which includes minced chicken with Malaysian spices and Thai-style pan-fried pomfret with chilli. *LD Reserve. OPEN to 23.30, to 23.00 Sun.* A.Ax.Dc.V. **£££+**

Poons   **4 E3**
4 Leicester St WC2. 071-437 1528. Wind-dried meats are a speciality at this

unpretentious, family-run Cantonese restaurant. Other branches. *LD Reserve. OPEN to 23.30.* A.Ax.Dc.V. **££**

Oriental   **4 B4**
Dorchester Hotel, 55 Park Lane W1. 071-629 8888. Exquisite Cantonese cuisine in sumptuous surroundings. Set menus or try one of the chef's specials. Correct dress essential. *LD Reserve. OPEN to 23.00. CLOSED L Sat & LD Sun.* A.Ax.Dc.V. **£££+**

Tai Wing Wah   **4 E3**
7-9 Newport Pl WC2. 071-287 2702. One of the best places for dim sum in London. A pleasant restaurant with friendly staff who are happy to explain the Chinese menu. The deep-fried crispy Peking chicken is exquisite. *LD Reserve. OPEN to 23.30 Mon-Thur, to 24.00 Fri & Sat, to 22.30 Sun.* A.Ax.Dc.V. **££**

East European

Covering the cuisines of Hungary, Russia and Poland. Hungarian food is distinguished by unusual but extremely tasty dishes. Paprika is a popular ingredient and freshwater fish, such as carp and pike, are widely used. If you like fish, try one of the Russian restaurants listed below. They also serve such delights as borscht (cold beetroot soup) and blinis (savoury or sweet pancakes). Polish food is hearty and filling. Meat dumplings and boiled beef will almost certainly be on the menu; and you can accompany your meal with native Polish vodkas.

Borshtch 'n' Tears   **3 G6**
46 Beauchamp Pl SW3. 071-589 5003. Crowded, informal, lively Russian restaurant. Try the borscht, beef Stroganoff, chicken Dragomiroff, golubtsy (stuffed cabbage leaves) or blinis. Russian music. *LD OPEN to 01.00.* Ax. **££**

Daquise   **6 D2**
20 Thurloe St SW7. 071-589 6117. Very popular with Polish émigrés, this restaurant serves simple, but very well prepared dishes. Borscht, stuffed cabbage, sausages and shashlik. Also open for morning coffee and afternoon tea, with some of the most delicious pastries in London. *LD OPEN to 22.45.* No credit cards. **££**

Gay Hussar   **4 E2**
2 Greek St W1. 071-437 0973. Intimate, cosy, much-loved Hungarian restaurant. Cold wild cherry soup, pike with beetroot sauce, roast saddle of carp, goulash. To follow, sweet cheese pancakes and poppy seed strüdel. Hungarian wines. *LD*

Reserve. OPEN to 22.45. CLOSED Sun. No credit cards. **£££**

Kaspia   **4 C3**
18 Bruton Place W1. 071-493 2612. In plush surroundings behind a caviar shop, this restaurant only serves fish and caviar. Three set-price menus, the Sanka, Troika and Trois Caviars, or specialities of smoked salmon, blinis and quail's eggs. Russian and Polish vodkas and champagnes. *LD Reserve. OPEN to 23.30. CLOSED LD Sun.* A.Ax.Dc.V. **£££+**

Luba's Bistro   **3 F6**
6 Yeoman's Row SW3. 071-589 2950. Individual, down-to-earth, spartan atmosphere. Seating at long tables. Bring your own wine. Authentic Russian cooking. Borscht, beef Stroganoff, kooliebaiaka (salmon pie), zrazra (chicken with vegetables), golubtsy, pojarsky. *D OPEN to 24.00. CLOSED Sun.* A.Ax.V. **££**

Nikita's   **6 B4**
65 Ifield Rd SW10. 071-352 6326. A cavernous basement restaurant serving imaginative Russian dishes. Try the scallops zubrovka (with ginger and saffron) or the borscht served hot with sour cream. Wide selection of vodkas. *D Reserve. OPEN to 23.30. CLOSED Sun.* A.Ax.V. **£££**

English

It is the quality of the ingredients in English restaurants that makes for good food – fresh meat and vegetables, salmon and game. Many restaurants now serve dishes using traditional ingredients but with a modern outlook. For traditional roasts, carveries offer set-price meals and customers are served generous portions from enormous succulent joints of beef, lamb or pork (starter and dessert is usually included in the price). Many pubs also serve good lunches based on traditional English cooking. See 'Pubs' section.

Beeton's
58 Hill Rise, Richmond, Surrey. 081-940 9561. A weekly-changing menu which may include tomato and basil soup, nut roast with mango chutney, lamb with peanut and curry sauce. Unlicensed. *LD Reserve. OPEN to 22.30.* No credit cards. **L £ D ££**

Betjeman's   **5 C1**
43 Cloth Fair EC1. 071-796 4981. Steeped in history – the restaurant is in what used to be the study of the former home of the Poet Laureate. Old-style atmosphere. Aberdeen Angus entrecôte, Scottish smoked salmon, wide selection of British cheeses. *LD Reserve. OPEN*

to 23.00. CLOSED D Sat & LD Sun. A.V. **££**

Betjeman Carving Restaurant
Charing Cross Hotel, Strand WC2. 071-839 7282. Carvery. *LD OPEN to 22.30 (to 22.00 Sun).* A.Ax.Dc.V. **££**

Bowlers Restaurant   **5 F1**
Great Eastern Hotel, Liverpool St EC2. 071-283 4363. Carvery. *LD OPEN to 22.00.* A.Ax.Dc.V. **££**

The English House   **6 F2**
3 Milner St SW3. 071-584 3002. Charming dining room in the style of an English country house. Classic English cooking. *LD Reserve. OPEN to 23.30 (to 22.00 Sun).* A.Ax.Dc.V. **£££+**

George & Vulture   **5 E2**
3 Castle Ct, off Cornhill EC3. 071-626 9710. Built in 1170 and restored after the Great Fire, this hostelry was one of Dickens' haunts. Traditional English fare like Dover sole, roast beef, liver and bacon, sherry trifle. *L OPEN to 14.45. CLOSED Sat & Sun.* A.Ax.Dc.V. **££**

The Greenhouse   **4 C4**
27a Hays Mews W1. 071-499 3331. White walls with lush green plants create a conservatory effect. Simple English cooking enlivened by French and Italian flavours. Wonderful choice of traditional puddings including bread and butter pudding and baked rice pudding. *LD Reserve. OPEN to 23.00. CLOSED L Sat & D Sun.* A.Ax.Dc.V. **£££**

Green's
Marsham Ct, Marsham St SW1. 071-834 9552. Richly panelled and dignified, close to the Houses of Parliament. Attractively presented traditional English dishes and an excellent oyster bar. Anything from caviar to bangers and mash. Fine wine list. *LD Reserve L. OPEN to 23.00. CLOSED Sat & Sun.* A.Ax.Dc.V. **£££**

Maggie Jones   **3 C5**
6 Old Court Pl, off Kensington Church St W8. 071-937 6462. Cosy and pleasant with its wooden settles and country atmosphere. Hearty portions of traditional English cooking. *LD Reserve. OPEN to 23.30 (to 22.30 Sun).* A.Ax.Dc.V. **£££**

Porters   **4 F3**
17 Henrietta St WC2. 071-836 6466. Well-established theme restaurant specialising in pies – lamb and apricot, turkey and chestnut. Good old bread and butter pudding, rhubarb crumble or Stilton to follow. Traditional Sunday lunch. *LD OPEN to 23.30.* A.Ax.V. **£**

Printer's Pie   **5 B2**
60 Fleet St EC4. 071-353 8861. Pretty, old house. Competently prepared simple English dishes; grills, pies and steak 'n'

kidney pudding. Traditional sweets. *LD Reserve L. OPEN to 22.00. CLOSED D Sat & LD Sun.* A.Ax.Dc.V. **££**

Quality Chop House   **2 D6**
94 Farringdon Rd EC1. 071-837 5093. A lovingly preserved 'working-class caff' where labourers came to eat for over a hundred years. Now serves traditional English fare plus some European dishes. Always busy and lively. *LD Reserve. OPEN to 24.00, to 23.30 Sun. CLOSED L Sat.* No credit cards. **££**

Rules   **4 F3**
35 Maiden La, Strand WC2. 071-836 5314. Rich in associations: Dickens, Thackeray, Edward VII and Lillie Langtry all dined here. Genuine Edwardian eating house with very good traditional English food like jugged hare, steak 'n' kidney pie or pudding, venison and grouse. Seasonal menu. *LD Reserve. OPEN to 24.00.* A.Ax.V. **£££**

Simpson's-in-the-Strand   **4 F3**
100 Strand WC2. 071-836 9112. A famous restaurant with an Edwardian club atmosphere. Large carvings from enormous joints of beef and lamb are excellent. Correct dress essential. *LD Reserve. OPEN to 22.45.* A.Ax.Dc.V. **£££**

Strand Palace Hotel   **4 F3**
Strand WC2. 071-836 8080. Carvery. *LD OPEN to 22.00 (to 21.00 Sun).* A.Ax.Dc.V. **££**

Throgmorton Restaurants   **5 E2**
27a Throgmorton St EC2. 071-588 5165. Huge establishment comprising three underground restaurants; the Long and Short Rooms and the Oak Room. Generous portions of roast beef, fried fish, and steak 'n' kidney pie. *L Reserve. OPEN to 15.00. CLOSED Sat & Sun.* A.Ax.Dc.V. **££**

Tiddy Dols   **4 C4**
55 Shepherd Market W1. 071-499 2357. Occupying eight, quaint 18thC houses in Shepherd Market. Dishes include roast fillet of beef, roast highland pheasant, beef Wellington and the original ginger-bread Tiddy Dol. *D OPEN to 23.30.* A.Ax.Dc.V. **£££**

Tower Thistle Hotel   **5 G4**
St Katharine's Way E1. 071-481 2575. Carvery. *LD OPEN to 22.30, to 24.00 Sat & Sun.* A.Ax.Dc.V. **£££**

Wiltons   **4 D4**
55 Jermyn St SW1. 071-629 9955. Fine food and unyielding tradition. Baby lobsters, crabs, salmon, halibut, sole and turbot. Chops, grills, marvellous game. Stilton to follow. Fine wine list, good port. *LD Reserve. OPEN to 22.30. CLOSED L Sat & LD Sun.* A.Ax.Dc.V. **£££+**

Fish

As well as those restaurants that specialise in elaborately cooked fish dishes, London has a large number of fish and chip 'take away' shops, mostly to be found in residential areas, but too numerous to list here. Fish and chips is a national dish which you can take away soused in vinegar, salt and pepper. Eaten hot it can be delicious and good value.

Bentley's   **4 D3**
11-15 Swallow St W1. 071-734 4756. Famous seafood restaurant and oyster bar offering a wide variety of excellent fish dishes, plus oysters, prawns and crab. *LD Reserve. OPEN to 22.30. CLOSED Sun.* A.Ax.Dc.V. **£££**

Bibendum Oyster Bar   **6 E2**
Michelin House, 81 Fulham Rd SW3. 071-581 5817. Friendly atmosphere in this elegant oyster bar. Plateau de fruits de mer, langoustines, four varieties of oyster. Queuing often necessary. *LD Reserve. OPEN to 23.00, to 22.30 Sun.* A.V.

Café Fish   **4 E3**
39 Panton St SW1. 071-930 3999. Blackboard menus list wide selection of fish which you can have shallow or deep fried, charcoal grilled or steamed. Cover charge includes fish pâté and French bread. Good cheeseboard and wine list. Pianist every night. Downstairs restaurant. *LD Reserve. OPEN to 23.30. CLOSED LD Sun.* Wine bar *OPEN to 23.00.* A.Ax.Dc.V. **££**

La Gaulette   **1 E6**
53 Cleveland St W1. 071-580 7608. Delightful and friendly restaurant specialising in tropical fish prepared Mauritian style. Red snapper with wine sauce, crab flavoured with ginger and coriander. *LD Reserve. OPEN to 23.00. CLOSED L Sat & LD Sun.* A.Ax.Dc.V. **£££**

L'Hippocampe   **4 E2**
63 Frith St W1. 071-734 4545. Imaginative decor; the walls and floor are etched with fish motifs. Short, changing menu features delicately cooked fish and crustacea. The bouillabaisse is legendary, but is only on the menu when the ingredients are available. *LD Reserve. OPEN to 23.15. CLOSED L Sat & LD Sun.* A.Ax.Dc.V. **£££**

Lobster Pot
3 Kennington Lane SE11. 071-582 5556. French restaurant full of nautical knick-knacks. Changing menu; rock salmon served with crayfish, poached lobster. *LD OPEN to 23.30. CLOSED LD Mon.* A.Ax.Dc.V. **££**

Lucullus   **3 F5**
48 Knightsbridge SW1. 071-245 6622. Superb array of fresh fish at the entrance. Speciality is salmon stuffed with broccoli mousse wrapped in filo pastry with champagne sauce. Seafood platter. Also lamb, steaks, chicken. *LD Reserve. OPEN to 23.30.* A.Ax.Dc.V. **£££**

Manzi's   **4 E3**
1-2 Leicester St WC2. 071-734 0224. Old-established Italian fish restaurant on two floors. Wide range of fish and shellfish as well as simpler dishes such as poached salmon or grilled turbot. *LD Reserve. OPEN to 23.30. CLOSED L Sun (upstairs CLOSED LD Sun).* A.Ax.Dc.V.

Poissonnerie de l'Avenue   **6 E2**
82 Sloane Av SW3. 071-589 2457. Beautifully cooked fresh dishes; fish comes from the restaurant's own fish shop next door. Coquilles St Jacques au vin blanc, moules, sole, turbot, oysters, Dublin Bay prawns. *LD Reserve. OPEN to 23.30. CLOSED Sun.* A.Ax.Dc.V. **£££**

Sheekey's   **4 F3**
28-32 St Martin's Ct WC2. 071-240 2565. Established since 1896, it is noted for its shellfish and seafood. Fresh salmon, steamed turbot with lobster sauce, stewed eels. Crowded and theatrical. *LD Reserve. OPEN to 23.15. CLOSED L Sat & LD Sun.* A.Ax.Dc.V. **£££**

Sweetings   **5 D2**
39 Queen Victoria St EC4. 071-248 3062. Tiny 150-year-old City eatery. Fish parlour, with excellent service. Sit at the bar and eat herrings with mustard, whitebait, excellent fish pie. Quieter restaurant at the back. Queuing often necessary as they don't take bookings. *L OPEN to 15.00. CLOSED Sat & Sun.* No credit cards. **££**

Wheeler's
Chain of restaurants dating back over 100 years to the fish shop in Old Compton St which today is one of the many branches. Welcoming atmosphere with sophistication. Scallops, lobster Normande, sole Egyptian and shellfish. Some branches are listed below:

Alcove   **3 B6**
17 Kensington High St W8. 071-937 1443. *LD Reserve. OPEN to 22.45, to 22.15 Sun.* A.Ax.Dc.V. **£££**

Wheeler's Old Compton Street 4 E2
19 Old Compton St W1. 071-437 2706. *LD Reserve. OPEN to 23.15, to 22.30 Sun.* A.Ax.Dc.V. **£££**

Wheeler's St James's   **4 D4**
12a Duke of York St SW1. 071-930 2460. *LD Reserve. OPEN to 22.30. CLOSED Sun.* A.Ax.Dc.V. **£££**

French

The following all serve French cuisine; some specialise in simple French provincial dishes, others in highly sophisticated haute cuisine. It should also be noted that French cuisine is amongst the most expensive in the world.

Ark   3 C4
122 Palace Gdns Ter W8. 071-229 4024. Cosy and friendly atmosphere with good provincial French food. Champignons de campagne, fruits de mer, chicken pilaf. Another branch at 35 Kensington High St W8 which serves modern French cuisine. 071-937 4294. *LD Reserve. OPEN to 23.15. CLOSED L Sun.* A.V. **££**

Auberge de Provence   4 D6
St James's Court Hotel, 41 Buckingham Gate SW1. 071-821 1899. Rustic hotel dining room. Mediterranean herbs and flavourings add zest to the provençal inspired cooking. Steamed sea bass with tomato, basil and olive oil, noisettes of lamb with basil and creamed aubergines. Provençal wines. Vegetarian dishes. *LD Reserve. OPEN to 23.00. CLOSED L Sat & LD Sun.* A.Ax.Dc.V. **£££**

Le Bistingo   4 E2
57 Old Compton St W1. 071-437 0784. Excellent Soho bistro serving provincial French cooking. Blackboard menu usually includes moules marinières, coq au vin and steak au poivre. Carafe wines. Other branches. *LD OPEN to 23.30. CLOSED Sun.* A.Ax.Dc.V. **££**

Boulestin   4 F3
1a Henrietta St WC2. 071-836 7061. There are many interesting specialities on the menu of this famous old restaurant. Sumptuous dishes such as crabe à l'artichaut, ballotine de turbot farcie au homard. Fine wines, dignified service. *LD OPEN to 23.15. CLOSED L Sat & LD Sun.* A.Ax.Dc.V. **£££+**

Café des Amis du Vin   4 F2
11 Hanover Place, off Long Acre WC2. 071-379 3444. Popular, lively spot with a wine bar in the basement, café on the ground floor and restaurant on the first floor. Intimate atmosphere in which to enjoy regional French cuisine. *LD Reserve. OPEN to 23.30. CLOSED LD Sun.* A.Ax.V. **££**

Claridge's Restaurant   4 C3
Brook St W1. 071-629 8860. Distinguished French cooking in luxurious surroundings. The atmosphere is typical of the sedate thirties. Polished service. Large and notable wine list. *LD Reserve. OPEN to 23.30.* A.Ax.Dc.V. **£££+**

Connaught Restaurant   4 B3
Carlos Pl W1. 071-499 7070. Known as one of the grandest hotel dining rooms in the world. Old-fashioned panelling, mirrors and chandeliers are the setting for the famous Connaught terrine, oeuf de cailles Maintenon, langoustines and excellent game. Impeccable food, fine wines and a formal atmosphere – jacket and tie must be worn. *LD Reserve. OPEN to 22.30.* Grill room *CLOSED Sat & Sun.* A.Ax.V. **£££+**

L'Epicure   4 E2
28 Frith St W1. 071-437 2829. Something of a Soho institution. First-class cuisine with excellent flambéd dishes. Châteaubriand, crêpes de volaille, crêpes Suzette to follow. *LD OPEN to 23.15. CLOSED L Sat & LD Sun.* A.Ax.Dc.V. **£££**

L'Escargot   4 E2
48 Greek St W1. 071-437 2679. A secluded dining room upstairs and a brasserie on the ground floor. First-class cuisine from a frequently changing menu. Excellent wine list and efficient service. *LD Reserve. OPEN to 23.15. CLOSED L Sat & LD Sun.* A.Ax.Dc.V. Restaurant **£££** Brasserie **££**

L'Etoile   4 D1
30 Charlotte St W1. 071-636 7189. One of the oldest French restaurants in London. Old-fashioned service and atmosphere with traditional dishes on the menu; rognons, ris de veau and tripes à la mode de Caen. *LD Reserve. OPEN to 23.00. CLOSED L Sat & LD Sun.* A.Ax.Dc.V. **£££**

Le Gavroche   4 B3
43 Upper Brook St W1. 071-408 0881. One of the best restaurants in London, renowned for its luxurious atmosphere and imaginative *haute cuisine.* Cooking and service faultless. *D Reserve. OPEN to 23.00. CLOSED Sat & Sun.* A.Ax. Dc.V. **£££+**

Harvey's
2 Bellevue Rd SW17. 081-672 0114. South London restaurant with excellent reputation. Menu changes every month; classic French cuisine. Leek terrine stuffed with scallops and langoustines, roast rabbit with wild mushrooms. Terrine of fresh fruit. *LD Reserve. OPEN to 23.00. CLOSED LD Sun & Mon.* A.V. **£££+**

Au Jardin des Gourmets   4 E2
5 Greek St W1. 071-437 1816. Famous for its climate-controlled cellar which harbours old and rare clarets. Ambitious menu in elegant surroundings; modern and traditional dishes. *LD Reserve. OPEN to 23.15. CLOSED L Sat & LD Sun.* A.Ax.Dc.V. **£££**

Mon Plaisir   **4 F2**
21 Monmouth St WC2. 071-836 7243.
Small, typically French restaurant. Friendly
atmosphere and helpful service. Short,
unpretentious menu: cassoulet, suprême
de volaille au bleu bresse, coq au vin.
Other branches. LD Reserve. OPEN to
23.15. CLOSED L Sat & LD Sun.
A.Ax.Dc.V. **££-£££**

Nico at Ninety   **4 B3**
90 Park Lane W1. 071-409 1290. Nico
Ladenis is one of London's most well-
known and inventive chefs, formerly of
Chez Nico and Simply Nico. Classic
French dishes in sumptuous surround-
ings. LD Reserve. OPEN to 23.00.
CLOSED Sat & Sun. A.Ax.Dc.V. L **£££**
D **£££+**

Le Poulbot   **5 D2**
45 Cheapside EC2. 071-236 4379.
Expense-account lunches downstairs,
less expensive fare upstairs in the
brasserie. Excellent food. Polished service
and fine wine list. L Reserve. OPEN
to 15.00. CLOSED Sat & Sun. A.Ax.
Dc.V. **£££**

La Poule au Pot   **7 A2**
231 Ebury St SW1. 071-730 7763.
Cheerful and crowded. Rustically furnished with brick walls and copper knick-
knacks. Robust, provincial cooking. Set
lunch menu. LD Reserve. OPEN to 23.15.
A.Ax.Dc.V. **£££**

Au Provençal
295 Railton Rd SE24. 071-274 9163.
Fine French provincial cooking in a popular local restaurant. Moules marinières,
wild duck, chicken with tarragon.
Vegetarian dishes on the menu. D
Reserve. OPEN to 22.30. A.V. **££**

Le Renoir   **4 E3**
79 Charing Cross Rd WC2. 071-734
2515. Friendly, efficient and right in the
heart of theatreland. Good French cooking; the menu is arranged in price brack-
ets so all starters cost the same, as do
main courses and desserts. Grilled trout,
grilled duck, steak frites and simpler dishes such as croque-monsieur and
omelettes. LD OPEN to 01.30, to 24.00
Sun. A.Ax.Dc.V. **££**

St Quentin   **6 E1**
243 Brompton Rd SW3. 071-589 8005.
Lively Knightsbridge restaurant in the style
of a Parisian brasserie. Classic French
cooking; foie gras, beef tournedos.
Cheeses and pâtisseries supplied by a
nearby gourmet shop. LD OPEN to
23.30, to 23.00 Sun. A.Ax.Dc.V. **£££**

La Tante Claire   **6 F4**
68 Royal Hospital Rd SW3. 071-352
6045. Highly regarded and beautiful

restaurant offering innovative, perfectly
executed French cuisine. Pig's trotters
stuffed with sweetbreads are chef Pierre
Koffman's speciality. LD OPEN to 23.00.
CLOSED LD Sat & Sun. A.Ax.Dc.V. **£££+**

Thierry's   **6 D4**
342 King's Rd SW3. 071-352 3365.
Authentic cooking. Robust dishes like
rack of lamb, confit de canard, cassoulet,
moules, soufflé au fromage. LD Reserve
D. OPEN to 23.00, to 22.30 Sun.
A.Ax.Dc.V. **££**

Villandry Dining Room   **4 B1**
89 Marylebone High St W1. 071-224
3799. Excellent food on the daily changing menu at this popular lunchtime dining
room. Dishes are simply prepared and
made with the freshest ingredients;
French ham with potatoes lyonnaise, red
pepper and pesto tart, cassoulet. L
Reserve. OPEN to 15.00. CLOSED Sun.
A.Dc.V. **££**

Greek, Turkish & Cypriot

There is more to Greek and Cypriot food
than moussaka and kebabs; the use of
fresh ingredients and interesting herbs
and spices produce sizzling meat dishes
and meze offers a multi-course meal with
a selection of samplers from the menu.
A new style of cooking – ocakbasi – has
become popular in London's Turkish
restaurants. Similar to a barbecue, meat
is grilled over charcoal in a narrow pit, in
front of which you can sit.

Café Grec   **4 D1**
18 Charlotte St W1. 071-436 7411.
Authentic cuisine; the owner and chef are
both from the Greek mainland. Unusual
dishes; menu often includes a recipe from
Ancient Greece. Vegetarian dishes.
Excellent service. LD Reserve. OPEN to
23.00. CLOSED L Sat & LD Sun.
A.Ax.Dc.V. **££**

Cypriana   **4 D1**
11 Rathbone St W1. 071-636 1057.
Traditional Cypriot food in airy surroundings. Specialities are kleftiko, afelia,
stifado, dolmades. LD OPEN to 23.30.
CLOSED L Sat & LD Sun. A.Ax.Dc.V. **££**

Istanbul Iskenbecisi
9 Stoke Newington Rd N16. 071-254
7291. Attractive surroundings in this late-
night Turkish restaurant. The menu is for
the strong-stomached – boiled brain, roast
head of sheep and lamb's tongue. You
can of course choose a more conventional
shish kebab or goulash. LD Reserve.
OPEN to 05.00. No credit cards. **£**

Mangal
10 Arcola St E8. 071-249 0400. Tiny,

busy establishment run by one of the best Turkish chefs in London. Specialise in ocakbasi. Also serves Lahmacun (a Turkish pizza covered with spicy minced lamb). *LD Reserve. OPEN to 24.00.* No credit cards. **£**

Mega Kalamaras 3 C3
76-78 Inverness Mews, off Inverness Pl W2. 071-727 9122. Also smaller and less expensive **Micro Kalamaras** 66 Inverness Mews W2. 071-727 5082. True taverna atmosphere. Superb national dishes ranging from dolmades to baklava. Micro is unlicensed. *D Reserve. OPEN to 23.00. CLOSED Sun.* A.Ax.Dc.V. **£**

Psistaria 4 D6
82 Wilton Rd SW1. 071-821 7504. Psistaria means grill, and grilled meat and fish are the specialities in this Cypriot restaurant. Attractive and spacious with friendly service. *LD OPEN to 23.30, to 23.00 Sat. CLOSED LD Sun.* A.Dc.V. **££**

White Tower 4 E1
1 Percy St W1. 071-636 8141. Old-fashioned, refined atmosphere. First-class cuisine with Middle Eastern influences. *LD Reserve. OPEN to 22.30. CLOSED Sat & Sun.* A.Ax.Dc.V. **£££**

Indian

Although most of London's Indian restaurants are run by Bangladeshis, you will find various influences in the cooking. Hindu cooking uses fish and vegetables in rich liquid juices; Muslims use more meat and the food is drier. Moghul influences bring ingredients from the Middle East and also tandoori food (fish and meat marinated in yoghurt and spices and cooked in a clay oven). As a general rule, north Indian food comprises spicy curries eaten with rice and breads, while food from the south is predominantly vegetarian. In all Indian cooking classic spices and flavourings are used generously.

Bombay Brasserie 6 C2
Courtfield Close, Courtfield Rd SW7. 071-370 4040. Large, fashionable, colonial-style venue, with plants, fans and wicker chairs. Dishes from several regions including Bombay thali, Goan fish curry. Cobra coffee flambé to finish. Excellent lunchtime buffet. *LD Reserve D. OPEN to 24.00.* A.Dc.V. **£££**

Chutney Mary 6 C5
535 King's Rd SW10. 071-351 3113. London's first Anglo-Indian restaurant where chefs from different regions recreate the dishes from colonial days. Curried mango soup, lamb patties with chutney. Bombay bangers. *LD Reserve. OPEN to 23.30, to 22.00 Sun (buffet only).* A.Ax.Dc.V. **£££**

Covent Garden Rickshaw 4 F3
11 Henrietta St WC2. 071-379 5555. Pleasantly decorated dining room offering a lunchtime buffet which is great value. Chicken tikka, vegetarian korma, moong dhal. *LD OPEN to 23.00 Sun.* A.V. **££**

Diwan-E-Khas 1 E5
45 Grafton Way W1. 071-388 1321. Cavernous interior in which to sample excellent tandoori dishes from northern India. Also Mogul chicken or lamb. *LD OPEN to 23.45.* A.Ax.Dc.V. **£**

Khan's 3 C2
13-15 Westbourne Gro W2. 071-727 5420. The vast dining hall with oriental arches and palm tree pillars was formerly a Lyons tea house. Cheap, cheerful and noisy with excellent north Indian cuisine. Kofti dilruba – spiced curried meatballs – is one of the specialities. *LD Reserve D. OPEN to 24.00.* A.Ax.Dc.V. **£**

Lahore Kebab House
2 Umberston St E1. 071-481 9737. Unlicensed 'caff' widely known for its authentic food and huge portions. Curried quails, tikka, tandoori and kebabs. Freshly baked breads, hot rice pudding. Vegetarian dishes. *LD OPEN to 24.00.* No credit cards. **£**

Last Days of the Raj 4 F2
22 Drury La WC2. 071-836 1628. Bengali specialities in crowded theatreland restaurant. Meat thali, lamb tandoori, hot and sour chicken. *LD Reserve. OPEN to 23.30, to 22.00 Sun. CLOSED L Sun.* A.Ax.Dc.V. **££**

Mumtaz 1 A4
4-10 Park Rd NW1. 071-723 0549. One of the most lavishly decorated Indian eateries in London. Good tandoori dishes and wide vegetarian selection. *LD OPEN to 23.30, to 23.00 Sun.* A.Ax.Dc.V. **£££**

Ragam 1 E6
57 Cleveland St W1. 071-636 9098. Popular, friendly restaurant serving dishes from southern India. The kalan is a Keralan dish made from buttermilk, coconut and sweet mangoes. Avial is made from mixed vegetables cooked with yoghurt and curry leaves; both are delicious. *LD Reserve. OPEN to 23.30.* A.Ax.Dc.V. **££**

Ravi Shankar 1 E5
133-135 Drummond St NW1. 071-388 6458. Inexpensive southern Indian restaurant serving authentic vegetarian dishes. Excellent Mysore masala dosai, thali and tasty snacks. Shares a kitchen with **Chutneys**, 124 Drummond St NW1 (1 E5). 071-388 0604. *LD OPEN to 23.00.* A.Ax.Dc.V. **£**

The Red Fort   4 **E2**
77 Dean St W1. 071-437 2115. A trend-setter in Bangladeshi fish dishes and now one of the most acclaimed Indian restaurants in the world. Luxurious surroundings and excellent cooking. Try quails in mild spice or chicken karahi. Have a cocktail in the elegant bar while waiting for your table. *LD Reserve. OPEN to 23.15.* A.Ax.Dc.V. **££**

Salloos   4 **B5**
62 Kinnerton St SW1. 071-235 4444. Luxurious Pakistani restaurant tucked away in a mews in Knightsbridge. Tandoori dishes are marinated for 24 hours and are always cooked to order. Some excellent 'special' recipes; try the chicken taimuri, pieces of chicken marinated, cooked in various sauces and deep-fried in batter. *LD OPEN to 23.15. CLOSED Sun.* A.Ax.Dc.V. **£££**

Star of India   6 **C3**
154 Old Brompton Rd SW5. 071-373 2901. Unusual Renaissance setting for excellent Indian food. Prawn biryani, whole stuffed tandoori chicken, kebabs. *LD OPEN to 23.45, to 23.15 Sun.* A.Ax.Dc.V. **££**

Tandoori of Chelsea   6 **D3**
153 Fulham Rd SW3. 071-589 7617. Elegant furnishings and a high standard of regional cooking using traditional tandoor clay ovens. Lamb and chicken are marinated in herbs and spices before cooking. *LD Reserve. OPEN to 24.00, to 23.30 Sun.* A.Ax.Dc.V. **££**

Veeraswamy's   4 **D3**
99-101 Regent St (entrance in Swallow St) W1. 071-734 1401. Authentic food in London's oldest Indian restaurant. Moglai, Delhi, Madras, Ceylon and Vindaloo curries. Lunch buffet. *LD Reserve. OPEN to 23.30. CLOSED Sun.* A.Ax.Dc.V. **££**

Inexpensive eating

There are lots of inexpensive restaurants and diners in London where you can eat a three-course meal for around £10. Those listed here do not include the cafés serving 'sausage, egg and chips', nor the international 'fast food' chains which can be found on nearly every high street. This list prizes all styles of cooking and features restaurants where you will find a good atmosphere and which offer good value for money.

Alpino   1 **C6**
42 Marylebone High St W1. 071-935 4640. Alpine-style restaurant. Busy at all times. Quick service. Generous portions of pasta, fish and chicken dishes. *LD*

OPEN to 23.00. CLOSED Sun. A.Ax.Dc.V.

Barocco   4 **E2**
13 Moor St W1. 071-437 2324. Unlicensed café serving mainly Italian dishes, but some British choices too. Dish of the day and excellent trifle for dessert. *LD OPEN to 22.45. CLOSED Sun.* No credit cards.

Boggi's   2 **C5**
34 Topham St EC1. 071-837 8392. This cheerful restaurant has a daily variety of specials such as fettuccini with cream and mushrooms and spaghetti bolognese. Choice of desserts. Unlicensed. *L OPEN to 15.00. CLOSED Sat & Sun.* No credit cards.

Café in the Crypt   4 **F3**
Crypt of St Martin-in-the-Fields, Duncannon St WC2. 071-839 4342. Friendly restaurant serving wholesome food to tourists and office workers. Beef bake, spinach and cheese pancakes, cappuccino. Licensed. *LD OPEN to 20.30. CLOSED Sun.* A.V.

Centrale   4 **E2**
16 Moor St W1. 071-437 5513. Consistently good Italian cooking at this West End restaurant. Vegetarian dishes. Unlicensed. *LD OPEN to 21.45.* No credit cards.

Charlotte Restaurant
221 West End Lane NW6. 071-794 6476. Intimate restaurant serving breakfast, lunch and dinner. Predominantly French menu; cabillaud aux poivres (cod in pepper sauce) comes with légumes vertes au beurre or pommes lyonnaise. Licensed. *BLD OPEN to 23.30. CLOSED Sun.* No credit cards.

Chelsea Kitchen   6 **E3**
98 King's Rd SW3. 071-589 1330. The daily menu offers healthy portions of moussaka, goulash or spaghetti; followed by home-made puddings. Licensed. *LD OPEN to 23.45, to 23.30 Sun.* No credit cards.

Costas Grill   3 **B4**
14 Hillgate St W8. 071-229 3794. Good, friendly Greek restaurant specialising in charcoal grills. Eat outside in the summer. Costas Fish Restaurant next door. *LD OPEN to 22.30. CLOSED Sun.* Fish shop also *CLOSED Mon.* No credit cards.

Diana's Diner   4 **F2**
39 Endell St WC2. 071-240 0272. Good, traditional British and Italian cuisine; two choices from the menu are braised liver with mash, or onions and spaghetti napoli. Unlicensed. *BLD OPEN to 20.30, to 17.00 Sun.* No credit cards.

Diwana Bhel Poori House   1 **E5**
121 Drummond St NW1. 071-387 5556.

Good value vegetarian Indian food. Try the thali, a set meal which includes a variety of delicacies, or bhel poori which are small snacks sold from street stalls in Bombay. *LD OPEN to 23.30. A.Ax.V.*

Gaby's Continental Bar   4 E2
30 Charing Cross Rd WC2. 071-836 4233. Busy Middle Eastern café serving salt beef, pastrami, felafels, houmous and baklava in generous portions. Licensed. *LD OPEN to 24.00, to 22.00 Sun.* No credit cards.

Geales   3 B4
2-4 Farmer St W8. 071-727 7969. Large selection of excellent fish and chips; cod's roe, clams, sole. Varied wine list. *LD OPEN to 23.00. CLOSED Sun & Mon.* A.V.

Jimmy's   4 E2
23 Frith St W1. 071-437 9521. Greek-Cypriot basement restaurant, especially popular with students. Huge helpings at very reasonable prices. Beef stew, moussaka, lamb tava, plus fresh salads, baklava, kataifi. *LD OPEN to 23.00. CLOSED Sun.* No credit cards.

Mustoe Bistro   1 B1
73 Regent's Park Rd NW1. 071-586 0901. Small, intimate bistro popular with locals. Aubergine and yoghurt, eggs madras, garlic or pepper steak. Vegetarian dishes. Good desserts. *D Reserve. OPEN to 23.00, to 22.30 Sun.* No credit cards.

The Nautilus
27-29 Fortune Green Rd NW6. 071-435 2532. As its name suggests, seafood is the order of the day – 18 different sorts including scampi and sole. Soups and salads, too, and a wide range of ice-creams. *LD OPEN to 22.30. CLOSED Sun.* No credit cards.

Pollo   4 E3
20 Old Compton St W1. 071-734 5917. Very busy ground floor and basement restaurant. Huge varied menu – pasta, chicken, steaks, burgers. *LD OPEN to 23.30. CLOSED Sun.* No credit cards.

Le Shop   6 D4
329 King's Rd SW3. 071-352 3891. Large range of sweet and savoury crêpes. Normandy cider, constant classical music. *LD OPEN to 24.00.* A.V.

Spaghetti House   4 E3
24 Cranbourn St WC2. 071-836 8168. There are several branches of this restaurant. Genuine Italian spaghetti houses, friendly and busy. Minestrone, pasta, veal, steak and chicken dishes. Delicious pastries or ice-cream to follow. *LD OPEN to 23.00, to 22.30 Sun. A.Ax.Dc.V.*

Standard   3 C2
23 Westbourne Gro W2. 071-727 4818. Large, popular Indian restaurant serving over 80 specialities including tandoori and vegetarian dishes. Also fish masala. *LD Reserve. OPEN to 23.45. A.Ax.Dc.V.*

Star Café   4 E2
22b Great Chapel St W1. 071-437 8778. Relaxed and friendly restaurant on two floors. Excellent menu featuring unusual dishes such as cauliflower, asparagus and aubergine gratin and poached salmon hollandaise. Licensed. *BLD OPEN to 18.00 Mon-Thur, to 16.00 Fri. CLOSED Sat & Sun.* No credit cards.

Stockpot   4 E3
40 Panton St SW1. 071-839 5142. Crowded, noisy and excellent value. Home-made soups, casseroles and puds at popular prices. *LD OPEN to 23.30, to 22.00 Sun.* Also at 6 Basil St SW3 (**3 G5**). 071-589 8627. *LD OPEN to 22.30, to 22.30 Sun.* No credit cards.

The Three Lanterns   4 E3
5 Panton St SW1. 071-839 5031. Always busy with tourists and theatre-goers. Spanish omelette, chicken and mushroom vol-au-vents and a fabulous mixed grill. Licensed. *LD OPEN to 23.00, to 20.30 Sun.* No credit cards.

Up All Night   6 C4
325 Fulham Rd SW10. 071-352 1996. True to its name. Steaks, hamburgers, chilli, spaghetti, kebabs. *LD OPEN to 06.00.* A.Ax.V.

Wong Kei   4 E3
41-43 Wardour St W1. 071-437 8408. Cheap and cheerful Cantonese restaurant on four floors. Always busy and bustling. *LD OPEN to 23.15.* No credit cards or cheques.

International

These restaurants master a number of different cooking styles and offer an array of authentic tastes from all corners of the globe. Some pick from the best dishes of the world, blending styles and flavours to create distinctive new ones.

Bateaux London   5 A3
Departs from Temple Pier, Victoria Embankment WC2. 071-925 2215. The luxury restaurant cruiser 'Symphony' combines fine dining in a luxurious setting with magnificent views of London from the river. The international menu is freshly prepared on board by the ship's own chef. Music and dancing on dinner cruises. *LD (Reserve).* Lunch cruises depart 12.45, dinner cruises 20.00. *Phone 071-925 2215 for details and reservations.*

Belgo   1 D1
72 Chalk Farm Rd NW1. 071-267 0718.

This is actually a Belgian restaurant which you enter through a tunnel and where the waiters wear habits! Moules au gratin, wild boar sausages with stoemp. Belgian beers. *LD OPEN to 23.30.* A.Ax.V. **££**

The Canteen　　　　　　**6 C6**
Unit 4G Harbour Yard, Chelsea Harbour SW10. 071-351 7330. Owned by Michael Caine and Marco Pierre White. Magnificent views of the marina. Varied menu includes sea-bass, lobster, rump of lamb, with bisquit glacé or lemon tart to follow. *LD Reserve. OPEN to 23.45, to 22.45 Sun.* A.V. **£££**

dell 'Ugo　　　　　　**4 E2**
56 Frith St W1. 071-734 8300. Soho restaurant on three floors. On street level is a café serving salads with Mediterranean produce. Upstairs the restaurant is dominated by one wall of abstract painting. Menu includes squid with lentils, a choice of one-pot dishes and delicious puddings. *LD Reserve. OPEN to 00.15. CLOSED Sun.* A.Ax.V.

East of the Sun West of the　　**5 B4**
Moon
Gabriel's Wharf, Upper Ground SE1. 071-620 0596. Restaurant on two floors overlooking the River Thames. A huge choice of dishes from China, South East Asia, eastern Europe and the Middle East. Also unusual vegetarian dishes. *LD OPEN to 24.00, to 01.00 Fri & Sat.* A.Ax.Dc.V. **£££**

Phood　　　　　　**4 D2**
31 Foubert's Place W1. 071-494 4192. Pale pink and matt black interior; in *summer* the front opens for al fresco dining. Eclectic menu includes Thai fishcakes, eggs Benedict and several vegetarian choices. Snack menu *17.30-19.30. BLD OPEN to 24.00.* A.Ax.V. **££**

Pomegranates　　　　　**7 C4**
94 Grosvenor Rd SW1. 071-828 6560. Highly original and adventurous restaurant with truly international menu. Welsh, Turkish, Malaysian, Greek, French, Italian and Chinese dishes all prepared from first-class ingredients. Multi-national wine list too. *LD Reserve D. OPEN to 23.15. CLOSED L Sat & LD Sun.* A.Ax.Dc.V. **£££**

Quaglino's　　　　　　**4 D4**
16 Bury St SW1. 071-930 6767. Terence Conran's large and glamorous brasserie seating 400. A sweeping staircase descends from the entrance foyer (where a shop sells foodstuffs offered on the menu) to a bar and antipasti bar. From there a marble staircase descends to the main restaurant. Varied menu; crustacea,

plateau de fruits de mer, black pudding, roast duck with coriander and ginger. Live music and dancing to *03.00 Fri & Sat. LD Reserve. OPEN to 24.00, to 02.00 Fri & Sat, to 23.00 Sun.* A.Ax.Dc.V. **£££**

South of the Border　　　**5 C4**
8 Joan St SE1. 071-928 6374. Converted warehouse with a bar on the ground floor overlooked by a balcony. Outside terrace for dining in summer. Indonesian food such as rijstafel, Japanese-style tempura prawns and some Australian dishes including Carpet Bag Australasian. Home-made desserts, ice-cream or cheese. *LD OPEN to 23.30. CLOSED L Sat & LD Sun.* A.Ax.Dc.V. **££**

The Wilds　　　　　　**6 B5**
356 Fulham Rd SW10. 071-376 5553. An unusual mixture of African and European cuisine is reflected in the burnished walls and swagged wall-hangings. Memorable dishes such as Gruyere and spinach crêpes, spicy shrimp salad with chillis. *L (Fri-Sun only) D (Mon-Sat) OPEN to 23.30.* A.V. **£££**

Italian

There are plenty of places to eat Italian food in London, from old-fashioned ristorantes and trattorias to the new style of restaurants where chefs draw on Italian ingredients to produce their own interpretations of traditional dishes.

L'Accento　　　　　　**3 C2**
16 Garway Rd W2. 071-243 2201. Excellent food at this busy restaurant. Tagliatelle with walnut sauce, ravioli filled with pumpkin purée, gnocchi with saffron and courgettes. All-Italian wine list. *LD OPEN to 23.30. CLOSED L Sat & LD Sun.* A.V. **££**

Biagi's　　　　　　**4 A2**
39 Upper Berkeley St W1. 071-723 0394. Well-run, intimate trattoria decorated with fishing nets. Good varied Italian dishes. Scalloppine alla crema, entrecôte alla pizzaiola, saltimbocca. *LD Reserve. OPEN to 23.00.* A.Ax.Dc.V. **££**

Café Italien des Amis du Vin　**4 D1**
19 Charlotte St W1. 071-636 4174. Brasserie and more formal dining rooom in which to sample classic Italian dishes. Tables on a raised platform outside during *summer.* Vegetarian dishes. Italian wines. *LD OPEN to 23.00.* Restaurant *CLOSED LD Sun.* A.Ax.Dc.V. **££**

Cibo
3 Russell Gdns W14. 071-371 6271. Modern, elegant dining room serving regional dishes. Menu changes weekly and may include gnocchi in duck sauce,

baked sea bass with herbs or grilled scallop kebab in basil and lemon sauce. *LD OPEN to 23.00. CLOSED L Sat & LD Sun.* A.Ax.Dc.V. **£££**

La Famiglia   6 C4
5 Langton St SW10. 071-351 0761. Lively and very popular. High standard of cooking – pasta and fagioli, sea bream with fennel, tiramisu. Tables in the garden during summer. *LD OPEN to 24.00.* A.Ax.Dc.V. **£££**

L'Incontro   7 A3
87 Pimlico Rd SW1.071-730 6327. Sumptuous, comfortable restaurant with a wealthy clientele enjoying Venetian cooking. Salt cod with olive oil, cuttlefish in ink with polenta. Excellent Italian wines. *LD Reserve. OPEN to 23.30, to 22.30 Sun. CLOSED L Sat & Sun.* A.Ax.Dc.V. **£££+**

Leoni's Quo Vadis   4 E2
26-29 Dean St W1. 071-437 4809. Pretty pastel dining room in one of Soho's oldest buildings where Karl Marx lived while he was writing *Das Kapital*. The specialities are rich, traditional Italian dishes. Excellent courteous service. *LD Reserve. OPEN to 23.15, to 22.30 Sun. CLOSED L Sat & Sun.* A.Ax.Dc.V. **£££**

Luigi's
15 Tavistock St WC2. 071-240 1795. Something of an institution now. Luigi's is crowded and popular with after-theatre diners. Photographs of entertainment personalities decorate the walls. Good, authentic food: cannelloni, mussels grilled with garlic and breadcrumbs, veal and chicken dishes. Extensive wine list. *LD Reserve. OPEN to 23.30. CLOSED Sun.* A.Dc.V. **£££**

Mezzaluna   4 F2
Thomas Neal Centre, 22 Shorts Gdns WC2. 071-379 3336. One of the new style of Italian restaurants, serving innovative pastas and salads, and pizzas baked in a wood-fire stove. Welcoming and friendly. *LD OPEN to 23.00, to 24.00 Fri & Sat.* A.Ax.Dc.V. **££**

Mimmo d'Ischia
61 Elizabeth St SW1. 071-730 5406. Bright, exciting restaurant on two floors. Original and imaginative dishes. Good spigola. *LD Reserve. OPEN to 23.15. CLOSED Sun.* A.Ax.Dc.V. **£££**

Opera Terrazza!   4 F3
45 East Terrace, Covent Garden WC2. 071-379 0666. Informal conservatory-style trattoria with large outdoor terrace overlooking Covent Garden piazza. Serves new-wave Italian cuisine; fresh pasta dishes, chargrilled chicken and fish. Live music. *LD OPEN to 23.30.* A.Ax.Dc.V. **££**

Orso   4 G3
27 Wellington St WC2. 071-240 5269. Trendy restaurant serving modern Italian food. Daily-changing menu may include grilled scallops with red and yellow peppers, venison with polenta and small pizzas with various toppings. *LD Reserve. OPEN to 24.00.* No credit cards. **£££**

Osteria Antica Bologna
23 Northcote Rd SW11. 071-978 4771. Lively restaurant serving up innovative regional dishes. You can have your starters as an Italian version of meze (a selection of dishes at once). *LD Reserve. OPEN to 23.00, to 22.30 Sun. CLOSED L Mon & Tue.* A.Ax.V. **££**

Portofino   2 D2
39 Camden Pas N1. 071-226 0884. Small, popular. Good friendly service and excellent cooking. Generous portions. Fresh fish in season. Guitarist *Thur, Fri & Sat. LD OPEN to 23.30. CLOSED Sun & B.hols.* A.Ax.Dc.V. **£££**

Riva
169 Church Rd SW13. 081-748 0434. Dishes inspired by ingredients and cooking methods of northern Italy. Grilled polenta topped with stewed eel and olives, snails cooked with nuts and wild fennel. Pavement seating in *summer. LD Reserve. OPEN to 23.00, to 21.30 Sun. CLOSED L Sat.* A.V. **£££**

River Café
Thames Wharf, Rainville Rd W6. 071-381 8824. Light and airy restaurant serving modern Italian food. Only the freshest possible ingredients are used and the menu changes daily. Superb dishes include chicken stuffed with parsley and garlic, and char-grilled peppers with anchovies. *LD Reserve. OPEN to 21.30. CLOSED D Sun.* A.V. **£££**

San Lorenzo   3 G6
22 Beauchamp Pl SW3. 071-584 1074. One of London's best known Italian restaurants offering a different menu every day. Fashionable clientele who enjoy excellent pasta and bollito misto. Unusual veal and chicken dishes. *LD Reserve. OPEN to 23.30. CLOSED Sun & B.hols.* **£££+**

Terrazza Est   5 B2
109 Fleet St EC4. 071-353 2680. Lively atmosphere in this basement restaurant where opera singing begins around *20.00 Mon-Fri.* Set à la carte menu, salads and pasta dishes are the mainstay. Good desserts. *LD Reserve. OPEN to 23.30. CLOSED Sat & Sun.* A.Ax.Dc.V. **££**

Topo Gigio   4 D3
46 Brewer St W1. 071-437 8516. Appetising Italian food; good minestrone,

cannelloni, petto di pollo, veal escalopes. Helpful service, large portions. *LD Reserve. OPEN to 23.30. CLOSED Sun.* A.Ax.Dc.V. **££**

Japanese

In Japanese cooking only the freshest ingredients are used as a high proportion of food is eaten raw. Ingredients are cooked separately to preserve flavours and are cut to emphasise the natural shape and texture of the food. Plain rice, noodles and miso soup form the basis of any meal; noodle bars are the latest trend. Etiquette is important, however restaurant staff will usually be happy to explain the 'rules'.

Benihana
100 Avenue Rd NW3. 071-586 7118. Lively restaurant where diners are seated round a rectangular grill, facing the chef, as he prepares, with much twirling and flashing of blades, grilled vegetables, seafood, chicken and beef. 12-course Kaiseki meal available. *LD Reserve. OPEN to 24.00, to 22.45 Sun.* A.Ax.Dc.V. L **££** D **£££**

Masako   **4 B2**
6-8 St Christopher's Pl W1. 071-935 1579. Authentic Japanese restaurant with private dining rooms attended by charming waitresses in kimonos. Completely oriental atmosphere. Try the set sukiyaki or tempura meals. *LD OPEN to 22.00. CLOSED Sun.* A.Ax.Dc.V. **£££+**

Miyama   **4 C4**
38 Clarges St W1. 071-499 2443. Extensive menu at this friendly Japanese restaurant. Teppan-yaki counter, sushi bar and private tatami rooms. *LD OPEN to 22.30. CLOSED L Sat & LD Sun.* A.Ax.Dc.V. L **££** D **£££+**

Ninjin   **1 D5**
244 Great Portland St W1. 071-388 4657. This restaurant below a Japanese supermarket is inexpensive, comfortable and friendly. Comprehensive menu and generous portions. Good selection of Kushiyaki (meat skewers). *LD Reserve. OPEN to 22.00. CLOSED LD Sun.* A.Ax.Dc.V. L **££** D **£££**

Suntory   **4 D4**
72 St James's St SW1. 071-409 0201. Elegant restaurant with traditional touches. Try teppan-yaki, sushi or sashimi, all exquisitely prepared. Private tatanu rooms. *LD Reserve. OPEN to 22.00. CLOSED LD Sun.* A.Ax.Dc.V. L **££** D **£££+**

Wagamama   **4 F1**
4 Streatham St WC1. 071-323 9223. A basement noodle bar with simple decor. Emphasis on the menu is on health and balance. Huge bowls of ramen noodle soup and fried rice or noodles topped with vegetables, chicken or seafood. Super-efficient waiters and waitresses send your order direct to the kitchen via hand-held computer pads. Be prepared to queue to get in. Non-smoking. *LD (no reservations). OPEN to 23.00.* No credit cards. **£**

Jewish

Orthodox Jews are allowed to eat only fish with scales and cloven-hoofed animals which chew the cud, and may not mix dairy products with meat. Menus usually show an East European and Middle Eastern influence although American/Jewish cuisine, served in New-York style delis, is becoming more popular.

Bloom's   **5 G2**
90 Whitechapel High St E1. 071-247 6835. And 130 Golders Green Rd NW11. 081-455 1338. Bustling Kosher restaurants. Large helpings; lockshen soup and meatballs, salt beef, stuffed kishka. *LD OPEN to 21.30. CLOSED D Fri, LD Sat & Jewish hols.* A.Ax.V. **££**

Harry Morgan's
31 St John's Wood High St NW8. 071-722 1869. All-Jewish menu care of Mrs Morgan. Very reasonable prices. Gefilte fisch, latkes (sweet, fried, crisp potato pancakes), blintzes, Hungarian goulash, black cherry cheesecake. *LD OPEN to 22.00. CLOSED D Fri.* No credit cards. **££**

The Kosher Luncheon Club
Morris Kasler Hall, 13 Greatorex St E1. 071-247 0039. The last of a tradition of East End Kosher lunch clubs, originally soup kitchens for Jewish workers. Now serves good-quality, inexpensive dairy and fish meals. *L OPEN to 15.00. CLOSED Sat.* No credit cards. **£**

Reuben's   **4 B1**
20a Baker St W1. 071-935 5945. Simple, kosher deli and take-away with first-floor restaurant, in the oldest building in Baker Street. Salt beef, chopped liver, gefilte fisch, lockshen pudding. *LD Reserve Sun. OPEN to 22.00. CLOSED D Fri & LD Sat.* A.V. **££**

Widow Appelbaum's   **4 C2**
46 South Molton St W1. 071-629 4649. American-Jewish deli offering 101 dishes. Mirrors and photos of New York in the jazz age. Wooden bench seating with tables outside in *summer*. Matzo balls,

hot salt beef and pastrami, apfelstrüdel and ice-cream sodas. *LD OPEN to 22.00.* A.Ax.Dc.V. **£**

Korean

Bulgogi is the Korean speciality – meat marinated in a spicy sauce and barbecued at the table. Seafood and fish also feature strongly. Kim chee (preserved cabbage dish) accompanies everything; other common ingredients are garlic, ginger and soy sauce. Desserts are simple, but fruit-cutting is a dazzling Korean art.

Arirang   **4 D2**
31-32 Poland St W1. 071-437 9662. This was the first Korean restaurant in London. Waitresses in national dress steer you through the large menu which includes yuk kwe (beef strips with sugar, pears and spices), ojingo pokum (hot, sweet squid) and tangsaoyuk (sweet and sour meatballs). *LD Reserve. OPEN to 23.00. CLOSED Sun.* A.Ax.Dc.V. **££**

Jin   **4 E2**
16 Bateman St W1. 071-734 0908. Authentic restaurant with smart white and gold frontage and a glamourous interior. Specialise in set meals which are barbecued at the table. Formal but friendly service. *LD OPEN to 23.00. CLOSED L Sun.* A.Ax.Dc.V. **££**

You Me House
510a Hornsey Rd N19. 071-272 6208. And 33 Pratt St NW1 (**1 E2**). 071-485 7899. Charming family-run bistro offering good-value set menus which may include bintatok (Korean pizza), deep-fried prawns, kim chee and beef dumplings. *D OPEN to 23.30. CLOSED Sun.* No credit cards. **££**

Malaysian, Indonesian & Singaporean

Coconut, peanut and coriander are some of the characteristic flavours in this cuisine. For hotter tastes try sambals (fiery pickles served as condiments). Malaysian specialities include satay – a spicy peanut dip. Singapore boasts mild and creamy curries; Indonesia is famous for rijstafel (a collection of small dishes served with rice).

Bintang
93 Kentish Town Rd NW1. 071-284 1640. Bamboo walls, Malaysian artefacts and crisp white linen. Specialise in seafood. Set menus. Tiger beer available. Friendly service. *LD OPEN to 24.00, to 02.00 Fri & Sat.* A.V. **££**

Melati   **4 E3**
1 Great Windmill St W1. 071-437 2745. Very popular Indonesian restaurant. Rice and noodle dishes, meat and seafood specialities. Fried rice with shredded chicken and shrimps, fish cutlets in coconut sauce. *LD Reserve. OPEN to 23.30, to 00.30 Fri & Sat.* A.Ax.Dc.V. **££**

Nusa Dua   **4 E2**
11-12 Dean St W1. 071-437 3559. Cheerfully decorated restaurant. Crispy prawns in hot dip, grilled fish with ginger and garlic, coconut pancake roll. Very good value set menu. *LD OPEN to 23.30. CLOSED L Sat & Sun.* A.Ax.Dc.V. **£**

Rasa Sayang   **4 E2**
10 Frith St W1. 071-734 8720. Unpretentious restaurant serving authentic Singaporean and Malaysian food. Try the beef satay, prawns, orange chicken. *LD Reserve D. OPEN to 23.30. CLOSED L Sat.* A.Ax.Dc.V. **££**

Singapore Garden
83 Fairfax Rd NW6. 071-328 5314. Friendly atmosphere in this homely restaurant decked out with plants and flowers. Seafood is a speciality, as are the traditional ironpot dishes with chicken, lamb or beef. *LD Reserve. OPEN to 22.45, to 23.15 Fri & Sat.* A.Ax.Dc.V. **££**

Mexican & Tex-Mex

Mexican dishes are largely variations of tortillas (thin corn or flour pancakes), minced or shredded meats, frijoles (red beans cooked until soft and mushy) and chilli. Ceviche (raw fish marinated in lime juice), chicken mole (in a spicy chilli and bitter chocolate sauce) and tamales (pancakes of meat slow-baked in corn husks) are also popular dishes. Rice, avocados and tomatoes are common accompaniments.

Café Pacifico   **4 F2**
5 Langley St WC2. 071-379 7728. Crowded cantina in a converted warehouse. No booking at night, just have a Mexican cocktail while you wait. Young clientele. Guacamole, nachos, tacos, enchiladas, quesadillas, tostados, chilaquiles. Fresh pineapple or helados to follow. *LD Reserve L. OPEN to 23.45, to 22.45 Sun.* A.Ax.V. **££**

Chiquito   **4 E3**
20 Leicester Sq WC2. 071-839 6925. Large, bright restaurant decorated with artefacts and colourful wall-hangings. Fresh ingredients and mild spices are used to prepare north Mexican cuisine; pollo moterez, enchiladas, chimichangas. Mexican fried ice-cream. Margaritas,

Mexican beer. *LD OPEN to 23.45, to 22.45 Sun.* A.Ax.Dc.V. **££**

La Cucaracha   4 E2
12-13 Greek St W1. 071-734 2253. London's first Mexican restaurant, in the cellars of a converted monastery. Hacienda-style decoration with sunny covered terrace at the back. Ceviche, tacos, burritos, avocado Mexicana (baked and stuffed with crabmeat), enchiladas. Spicy and delicious. *LD OPEN to 23.30.* A.Ax.Dc.V. **££**

Down Mexico Way   4 D3
25 Swallow St W1. 071-437 9895. Elaborately decorated with hand-painted tiles and a grand fireplace. An interesting menu including nachos, ceviche, jalapeno muffins, mesquite smoked dishes and marvellous Mexican soup. Occasional live music. *LD OPEN to 23.45, to 22.30 Sun.* A.Ax.Dc.V. **££**

Los Locos   4 F3
24 Russell St WC2. 071-379 0220. Mexican bar and restaurant with lots of Tex-Mex specials. Nachos, tacos, carnitas, steaks, alligator, enchiladas, grilled shrimps, fajitas – cooked over mesquite wood. Limited wine list, Mexican beer and cocktails. Disco *from 23.30 every night. D OPEN to 21.30. Disco to 03.00. CLOSED Sun.* A.Ax.Dc.V. **££**

Middle Eastern

Charcoal grilling is a popular method of cooking throughout the area, and dishes are often spicy. Yoghurt is a common ingredient. Ginger, almonds, nutmeg, coriander and cinnamon are also widely used.

Al Hamra   4 C4
31-33 Shepherd Market W1. 071-493 1954. Elegant Lebanese restaurant. The meze is excellent and features several dishes not commonly available. Also a variety of charcoal-grilled meats and sweet, sugary desserts to follow. Lebanese wine or arak. *LD OPEN to 24.00.* A.Ax.Dc.V. **£££**

Fakhreldine   4 C4
85 Piccadilly W1. 071-493 3424. This huge and elaborately decorated restaurant overlooks Green Park. Extensive list of meze dishes, felafel and pitta, kibbeh, charcoal grills. *LD OPEN to 24.00.* A.Ax.Dc.V. **££-£££**

Hafez   3 B2
5 Hereford Rd W2. 071-229 9398. A small Persian restaurant full of character. Traditional flat breads are baked in the huge mosaic oven at the front. Chelo kebabs are Hafez's speciality. Vegetarian

dishes. *LD OPEN to 24.00.* No credit cards. **££**

La Reash Cous-Cous House   4 E2
23 Greek St W1. 071-439 1063. Not all cous-cous, despite the name; a variety of other dishes popular throughout the Middle East. Try chicken tagine which is served piping hot in a traditional Moroccan cooking pot. Vegetarian dishes. *LD OPEN to 24.00.* A.V. **££**

Tageen   4 F3
12 Upper St Martin's Lane WC2. 071-836 7272. Decorated in true Moroccan style – tiles, mirrors and glass lamps – and the food arrives at your table in tagines (traditional Moroccan cooking pots). Main dishes are all wonderfully marinated. Try the lamb tagine, cooked with prunes and almonds, and seasoned with cinnamon, saffron, pepper and ginger. Moroccan music on *Fri & Sat. LD OPEN to 23.30. CLOSED L Sat & LD Sun.* A.Ax.Dc.V. **££**

Modern European

These restaurants combine the techniques of French and English cooking whilst incorporating ideas and ingredients from around the world. Attractive and fairly expensive, they are pleasant and relaxing places in which to eat.

Alistair Little   4 E2
49 Frith St W1. 071-734 5183. Fashionable restaurant with an imaginative, frequently-changing menu. Asparagus hollandaise, salmon fishcakes, rhubarb and pistachio trifle to follow. *LD Reserve. OPEN to 23.30. CLOSED L Sat & LD Sun.* A.Ax.Dc.V. **£££+**

Bibendum   6 E2
Michelin House, 81 Fulham Rd SW3. 071-581 5817. Lofty dining room in the unusual 1910 Michelin building. Long menu of elegant and inventive French and English dishes is renowned. *LD Reserve. OPEN to 23.30, to 22.30 Sun.* A.V. **£££+**

Chanterelle   6 C3
119 Old Brompton Rd SW7. 071-373 7390. Attractive fresh decor in this crowded restaurant. Generous portions of distinctive Anglo-French dishes. Rack of lamb with mint and olive crust, Arbroath smokie with cream and cheese. Set-price menus change regularly and are excellent value. *LD Reserve. OPEN to 23.30.* A.Ax.Dc.V. **££**

Clarke's   3 B4
124 Kensington Church St W8. 071-221 9225. Cool, modern restaurant offering set lunch and dinner menus. Main courses are often char-grilled; breast of chicken comes served on a rosemary and potato

pancake. Excellent desserts. *LD OPEN to 22.00. CLOSED Sat & Sun*. A.V. **L £££ D £££+**

Hilaire   **6 D2**
63 Old Brompton Rd SW7. 071-584 8993. Bryan Webb, the chef here, is renowned for his excellent cuisine which combines Mediterranean influences and classic cooking. Set and à la carte menus. *LD Reserve. OPEN to 23.30. CLOSED L Sat & LD Sun*. A.Ax.Dc.V. **£££+**

The Ivy   **4 F3**
1 West St WC2. 071-836 4751. Nostalgic dining room serving excellent cuisine. Classic dishes with added modern touches. Impeccable service. European wine list. *LD Reserve. OPEN to 24.00*. A.Ax.Dc.V. **££-£££**

Langan's Bistro   **1 D6**
26 Devonshire St W1. 071-935 4531. Peter Langan's first restaurant, decorated with original Hockneys and Proctors, and inverted parasols. Gratin of Arbroath smokies, avocado and tomato salad with hazelnut sauce, poached salmon trout with dill sauce, breast of chicken with tarragon sauce. Mrs Langan's chocolate mousse is an unmissable dessert. *LD Reserve. OPEN to 23.30. CLOSED L Sat & LD Sun*. A.Ax.Dc.V. **£££**

Langan's Brasserie   **4 C4**
Stratton St W1. 071-493 6437. Buzzing atmosphere and stylish surroundings. Changing menu may include oyster mushrooms, spinach. Soufflé with anchovies, black pudding. Live music *every night*. *LD Reserve. OPEN to 23.30. CLOSED L Sat & LD Sun*. A.Ax.Dc.V. **£££**

Museum Street Café   **4 F1**
47 Museum St WC1. 071-405 3211. Charming decor and piles of freshly-baked bread. Excellent weekly-changing set menu may include tomato and salmon soup, beef sirloin au poivre with spinach gratin, baked red mullet with wild rice. Unlicensed. *LD Reserve. OPEN to 23.00. CLOSED Sat & Sun*. No credit cards. **££**

Odin's   **1 D6**
27 Devonshire St W1. 071-935 7296. Stylish, luxurious restaurant decorated with interesting photographs, prints and paintings. Frequently changing à la carte dishes. Roast duck, rack of lamb, plus seasonal specialities such as game, lobster and mussels. Home-made ice-cream or lemon curd tart to follow. *LD Reserve. OPEN to 23.30. CLOSED L Sat & LD Sun*. A.Ax.Dc.V. **£££**

One Nine Two   **3 A3**
192 Kensington Park Rd W11. 071-229 0482. Trendy wine bar and restaurant.

Daily menu may include fish soup, grilled quail, calves' liver, cheesecake, chocolate truffle cake. Carefully selected wine list. *LD OPEN to 23.30. CLOSED L Mon*. A.Ax.V. **££**

Savoy Grill   **4 G3**
The Savoy Hotel, Strand WC2. 071-836 4343. World-famous, well-deserved reputation for classic English and French cooking. Delightful panelled room, soft lighting and a very fine wine list. *LD Reserve. OPEN to 23.15. CLOSED L Sat & LD Sun*. A.Ax.Dc.V. **£££+**

Stephen Bull   **4 A2**
5 Blandford St W1. 071-486 9696. Black and white decor and artful lighting. Innovative menu changes daily. Good fish dishes, twice-cooked goat's cheese soufflé, langoustines with noodles, ginger and soy, pear and pistachio tart. *LD Reserve. OPEN to 22.45. CLOSED L Sat & LD Sun*. A.V. **£££**

Open-air

More and more London restaurants are providing outdoor seating areas. The following places have pavement or terrace seating or tables in a garden, enclosed courtyard or conservatory.

Anemos   **4 D1**
32 Charlotte St W1. 071-580 5907. Friendly, crowded and noisy. Eat outside at the pavement tables in *summer*. Humous, excellent kebabs, moussaka. *LD Reserve D. OPEN to 01.00. CLOSED Sun*. A.Ax.Dc. **£**

Au Bon Accueil   **6 E2**
19-21 Elystan St SW3. 071-589 3718. Tables set out on the pavement in *summer*. Comfortable French restaurant with good unpretentious cooking – seafood crêpes, venison casserole, jugged hare, pheasant in red wine. *LD Reserve. OPEN to 23.30. CLOSED L Sat & LD Sun*. A.Ax.Dc.V. **££**

Barbican, Waterside Café   **2 E6**
Level 5, Barbican Centre EC2. 071-638 4141. Modern self-service café by the man-made lake of the arts centre. Snacks or full meals. *LD OPEN to 20.00*. No credit cards. **£**

Dan's   **6 E3**
119 Sydney St SW3. 071-352 2718. Bright, airy room with hanging plants and seating for 20 in the garden. Modern European cuisine – warm spinach mousse with basil, rack of lamb with honey and mustard, chocolate truffle cake to follow. *LD OPEN to 22.30. CLOSED L Sun*. Ax.Dc.V. **£££**

La Famiglia   **6 C4**
7 Langton St SW10. 071-351 0761.

Attractive, with pretty rear garden seating 100. Southern Italian cooking. Fourteen types of pasta. Italian wine. *LD OPEN to 24.00.* A.Ax.Dc.V. **££**

Glaisters 6 **C4**
4 Hollywood Rd SW10. 071-352 0352. Pretty walled garden at the back. Wide-ranging menu; anything from burgers to Dover sole. *LD OPEN to 23.30, to 22.30 Sun.* A.V. **££**

San Lorenzo Fuoriporta
Worple Rd Mews SW19. 081-946 8463. Cheerful, lively trattoria with tables in the garden during *summer.* Traditional menu – scalloppine di vitello alla San Lorenzo, petti di pollo, good fresh vegetables and home-made pasta. *LD Reserve. OPEN to 23.00, to 22.30 Sun.* A.Ax.Dc.V. **£££**

Scandinavian

Fish, salads, fruit, cheese and wholegrain bread make this type of cooking extremely healthy. The traditional smørgasbørd is a good way to sample lots of dishes at once.

Anna's Place
90 Mildmay Pk N1. 071-249 9379. Small, intimate restaurant offering excellent home-made Swedish cooking and hospitable service. For starters, camembert with parsley, then gravadlax, beef or herring, duck breast with Swedish cabbage. *LD Reserve. OPEN to 22.45. CLOSED Sun & Mon.* No credit cards. **££**

Copenhagen Pâtisserie
196 Haverstock Hill NW3. 071-435 7711. A variety of open sandwiches, cakes and pastries. Pavement seating. *OPEN to 20.00, to 22.00 Sat & Sun.* No credit cards. **£**

Garbo's 4 **A1**
42 Crawford St W1. 071-262 6582. Also at 14 Little Chester St SW1 (4 **C6**). Pleasant restaurant serving Scandinavian home cooking. Try the herring salad Baltic, cabbage stuffed with minced pork, beef and rice or the smoked eel. Lunchtime smørgasbørd. Imported Swedish beer and schnapps. *LD Reserve D. OPEN to 24.00. CLOSED L Sat & Sun.* A.Ax.V. **££**

Spanish & Portuguese

Although Spanish cuisine varies from region to region, fish and seafood are the common ingredients, often cooked in garlic and olive oil. Tapas bars, serving simple snacks, are still popular in London. Stews, soups and simple fish dishes form the basis of Portuguese cooking.

Bar Gansa 1 **D2**
2 Inverness St NW1. 071-267 8909. One of the best tapas bars in London with a lively crowd and occasional live music. *OPEN to 24.00, to 22.30 Sun.* A.V. **£**

El Bodegon 6 **C4**
9 Park Wlk SW10. 071-352 1330. Small tapas bar in the basement and a restaurant on the ground floor. The food is well presented. Gambas al pil-pil (prawns in a hot garlic sauce), paella, zarzuela. Year-round patio seating. *LD OPEN to 24.00.* A.Ax.Dc.V. **££**

Caravela 3 **F5**
39 Beauchamp Pl SW3. 071-581 2366. Small, intimate, Portuguese restaurant. King prawns piri piri, fresh grilled sardines. Delicious orange roll dessert. Wine list exclusively Portuguese. Guitarists or fado singer *Tue-Sun. LD Reserve. OPEN to 01.00, to 24.00 Sun. CLOSED L Sun.* A.Ax.Dc.V. **£££**

Casa Santana
44 Golborne Rd W10. 081-968 8764. Lively, jolly Portuguese restaurant with a rustic feel. Hearty servings of traditional stews and fish dishes. Live guitar music *Fri-Sun. LD OPEN to 23.00.* A.Ax.Dc.V. **££**

Galicia 3 **A2**
323 Portobello Rd W10. 081-969 3539. Crowded restaurant where tapas are served at the bar. The Spanish chef prepares authentic dishes which include marinated anchovies and pulpo a la Gallega (octopus served on a wooden plate with rock salt and pimentos). Good selection of Galician wines. *LD OPEN to 23.30. CLOSED Mon.* A.Ax.V. **££**

Triñanes
298 Kentish Town Rd NW5. 071-482 3616. Serves tapas divided into vegetable, meat and seafood varieties. Small selection of more substantial dishes. Live music and flamenco dancing. *LD OPEN to 02.00, to 01.00 Sun. CLOSED L Sat.* No credit cards. **££**

El Rincon Latino
148 Clapham Manor St SW4. 071-622 0599. Very popular restaurant run by two half-Spanish, half-Colombian sisters. Authentic Spanish and Latin American food. Excellent wine list. Spanish breakfast of chocolate con churros is served *11.00-14.00 Sat. LD Reserve. OPEN to 24.00. CLOSED Sun.* A.Ax.V. **££**

Thai & Vietnamese

Thai cuisine encompasses many different flavours and styles of cooking, and uses interesting mixtures of meat, seafood and vegetables. Dishes tend to be spicy with either sweet and sour or hot chilli sauces, and are always beautifully presented. Vietnamese cuisine is a combination of Chinese and French cooking. Root ginger, coriander, coconut milk, chilli and lemon grass are common ingredients.

Bahn Thai   **4 E2**

21a Frith St W1. 071-437 8504. High-quality authentic Thai food make this a very popular restaurant where the dishes are chilli-rated for spiciness! Thai specialities like crispy frog's legs and Thai blue swimming crab. *LD OPEN to 23.15, to 22.30 Sun.* A.Ax.Dc.V. **££**

Blue Elephant   **6 A5**

4-6 Fulham Bdwy SW6. 071-385 6595. One of London's best Thai restaurants. The surroundings resemble a tropical jungle and the food is beautifully presented, Royal Thai style, by unobtrusive waiters and waitresses in Thai costume. Excellent *Sun* brunch buffet. *LD OPEN to 00.30. CLOSED L Sat.* A.Ax.Dc.V. **£££**

Bonjour Vietnam   **6 A5**

593-599 Fulham Rd SW6. 071-385 7603. One of the Zen chain of restaurants. A huge 30ft fish tank is part of the relaxed, welcoming atmosphere. Sample traditional and new-wave Vietnamese dishes such as Saigon spicy chicken with chilli or steamed scallops. *LD OPEN to 23.30, to 23.00 Sun.* A.Ax.Dc.V. **££**

Chiang Mai   **4 E2**

48 Frith St W1. 071-437 7444. Light, airy restaurant serving authentic Thai cuisine. Chilli-hot grated papaya salad, pad Thai noodles, khao soi (chicken curry soup with noodles). Set menus. *LD Reserve. OPEN to 23.00.* A.Ax.V. **££**

Pho   **4 E3**

2 Lisle St W1. 071-437 8265. A very popular, thriving café-style restaurant serving freshly-cooked food. Try the Vietnamese soup (Pho) which is a wonderful blend of flavours and textures. *LD OPEN to 23.30.* No credit cards. **£**

Sri Siam   **4 E3**

14 Old Compton St W1. 071-434 3544. Also at 85 London Wall EC2 **5 E1**). Popular Thai restaurant, attracting a fashionable crowd. The food is excellent; beautifully cooked and presented. The soups and stir-fry dishes are particularly popular. Set lunch menu. *LD OPEN to 23.15, to 22.30 Sun. CLOSED L Sun.* A.Ax.Dc.V. **££**

Van Long   **4 E2**

40 Frith St W1. 071-434 3772. Attractive, modern Vietnamese restaurant. Excellent soups and superior seafood dishes. Long menu but set meals help the uninitiated. *LD OPEN to 23.30. CLOSED Sun.* A.Ax.Dc.V. **££**

Vegetarian & wholefood

Vegetarian restaurants are very popular in London and some of the best are listed below. See also the 'Indian' and 'Inexpensive' sections. For further information contact the Vegetarian Society: 061-928 0793. It publishes the International Vegetarian Travel Guide, *which includes a directory of vegetarian restaurants, shops, guest houses and hotels throughout the UK and the world.*

Café Santé   **4 F3**

17 Garrick St WC2. 071-240 7811. New-style vegetarian café with sleek black tables and chairs. Interesting salads, hot dishes which change daily, plus a few non-vegetarian meals. Unlicensed. *LD OPEN to 23.30, to 19.00 Sun.* No credit cards. **£**

Cranks   **4 D2**

8 Marshall St W1. 071-437 9431. This branch was the first of London's original healthfood restaurants. Having been bought out of receivership, the chain has been re-launched and is once again serving innovative vegetarian dishes. Try the vegan tofu-topped lentil quiche or the nut burger with couscous, beans and almonds. Other branches. *LD Reserve D. OPEN to 20.00. CLOSED Sun.* A.V. **£-££**

Food For Thought   **4 F2**

31 Neal St WC2. 071-836 0239. Daily-changing menu always features a soup, a salad, stir-fried vegetables and a few hot dishes. Good choice of puddings too. Always busy. Unlicensed. Non-smoking. *BLD OPEN to 20.00, to 16.30 Sun.* No credit cards. **£**

Fungus Mungus

Not the most attractive name for this 1960s-style cluttered bar but the food is surprisingly good. International vegetarian dishes, wholesome puddings, exotic beers. *L (Sun only) D OPEN to 24.00, to 23.00 Sun.* No credit cards. **££**

The Gate

51 Queen Caroline St W6. 081-748 6932. Tucked behind the Hammersmith Apollo above a Christian Community Centre, this is an airy, spacious restaurant. Innovative dishes like pea and mint soup and shiitake mushroom and spinach lasagne. Organic wines and beers. *LD OPEN to 22.45. CLOSED Sun.* A.Ax.Dc.V. **££**

de Las Casas

153 Clapham High St SW4. 071-738 8760. A trendy, brightly-decorated restaurant/café. Newspapers, chess and

backgammon boards provided on request. Soups are a must, blue cheese and celery, followed by tofu and fennel goulash with rice or apple. Tempting cheesecakes and trifles. Occasional evening entertainment. *LD OPEN to 23.00 (to 18.00 Sun & Mon).* No credit cards. **£**

Leith's   **3 A3**
92 Kensington Park Rd W11. 071-229 4481. Up-market restaurant with an excellent vegetarian menu. Hot and cold starters such as artichoke pie and asparagus mousse. Beautifully presented main courses and hand-made sweets. *D Reserve. OPEN to 23.30.* A.Ax.Dc. V. **£££+**

Mandeer   **4 E2**
21 Hanway Pl W1. 071-323 0660. Highly-acclaimed pioneering Indian vegetarian and wholefood restaurant. Specialities include aubergine bhajis, thali Mandeer or puffed lotus savoury. Generous set menu available. Also a very reasonable self-service cafeteria. Licensed. *LD OPEN to 21.45. CLOSED Sun.* A.Ax.Dc.V. **£**

Mildred's   **4 E2**
58 Greek St W1. 071-494 1634. Trendy glass-fronted café with an excellent vegetarian and vegan menu. Organic produce is used wherever possible. Also fish and seafood dishes. The vegetable stir-fry with satay sauce is popular. Organic wines and beers. Herbal teas. *LD OPEN to 23.00. CLOSED Sun.* No credit cards. **£**

Neal's Yard Dining Rooms   **4 F2**
14 Neal's Yard WC2. 071-379 0298. A light, airy vegetarian restaurant where you can either sit at the bar or at large shared tables. International dishes include Egyptian pitta, Indian thali, Turkish meze and Indonesian sambal. Unlicensed. Non-smoking. *LD OPEN to 20.00 (to 17.00 Mon, to 18.00 Sat). CLOSED Sun.* No credit cards. **£**

The Place Below   **5 D2**
St Mary-le-Bow, Cheapside EC2. Situated in the crypt of St Mary-le-Bow, this is an excellent café which offers a short menu of lunch dishes and a gourmet vegetarian menu on *Thur & Fri* evenings. Roquefort terrine, aubergine and fennel casserole, fresh exotic fruit. Home-made olive and garlic bread, home-made lemonade. Unlicensed. Non-smoking. *LD Reserve D. OPEN to 15.00 Mon-Wed, to 22.30 Thur & Fri.* No credit cards. L **£** D **££**

Vijay
49 Willesden La NW6. 071-328 1087.

Traditional south Indian vegetarian food served here as well as tasty meat curries for any non-vegetarian friends. Try their masala dosai, sambar or vegetables cooked in yoghurt and coconut. Genuine Indian sweets – almond cakes and kulfi. *LD Reserve. OPEN to 22.45, to 23.45 Fri & Sat.* A.Ax.Dc.V. **£**

Breakfast and brunch

'Hot bread' and pastries can be obtained as early as 06.00 from bakeries. Continental-style cafés, brasseries and pâtisseries serve fresh croissants and coffee and more substantial brunches. For a traditional English breakfast try the cafés around markets and main-line stations or splash out at one of the traditional hotels. Times are given for breakfast or brunch only. Price symbols for this section only are: £ under £5; ££ £5-£10; £££ over £10.

Cafés, brasseries and pâtisseries

Bartholomew's   **5 C1**
57a West Smithfield EC1. 071-606 3903. Traditional English. *OPEN 07.00-11.00. CLOSED Sat & Sun.* A.Ax.Dc.V. **£-££**

La Brasserie   **6 E2**
272 Brompton Rd SW3. 071-584 1668. French-style café serving continental breakfast. *OPEN all day from 08.00 Mon-Sat, & 10.00 Sun.* A.Ax.Dc.V. **£££**

Fleur de Lys   **6 C1**
13a Gloucester Rd SW7. 071-589 4045. Pâtisserie where everything is baked on the premises. *OPEN from 08.00 Mon-Sat.* No credit cards. **£**

Hotels

Serve breakfast to non-residents from around 07.00 (08.00 Sun).

Brown's Hotel   **4 C3**
Dover St W1. 071-493 6020. English or Continental. A.Ax.Dc.V. **£££**

Cadogan   **6 F1**
75 Sloane St SW1. 071-235 7141. English or Continental. A.Ax.Dc.V. **£££**

Claridge's   **4 C3**
Brook St W1. 071-629 8860. English, à la carte or Continental. A.V. **££-£££**

Hyde Park Hotel   **4 B5**
66 Knightsbridge SW7. 071-235 2000.

English, Continental or à la carte. A.Ax.Dc.V. **£££**

Ritz 4 D4
Piccadilly W1. 071-493 8181. English, à la carte or Continental. A.Ax.Dc. V. **£££**

Savoy 4 G3
Strand WC2. 071-836 4343. English or Continental. A.Ax.Dc.V. **£££**

Afternoon tea

Afternoon tea is a British institution; at one time very fashionable. Most large department stores such as Fortnum & Mason, Selfridges and Harrods serve afternoon tea in their restaurants but if you want to avoid the hustle and bustle of busy shopping areas, the following pâtisseries and hotels are your best bet.

Tea & cakes

Maison Sagne 1 C6
105 Marylebone High St W1. 071-935 6240. Traditional tea shop with its own bakery and delicious pâtisserie. Afternoon tea served *15.00-17.00 Mon-Fri*.

The Muffin Man 6 B1
12 Wright's La W8. 071-937 6652. A range of set teas: Devon, 'Muffin Man', traditional. Served *all day Mon-Sat*.

Pâtisserie Valerie 4 E2
44 Old Compton St W1. 071-437 3466. Soho pâtisserie with tea, coffee and hot chocolate. Excellent cream cakes and sandwiches. Served *all day Mon-Sun*. Other branches.

Tea in hotels

Excellent service and a comfortable sense of welcome. Expect to pay between £10-£15 for a full tea.

Brown's 4 D3
Dover St W1. 071-493 6020. Very English, country house setting. Sandwiches, cakes, tarts. Served *15.00-18.00*.

Claridge's 4 C3
Brook St W1. 071-629 8860. A touch of class in the comfortable reading room, where liveried footmen serve sandwiches and assorted pastries. *Reserve*. Served *15.00-17.30*.

Dorchester 4 B4
Park La W1. 071-629 8888. Dainty sandwiches, cakes and pastries in opulent surroundings. Served *15.00-17.45*.

Ritz 4 D4
Piccadilly W1. 071-493 8181. A good comfortable hotel. Tea in the Palm Court, with dainty sandwiches, pastries and cream cakes. *Reserve*. Served at 15.15 & 16.30.

Thé dansant

Waldorf Hotel 4 G3
Aldwych WC2. 071-836 2400. Opulent Palm Court tea lounge with comfort and good service. Edwardian elegance. Dancing to the band and full set tea *Sat & Sun 15.30-18.30 (Reserve).*

Ice-cream

Baskin-Robbins
Delicious American ice-cream, 31 flavours. OPEN 11.00-23.00.
Empire Cinema, Leicester Sq WC2. 4 E3 071-734 8222.
Plaza Cinema, Lower Regent St W1. 4 E3 071-930 0144.

Dayvilles
More delicious ice-cream. 32 flavours.
264a Earl's Court Rd SW5. 6 A3 071-370 0083. OPEN 09.00-23.00.
2 The Mall W5. 081-567 3778.
OPEN 11.00-24.00 (to 01.00 Fri).

Haagen-Dazs
16 flavours of American ice-cream.
75 Hampstead High St NW3. 071-794 0646. OPEN 10.00-23.00.
138a Kings Rd SW3. 071-823 5 F3 9326. OPEN 10.00-23.00.
The Piazza WC2. 071-240 0436. 4 F3 OPEN 10.00-23.00.
Leicester Sq WC2. 071-287 9577. 4 E3 OPEN 10.00-24.00.

Marine Ices 1 C1
8 Haverstock Hill NW3. 071-485 3132. Huge choice of Italian ice-cream and water ices. Also restaurant. OPEN 10.30-23.00 (to 19.00 Sun).

Pubs

The British pub is an institution which has evolved from the Saxon alehouse, the medieval tavern and inn, to the Victorian 'public house'. For centuries London was one of the great brewing capitals; in the 11thC the Domesday Book recorded that the monks of St Paul's Cathedral brewed 67,000 gallons of ale annually. In the 12thC children drank beer as a preventative to typhoid. In 1437 a Brewers' Company was set up and many breweries were established alongside the Thames. In the 16thC workmen's wives blended malt, yeast, water and sugar at home. By the end of the 17thC there was a switch from unhopped, heavy and sweet ale to lighter and more bitter hopped beer. By 1733 there were almost 100 gin shops (drinking houses) in St Giles next to tuppenny brothels. A publican's placard in Southwark promised: 'Drunk for 1d. Dead drunk for 2d. Clean straw for nothing'. The rise of gin palaces resulted from the Beerhouse Act of 1830 which permitted the unlicensed sale of beer. Throngs of gin palace patrons spurred the brewers into improving their premises and it was out of these gin mills, taverns and inns that London's 7000 pubs evolved.

The British pub has always been a great meeting place and a venue for games (such as darts and dominoes) and entertainment (Shakespeare presented his plays in taverns, and Music Hall was born in Victorian pubs). Today London's thriving fringe theatre and music scene is largely based in pubs.

The variety of London's pubs is enormous; historic pubs in the City, modern pubs of unusual design and decor, riverside pubs, theatre pubs.

Traditional pub hours are 11.00-15.00 & 17.30-23.00 Mon-Sat, 12.00-14.30 & 19.00-22.30 Sun. However, these have been relaxed and pubs are officially allowed to open 11.00-23.00 Mon-Sat (no change to Sun hours). Not all pubs take advantage of the new opening hours so it is advisable to check in advance. Many pubs in the City are closed on Sat & Sun and also close early at around 21.00.

L lunch **D** *dinner* **B** *bar food. Most pubs serve snacks.*

🢒 *sign means open all day, 11.00-23.00 Mon-Sat, 12.00-14.30 & 19.00-22.30 Sun.*

Nicholson's London Pub Guide *gives more detailed information on where to drink in the capital.*

Argyll Arms   **4 D2**
18 Argyll St W1. 071-734 6117. 300-year-old pub which has retained all its traditional features. The old manager's pulpit-like office still stands in the middle of the main bar. **B L D**

Barley Mow   **5 C1**
50 Long La EC1. 071-606 6591. Built on the site of a monastery, this 400-year-old inn specialises in real ale and bitter. Stylish Edwardian interior, exposed beams. **B**

Blackfriar   **5 C3**
174 Queen Victoria St EC4. 071-236 5650. Triangular building near Blackfriars

station. Stunning art nouveau temple of marble and bronze; lunchtime hot and cold bar food and cold buffet in the evening. **B**

🢒 **Buckingham Arms**   **4 D6**
62 Petty France SW1. 071-222 3386. Attractive mid-Victorian pub. Gathering place for business people. **B**

🢒 **Bunch of Grapes**   **6 E1**
207 Brompton Rd SW3. 071-589 4944. Victorian pub with finely engraved snob-screens separating the bars and impressively carved wooden pillars. Traditional ales. **B L D**

🢒 **Captain's Cabin**   **4 E3**
4-7 Norris St, Haymarket SW1. 071-930 4767. A cosy nautical pub well situated for a pre-theatre drink. **B**

Cartoonist   **5 B2**
76 Shoe La EC4. 071-353 2828. In the heart of the old newspaper world, this Victorian pub is wallpapered with cartoons. Its outside sign is changed every year, the design being chosen from those submitted by cartoonists. Headquarters of the International Cartoonist Club. **B**

🢒 **Chelsea Potter**   **6 E3**
119 King's Rd SW3. 071-352 9479. Trendy meeting place for the locals with an alternative juke box in the bar. **B L**

🢒 **Cheshire Cheese**   **5 B3**
5 Little Essex St WC2. 071-836 2347. Intimate Jacobean pub with original oak beams and three bars. **B L**

Cheshire Cheese, Ye Olde   **5 B2**
145 Fleet St EC4. 071-353 6170. Rebuilt after the Great Fire with low-ceilinged interiors, oak tables, sawdust on the floor. Although new bars have been added, most of this pub hasn't changed much since Dr Johnson used to drop in. Snacks and good traditional English cooking. **L D**

🢒 **Cittie of York**   **5 A1**
22-23 High Holborn WC1. 071-242 7670. A huge pub in the Victorian grand manner with cosy cubicles where lawyers used to have confidential chats with their clients. Cellar bar. **B D**

🢒 **Cock Tavern, Ye Olde**   **5 B2**
22 Fleet St EC4. 071-353 8570. Lawyers have replaced the journalists who used to frequent this tavern with literary and Dickensian associations and mementoes. Nell Gwynne, Pepys and Garrick once drank here. Carvery restaurant which also serves fish, puddings, pies and vegetarian dishes. **B L**

🢒 **Crown & Two Chairmen**   **4 E2**
31 Dean St W1. 071-437 8192. Earned its name nearly 200 years ago by playing host to royalty who arrived by sedan chair – a crown carried by two chairmen. Real

ale, hot and cold bar food. Rub shoulders with writers and people from the film world. **B**

Dirty Dick's   **5 F1**
202-204 Bishopsgate EC2. 071-283 5888. The original pub named after Nat Bentley, well-known 18thC miser of the ballad. Remnants of mummified cats and mouse skeletons are preserved behind glass. **B L**

Dover Castle   **1 D6**
43 Weymouth Mews W1. 071-636 9248. Mews pub patronised by BBC staff. Fourteen different types of sausage available. **B**

Duke of Cumberland
235 New King's Rd SW6. 071-736 2777. Edwardian elegance prevails. Popular with the young and trendy. Summertime drinking on Parson's Green. Real ale. **B**

Duke of Wellington   **7 A2**
63 Eaton Ter SW1. 071-730 3103. Traditional pub – pictures of the Iron Duke abound as do brass and copperware. Used by shoppers and workers as well as Chelsea locals. Good snacks. **B**

Eagle   **2 E4**
2 Shepherdess Wlk N1. 071-253 4715. Victorian music hall immortalised in the song *Pop goes the Weasel*. People used to spend their money here after 'popping the weasel', ie after pawning their possessions. Barbecues in *summer*. **B**

Edgar Wallace   **5 B3**
40 Essex St WC2. 071-353 3120. On an original Elizabethan site but now with the famous writer as the theme of the pub. Dr Johnson and his circle used to meet here regularly once a week. Small upstairs restaurant. **B L**

Fox & Grapes
Camp Rd, Wimbledon Common SW19. 081-946 5599. Julius Caesar camped near here. Mock Tudor pub rambling right on to the common. Good lunches, though limited menu on *Sun*. **B L**

Flask
77 Highgate West Hill N6. 081-340 3969. Dating back to 1663, this tavern is named after the flasks which people used to buy here to fill with water at the Hampstead wells. Highwayman Dick Turpin once hid in the cellars and William Hogarth and Karl Marx both drank here. Crowded forecourt for outdoor drinking. **B L**

French House   **4 E2**
49 Dean St W1. 071-437 2799. Centre for the Free French during the war. De Gaulle drank here as did Brendan Behan and Dylan Thomas. Good wines. **B L D**

George   **5 B2**
213 Strand WC2. 071-353 9238. Fine old

timbered inn built in 1723. Stands opposite the Royal Courts of Justice. Upstairs carvery. **B L**

George Inn   **5 E4**
77 Borough High St SE1. 071-407 2056. Unique galleried coaching inn rebuilt in 1676 after the Great Fire of Southwark. Featured in Dickens' *Little Dorrit*. Courtyard entertainment in *summer*. Wine bar with good selection of wines, pâtés and cheeses. Restaurant. **B L D**

Globe   **4 F2**
37 Bow St WC2. 071-836 0219. Nearest pub to the Royal Opera House, frequented by members of the orchestra. Used in Hitchcock's *Frenzy*. **B**

Golden Lion   **4 D4**
25 King St SW1. 071-930 7227. Traditional Victorian pub with Oscar Wilde and Lillie Langtry associations. **B L**

Green Man
Putney Heath SW15. 081-788 8096. 15thC ale house overlooking the Heath. Associated with duels and highwaymen. Barbecues in *summer*. **B L**

Grenadier   **4 B5**
18 Wilton Row SW1. 071-235 3074. Once an officers' mess for the Duke of Wellington's soldiers. Full of military bric-à-brac. **B L D**

The Guinea   **4 C3**
30 Bruton Pl W1. 071-409 1728. Pleasant old pub hidden away in a narrow, cobbled Mayfair mews. Originally known as the One Pound One, probably because of the cattle pound that once stood nearby. Became The Guinea in the reign of Charles II when the gold coin of the same name was first minted. Good but pricey English dining room. **B L D**

Holly Bush
22 Holly Mount, Heath St NW3. 071-435 2892. Unspoiled, pleasant pub in picturesque setting. Olde-worlde with gas lighting and open fires in winter. *Sun* lunches. **B**

Island Queen   **2 D3**
87 Noel Rd N1. 071-226 5507. Has without doubt the most outlandish decor of any pub in London; giant papier-mâché caricatures of politicians and famous figures are suspended from the ceiling! **B D**

King of Bohemia
10 Hampstead High St NW3. 071-435 6513. Bow- fronted Georgian pub – a fashionable local. **B**

King's Head & Eight Bells   **6 E4**
50 Cheyne Wlk SW3. 071-352 1820. 18thC decor with pots, jugs and prints of old Chelsea. Quite a few famous regulars. **B**

Lamb   **2 B5**
94 Lamb's Conduit St WC1. 071-405

0713. A busy Bloomsbury local with some intriguing music hall photographs and Hogarth prints. Original snob-screens. Non-smoking area. **B**

🍷 Lamb & Flag 4 F3
33 Rose St WC2. 071-497 9504. A 300-year-old pub, originally called 'The Bucket of Blood' because of the bare fist fights in the upstairs room (Dryden apparently got the 'once-over' here). **B**

🍷 Marquess of Anglesey 4 F2
39 Bow St WC2. 071-240 3216. A pub with a chequered history. It was changed from an inn to a coffee house in the 18thC, converted back to a pub in the 19thC, extended in 1858, demolished in 1941 and rebuilt in 1953. **B L D**

The Mayflower
117 Rotherhithe St SE16. 071-237 4088. This famous Tudor riverside inn was originally called The Shippe, but changed its name when The Mayflower, which carried the Pilgrim Fathers from this part of the Thames, reached America. **B**

🍷 Museum Tavern 4 F1
49 Great Russell St WC1. 071-242 8987. Opposite the British Museum, this tavern attracts students and sightseers. Karl Marx wrote and drank here. **B**

🍷 Nag's Head 4 F3
10 James St WC2. 071-836 4678. Famous and lively Edwardian pub with a strongly theatrical flavour. **B**

Old Bull & Bush
North End Rd NW3. 081-455 3685. The pub made famous by the Florrie Forde song. The 17thC building was once the country home of the painter William Hogarth. **B**

🍷 Olde Butler's Head 5 E2
Mason's Av, Coleman St EC2. 071-606 3504. Pleasant, renovated 17thC inn with English cooking. **B L D**

🍷 Olde Mitre Tavern 5 B1
1 Ely Ct EC1. 071-405 4751. Built in 1546 by the Bishop of Ely for his servants. Associations with Elizabeth I and Dr Johnson. **B**

🍷 Printer's Devil 5 B2
98 Fetter La EC4. 071-242 2239. A printers' and journalists' pub taking its title from the traditional nickname for a printer's apprentice. Notable collection of early printing curios. **B L**

🍷 Queen's Elm 6 D3
241 Fulham Rd SW3. 071-352 9157. So-called because Elizabeth I took shelter under a nearby elm in 1567. Lively and popular with writers and publishers. **B**

🍷 Red Lion 4 D4
2 Duke of York St SW1. 071-930 2030. Plenty of Victoriana in this friendly pub.

Beautifully preserved mirrors and rich mahogany panelling. **B**

🍷 Red Lion 4 C4
1 Waverton St W1. 071-499 1307. Lovely 17thC Mayfair inn with forecourt. Frequented by models, actors and young businessmen. Restaurant serving international cuisine. **B L D**

🍷 Roebuck
130 Richmond Hill, Richmond. 081-948 2329. Large ground floor with wood beams and prints of old Richmond. Upstairs restaurant. Terrific Thames views. **B L D**

🍷 Rose & Crown 4 C5
2 Old Park La W1. 071-499 1980. 200-year-old country pub now surrounded by Park Lane houses. Tyburn associations. Five hot dishes every lunchtime. **B L**

Rossetti
23 Queen's Gro NW8. 071-722 7141. Airy pub with Rossetti etchings on the walls. English beer, good Thai food. **B L D**

🍷 Running Footman 4 C4
5 Charles St W1. 071-499 2988. Pub which once had the longest name in London, 'I am the Only Running Footman'. Popular with croupiers from the clubs nearby. **B L D**

🍷 Salisbury 4 F3
90 St Martin's La WC2. 071-836 5863. Glittering Edwardian pub in the heart of theatreland. Cut-glass mirrors, illuminated gilt statuettes and sumptuous red velvet seats. A famous meeting place for theatre people. **B**

Seven Stars 5 A2
53 Carey St WC2. 071-242 8521. Behind the Law Courts stands this small 17thC pub, one of the smallest in London. **B**

🍷 Sherlock Holmes 4 F4
10 Northumberland St WC2. 071-930 2644. Upstairs is a perfect replica of Holmes' study at 221b Baker St. The whole pub is saturated with relics of the legendary fictitious detective. **B L D**

🍷 Spaniards Inn
Spaniards Rd NW3. 081-455 3276. Famous 16thC inn with literary and Dick Turpin associations. Pretty garden. **B**

Spotted Dog, The Old
212 Upton La E7. 081-472 1794. 17thC inn used by City merchants during the Great Plague. Oak beams, plaster white-wash, prints. **B L D**

🍷 Still & Star 5 G2
1 Little Somerset St, Aldgate E1. 071-488 3761. The only one of its name in England, and set in 'blood alley' where Jack the Ripper struck. IPA on two pumps. **B**

🍷 **Watling, Ye Olde**   **5 D2**
29 Watling St EC4. 071-248 6252. Oak-beamed tavern rebuilt by Wren after the Great Fire of 1666. Stands on one of the oldest roads in London. **B L** in upstairs bistro.

🍷 **Williamson's Tavern**   **5 D2**
1-3 Groveland Ct, Bow La EC4. 071-248 6280. Inviting City tavern built after the Great Fire. This was the original residence of the Lord Mayor of London before Mansion House was built. **B**

Wrestlers, Ye Olde
98 North Rd N6. 081-340 4297. L-shaped bar with leaded glass windows, named after the wrestling that was once a regular event here. **B L D**

Outdoor drinking

Cross Keys   **6 E4**
2 Lawrence St SW3. 071-352 1893. Popular Chelsea local with friendly staff and excellent hot and cold food. Walled garden. **B**

🍷 **Duke of Clarence**   **3 A4**
203 Holland Park Av W11. 071-603 5431. Medieval-style interior with typically Victorian bar. Beautiful flagged courtyard with conservatory bar. Barbecues in summer. **B**

🍷 **Jack Straw's Castle**
North End Way NW3. 071-435 8885. Unusual weatherboard frontage and marvellous views over Hampstead Heath. Courtyard with tables and chairs. **B L D**

Scarsdale Arms   **3 A6**
23a Edwardes Sq W8. 071-937 1811. Pretty terrace surrounded by plane trees at the front. Good bar food and real ales. **B**

🍷 **Spaniard's Inn**
Spaniard's Rd NW3. 081-455 3276. Once the residence of the Spanish Ambassador to the Court of James I, then a pub run by two Spanish brothers who took it over in 1620. Shelley, Keats, Byron and Dickens drank here; a scene of *The Pickwick Papers* was set in the large garden, which has its own bar. **B**

🍷 **Swan Tavern**   **3 E3**
55 Bayswater Rd W2. 071-262 5204. Popular beer garden opposite Hyde Park. Illuminated from dusk on. **B**

🍷 **Waterside Inn**   **1 G2**
82 York Way N1. 071-837 7118. Red-brick pub with olde-worlde feel inside and seating along the Regent's Canal outside. **B L**

🍷 **Windmill Inn, Ye Olde**
Clapham Common South Side SW4. 081-673 4578. Popular and lively Victorian pub with two patios. **B L D**

🍷 **Windsor Castle**   **3 B4**
114 Campden Hill Rd W8. 071-727 8491. Built in 1835 when you could see Windsor Castle from here. Large walled garden with bar and snack bar. **B L D**

Real ale specialists

🍷 **Bricklayer's Arms**   **2 G5**
63 Charlotte Rd EC2. 071-739 5245. More than 50 real ales on hand pumps. At lunchtime a City pub and in the evening a traditional East End boozer. **B L**

🍷 **Goose & Firkin**   **5 C6**
47 Borough Rd SE1. 071-403 3590. The first of the Firkin chain of pubs which were opened to revive the ancient craft of brewing on the premises. Friendly, casual with good bar food. **B**

🍷 **Hole in the Wall**   **5 B4**
5 Mepham St SE1. 071-928 6196. Built into the arches by Waterloo Station. Thirteen real ales. **B**

Three Kings
171 North End Rd W14. 071-603 6071. Once the Nashville Rooms, known for its visiting bands, and now a huge temple of real ale with 29 handpumps, 7 real ales, lagers and ciders.

Riverside pubs

🍷 **Anchor**   **5 D3**
1 Bankside/34 Park St SE1. 071-407 1577. 18thC replacement of original destroyed by Great Fire of 1666. Exposed beams, large open fireplace and general Olde-English decor. **B L D**

Angel
101 Bermondsey Wall East SE16. 071-237 3608. 15thC Thames-side pub on piles, with extensive views over the river and the Pool of London. English cooking. **B L D**

Black Lion
2 South Black Lion La W6. 081-748 7056. Lovely 400-year-old riverside pub with a prize-winning paved garden. **B**

🍷 **Blue Anchor**
13 Lower Mall W6. 081-748 5774. Right on the river by Hammersmith Bridge where you can watch the rowers from the nearby clubs. **B**

🍷 **Bull's Head**
Strand on the Green W4. 081-994 0647. 350-year-old Chiswick waterfront tavern with Cromwellian links. **B**

🍷 **City Barge**
27 Strand on the Green W4. 081-994 2148. 15thC Elizabethan charter inn on Chiswick waterfront. **B L**

🍷 **Cutty Sark**
Ballast Quay, Lassell St SE10. 081-858

3146. Quiet Georgian pub with wooden interior. Overlooks river and wharves near Cutty Sark in dry-dock. **B L D**

☞ **Dickens Inn**   5 G3
St Katharine's Way E1. 071-488 2208. Pub in Dickensian style. Fine views of diverse craft in St Katharine's Dock. Two restaurants. **B L D**

☞ **Dove**
19 Upper Mall W6. 081-748 5405. 18thC pub with a terrace overlooking the river. James Thomson wrote *Rule Britannia* here. **B L**

Grapes
76 Narrow St E14. 071-987 4396. Traditional atmospheric pub with balcony overlooking river. **B L D** in fish restaurant upstairs.

London Apprentice
62 Church St, Old Isleworth, Middx. 081-560 1915. Famous 16thC Thames-side pub with fine Elizabethan and Georgian interiors. Prints of Hogarth's 'Apprentices'. **B L D**

Mayflower
117 Rotherhithe St SE16. 071-237 4088. Tudor inn connected historically with the Pilgrim Fathers. The only pub in England licensed to sell British and American stamps. Drink on the jetty in good weather. **B L D**

Prospect of Whitby
57 Wapping Wall E1. 071-481 1095. Historic dockland tavern with many famous and infamous associations. Decorated with nautical souvenirs and fine pewter. Excellent English menu in upstairs restaurant. Food bar overlooking the river. Beer garden. **B L D**

Ship
10 Thames Bank SW14. 081-876 1439. 16thC pub with terrace at the Mortlake end of the Oxford and Cambridge boat race course. **B L**

☞ **Ship Inn**
41 Jew's Row SW18. 081-870 9667. Just beside Wandsworth Bridge, this pub is at its best in *summer* when you can sit out on the patio overlooking the river. **B**

PS Tattershall Castle   4 F4
Victoria Embankment WC2. 071-839 6548. Several bars on board London's only paddle-steamer pub. Outside drinking on deck. Restored engine room on view. **B D**

☞ **Town of Ramsgate**
62 Wapping High St E1. 071-488 2685. 15thC tavern with a grisly past; the riverside garden was once the hanging dock for petty criminals. **B**

Trafalgar Tavern
Park Row SE10. 081-858 2437. Smart Thames-side inn close to Wren's impos-

ing Royal Naval College. Good English cooking in the restaurant. **B L D**

White Swan
Riverside, Twickenham, Middx. 081-892 2166. Attractive black-and-white balconied pub overlooking the river. Excellent lunchtime food. **B**

Music pubs

These vary enormously, from pubs with a pianist who plays old-time favourites to those with professional facilities and large audience capacity for rock and jazz bands. The pubs listed below are all established live music venues, but it's best to check in advance what is happening each night. Most pubs with a separate music room ask for gate money; you should expect to pay around £5.

Bull & Gate
389 Kentish Town Rd NW5. 071-485 5358. Jazz, R & B or blues, *seven nights a week.*

Bull's Head
373 Lonsdale Rd SW13. 081-876 5241. Modern jazz by top English and international musicians *every night, plus Sun L.*

Dublin Castle   1 D2
94 Parkway NW1. 071-485 1773. Music *seven nights a week.* Anything from rockabilly to R & B.

Half Moon
93 Lower Richmond Rd SW15. 081-780 9383. Music *every night* including rock, folk and jazz bands; jazz *Sun L* too.

King's Head   2 D2
115 Upper St N1. 071-226 1916. Live music *Mon-Sat* after the stage performance. Folk, rock or jazz.

Minogues   2 C2
80 Liverpool Rd N1. 071-354 4440. Live music *Wed-Sun*, generally traditional Irish, but occasionally other styles as well.

New Pegasus
109 Green Lanes N16. 071-226 5930. Live music *every night* – mostly rock, occasionally country.

Ruskin Arms
386 High St North E12. 081-472 0377. Visiting bands play heavy rock *Thur-Mon*. Boxing gym upstairs.

Sir George Robey
240 Seven Sisters Rd N4. 071-272 5356. Live music *every eve.*

Station Tavern
41 Bramley Rd W10. 071-727 4053. Blues played *seven nights a week.*

Swan   6 A5
1 Fulham Bdwy SW6. 071-385 1840. Mixed bands and R & B *six nights a week Mon-Sat & Sun L.*

Swan Tavern   3 **E3**
66 Bayswater Rd W2. 071-262 5204.
Illuminated at night, this popular beer
garden opposite Hyde Park is a busy
rendezvous for tourists. Honky-tonk piano
every eve except Sun.

Torrington
4 Lodge La N12. 081-445 4710. Visiting
bands play wide range of music on *Fri &
Sun eve.*

Tufnell Park Tavern
Tufnell Park Rd N7. 071-272 2078.
1930s decor provides a suitable back-
drop for live jazz *Thur-Sun eve.*

White Horse
154 Fleet Rd NW3. 071-485 2112. Indie
rock downstairs *Wed-Sat eve.*

White Lion   2 **E5**
37 Central St EC1. 071-253 4975. Real
East End pub where punters can sing
along to the piano played *Fri-Mon eve.*

Gay pubs & bars

*Gay and drag pubs have been combined
because while not all gay pubs offer drag
acts, all pubs with drag acts attract an at
least partially gay clientele. For further
information contact Gay Switchboard 071-
837 7324 (24 hrs). See also 'Gay nightlife'.*

Black Cap
171 Camden High St NW1. 071-485
1742. Two bars. Second offers drag
shows *every night & Sun L.*

Crews   4 **F3**
14 Upper St Martin's La WC2. 071-379
4880. Huge, busy pub with a dark, club-
like atmosphere.

The Edge   4 **E2**
11 Soho Sq W1. 071-439 1223. Smart
gay/straight bar on two levels. **B L D**

King's Arms   4 **D2**
23 Poland St W1. 071-734 5907. Busy,
friendly gay men's pub in central
position. **B**

Market Tavern   7 **E4**
Market Towers, 1 Nine Elms La SW8.
071-622 5655. Atmospheric and friendly
pub with separate, quieter bar. Different
theme nights. **B**

Recessions   1 **G5**
Brunswick Centre, Russell Sq WC2. 071-
833 8554. Friendly gay-owned pub open
to a mixed crowd *(women only Sat).* **B**

Royal Oak
62 Glenthorne Rd W6. 081-748 2781.
Large, busy pub with drag cabaret *Mon,
Thur-Sun eve & Sun lunchtime.* **B**

Royal Vauxhall Tavern   7 **F3**
372 Kennington La SE11. 071-582 0833.
Drag shows *every night of the week &
Sun lunchtime.* **B**

Theatre pubs

*You normally need to become a member
(**M**) of the theatre club; if so, membership
can be bought before the performance,
and the cost is usually nominal.*

The Bear and Staff   4 **E3**
37 Charing Cross Rd WC2. 071-724
3208. Small and friendly pub theatre
staging open-ended runs of popular
fringe shows.

Bush Theatre
See 'Fringe, pub & experimental theatre'.

DOC Theatre Club
Duke of Cambridge, 64 Lawford Rd
NW5. 071-485 4303. Stages classical
and modern plays with an emphasis on
European theatre. **M**

Etcetera Theatre
Oxford Arms, 265 Camden High St
NW1. 071-482 4857. General fringe
shows with a lot of new work from
visiting companies. Also in-house productions. **M**

The Finborough
Finborough Arms, Finborough Rd SW10.
071-373 3842. Innovative 'new writing'
theatre where the policy is to produce
new work only. **M**

The Gate
See 'Fringe, pub & experimental theatre'.

Grace Theatre   6 **F6**
See 'Fringe, pub & experimental theatre'.

Hen & Chickens
Highbury Cnr N5. 071-704 2001. Regular
Mon eve Theatresports. Also productions
by visiting theatre companies.

King's Head   2 **D2**
See 'Fringe, pub & experimental theatre'.

Man in the Moon   6 **D4**
See 'Fringe, pub & experimental theatre'.

Orange Tree
See 'Fringe, pub & experimental theatre'.

Pentameters
Three Horseshoes Pub, 28 Heath St
NW3. 071-435 3648. Classics, new work
and occasional poetry readings. **M**

Wine bars

*Cheaper and more informal than restau-
rants and an alternative to the pub, wine
bars are excellent meeting places. Wine is
served by the glass or bottle (a bottle is
usually the cheaper way of doing it) and a
selection of cheeses, pâtés and salads is
usually available. Below we list a selection
of well-established wine bars, many of
which have their own restaurants.
Assume that the bars listed here are open
traditional pub hours except where there*

is the ● sign which means open all day 11.00-23.00 Mon-Sat, 12.00-14.30 & 19.00-22.30 Sun.

L lunch **D** dinner **B** bar food

Andrew Edmunds   **4 D3**
46 Lexington St W1. 071-437 5708. Small but charming wine bar/restaurant which serves excellent wines and imaginative food. Daily specials. **B L D**

● **Archduke**   **5 A4**
Concert Hall Approach SE1. 071-928 9370. Underneath the railway arches. Good range of wines, live jazz and blues *nightly*. Upstairs restaurant specialises in sausages from around the world. *CLOSED L Sat & LD Sun.* **L D**

L'Artiste Musclé   **4 C4**
1 Shepherd Market W1. 071-493 6150. Cheerful French wine bar with seating outside in *summer*. Fine selection of cheeses. **B L D**

Balls Bros
One of the oldest wine bar chains in London, especially useful for City workers. Other branches. *OPEN to 20.30 (unless otherwise stated). CLOSED Sat & Sun.* **B L**
Hay's Galleria, Tooley St SE1.   **5 F4**
071-407 4301.
2 Old Change Ct, St Paul's   **5 D2**
Churchyard EC4. 071-248 8697.
St Mary-at-Hill EC3. 071-626   **5 F3**
0321. *CLOSES 19.00.*
6 Cheapside EC2. 071-248 2708.   **5 D2**
Moor House, London Wall EC2.   **5 E1**
071-628 3944.
42 Threadneedle St EC2. 071-283   **5 E2**
6701.

● **Le Beaujolais**   **4 E3**
25 Litchfield St WC2. 071-836 2277. Lively, mixed clientele in this popular, yet intimate wine bar. Good French wines and authentic French cooking. *CLOSED L Sat & LD Sun.* **L D**

● **Bill Bentley's**   **3 F6**
31 Beauchamp Pl SW3. 071-588 2655. Dark, cosy bar in the old-fashioned tradition with an excellent fish restaurant upstairs. The wine, mostly good quality French, is reasonably priced and complemented well by the delicious snacks from the oyster bar. Other branches. *OPEN to 21.30. CLOSED Sat & Sun.* **B L**

● **Brahms & Liszt**   **4 F3**
19 Russell St WC2. 071-240 3661. Lively, crowded Covent Garden wine bar. Music is loud, food varied, with the emphasis on cheeses and salads. Some hot dishes. *OPEN to 01.00, to 22.30 Sun.* **L D**

Cork & Bottle   **4 E3**
44-46 Cranbourn St WC2. 071-734

7807. Spacious basement with unusual variety of top-class bargain wines. The walls are covered with prints and posters about wines and champagnes. *OPEN to 24.00.* **B**

Davy's Wine Bars
Dusty barrels, old prints and sawdust-covered floors create the Victorian image of these houses, the names of which date back to the wine trade of 100 years ago. The chain offers a good selection of wines and tasty fresh appetisers plus other light dishes. *Phone to check opening times.* The City bars *CLOSE at 20.00 or 20.30.* Most branches are *CLOSED Sat & Sun.* The following list is a selection:

Boot & Flogger   **5 D4**
10-20 Redcross Way SE1. 071-407 1184.

Bung Hole   **5 A1**
57 High Holborn WC1. 071-242 4318.

City Boot   **5 E1**
7 Moorfields High Wlk EC2. 071-588 4766.

● **Crusting Pipe**   **4 F3**
27 The Market, Covent Garden WC2. 071-836 1415.

Davy's Wine Vaults
165 Greenwich High Rd SE10. 081-858 7204.

Tappit Hen   **4 F3**
5 William IV St WC2. 071-836 9811.

Dover Street Wine Bar   **4 D4**
8-9 Dover St W1. 071-629 9813. Basement wine bar. Live jazz, funk or soul bands *every night. OPEN to 03.00. CLOSED Sun.* **L D**

● **Ebury Wine Bar**   **7 A2**
139 Ebury St SW1. 071-730 5447. Wine bar/restaurant serving nouvelle cuisine and 70 different wines. **L D**

Gordon's Wine Bar   **4 F4**
47 Villiers St WC2. 071-930 1408. 300-year-old wine cellar where the ancient stone walls and ceilings drip with water! Excellent selection of wines, ports and sherries. *CLOSED Sat & Sun.* **B**

● **Pitcher & Piano**
Pleasant and airy wine bars with well-chosen wine lists and a range of snacks.
8 Balham Hill SW12. 081-673 1107.
18-20 Chiswick High Rd W4. 081-742 7731.
214-216 Fulham Rd SW10. 071-   **6 C4**
352 9234.
871-873 Fulham Rd SW6. 071-736 3910.

● **Shampers**   **4 D3**
4 Kingly St W1. 071-437 1692. Always a congenial atmosphere here. A hundred and sixty different varieties of wine and 20 different champagnes. Brasserie down-

stairs. Taped jazz. *CLOSED D Sat & LD Sun.* **B**

Soho Soho **4 E2**

11-13 Frith St W1. 071-494 3491. Spacious, colourful French wine bar, café and brasserie. French food. *CLOSED L Sat & LD Sun.* **B L D**

El Vino **5 B2**

47 Fleet St EC4. 071-353 6786. Something of an institution. Thoroughly masculine atmosphere. Women were not allowed to buy drinks at the bar until 1982. Downstairs restaurant. *OPEN to 20.30. CLOSED Sat & Sun.* **B L**

Brasseries & cafés

Continental-style brasseries and cafés offer informal, stylish surroundings where you will find good food (from snacks to full meals) and alcoholic drinks (which you can consume without having to eat).

All the bars listed below are open all day.

La Brasserie **6 E2**

272 Brompton Rd SW3. 071-584 1668. The most authentic French-style brasserie in London. Sophisticated but unpretentious. *OPEN to 24.00, to 23.30 Sun.*

Brasserie du Coin **2 B5**

54 Lamb's Conduit St WC1. 071-405 1717. Typical French brasserie with wooden floors and candlelit tables. Wine list is mostly French with some Portuguese and Italian choices. *OPEN to 23.30. CLOSED Sat & Sun.*

Café des Amis du Vin **4 F2**

11 Hanover Pl, Long Acre WC2. 071-379 3444. Sandwiched between a wine bar in the basement and an elegant restaurant upstairs. The walls are adorned with photographs from the nearby Royal Opera House. *OPEN to 23.30. CLOSED Sun.*

Café Bohème **4 E2**

13 Old Compton St W1. 071-734 0623. Perennially popular French-style brasserie/bar in the heart of Soho. *OPEN to 01.00, to 23.00 Sun.*

Café Flo

A growing chain of chic Parisian-style cafés. Reasonably-priced à la carte menus plus well-prepared set menus.

676 Fulham Rd SW6. 071-371 9673.

205 Haverstock Hill NW3. 071-435 6744.

127-129 Kensington Church St W8. **3 B4** 071-727 8142.

51 St Martin's La WC2. 071-836 **4 F3** 8289.

334 Upper St N1. 071-226 **2 D2** 7916.

Café Pelican **4 F3**

45 St Martin's La WC2. 071-379 0309. Renowned for impeccable service. Relaxed atmosphere, piano jazz in the background. *OPEN to 02.00.*

Café Rouge **5 F4**

Hay's Galleria, Tooley St SE1. 071-378 0097. Sister to Café Pelican, this brasserie is run on similar lines with wooden tables and classical French paintings adorning the walls. *CLOSED Sat & Sun.*

Camden Brasserie **1 D2**

216 Camden High St NW1. 071-482 2114. Relaxed ambience. Open fire in winter. Serves quality Mediterranean food. *OPEN to 23.30, to 22.30 Sun.*

Covent Garden Brasserie **4 F3**

1 Covent Garden Piazza WC2. 071-240 6654. This Parisian-style brasserie provides a refuge from the hustle and bustle of the piazza. Snacks and substantial French and Italian dishes. French, Chilean and Californian wines.

Dôme

Successful chain of brasseries named after the Paris Dôme. Friendly, lively atmosphere and standard brasserie fare.

38-39 Hampstead High St NW3. 071-435 4240.

354 King's Rd SW3. 071-352 7611. **6 D4**

98-100 Shepherd's Bush Rd W6. 071-602 7732.

85 Strand on the Green W4. 081-995 6575.

341 Upper St N1. 071-226 3414. **2 D2**

34 Wellington St WC2. 071-836 **4 G3** 0701.

PJ's **6 E2**

52 Fulham Rd SW3. 071-581 0025. A huge trendy brasserie/bar with an international menu and a wine list spanning the globe from American to Australia.

Soho Brasserie **4 E2**

23-25 Old Compton St W1. 071-439 9301. Arty French interior and a smart clientele. Outside tables in *summer*. Good bar snacks.

Tuttons Brasserie **4 F2**

11-12 Russell St WC2. 071-836 4141. Right on the edge of Covent Garden piazza, this is a large, airy brasserie with a relaxed atmosphere. International menu. *OPEN to 23.30, to 24.00 Fri & Sat.*

Shops and services

London has an amazing array of shops from the world-renowned department stores to smaller specialist outlets, selling anything from up-to-the-minute fashions to antiques and unusual crafts.

Consumer protection

Always keep the receipt for goods you buy and, if you're not satisfied, take them back to the shop and ask to speak to the manager. If the fault is entirely theirs you don't have to accept a credit note: ask for cash.

The *Trade Descriptions Act* protects the consumer against fraudulent claims made for goods, and the *Sale of Goods Act* against merchandise not up to standard – contact the Trading Standards Officer at your local Town Hall, your local Consumer Advice Centre or the Citizens Advice Bureau.

Opening times

Generally shops *open 09.00/10.00-17.30/18.00 Mon-Sat and are closed on Sun and B.hols*. West End shops stay *open late on Thur to 19.30/20.00, and until the same time on Wed* in Knightsbridge, King's Rd and Sloane Sq. A lot of Bond Street shops *do not open on Sat*. In cases where a shop's hours differ from the standard times above, the opening hours appear in italic at the end of the entry.

Shopping areas

The West End   4 D2
The capital's biggest shopping area consisting of three main streets. **Oxford Street** (4 C2) is over a mile long and has nearly all the major department stores including Selfridges, London's largest Marks & Spencer and an overwhelming assortment of individual fashion shops. It gets very crowded here, especially on *Sat* and at *lunchtime*. **Regent Street** (4 D3) is less hectic and offers luxurious items at Liberty, plus several china, glass and clothing stores. **Carnaby St** (4 D3) is still worth a visit. World-renowned in the 1960s, it has retained its busy and lively atmosphere, with frequent pavement shows and interesting clothes and

souvenir shops. Some of the high street chains have now also moved in. For real luxury try **New Bond Street** (4 C3) where you'll find shoes, jewellery, pictures, prints and designer clothes. Two pedestrianised streets just off Oxford St are well worth exploring – **St Christopher's Place** (4 B2) and **South Molton St** (4 C2). Both are packed with stylish small shops and attractive eating places.

Brent Cross
This vast shopping complex at the head of the M1 on the North Circular is north London's 'West End'. Ample free parking so the ideal way to avoid central London traffic and still visit branches of the main central London stores. Also has smaller, more individual, shops. *OPEN 10.00-20.00 Mon-Fri, 09.00-18.00 Sat*.

Camden   1 D1
Trendy and popular canalside area lined with shops and a huge, sprawling market. Very busy on a *Sat afternoon*. Shops deal in period clothes, alternative books, imported records, pine furniture and artefacts.

Charing Cross Road   4 E2
& Bloomsbury   4 F1
This is the area for books – new, second-hand, antique, specialist or best-sellers. Also prints and maps.

Covent Garden   4 F3
Once the site of the famous fruit and vegetable market, this is now a fashionable pedestrianised piazza. The arcades are lined with small specialist fashion and gift shops, plus plenty of places to eat and drink. There are also open-air craft stalls, an antiques market and an occasional craft market. Leading off the piazza in every direction, the streets reveal an interesting variety of shops and restaurants with the latest in fashion, hi-tech household equipment and exotic foods.

Hampstead
A quaint and pleasant place to browse. As well as the usual chain stores there are a number of exclusive clothes shops and narrow streets with arcades of antique and art dealers. Also plenty of wine bars, cafés and brasseries.

Hay's Galleria   5 F4
Tooley St SE1. Shopping and leisure complex near London Bridge. Lots of the main chain stores, plush coffee houses and wine bars.

Kensington High Street   3 C5
Less hectic than Oxford Street, though a similar range of shops, plus Barkers of Kensington – its own department store. Delve into the roads leading off for more individual fashion shops.

King's Road/Chelsea   6 F3
Still as much a place to be seen as to see; this area comes alive on *Sat*. One of the centres for up-to-the-minute fashion, it is particularly good for shoes and men's clothing.

Knightsbridge   4 A5
A fashionable area for the rich and famous, dominated by Harvey Nichols and Harrods, which can supply almost any demand if you are willing to pay the price. Exclusive furniture, jewellery and clothes can also be found in Beauchamp Place.

Piccadilly/Trocadero/   4 E3
London Pavilion
Quality and tradition at Fortnum & Mason, Hatchard's, Simpson and Lillywhites; also the historic Burlington Arcade. The Trocadero and the London Pavilion cater for the more up-to-date market, providing one-stop shopping, refreshment and entertainment; while Tower Records now dominates Piccadilly Circus from the old Swan & Edgar building.

Portobello Road   3 A2
Most famous for its huge market where you can alternate from the expensive antique dealer to the rag-and-bone merchant. A variety of household goods and second-hand clothes. Also unusual art deco and craft shops in the surrounding streets. Excellent delis.

Soho   4 E2
Sex shops and porno cinemas are now giving way to excellent specialist food shops, oriental supermarkets, designer clothes shops, restaurants and wine bars. Berwick Street Market and Chinatown are definitely worth a visit.

Tottenham Court Road   4 E1
Stretching north from the end of Oxford Street, this area is buzzing with shops selling electronic equipment (stereos, videos, cameras and computers). Furniture and modern design also feature at Heal's and Habitat, with many smaller shops also selling sofas, sofa-beds and futons.

Whiteleys   3 C3
Queensway W2. One of the first department stores, now transformed into a lively, smart, cosmopolitan complex of shops, cafés, restaurants, bars and an eight-screen cinema.

Department stores

There are several large stores in London where you can buy practically anything. Others are slightly more specialised, but still offer a wide choice of goods. Most have coffee shops and restaurants serving good, reasonably-priced lunches and teas; many also have hairdressing salons.

Army & Navy   7 C1
101-105 Victoria St SW1. 071-834 1234. Excellent wine department. Clothes, cosmetics, household goods, toys, books, china and glass. Hairdress- ing salon, coffee shop, restaurant.

Barkers of Kensington   3 C5
63 Kensington High St W8. 071-937 5432. Good general store selling fashionable clothes, household and electrical goods. Hairdressing/beauty salon.

British Home Stores (BHS)   4 C2
252 Oxford St W1. 071-629 2011. Inexpensive high street chain for clothes and household goods. Extensive home lighting department.

Debenhams   4 C2
344-348 Oxford St W1. 071-580 3000. Fashion clothes at reasonable prices. Good departments for kitchenware, lingerie, hosiery, cosmetics.

D.H. Evans   4 C2
318 Oxford St W1. 071-629 8800. Straightforward store with an excellent fashion and lingerie department. Unusual sizes well catered for in the dress department. Perfumery, furniture and household goods. Olympus Sports in the basement.

Dickins & Jones   4 D2
224 Regent St W1. 071-734 7070. Fashionable store selling high-quality clothing, accessories and haberdashery. Excellent dress fabrics. China and glass. Coffee shop.

Fenwicks   4 C3
63 New Bond St W1. 071-629 9161. Good fashions and accessories. Imaginative gifts and stationery. Books. Also large store at Brent Cross Shopping Centre NW4. 081-202 8200.

Fortnum & Mason   4 D4
181 Piccadilly W1. 071-734 8040. World-famous. Luxury goods and exotic foods. Superb hampers for all occasions. Designer collection clothes.

Harrods   3 G6
Knightsbridge SW1. 071-730 1234. The world's most famous department store. Superb men's, ladies' and children's fashions and accessories. Perfumery, gifts, china and glass, pets, toys, books, furniture, fabrics. Edwardian marble food halls. Hairdressing/beauty salon, gentle-

men's barber. Restaurants, tea and coffee shops. Also a wide range of services.

Harvey Nichols   **4 A5**
Knightsbridge SW1. 071-235 5000. Stylish clothes from top British, Continental and American designers. Home furnishing and household goods. *Restaurant. OPEN 10.00-19.00 Mon-Fri (to 20.00 Wed), to 18.00 Sat.*

John Lewis   **4 C2**
278-306 Oxford St W1. 071-629 7711. One of the largest dress fabric departments in Europe. Furniture, furnishings, china and glass, fashions. Good haberdashery and craft materials. Bureau de change, export bureau and interpreters. Branch at Brent Cross Shopping Centre NW4. 081-202 6535.

Liberty   **4 D2**
210-220 Regent St W1. 071-734 1234. Fashionable and famous, especially for its distinctive fabrics and unusual luxury goods. Fashion jewellery, wide range of glass and china, oriental rugs, prints and gifts. Designer collection clothes.

Littlewoods   **4 B2**
508-520 Oxford St W1. 071-629 7847. Inexpensive high street chain for clothing and household goods.

Marks & Spencer   **4 B2**
458 Oxford St W1. 071-935 7954. Excellent quality clothes and accessories for men, women and children. Wide range of foods, home furnishings, cosmetics. Bureau de change. Numerous other branches. *OPEN 09.00-19.00 Mon-Wed & Sat, to 20.00 Thur & Fri.*

Peter Jones   **6 F2**
Sloane Sq SW1. 071-730 3434. Quality clothing, accessories and household goods. Also modern and antique furniture, glass and china. Large furnishing fabric department. Excellent linens: wide range of plain coloured sheets and towels in all sizes. Fashion clothes, hairdressing salon. Interpreters available. Restaurant, coffee shop.

Selfridges   **4 B2**
400 Oxford St W1. 071-629 1234. Limitless household department. Furniture, men's and women's fashions, toys, food hall, sports clothing and equipment. Bank, information desk, garage with parking facilities for 700 cars.

Clothes: general

The following shops cater for men and women, unless otherwise stated. See 'Men's clothes' and 'Women's clothes' for specialist shops.

Clothes stores

For a good selection of quality clothing try the following well-known stores. Nearly all London's department stores also have extensive collections of clothes and accessories.

Aquascutum   **4 D3**
100 Regent St W1. 071-734 6090. Fine quality British raincoats, suits, knitwear and accessories for men and women.

Austin Reed   **4 D3**
103 Regent St W1. 071-734 6789. English and Continental suits and accessories for men. Accent on quality. Valet service and barber. Options department for ladies, selling executive and designer wear suits and classic dresses.

Burberrys   **4 E3**
18 Haymarket SW1. 071-930 3343. Classic raincoats for men and women cut in English style. Hats, scarves, knitwear, suits and accessories. Other branches.

C & A   **4 A2**
501-519 Oxford St W1. 071-629 7272. Vast selection of reasonably-priced fashions and classics for all the family. Skirts, dresses, coats, knitwear, suits and leathers. Avanti collection for young men. Sportsworld department includes large seasonal collection of ski-wear. Full fashion range for 14-25 year-olds in the Clock House. Other branches.

Jaeger   **4 D3**
200-206 Regent St W1. 071-734 8211. Four floors of well-cut fashionable English clothes. Suits, coats, knitwear and casual wear for men. Dresses, suits and separates for women in colour co-ordinated departments. Cashmere, camel and knitted garments. Original accessories, jewellery.

Moss Bros   **4 F3**
88 Regent St W1. 071-494 0666. Famous for classic menswear. Women's designer clothes, jewellery and accessories. Other branches.

Simpson   **4 D3**
203 Piccadilly W1. 071-734 2002. High-quality clothing for men and women. Suits, knitwear, dresses, separates. Daks country clothes, Squadron sportswear, luggage and accessories. Wine bar, restaurant, gentlemen's barber.

Fashion shops

Many of the following have several branches. Only the main ones are listed below.

Benetton   **4 C2**
255-259 Regent St W1. 071-355 4881. Large range of colourful Italian knitwear and separates.

Boy   **6 E3**
153 King's Rd SW3. 071-351 1115.

Slightly off-beat and trendy fashions for men, women and children.

Dash 4 C2
266 Oxford St W1. 071-408 1131. Smart sportswear for everyday and sporting use. Colourful tracksuits and co-ordinating accessories.

French Connection 4 D2
10 Argyll St W1. 071-287 2046. Colourful, fashionable styles. Other branches.

The Gap 4 D2
210 Regent St W1. 071-287 3851. American-style casual wear for men, women and children. Co-ordinated colours.

Hennes 4 B2
481 Oxford St W1. 071-493 8557. Also at 238 Oxford St W1 (4 C2). 071-493 4004. High fashion clothes for men, women and children.

Jigsaw 4 F3
21 Long Acre WC2. 071-240 3855. Casual, sporty styles in natural fibres. Limited number of co-ordinating colours available but stock changes frequently. Accessories, lingerie and shoes.

Marc O'Polo 3 C5
Barkers Centre, Kensington High St W8. 071-938 3558. Quality clothing made only from natural materials.

Naf-Naf 6 F2
13-15 King's Rd SW3. 071-730 8752. Casual and very popular French clothing. Tracksuits, sweatshirts, rompersuits, bomberjackets in bright colours with Naf-Naf slogan on everything.

Next 4 D3
160 Regent St W1. 071-434 2515. Colour co-ordinated fashion separates. Suits and casual wear. Shoes, accessories and cosmetics.

River Island 3 C5
124 Kensington High St W8. 071-937 0224. Popular young styles for men and women at very reasonable prices.

Top Shop & Top Man 4 D2
Oxford Circus W1. 071-636 7700. Large shop for variety of inexpensive fashions in styles to suit most tastes.

Way In 3 G6
Harrods, Knightsbridge SW1. 071-730 1234. Fashionable clothes department within the famous store.

Designer wear

The following shops have been chosen for the quality and individuality of their goods. Prices vary – the South Molton Street and Knightsbridge areas tend to be expensive.

Arte 6 F3
55 King's Rd SW3. 071-730 3607. Bold and unusual fashions for the daring dresser.

Browns 4 C2
23-27 South Molton St W1. 071-491 7833. The very best of British and international designer clothing exclusive to the shop.

Christopher New 4 E3
52 Dean St W1. 071-734 5363. Classic-cut menswear with unusual trimmings. Coins, buttons, medals and stars. Jazzy embroidery.

Feathers 3 G6
40 Hans Cres SW1. 071-589 0356. Well-chosen collection of Continental clothes and accessories for women. Good knits, shoes, bags and belts.

Giorgio Armani 3 G6
178 Sloane St SW1. 071-235 6232. Beautiful designs by Armani for men and women. Chic and expensive.

Hyper Hyper 3 C5
26-40 Kensington High St W8. 071-937 6964. A fashion forum on two floors featuring the work of exciting young designers in individual units. A large variety of avant garde clothing for men and women. Also shoes and accessories for all occasions. Café on ground floor.

Issy Miyake 6 E2
270 Brompton Rd SW3. 071-581 3760. Everything from tailored skirts to ethnic-looking scarves are carefully designed. Stocks a classic line for men as well as Issy Woman for the younger woman.

Joseph Tricot 3 G6
26 Sloane St SW3. 071-235 5470. Joseph's fashions converted into wool. Some suede and leather garments.

Karl Lagerfeld 4 D3
173 New Bond St W1. 071-493 6277. Excellent quality clothes for women. Soft fabrics and bold colours at bold prices. Jewellery also.

Katharine Hamnett 3 G6
20 Sloane St SW1. 071-823 1002. Strong on unfussy casual wear for men and women. All her latest themes are stocked here.

Kenzo Paris 3 G6
15 Sloane St SW1. 071-235 4021. Unusual clothes for women in colours that change every season.

Malcolm Levene 4 B1
13-15 Chiltern St W1. 071-487 4383. Men's classic fashion and contemporary chic. Hand-made shoes, designer suits, trousers and jackets. Exclusive UK stockists of Kiehls – a range of skin and hair products.

Piero de Monzi 6 D2
68-70 Fulham Rd SW3. 071-581 4247. Sporty but expensive clothes from Italy for men and women. Excellent knitwear.

Polo Ralph Lauren   **4 C3**
143 New Bond St W1. 071-491 4967.
Expensive American designer collection,
ready-to-wear classic range and casual
wear for men and women. Accessories.

St Laurent 'Rive Gauche'   **4 C3**
137 New Bond St W1. 071-493 1800.
Exclusive own-label Paris clothes for men
and women.

Valentino   **4 C3**
160 New Bond St W1. 071-493 2698. A
shop for the woman who loves to dress
well and has the money to indulge her
tastes. The grand evening dresses take
some beating.

Vincci   **4 D4**
60-67 Jermyn St SW1. 071-629 0407.
Range of shops which provide top Italian
designs in unusual fabrics. Formal and
casual menswear.

Wardrobe   **4 B1**
17 Chiltern St W1. 071-935 4086. Also at
3 Grosvenor St W1 (**4 C3**). 071-629
7044. Good quality fashion for all ages.
Consultancy service for working women
with advice on clothes, make-up and hair.

Whistles   **4 F3**
20 Covent Garden Mkt WC2. 071-379
7401. Expensive, up-market clothes for
women.

World's End   **6 D4**
430 King's Rd SW3. 071-352 6551.
Designer Vivienne Westwood's eccentric
shop. Unpredictable and often humorous
fashions.

Shoe shops

*There are many good shoe shop chains
in addition to the more expensive individual shops. This is a selection of both:*

Anello & Davide   **4 F2**
35 Drury La WC2. 071-836 1983.
Specialise in dance and bridal shoes.

Bally   **4 D3**
30 Old Bond St W1. 071-493 2250.
Good quality shoes for men and women.

Bertie   **4 B2**
409 Oxford St W1. 071-629 5833.
Imaginative styles and unconventional
colours.

Charles Jourdan   **3 G5**
39-43 Brompton Rd SW3. 071-581
3333. Beautiful shoes imported from
France for men and women.

Church's   **4 D3**
58-59 Burlington Arc W1. 071-493 8307.
The famous high-quality classic men's
and women's shoes. Wide range of
fittings.

Deliss   **6 F1**
41 Beauchamp Pl SW3. 071-584 3321.

Exclusive designs in all kinds of shoes
and boots, made-to-measure from fabrics
and leather. Bags and accessories.

Derber   **3 C5**
80 Kensington High St W8. 071-937
1578. Popular and stylish shoes and
boots for women. High fashion range for
men.

Clark's   **4 E2**
15 Oxford St W1. 071-437 2593. Stock
quality shoes in wide fittings as well as
fashion shoes and children's footwear.
Other branches.

Dolcis   **4 D2**
181 Oxford St W1. 071-437 6401.
Popular chain with many branches.

Faith   **4 C2**
383 Oxford St W1. 071-499 2176.
Reasonably-priced classic everyday
styles.

Ferragamo   **4 D3**
24 Old Bond St W1. 071-629 5007.
Italian shoemakers. Smart, comfortable
shoes.

Freed   **4 F3**
94 St Martin's La WC2. 071-240 0432.
Specialists in theatrical and ballet shoes.
Also make excellent boots to order.
Contact 081-985 6121.

Gamba Shoes   **4 F3**
3 Garrick St WC2. 071-437 0704. Ballet
shoes, character shoes, pumps in satin
and leather. Dyeing service for their own
satin shoes – can match almost any
colour.

Gucci   **3 G6**
17-18 Sloane St SW1. 071-235 6707.
Pricey, but well-made and distinctive
styles.

Hobbs   **4 C2**
47 South Molton St W1. 071-629 0750.
Classic and fashion shoes for women in a
good range of colours.

John Lobb   **4 D4**
9 St James's St SW1. 071-930 3664.
Top-quality, hand-made, made-to-
measure shoes.

Kurt Geiger   **4 C2**
95 New Bond St W1. 071-499 2707.
Exclusive women's shoes and handbags.
Also at Harrods, Dickins & Jones and
other big stores.

Lilley & Skinner   **4 B2**
360 Oxford St W1. 071-629 6381. One
of many branches for fashion shoes at
reasonable prices.

Maxwell's   **4 D3**
11 Savile Row W1. 071-734 9714. Hand-
made bespoke boots and shoes of the
highest quality.

Natural Shoe Store   **4 F2**
21 Neal St WC2. 071-836 5254. Ultra-

comfortable, foot-shaped shoes for men, women and children.

Pied à Terre　　　　**4 C2**
19 South Molton St W1. 071-493 3637. Unusual styles for men and women, including exotic suede slippers. Also do a cheaper range called Basics.

Pinet　　　　**4 C3**
47 New Bond St W1. 071-629 2174. Shoes in all kinds of skins exclusive to the shop.

Ravel　　　　**4 C2**
248 Oxford St W1. 071-499 1949. Fashion shoe chain with many branches.

Russell & Bromley　　　　**4 C3**
24-25 New Bond St W1. 071-629 6903. Fine hand-made shoes from Spain, France and Italy. Other branches.

Sacha　　　　**4 D3**
22 Carnaby St W1. 071-439 0012. Modern shoes in up-to-date styles.

Saxone　　　　**4 B2**
502-504 Oxford St W1. 071-629 2138. Fashion shoe shop with many branches.

Trickers　　　　**4 D4**
67 Jermyn St SW1. 071-930 6395. Quality hand-made shoes for women and ready-made shoes for men at reasonable prices.

Leather, suede & sheepskin clothes

Leather Rat　　　　**4 C2**
37 South Molton St W1. 071-499 2284. Stocked with a wide variety of styles

Lewis Leathers　　　　**4 C1**
122 Great Portland St W1. 071-636 4314. Masses of leather wear for men and women at reasonable prices.

Loewe　　　　**4 C3**
130 New Bond St W1. 071-493 3914. Quality hand-made Spanish leather and suede coats, dresses and suits for men and women.

Natural Leather　　　　**4 F2**
62 Neal St WC2. 071-240 7748. A safe bet if you want to buy a straightforward, good quality designer leather jacket. *OPEN 11.00-19.00 Mon-Sat.*

Rivaaz　　　　**6 E3**
113 King's Rd SW3. 071-352 2480. Leather, suede and sheepskin fashions. *OPEN 10.00-19.00 Mon-Sat.*

Second-hand clothes

Markets are your best bet for period clothes – especially Portobello Rd, Kensington Market and Camden Lock. See also 'Charity Shops'.

Angels & Bermans　　　　**4 E2**
119-123 Shaftesbury Av WC2. 071-836 5678. Military full dress uniform 1800 onwards for professional use. Hire only.

Annie's　　　　**2 D2**
10 Camden Pas N1. 071-359 0796. Original clothes and accessories of the '20s, '30s and '40s, plus large selection of antique lace dresses, blouses, etc.

Antiquarius Antique Market　　**6 E3**
131-141 King's Rd SW3. 071-351 5353. Victorian nighties, '20s flapper dresses and crepe dresses, '30s velvet evening dresses and more recent items. Quite expensive.

Cornucopia　　　　**7 C2**
12 Upper Tachbrook St SW1. 071-828 5752. Good range of second-hand clothes, shoes, jewellery and accessories, dating from 1910 into the 1960s, at reasonable prices.

Flip　　　　**4 F3**
125 Long Acre WC2. 071-836 7044. Also at 5 Southampton St WC2 (**4 F3**). 071-379 5098. Large selection of second-hand American clothing.

The Frock Exchange　　　　**6 B5**
450 Fulham Rd SW6. 071-381 2937. Nearly new clothes and accessories.

Gallery of Antique Costume & Textiles
2 Church St, Lisson Gro NW8. 071-723 9981. Selection of period clothes spanning three centuries. Some reproductions. Also large stock of decorative textiles including wall hangings and quilts. Film and theatre suppliers.

Lawrence Corner　　　　**1 E4**
62-64 Hampstead Rd NW1. 071-813 1010. Uniforms and Army/Navy surplus from World War II onwards. To hire or buy.

Nologo　　　　**1 C6**
91 Marylebone High St W1. 071-487 3570. Designer revamped seconds.

Pandora Dress Agency　　　　**3 F6**
16-22 Cheval Pl SW7. 071-589 5289. Very good used model garments bought and sold on commission.

Men's clothes

Bespoke tailors

Savile Row for expensive but long-lasting hand-tailored clothes in the finest cloths.

Anderson & Sheppard　　　　**4 D3**
30 Savile Row W1. 071-734 1420.

Blades　　　　**4 D3**
8 Burlington Gdns, Savile Row W1. 071-734 8911.

Buckleigh　　　　**6 G3**
83 Lower Sloane St SW1. 071-730 0770.

Men's formal wear, bespoke and ready-made.

Douglas Hayward   **4 B3**
95 Mount St W1. 071-499 5574.

Gieves & Hawkes   **4 D3**
1 Savile Row W1. 071-434 2001. Classic but fashionable bespoke and ready-made clothes.

Henry Poole   **4 D3**
15 Savile Row W1. 071-734 5985.

Huntsman & Sons   **4 D3**
11 Savile Row W1. 071-734 7441. King of Savile Row from before 1800.

Kilgour, French & Stanbury   **4 D3**
8 Savile Row W1. 071-734 6905.

Nutters of Savile Row   **4 D3**
35a Savile Row W1. 071-437 6850. Exclusive but adventurous men's tailor.

Tom Gilbey   **4 D3**
2 New Burlington Pl W1. 071-734 4877. An appointment is necessary at this design house where any type of suit can be made to measure. Women are also catered for. Tom Gilbey's Waistcoat Gallery has a large selection of bespoke and ready-to-wear waistcoats.

Fashion shops

Burtons   **4 D3**
114-120 Regent St W1. 071-734 1951. Suits and accessories at reasonable prices.

Dunn & Co   **4 D3**
56-58 Regent St W1. 071-494 2010. Classic suits and tweed jackets with a modern influence.

Hackett
65b New King's Rd SW6. 071-371 7964. Well known for classic English style but stock ranges from formal to sportswear. Good selection. Other branches.

Herbie Frogg   **4 C3**
38 New Bond St W1. 071-499 2029. Stylish, classic suits by Hugo Boss. High fashion casual wear by Jino Cchietti.

Hornes   **4 E2**
4 Oxford St W1. 071-580 9104. Casual wear, suits and shoes with the emphasis on co-ordination.

Jones   **4 F3**
13 Floral St WC2. 071-352 5323. Exciting designer wear at average prices. Jeans, leather jackets, shirts, shoes.

Les 2 Zebras   **4 F3**
38 Tavistock St WC2. 071-836 2855. Specialise in very chic, casual clothes for men by French, Italian and English designers. Knitwear, accessories, shoes and leather goods.

Tie Rack   **3 C5**
Kensington Arcade, Kensington High St

W8. 071-937 5168. Chain of small shops selling ties in a range of different fabrics.

Woodhouse   **4 E2**
99-101 Oxford St W1. 071-437 2809. Extensive range of fashionable clothes.

Shirts

These firms make top-quality shirts to measure:

Coles Ltd   **6 F2**
131 Sloane St SW1. 071-730 7564.

Harvie & Hudson   **4 D4**
77 & 97 Jermyn St SW1. 071-930 3949.

Hilditch & Key   **4 D4**
73 Jermyn St SW1. 071-930 5336.

Turnbull & Asser   **4 D4**
71 Jermyn St SW1. 071-930 0502. Also at 23 Bury St SW1 (**4 D4**). Ready-made and bespoke English cottons and silks.

Knitwear

W. Bill   **4 D3**
28 Old Bond St W1. 071-629 2554. Wide range of British knitwear including lambswool, cashmere, intarsia and Argyll sweaters. Hand-knitted Icelandic, Fair Isle, Arran and cricket sweaters. Shetland Everests exclusive to the shop.

The Scotch House   **3 G5**
2 Brompton Rd SW1. 071-581 2151. Also at 84 Regent St W1 (**4 D3**). 071-734 0203. A wide selection of Fair Isle, Shetland and Pringle knitwear. Tartans too.

S. Fisher of Burlington Arcade   **4 D3**
22-23 & 32-33 Burlington Arcade W1. 071-493 4180. Very popular with overseas visitors for cashmere, lambswool and classic knitwear.

Sportswear

Lillywhites and Simpson have very extensive stocks of sports and casual wear. See also 'Sports equipment' under 'Specialist shops and services'.

J.C. Cording   **4 D3**
19 Piccadilly W1. 071-734 0830. Weatherproof and country clothing plus typical English fashion. Famous for old-fashioned, classic look cords and trousers. Exclusive luggage.

R.M. Williams   **4 D3**
179-181 Regent St. 071-434 0061. Authentic Australian clothing for men and women. Range of moleskin trousers and skirts. Also jackets, shoes and accessories.

Swaine, Adeney, Brigg   **4 D4**
185 Piccadilly W1. 071-734 4277. Wide selection of English country and shooting clothes. Saddlery.

Military & naval dress

Moss Bros　　　　　　**4 D3**
88 Regent St W1. 071-494 0666. Make uniforms for officers in any of the services. War medals and ribbons. Ceremonial accoutrements can be hired.

Unusual sizes

Cooper's All Size　　　　**3 F2**
72 & 74 Edgware Rd W2. 071-402 8635. Ready-to-wear clothes for the tall and small. Chest sizes 34-60in (86-152cm). Alterations service.

High & Mighty　　　　　**4 A5**
83 Knightsbridge SW1. 071-589 7454. Everything ready-to-wear for the big or tall man. Chest sizes 44-58in (112-147cm) up to 6ft 11in (2.06m) in height. Shoes up to size 15.

Magnus
63 Southend Rd NW3. 071-435 1792. Outsize shoes for men sizes 11-15 and women sizes 8-11.

Clothes hire

Kritz　　　　　　　　　**1 B5**
19 Melcombe St NW1. 071-935 0304. Gents' dress-wear hire service since 1904.

Moss Bros　　　　　　**4 D3**
88 Regent St W1. 071-494 0666. Men's ceremonial and formal wear. Arrange to hire a week in advance.

Young's Dress Hire　　　**4 C2**
19-20 Hanover St W1. 071-493 9153. Formal wear with a difference. A full range of morning suits, dinner suits, lounge suits, daywear and white tuxedos.

Women's clothes

Classic styles

Belville-Sassoon　　　　**6 F2**
18 Culford Gdns SW3. 071-581 3500. Extravagant and elegant dresses for day, cocktail and evening wear.

Caroline Charles　　　　**6 E1**
56-57 Beauchamp Pl SW3. 071-589 5850. Pretty feminine clothes exclusively designed. All ages.

Galicia　　　　　　　　**4 F3**
24 Wellington St WC2. 071-836 2961. Classic and fashion clothes. Separates, dresses, suits, coats and rainwear.

Panache　　　　　　　**6 F1**
24 Beauchamp Pl SW3. 071-584 9807. A selection of the best designs from top

international ready-to-wear collections. Printed silks, jersey, and French and Italian knits. Day and evening wear.

Peal & Co　　　　　　**4 D3**
37 Burlington Arc W1. 071-493 5378. Fashionable and classic knitwear and separates. Also cater for men.

The White House　　　　**4 C3**
51-52 New Bond St W1. 071-629 3521. Famous for their beautiful linen but also specialise in lovely clothes for women and children from little-known French, Italian and Swiss designers. Also exquisite lingerie.

Fashion shops

Up-to-date fashion without the expensive price tags of more exclusive designs. Many have more than one branch but main branches only are listed below.

Boules　　　　　　　　**4 F3**
22-23 James St WC2. 071-379 7848. Own-label fashions and accessories at affordable prices. *OPEN 10.30-19.30 Mon-Fri, 10.30-19.00 Sat, 13.00-18.00 Sun.*

Country Casuals　　　　**4 D2**
Dickins & Jones, 226 Regent St W1. 071-434 3633. Colour co-ordinated separates in classic and high fashion ranges. Matching accessories.

Dorothy Perkins　　　　**4 C2**
267 Oxford St W1. 071-499 2084. Women's fashions, dresses, co-ordinates, separates, shoes by Faith. Smart and casual wear.

Esprit　　　　　　　　**3 G5**
6 Sloane St SW1. 071-245 9139. Casual clothes for women. Attractive styles and colours.

Hobbs　　　　　　　　**4 C2**
47 South Molton St W1. 071-629 0750. Classic, easy-to-wear separates. Well made suits and co-ordinates.

Laura Ashley　　　　　**4 D2**
256 Regent St W1. 071-437 9760. Distinctive cotton print dresses and separates in romantic styles. Nighties, evening and wedding dresses. Also corduroy and woollens for winter. Accessories include boots, shoes, hats and jewellery.

Miss Selfridge　　　　　**4 B2**
40 Duke St W1. 071-629 1234. Enormous selection of fashionable clothes. Excellent sweaters and shirts. Tights, jewellery, cosmetics and a good shoe shop.

Monsoon　　　　　　　**4 F3**
23 Covent Garden Mkt WC2. 071-836 9140. Up-market Indian cottons, silks and velvets. Good for party clothes. Visit

the Monsoon accessories shop 'Accessorize' next door for co-ordinating belts, hats, jewellery and shoes.

Richards   **4 C2**
263-265 Oxford St W1. 071-499 5223. Large selection of dresses, separates, coats and leisurewear.

Stefanel   **4 C2**
15 South Molton St W1. 071-499 9907. Italian knitwear and separates in bright fashion colours.

Wallis   **4 D2**
215 Oxford St W1. 071-439 8669. Large range of dresses and well-cut quality fashions. Specialise in colour co-ordinates.

Warehouse   **4 D2**
19-21 Argyll St W1. 071-437 7101. Young fashion from young designers at reasonable prices.

Knitwear

Crochetta   **4 C2**
68 South Molton St W1. 071-493 1500. Hand-made exclusive knitwear in silk, wool, cotton. Dresses and separates.

Jaeger   **4 D3**
204 Regent St W1. 071-734 8211. Fashion and classic knitwear.

Patricia Roberts   **4 B5**
60 Kinnerton St SW1. 071-235 4742. Beautiful and imaginative designer knitwear. An extensive collection of mohairs, Shetlands, cashmeres and cotton boucles in bright primary colours.

The Scotch House   **3 G5**
2 Brompton Rd SW1. 071-581 2151. Enormous range of Scottish knitwear – Shetland, cashmere and lambswool.

Westaway & Westaway   **4 F1**
65 Great Russell St WC1. 071-405 4479. Specialists in woollens and cashmere.

Lingerie, hosiery & nightwear

Marks & Spencer, Littlewoods and Fenwicks carry good, inexpensive lingerie and nightwear, while Harvey Nichols, Harrods and Fortnum & Mason are excellent for more elegant styles.

Bradleys   **4 A5**
85 Knightsbridge SW1. 071-235 2902. Speciality shop for fine lingerie, nightwear and beachwear.

Courtenay   **4 C3**
22 Brook St W1. 071-629 0542. Pretty lingerie in silk, cotton, lace; also evening wear and accessories.

Fogal   **3 G5**
51 Brompton Rd SW3. 071-225 0472. Tights, stockings and socks made from silk, cashmere and other exotic fabrics in all sizes, colours and patterns.

Janet Reger   **6 E1**
2 Beauchamp Pl SW3. 071-584 9368. Glamorous, expensive nightwear and lingerie. Collectors' item catalogue also available.

Knickerbox   **4 C2**
469 Oxford St W1. 071-355 1347. High street chain selling various styles of underwear for men and women.

Night Owls   **6 D3**
78 Fulham Rd SW3. 071-584 2451. Unique little shop selling exquisite nightwear.

Rigby & Peller   **6 F1**
2 Hans Rd SW3. 071-589 9293. Exclusive corsetières. Made-to-measure underwear and high-class Continental beachwear.

Sock Shop   **4 E2**
89 Oxford St W1. 071-437 1030. High street chain of small shops stocked full with all colours and styles of socks, tights and stockings. *OPEN 08.30-19.30 Mon-Sat (to 20.00 Thur).*

Maternity clothes

It is worth looking in the chain stores because they often stock their own range of maternity clothes.

Balloon   **6 E2**
77b Walton St SW3. 071-584 3668. Elegant, expensive maternity wear.

Great Expectations   **6 D3**
78 Fulham Rd SW3. 071-584 2451. Stylish, youthful and quite trendy maternity clothes.

Mothercare   **4 B2**
461 Oxford St W1. 071-629 6621. (Main branch.) Good quality maternity and baby clothes and equipment at practical prices.

Unusual sizes

Base   **4 F2**
55 Monmouth St WC2. 071-240 8914. Half the clothes here are designed by Yugoslav Rushka Murganovic and the rest come from Europe or America. Bold designs and fun colours.

Buy & Large   **6 G2**
4 Holbein Pl, Sloane Sq SW1. 071-730 6534. Full selection of clothes in fittings from 16-24. Good for evening wear.

Crispins   **1 C6**
28-30 Chiltern St W1. 071-935 7984. Court shoes, boots, sandals and espadrilles in large sizes (8-11); plus narrow fittings in sizes 4-11.

Evans   **4 A2**
538-540 Oxford St W1. 071-499 5372.

General selection of clothes for the larger woman from size 14.

Lilley & Skinner 4 B2
360 Oxford St W1. 071-629 6381. Special department for large and small size fashion shoes at reasonable prices.

Long Tall Sally 1 C6
21 Chiltern St W1. 071-487 3370. Specialise in elegant clothes for tall women, sizes 12-20. Lingerie, separates, specially-designed evening wear.

Mary Fair 1 B6
61 Crawford St W1. 071-262 9763. Individually-designed clothes in small sizes.

Bridalwear

Most large department stores have good bridalwear departments. There are also large specialist shops with extensive collections and fitters on hand to advise. Smaller, even more specialised shops deal in exclusive styles, sometimes using antique fabrics.

Berkertex Brides 4 C2
81 New Bond St W1. 071-629 9301. Biggest bridal store in the country. Lots of satins, taffetas and lace. Good stock of formal registry office wedding dresses.

Catherine Buckley 3 A3
302 Westbourne Gro W11. 071-229 8786. Designer of exclusive, elaborate wedding gowns often made in antique textiles to Edwardian styles. New and antique lace used with embroidery and beading.

David Fielden
071-376 8148. Glamorous wedding dresses and evening wear made to order using an exotic array of materials. *By appt only.*

Laura Ashley 4 B2
451 Oxford St W1. 071-355 1363. Tradition, nostalgia and femininity are Laura Ashley's trademarks in wedding dresses. Natural fabrics and reasonably priced.

Liberty 4 D2
210-220 Regent St W1. 071-734 1234. Liberty has 12 designers working on its wedding dresses. Sample stock from which stock sizes made up, although made-to-measure service available from some designers.

Pronuptia de Paris 4 C2
19-20 Hanover St W1. 071-493 9152. Large collection of bridalwear which changes every season. Full fitting service by specialists.

Dress Hire

One Night Stand 7 A3
44 Pimlico Rd SW1. 071-730 8708.

Ballgowns, cocktail and dinner wear. Over 400 garments in stock with new styles each season.

Contemporary Wardrobe 2 A5
The Horse Hospital, Colonnade, Herbrand St WC1. 071-713 7370. Full-length gowns and cocktail dresses. Silk, taffeta, chiffon. Jewellery and gloves for hire. Make dresses to order.

Simpsons
158 Munster Rd SW6. 071-836 5993. Specialise in ballgowns and evening attire generally.

Twentieth Century Frox
614 Fulham Rd SW6. 071-731 3242. Ballgowns and cocktail dresses.

Children's clothes

See 'Children's shopping' section in 'Children's London'.

Accessories

General

Accessorize 4 F3
Unit 22, Covent Garden Mkt WC2. 071-240 2107. A large selection of earrings, costume jewellery, bags, belts, shoes and watches. *OPEN 10.00-20.00 Mon-Sat, 12.00-18.00 Sun.*

American Retro 4 E3
35 Old Compton St W1. 071-734 3477. Sells original '50s American garb and natty accessories.

Brats 6 D4
281 King's Rd SW3. 071-351 7674. An up-market accessory shop; all good designs and value for money.

Cobra
5 Portobello Grn, 281 Portobello Rd W10. 081-960 4874. Own label flamboyant designer jewellery, bags, belts and wallets.

Gallery 4 D4
1 Duke of York St, off Jermyn St SW1. 071-930 5974. Specialise in high quality accessories for men – blazer buttons and crests for various schools, universities and regiments. Also shirts, ties, cuff links, belts and braces.

Gucci 4 D3
33 Old Bond St W1. 071-629 2716. Classic, matching accessories all emblazoned with the recognisable Gucci 'G's.

Hermes 4 C3
155 New Bond St W1. 071-499 8856. Expensive, chic quality bags, scarves, jewellery and perfumes.

Mary Quant   4 **D3**
21 Carnaby St W1. 071-494 3277.
Bursting with novel accessories, including
fancy tights, make-up and undies. Stock
changes regularly.

Next Accessories   3 **C5**
123c Kensington High St W8. 071-938
4211. Accessories in sophisticated
colours and styles. 'Essentials' are a
range of useful, well-designed objects
which make great gifts – torches, diaries,
luggage etc.

Filofax

Faxcessory   4 **F4**
Unit 5, Villier St WC2. 071-321 0074.
Filofaxes, inserts, briefcases.

Filofax Centre   4 **D3**
21 Conduit St W1. 071-499 0457.
Filofaxes to fit every pocket and an amazing range of inserts.

Just Facts   4 **D2**
43 Broadwick St W1. 071-734 5034.
Stocks the entire Filofax range.

Handbags & luggage

*Most fashion and shoe shops carry a good
range of handbags. For a selection of
luggage, try the large department stores.*

Alba Handbags   1 **B6**
189 Baker St NW1. 071-935 3410. Good
modern bags; exciting shapes and
colours.

The City Bag Store   4 **C2**
3 South Molton St W1. 071-499 2549.
Wide range of bags including 'le sport
sac' of New York, and Enny of Italy.

Mulberry   4 **B2**
12 Gees Court, St Christopher's Pl W1.
071-493 2546. Full range of Scotch grain
and leather luggage, fashion handbags
and briefcases.

Salisburys   4 **A2**
530 Oxford St W1. 071-355 1391. High
street chain selling wide range of inexpensive bags, handbags and luggage.

Hats

Bates   4 **E3**
21a Jermyn St SW1. 071-734 2722.
Edwardian-fronted men's hat shop, also
favoured by the ladies.

David Shilling   3 **F1**
5 Homer St W1. 071-262 2363. Famous
and exclusive hat creations; as immortalised by Mr Shilling's mother at Ascot.
Chic and elegant hats for everyday wear.

The Hat Shop   4 **F2**
58 Neal St WC2. 071-836 6718. A wide
variety of hats for men and women, ranging from classic panamas and boaters to
designer specials.

Herald & Hart Hatters
131 St Philip St SW8. 071-627 2414.
Amazing selection of straw hats and pins
to keep them on.

Herbert Johnson   4 **C3**
30 New Bond St W1. 071-408 1174. A
fine range of hats for men and women to
suit all occasions. Everything from crash
helmets to yachting caps.

James Lock   4 **D4**
6 St James's St SW1. 071-930 5849.
Hats for every occasion. Felt hats, tweed
hats and caps. Famous for bowlers. Also
top-quality riding and polo hats.

Specialist shops and services

*London is an international centre of art,
fashion, antiques and collectors' items.
Many shops have specialised in certain
goods and have become world-famous
names. The list below represents only a
selection of some of the best shops in
each category. Some shops close on Sat
afternoon and stay open late on Wed or
Thur evenings.*

'Which?' Magazine   1 **D5**
Consumers' Association, 2 Marylebone
Rd NW1. 071-486 5544. The best subscription periodical for unbiased testing of
everyday products and services. Available
at libraries for reference.

Animals

Animal Fair   3 **B6**
17 Abingdon Rd W8. 071-937 0011.
Animals and services such as boarding
(for small animals) and grooming. Agency
for kennels in the country.

Battersea Dogs Home   7 **B5**
4 Battersea Park Rd SW8. 071-622
3626. Dogs and cats, some with pedi-
grees, all available for adoption.

Christopher Dog Consultants
30 Crooked Billet, Wimbledon Common
SW19. 081-947 3065. Long-established
dog agency. Specialise in Yorkshire
Terriers and Shihtzu but will direct you to
the breeder of any dog. Also clipping and
shampooing, and help with exporting.

Friends of Animals League
Foal Farm, Jail La, Biggin Hill, Kent.
(0959) 572386. Mainly dogs, cats, and
other domestic animals, rescued and
available for adoption by carefully vetted
homes.

National Canine Defence   **1 E2**
League
1 Pratt Mews NW1. 071-388 0137. Re-houses abandoned dogs and provides information on canine problems and care.

Antiques

There are hundreds of antique shops in London selling 18th and 19thC furniture, china and objets d'art. Good hunting grounds are the King's Rd, Portobello Rd, Camden Passage in Islington, Kensington Church St, Fulham Rd and Camden Town.

Antique fairs

Antiquarian Book Fair   **4 C4**
Park Lane Hotel, Piccadilly W1. 071-499 6321. International fair with books, documents, musical scores. *Late Jun.*

Chelsea Antiques Fair   **6 E3**
Chelsea Old Town Hall, King's Rd SW3. 071-937 5464. Held from *Mar-Sep*, this well-established fair offers a wide range of antiques and works of art.

Antique shops

Bluett & Sons   **4 C3**
60 Brook St W1. 071-629 4018. Mainly Chinese, and some south-east Asian, ceramics and works of art.

T. Crowther & Son
282 North End Rd SW6. 071-385 1375. Period lead, bronze and stone figures, gates, mantelpieces, wrought-iron work, panelling and beautiful furniture.

Gallery of Antique Costume and Textiles
2 Church St NW8. 071-723 9981. One of Europe's largest suppliers of antique costumes and textiles. Pillows of London is part of the Gallery.

Jeremy   **6 F1**
29 Lowndes St SW1. 071-823 2923. English and French furniture and objets d'art.

Jonathan Harris   **3 B5**
54 Kensington Church St W8. 071-937 3133. Fine quality and unusual European and Oriental furniture and works of art.

Mayorcas   **4 D4**
38 Jermyn St SW1. 071-629 4195. Well-known dealers in antique textiles – costumes, embroidery, vestments, tapestry.

Myriad
131 Portland Rd W11. 071-229 1709. Painted and decorative furniture and general antiques.

Pelham Galleries   **4 B3**
24-25 Mount St W1. 071-629 0905.

Specialists in English and Continental furniture, works of art, musical instruments and tapestries.

Spink & Son   **4 D4**
5-7 King St SW1. 071-930 7888. English paintings and watercolours. Silver, jewellery, paperweights, Oriental, Asian and Islamic art, textiles, medals and coins.

Antique markets

Covered antique markets can be found in Camden Passage, Portobello Rd, King's Rd and as follows:

Alfie's Antique Market
13-25 Church St NW8. 071-723 6066. Five floors of antique stalls selling just about everything, also some repairs done. Coffee bar.

Antiquarius   **6 E3**
137 King's Rd SW3. 071-352 7989. All aspects of fine, applied and decorative arts. Also worth visiting for the antique clothing.

Chelsea Antique Market   **6 E4**
245-253 King's Rd SW3. 071-352 5581. A large, busy market covering all collectors' items.

Furniture Cave   **6 C5**
533 King's Rd SW10. 071-352 4229. Several companies under one roof selling a wide range of non-contemporary furniture. Also have a large architectural and sculpture range.

Grays Market   **4 C3**
1-7 Davies Mews W1. 071-629 7034. Two giant covered markets selling a huge selection of antiques.

Antiquities

Charles Ede   **4 C3**
20 Brook St W1. 071-493 4944. Roman, Greek, Egyptian and Near Eastern antiquities. *OPEN Tue-Fri 12.30-16.30, or by appt.*

Aquaria

Aquapets
17 Leeland Rd W13. 081-567 2748. Excellent general stock of fish, tanks and equipment.

Queensborough Fisheries
111 Goldhawk Rd W12. 081-743 2730. Excellent selection of various tropical and pond fishes. Also equipment, tanks and water plants. *CLOSED Thur.*

Tachbrook Tropicals   **7 C2**
244 Vauxhall Bridge Rd SW1. 071-834 5179. Importers and growers of over 200 species of tropical water plants for the

aquarium. Also import fish. Accessories. Maintenance and servicing of aquaria.

Arts & crafts supplies

Alec Tiranti **1 E5**
27 Warren St W1. 071-636 8565. Large range of tools and material for wood and stone carving. Also plaster, resins, fibreglass and cold-pouring rubbers.

J. Blundell & Sons **4 D2**
199 Wardour St W1. 071-437 4746. Jewellery 'findings' and supplies. *OPEN 09.30-16.00 Mon, Tue, Thur & Fri.*

Candle Makers Supplies
28 Blythe Rd W14. 071-602 4031. Sell everything for making your own candles as well as equipment for batik and silk-painting. Also wax dye-craft and resin casting. Candle-making, batik and silk-painting classes *some Sat.* Vast range of candles.

Cornelissen **4 F1**
105 Great Russell St WC1. 071-636 1045. Fine art, restoration and print-making materials.

Daler Rowney Ltd **4 E1**
12 Percy St W1. 071-636 8241. Large and varied stock of general artists' paints and materials.

Green & Stone **6 E4**
259 King's Rd SW3. 071-352 0837. Established over 60 years ago. Modern equipment and a collection of Victorian materials such as easels, pens and 19thC watercolour paper.

The Handweaver's Studio & Gallery
29 Haroldstone Rd E17. 081-521 2281. Fleece, yarns, dyes and other equipment for weaving and spinning. Books. Also tuition.

Langford & Hill **4 D3**
10 & 38-40 Warwick St W1. 071-437 9945. The place in London to find a selection of the latest American and German commercial art materials, films, coloured papers, special inks, drawn curves, etc. Expert advice.

T.N. Lawrence **2 C5**
119 Clerkenwell Rd EC1. 071-242 3534. Everything for the engraver, etcher and print-maker.

Paperchase **4 E1**
213 Tottenham Court Rd W1. 071-580 8496. Exciting collection of papers and card. All types of artists' papers, book papers, Japanese papers, foils and display papers.

Reeves Dryad **3 B5**
178 Kensington High St W8. 071-937 5370. Think of a craft and they'll sell you the materials for it.

Russell & Chapple **4 F2**
23 Monmouth St WC2. 071-836 7521. Supply artists' fabrics.

Thorpe Modelmakers **5 B1**
98 Gray's Inn Rd WC1. 071-405 1016. Balsa wood, trees, cars and people for modelmaking.

Winsor & Newton **4 E2**
51-52 Rathbone Pl W1. 071-636 4231. Good general selection of artists' materials, papers and paints.

Auctioneers: general

W. & F.C. Bonham & Sons **3 F6**
Montpelier Galleries, Montpelier St SW7. 071-584 9161. Paintings, furniture, carpets, porcelain, jewellery and silver.

Christie's **4 D4**
8 King St, SW1. 071-839 9060. Internationally famous. Comprehensive fine art auctioneers since 1766.

Christie's South Kensington **6 D2**
85 Old Brompton Rd SW7. 071-581 7631. All sorts of antique and antiquarian objects, including pictures, jewellery, silver, glass, ceramics, furniture and books.

Croydon Auction Rooms
144-150 London Rd, West Croydon, Surrey. 081-688 1123. Miscellaneous sales *10.00 Sat.*

Lots Road Galleries **6 C5**
71 Lots Rd SW10. 071-351 7771. General assorted sales *18.00 every Mon.* View *09.00-17.00 Mon, 09.00-15.00 Fri, 10.00-13.00 Sat & Sun.*

Phillips **4 C2**
101 New Bond St W1. 071-629 6602. Fine arts auctioneers and valuers.

Phillips Marylebone Auction Rooms **3 C3**
10 Salem Rd W2. 071-229 9090. Sale of paintings only *11.00 Fri.* Viewing *09.00-19.00 Thur.*

Sotheby's **4 C3**
34-35 New Bond St W1. 071-493 8080. Internationally famous for antiques and works of art. Paintings, ceramics, glass, furniture, silver, jewellery, books, manuscripts, photographic material and collectors' items.

Auctions: stamps & coins

Glendining **4 C2**
101 New Bond St W1. 071-493 2445. Coins, military and naval medals. *About 20 sales a year.*

London Stamp and Coin Exchange **4 C3**
5 Buckingham St, Strand WC2. 071-930 1413. *One or two auctions a year.*

Royale Stamp Co　　　　**4 F3**
42 Maiden La WC2. 081-991 1872.

Stanley Gibbons　　　　**4 F3**
399 Strand WC2. 071-836 8444.
Stamps, postal history, albums and catalogues. *Sixteen auctions a year.*

Bath repair

Renubath
248 Lillie Rd SW6. 071-381 8337. Bath
resurfacing. Chemical cleaning, specialist
repairs to enamel and porcelain. Good
range of colours.

Bathrooms

Bathroom Discount Centre
297 Munster Rd SW6. 071-381 4222.
Suites by Ideal, Twyfords and Armitage
Shanks, all at a discount.

Czech & Speake　　　　**4 D4**
39c Jermyn St SW1. 071-439 0216. Brass
taps and shower fittings (some thermostat-
ic) moulded from Edwardian originals. Also
sell accessories and toiletries.

Sitting Pretty
131 Dawes Rd SW6. 071-381 0049.
Lavatory seats in mahogany or obeche
(the latter can be stained to any colour).
Also unfinished mahogany seats for the
DIY enthusiast and reproduction, period
suites.

Beauty specialists

Alternative & Orthodox　　　**1 C5**
Medicine Clinic
56 Harley House, Marylebone Rd NW1.
071-486 8087. Treatments include aromatherapy, reflexology, facials, scarring
treatments and stress alleviation. Own
range of natural products designed to
treat specific skin problems and types.

The Body Shop　　　　**3 B6**
137 Kensington High St W8. 071-376
0771. Sell a large range of preparations
based on fruit, flowers, spices and
woods, formulated by herbalists. Non-
animal derived products. Other branches.

Cosmetics à la Carte　　　**6 G1**
19b Motcomb St SW1. 071-235 0596.
'Beauty workshop' with advice and a
chance to experiment.

Delia Collins　　　　**3 F6**
19 Beauchamp Pl SW3. 071-584 2423.
Well-known and long-established beauty
specialists. Sell their own preparations.

Helena Harnik　　　　**4 A2**
19 Upper Berkeley St W1. 071-724 1518.
Specialise in electrolysis and the treatment of problem skins.

Joan Price's Face Place　　　**6 F2**
33 Cadogan St SW3. 071-589 9062.
Make-up lessons using many different
products from various ranges. Also body
and facial massages, pedicure and
manicure, waxing, lash tinting, electrolysis, cathiodermie.

Ray Cochrane Beauty School　**4 A1**
118 Baker St W1. 071-486 6291. Deal
with skin troubles, figure problems and
unwanted hair. Facials, manicures and
pedicures by advanced students under
supervision. Consultants very capable.

Yves Rocher　　　　**4 B2**
7 Gees Ct W1. 071-409 2975. Shop
packed with their famous beauty products
– everything from shampoo to perfume.
The emphasis is on natural beauty.

Bedroom shops

And So To Bed. . .
638-640 King's Rd SW6. 071-731 3593.
Specialists in antique, modern and
designer beds. Brass headboards and
wood and brass bedsteads. Complete
range of bedlinen.

West London Bedding
313-321 North End Rd SW6. 071-385
2000. Huge warehouse with brass, pine,
sofa beds, divans. Very good value.

Books: new

*Most major department stores have book
departments, the better ones being
Harrods, Selfridges and Liberty. The
following bookshops are recommended:*

Barbican Business Book　　　**5 E1**
Centre
9 Moorfields EC2. 071-628 7479. Wide
range of business and finance books.

Books Etc　　　　**4 E2**
120 Charing Cross Rd WC2. 071-379
6838. Well-organised general bookstore.

Cinema Bookshop　　　　**4 E2**
13-14 Great Russell St WC1. 071-637
0206. Specialists in books relating to the
cinema, including out-of-print titles and
magazines.

Collet's　　　　**4 F1**
40 Great Russell St WC1. 071-580 7538.
Specialise in Russian and Eastern
European books.

Compendium　　　　**1 D2**
234 Camden High St NW1. 071-485
8944. Contemporary bookshop specialising in political and feminist literature. US
fiction. Also the occult, mysticism,
psychology and fringe subjects.

Countryside Bookshop　　　**4 D1**
39 Goodge St W1. 071-636 3156.

Collection of books, maps and field guides about the British country~ide.

Dillon's   **1 F5**
82 Gower St WC1. 071-636 1577. Large academic and general stock including science and language. Some antiquarian and second-hand books. Other branches.

The Economists' Bookshop   **5 A2**
Clare Market, Portugal St WC2. 071-405 5531. Specialists in social science and business books. Second-hand dept.

European Bookshop   **4 D3**
4 Regent Pl, off Regent St W1. 071-734 5259. Mainly French books but also Spanish, German and Italian, plus European periodicals.

Forbidden Planet   **4 E2**
71 New Oxford St WC1. 071-379 6042. Specialists in science fiction, fantasy and horror. Large stock of comics and posters.

Foyles   **4 E2**
119-125 Charing Cross Rd WC2. 071-437 5660. The biggest – has practically every English book in print.

French's Theatre Bookshop   **1 E5**
52 Fitzroy St W1. 071-387 9373. Books on the theatre and play scripts.

Gay's the Word   **2 A5**
66 Marchmont St WC1. 071-278 7654. Gay and feminist bookshop. New and second-hand. *OPEN 11.00-19.00 Mon-Sat, 14.00-18.00 Sun.*

Grant & Cutler   **4 D2**
55-57 Great Marlborough St W1. 071-734 2012. New and second-hand books in German, French, Spanish, Portuguese and Italian.

Hatchards   **4 D3**
187 Piccadilly W1. 071-439 9921. Something of an institution. Comprehensive selection of general books. Knowledgeable staff.

HMSO Bookshop   **5 A1**
49 High Holborn WC1. 071-873 0011. HMSO publications on every subject from cooking to parliament. No fiction.

Motor Books   **4 F3**
33-36 St Martin's Ct WC2. 071-836 5376. Specialists in books on cars and aviation. Also military and railway books. Worldwide mail order service.

Pan Bookshop   **6 D3**
158-162 Fulham Rd SW10. 071-373 4997. Wide selection of paperbacks and most new hardbacks. *OPEN long hours: 10.00-22.00 Mon-Sat, 12.00-21.30 Sun.*

The Penguin Bookshop   **4 F3**
10 Covent Garden Mkt WC2. 071-379 7650. Almost complete range of Penguin titles and a good range of other paperbacks and hardbacks.

Silver Moon   **4 E3**
64-68 Charing Cross Rd WC2. 071-836

7906. Good selection of feminist literature.

W.H. Smith
General books. Branches throughout London and at railway stations.

Sportspages   **4 E2**
94-96 Charing Cross Rd WC2. 071-240 9604. Sports bookshop covering all aspects of sport and fitness. Also stocks magazines and videos.

Stanfords   **4 F3**
12-14 Long Acre WC2. 071-836 1321. World's largest map and travel bookshop. Also wall maps of the world, globes and ancient plans of towns.

Travel Bookshop
13 Blenheim Cres W11. 071-229 5260. Books for every type of travel experience.

Travis & Emery   **4 F3**
17 Cecil Ct WC2. 071-240 2129. New and second-hand books on music. Theatrical and musical prints. Catalogues issued.

Waterstone's   **3 B6**
193 Kensington High St W8. 071-937 8432. Good general bookshop. Other branches.

Watkins Books Ltd   **4 F3**
19-21 Cecil Ct WC2. 071-836 2182. Mysticism, the occult, religions and astrology.

Wholefood   **4 B1**
24 Paddington St W1. 071-935 3924. Books on nutrition and health, diets, natural childbirth, ecology and agriculture.

A. Zwemmer   **4 E2**
80 Charing Cross Rd WC2. 071-379 7886. Also at 24 Litchfield St WC2 (**4 E3**). 071-836 4710. Comprehensive stock of international books on art, architecture, design, fashion, film and photography.

Books: rare & antiquarian

The book collector is fortunate in having over 250 bookshops in London, many specialising in particular subjects. Charing Cross Rd, Cecil Ct and around the British Museum are good areas for browsing.

Bell Book & Radmall   **4 F3**
4 Cecil Ct WC2. 071-240 2161. Modern first editions of English and American literature. Plus detective, science and fantasy fiction.

Bernard Quaritch   **4 D3**
5-8 Lower John St, Golden Sq W1. 071-734 2983. Illuminated manuscripts, early printed books, English literature pre-1900, natural history, science and travel.

Dance Books   **4 F3**
9 Cecil Ct WC2. 071-836 2314. All aspects of dancing and human move-

ment. Also posters, photos, records and video cassettes.

David Drummond   4 F3
11 Cecil Ct WC2. 071-836 1142. Rare and out-of-print books on the performing arts, and ephemera including circus, music hall and theatrical souvenirs. Also early children's books and Victorian valentines. *Unusual hours: 11.00-14.30 & 15.30-17.45 Mon-Fri, 11.00-14.15 first Sat in month (other Sats by appt only).*

Hatchards   4 D3
187 Piccadilly W1. 071-439 9921. Fine, illustrated second-hand books above a modern bookshop. Search facility.

G. Heywood Hill   4 C4
10 Curzon St W1. 071-629 0647. Books with fine colour plates. Also an extensive collection of 19th and early 20thC children's books and general second-hand books. New books stocked as well.

Maggs Bros   4 C3
50 Berkeley Sq W1. 071-493 7160. Rare and fine books, illuminated manuscripts, autographed letters.

Marlborough Rare Books   4 C3
144-146 New Bond St W1. 071-493 6993. Illustrated books, bibliography and architecture.

Otto Haas
49 Belsize Park Gdns NW3. 071-722 1488. One of the best stocks of music, musical literature and autographs in the world. *By appt only.*

Pickering & Chatto   4 E4
17 Pall Mall SW1. 071-930 2515. Rare and antiquarian books. English literature, science, medicine, economics. Literary manuscripts.

Sotherans   4 D3
2-5 Sackville St W1. 071-439 6151. Established in London 1815. Antiquarian books, prints, periodicals and some modern books. Also binding and restoration. Separate Print Gallery at 80 Pimlico Rd SW1 (**7 A3**). 071-730 8756.

Turret   4 F2
36 Great Queen St WC2. 071-405 6058. Engagingly chaotic with rare, antiquarian and new tomes. Beckett, Auden, Hughes and Sillitoe.

Book binding & restorations

Sangorski & Sutcliffe   5 F5
Zaehnsdorf
175r (entrance at 159) Bermondsey St SE1. 071-407 1244. Two companies at the same address. Hand binding in all styles and materials, design service. Repair and restore leather bindings.

Buttons

Try the markets – Camden Lock for art deco styles.

Button Queen   4 B2
19 Marylebone La W1. 071-935 1505. Specialise in antique, old and modern buttons, buckles, etc.

Taylors Buttons   4 D3
1 Silver Pl W1. 071-437 1016. Largest variety of buttons in London.

Cameras

See under 'Photographic equipment'.

Camping

See under 'Sports equipment'.

Carpets: antique & oriental

Bernardout & Bernardout   6 D2
7 Thurloe Pl SW7. 071-584 7658. Oriental rugs and carpets, tapestries and needlework. Some French and English stock. Expert cleaners and repairers.

David Black Oriental Carpets
96 Portland Rd W11. 071-727 2566. Specialists in antique tribal rugs, carpets, kilims, embroideries, Indian dhurries and rare textiles. Valuations, restoration, cleaning. Also new carpets and kilims. Publish 7 volumes on antique carpets and sell books by other publishers on antique carpets. *OPEN 10.00-18.00 Mon-Fri & 11.00-17.30 Sat, or by appt.*

C. John   4 B4
70 South Audley St W1. 071-493 5288. Oriental and Persian carpets.

Kilim Warehouse
28a Pickets St SW12. 081-675 3122. A vast selection of antique, decorative and new kilims from all parts of the world. Cleaning and restoration service.

Mayorcas   4 D4
38 Jermyn St SW1. 071-629 4195. Outstanding stock of European carpets, textiles and tapestries.

Samad's   4 B5
33a Knightsbridge SW1. 071-235 5712. Variety of oriental carpets and rugs.

Carpet & textile restorers

Anglo-Persian Carpet Co   6 D2
6 South Kensington Station Arc SW7. 071-589 5457. Oriental carpets and tapestries.

David Black Oriental Carpets
96 Portland Rd W11. 071-727 2566. Cleaning and repair service for oriental and other antique carpets.

Ceramics: antique

The principal areas for antique ceramic shops are Kensington Church St and Knightsbridge – remember to look in the back streets.

Alistair Sampson Antiques   6 **E1**
156 Brompton Rd SW3. 071-589 5272. Early English pottery. Also 17th and 18thC oak furniture, English brass, needlework, primitive pictures and treen.

Haslam and Whiteway   3 **B4**
105 Kensington Church St W8. 071-229 1145. Late 19thC Arts and Craft Movement pieces.

Ceramic restorations

China Repairers
64 Charles La NW8. 071-722 8407. Specialise in repairing antique and modern china and glass.

Robin Hood's Workshop   6 **G2**
18 Bourne St SW1. 071-730 0425. China repairs and tuition in ceramic restoration. By appt only.

Charity shops

Charitable organisations such as Oxfam, Notting Hill Housing Trust and Sue Ryder Foundation run shops (numerous branches – check in telephone directory for your nearest one) selling second-hand clothes, books and bric-à-brac in good condition. Some also sell ethnic handicrafts. School and church halls often hold beneficiary jumble sales where both donations and buyers are welcome.

China, glass & porcelain

Casa Fina   4 **F3**
9 Central Av, Covent Garden Mkt WC2. 071-836 0289. Ceramics from Italy – lamp-bases, tableware, chandeliers.

Chinacraft   4 **B3**
121 Park St W1. 071-499 9881. Fine English china, crystal and figurines. Over 15 branches, most in central London.

Craftsmen Potters Shop   4 **D2**
William Blake House, 7 Marshall St W1. 071-437 7605. Only members of the Craftsmen Potters Association can sell work here. This demands a high standard.

General Trading Company   6 **F2**
144 Sloane St SW1. 071-730 0411. Some of the best designs in contemporary English and Continental glass and china. Large stock.

Gered   4 **D4**
173-174 Piccadilly W1. 071-629 2614. Large showroom displaying and selling Spode, Royal Crown Derby, Royal Doulton and Wedgwood.

The Glasshouse   4 **F2**
65 Long Acre WC2. 071-836 9785. Here you can see craftsmen making glass – and everything is for sale. Restoration work undertaken.

Lalique Ltd   4 **C3**
162 New Bond St W1. 071-499 8228. Elegant displays of Lalique crystal, Limoges porcelain and Christofle silver.

Lawleys   4 **D3**
154 Regent St W1. 071-734 2621. Popular chain selling Wedgwood, Royal Doulton, Waterford crystal and other top names.

Reject China Shop   6 **E1**
33-35 Beauchamp Pl SW3. 071-581 0737. Also at 134 Regent St W1 (4 **D3**). 071-434 2502. Reject china at low prices – the flaws tend to be hardly noticeable.

Rosenthal China Shop   4 **D3**
139 Regent St W1. 071-734 3076. Specialise in Rosenthal china, glass and porcelain.

Villeroy & Boch   4 **D3**
203 Regent St W1. 071-434 0249. Villeroy & Boch were established in 1748. Only English showroom stocking own china, porcelain and cutlery, plus Atlantis crystal.

Chocolates & confectionery

Fortnum & Mason, Harrods and Selfridges all have excellent confectionery departments selling hand-made English and Continental chocolates.

Bendicks   4 **G3**
7 Aldwych WC2. 071-836 1846. Famous for their bittermints, but also stock a wide range of chocolates.

Charbonnel et Walker   4 **D3**
28 Old Bond St W1. 071-491 0939. Hand-made, mainly soft-centred chocolates. Exotic, extravagant presentation boxes in silk or satin, but they will fill anything with their chocolates!

Prestat   4 **D4**
14 Princes Arc, Piccadilly SW1. 071-629 4838. Delicious hand-made chocolates and fresh cream truffles. Seasonal novelties.

Rococo   6 **D4**
321 King's Rd SW3. 071-352 5857. Traditional chocolatier. Over 50 types of loose hand-made chocolates. Delicious fresh cream truffles. Will design anything in chocolate.

Thornton's   4 **F3**
2 Covent Garden Mkt WC2. 071-836 2173. Continental chocolates, toffee and seasonal novelties.

Clocks & watches: antique

Aubrey Brocklehurst 6 **C2**
124 Cromwell Rd SW7. 071-373 0319.
Specialise in longcase and bracket
clocks; also barometers. Clock and furniture restorations.

Camerer Cuss 4 **D4**
17 Ryder St W1. 071-930 1941. Antique
watches and clocks.

Garrard & Co 4 **D3**
112 Regent St W1. 071-734 7020.
Pieces by the great English clockmakers
of the past and an extensive range of
French period carriage clocks. Top quality.

Pearl Cross 4 **F3**
35 St Martin's Ct WC2. 071-836 2814.
Antique jewellery, silver and presentation
gold watches from 1880 onwards. Also
antique pocket and wrist watches.

Peter K. Weiss 5 **A1**
18 Silver Vaults, Chancery La WC2. 071-
242 8100. Antique clocks and watches.

Ronald A. Lee 4 **C3**
1-9 Bruton Pl W1. 071-629 5600. 17th
and 18thC clocks of very high quality.
Also furniture and fine art.

Clock restoration

See also under 'Clocks & watches:
antique'.

Clerkenwell Glass 2 **D5**
29 Britton St EC1. 071-253 3110.

Clock Clinic
85 Lower Richmond Rd SW15. 081-788
1407.

J. Walker 4 **C2**
1st Floor, 64 South Molton St W1. 071-
629 3487. Modern clock repairs too.

Coffee & tea

Algerian Coffee Stores 4 **E3**
52 Old Compton St W1. 071-437 2480.
Established in 1887, the shop sells 30
different blends of coffee and over 100
leaf, flavoured and herb teas. Also coffee-
making equipment.

Drury Tea & Coffee Co 4 **F2**
37 Drury La WC2. 071-836 2607. Also at
New Row WC2 (4 **F3**). 071-836 1960.
Long-established company •offering 32
different types of coffee and 35-40 types
of tea. Also coffee-making equipment and
good quality biscuits and preserves.

Ferns 4 **E2**
27 Rathbone Pl W1. 071-636 2237. Old-
established firm selling 14 blended
coffees and a good selection of leaf,
flavoured and herb teas. All own-label.

H.R. Higgins (Coffee man) 4 **B2**
79 Duke St W1. 071-629 3913. Over 40

different types of coffee including original
and blended, light, medium and dark
roasts. Also over 20 teas.

The Tea House 4 **F2**
15a Neal St WC2. 071-240 7539. More
than 50 own-label leaf teas and tisanes in
this striking red and black shop devoted
to tea and 'teaphernalia'. Vast selection of
teapots including unusual and novelty;
caddies, preserves, biscuits.

Coins & medals

See also 'Auctions: stamps & coins'.
A.H. Baldwin 4 **F3**
11 Adelphi Ter WC2. 071-930 6879.
Good general selection. Ancient,
medieval and modern; commemorative
and military.

Dolphin Coins
2c Englands La NW3. 071-722 4116.
Hammered coins in gold and silver. Rare
colonial coins. Foreign coins, banknotes
and medals.

B.A. Seaby 4 **C3**
7 Davies St W1. 071-495 2590. One of
the largest coin shops in the world and
publishers of standard coin catalogues for
British, Roman and Greek coins.

Spink 4 **D4**
5-7 King St SW1. 071-930 7888. They
stock or can acquire any coin wanted by
a collector. Also mint commemorative
medals.

Computers

Lots of high street chain stores now sell
computers but their selection of software
can be limited. The heart and soul of
London's computer world is Tottenham
Court Rd (4 **E1**) where dozens of shops
sell computers, printers and electronic
gear.
See also 'Electronics shops'.

Centre Point Software 4 **E2**
20-21 St Giles High St WC2. 071-836
0599. Huge selection of computer
software, including all top computer
games.

Copper & brass

Jack Casimar 3 **B3**
23 Pembridge Rd W11. 071-727 8643.
Large stock of antique brass, copper and
pewter.

Knobs & Knockers 6 **B5**
385 King's Rd SW10. 071-352 5693.
A huge selection of brass furniture and
fittings.

Crafts: national

Africa 4 F3
Kikapu, The Africa Centre, 38 King St
WC2. 071-240 6098. Baskets, jewellery,
clothes.

Australia 5 A3
Australian Gift Shop, Western Australia
House, 113-116 Strand WC2. 071-836
2292. Aboriginal crafts and Australian-
made gifts and souvenirs; books and
food products including Vegemite.

Britain
Craft Council Gallery Shop 2 C3
44a Pentonville Rd N1. 071-278 7700.
High-quality British crafts. Glass, ceramics,
jewellery, textiles, basketry.
Naturally British 4 F3
13 New Row WC2. 071-240 0551.
Hand-made British goods. Pottery, toys,
gifts, clothes, hand-knits and jewellery.

Denmark 4 C3
Royal Copenhagen Porcelain and Georg
Jensen Silver, 15 New Bond St W1. 071-
499 6541. Also Holmegaard glass.

France 6 E2
Souleiado, 171 Fulham Rd SW3. 071-589
6180. Provençal fabrics and accessories.

Ireland 4 D4
The Irish Shop, 11 Duke St W1. 071-935
1366. Waterford crystal, Donegal tweed,
Irish linen, Belleek china, Arran sweaters,
Celtic jewellery.

Japan
Asahi, 110 Golborne Rd W10. 081-960
7299. Authentic Japanese kimonos and
fans.

New Zealand 4 F3
Kiwifruits, 25 Bedfordbury WC2. 071-240
1423. Gifts, crafts, books. Kiwifruits New
Zealand Book Shop, 6 Royal Opera Arc,
Pall Mall SW1 (4 **E4**). 071-930 4587.

Peru 7 A2
Inca, 45 Elizabeth St SW1. 071-730
7941. Colourful, hand-made Peruvian
clothes, sweaters, accessories and gifts.

Russia 5 A3
The Russian Shop, 99 Strand WC2. 071-
497 9104. Russian dolls, painted trays,
lacquered boxes and other handicrafts.

Scotland 4 A5
The Scotch House, 2 Brompton Rd SW1.
071-581 2151. Also 86 and 191 Regent
St W1 (4 **D3**). Excellent tartans, kilts,
rugs, foods and Fair Isle, Arran and
Shetland woollens.

Spain
Casa Fina 4 F3
9 Covent Garden Mkt WC2. 071-836
0289. Spanish porcelain.
Casa Pupo 7 A2
56 Pimlico Rd SW1. 071-730 7111.
Spanish, Italian and Portuguese furniture.

Switzerland 4 E3
Swiss Centre, Leicester Sq WC2. 071-
734 0444. Cuckoo clocks, army knives,
cheese raclettes, dolls, chocolates.

Cycles

Edwardes
223 Camberwell Rd SE5. 071-703 3676.
Wide range of cycles for children and
adults. Cycling accessories, second-hand
bikes and repair service.

F.W. Evans Cycles
77-79 The Cut SE1. 071-928 4785. One
of the largest stockists of bikes and
accessories. Also build touring bikes.

Freewheel
275 West End La NW6. 071-435 3725.
All kinds of bikes plus clothing and accessories.

W.F. Holdsworth
132 Lower Richmond Rd SW15. 081-788
1060. A wide range of bikes and accessories.

Stuart Cycles
1 Ascot Pde, Clapham Park Rd SW4.
071-622 4818. Hand-built and production bikes. Full range of services.

Cycle hire

See under 'Transport in London'.

Discount shopping

*Cheap buys and bargains can often be
found by looking in the local newspapers,
at newsagents' notice-boards or in* Time
Out, Exchange & Mart *and the* Evening
Standard. *Charity shops, jumble sales
and markets are also useful for the low-
budget shopper.*

Domestic help

Also refer to the classified adverts in The
Lady *magazine, 40 Bedford St WC2
(4* **F3**). *071-379 4717.*

Babysitters Unlimited
081-892 8888. Can provide cleaners and
babysitters.

Belgravia Bureau 6 E2.
35 Brompton Rd SW3. 071-584 4343.
Supply cooks, cleaners, housekeepers,
secretaries, chauffeurs, butlers and
gardeners. Can supply couples who work
as a team.

Childminders 1 C6
9 Paddington St W1. 071-935 4386.
Babysitters (mostly trained nurses)
supplied to the home and to hotels in
central London and most suburban areas.

Curzon Cleaning Services
598 Kingston Rd SW20. 081-643 7405. For all kinds of household, window and specialist cleaning. Not daily cleaning.

Lumley Employment   **7 C3**
85 Charlwood St SW1. 071-630 0545. If you want a Cordon Bleu cook for a special occasion, this is the place to come. Catering services agency.

The Nanny Service   **1 C6**
9 Paddington St W1. 071-935 3515. Temporary, permanent and maternity nannies. Residential and non-residential available for positions in London and the Home Counties.

Thames Cleaning Company
16 Hatherley Rd, Sidcup, Kent. 081-300 5888. Clean carpets, dry-clean curtains, polish hard floors and clean windows and venetian blinds. A full cleaning service.

Universal Aunts
PO Box 304, Clapham SW4. 071-738 8937. A well-known agency that will provide all kinds of domestic help, including house-keepers, cooks, nannies, drivers, shopping, caretaking, secretarial work, gardening, babysitting, and a special 'meet and greet' service at all stations and airports. Office OPEN 09.30-17.00.

Dry-cleaning & laundry

There are many reliable dry-cleaners and launderers in London. Sketchley Cleaners is one of the largest chains, with branches on most high streets. For specialist treatment go to:

Dry Cleaning Information Bureau (DIB)
c/o 7 Churchill Ct, 58 Station Rd, Nth Harrow, Middx. Operates the 24-hr DIB Hotline: 081-863 8658, offering free advice on just about any cleaning problem or disaster.

Elegant Cleaners   **3 F2**
30-31 Kendal St W2. 071-402 6108. Specialists in silk, evening gowns, suede, leather and fur.

Jeeves   **6 F1**
8-10 Pont St SW1. 071-235 1101. A personal service. Everything is hand-finished and the prices are reasonable. They collect and deliver in central London and have a postal service. Also carry out repairs and various other services.

Lewis & Wayne Ltd   **6 E2**
13-15 Elystan St SW3. 071-589 5730. For garment cleaning and hand-finishing of evening gowns and bridalwear. Taking down and rehanging curtains, on-site carpet cleaning. All types of hand-finished laundry.

Liliman & Cox   **4 C3**
34 Bruton Pl W1. 071-629 4555. Highest quality cleaning of special garments such as beaded and embroidered dresses.

Suede Services
2a Hoop La NW11. 081-455 0052. Specialise in cleaning, restoring, remodelling and repairing all skin garments, including pigskin.

Textile Services Association
7 Churchill Ct, 58 Station Rd, Nth Harrow, Middx. 081-863 7755. A national trade body with about 350 parent company members who are themselves responsible for approx 2000 dry-cleaners and 500 laundries, all of whom display an LTSA code of practice sign. The association also operates a consumer complaints service.

Electrical

Electrical Contractors' Association   **3 C3**
32-34 Palace Ct W2. 071-229 1266. 450 member firms in London area. High standard of work guaranteed.

Electronics shops

The area around Tottenham Court Rd and St Giles Circus is packed with shops selling electronic, video, radio and tape recording equipment at competitive prices. Edgware Rd also has a good selection. See also 'Computers'.

Henry's   **3 E1**
404 Edgware Rd W2. 071-723 1008. Electronic and radio components, amplifiers. Specialise in test equipment. Prompt mail order service and personal computing.

Sonic Foto Centre   **4 E1**
256 Tottenham Court Rd W1. 071-580 5826. Extensive selection of audio and video equipment.

Tandy   **4 E1**
224 Tottenham Ct Rd W1. 071-436 8837. Chain selling a range of audio and video equipment. Many branches.

Estate Agents

National Association of Estate Agents
Arbon House, 21 Jury St, Warwick, Warks. (0926) 496800. Can give you the names of estate agents in a particular area.

Fancy dress hire

Angels & Bermans   **4 E2**
119 Shaftesbury Av WC2. 071-836 5678.

Vast range of costumes for men and women.

Theatre Zoo **4 E2**
21 Earlham St WC2. 071-836 3150. All types of animal costumes and masks. Also wigs, jewellery and make-up.

Fish

See under 'Aquaria'.

Fishing tackle

See under 'Sports equipment'.

Flowers

See also under 'Gardening'.

The Flower Gallery **7 A2**
114 Ebury St SW1. 071-730 2375. Fresh and dried flowers delivered daily. Herbs also available.

Flower House **6 D2**
315 Brompton Rd SW3. 071-584 4141. Good exotic plants and flowers.

Interflora
Interflora House, Sleaford, Lincs (Head Office). (0529) 304545. Will deliver flowers locally, nationwide or worldwide. Linked to 136 countries. Telephone order service for credit card holders (A.Ax.Dc.V.). *Check in telephone directory for your nearest Interflora florist.*

Jane Packer Floral Design **4 B2**
56 James St W1. 071-935 2673. Bouquets, baskets, fresh and dried flowers. Delivery service.

Joan Palmer **4 E6**
31 Palmer St SW1. 071-222 4364. Bouquets, baskets, fresh flowers. Same-day delivery in London area.

Moyses Stevens Floral Arts **4 C3**
6 Bruton St W1. 071-493 8171. Fresh and dried flowers. Delivery service. Also at 157-158 Sloane St SW1 (**6 F2**). 071-259 9303.

Food: health shops

Ceres Grain Shop **3 A2**
269a Portobello Rd W11. 071-229 5571. Vegetarian, including macrobiotic, food. Complete range of chemical-free herbs, vegetables and grains. Wholefood take-away food cooked on the premises.

Cranks **4 D2**
8 Marshall St W1. 071-437 2915. Appetising health foods, dried fruits and grains. Restaurant next door.

Health Foods
767 Fulham Rd SW6. 071-736 8848. Specialise in honeys and homoeopathic

and back remedies. Also a wide selection of vitamins, minerals and health foods.

Holland & Barrett **4 C2**
Unit C12/C13, West One Shopping Centre, Oxford St W1. 071-493 7988. Complete range of wholefoods and cooking herbs. Cosmetics made with natural ingredients, natural vitamin supplements. Wide range of take-aways.

Neal's Yard Wholefood Warehouse **4 F2**
21-23 Short's Gdns WC2. 071-379 8553. Huge variety of health foods, nuts, dried fruit.

Wholefood **4 B1**
24 Paddington St W1. 071-935 3924. Organically-grown products, free-range eggs, groceries and even wines. Vitamins, nutrition books.

Food shops

Soho is an area full of small Continental shops crammed with exotic foods, wines and spices. See under 'Markets' for cheaper buys and fresh foods.

T. Adamou
124-126 Chiswick High Rd W4. 081-994 0752. Established for 30 years, sells a wide range of foods from Greece and the Middle East.

Carluccio's **4 F2**
28a Neal St WC2. 071-240 1487. Next door to Antonio Carluccio's Neal Street Restaurant. Sells ready-cooked Italian delicacies.

Cheong-Leen **4 F2**
4-10 Tower St WC2. 071-836 5378. Chinese supermarket with a large selection of groceries.

Fortnum & Mason **4 D4**
181 Piccadilly W1. 071-734 8040. Exotic and unusual tinned and bottled foods from all over the world. Famous for hampers.

Fratelli Camisa **4 E3**
1a Berwick St W1. 071-437 7120. Good Continental delicatessen. Wines, fresh pasta and seasonal delicacies such as truffles.

Harrods **4 A6**
Knightsbridge SW1. 071-730 1234. International selection of top-quality fresh, tinned and bottled foods.

International Cheese Centre **1 E6**
21 Goodge St W1. 071-631 4191. Over 400 cheeses. Wines and fresh sandwiches.

Justin de Blank **7 A2**
42 Elizabeth St SW1. 071-730 0605. Wide range of freshly-prepared dishes and prime fruit and vegetables. Fresh home-made bread daily.

Lina Stores   **4 E3**
18 Brewer St W1. 071-437 6482.
Amazing selection of Italian foods.
Excellent fresh pasta, bread and olives.

Maison Sagne   **1 C6**
105 Marylebone High St W1. 071-935
6240. Croissants, superb sausage rolls,
pastries. Excellent gateaux and special
occasion cakes made to order.

Neal's Yard Dairy   **4 F2**
17 Short's Gdns WC2. 071-379 7646.
Up to 30 cheeses from Ireland and Britain
in stock at any one time. Delivery and mail
order service.

Ninjin Food Store   **1 D5**
244 Great Portland St W1. 071-388
2511. Japanese food specialists. Fresh
meat and fish too.

Pak Continental Food Stores
191 Shepherds Bush Mkt W12. 081-743
5389. Specialise in African and West
Indian food.

Pâtisserie Valerie   **4 E3**
44 Old Compton St W1. 071-437 3466.
Excellent cakes and pâtisseries. Also
sandwiches, tea and coffee.

Paxton & Whitfield   **4 D4**
93 Jermyn St SW1. 071-930 0259.
Famous for superb English and
Continental cheeses, traditional hams,
teas, home-made pies and pâtés. Small
selection of wines.

Products from Spain   **4 D1**
89 Charlotte St W1. 071-580 2905.
Importers of a vast range of Spanish
foods – retail and wholesale.

Randall & Aubin   **4 E3**
16 Brewer St W1. 071-437 3507/8.
Pâtés, cheeses of all sorts, assorted
cooked and fresh meats and game.

Viniron   **1 E4**
119 Drummond St NW1. 071-387 8653.
Drummond Street is full of Indian shops
and restaurants. Viniron is one of the best –
spices, curries and vegetables from India.

Vivian's   **6 D4**
360 King's Rd SW3. 071-351 3180.
Delicatessen selling 80 French cheeses,
eight types of olive, hams, salami, over 20
varieties of coffee.

Foreign newspapers & periodicals

*Many of the Soho and Queensway
newsagents deal in foreign papers.
European magazines are usually available
at the larger newsagents and at the
station and airport branches of W.H.
Smith and John Menzies. The following
shops stock a good selection of both:*

Harrods   **4 A6**
Knightsbridge SW1. 071-730 1234.

Capital Newsagents   **4 E3**
48 Old Compton St W1. 071-437 2479.

NSS Newsagents
6 Pembridge Rd W11. 071-229 8020.

Selfridges   **4 B2**
400 Oxford St W1. 071-629 1234.

Solosy   **4 E3**
50 Charing Cross Rd WC2. 071-836 6313.

Furnishing: fabrics & wallpapers

*The big stores, particularly Peter Jones,
John Lewis, Heal's and Liberty, have a
large range of furnishing fabrics and
wallpapers.*

Afia   **4 A1**
96-97 Crawford St W1. 071-402 8201.
Huge comprehensive stock of fabrics.

Cole & Son (Wallpapers)   **4 D1**
18 Mortimer St W1. 071-580 1066.
Exclusive and unusual French and
Continental prints. Fine modern and
traditional English hand-blocked designs.
Complementary fabrics. Telephone
orders 071-580 2288.

Colefax & Fowler   **4 C3**
39 Brook St W1. 071-493 2231.
Exclusive screen-printed wallpapers and
co-ordinating chintzes based on 18th and
19thC country house designs.

Designers Guild   **6 D4**
271 & 277 King's Rd SW3. 071-351
5775. Beautiful fabrics, wall-coverings,
furniture and accessories in plain, floral or
abstract designs.

Elizabeth Eaton   **7 A2**
30 Elizabeth St SW1. 071-589 0118.
Pretty American and French wallpapers in
cottagey prints. Fabrics, upholstery and
furniture too.

Osborne & Little   **6 D4**
304 King's Rd SW3. 071-352 1456. Wallpapers and fabrics. Exclusive designs.

Sanderson
No longer a retail outlet but their wide
selection of floral and co-ordinated
furnishing fabrics and wallpapers are
available at John Lewis, D.H. Evans and
Selfridges.

G. Thornfield   **2 B5**
321 Gray's Inn Rd WC1. 071-837 2771.
Large selection of well-known brands of
wallpaper at up to half list prices.

Watts & Co   **7 D1**
7 Tufton St SW1. 071-222 2893. Unique
and elegant patterns made up in the
colour of your choice from original
Victorian wallpaper blocks. They have
about 32 designs and an unlimited range
of colours.

Furniture: antique

See under 'Antique shops'.

Furniture: modern

The big stores such as D.H. Evans, Harrods, John Lewis and Selfridges have good selections. Marks & Spencer and Next sell their own range of stylish and co-ordinated furniture and accessories.

Ciancimino International   **6 D4**
307-311 King's Rd SW3. 071-352 2016. Sculptor-turned-furniture designer – tables and chairs of aluminium and wood in an interlocking system that allows for adaptation in shape and size; office or residential. Made to order.

Futon Company   **1 E5**
169 Tottenham Court Rd W1. 071-636 9984. Sell the traditional Japanese mattresses and a range of furniture with elements of Japanese design.

Habitat   **4 E1**
196 Tottenham Court Rd W1. 071-631 3880. Popular international and reasonably-priced furniture; colourful household goods.

Heal's   **4 E1**
196 Tottenham Court Rd W1. 071-636 1666. Big selection of the best British and Continental designs.

Ikea
Brent Park, 255 North Circular Rd NW10. 081-451 5611. Vast range of inexpensive and functional furniture. DIY and ready-made. Very good value. Restaurant. Good facilities for children.

Maples   **1 E5**
145 Tottenham Court Rd W1. 071-387 7000. 50,000sq ft of furniture; all types and styles, including reproduction, futuristic and office furniture. Huge range of soft furnishings. Curtain-making service from Maples' own range of fabrics. English and Oriental carpets and rugs. Contract and design service.

Sofas & Sofa-Beds   **4 E1**
219 Tottenham Court Rd W1. 071-636 6001. Wide range of sofas, in many different fabrics, which convert into double beds.

Wesley-Barrell   **4 D2**
60 Berners St W1. 071-580 6979. Sell own-make settees, sofa-beds, beds and chairs, but also stock other makes of dining-room furniture.

Zarach Design   **7 B2**
13 Eccleston St SW1. 071-730 3339. Ultra-modern furniture and fittings in chrome, leather, etc. More an interior design service but will order from catalogue.

Furniture restorers

Clifford Tracy
6/40 Durnford St N15. 081-800 4774. Antique furniture restorers and cabinet makers. Excellent personal service.

W.R. Harvey & Co (Antiques)   **1 C1**
67-70 Chalk Farm Rd NW1. 071-485 1504. Specialist restorers of fine antique furniture.

Phoenix Antique Furniture   **5 C5**
Restoration Ltd
96 Webber St SE1. 071-928 3624. Cabinet work, polishing, upholstery; pieces made to commission.

Gadgets

Innovations
19 Paradise Rd, Richmond, Surrey. 081-948 3792. New products on the market; anything from electric scissors to Italian water sandals. Mail order service available.

Galleries: prints, paintings & sculpture

Most picture galleries are grouped in and around Bond St, South Kensington and St James's. Camden Lock is an interesting area for contemporary pictures and pottery, as are the open-air exhibitions by London's major parks.
This is a selection of specialist galleries often showing exhibitions of individuals' work. See the daily papers, Time Out and the art press for current listings.

Agnew   **4 D4**
43 Old Bond St W1. 071-629 6176. Outstanding selection of old masters.

Annely Juda Fine Art   **4 C2**
23 Dering St W1. 071-629 7578. Russian constructivism and contemporary paintings, drawings and sculpture.

Browse & Derby   **4 D3**
19 Cork St W1. 071-734 7984. 19th and 20thC French and English paintings, drawings and sculpture.

Contemporary Applied Arts   **4 F2**
43 Earlham St WC2. 071-836 6993. Comprehensive display of work by craftsmen in many materials including many British pieces.

Crane Kalman   **6 E1**
178 Brompton Rd SW3. 071-584 7566. 20thC British and European paintings and sculpture.

Curwen Gallery   **4 E1**
4 Windmill St, off Charlotte St W1. 071-636 1459. Originals and prints by young

British artists; also original prints by Henry Moore and Barbara Hepworth.

Editions Alecto   **3 C6**
46 Kelso Pl W8. 071-937 6611. Contemporary and historical original prints including the official facsimile of the *Domesday Book*.

Editions Graphiques   **4 D3**
3 Clifford St W1. 071-734 3944. 19th and 20thC prints, graphics and paintings from 1880. Art nouveau and art deco objects.

Gimpel Fils   **4 C3**
30 Davies St W1. 071-493 2488. Contemporary British, American and European art.

Grosvenor Prints   **4 F2**
28-32 Shelton St WC2. 071-836 1979. A huge selection of antique prints and engravings.

Malcolm Innes Gallery   **6 E2**
172 Walton St SW3. 071-584 0575. Paintings, watercolours and prints of the 19th and 20thC, specialising in Scottish and sporting subjects.

Marlborough Fine Art   **4 D3**
6 Albemarle St W1. 071-629 5161. 19th and 20thC 'master' paintings, contemporary art and sculpture.

Marlborough Graphics   **4 D3**
6 Albemarle St W1. 071-629 5161. Large selection of graphics: Kokoschka, Moore, Richards, Sutherland, Nolan, Kitaj, Pasmoore. Also contemporary graphics and photography.

Mayor Gallery   **4 D3**
22a Cork St W1. 071-734 3558. Contemporary paintings, drawings and sculpture.

Redfern Gallery   **4 D3**
20 Cork St W1. 071-734 1732. 20thC paintings, drawings, sculpture and graphics.

Tyron & Moorland Gallery   **4 D3**
23 Cork St W1. 071-734 6961. Sporting and natural history pictures and paintings.

Waddington   **4 D3**
5, 11, 12 & 34 Cork St W1. 071-437 8611. 20thC painting, works on paper, sculpture and graphics.

Zella 9   **6 C4**
2 Park Wlk SW10. 071-351 0588. Limited edition contemporary prints and watercolours.

Games

Games Workshop
1 Dalling Rd W6. 081-741 3445. Science fiction and military board games. Role-playing games and lead miniatures.

Just Games   **4 D3**
71 Brewer St W1. 071-437 0761. Up-to-date selection of board and card games and executive toys. More traditional games too.

Virgin Games Centre   **4 D2**
100 Oxford St W1. 071-637 7911. Renowned for its incredible fantasy games. Department dedicated to war games. Stock the complete Trivial Pursuit range.

Gardening

See also under 'Flowers'.

Camden Garden Centre   **1 E1**
2 Barker Drive, St Pancras Way NW1. 071-485 8468. Garden and indoor plants. Terracotta pots and troughs.

Chelsea Gardener   **6 E3**
125-147 Sydney St SW3. 071-352 5656. Trees, shrubs, roses, house plants. Garden furniture.

Clifton Nurseries   **3 C1**
5a Clifton Villas W9. 071-289 6851. A very comprehensive range of gardening plants; specialists in town gardens and window boxes. Landscaping service.

Dial A Gardener
The Old Factory, Carpenter's Pl, 111 Clapham High St SW4. 071-498 0500. Young and enthusiastic firm tackling garden design. They'll take on any size job down to window boxes and just tidying up a scruffy corner.

New Covent Garden Market
Vauxhall SW8. 071-720 2211. Cheapest way to buy plants in London – but you must buy by the box. Flower market *OPEN Mon-Fri until 11.00.*

Rassells   **4 A1**
80 Earl's Court Rd W8. 071-937 0481. Everything for the greenfingered; terracotta pots and fibreglass tubs, trelliswork, hanging baskets, window boxes, house plants and herbs, perennials, bulbs and bedding plants. Fresh cut flowers.

Suttons Seeds   **4 G3**
33 Catherine St WC2. 071-836 0619. The showplace of the famous seed company, offering a very wide selection. Also bulbs and garden supplies. Mail order and export service.

Syon Park Garden Centre
Syon Park, Brentford, Middx. 081-568 0134. Housed in the old riding school are all the implements needed for gardening, plus a large selection of garden plants.

Thompson & Morgan
Poplar Rd, Ipswich, Suffolk. (0473) 688588. Seeds usually ordered by mail – this is one of the very best for quality. Particularly good for vegetables and unusual varieties.

Garden furniture & ornaments

John Lewis and Peter Jones both have good garden furniture departments, but they only stock the full range from Mar-Sep. Some garden centres (see under 'Gardening') also stock garden furniture.

Chelsea Gardener   **6 E3**
125-147 Sydney St SW3. 071-352 5656. Full range of garden furniture.

Crowther of Syon Lodge
Syon Lodge, London Rd, Busch Corner, Isleworth, Middx. 081-560 7978. Vast selection of period and period-style garden ornaments. Furniture and chimneypieces.

Julian Chichester Designs
202 Dawes Rd SW6. 071-381 0243. Fine English 18th and 19thC-style garden furniture.

Mallet at Bourdon House   **4 C3**
2 Davies St W1. 071-629 2444. Garden statuary and furniture. Antique dealers.

Gemmology

Gemmological Association   **5 B1**
1st Floor, 27 Greville St EC1. 071-404 3334. Supply crystal specimens and ornamental materials for students. Gem-testing equipment. Also run courses.

R. Holt & Company   **2 C6**
98 Hatton Gdn EC1. 071-405 0197. Semi-precious and precious stones, cut and uncut. Facilities provided for testing stones. Some jewellery. Bead-stringing and stone-cutting on the premises.

Genealogy & heraldry

To help you trace your predecessors and make up the 'family' coat of arms try:

College of Arms   **5 C3**
Queen Victoria St EC4. 071-248 2762. Will undertake research and help identify coats of arms. House official records of all coats of arms ever granted in England.

The Heraldry Society   **4 F1**
44-45 Museum St WC1. 071-430 2172. Membership open to all. Small library. Sell heraldic books.

Society of Genealogists   **2 E5**
14 Charterhouse Bldgs, off Goswell Rd EC1. 071-251 8799. Help to trace your ancestors. Library if you want to do your own research.

Geology

Gregory, Bottley & Lloyd   **6 A4**
8-12 Rickett St SW6. 071-381 5522. Fascinating stock of minerals, fossils, meteorites. Geology equipment.

Gifts

Covent Garden General Store   **4 F2**
111 Long Acre WC2. 071-240 0331. Well-established shop on two floors selling a huge range of tasteful gifts including pottery, comestibles, caneware and ornaments.

Crabtree & Evelyn   **3 C5**
6 Kensington Church St W8. 071-937 9335. Unusual range of comestibles, toiletries and soaps, all delightfully packaged. Books and cards. Mail order service.

The Gift Centre   **4 F1**
140 Southampton Row WC1. 071-837 4084. Wide selection of gift ideas.

Graham & Green   **3 A2**
4 & 7 Elgin Cres W11. 071-727 4594. Cushions covered in Victorian and Edwardian lace. Basketware specialists.

Halcyon Days   **4 C3**
14 Brook St W1. 071-629 8811. Beautiful enamelware, little boxes for all occasions, thimbles, pin-cushions and needlecases. Some small antique items and antique enamel boxes. Catalogue.

Neal Street East   **4 F2**
5 Neal St WC2. 071-240 0135. Interesting and enterprising gifts with a definite Chinese flavour: books, prints, clothes, ceramics, baskets, toys.

Past Times   **3 F6**
146 Brompton Rd SW3. 071-581 7616. Reproduction jewellery, crafts and cards from 4000 years of British history. Curiosities and books also.

Glass: antique

Most antique dealers have good 18th-19thC glass as part of their stock in trade. See also under 'Antique shops' and 'Antique markets'.

W.G.T. Burne   **6 E2**
11 Elystan St SW3. 071-589 6074. English and Irish glass. Wine glasses, candelabra and chandeliers from the early 18th and early 19thC.

Lloyd   **4 B6**
5a Motcomb St SW1. 071-235 1010. Good stock of glass of all periods, including a selection of 18th and 19thC decanters. *By appt.*

Glass: modern

See under 'China, glass & porcelain'.

Guns: antique

Peter Dale   **4 E4**
11-12 Royal Opera Arc, Pall Mall SW1.
071-930 3695. Antique weapons and
armour for the collector.

Guns: modern

Boss   **4 E4**
13 Dover St W1. 071-493 0711.
Manufacturers of top-quality sporting shot
guns. A long waiting list for purchasers.

Holland & Holland   **4 C3**
33 Bruton St W1. 071-499 4411. The top
London gunsmiths.

James Purdey & Sons   **4 B3**
57 South Audley St W1. 071-499 1801.
Fine gunsmiths.

John Rigby & Co (Gunmakers)   **5 C5**
66 Great Suffolk St SE1. 071-734 7611.
Manufacturers and dealers of high-quality
hand-made modern sporting guns and
rifles.

Swaine, Adeney, Brigg   **4 D3**
185 Piccadilly W1. 071-734 4277.
Piccadilly Gun Rooms. Agents for Westley
Richards and Atkin, Grant, Lang. Stock
modern and antique guns and accessories.

Hairdressers: men

Gavin Hodge at Sweenys   **6 F1**
48 Beauchamp Pl SW3. 071-589
3066/7. Fashionable barber in an elegant
club atmosphere. Women's hairdressing
too.

Stanley Alwin   **4 E3**
110 Shaftesbury Av W1. 071-437 8933.
Some of the leading London hairdressers
come here to get their own hair cut.

Trumper   **4 C4**
9 Curzon St W1. 071-499 1850. A very
famous establishment. Superb shopfront
and interior.

Hairdressers: women & unisex

*Nearly all the big department stores have
hairdressing salons which will cater for
men and women.*

Antenna   **3 B4**
27a Kensington Church St W8. 071-938
1866. Synonymous with hair extensions.
Also cutting, colouring and perming.

Hair by Alan D   **4 C3**
215 Regent St W1. 071-734 3381.
Fashionable styles, beauty treatments.
Many branches.

Hebe   **4 F3**
38 William IV St WC2. 071-836 1132. Full
range of perms, colours and highlighting
products. Other branches.

Michaeljohn   **4 D3**
25 Albemarle St W1. 071-629 6969.
Modern and fashionable.

Molton Brown   **4 C2**
58 South Molton St W1. 071-629 1872.
Creative cutting; specialise in hand-drying
techniques. Hair products, accessories
and cosmetics. Men's cutting: 071-493
5236.

Sissors   **6 F3**
69a King's Rd SW3. 071-352 0606.
High-fashion styles for men and
women.

Steiner   **4 C3**
66 Grosvenor St W1. 071-493 1144.
A world-famous salon linked with high-
quality hair-care products.

Toni & Guy   **4 C3**
10-12 Davies St W1. 071-629 8348.
Ultra-modern and stylish salon.
Hairdressing to a high standard by well-
trained stylists.

Trevor Sorbie   **4 F3**
10 Russell St WC2. 071-379 6901.
Innovative and excellent cutting, colouring
and perming.

Vidal Sassoon   **4 A5**
54 Knightsbridge SW1. 071-235 7791.
Also at 60 South Molton St W1 (**4 C2**).
071-491 8848. And 130 Sloane St SW3
(**6 F2**). 071-730 7288. Famous avant-
garde styles.

Handbag & luggage repairs

Jeeves   **6 F1**
8 Pont St SW1. 071-235 1101.
Handbag, luggage and shoe repairs and
renovations.

Herbalists

G. Baldwin & Co
171-173 Walworth Rd SE17. 071-703
5550. Locally renowned, long-established
shop with huge range and helpful advice.
Sells health foods too.

Culpeper   **4 C3**
21 Bruton St W1. 071-629 4559. Also at
8 Covent Garden Mkt WC2 (**4 F3**). 071-
379 6698. Also specialists in pure
cosmetics, pot pourri and pomanders.

Neal's Yard Apothecary   **4 F2**
& Therapy Rooms
15 Neal's Yd WC2. 071-379 7222.
Herbal remedies. Bach flower remedies
and natural cosmetics, books and
leaflets.

Household & kitchen equipment

Habitat, Heal's and Selfridges have excellent household and kitchen departments.

Casa Pupo 7 **A3**
56-60 Pimlico Rd SW1. 071-730 7111. Spanish ceramics, glassware, rugs, ornaments and bedcovers at fairly reasonable prices.

Covent Garden Kitchen Supplies 4 **F3**
3 Covent Garden Mkt WC2. 071-836 9167. Wide range of kitchen equipment from France. Other ranges as well.

David Mellor 6 **G2**
4 Sloane Sq SW1. 071-730 4259. All sorts of kitchen equipment, some pottery, basketware.

Divertimenti 4 **B2**
45-47 Wigmore St W1. 071-935 0689. Wide selection of cookware and table-ware.

Elizabeth David 4 **F3**
3 North Row, Covent Gdn Mkt WC2. 071-836 9167. Complete range of kitchen pots, pans, knives and pastrycook's equipment from France and elsewhere.

General Trading Company 6 **F2**
144 Sloane St SW1. 071-730 0411. A miscellany of antiques, china, glass and soft furnishings – all in elegant 'private house' setting.

The Reject Shop 4 **E1**
209 Tottenham Court Rd W1. 071-580 2895. Also at 245 Brompton Rd SW3 (6 **E1**). 071-584 7611. And 234 King's Rd SW3 (6 **E3**). 071-352 2750. Big selection of home accessories and furniture, lighting, cookware, etc. Low prices.

William Page 4 **E2**
121 Shaftesbury Av WC2. 071-379 6334. Excellent functional 'down-to-earth' pots, pans and cutlery as used by the local restaurant trade.

Icons

Maria Andipa's Icon Gallery 6 **E2**
162 Walton St SW3. 071-589 2371. Byzantine, Greek, Russian and Ethiopian icons. Also ethnic jewellery.

Ironwork

G. & S. Allgood 1 **E5**
297 Euston Rd NW1. 071-387 9951. Well-designed architectural ironmongery.

J.D. Beardmore 4 **E1**
3-4 Percy St W1. 071-637 7041. Very large selection of good reproduction and architectural ironmongery and cabinet fittings.

Comyn Ching 2 **E5**
110 Golden La EC1. 071-253 8414. An enormous range of ironmongery designs still produced from old patterns. Architectural and builders' ironmongers.

Jewellery & silver: antique

Many antique shops deal in silver and jewellery, particularly those in the Burlington Arcade. Also try the antique markets for a variety of choice and price.

Ann Bloom 4 **D3**
10a New Bond St W1. 071-491 1213. Exclusive collection of fine period jewellery and period silver photograph frames.

Armour-Winston 4 **D3**
43 Burlington Arc W1. 071-493 8937. Fine jewels and clocks.

Asprey 4 **D3**
165 New Bond St W1. 071-493 6767. Unusual antique and modern jewellery. Also an excellent range of luxury gifts.

Beau Gems 5 **E2**
26 Royal Exchange EC3. 071-623 7634. Stock mainly Victorian and art deco pieces, although they also have pieces from other periods. Another branch at 418 Strand WC2 (4 **F3**). 071-836 7356.

Bentley 4 **D3**
8 New Bond St W1. 071-629 0651. Long-established. Superb jewels and antique silver. Also Fabergé pieces. Buy as well as sell.

Bond Street Silver Galleries 4 **C3**
111-112 New Bond St W1. 071-493 6180. 15 showrooms of antique, modern and second-hand jewellery and silver.

Collingwood 4 **D3**
171 New Bond St W1. 071-734 2656. Long-established jewellers to the Queen – antique and modern gold and silverware.

Garrard 4 **D3**
112 Regent St W1. 071-734 7020. Jewellers to the Queen. Fine antique and modern silver.

Green's Antique Galleries 3 **B4**
117 Kensington Church St W8. 071-229 9618. Victorian jewellery and rings. Also silver.

The London Silver Vaults 4 **B2**
Chancery House, 53-64 Chancery La WC2. 071-242 5106. Underground vaults like an Aladdin's cave crammed with antique and modern silver and plate.

Paul Longmire 4 **D4**
12 Bury St SW1. 071-930 8720. Suppliers of jewellery to the Queen and Queen Mother. Vast selection of cuff links;

seal engraved rings. Extensive display space as this shop has the largest windows of any privately-owned jewellers in the West End.

Philip Antrobus   **4 D3**
11 New Bond St W1. 071-493 4557. Fine gold and gem-set jewellery ranging from antique to modern.

S.J. Phillips   **4 C3**
139 New Bond St W1. 071-629 6261. Fine jewels, silver and objets d'art from England and the Continent.

Shrubsole   **4 F1**
43 Museum St WC1. 071-405 2712. Fine antique English silver and old Sheffield plate for the discerning collector.

Tessiers   **4 D3**
26 New Bond St W1. 071-629 0458. Fine old firm of silversmiths. Antique jewels. Valuations and repairs of modern and antique jewellery.

Jewellery & silver: modern & costume

London is rich in fine specialist jewellery shops. Many are world famous. Good areas to shop are: Bond St, the Burlington Arcade, Knightsbridge.

Argenta   **6 D3**
82 Fulham Rd SW3. 071-584 1841. Stunning modern silverware from Scandinavia and modern English designs. Their silversmith will make up individual pieces.

Butler & Wilson   **6 E2**
189 Fulham Rd SW3. 071-352 3045. Selection from art deco and Celtic pieces to modern jewellery.

Cartier   **4 D3**
175 New Bond St W1. 071-493 6962. Top-class internationally famous jewellers.

Ciro Pearls   **4 D3**
9 New Bond St W1. 071-491 7219. Specialists in cultured and imitation pearl jewellery of all kinds. Also large selection of superior costume jewellery.

Cobra & Bellamy   **6 F2**
149 Sloane St SW1. 071-730 2823. Specialise in art deco silver and costume jewellery from the 1920s to 1950s.

Electrum Gallery   **4 C2**
21 South Molton St W1. 071-629 6325. Exhibit and sell contemporary designer jewellery to suit all the latest tastes.

Georg Jensen Silver   **4 D3**
15 New Bond St W1. 071-499 6541. Modern Danish jewellery and silver.

Ken Lane   **6 E1**
58 Beauchamp Pl SW3. 071-584 5299.

Wide range of exciting and daring costume jewellery.

Kutchinsky   **6 F1**
73 Brompton Rd SW3. 071-584 9311. Fine jewels, and top-quality Swiss watches.

Mappin & Webb   **4 D3**
170 Regent St W1. 071-734 3801. High-quality jewellery and silver.

Jewellery: hire

Charles Fox   **4 F3**
22 Tavistock St WC2. 071-240 3111. Magnificent artificial jewellery for hire.

Jewellery: repairs & restorations

National Association of   **2 G5**
Goldsmiths
78a Luke St EC2. 071-613 4445. Can supply a list of jewellers who carry out repair and restoration work.

Jewellery: valuations

Garrard   **4 D3**
120 Regent St W1. 071-734 7020. Registered valuer.

Mappin & Webb   **4 D3**
170 Regent St W1. 071-734 3801. Registered valuer.

Key cutting

Selfridges, Harrods, many branches of Woolworths and other big stores have a while-you-wait service; as do many small local ironmongers, shoe repairers and some of the larger tube stations.

Kites

High as a Kite
153 Stoke Newington Church St N16. 071-275 8799. Single line, box and stunt kites. Also frisbees, boomerangs and juggling equipment.

Kite Store   **4 F2**
48 Neal St WC2. 071-836 1666. Kites of every imaginable design, including models you can assemble yourself. Also frisbees and boomerangs. Mail order service.

Knitting yarns

Most of the big department stores stock a range of knitting yarns and patterns.

Harrods, John Lewis and Dickins & Jones are particularly good.

Colourway 3 B2
112a Westbourne Gro W2. 071-229 1432. Yarns are mainly by Rowan and Christian de Falbe. Also have tapestry kits, designer sweaters and books.

Patricia Roberts 4 B5
60 Kinnerton St SW1. 071-235 4742. Pure yarns in a vast range of seasonally changing colours. Patricia Roberts original patterns or buy the ready-knitted jumpers.

Ries Wools of Holborn 4 G1
242-243 High Holborn WC1. 071-242 7721. Knitting wools and homecrafts.

Left-handed

Anything Left-handed 4 D3
65 Beak St W1. 071-437 3910. Potato peelers, pen nibs, scissors – every gadget is designed for the left-handed. Mail order service and catalogue.

Lighting

Good lighting departments at Heal's, Harrods, Habitat, John Lewis, Selfridges and BHS.

Christopher Wray's Lighting Emporium 6 B6
600 King's Rd SW6. 071-736 8434. Over 2000 genuine, restored oil and gas lamps. Also a lamp workshop to service, restore, repair or convert to electricity any oil or gas lamp.

London Lighting 6 E2
135 Fulham Rd SW3. 071-589 3612. Excellent, pricey collection of modern light fittings.

Mr Light 6 D3
275 Fulham Rd SW10. 071-352 7525. Large range of indoor and outdoor lights including desk lamps, corner lamps and spotlights. Designs very modern or traditional.

Thorn EMI 4 C2
4 Tenterden St, Hanover Sq W1. 071-355 4848. Customer advisory service on lighting and all things electrical.

Linen

Givans Irish Linen Stores 6 E3
207 King's Rd SW3. 071-352 6352. Top-quality linen from this well-stocked shop with an air of old-fashioned gentility.

Irish Linen 4 D3
35 Burlington Arc W1. 071-493 8949. Tiny shop with expensive, beautifully-made table cloths, napkins, pillowcases, etc.

Linen Cupboard 4 C2
21 Great Castle St W1. 071-629 4062. Cut-price household linen and baby linen. Stock all the famous names.

The White House 4 C3
51 New Bond St W1. 071-629 3521. Stock the most luxurious and expensive linen in London. Exquisite hand-embroidery and hand-made lace edges. Also silk and satin lingerie and regal childrenswear.

Locksmiths

Barry Bros 3 E2
121-123 Praed St W2. 071-262 9009. Wide range of fire and crime prevention equipment. Operate an emergency service *08.00-24.00 Mon-Sun.*

Magazines & comics

Comic Showcase 4 F2
76 Neal St WC2. 071-240 3664. New and second-hand comics, cartoon strips, calendars and original comic art work.

The Vintage Magazine Shop 4 D3
39-41 Brewer St W1. 071-439 8525. Vintage magazines from the turn of the century, especially '30s, '40s and '50s, sheet music, theatre programmes, children's annuals. Also movie shop with film star mags and posters. American comic shop, and vintage pop and rock ephemera shop.

Maps: antique

Cartographia 4 F1
Pied Bull Yd, Bury Pl WC1. 071-404 4050. Antique maps and engravings from the 15thC onwards. Framing service.

The Map House 6 E1
54 Beauchamp Pl SW3. 071-589 4325. Antique maps, engravings, prints, atlases and globes.

Maps: modern

Geographia Map Shop 5 C2
58 Ludgate Hill EC4. 071-248 3554. Stocks an extensive range of maps of all parts of the world, including Ordnance Survey maps, atlases, and globes. Good choice of guide books as well.

London Map Centre 4 E6
22-24 Caxton St SW1. 071-222 2466/4945. Stockists of Ordnance Survey and other maps.

Stanfords   4 F3
12-14 Long Acre WC2. 071-836 1321. Maps of GB and the rest of the world; Ordnance Survey maps, globes. Will obtain any map, to any scale, of any part of the world – but it may take time. Also guide books and foreign geology section.

Media

BBC World   4 G3
Bush House, Strand WC2. 071-257 2576. Information centre and shop – geared mainly to the World Service, but also deals with home radio and TV. London showroom for BBC English courses. Large range of technical manuals and media books. Sell BBC publications, records, cassettes and videos. *CLOSED Sat & Sun.*

Militaria shops

See also under 'Antiques', 'Guns: antique' and 'Models'.
Collectors Corner
127a Crofton Rd SE5. 071-703 1856. Militaria of the world, covering all aspects. Parachutist wings and worldwide elite forces. Reference books.
Tradition   4 C4
10 White Horse St W1. 071-491 7077. Also at 2 Shepherd St W1 (4 **C4**). Antique weapons and uniforms. Buttons, badges, buckles, helmets and belt plates. Paintings, prints and postcards. Model soldiers.

Military war medals

Services war medals can be bought at Moss Bros military department. Also:
Armoury of St James   4 D4
17 Piccadilly Arc SW1. 071-493 5082.

,Models

Beatties of London   4 F2
202 High Holborn WC1. 071-405 6285. Model trains, cars, kits, boats, games, radio-controlled toys, diecast aircraft, jigsaws, tools, electronic games.
Hamleys   4 D3
188-196 Regent St W1. 071-734 3161. Good stocks of remote-controlled toys and train sets. Impressive working train system on show from time to time.
Hobby Stores   1 D2
39 Parkway NW1. 071-485 1818. Wide range of kits and accessories. Mostly remote-controlled. Expert staff.

Julip Model Horses   6 E1
18 Beauchamp Pl SW3. 071-589 0867. Every breed of horse and pony available, together with tack and other equipment.
Model Aircraft Supplies
207 Camberwell Rd SE5. 071-703 4562. Specialists in working model kits – not only aircraft.
W. & H. Models   4 C4
14 New Cavendish St W1. 071-935 5810. Train sets, scale models, plastic kits, and remote-controlled cars. English and Continental stocks. Experienced staff.
Parker Gallery   7 A3
28 Pimlico Rd SW1. 071-730 6768. Many kinds of ship models. Specialise in military, naval and topographical prints, oils and watercolours.
Tradition   4 C4
5a Shepherd St W1. 071-493 7452. The best selection of old and new model soldiers in London. Make their own. Militaria and military books.

Motorbikes & accessories

Gambier Reeks
120 New King's Rd SW6. 071-736 3096. The full range of Yamaha motorbikes plus spare parts and accessories can be found here. Also good selection of second-hand bikes and an efficient workshop for repairs.
Lewis Leathers   4 C1
122 Great Portland St W1. 071-636 4314. Motorbike leather specialists.
Motorcycle City
30-32 Clapham High St SW4. 071-720 6072. Kawasaki and Honda specialists. Also range of second-hand motorbikes and accessories. Large workshop for repairs and services.

Motoring organisations

Automobile Association (AA)
30-31 Haymarket SW1. 071-839 4355. Join the AA at any of the 30 centres in Greater London (check the telephone directory for the nearest). Provide various breakdown and recovery services, as well as legal advice, route details and discounts on various services and publications.
Royal Automobile Club (RAC)
RAC House, Bartlett St, South Croydon. 081-686 0088. Membership offers' a recovery breakdown service and access to insurance schemes and publications at a reduced rate.

Musical automata & boxes

Jack Donovan   **3 A2**
93 Portobello Rd W11. 071-727 1485.
Musical boxes.

Talking Machine
30 Watford Way NW4. 081-202 3473.
Deal in early gramophones, phono-
graphs, Victorian sewing machines,
primitive typewriters, classic jukeboxes,
early radio and TV equipment and old
records.

Musical instruments

Andy's Guitar Centre   **4 E2**
27 Denmark St WC2. 071-836 0899.
New and second-hand electric guitars
and basses. Semi-acoustic and classical.
Workshop where guitars are made and
repaired. Many major pop groups among
their customers.

J. & A. Beare   **4 D2**
7 Broadwick St W1. 071-437 1449.
Fine old violins, violas and cellos. Also
restorers.

Bill Lewington   **4 E2**
144 Shaftesbury Av WC2. 071-240 0584.
New and second-hand wind and brass
instruments.

Bluthner   **4 C3**
8 Berkeley Sq W1. 071-753 0533.
Pianos.

Boosey & Hawkes   **4 C2**
295 Regent St W1. 071-580 2060.
Manufacture whole range of brass
and woodwind instruments. Sell instrumental accessories, music and books
but no instruments from here. Music
publishers.

Early Music Shop at Schott   **4 D2**
& Co
48 Great Marlborough St W1. 071-437
1246. Reproduction instruments mainly
from the Renaissance and Baroque
periods.

T.W. Howarth   **4 B1**
31 Chiltern St W1. 071-935 2407.
Manufacturers of oboes d'amore and
cor anglais. Woodwind specialists. Music,
accessories, woodwind repairs.

Ivor Mairants Musicentre   **4 E2**
56 Rathbone Pl W1. 071-636 1481.
Specialise in guitars, of which they have a
huge range, and other fretted instruments
such as mandolins, banjos and ukuleles.
1001 accessories.

N.P. Mander
St Peter's Organ Works, St Peter's Clo,
Warner Pl E2. 071-739 4747. Antique
organs supplied all over the world. Also
restorations carried out and new organs

built for churches, cathedrals and home
use.

Morley Piano & Harpsichord
Workshops
34 Engate St SE13. 081-318 5838.
Antique, reproduction, second-hand and
modern pianos, and early keyboard
instruments. Domestic long-term piano
rental. Also tune, repair, recondition and
restore any keyboard instrument.

Paxman   **4 F3**
116 Long Acre WC2. 071-240
3642/3647. One of the most famous horn
makers in the world. They sell all types,
both new and second-hand. Sheet music
and repairs.

Peter Coutts
43 Perryn Rd W3. 081-743 8727. Hand-
made harpsichords.

Professional Percussion   **1 D1**
205 Kentish Town Rd NW5. 071-485
0822. Vast selection of drums, drum
kits and other percussion instruments.
Accessories and second-hand equipment
too.

Ray Man Eastern Musical   **4 F2**
Instruments
64 Neal St WC2. 071-240 1776. Eastern
and Indian instruments. Also a selection
of Chinese, African, Japanese, Balinese
and Indian records. Lessons on Chinese
instruments. Hiring service too.

Roka   **4 E2**
5 Denmark St WC2. 071-240 2610.
Repairs carried out on acoustic and
electric guitars, amplifiers. Comprehensive
stock of spares and second-hand guitars.

Salvi Harps   **5 C4**
58 Hopton St SE1. 071-928 8451. Italian
firm which makes and sells harps and
everything to go with them.

Schott   **4 D2**
48 Great Marlborough St W1. 071-437
1246. Music publishers and sellers of
educational and classical sheet music.
Sell recorders.

Steinway & Sons   **4 B2**
Steinway Hall, 44 Marylebone La,
Wigmore St W1. 071-487 3391. Wide
variety of Steinway pianos.

Musical instrument restorations

Fiddles & Sticks   **3 A2**
13 All Saints Rd W11. 071-221 4040.
Stringed and brass instruments restored.

Impact Percussion   **5 F5**
120-122 Bermondsey St SE1. 071-403
5900. Percussion hire, retail and repair.

Munson & Harbour
Masterpiece Works, Hampshire St NW5.
071-267 1610. Harp repairers.

Music: printed, antique

Otto Haas
49 Belsize Park Gdns NW3. 071-722 1488. Rare collectors' items – manuscripts and printed music from the Middle Ages to the 20thC. *By appt only.*

Travis & Emery   **4 E3**
17 Cecil Ct, Charing Cross Rd WC2. 071-240 2129. Printed music from the 1700s. Also books on music.

Music: printed, modern

Chappell of Bond Street   **4 C3**
50 New Bond St W1. 071-491 2777 Established 1811. Publishers with a worldwide reputation. Sheet music. Also sell a variety of instruments.

Cramer Music   **4 F3**
23 Garrick St WC2. 071-240 1612. Mail order number for classical, educational and popular music.

Novello   **1 B1**
3 Primrose Mews, 1a Sharpleshall St NW1. 071-483 2161. Famous publishers of educational, church, vocal, instrumental and orchestral music.

Needlework & embroidery

Harrods, Selfridges, John Lewis and Peter Jones have excellent needlework departments.

Ellis & Farrier   **4 D3**
20 Beak St W1. 071-629 9964. Sell all kinds of beads mostly for the embroidery trade; sequins, bugle beads; pearl drops, shaped stones; all colours and sizes. Will dye beads especially to customers' requirements.

Luxury Needlepoint
324 King St W6. 081-741 1314. Everything to do with tapestries, either to make yourself or ready-made. Furniture to accommodate the tapestries.

Royal School of Needlework
Appt 12a, Hampton Ct Pal, East Molesey, Surrey. 081-943 1432. Cleaning and restoration of all embroideries and textiles. New commissions also undertaken. Classes in all aspects of embroidery and related textile crafts. Mail order embroidery material and equipment (0451) 844433.

Party services

Moveable Feasts
83-85 Holloway Rd N7. 071-607 2202. Vast selection of three-course lunch and dinner menus. Cater for weddings, parties, etc; supply staff, cutlery and plates.

Party Planners   **3 A2**
56 Ladbroke Gro W11. 071-229 9666. Run by the Queen's cousin. Organise all types of parties from dinners to balls. Also conferences, overseas groups and weddings.

Searcy Tansley & Co   **6 E1**
136 Brompton Rd SW3. 071-584 9207. High-class catering for cocktail parties, dances, etc.

Toastmasters Incorporated
6 Gladstone House, High Rd N22. Answering service: 081-888 7098/2398. After-dinner speakers and professional toastmasters to officiate at any type of function can be supplied at short notice.

Walton Street Stationery   **6 E2**
Company
97 Walton St SW3. 071-589 0777. For printing of party invitations, wedding lists and stationery.

Pens

Pencraft   **4 G2**
91 Kingsway WC2. 071-405 3639. Very wide range of ballpoints and fountain pens.

Penfriend   **4 G3**
Bush House Arc, Bush House, Strand WC2. 071-836 9809. Large selection.

W.H. Smith   **4 G2**
11 Kingsway WC2. 071-836 5951. Repairs and sales of Parker pens.

Perfume

Stores and chemists usually stock a large range of the most popular perfumes. For something more unusual try the shops listed below. Large shops like Selfridges, Harrods and Dickins & Jones stock 'The Perfumer's Workshop' range which enables you to blend your own.

Chanel   **4 D3**
26 Old Bond St W1. 071-493 5040. The whole perfume and cosmetics range.

Floris   **4 D4**
89 Jermyn St SW1. 071-930 2885. Perfumers to the Court of St James since George IV, specialising in English flower perfumes, matching toiletries and preparations for men.

Penhaligon's   **4 C3**
20b Brook St W1. 071-493 0002. Traditional toilet waters and hand-made fragrances. Also deal in old English silver scent bottles. Other branches.

Pest control

Your local council offers a free service for the disposal of vermin and insects, or try:

Rentokil   4 D2
37-38 Margaret St W1. 071-493 0061. Give free surveys for pest control. They do the remedial work as well as clearing them out.

Photographic equipment

Dixons   4 E2
88 Oxford St W1. 071-636 8511. Photographic as well as audio-visual equipment. Over 90 branches in London, all with excellent stocks.

Fox Talbot   4 F3
443 Strand WC2. 071-379 6522. Large selection of top names.

Jessops   4 E2
67-69 New Oxford St W1. 071-240 6077. Wide range of photographic and dark-room equipment at competitive prices.

Keith Johnson & Pelling   1 E5
93-103 Drummond St NW1. 071-380 1144. Large stocks of professional photographic and audio-visual equipment. Rental and repair service.

Leeds Photovisual   1 G5
20-22 Brunswick Centre, Bernard St WC1. 071-833 1661. Cameras, films and all accessories. Hire service also available.

R.G. Lewis   4 F2
217 High Holborn WC1. 071-242 2916. Developing, enlargements and photographic equipment.

Morgans   4 E1
179 Tottenham Court Rd W1. 071-636 1138. Extensive selection of good second-hand cameras and photographic equipment.

Wallace Heaton   4 C3
127 New Bond St W1. 071-629 7511. High-quality new photographic, cine and projection equipment.

Photography services

Atlas Photography
6 Blundell St N7. 071-607 6767. All aspects of photographic services. Can enlarge, provide exhibition display prints, print T-shirts, supply film.

Joe's Basement   4 E2
113 Wardour St W1. 071-434 9313. A professional photographic laboratory open *24 hrs*. Colour transparency film back in *2 hrs*, black and white in *6 hrs*; colour print film in *24 hrs*.

Picture framing & restoring

Blackman Harvey   4 F2
36 Great Queen St WC2. 071-836 1904. *48-hr* framing service. Also do picture and frame restorations.

Bourlet Frames   3 F2
32 Connaught St W2. 071-724 4837. Large range of styles and some handmade frames. Watercolour and oil restoration also undertaken.

F.A. Pollak   5 C1
3-4 Faulkner's Alley, Cowcross St EC1. 071-250 1050. High-quality bespoke framing service.

J. & L. Tanous   6 B6
115 Harwood Rd SW6. 071-736 6497. Modern and antique framing of quality. Fine art picture frame makers; gilders, restorers.

Plants

See under 'Flowers' and 'Gardening'.

Postcards

Memories
18 Bell La NW4. 081-202 9080. Large collection of turn-of-the-century to pre-war postcards.

Pleasures of Past Times   4 E3
11 Cecil Ct WC2. 071-836 1142. Extremely large classified collection of early postcards, greetings cards, early children's books and theatre ephemera.

Posters & reproductions

Art galleries sell reproductions of their more popular paintings, and museum shops normally have a good seleciton of posters.

Athena   4 E3
1 Leicester Sq WC2. 071-437 6780. Good selection of posters and reproductions. Other branches.

Dillons Arts Shop   4 F3
8 Long Acre WC2. 071-836 1359. Sell a wide range of posters on the performing and visual arts.

Medici Gallery   4 C3
7 Grafton St W1. 071-837 7099. Reproductions, limited editions, graphics and greetings cards. Exhibitions *Mar-Aug*.

Paperchase   1 F6
213 Tottenham Court Rd W1. 071-580 8496. Modern posters. Also prints and art books.

The Poster Shop   4 F3
28 James St WC2. 071-240 2526. Posters from all over the world covering

every subject. Huge selection. Framed posters too. Other branches.

Press cutting agencies

International Press Cutting Bureau
224-236 Walworth Rd SE17. 071-708 2113. Monitoring service for worldwide press.

Romeike & Curtice
Hale House, 290-296 Green Lanes N13. 081-882 0155. Extensive cuttings from newspapers, magazines, trade journals, as well as advert checking and a foreign department.

Records, cassettes, CDs & videos

Alto   **4 D2**
39 Carnaby St W1. 071-821 5536. Vast range of compact discs and videos. Latest sounds and oldies.

Caruso & Co   **4 E2**
35 New Oxford St WC1. 071-379 5839. English and foreign, vocal and operatic, and a large selection of classical records. Also nostalgia, 78s and second-hand records.

Cassettes Plus   **4 F3**
9 St Martin's Ct WC2. 071-836 8514. Specialist cassette shop offering London's largest selection – 10,000 titles. Also compact discs.

Cheapo Cheapo Records   **4 E3**
53 Rupert St W1. 071-437 8272. Jazz, rock, classical and blues – and the name does not lie. All second-hand stock.

HMV   **4 D2**
150 Oxford St W1. 071-631 3423. Comprehensive stock of all types of music in a very large store.

James Asman   **4 F3**
23a New Row WC2. 071-240 1380. Long-established jazz, blues and nostalgia records specialist run by jazz critic James Asman. Lots of imports and second-hand bargains. Collections bought.

Minus Zero   **3 A2**
2 Blenheim Cres W11. 071-229 5424. New wave, punk, American and British sixties psychedelia, and rare and re-issued records.

Music Discount Centre   **4 F3**
437 Strand WC2. 071-240 2157. Huge selection of classical cassettes and compact discs ranging from the very specialist to the more popular. Inexpensive. Other branches.

Our Price Records   **4 E1**
12 Tottenham Court Rd W1. 071-636

4631. Every taste catered for, though they specialise in pop and rock. Competitively priced.

Ray's Jazz Shop   **4 F2**
180 Shaftesbury Av WC2. 071-240 3969. Jazz records, cassettes and compact discs.

Music & Video Exchange   **3 B4**
38 Notting Hill Gate W11. 071-243 8573. Exchange or select from thousands of second-hand records, cassettes, compact discs and videos. Rare deletions. Also at 229 Camden High St NW1 (**1 D2**). 071-267 1898. And 90 Goldhawk Rd W12. 081-749 2930.

Tower Records   **4 D3**
1 Piccadilly W1. 071-439 2500. Housed in the old Swan & Edgar building, this is said to be the 'greatest record store in the known world'. Full range of sounds and large selection of compact discs, videos and US imports.

Virgin Megastore   **4 E2**
14-16 Oxford St W1. 071-631 1234. Progressive and popular music, blues, jazz, classical – almost everything at below the recommended price. Other branches.

Sex supermarkets

Ann Summers   **4 D3**
26 Brewer St W1. 071-437 4016. The original sex supermarket, with all types of contraceptives, gadgets, and sex aids. Helpful staff; demonstrations.

Lovecraft   **4 E3**
46 Cranbourn St WC2. 071-437 2105. 'Amusement arcade' sex supermarket. Wide selection of products.

Shells

Eaton's Shell Shop   **4 F2**
30 Neal St WC2. 071-379 6254. Very varied shop offering as its main line an awe-inspiring selection of shells, minerals, crystals and fossils, costing anything from a few pence to hundreds of pounds. Popular with collectors, and theatre and cinema prop hunters. Also shell and semi-precious stone jewellery. Natural woven matting, bamboo poles, cane roller blinds made-to-measure and chair cane.

Shoe repairs

Most of the large tube and mainline stations have heel bars for quick repairs.

Jeeves Snob Shop   **6 F1**
7 Pont St SW1. 071-235 1101. Superlative repairs and shoe services.

Also take on sports footwear and hand-bag and luggage repairs. Collect and deliver within London postal area and operate nationwide postal service. Other branches.

Shoe shine

Traditional Victorian Shoeshine Company
081-964 5624. Re-introducing the art of the London Shoeblack. All methods of shoe care; cleaning of leather, suede and synthetic footwear by red-jacketed shoeshine boys and girls. Sites at Burlington Arcade W1 (**4 D3**), Charing Cross WC2 (**4 F4**) and the May Fair Hotel, Stratton St W1 (**4 C4**). Other sites around central London.

Silver

See under 'Jewellery & silver'.

Souvenirs

It's no problem finding souvenir shops in London. Try around Oxford St, Carnaby St and Leicester Sq. More sophisticated gifts can be found at a number of museums, and Covent Garden is an oasis for up-market and quirky gift ideas.
See also 'Gifts'.

Sponges

Maitlands   **4 D4**
175 Piccadilly W1. 071-493 1975. Marvellous selection of natural sponges in all sizes. Also hairbrushes, shaving brushes and perfumes.

Sports: general

Lillywhites   **4 E3**
Lower Regent St SW1. 071-930 3181. Excellent general stock of top English and Continental equipment for most sports.
Olympus Sports   **4 C2**
301 Oxford St W1. 071-409 2619. Wide range of tennis, squash and badminton equipment, swimwear, ski-wear; large training shoe department. Also hand luggage and sports bags.
Sports City   **4 E1**
22 Tottenham Court Rd W1. 071-631 1410. Complete range of Adidas, Reebok and Nike sports clothing, footwear and equipment, plus other brands.
Sportspages   **4 E2**
94-96 Charing Cross Rd WC2. 071-240

9604. Sports bookshop covering all aspects of sport and fitness. Also stocks magazines and videos.

Sports equipment: archery

Quicks Archery Specialists
Hampton Court Rd, Kingston, Surrey. 081-977 5790.

Sports equipment: boating & yachting

Arthur Beale   **4 F2**
194 Shaftesbury Av WC2. 071-836 9034. Excellent small yacht chandler. Nautical clothing and books.
Force 4   **7 C1**
30 Bressenden Pl SW1. 071-828 3900. Full range of boating equipment, hardware and clothing. Dinghies and small inflatables in stock. Nautical gifts, books and charts.
London Yacht Centre   **5 F1**
13 Artillery La E1. 071-247 0521. Very large stock of boating equipment with the advantage of being near Liverpool Street station – gateway to the east coast yachting resorts.
Thomas Foulkes
6a Sansom Rd (off Lansdowne Rd) E11. 081-539 5084. One of the best selections in London of all types of gear and equipment.

Sports equipment: boxing

Lonsdale   **4 D3**
21 Beak St W1. 071-437 1526. Punch bags, mouth guards, clothing. Also boxing videos and books.

Sports equipment: camping & mountaineering

In addition to those listed below, Simpson and Lillywhites also have small camping sections.
Adventure Shops   **4 F3**
14-16 Southampton St WC2. 071-836 8541. Large stocks of climbing, skiing and camping clothes and equipment.
Blacks Camping & Leisure   **4 E2**
53 Rathbone Pl W1. 071-636 6645. Probably the most versatile camping shop in London. Supply the best British and Continental equipment and clothing: have equipped many mountaineering expeditions. Specialists in climbing and mountaineering.

Camping Centre
44-48 Birchington Rd NW6. 071-328 2166. Possibly the largest exhibition of tents in the country – also trailer tents. Backpacking and outdoor clothing.

Camping & Outdoor Centre **7 B1**
27 Buckingham Palace Rd SW1. 071-834 6007. Everything you could need to camp, climb or walk.

Survival Shop **1 F4**
Euston Station. 071-388 8353. Everything you need to survive in the wilds. Swiss army knives, Mag-Lite torches, polythene map cases, first-aid kits, compasses, back packs, tents, boots and hats.

Sports equipment: fencing

Leon Paul Equipment **2 B6**
14 New North St WC1. 071-405 3832. World-famous fencing equipment, designed and tested to Olympic standards.

Sports equipment: fishing

Don's of Edmonton
239 & 246 Fore St N18. 081-807 5396. Knowledgeable proprietor. Good stock. 239 specialises in game fishing, salmon and trout; 246 in salt water and big game tackle.

C. Farlow **4 E4**
5 Pall Mall SW1. 071-839 2423. Modern approach to anglers' needs. Specialists in trout and salmon fishing tackle. Large country clothing section. Staff are all anglers. Established 1840.

House of Hardy **4 E4**
61 Pall Mall SW1. 071-839 5515. Finest hand-made rods in the world and general fishing tackle.

Sports equipment: football

Soccer Scene **4 D3**
24 Carnaby St W1. 071-439 0778. Vast selection of team shirts including all the UK teams, top Continental clubs and national squads. Also footballs and all clothes and accessories.

Sports equipment: golf

Golf City **5 C2**
13 New Bridge St EC4. 071-353 9872. Clubs, trolleys, balls, shoes, clothes and accessories. Half sets of clubs available for the beginner.

Sports equipment: gym & fitness

Weider Health & Fitness **4 F4**
Charing Cross Concourse, Charing Cross underground station WC2. 071-240 1363. Gym equipment and clothing, body-building foodstuffs, videos and books.

Sports equipment: martial arts

Bernard Weatherill **4 D3**
8 Savile Row W1. 071-734 6905. Excellent sporting tailors. Specialists in breeches.

Giddens of London **4 D3**
15d Clifford St W1. 071-734 2788. Top-quality riding clothes. Manufacture their own saddles, harnesses and equestrian accessories.

Swaine, Adeney, Brigg **4 D4**
185 Piccadilly W1. 071-734 4277. Complete range of equestrian equipment and clothing.

Sports equipment: riding & saddlery

Shaolin Way **4 E3**
10 Little Newport St WC2. 071-734 6391. Judo suits, karate outfits, videos and books.

Sports equipment: running

Run and Become, Become and Run **4 E6**
42 Palmer St SW1. 071-222 1314. Specialist running shop. Vast range of running shoes and shoes for many other sports. Plus comprehensive stock of running clothes and accessories. Help and advice from running experts.

Sports equipment: shooting

See under 'Guns: modern'.

Sports equipment: skating

Skate Attack
95 Highgate Rd NW5. 071-267 6961. Roller skates, ice skates and skateboards.

Sports equipment: skiing

Lillywhites, Simpson, C & A and Harrods have good ski clothes and equipment.

Alpine Sports 3 **B6**
215 Kensington High St W8. 071-938
1911. All ski equipment and clothing.

Ellis Brigham 4 **F3**
30-32 Southampton St WC2. 071-240
9577. Large specialist ski shop with a full
range of ski-wear and equipment. Also
hire of ski equipment and ski repair workshop. Mountaineering equipment and
sportswear.

Snow & Rock 3 **B6**
188 Kensington High St W8. 071-937
0872. Clothes and equipment for skiing
and mountaineering.

Sports equipment: sub aqua

Collins & Chambers
197-199 Mare St E8. 081-985 0752.
Seibe-Gorman, Farallon, Aquastar and
Pirelli concessionaires. Wide range of
quality gear. 10% discount to BSAC
members.

Sports equipment: tennis

The Racquet Shop
22 Norland Rd W11. 071-603 0013.
Racquets for badminton and squash as
well as tennis. Accessories. Regripping
and restringing service.

Sports equipment: watersports

Activ
557-561 Battersea Park Rd SW11. 071-
223 2590. Full range of windsurfers and
windsurfing gear, and clothing to buy or
hire; windsurfing courses. Water skis.
Seasonal stock of snow skis and ski-
wear.

Windsurfer's World
146 Chiswick High Rd W4. 081-994
6769. Boards, sails, board accessories,
harnesses. Wetsuits and steamers.
Windsurfer hire.

Stained glass

Goddard & Gibb Studios
41-49 Kingsland Rd E2. 071-739 6563.
Make and repair stained glass for all kinds
of windows, door panels and Tiffany
lampshades.

Stamps

See also 'Auctions: stamps & coins'.
Cameo Stamps 4 **F3**
6 Buckingham St WC2. 081-742 3202.
Vast selection of British and worldwide
thematics/topicals. Wants lists welcomed.
Mail order catalogue.

Georges Korel 4 **E3**
2 Irving St WC2. 071-930 4727.
Specialise in collections of all countries,
British, foreign and colonial sets and
singles, thematics/topicals and Masonic
covers and stamps. Children especially
welcome.

Leo Baresch 4 **F3**
110 St Martin's La WC2. 071-240 1963.
Deal in all world collections, covers and
stamps.

Royale Stamp Co 4 **F3**
42 Maiden La WC2. 071-836 6122.
British and Commonwealth stamps from
1840.

Stanley Gibbons International 4 **F3**
399 Strand WC2. 071-836 8444. World-
famous for stamps and catalogues. New
issues to classics.

Stationery shops

*W.H. Smith has branches at the main
stations and throughout the suburbs, and
most of the big stores have good
selections.*

Frank Smythson 4 **C3**
44 New Bond St W1. 071-629 8558. The
absolute tops in posh diaries, stationery
and leather goods.

Italian Paper Shop 3 **G6**
11 Brompton Arc SW3. 071-589 1668.
Beautiful, marbled stationery and desk
accessories.

Paperchase 1 **F6**
213 Tottenham Court Rd W1. 071-580
8496. Exciting collection of paper
products including stationery, cards, gifts
and wrapping paper.

Rymans 4 **D2**
6-10 Great Portland St W1. 071-636
3468. Stationery, office equipment,
business machines, furniture and many
other useful things. Branches throughout
London.

Tea

See under 'Coffee & tea'.

Theatrical supplies

See also 'Fancy dress hire'.
MBA Costumes 1 **D5**
52-56 Osnaburgh St NW1. 071-388
4994. Manufacturers of theatrical
costumes.

Stagesets
Unit L, Delta Wharf, Tunnel Av SE10. 081-

853 2370. Hire or sales of scenery, furniture, backcloths.

Theme shops

The Disney Store   **4 D3**
140 Regent St W1. 071-287 6558. Huge range of Disney products; videos, books, toys, stationery, clothing, jewellery, homeware.

Sherlock Holmes   **1 B5**
Memorabilia Company
230 Baker St NW1. 071-486 1486. Sherlock Holmes related objects – mugs, T-shirts, posters, postcards, antique books and period magazines.

Tintin Shop   **4 F3**
34 Floral St WC2. 071-836 1131. Packed with all Hergé's books about the young hero, plus T-shirts, postcards and other novelties.

Tobacconists: pipes, cigars, tobacco & snuff

Astleys   **4 D4**
109 Jermyn St SW1. 071-930 1687. Established since 1862. Specialise in briar and meerschaum pipes.

Dunhill   **4 D4**
30 Duke St SW1. 071-499 9566. Exclusive masculine luxury goods including pipes, lighters, cigars, writing instruments and leather goods.

Inderwick   **4 D3**
45 Carnaby St W1. 071-734 6574. Established in the 18thC. Made pipes for Edward VII. Tobaccos blended for individual tastes.

James J. Fox (Cigar   **4 D3**
Merchants)
2 Burlington Gdns, Old Bond St W1. 071-493 9009. Specialise in finest cabinet selections of all the choicest Havana cigars. Also wide range of cigars, tobaccos and all smoking accessories.

Robert Lewis   **4 D4**
19 St James's St SW1. 071-930 3787. The best Havana cigars, as well as Turkish and Virginia cigarettes. Own mixtures. One of the biggest cigar merchants in Europe.

Smith's Snuff Shop   **4 E3**
74 Charing Cross Rd WC2. 071-836 7422. Colourful blue and gold 19thC shopfront. Inside has old Victorian tobacco adverts. A great snuff house. Full range of Havana and Continental cigars. Finest selection in UK of Turkish and Egyptian cigarettes.

Toys

See under 'Children's shopping'.

Umbrellas & walking sticks

Burberrys   **4 E3**
18 Haymarket SW1. 071-930 3343. Also at 165 Regent St W1 (4 **D3**). 071-734 4060. Good selection of umbrellas and raincoats.

James Smith   **4 F2**
53 New Oxford St WC1. 071-836 4731. Famous store (established in 1830) for umbrellas, shooting sticks, walking sticks.

Swaine, Adeney, Brigg   **4 D3**
185 Piccadilly W1. 071-734 4277. World-famous hand-made Brigg umbrellas and luxury leather goods.

Umbrella repairs

Carter's Umbrellas   **5 E2**
30 Royal Exchange Bldgs, Threadneedle St EC3. 071-626 7724. Sale, repair and refurbishment of umbrellas.

T. Fox & Co   **5 E1**
118 London Wall EC2. 071-606 4720. Manufacture, sales and repairs. Will undertake repairs of British-framed umbrellas.

Veterinary clinics

Beaumont Animals Hospital   **1 F2**
Royal Veterinary College, Royal College St NW1. 071-387 8134. Clinic for domestic animals.

Blue Cross Animals Hospital   **7 B2**
1 Hugh St SW1. 071-834 5556. Clinic for domestic animals.

Wine

Most chain store wine merchants in London belong to big organisations who buy in bulk and offer competitive prices. Also listed are some completely independent shops specialising in individual service and small excellent parcels of wine. Harrods has a good wine department which buys selectively and independently.

Les Amis du Vin   **1 C6**
51 Chiltern St W1. 071-487 3419. Large selection of over 500 ports, sherries, wines and champagnes, including 20 own-label varieties bottled in the country of origin. Wine club offering good discounts to members.

Berry Bros & Rudd   **4 D4**
3 St James's St SW1. 071-396 9600.

Charming old wine merchant's shop. First-class list. Independent merchant.

Bow Wine Vaults   **5 D2**
10 Bow Churchyard EC4. 071-248 1121. Old-fashioned wine merchant adjoining a popular City wine bar.

Christie's   **4 D4**
8 King St SW1. 071-839 9060. Wine auctions usually held on *Thur.*

Justerini & Brooks   **4 D4**
61 St James's St SW1. 071-493 8721. Wine and spirit merchants. Will advise on laying down a cellar.

Oddbins   **5 C2**
41a Farringdon St EC4. 071-236 7721. Wide range of drinkable wines from throughout the world as well as bargains in more illustrious wines. Other branches.

Soho Wine Market   **4 E2**
3 Greek St W1. 071-437 9311. Cut-price wines and spirits – some excellent bargains.

Sotheby's   **4 C3**
34-35 New Bond St W1. 071-493 8080. Auctions of fine and rare wines, spirits and vintage port.

La Vigneronne   **6 D2**
105 Old Brompton Rd SW7. 071-589 6113. Rare vintages of claret, burgundy and Madeira. Also specialise in Alsace wines and wines from the South of France.

Wine accessories

Richard Kihl   **1 B1**
164 Regent's Park Rd NW1. 071-586 3838. Wine accessories of all types such as antique decanters, corkscrews, claret jugs and glasses.

Wine by the case

You have to buy in bulk from the following – a minimum of 12 bottles – but the wines tend to be correspondingly cheaper and a wide choice is offered.

Bibendum   **1 C1**
113 Regent's Park Rd NW1. 071-722 5577. Large selection of fine vintage clarets and ports. Also good general stock at wide range of prices, and wine accessories. *OPEN 10.00-20.00 Mon-Sat.*

Majestic Wine Warehouse   **6 E5**
Unit 2, Albion Wharf, Hester Rd SW11. 071-223 2983. Vast selection of wines at varying prices. Good value. Hire of glasses. *OPEN 10.00-22.00 Mon-Sun.* Other branches.

Wine clubs

Berry Bros, Justerini & Brooks and some others (see under 'Wine') will lay down wine and help customers invest in good wines.

The Wine Society
Gunnels Wood Rd, Stevenage, Herts. (0438) 740222. A wine-selling co-operative owned by its members, who receive regularly-updated lists. The range offered is wide and reliable.

Wine-making & brewing supplies

Larger branches of Boots sell wine- and beer-making supplies.

The Beer Shop   **2 G4**
8 Pitfield St N1. 071-739 3701. Will supply all equipment and ingredients for wine and beer-making.

Markets

There are hundreds of markets in London ranging from open-air craft markets to Sunday morning street markets selling clothes and general household goods. You can also visit the wholesale markets; officially they sell only in bulk but they are interesting to look around. Food stalls and street entertainers are to be found around many of the markets, and cockney hype-artists can be very entertaining.

Remember that on wet days and Mon markets tend to be fairly dead. Opening times given here are a guide only. Markets often close early, depending on the state of business. EC = early closing.

Also see 'Markets' under 'Antiques'.

Bermondsey and New   **5 F5**
Caledonian Market
Between Tower Bridge Rd and Bermondsey St SE1. One of the most famous antiques market in southern England. Around 350 stalls outside plus 150 indoors. Mostly aimed at collectors and dealers, although the large variety and specialist goods make for fascinating browsing. Snack bars and cafés. *OPEN 05.00-13.00 Fri only.*

Berwick Street W1   **4 E2**
Busy and boisterous general market in the heart of Soho: the fruit and vegetables are good, and prices reasonable. Also meat, cheeses, fresh fish and household goods. *OPEN 09.00-18.00 Mon-Sat.*

Bethnal Green Road E1
General high street market. *OPEN 08.30-17.00 Mon-Sat.*

Billingsgate (wholesale)
North Quay, West India Dock Rd E14. Europe's principal inland fish market moved from the City to Docklands in 1982. Plenty of activity but can be a very wet and smelly experience! OPEN 05.30-12.00 Tue-Sat, 05.30-10.00 Sun (shellfish only).

Borough Market (wholesale)   5 E4
8 Southwark St SE1. Wholesale fruit and vegetables under the railway arches of London Bridge. OPEN 02.00-09.00 Mon-Sat.

Brick Lane E1   5 G1
An exciting place to go to on a Sun morning when Brick La and the surrounding streets – Cheshire St, Sclater St, Cygnet St and Bacon St – come alive with stalls, stall-holders and potential customers jostling for space. Famous for second-hand furniture but come here for almost anything.

Brixton
Radiating from Atlantic Rd SW9. Large general market with a distinct West Indian flavour; exuberant atmosphere heightened by the loud reggae music reverberating around the railway arches. OPEN 08.00-18.00 Mon-Sat, EC Wed.

Camden Lock   1 D1
Where Chalk Farm Rd crosses Regent's Canal NW1. Amongst the cobbled courtyards and warehouses of the lock is a huge expanse of market selling everything from designer clothes and pine furniture to antique clothing, junk and bric-à-brac. Also a number of interesting food stalls. Refreshments. OPEN 10.00-18.00 Sat & Sun.

Camden Passage   2 D3
Islington High St N1. A paved walk lined with shops and stalls; selling a mixture of antiques and attractive, but expensive, bric-à-brac. Also second-hand records and books, old clothes, prints and furniture. OPEN 09.00-18.00 Mon-Sat. Market stall days OPEN 06.45-16.00 Wed & Sat.

Camden Town   1 D2
Inverness St NW1. Fruit, vegetables and a few junk stalls. OPEN 09.00-13.00 Mon-Sat.

Chapel Market   2 C3
White Conduit St, off Liverpool Rd N1. General market selling cheap fruit and vegetables and tat; also pet stall. OPEN Tue-Sun, EC Thur & Sun.

Chelsea Antiques Market   6 E4
245-253 King's Rd SW3. 071-352 9695. Large, bustling market spreading back from the King's Rd. Mostly general stock, but some specialists. OPEN 10.00-18.00 Mon-Sat.

Columbia Road E2
Flowers and plants. OPEN 08.00-13.00 Sun only.

Covent Garden WC2   4 F3
The Piazza is host to an antiques market on Mon and a gimmicky market selling crafts and gifts Tue-Sat. See also 'Jubilee Market'.

The Cut   5 B5
Lower Marsh Rd, off Waterloo Rd SE1. Fruit, vegetables and all sorts of household items. Best times 12.00-14.00 Mon-Sat.

East Street SE17
General items sold in the week, but mainly fruit, vegetables, plants and flowers Sun. OPEN 07.00-14.00 Tue-Sun.

Farringdon Road EC1   2 C5
Old and rare books, manuscripts and newspapers. OPEN Mon-Fri.

Gabriel's Wharf   5 B4
56 Upper Ground SE1. The South Bank's answer to Covent Garden – a collection of craft workshops including jewellery, fabric and leather designers, plus a restaurant bar and a garden centre. At weekends there is a market which also sells flowers, vegetables, designer gimmicks and clothes all to the accompaniment of live street entertainment. Market OPEN 09.30-18.00 Sat & Sun. Workshops OPEN 11.00-17.00 Tue-Sun.

Greenwich Market
Greenwich High Rd SE10. Second-hand clothes, books and jewellery Sat & Sun, fruit and vegetables Mon-Fri.

High Street, Walthamstow E17
Over a mile of stalls and shops selling literally everything. Crowded and noisy. OPEN Thur, Fri & Sat.

Jubilee Market   4 F3
Jubilee Hall, Covent Garden WC2. Smallish market beside the paved shopping and market complex. Antiques 05.00-17.00 Mon, general 09.00-17.00 Tue-Fri, crafts 10.00-17.00 Sat & Sun.

Kensington Market   3 C5
Kensington High St W8. A maze of off-beat clothes mingled with jewellery, antiques and records. Stall-holders prepared to buy, sell and barter. OPEN 10.00-18.00 Mon-Sat.

Kingsland Waste E8
For the DIY enthusiast – hardware, tools and timber. OPEN 07.00-17.00 Sat.

Kingston Markets
Kingston-on-Thames, Surrey. General market on Mon on Cattle Market Car Park, Fairfields Rd. OPEN 08.00-14.00. Ancient and Apple Market, Market Pl is mainly fruit, vegetables and fish but has some general stalls. OPEN 08.00-17.30 Mon-Sat, EC Wed (to 14.00).

SHOPS

Aquascutum 734 6090
Army & Navy 834 1234
Asprey 493 6767
Austin Reed 734 6789
BHS (Kensington High St) 937 0919
BHS (Oxford St) 629 2011
Barkers 937 5432
C & A 629 7272
C & A 493 6962
Christie's 839 9060
Conran Shop 589 7401
DH Evans 629 8800
Debenhams 580 3000
Dickins & Jones 734 7070
Dillons 636 1577
Fenwick 629 9161
Fortnum & Mason 734 8040
Foyles 437 5660
General Trading Company 730 0411
Habitat (King's Rd) 351 1211
Habitat (Tottenham Court Rd) 631 3880
Hamleys 734 3161
Harrods 730 1234
Harvey Nichols 235 5000
Hatchards 439 9924
Heal's 636 1666
HMV 631 3423
Jaeger 734 8211
John Lewis 629 7711
Laura Ashley 437 9760
Liberty 734 1234
Lillywhites 930 3181
Littlewoods 434 4301
London Pavilion 437 1838
Maples 387 7000
Marks & Spencer (Ken. High St) 938 3711
Marks & Spencer (Marble Arch) 935 7954
Marks & Spencer (Oxford St) 437 7722
Mothercare 629 6621
Next (Kensington High St) 938 4211
Next (Regent St) 434 2515
Peter Jones 730 3434
Plaza on Oxford St 637 8811
Selfridges 629 1234
Simpson 734 2002
Sotheby's 493 8080
Top Shop 636 7700
Tower Records 439 2500
Trocadero 439 1791
Victoria Place Shopping Centre 931 8811
Virgin Megastore 631 1234
Whiteleys Shopping Centre 229 9844

SHOPPING IN LONDON

Shaded areas denote main shopping streets
Numbers given at stations
indicate useful bus transport to
shopping areas

© Nicholson

Lambeth Walk SE11   **7 F2**

General market. Vegetables and fruit, clothing, electrical goods, materials. *OPEN 10.00-18.00 Mon-Sat, EC Thur (to 13.30).*

Leadenhall Market   **5 F2**

Gracechurch St EC3. General retail market: vegetables, poultry, plants, fish and endless other items. The late Victorian glass and ironwork of the building is superb. *OPEN 07.00-17.00 Mon-Fri.*

Leather Lane EC1   **2 C6**

Vast range of goods, very few leather stalls nowadays. Lively patter. Close to London's diamond trade in Hatton Garden. *OPEN 11.00-15.00 Mon-Fri.*

London Silver Vaults   **5 A1**

Chancery La WC2. Underground vaults like an Aladdin's cave crammed with antique and modern silverware. *OPEN 09.00-17.30 Mon-Fri, 09.00-12.30 Sat.*

New Covent Garden (wholesale)   **7 D5**

Nine Elms SW8. London's foremost wholesale fruit, vegetable and flower market which has been in its present location since the end of 1974. Some of the old charm and vitality has been lost in the move from the age-old site in the centre of London, but it is still extremely lively and well worth a visit if you can get up in time. *OPEN 04.00-11.00 Mon-Fri, 04.00-09.00 Sat.*

North End Road SW6

Variety of stalls. Plants and flowers in *summer. OPEN 09.00-18.00 Mon-Sat, EC Thur.*

Northcote Road SW11

Busy market, selling mainly fruit and vegetables, near Clapham Junction. *OPEN 09.00-17.00 Mon-Sat.*

Petticoat Lane   **5 G2**

Petticoat Lane as such does not exist but is the name given to the market which radiates from Middlesex St E1 on *Sun mornings.* Some of the streets – Goulston St (good for fashion), Toynbee St and Wentworth St – are open during the week too. The other streets involved are Bell La, Strype St, Cobb St, Leyden St, New Goulston St and Old Castle St. Petticoat Lane is London's biggest market with 850 stalls. Well known for selling clothes, the choice extends from designer fashion to tack. The range of other goods on sale is very wide – china, electrics, linens, toys. *OPEN 08.00-14.00 Sun.*

Portobello Road W11   **3 A2**

Very well-known and much-frequented market extending into Golborne Rd and Westbourne Grove. Fruit, vegetables and new goods sold *09.00-18.00 Mon-Wed,*

EC Thur (to 13.00). Second-hand junk and bric-à-brac sold *08.00-17.00 Fri* and on *Sat* the famous antiques market is held, though it is now too established for many bargains to exist. The arcades off Portobello Rd open on *Sat only.* Antique market *OPEN 08.00-sunset Sat.*

Ridley Road E8

Famous East End market with Jewish and West Indian influences. *OPEN Tue-Sat, EC Thur.*

Roman Road E3

Traditional East End market, more than 160 years old. Large, busy, with lots of discount fashion stalls. Also fruit and vegetables. *OPEN 08.00-14.00 Tue & Thur, 08.00-17.00 Sat.*

Shepherd's Bush W12

Large, general open-air market alongside the railway arcade. Food stalls have a strong West Indian bias. Pets, household goods and the usual market tat. *OPEN 09.30-17.00 Mon-Sat, EC Thur.*

Smithfield (wholesale)   **5 C1**

Charterhouse St EC1. World's largest meat market; some interesting architecture and storage techniques but not for the squeamish. *OPEN 05.00-12.00 Mon-Fri.*

Spitalfields, New (wholesale)

23 Sherrin Rd E10. London's premier horticultural market, moved from the City to this modern market complex.

Spitalfields, Old   **5 G1**

Commercial St E1. Original home of the wholesale market. Now houses an organic market on *Sun,* where visiting farmers from around the country sell their produce. Also crafts and plants. *OPEN 09.00-15.00 Sun.*

Trafalgar Rd SE10

General street trading in Colom Rd, Tyler St and Earlswood St. *OPEN 09.00-17.00 Mon-Sat, EC Thur.*

Wembley

Stadium Way NW10. Mainly clothes stalls but good range of household goods, from china to three-piece suites. *OPEN 09.00-15.00 Sun.*

Wentworth Street E1   **5 G2**

Part of Petticoat Lane market on Sun. Fruit, vegetables and bric-à-brac. *OPEN 08.30-14.00 Sun-Fri.*

Whitechapel Market

Whitechapel Rd E1. Famous East End high street market. Huge array of stalls. *OPEN 08.30-17.00 Mon-Sat.*

Woolwich

Beresford Sq SE18. Variety of goods sold in this well-known south London market and in the adjacent covered market in Plumstead Rd. *OPEN 09.00-17.00 Mon-Sat, EC Thur.*

Money and business services

Money

Currency

The unit of currency is the pound sterling (£) divided into 100 pence (p). There are coins for 1p, 2p, 5p, 10p, 20p, 50p and £1, with notes for £5, £10, £20 and £50.

Exchange facilities

There is no exchange control in Britain, so you can carry any amount of money through customs, in or out of the country. The best rate of exchange is always to be found in a bank. Bureaux de change will exchange most currencies and will cash cheques, but charge more to do so. They can be found at airports, main-line train stations, central tube stations and in the larger department stores. Bureaux de change stay open outside banking hours. The larger hotels sometimes have facilities for changing major currencies, and will accept travellers' cheques in payment of bills. Most restaurants will also accept travellers' cheques as long as they are accompanied by a valid form of identification.

Chequepoint Bureau de Change
13 Davies St W1. 071-409 1122.   **4 C3**
220 Earl's Court Rd SW5.   **6 B2**
071-373 9515.
Marble Arch, 548 Oxford St W1.   **4 A2**
071-723 2646.
Eurochange Bureaux Ltd
95 Buckingham Palace Rd SW1.   **7 B1**
071-834 3330.
Leicester Sq Tube Stn, 45 Charing   **4 E3**
Cross Rd WC2. 071-439 2827.
Paddington Tube Stn, 179 Praed   **3 E2**
St W2. 071-258 0442.
Tottenham Court Rd Tube Stn W1.   **4 E2**
071-734 0279.
Thomas Cook Ltd
39 Tottenham Court Rd W1.   **4 E1**
071-323 5445.
123 High Holborn WC1. 071-831   **4 G1**
4408.
104 Kensington High St W8.   **3 C5**
071-376 2588.
100 Victoria St SW1. 071-828 8985.**7 C1**
Selfridges, 400 Oxford St W1.   **4 B2**
071-629 1234.

Banks

Banks are traditionally open 09.30-15.30 Mon-Fri although some branches are open until 16.30. They are closed B.hols and often close early on the day before a B.hol. Some selected branches open on Sat. Longer banking hours at Heathrow and Gatwick Airports: 24-hr opening all year; and at Luton Airport: OPEN 06.00-23.00 in summer.

England's main high street banks are Barclays, Lloyds, Midland, National Westminster and the TSB (Trustee Savings Bank). Their head offices are listed below together with several other British banks and international departments.

Barclays Bank plc   **5 E2**
54 Lombard St EC3. 071-626 1567.
Bank of Ireland   **5 D3**
36 Queen St EC4. 071-329 4500.
Bank of Scotland   **5 E2**
38 Threadneedle St EC2. 071-601 6666.
Coutts & Co   **5 E3**
International Dept, 27 Bush La, Cannon St EC4. 071-623 3434.
Lloyds Bank plc   **5 E2**
71 Lombard St EC3. 071-626 1500.
Lloyds Bank International Ltd   **5 E3**
11-15 Monument St EC3. 071-775 2000.
Midland Bank plc   **5 E2**
Poultry EC2. 071-260 8000.
National Westminster Bank plc   **5 E2**
41 Lothbury EC2. 071-726 1000.
National Westminster Bank   **5 F2**
International Division, 25 Old Broad St EC2. 071-920 5555.
Royal Bank of Scotland   **5 E2**
67 Lombard St EC3. 071-623 4356.
TSB   **5 E2**
60 Lombard St EC3. 071-623 6000.

Credit cards

The major credit cards – Access, American Express, Diners Club, Visa – are accepted in most places as a form of payment. Carte Blanche is less popular.

Access and Visa
To report lost or stolen cards contact the emergency number of the issuing bank (24-hr emergency service):
Barclays   (0604) 230230
Lloyds   (0702) 362988

Midland	081-450 3122
National Westminster	(0532) 778899
Royal Bank of Scotland	(0702) 362988
TSB	(0273) 204471
Visa cards issued abroad:	(0604) 230230

American Express   4 E3

6 Haymarket SW1. 071-930 4411. OPEN 09.00-17.00 Mon-Fri, 09.00-12.00 Sat. Customer service handles any enquiry or billing problem. Acts as travel agent, sells and cashes personal cheques on an emergency basis if customer has an American Express card. If card is lost the company can issue an emergency replacement card. To report lost or stolen cards call (0273) 696933 for a *24-hr emergency service.*

Barclaycard

Barclaycard Centre Dept G, Northampton, Northants. (0604) 230230. To report lost or stolen cards during office hours contact any Barclays bank or ring the above number *(24-hr service)* and write a confirming letter within seven days.

Diners Club

Diners Club House, Kingsmead, Farnborough, Hants. (0252) 516261. *24-hr service* for reporting lost cards and the telephone call should, within seven days, be followed by a confirming letter.

Eurocard

See under 'Access and Visa' above.

Eurocheque card

In case of loss contact issuing branch or telephone this emergency number: 071-588 3600. Confirm the loss in writing within seven days.

Mastercard

To report lost or stolen cards contact (0702) 362988 *(24-hrs).*

Taxes

Most goods and services purchased in the UK are subject to VAT (value added tax) at the standard rate of 17½ %. Luxury items – tobacco, perfume, alcoholic beverages and motor vehicles – are subject to higher rates. Overseas visitors can reclaim the VAT paid on high value items by obtaining a VAT 407 form from the retailer. On returning home the goods must be certified by the customs officer. Evidence of this plus the form must then be returned to the retailer, who will send the refund to the visitor's country of origin. However, this procedure can be lengthy. A good alternative is to shop in stores showing the London Tax Free Shopping sign. This system entails filling in a voucher, presenting it to customs with the goods and returning it to the London Tax

Free Shopping organisation who will then immediately refund your money in the currency of your country of residence.

Tipping

Should be an expression of pleasure for service rendered and never a duty; it is still possible not to tip at all if the circumstances justify this. These guidelines give some idea of the average tip:

Restaurants Many now add on a service charge, usually 12½%, but do not always say so – if in any doubt ask them. They usually say if it is *not* included. 12½% is the minimum; give up to 15% for above-average service.

Taxis 10-15%.

Women's hairdressers 15% to the hairdresser, 5% to the shampooer.

Men's hairdressers 15%.

Cloakroom attendants 10p per article when collected.

Washroom services 10p if individual attention is given.

Commissionaires For getting a taxi; up to 50p depending on the effort expended.

Pubs & bars Never at the bar, but buy the barman a drink if you wish. For waiter service in the lounge, from 10p per drink.

Hotels Almost all add it to your bill, usually 10%. Give extra to individuals for special service, from 50p.

Porters 50p-£1 per case depending on how far it is carried.

Business services

London offers a number of back-up services to make life easier for the travelling business man or woman. There are organisations which hire out offices or conference rooms by the hour, day or month along with complete secretarial and communication services. They will provide you with a London address while you are overseas and a message service whereby someone will handle telephone calls and forward your telexes. Other agencies deal with secretarial and staffing services only. It is worth enquiring about the amenities available at your hotel, as most of the major ones help their business guests by providing communication facilities.

Angela Pike Associates   4 D3

Meridian Hotel, Piccadilly W1. 071-434 4425. *24-hr* secretarial business bureau. 7 days a week.

Business Space   4 D3

211 Piccadilly W1. 071-439 8985. Luxury

offices and conference rooms for hire with all the necessary services.

Extel Financial   **2 F5**
Fitzroy House, 13-17 Epworth St EC2. 071-253 3400. Deals with all kinds of queries and problems. Also publishes financial data on more than 7000 British and foreign businesses. *Charge.*

Heathrow Business Centre
Heathrow Airport Terminal 2. 081-759 2434. For high-flyers between flights. Private office accommodation, work cubicles and services including the use of a personal computer.

Nightingale London Secretariat 4 C3
3 Berkeley Sq W1. 071-629 6116. Office hire and all business requirements. *Membership required.*

Conference services

Conference Associates &   **4 C1**
Services Ltd
Congress House, 55 New Cavendish St W1. 071-486 0531. Professional conference organisers who arrange everything from the budgeting to the hosting of any size meeting or conference.

Video/Audio Conferencing
British Telecom organises national and international video conferencing. Phone the Conference Booking Centre on 071-606 0541 for details.

Conference centres

Alexandra Palace & Park
Wood Green N22. 081-365 2121.

Barbican Arts and Conference 2 E6
Centre
Barbican EC2. 071-638 4141.

Earl's Court Exhibition Centre 6 A3
Warwick Rd SW5. 071-385 1200.

Olympia Exhibitions
Hammersmith Rd W14. 071-603 3344.

Queen Elizabeth II Conference 4 E5
Centre
Broad Sanctuary SW1. 071-222 5000.

Wembley Conference Centre
Wembley Complex, Empire Way, Wembley, Middx. 081-902 8833.

Courier services: international

The following all offer door-to-door collection and delivery services around the world.

Datapost
Head Office: 33 Grosvenor Pl SW1. (0800) 884422. Freephone Datapost for a speedy door-to-door collection and delivery service.

DHL
081-890 9000.

IML Air Couriers
081-890 8888.

Intelpost
Royal Mail, Mount Pleasant, Farringdon Rd EC1. 071-239 2495. Public facsimile system enabling copies of documents to be transmitted to 29 countries in four continents.

TNT Skypack
081-561 2345.

Courier services: nationwide

See Yellow Pages *for extensive listings of local and national messengers.*

Employment agencies

There are many different agencies all over London (see Yellow Pages *for listings). The ones given below are the main offices of some of the largest firms, which have branches in most commercial districts.*

Alfred Marks Group
16 Maddox St W1. 071-491 4645.   **4 C3**

Brook Street
353 Oxford St W1. 071-493 8531.   **4 C2**
131 Cannon St EC4. 071-623 3966. **5 E3**

Kelly Temporary Services
82-83 Strand WC2. 071-836 3856.   **4 F3**

Office Angels
25 Oxford St W1. 071-434 9545.   **4 E2**
71-75 Buckingham Palace Rd SW1. **7 B1**
071-630 0844.

Reed Employment
87 Moorgate EC2. 071-638 1021.   **5 E1**
309 High Holborn WC1. 071-404   **5 A1**
0174.

Financial information

Citycall
Dial (0898) 121230 for information from the London and international stock exchanges and for sterling and other currency conversion rates.

Storage

Berkley Safe Deposit Co   **4 C3**
13-15 Davies St W1. 071-409 1122. Rental of strong boxes.

Metro Store
81-89 Carnwath Rd SW6. 071-736 5433. Rents out warehouse space by the week.

Translation

Conference Interpreters Group
10 Barley Mow Pass W4. 081-995 0801.

Internationally-recognised interpreters in most widely-spoken languages.

Interlingua/TTI

Rothschild House, Whitgift Centre, Croydon, Surrey. 071-240 5361. Rapid translations done in over 70 languages. Also interpreters for meetings and conferences. Typesetting, printing and executive language tuition done in-house. *OPEN 09.00-17.30 Mon-Fri.*

Transport

For taxis and car hire see 'Transport in London' section.

Air London

(0293) 549555. Can organise any plane from executive jets to air ambulances, from air taxis to 747s.

Business information

These are the major organisations available to help the business man or woman with trade enquiries and export and import information. Do not overlook the assistance you can get from your bank, your own trade association, or the trade sections of embassies and chambers of commerce who do much to promote trade between countries.

Association of British   7 D1
Chambers of Commerce
9 Tufton St SW1. 071-222 1555.

British Exporters Association   4 E5
16 Dartmouth St SW1. 071-222 5419.

Central Office of Information   5 B6
Hercules Rd SE1. 071-928 2345.

Chamber of Commerce   5 D3
69 Cannon St EC4. 071-248 4444.

Companies House   2 F5
55-71 City Rd EC1. 071-253 9393. Searches undertaken for information on any company registered under the Companies Act for £1 fee.

Confederation of British   4 E2
Industry (CBI)
Centrepoint, 103 New Oxford St WC1. 071-379 7400.

Department of Trade   7 C1
Ashdown House, 123 Victoria St SW1. 071-215 5000. The Enquiry Service will put you through to the appropriate officer of the DTI's Export Services for information and advice on exporting. Market assessments; Export Intelligence Service (subscribers are informed of export opportunities in their area of business as they arise); appointment of overseas agents; reports on standing of overseas traders; foreign tariff and import regulations; assistance for companies at overseas trade fairs and exhibitions; service for foreign business visitors wishing to buy British goods.

Design Council   4 E3
28 Haymarket SW1. 071-839 8000.

Institute of Export   2 G5
Clifton House, 64 Clifton St EC2. 071-247 9812.

Institute of Practitioners in   4 B6
Advertising
44 Belgrave Sq SW1. 071-235 7020.

National Economic   7 E2
Development Office
Millbank Tower, Millbank SW1. 071-211 3000.

Travel and holiday information

Passports

Applications for, and renewals of, full 10-year passports can be handled by your bank or travel agency for a small charge. Personal applications only to the Passport Office and a birth certificate must be produced. British Visitors passports, valid for one year, can be obtained from main post offices. These are for holiday-makers only and are valid in Canada and many European countries, usually those that don't require visas.

They are issued on production of a medical card, birth certificate or expired but uncancelled passport.

Passport Office   4 D6
Clive House, Petty France SW1. 071-279 3434. *OPEN 09.00-16.00 Mon-Fri. OPEN Sat for emergencies only (phone 071-279 4000 for appt).*

Home Office   4 E5
50 Queen Anne's Gate SW1. 071-273 3000.

Immigration Office

Lunar House, Wellesley Rd, Croydon, Surrey. 081-686 0688. Deals with questions concerning the granting of British visas to foreigners and entry under the Commonwealth Immigration Act. Subject to approval, visas are then supplied by the Foreign Office.

Passport photographs

These can be done by any photographer, who will know the size and other requirements. Basically you should submit two identical black and white (certain colour photos are also acceptable), full face photographs of yourself without a hat. The size should be no more than 2in by 1½in (50mm by 38mm). The paper should be ordinary photographic paper, unglazed and unmounted. It is possible to have the photos taken in one of the street or station photograph machines (those that have the words 'Passport' or 'Passport approved' marked on them).

Inoculations and vaccinations

These can be carried out by your own doctor under the National Health Scheme free – though the doctor may make a charge for signing the certificate. The certificate should then be taken for stamping to the Health Department of the local authority in which the vaccinator practises. International certificates are required for cholera and yellow fever. Details of international requirements are given in 'Health Advice for Travellers' available at all post offices.

**British Airways Immunisation   4 D3
Clinic**
156 Regent St W1. 071-439 9584. All inoculations including yellow fever. *OPEN 09.00-16.15 Mon-Fri, 10.00-16.00 Sat. Also at Heathrow Airport 081-562 5825. OPEN 09.00-12.30 & 14.00-16.30 Mon-Fri (appt only); 101-102 Cheapside EC2 (5 **D2**). 071-606 2977. OPEN 09.00-13.00 & 14.00-16.30 (appt only). British Airways Victoria Station SW1 (7 **B2**). 071-233 6661. OPEN 08.15-11.30 & 12.30-15.45 Mon-Fri (appt only). Charge.*

**Hospital for Tropical   1 E5
Diseases Travel Clinic**
Queen's House, 180-182 Tottenham Court Road W1. 071-637 9899. Provides medical kits, mosquito nets, water purification devices, medication and travel products. All inoculations. *OPEN 09.00-17.00 Mon-Fri. Charge.*

Unilever House   5 C3
Blackfriars EC4. 071-822 6017. *Appt only. OPEN 14.10 & 16.00 Mon-Fri for all main inoculations required for travelling. Charge.*

Vaccinating Centre   3 G2
53 Great Cumberland Pl W1. 071-262 6456. A centre for vaccinations and inoculations. *OPEN Mon-Fri 09.00-16.45. No appt necessary. Charge.*

Money: currency exchange

For full details on currency and exchange facilities see 'Money' section of 'Money and business services'.

Embassies & High Commissions

*Embassies have consulates in the same building unless a separate address is given. All these offices deal with emigration. A full list of embassies and high commissions is in the London Diplomatic List, available from the HMSO Bookshop, 49 High Holborn WC1 (5 **A1**).*

Australia   4 G3
Australia House, Strand WC2. 071-379 4334.

Austria   4 B6
18 Belgrave Mews West SW1. 071-235 3731.

Bahamas   4 C4
10 Chesterfield St W1. 071-408 4488.

Bangladesh   3 D6
28 Queen's Gate SW7. 071-584 0081.

Barbados   4 E2
1 Great Russell St WC1. 071-631 4975.

Belgium   4 B6
103 Eaton Sq SW1. 071-235 5422.

Brazil   4 A3
32 Green St W1. 071-499 0877.
Consulate: 6 St Alban's St SW1.   4 E3
071-930 9055.

Bulgaria   3 D6
186-188 Queen's Gate SW7. 071-584 9400.

Canada   4 C3
MacDonald House, 1 Grosvenor Sq W1. 071-629 9492.

Chile   1 D6
12 Devonshire St W1. 071-580 6392.
Consulate: 071-580 1023.

China   1 D6
49 Portland Pl W1. 071-636 5726.

Croatia (Republic of)   4 D4
18-21 Jermyn St SW1. 071-434 2946.

Cuba   4 **F2**
167 High Holborn WC1. 071-240 2488.

Cyprus   4 **B3**
93 Park St W1. 071-499 8272.

Czech Republic   3 **C4**
26 Kensington Palace Gdns W8. 071-727 4918.

Denmark   5 **G6**
55 Sloane St SW1. 071-235 1255.

Egypt   4 **B4**
75 South Audley St W1. 071-499 2401.

Finland   4 **B6**
38 Chesham Pl SW1. 071-235 9531.

France   4 **A5**
58 Knightsbridge SW1. 071-235 8080.
Consulate: 21 Cromwell Rd SW7.   6 **D2**
071-581 5292.

Germany   4 **B6**
23 Belgrave Sq SW1. 071-235 5033.

Ghana
104 Highgate Hill N6. 081-342 8686.

Greece   3 **A4**
1a Holland Park W11. 071-221 6467.

Guyana   3 **C3**
3 Palace Ct, Bayswater Rd W2. 071-229 7684.

Hong Kong Government Office   4 **C3**
6 Grafton St W1. 071-499 9821.

Hungary   4 **B6**
35 Eaton Pl SW1. 071-235 4048.
Consulate: 35b Eaton Pl SW1.   7 **A1**
071-235 2664.

Iceland   4 **C5**
1 Eaton Ter SW1. 071-730 5131.

India   4 **G3**
India House, Aldwych WC2. 071-836 8484.

Iran   3 **E5**
27 Prince's Gate SW7. 071-584 8101.
Consulate: 50 Kensington Court   3 **C5**
W8. 071-937 5225

Iraq   3 **D6**
21-22 Queen's Gate SW7. 071-584 7141.

Ireland   4 **C5**
17 Grosvenor Pl SW1. 071-235 2171.
Passport office: 071-245 9033.

Israel   3 **C5**
2 Palace Grn W8. 071-957 9500.

Italy   4 **C3**
14 Three Kings Yd W1. 071-629 8200.
Passport office: 38 Eaton Pl SW1.   4 **B6**
071-235 9371.

Jamaica   3 **D6**
2 Prince Consort Rd SW7. 071-823 9911.

Japan   4 **C4**
101 Piccadilly W1. 071-465 6500.

Jordan   3 **B5**
6 Upper Phillimore Gdns W8. 071-937 3685.

Kenya   1 **D6**
45 Portland Pl W1. 071-636 2371.

Kuwait   6 **C1**
46 Queen's Gate SW7. 071-589 4533.

Lebanon   3 **C4**
15 Palace Gdns Mews W8. 071-229 7265.

Luxembourg   4 **B5**
27 Wilton Cres SW1. 071-235 6961.

Malaysia   4 **B5**
45 Belgrave Sq SW1. 071-235 8033.

Malta   3 **C6**
16 Kensington Sq W8. 071-938 1712.

Mexico   4 **B5**
8 Halkin St SW1. 071-235 6393.

Morocco   6 **C1**
49 Queen's Gate Gdns SW7. 071-581 5001.

Nepal   3 **C4**
12a Kensington Palace Gdns W8. 071-229 1594.

Netherlands   6 **C1**
38 Hyde Park Gate SW7. 071-584 5040.

New Zealand   4 **E4**
New Zealand House, 80 Haymarket SW1. 071-930 8422.

Nigeria   4 **F4**
Nigeria House, 9 Northumberland Av WC2. 071-839 1244.

Norway   4 **B6**
25 Belgrave Sq SW1. 071-235 7151.

Pakistan   3 **G6**
36 Lowndes Sq SW1. 071-235 2044.

Peru   3 **G6**
52 Sloane St SW1. 071-235 1917.
Consulate: 071-235 6867.

The Philippines   3 **C4**
9a Palace Grn W8. 071-937 3646.

Poland   1 **D6**
47 Portland Pl W1. 071-580 4324.
Consulate: 73 New Cavendish St   1 **D6**
W1. 071-580 0476.

Portugal   4 **B6**
11 Belgrave Sq SW1. 071-235 5331.
Consulate: 62 Brompton Rd SW3.   3 **F6**
071-581 8724.

Romania   3 **C5**
4 Palace Grn, Kensington Palace Grn W8. 071-937 9666.

Russian Federation   3 **C4**
13 Kensington Palace Gdns W8. 071-229 3628.

Saudi Arabia   4 **C4**
30 Charles St W1. 071-917 3000.

Sierra Leone   1 **D6**
33 Portland Pl W1. 071-636 6483.

Singapore   4 **B5**
9 Wilton Cres SW1. 071-235 8515.

Slovakia (Republic of)   3 **C4**
25 Kensington Palace Gdns W8. 071-243 0803.

Slovenia (Republic of)
Heather Lodge, Kingston Hill, Kingston-upon-Thames, Surrey. 081-974 8300.

South Africa   4 **F4**
South Africa House, Trafalgar Sq WC2.
071-930 4488.
Spain   4 **B6**
24 Belgrave Sq SW1. 071-235 5555.
Sri Lanka   3 **F3**
13 Hyde Park Gdns W2. 071-262 1841.
Sweden   4 **A1**
11 Montagu Pl W1. 071-724 2101.
Switzerland   4 **A1**
16 Montagu Pl W1. 071-723 0701.
Tanzania   4 **C4**
43 Hertford St W1. 071-499 8951.
Thailand   6 **C1**
30 Queen's Gate SW7. 071-589 0173.
Trinidad & Tobago   4 **B6**
42 Belgrave Sq SW1. 071-245 9351.
Tunisia   3 **E5**
29 Prince's Gate SW7. 071-584 8117.
Turkey   4 **B6**
43 Belgrave Sq SW1. 071-235 5252.
Consulate: Rutland Gdns SW7.   3 **F5**
071-589 0949.
USA   4 **B3**
24 Grosvenor Sq W1. 071-499 9000.
Venezuela   6 **D2**
1 Cromwell Rd SW7. 071-584 4206.
Consulate: 56 Grafton Way W1.   1 **E5**
071-387 6727 (Visas Dept).
Vietnam   3 **C6**
12 Victoria Rd, Kensington W8. 071-937
1912.
Yugoslavia (Federal Republic of)6 **B2**
5 Lexham Gdns W8. 071-370 6105.
Zambia   3 **D5**
2 Palace Gate W8. 071-589 6655.
Zimbabwe   4 **F3**
429 Strand WC2. 071-836 7755.

Tourist offices

Australia
Australian Tourist Commission, 10-18
Putney Hill SW15. 081-780 1424.
Austria   4 **C3**
Austrian National Tourist Office, 30 St
George St W1. 071-629 0461.
Bahamas   4 **C4**
Bahama Island Tourist Office, 10
Chesterfield St W1. 071-629 5238.
Barbados   4 **E1**
Barbados Tourist Board, 263 Tottenham
Court Rd W1. 071-636 0090.
Belgium
Belgian National Tourist Office, Premier
House, 2 Gayton Rd, Harrow, Middx.
081-861 3300.
Bermuda   6 **E5**
Bermuda Dept of Tourism, 1 Battersea
Church Rd SW11. 071-734 8813.
Britain   4 **E4**
British Tourist Authority Information

Centre, 12 Lower Regent St SW1.
Personal callers only.
Bulgaria   4 **C2**
Bulgarian National Tourist Office, 18
Princes St W1. 071-499 6988.
Canada   4 **E4**
Canadian Government Travel Bureau,
Canada House, Trafalgar Sq SW1. 071-
930 8540.
Czech Republic/Slovakia   5 **D4**
Cedok Independent Travel, 49 Southwark
St SE1. 071-378 6009.
Denmark   4 **D3**
The Danish Tourist Board, Sceptre
House, 169-173 Regent St W1. 071-734
2637.
Egypt   4 **D4**
Egyptian Tourist Centre, 168 Piccadilly
W1. 071-493 5282.
Finland   4 **E3**
Finnish Tourist Board, 66 Haymarket
SW1. 071-839 4048.
France   4 **D4**
French Government Tourist Office, 178
Piccadilly W1. 071-491 7622.
Germany   4 **C4**
German National Tourist Office,
Nightingale House, 65 Curzon St W1.
071-495 3990.
Gibraltar   4 **G3**
Gibraltar National Tourist Office, 179
Strand WC2. 071-836 0777.
Greece   4 **D3**
The National Tourist Organisation of
Greece, 4 Conduit St W1. 071-734 5997.
Holland   4 **D6**
The Netherlands National Tourist Office,
25-28 Buckingham Gate SW1. (0891)
200277.
Hong Kong   4 **E4**
Hong Kong Tourist Association, 125 Pall
Mall SW1. 071-930 4775.
Hungary   4 **D3**
Hungarian Travel Centre, 6 Conduit St
W1. 071-493 0263.
Iceland   1 **E5**
Iceland Tourist Information Bureau, 172
Tottenham Court Rd W1. 071-388 5599.
Ireland   4 **C3**
Irish Tourist Office, Ireland House, 150
New Bond St W1. 071-493 3201.
Israel   4 **D2**
Israel Government Tourist Office, 18 Great
Marlborough St W1. 071-434 3651.
Italy   4 **C2**
Italian State Tourist Dept (ENIT), 1 Princes
St W1. 071-408 1254.
Jamaica   3 **E6**
Jamaica Tourist Board, 1-2 Prince
Consort Rd SW7. 071-224 0505.
Japan   4 **D3**
Japan National Tourist Organisation, 167
Regent St W1. 071-734 9638.

Jersey   **4 C3**
Jersey Tourist Information Office, 38 Dover St W1. 071-493 5278.

Kenya   **4 C3**
Kenya Tourist Office, 25 Brooks Mews W1. 071-839 4477.

Lebanon   **4 D4**
Lebanese Tourist Office, 90 Piccadilly W1. 071-409 2031.

Luxembourg   **4 D3**
Luxembourg National Tourist Office, Kingsland House, 122 Regent St W1. 071-434 2800.

Malta   **4 D2**
Malta Government Tourist Office, Suite 300, Mappin House, 4 Winsley St W1. 071-323 0506.

Mexico   **4 E4**
Mexico Tourist Board, 60 Trafalgar Sq WC2. 071-734 1058.

Morocco   **4 D2**
Moroccan National Tourist Office, 205 Regent St W1. 071-437 0073.

New Zealand   **4 E4**
New Zealand Government Tourist Bureau, New Zealand House, 80 Haymarket SW1. 071-930 8422.

Northern Ireland   **4 C4**
Northern Ireland Tourist Board, 11 Berkeley St W1. 071-493 0601.

Norway   **4 E3**
Norwegian Tourist Board, Prince Charles House, Lower Regent St W1. 071-839 6255.

Poland   **4 D2**
Polish Travel Office, 82 Mortimer St W1. 071-580 8028.

Portugal   **4 D3**
Portuguese Tourist Office, 25 Sackville St W1. 071-494 1441.

Russia (Commonwealth of Independent States)
Intourist, Intourist House, 219 Marsh Wall, Isle of Dogs E14. 071-538 8600.

Scotland   **4 E4**
Scottish Tourist Board, 19 Cockspur St SW1. 071-930 8661.

Slovenia   **4 D3**
Yugotours, 150 Regent St W1. 071-734 7321.

South Africa
South African Tourism Board, 5 Alt Grove SW19. 081-944 6646.

Spain   **4 D4**
Spanish National Tourist Office, 57 St James's St SW1. 071-499 0901.

Sweden   **4 C2**
Swedish National Tourist Office, 73 Welbeck St W1. (0891) 200280.

Switzerland   **4 E3**
Swiss National Tourist Office, Swiss Centre, Coventry St W1. 071-734 1921.

Thailand   **4 D3**
Thailand Tourist Office, 49 Albemarle St W1. 071-499 7679.

Tunisia   **4 B2**
Tunisian National Tourist Office, 77a Wigmore St W1. 071-224 5561.

Turkey   **4 D4**
Turkish Tourism and Information Office, 170-173 Piccadilly W1. 071-734 8681.

USA   **4 B3**
United States Travel and Tourism Administration, 24 Grosvenor Sq W1. 071-495 4466. Telephone enquiries only.

Vietnam
Vietnam Tourist Office, 93 Chiswick High Rd W4. 081-961 0117.

Wales   **4 E4**
Wales Tourist Board, 12 Lower Regent St SW1. Personal callers only.

Zimbabwe   **4 F4**
Zimbabwe Tourist Office, 429 Strand WC2. 071-836 7755.

Travel agents and tour operators

Travel agents, who retail package holidays and travel tickets, can be found all over London. Most belong to the Association of British Travel Agents (ABTA); if they do they can only sell the holidays of tour operators who also belong to ABTA. Buying from ABTA agents is a good idea since any complaints can be addressed to the Association if the agent and operator do not give satisfaction. All-inclusive tours sold by ABTA tour operators are covered by a bond to safeguard holiday-makers' money. Agents and operators advertise in newspapers and magazines, and operators' brochures are available at travel agents. You can often book directly with the operator. Agents also sell insurance and travellers' cheques.

Association of British Travel   **4 D1**
Agents
55 Newman St W1. 071-637 2444.

London Tourist Board   **7 B1**
Information Centre
Victoria Station Forecourt SW1. Personal callers only. Information on travel and holidays in Britain.

Thomas Cook   **4 C4**
45 Berkeley St W1. 071-499 4000. The biggest travel agency and also a tour operator. Sell their own travellers' cheques.

Airports

London City Airport
King George V Dock, Connaught Rd E16. 071-474 5555.

London Gatwick Airport
West Sussex. (0293) 535353.
London Heathrow Airport
Bath Rd, Heathrow, Middx. 081-759 4321.
London Stansted Airport
Stansted, Essex. (0279) 680500.
Luton Airport
Luton, Beds. (0582) 405100.
Southend Airport
Southend-on-Sea, Essex. (0702) 340201.
Westland Heliport
Lombard Rd SW11. 071-228 0181.

Air services

Check-in facilities for most major airlines are at the airports. For information contact airline booking offices. See telephone directories for details.
British Airways   **7 B2**
Central London Air Terminal, Victoria
Station SW1. 071-834 9411. *OPEN
06.00-18.00 Mon-Sun.*

Airport bus services

London Transport
A1 Heathrow, Cromwell Rd, Knightsbridge, Victoria.
A2 Heathrow, Paddington, Marble Arch,
Baker St, Euston, Russell Sq.
Flightline
747 Gatwick, Heathrow, Luton, Stansted.
757 Luton, Victoria.
777 Gatwick, Victoria.

Airport river services

London City Airport Express Service
071-987 0311. From all Riverbus Piers
*(see 'Transport in London') every 20 mins
between 07.00-19.00 Mon-Fri; every 30
mins between 10.30-16.30 Sat; and
every 30 mins between 10.30-17.30 Sun.*

Cheap air tickets

*Considerable savings can be made on full
price air tickets – any travel agent can
give details of arrangements which vary
according to destination. ABC (Advance
Booking Charter) and APEX (Advance
Purchase Excursion) return tickets are
available to many worldwide destinations
including N. America and Australia; tickets
for these must be bought 21 or 30 days
in advance and neither outward nor return
dates can be altered. The classified ads in
Time Out are a source of other less official
cheap flights. If you are a student, special
rates are available – check with the student travel office (see 'Student London').*

Airlines

*Most of the world's airlines operate ser-
vices to London and many have booking
offices here (listed in the telephone directory). Travel agents will also make bookings.*
British Airways Sales Shops
081-897 4000. British Airways sell
tickets and make bookings for any airline
that belongs to IATA (International Air
Transport Association). If you book by
phone *(24 hrs)*, you can have your ticket
sent by mail or collect and pay for it at
one of the Sales Shops.
101-102 Cheapside EC2.   **5 D2**
OPEN 09.00-17.00 Mon-Fri.
156 Regent St W1.   **4 D3**
*OPEN 09.00-18.00 Mon-Fri, 09.00-17.00
Sat.*
Victoria BR Station SW1.   **7 B2**
*OPEN 08.00-20.00 Mon-Fri, 09.00-17.00
Sat.*
200 Buckingham Palace Rd SW1   **7 B2**
OPEN 09.00-18.00 Mon-Fri (Business
travel only).

Specialist air and helicopter charter

*All the big airlines also operate charter
flights for all purposes, subject to avail-
ability.*
Air Amiga Ltd
Stapleford   Aerodrome,   Stapleford
Tawney, Essex. (0708) 688361. Four Bell
Jet Rangers, three twin Squirrel, one Long
Ranger. Can supply many sizes of aircraft.
Alan Mann Helicopters
Fairoaks Airport, Chobham, Surrey.
(0276) 856177. Operate a fleet of six 4-
seater Jet Ranger helicopters, two 109s
and one Bell 47 for training.
Cabair
Elstree Aerodrome, Elstree, Herts. 081-
953 4411. Piper, Drummond-Kougar, Jet
Ranger and Navajo air-taxi operators and
helicopter charter.
Dollar Air Services
Hangar 6, Coventry Airport, Coventry.
(0203) 304231. Fleet of helicopters for all
types of charter.
Instone Air Transport   **5 E4**
Bridge House, 4 Borough High St SE1.
071-407 4411. Freight specialists, air
brokers and aviation consultants.
London Airtaxi Centre   **5 E4**
New City Court, 20 St Thomas St SE1.
071-378 6935. Helicopter and aircraft
charter. Will supply almost any size of
aircraft.

Accommodation

Hotel booking agents

Accommodation Service of   **7 C1**
the London Tourist Board
London Tourist Board Information Centre, Victoria Station Forecourt SW1. (0839) 123435. They give information and make bookings. *OPEN 08.00-18.00 Mon-Sun.* Also at Heathrow Airport. *Charge.*

Expotel Hotel Reservations
Dial 071-328 1790 to make hotel reservations. Covers the whole of Great Britain. *OPEN 08.00-18.00 Mon-Fri. Free.*

Hotel Booking Service   **4 D3**
4 New Burlington Place W1. 071-437 5052. Excellent and knowledgeable service to business firms and general public. All types of hotel reservations in London, UK and worldwide. *OPEN 09.30-17.30 Mon-Fri. Free.*

Hotel Finders
20 Bell La NW4. 081-202 7000. All kinds of hotels. *OPEN 09.00-17.30 Mon-Fri, 09.00-13.00 Sat. Free.*

Hotelpacc Group Services Ltd 4 B5
40-46 Headfort Pl SW1. 071-235 9696. Hotel accommodation for groups (10 people or more) in London, UK and worldwide. Facilities for coach and tour operators and conference organisers. *OPEN 09.00-18.00 Mon-Fri. Free.*

Hotel Reservations Centre   **4 C6**
10 Buckingham Palace Rd SW1. 071-828 2425. *OPEN 09.00-18.00 Mon-Fri* for bookings all over Britain. Also at Victoria Station, Platforms 7 & 8 (**7 B1**). 071-828 1849. *Free.*

Room Centre
Kingsgate House, Kingsgate Pl NW6. 071-328 1790. Worldwide hotel and conference booking service. *OPEN 08.30-18.00 Mon-Fri. Free.*

Thomas Cook   **7 B1**
All kinds of hotels in London, Britain and worldwide. Sales desk at Victoria Station, Platform 9/10. 071-828 4646. *OPEN 07.00-23.00 Mon-Sun.* Also desks at King's Cross Station, Paddington Station, Gatwick Airport and Waterloo Station. *Charge.*

Note

It is compulsory for hotels to display their prices. Visitors should make sure exactly what is included in the price, ie breakfast,
VAT, service, etc. Many hotels have facilities for conferences, banquets, receptions etc, but in each entry we refer to this as conference facilities. Capacity, where given in numbers, is approximate at the upper end of the scale – check first. Small conference facilities means capacity for 20 people or less. Large conference facilities means the capacity is flexible according to the requirements; air cond = air conditioning, conf cap = conference capacity, P = parking, s pool = swimming pool.

For inexpensive accommodation see 'Student London'.

Hotels: top price

Over £120 per night, single room with bath or shower. Prices should be checked because they may vary considerably within the category and breakfast, VAT and service may not be included in the charge.

Athenaeum   **4 C4**
116 Piccadilly W1. 071-499 3464. Comfortable and friendly traditional hotel with modern facilities. 112 rooms all with bath and TV. 3 conf rooms. Air cond. No-smoking rooms. A.Ax.Dc.V.

The Beaufort   **6 E1**
33 Beaufort Gdns SW3. 071-584 5252. Beautifully decorated small Victorian hotel. 28 rooms. All drinks and light snacks included in price. Air cond. Health club membership. Video. A.Ax.Dc.V.

Belgravia Sheraton   **6 G1**
20 Chesham Pl SW1. 071-235 6040. Small luxury hotel, personal service. 90 rooms. Health club. Air cond. Conf cap 20. A.Ax.Dc.V.

Berkeley   **4 B5**
Wilton Pl SW1. 071-235 6000. Modern building. Interior stylish and elegant. French and Italian restaurants. 160 rooms. TV. S pool. Air cond. P. Conf cap 200. A.Ax.Dc.V.

The Berkshire   **4 C2**
350 Oxford St W1. 071-629 7474. Country house style hotel. Charming decor. Restaurant. 147 rooms all with bath, TV and video. Air cond. A.Ax.Dc.V.

Britannia   **4 B3**
Grosvenor Sq W1. 071-629 9400. International hotel in listed building. Three

restaurants. 317 rooms. Satellite/cable TV. Conf cap 100. Air cond. A.Ax.Dc.V.

Brown's   **4 C3**
19-24 Dover St W1. 071-493 6020. Traditional English country house atmosphere. Courteous service. 150 rooms all with TV and bath. Air Cond. 8 conf rooms. A.Ax.Dc.V.

Cadogan   **4 A6**
75 Sloane St SW1. 071-235 7141. Comfortable and friendly. Restaurant. 69 rooms all with TV and bath. Small conf facilities. A.Ax.Dc.V.

Chelsea Hotel   **4 A6**
17 Sloane St SW1. 071-235 4377. Modern hotel. Restaurant. King-size beds. 220 rooms all with satellite TV and bath. Conf cap 100. Air cond. A.Ax.Dc.V.

Churchill   **4 A2**
30 Portman Sq W1. 071-486 5800. Modern international hotel. 452 rooms. Air cond. P. Conf cap 250. A.Ax.Dc.V.

Claridge's   **4 C3**
Brook St W1. 071-629 8860. Old-fashioned luxury and lavish traditional atmosphere. Haute cuisine in the restaurant and good smorgasbord in the Causerie. 200 rooms. Secretarial service. A.Ax.Dc.V.

Connaught   **4 C3**
16 Carlos Pl W1. 071-499 7070. Dignified and distinguished. Excellent service. Restaurant with unrivalled reputation. 90 rooms all with bath and TV. Book well in advance. A.

Conrad   **6 C6**
Chelsea Harbour SW10. 071-823 3000. Modern luxury hotel with wonderful harbour views. 160 rooms all with TV and bath. Fitness centre. S pool. Air cond. P. Conf facilities. A.Ax.Dc.V.

Dorchester   **4 B4**
Park La W1. 071-629 8888. Luxury with courteous, efficient service. Dinner dances in the Terrace Restaurant. Grill room and Cantonese restaurant. Good food. 252 rooms. 55 suites. P (limited). Conf cap 500. A.Ax.Dc.V.

Dukes   **4 D4**
35 St James's Pl SW1. 071-491 4840. Unique situation on secluded gas-lit courtyard. Good restaurant. Roof terrace. 62 rooms including 26 suites all with bath and TV. Banqueting and small conf facilities. A.Ax.Dc.V.

Forte Crest St James'   **4 D4**
81 Jermyn St SW1. 071-930 2111. Modern and sophisticated. Restaurant. 256 rooms with TV and bath. P. Small conf facilities. A.Ax.Dc.V.

Grosvenor House   **4 B3**
Park La W1. 071-499 6363. Unobtrusive

luxury and service. 390 rooms, 70 suites, 143 apartments. Air cond. S pool, saunas, gymnasium, health club and beauty salon. Banqueting and conf cap 1800. Bookshop, boutique, garage and restaurants. A.Ax.Dc.V.

Hilton (Park Lane)   **4 B4**
22 Park La W1. 071-493 8000. Modern luxurious hotel overlooking Hyde Park. Good roof restaurant with views and dancing. 452 rooms. Air cond. P. Sauna. Conf cap 1000. A.Ax.Dc.V.

Hilton (Regent's Park)   **1 A4**
18 Lodge Rd, St John's Wood NW8. 071-722 7722. Modern hotel overlooking Lord's Cricket Ground. Minski's Restaurant and Japanese Restaurant. 377 rooms. P. Air cond. Conf facilities. A.Ax.Dc.V.

Holiday Inn King's Cross   **2 B4**
1 King's Cross Rd WC1. 071-833 3900. 405 rooms all with bath and TV. No-smoking rooms. Conf cap for up to 200. Health and leisure club with sauna, solarium, fitness centre, beauty therapy room. S pool. Air cond. A.Ax.Dc.V.

Holiday Inn Mayfair   **4 C4**
3 Berkeley St W1. 071-493 8282. Modern hotel with elegant interior. 186 rooms. Conf cap 50. A.Ax.Dc.V.

Howard   **5 A3**
Temple Pl WC2. 071-836 3555. Modern luxury with traditional design. 135 rooms. Air cond. P. Conf cap 200. A.Ax.Dc.V.

Hyatt-Carlton Tower   **6 F1**
Cadogan Pl SW1. 071-235 5411. International standards of luxury and service in this sophisticated hotel. Good food in the Chelsea Room and the Rib Room. 224 rooms. Air cond. Health club. P. Conf facilities. A.Ax.Dc.V.

Hyde Park   **4 A5**
66 Knightsbridge SW1. 071-235 2000. Traditional standards of luxury and comfort. Restaurant and Grill. 186 rooms. Fitness centre. Air cond. A.Ax.Dc.V.

Inn on the Park   **4 B4**
Hamilton Pl, Park La W1. 071-499 0888. Luxurious modern hotel, with every comfort. Two haute cuisine restaurants. Views over Hyde Park. 228 rooms. Fitness centre. P. Air cond. Conf facilities. Secretarial services. A.Ax.Dc.V.

Inter-Continental   **4 B5**
1 Hamilton Pl W1. 071-409 3131. Good modern hotel. Excellent central location. 467 rooms. Two restaurants. Night club. Air cond. Sauna, health club. P. Conf facilities. A.Ax.Dc.V.

Marriott (Marble Arch)   **4 A2**
134 George St W1. 071-723 1277. Newly renovated hotel with fitness centre and

sauna. Air cond. P. 241 rooms. Conf cap 150. A.Ax.Dc.V.

May Fair Inter-Continental 4 C4
Stratton St W1. 071-629 7777. Traditional hotel with modern amenities. Air cond. S pool. Theatre. 287 rooms. Conf cap 300. A.Ax.Dc.V.

Meridien Hotel 4 D3
21 Piccadilly W1. 071-734 8000. Deluxe hotel with own health club attached. Three restaurants. 263 rooms. Air cond. Conf facilities. A.Ax.Dc.V.

Ritz 4 D4
Piccadilly W1. 071-493 8181. Grandeur and elegance. Period rooms. Unobtrusive efficient service. Beautiful restaurant. 24-hr currency exchange. Babysitting. 129 rooms. Air cond. A.Ax.Dc.V.

Royal Garden 3 C5
2-24 Kensington High St W8. 071-937 8000. Comfortably modern, pleasantly run. Two restaurants. Good food. 395 rooms. Valet and secretarial services. Conf cap 500. A.Ax.Dc.V.

Royal Lancaster 3 E3
Lancaster Ter W2. 071-262 6737. A tall modern block geared to business people and conferences. Magnificent views over Kensington Gardens and Hyde Park. La Rosette restaurant specialises in seasonal French and English dishes. 418 rooms. Air cond. P. Valet, secretarial and interpreting services. Conf cap 1000. A.Ax.Dc.V.

Savoy 4 G3
Strand WC2. 071-836 4343. World-famous in reputation and clientele. Edwardian in atmosphere and service, yet still faultlessly up-to-date. Impeccable standards. Outstanding cuisine. Fitness centre. S pool. Air cond. 202 rooms. Secretarial service. 24-hr currency exchange. Car hire. A.Ax.Dc.V.

Scandic Crown, Nelson Dock
265 Rotherhithe St SE16. 071-231 1001. Luxury hotel overlooking the River Thames. 390 rooms with bath and satellite TV. Restaurant. Fitness and leisure club with sauna, solarium and gymnasium. S pool. P. Conf facilities. Hotel riverboat to Canary Wharf. A.Ax.Dc.V.

Selfridge 4 B2
Orchard St W1. 071-408 2080. Traditional comfort plus modern facilities. All bedrooms are soundproofed with air cond, bath, TV, radio. Two restaurants. 298 rooms. Conf facilities. A.Ax.Dc.V.

Sheraton Park Tower 4 A5
101 Knightsbridge SW1. 071-235 0172. Modern hotel with beautiful glass-encased restaurant. P. 293 rooms

including 25 suites. Air cond. Secretarial service. Conf cap 250. A.Ax.Dc.V.

Stafford 4 D4
16-18 St James's Pl SW1. 071-493 0111. Elegant and comfortable. Good restaurant. Private dining rooms. 74 rooms (12 are housed in converted mews cottages). Small conf facilities. A.Ax.Dc.V.

Westbury 4 C3
Conduit St W1. 071-629 7755. Modern with American standards of luxury and efficiency. Restaurant. 243 rooms. Conf cap 120. A.Ax.Dc.V.

Hotels: medium price

£60-£120 per night, single room with bath or shower. Continental breakfast and inclusive of VAT and service charge. Prices should be checked as they may vary considerably within the category.

Academy 1 F5
17-21 Gower St WC1. 071-631 4115. Small, elegant Georgian hotel. Good service. 35 rooms. TV. Bar. A.Ax.Dc.V.

Basil Street Hotel 4 A5
Basil St SW3. 071-581 3311. Victorian decor, country house atmosphere. Two restaurants and wine bar. Women's Club. 95 rooms. Small conf facilities. A.Ax.Dc.V.

Blakes 4 C3
33 Roland Gdns SW7. 071-370 6701. Informal atmosphere. Showbiz clientele. Each room individually and luxuriously decorated. 50 rooms including 16 suites. Air cond. A.Ax.Dc.V.

Blandford Hotel 4 B1
80 Chiltern St W1. 071-486 3103. Small comfortable hotel. Good value. 33 rooms all with bath and TV. P. A.Ax.Dc.V.

Bloomsbury Crest 1 G5
Coram St WC1. 071-837 1200. Modern tourist hotel. Coffee shop and restaurant. Conf facilities. 284 rooms. A.Ax.Dc.V.

Bonnington 4 F1
92 Southampton Row WC1. 071-242 2828. Modernised well-established hotel. Restaurant. 215 rooms. Conf facilities. A.Ax.Dc.V.

Charing Cross 4 F4
Strand WC2. 071-839 7282. Spacious hotel. Victorian, but modernised and comfortable. Cocktail bar and carvery. 218 rooms. Conf facilities. A.Ax.Dc.V.

Cumberland 4 A2
Great Cumberland Pl, Marble Arch W1. 071-262 1234. Large, busy hotel. Valeting service. Coffee shop and restaurant. 900 rooms. Air cond. Conf cap 500. A.Ax.Dc.V.

De Vere Park 3 D5
1 De Vere Gdns, 60 Hyde Park Gate W8.

071-584 0051. Victorian, spacious and modernised. Restaurant. 100 rooms. A.Ax.Dc.V.

Drury Lane Moathouse　　**4 F2**
Drury La WC2. 071-836 6666. Ultra-modern hotel in the heart of theatreland. Maudie's Restaurant is good. 153 rooms. Air cond. Conf cap 100. A.Ax.Dc.V.

Durrants　　**4 B2**
George St W1. 071-935 8131. Elegant family-owned hotel. 96 rooms including 3 suites. Three restaurants. Conf facilities. A.Ax.V.

Forum Hotel　　**6 C2**
97 Cromwell Rd SW7. 071-370 5757. Modern hotel. Shops. 910 rooms with bath. P. Conf facilities. A.Ax.Dc.V.

Gloucester　　**6 C2**
Harrington Gdns SW7. 071-373 6030. Modern large hotel. Air cond and shopping arcade. 549 rooms. Conf cap 500. A.Ax.Dc.V.

Great Eastern　　**5 F1**
Liverpool St EC2. 071-283 4363. Spacious, modernised old-style hotel. Three restaurants. 164 rooms. Conf and beautiful banqueting facilities. A.Ax.Dc.V.

Great Northern　　**1 G3**
King's Cross N1. 071-837 5454. Spacious, comfortable old-style hotel. Modern decor. 90 rooms. Conf facilities. A.Ax.Dc.V.

Great Western Royal　　**3 E2**
Praed St W2. 071-723 8064. Traditional, spacious and modernised. Efficient service. Two restaurants. 238 rooms. Conf facilities. A.Ax.Dc.V.

Grosvenor　　**7 B1**
101 Buckingham Palace Rd SW1. 071-834 9494. The building is reputed to be the finest example of French Renaissance-style architecture in Britain. 366 rooms with bath. Conf cap 200. A.Ax.Dc.V.

Hilton (Kensington)
179-199 Holland Park Av W11. 071-603 3355. Modern, well-furnished building with sandstone finish and smoked glass windows. Shops. Entertainment. 606 rooms with bath. Air cond. P. Conf cap 300. A.Ax.Dc.V.

Hospitality Inn　　**3 D3**
104 Bayswater Rd W2. 071-262 4461. Competently-run modern hotel overlooking Hyde Park. 175 rooms. Air cond. P. Small conf facilities. A.Ax.Dc.V.

Hotel Russell　　**1 G5**
Russell Sq WC1. 071-837 6470. Victorian splendour. Shop. 328 rooms all with bath and TV. Two restaurants. 24-hr currency exchange. Conf facilities. Special week-end rates throughout the year. A.Ax.Dc.V.

Ibis Hotel　　**1 E4**
3 Cardington St NW1. 071-388 7777. Part of a French-run chain. Good value, quality hotel. 300 rooms all with bath and TV. Restaurant and bar. Conf cap 130. P. A.Ax.Dc.V.

Kensington Close　　**3 C6**
Wright's La W8. 071-937 8170. Good-value hotel with plenty of facilities. Two restaurants. S pool, saunas, sun-beds, gym and squash. Garden. 530 rooms. Conf facilities. A.Ax.Dc.V.

Kensington Palace　　**3 D5**
De Vere Gdns W8. 071-937 8121. Restful and modernised traditional hotel. Kensington Restaurant. 298 rooms. Large conf facilities. A.Ax.Dc.V.

Kingsley　　**4 F1**
Bloomsbury Way WC1. 071-242 5881. Modernised hotel for the business person and tourist. Restaurant. 146 rooms. Small conf facilities. A.Ax.Dc.V.

London Embassy Hotel　　**3 C3**
150 Bayswater Rd W2. 071-229 1212. Modern hotel overlooking Kensington Gardens. Restaurant and cocktail bar. 193 rooms all with TV. P. Conf facilities. A.Ax.Dc.V.

The Londoner　　**4 C2**
Welbeck St W1. 071-935 4442. Well-appointed, friendly and modern. 143 rooms. A.Ax.Dc.V.

London International Olympia
380 Kensington High St W14. 071-603 3333. Large, modern hotel, next to Olympia and near the motorail terminal. Brasserie/restaurant. 406 rooms with bath. P. Conf facilities. A.Ax.Dc.V.

Marriott (Regent's Park)　　**1 A1**
128 King Henry's Rd NW3. 071-722 7711. Modern building outside the centre but within easy access. S pool, sauna, gym, air cond, in-house movies. P. 304 rooms. Executive floor with own check-in facilities. Conf cap 200. A.Ax.Dc.V.

Mountbatten　　**4 F2**
Monmouth St WC2. 071-836 4300. Theatreland hotel with luxurious marble interior. Valet service. Restaurant, cocktail bar. 127 rooms including 7 suites. Conf facilities. A.Ax.Dc.V.

Norfolk　　**6 D2**
Harrington Rd SW7. 071-589 8191. Elegantly modernised Victorian hotel close to the Natural History Museum and the Victoria & Albert Museum. 97 rooms all with spa baths. Gym. Brasserie, winery, tavern. Conf cap 60. A.Ax.Dc.V.

Novotel
Shortlands W6. 081-741 1555. Concrete edifice near Hammersmith flyover. Traditionally furnished. 640 rooms. Air cond. P. Conf facilities. A.Ax.Dc.V.

Park Court **3 D3**
75 Lancaster Gate W2. 071-402 4272. Full range of services for guests with children. 365 rooms with bath. Conf facilities. A.Ax.Dc.V.

Regency Hotel **6 D2**
100 Queen's Gate SW7. 071-370 4595. Traditional, elegant and courteous. 210 rooms. Bar. International restaurant. Conf cap 200. Health spa. TV. A.Ax.Dc.V.

Regent Crest **1 D6**
Carburton St W1. 071-388 2300. Modern hotel which is very popular with tourists. Restaurant. 317 rooms all with bath. P. Conf facilities. A.Ax.Dc.V.

Regent Palace Hotel **4 D3**
12 Sherwood St W1. 071-734 7000. At the heart of the West End. Carvery, bars, games room. 891 rooms. A.Ax.Dc.V.

Rembrandt **6 D2**
11 Thurloe Pl SW7. 071-589 8100. Modernised, well run. Restaurant with carvery. Conservatory. Romanesque health club. 200 rooms. Conf cap 200. A.Ax.Dc.V.

Royal Court **6 G2**
Sloane Sq SW1. 071-730 9191. Attractive, luxurious, country house style hotel. 102 rooms all with bath or shower. 'Twelve Sloane Square' international restaurant. Wine bar and tavern. A.Ax.Dc.V.

Royal Horseguards **4 F4**
2 Whitehall Ct SW1. 071-839 3400. Victorian building facing across the Thames to the Festival Hall. Traditionally furnished and comfortable. 376 rooms all with bath and TV. Restaurant. Conf facilities. A.Ax.Dc.V.

Royal Trafalgar **4 E3**
Whitcomb St WC2. 071-930 4477. Hotel behind the National Gallery. Restaurant. Has its own pub 'The Battle of Trafalgar'. 108 rooms. Special weekend rates. A.Ax.Dc.V.

Sherlock Holmes **1 B6**
108 Baker St W1. 071-486 6161. Spacious modern hotel with its name as a theme. 126 rooms with bath. Restaurant. Conf facilities. A.Ax.Dc.V.

Strand Palace **4 G3**
372 Strand WC2. 071-836 8080. Large, international style hotel on the Strand. 783 rooms. Three restaurants. 24-hr currency exchange. Babysitting. Conf facilities. A.Ax.Dc.V.

Swallow International **6 B2**
147 Cromwell Rd SW5. 071-370 4200. Modern hotel with restaurant and the Fountain Brasserie. 417 rooms. P. Conf facilities. A.Ax.Dc.V.

Tara (Copthorne) **3 C6**
Scarsdale Pl, Wright's La W8. 071-937

7211. Modern hotel. Four restaurants. 831 rooms with bath. P. Conf facilities. A.Ax.Dc.V.

Tower Thistle **5 G4**
St Katharine's Way E1. 071-481 2575. Large and comfortable modern hotel next to Tower Bridge and the Tower of London. three restaurants, one overlooking the river. Discotheque. 826 rooms. Air cond. P. Conf facilities. A.Ax.Dc.V.

Waldorf **4 G3**
Aldwych WC2. 071-836 2400. Edwardian-style elegance. Suitable for the business executive. Modernised and central. Brasserie, restaurant, wine bar, tea dances in the 'Palm Court' Fri-Sun. 290 rooms. Conf facilities. A.Ax.Dc.V.

Washington **4 C4**
Curzon St W1. 071-499 7030. Up-to-date fashionable hotel. Efficient service. 173 rooms. Conf cap 100. A.Ax.Dc.V.

White House **1 D5**
Albany St NW1. 071-387 1200. Former apartment hotel now offering full service. Overlooks Regent's Park. First class public rooms. Restaurant with good reputation. Wine bar. Coffee shop. 577 rooms. Conf facilities. A.Ax.Dc.V.

White's **3 D3**
90-92 Lancaster Gate W2. 071-262 2711. Charming, balustraded exterior, unobtrusive and modernised. Overlooks Hyde Park. Restaurant. 55 rooms. Air cond. P. Conf facilities. A.Ax.Dc.V.

Hotels near Heathrow Airport

All these are air conditioned and provide free transport to and from the airport. Prices vary considerably. £70-£120 per night, single room with bath or shower. Breakfast is often extra. Inclusive of VAT and service charge.

Ariel
Bath Rd, Hayes, Middx. 081-759 2552. Circular in design. Restaurant OPEN all day. 180 rooms with bath and TV. Conf facilities. A.Ax.Dc.V.

Arlington
Shepiston La, Hayes, Middx. 081-573 6162. Transit hotel for the airport. Restaurant. 80 rooms. Bar. Special weekend rates. A.Ax.Dc.V.

Edwardian International
140 Bath Rd, Hayes, Middx. 081-759 6311. Luxurious hotel. Two restaurants. Health club. S pool. Business centre. 460 rooms all with bath and TV. P. Conf facilities. A.Ax.Dc.V.

Excelsior
Bath Rd, West Drayton, Middx. 081-759

6611. Fully soundproofed. Indoor pool. Three restaurants. *24-hr* service. 839 rooms. Health and fitness centre. Conf facilities. A.Ax.Dc.V.

Heathrow Park Hotel
Bath Rd, Longford, Middx. 081-759 2400. New hotel built as near as possible to the airport and geared to cater for transit visitors. Restaurant. Bar. Coffee shop. 306 rooms. Conf cap 500. A.Ax.Dc.V.

Heathrow Penta Hotel
Bath Rd, Hounslow, Middx. 081-897 6363. Pleasant modern exterior. S pool, leisure centre. Two restaurants. Two bars. 635 rooms with bath, TV, mini bar, air cond. Conf facilities. A.Ax.Dc.V.

Holiday Inn Heathrow
Stockley Rd, West Drayton, Middx. (0895) 445555. Modern hotel with 9-hole golf course, pool, sauna, gym. Two restaurants. All rooms have bath, TV, telephone, radio, in-house movies. 380 rooms. Conf facilities. A.Ax.Dc.V.

Master Robert
366 Great West Rd, Hounslow, Middx. 081-570 6261. 3 miles from Heathrow, 10 miles from central London. 100 rooms with bath and TV. Conf facilities. Restaurant and cocktail bar. A.Ax.Dc.V.

Forte Crest
Sipson Rd, West Drayton, Middx. 081-759 2323. All rooms have bath, TV, telephone, mini bars, babysitting service. 572 rooms. Three restaurants. Eight conference rooms. A.Ax.Dc.V.

Sheraton Heathrow
Colnbrook by-pass, West Drayton, Middx. 081-759 2424. Recently refurbished, with a well-designed interior. Two restaurants, shops, use of fitness centre, coffee shop. Free transport links with central London four times a day. 440 rooms, all with TV and soundproofing. Conf facilities. A.Ax.Dc.V.

Sheraton Skyline
Bath Rd, Hayes, Middx. 081-759 2535. Luxurious hotel. Quadrangular in design. Gourmet restaurant. S pool, babysitting service. 353 soundproofed rooms. 5 suites. A.Ax.Dc.V.

Hotels near Gatwick Airport

All these provide free transport to and from the airport. £70-£120 per night, single room with bath or shower. Breakfast is often extra. Inclusive of VAT and service charge.

Chequers Thistle Hotel
Brighton Rd, Horley, Surrey. (0293)

786992. Country house style hotel. Restaurant, snack bar. Outdoor s pool. 78 rooms. Conf facilities. A.Ax.Dc.V.

Holiday Inn
Langley Dri, Crawley, W. Sussex. (0293) 529991. Modern, efficient airport hotel recently refurbished. Two bars. Brasserie. 222 rooms. Fitness centre. S pool. Conf cap 230. A.Ax.Dc.V.

George Hotel
High St, Crawley, W. Sussex. (0293) 524215. 15thC building retaining original features yet providing modern, well-equipped bedrooms in the rear extension. Restaurant. 86 rooms. Conf facilities. A.Ax.Dc.V.

Post House
Povey Cross Rd, Horley, Surrey. (0293) 771621. New, spacious hotel. Heated outdoor s pool. Restaurant. 218 rooms. P. Conf facilities. A.Ax.Dc.V.

Bed and breakfast

Staying at a bed and breakfast is a good way to encounter English family life. They are good value; breakfasts are traditional English, and your host can give you tips on sightseeing. Many situated in streets around main line stations, but also scan notice boards outside newsagents and look in local papers or make a reservation through Bed-and-Breakfast (GB), PO Box 66, 94 Bell St, Henley-on-Thames, Oxon. (0491) 578803. There are hundreds of small guest-houses, many of them are to be found in Victoria, Earl's Court, Bayswater and Bloomsbury. It is much easier to find a room in winter than in summer. Beware of hotel touts who operate at the main stations, particularly Victoria; the accommodation they offer is usually inadequate and expensive.

Self-catering

Self-catering apartments are an ideal alternative to hotels if you are staying in London for a longer period. An apartment gives you flexibility and privacy and the use of a kitchen means you save on restaurant bills. You can choose between holiday lets (short-term accommodation in a rented flat) and serviced apartments which offer a higher level of facilities (eg maid, reception, security). The best way of finding such accommodation is through an agency:

Holiday Flat Services Ltd
140 Cromwell Rd SW7. 071-935 2412.

Serviced apartments and privately-owned holiday lets. Short or long-term let. All standards from economy to deluxe.

London Tourist Flats
17 St Mary's Rd SW19. 081-947 0573. Studio, one-bedroom and two-bedroom self-contained apartments in the Wimbledon area. Minimum two-week let.

Number One Apartments   **6 C2**
1 Harrington Gdns SW7. 071-370 4044. Studio, one-bedroom and two-bedroom serviced apartments in Kensington. Daily maid service, porterage, 24-hr reception and security. Short or long-term let.

Another option is a self-catering holiday resort:

Lawrence Wharf
273-301 Rotherhithe St SE16. 071-815 0815. London's first self-catering holiday resort situated in Docklands overlooking the Thames. 139 luxury one, two and three-bedroom apartments. Short or long-term let. Guests can share the facilities of the Scandic Crown International Hotel at a small charge.

Camping sites

Certainly the cheapest accommodation in London, camping can provide a pleasant alternative for the visitor. Book in advance in summer.

Crystal Palace Caravan Club
Crystal Palace Pde SE19. 081-778 7155. Own tent. *OPEN all year.*

Abbey Wood Caravan Club
Federation Rd, Abbey Wood SE2. 081-310 2233. Electric hook-ups available for caravans. Own tent. *OPEN all year.*

Hackney Camping
Millfields Rd E5. 081-985 7656. Own tent. *OPEN Jun-Aug.*

Lee Valley Park
Picketts Lock Centre, Picketts Lock La N9. 081-345 6666. Own tent. *OPEN all year.*

Tent City
Old Oak Common Lane W3. 081-743 5708. Shared accommodation in large tents or pitches for your own tent. *OPEN Jun-mid Sep.*

Property Rental

Publications like the Evening Standard, *the* Times, Loot *and* Time Out *are good sources for advertisements for flats and houses to rent, as are local newsagents' windows and local papers.*

Flats and Flat-sharing

Agencies will help you find a flat or a bed-sit, a place in a ready established flat, or else find you a kindred spirit to search with. They do try to match up carefully according to age, interests, background, etc and may charge a fee for their services.

Capital Radio   **1 E5**
Euston Tower, Euston Rd NW1. 071-608 6080. Flatshare list available from the foyer at *11.00 every Tue.*

Flatmates   **6 E2**
313 Brompton Rd SW3. 071-589 5491.

Jenny Jones   **4 C2**
40 South Molton St W1. 071-493 4801.

London Accommodation   **3 C3**
Bureau
102 Queensway W2. 071-727 5062.

Luxury Rentals

The following agencies specialise in good quality luxury properties and company lets.

Benham & Reeves Residential Letting Office
14 Upper Kingswell, Heath St NW3. 071-435 9681. Furnished and unfurnished flats and houses.

Claridges
West Heath House, 32 North End Rd NW11. 081-455 0007. Furnished and unfurnished properties. Visitors and company lets.

Cluttons   **6 E2**
48 Pelham St SW7. 071-584 3651. Mostly unfurnished properties.

Keith Cardale Groves   **4 B2**
1 Lumley St W1. 071-629 6604.

Marsh & Parsons   **3 B4**
5 Kensington Church St W8. 071-937 6091 (Head Office). Several other branches in West London.

Chestertons Residential   **3 B5**
Off Hornton St, Kensington High St W8. 071-937 7244. And in Mayfair, Hyde Park, Notting Hill Gate, Chelsea, Pimlico.

Taylor Rose   **3 F6**
185-7 Brompton Rd SW3. 071-589 5858. Good quality luxury furnished property to let for 6 months to 1 year.

Estate agents

Mainly deal in the sale of property but sometimes in rented property as well. Normally operate very much on a local basis and they advertise in the local papers which is a good source for assessing the market in any particular area.

Sport, health and fitness

Sports centres

Britannia Leisure Centre   **2 G2**
40 Hyde Rd N1. 071-729 4485. Large indoor centre. Squash, badminton, weight-training, table tennis, basketball, volleyball, martial arts, swimming pool with wave machine and slide, sauna, sunbed, spa bath. Also tennis courts, and five-a-side courts, all floodlit. Tuition in most activities, over-50s classes, activities for the disabled, clubs for children and adults. *No membership requirement.*

Brixton Recreation Centre
27 Brixton Station Rd SW9. 071-274 7774. Indoor sports centre. Squash, badminton, weight-training, swimming pool, bowls, sauna, solarium. Classes plus social and cultural activities. *No membership requirement. Reduced rates 14.00-16.00.*

Chelsea Sports Centre   **6 E3**
Chelsea Manor St SW3. 071-352 6985. Facilities for swimming, sub aqua, squash, badminton, table tennis, volleyball, weight-training, aerobics, roller-skating. Gymnasium, sauna, solarium. Sports injuries clinic. *No membership requirement.*

Crystal Palace National Sports Centre
Crystal Palace SE19. 081-778 0131. Opened in 1964, this is the largest multi-sports centre in the country. Superb facilities for over 50 different sports include a floodlit stadium (seating 16,000 spectators), Olympic-size swimming and diving pools, a large indoor sports hall and a dry-ski slope. National and international events are frequently staged, including swimming, water polo, athletics and basketball events. Courses in many sports including skiing, squash and swimming. *Modest annual membership fee.*

Elephant & Castle Leisure   **5 C6**
Centre
22 Elephant & Castle SE1. 071-582 5505. Facilities for badminton, basketball, cricket, five-a-side football, netball, squash and volleyball. Swimming pool and gymnasium. *No membership requirement.*

Finsbury Leisure Centre   **2 E4**
Norman St EC1. 071-253 4490. Indoor centre with facilities for netball, badminton, squash, weight-training, basketball, martial arts, roller-skating. Outdoor facilities for football, netball and tennis. Also swimming pool, Turkish bath, sunbeds and sauna. *No membership requirement.*

Jubilee Hall Recreation Centre   **4 F3**
The Piazza, Covent Garden WC2. 071-836 4835. Indoor centre offering aerobics, badminton, basketball, dance, football, martial arts, weight-training, weight-lifting. Sauna, solarium and jacuzzi for women only. Sports injury clinic with staff trained in acupuncture and reflexology. *No membership requirement.*

Jubilee Sports Centre
Caird St, Queens Park W10. 081-960 9629. Indoor facilities for most sports including cricket, martial arts, squash, swimming and tennis. Crèche. *No membership requirement.*

Latchmere Sports Centre
Latchmere Rd, Battersea SW11. 081-871 7470. Indoor centre with sports hall, projectile room, multi-gym, meeting rooms, crèche and bar. Also leisure pool and activity room. *No membership requirement.*

Michael Sobell Sports Centre
Hornsey Rd N7. 071-609 2166. Large indoor centre adaptable to most sports. Classes in badminton, basketball, climbing, cricket, gymnastics, martial arts, netball, five-a-side football, short tennis, snooker, squash, table tennis, volleyball, weight-lifting and yoga. There is also an ice rink, a sauna and a baby-bounce. *Modest annual membership fee.*

Picketts Lock Sports Centre
Picketts Lock La N9. 081-345 6666. Indoor facilities for soccer, gymnastics, badminton, basketball, hockey, netball, volleyball, martial arts, roller-skating, shooting, bowls and swimming. Outdoor facilities: soccer, hockey, tennis and golf (9-hole course). Tuition available in most sports. *No membership requirement.*

Queen Mother Sports Centre   **7 C2**
223 Vauxhall Bridge Rd SW1. 071-798 2125. Large indoor centre with multi-gym, sauna, solarium and swimming pool. Facilities for badminton, weight-training, squash, martial arts, aerobics, yoga, gymnastics and short tennis for children. Tuition available for most activities. *No membership requirement*

(except day membership for squash and weight-training).

Swiss Cottage Sports Centre
Winchester Rd NW3. 071 413 6490. Indoor facilities for badminton, basketball, netball, indoor football, volleyball, gymnastics, weight-training, keep fit, martial arts, squash and swimming. Outdoors: football and tennis. Sunbed. *No membership requirement*

Tottenham Sports Centre
703 High Rd N17. 081-801 6401. Facilities for archery, shooting, bowling, gymnastics, children's football, martial arts, table tennis, boxing, badminton, aerobics, yoga. *No membership requirement.*

YMCA: Central   **4 E2**
112 Great Russell St WC1. 071-637 8131. Indoor only. Badminton, basketball, gymnastics, keep fit, aerobics, sub aqua, swimming, table tennis, volleyball and yoga. Also weight-training, short tennis and sunroom. *Membership necessary. Day membership available.*
Also **YWCA**: Central Club, 16-22 Great Russell St WC1 (**4 E2**). 071-636 7512. Gymnasium, swimming. *Membership fee for gymnasium.*

Sports venues

Lord's Cricket Ground
St John's Wood Rd NW8. 071-289 1615. Famous cricket ground built in 1814. Home of Middlesex County Cricket Club. Stages county and international test matches *May-Sep.*

The Oval   **7 F4**
Kennington SE11. 071-582 6660. Originally a market garden, this has been a cricket ground since 1845. Surrey County Cricket club and the English international team play here *May-Sep.*

Twickenham
Whitton Rd, Twickenham, Middx. 081-892 8161. Venue for rugby internationals, home internationals and finals of club, county and divisional competitions. Matches mainly *Jan-Mar.*

Wembley Stadium
Wembley Way, Middx. 081-900 1234. Vast, impressive venue for various major sporting events including international football and hockey matches, American football, the Rugby League Challenge Cup Final and the FA Cup Final.
Wembley Arena, which also stages sporting events, is part of the same complex.

Wimbledon
All England Lawn Tennis Club, Church Rd SW19. Recorded information: 081-946 2244. Venue for the famous tennis championships which take place *last week Jun-first week Jul.* Advance seats for Centre Court and No 1 Court are allocated by public ballot. To enter, write *Sep-Dec* for an application form.

Ticket agents: sport

Tickets are available for most events but sometimes they must be bought months in advance. Apply to the box office of the venue concerned or try:

Keith Prowse
Atlantic House, 1 Rockley Rd W14. 081-795 2222. Head office. Contact for the address of their nearest ticket agency.

Sport

London has facilities for nearly all types of sport and has a formidable number of clubs, sports grounds and associations. This list gives the main authorities, places and events not only for the spectator but also for those who want to take part. There are numerous facilities for inexpensive tuition and training; the Sports Council runs hundreds of courses all over London. For sports equipment see the 'Specialist shops & services' section.

Greater London & SE Region Sports Council
PO Box 480, Ledrington Rd SE19. 081-778 8600. Answers individual enquiries about sport in the London and SE areas. Information on grants and loans, facilities and events.

Sports Council   **1 F5**
Information Centre, 16 Upper Woburn Pl WC1. 071-388 1277. Answers all kinds of enquiries about sport and physical recreation nationally and internationally. Also produces a calendar of events.

Sportsline
071-222 8000. Gives details of clubs and events in the London area.

American Football

American Football
American football is now immensely popular in Britain. As well as national league division games, American league sides have exhibition games at Wembley Stadium. If you want to play or watch the great gridiron game, contact the:

SPORT, HEALTH AND FITNESS   203

British American Football   **3 B4**
Association
92 Palace Gardens Terr W8. 071-727
7760.

Archery

There are about 20 archery clubs in
London each of which has some facilities
for shooting. The County of London out-
door championships are held in Aug.
Indoor championships in Feb. Numerous
inter-county matches throughout the
year.
County of London Archery
Association
Hon Sec, Mr Miller, Flat 9/N, Peabody Av,
Sutherland St SW1. 071-821 1735. For
information on the sport in London.
Grand National Archery Society
National Agricultural Centre, 7th St,
Stoneleigh, Kenilworth, Warks. (0203)
696631. Will supply information about
national and international archery.
Southern Counties Archery Society
Hon Gen Sec, Mr A.L. Francis,
5 Fordington Rd, Winchester, Hants.
(0962) 854932. For information about
archery in all the southern counties and
London.

Athletics

The major events are held at Crystal
Palace.
British Athletics Federation
Edgbaston House, 3 Duchess Pl, Hagley
Rd, Edgbaston, Birmingham, West
Midlands. 021-456 4050. For all informa-
tion on athletics.

Badminton

All England championships at Wembley in
Mar; also many other tournaments
throughout the country during the year.
All England junior championships held at
Watford, Herts.
Badminton Association of England
National Badminton Centre, Bradwell Rd,
Loughton Lodge, Milton Keynes, Bucks.
(0908) 568822. Gives information on local
clubs, promotes all national and interna-
tional events in England, and supplies a
diary of events and handbook.

Baseball

There are National League and Southern
Baseball League clubs at Sutton,
Croydon, Hendon, Purfleet and
Wokingham.

Basketball

Championship play-offs take place at
Wembley, which also hosts the occasional visit by the internationally-renowned
Harlem Globetrotters.
English Basketball Association
48 Bradford Rd, Stanningley, Leeds.
(0532) 361166. Will supply a club list.

Billiards & snooker

Over 300 clubs in London and a variety
of leagues and competitions.
New World Snooker Clubs
A chain of London snooker clubs which
will remain open up to 24 hrs if there are
people still playing. Check the phone
book for your nearest club.
Centre Point Snooker Club   **4 E2**
Centre Point, New Oxford St WC1. 071-
240 6886. Open to 06.00.
Kilburn Snooker Club
50 Kilburn High Rd, Kilburn NW6. 071-
328 6926. Open 24 hrs.
Wandsworth Billiards & Snooker
Centre
63 Wandsworth High St, Wandsworth
SW18. 081-874 1252. Open 24 hrs.

Bowls

National championships held at Beach
House Park, Worthing, W. Sussex in Aug.
Public greens in Battersea Park, Finsbury
Park, and many other London parks.
English Bowling Association
The Secretary, Lyndhurst Rd, Worthing,
W. Sussex. (0903) 820222. For informa-
tion.

Boxing

ABA championships held in May. Bouts
take place at Wembley and the Royal
Albert Hall. For detailed listings, consult
Boxing News.
British Boxing Board of   **5 D5**
Control
52a Borough High St SE1. 071-403
5879. Controls and administers profes-
sional boxing.
London Amateur Boxing
Association
58 Comber Grove SE5. 071-252 7008.
Supplies a list of London clubs.

Canoeing

Various suitable rivers such as the
Thames, Kennet, Wey, Medway, Rother

and Stour – all within easy reach of London.

British Canoe Union
Adbolton La, West Bridgeford, Nottingham, Notts. (0602) 821100. For information and advice.

Clay pigeon shooting

Clay Pigeon Shooting Association
107 Epping New Rd, Buckhurst Hill, Essex. 081-505 6221. For a list of clubs. Organises home and overseas championships.

Cricket

Many amateur clubs throughout London and first-class cricket at Lord's and the Oval *(see 'Sports venues')*. *The season is* Apr-Sep.

National Cricket Association
Lord's Cricket Ground, St John's Wood Rd NW8. 071-289 6098. Gives information on amateur clubs and coaching facilities.

Croquet

Croquet Association
Mr B.C. Macmillan, The Secretary, Hurlingham Club, Ranelagh Gdns SW6. 071-736 3148. For information and advice.

Cycling

The spectacularly fast 6-day indoor event is held at Wembley Arena and the Round-Britain Milk Race takes place in May-Jun.

British Cycling Federation
36 Rockingham Rd, Kettering, Northants. (0536) 412211. Information on road, track and circuit racing.

Eastway Cycle Circuit
Temple Mills La E15. 081-534 6085. An enclosed road circuit with facilities for recreational riding, racing, training and coaching. BMX track. Camp site. Mountain bike course.

Drag racing

Events take place infrequently at various airfields around London.

British Drag Racing Association
29 Westdrive, Caldicott, Cambs. (0954) 210028. Arranges meetings at Santa Pod and Avon Park.

Santa Pod Raceway
c/o National Dragways, 101 Farm Lane, Fulham SW6. 071-386 8777. Meetings are held regularly at England's only permanent drag racing venue, Santa Pod Raceway, Podington, Nr. Wellingborough, Northants.

Fencing

Amateur Fencing Association
1 Baron's Gate, 33 Rothschild Rd W4. 081-742 3032. For information and lists of events and clubs.

Fishing

To fish anywhere in the Thames area it is necessary to hold a Thames Water Authority Rod Licence. An additional permit is needed to fish in royal parks. The season is between 16 Jun-14 Mar.

London Anglers' Association
Forest Road Hall, Hervey Park Rd E17. 081-520 7477. Gives information on clubs and offers associate membership.

National Rivers Authority (NRA)
For information on obtaining a fishing licence in your area.
For Anglian region (Norfolk, Suffolk and Essex): Kingfisher House, Goldhay Way, Orton Goldhay, Peterborough. (0733) 371811.
For South East region: Guildborne House, Chatsworth Rd, Worthing, W Sussex. (0903) 820692.

Fishing: lakes & ponds

To fish in lakes or ponds you must hold a permit or day ticket from the local borough councils, unless marked free. Reductions for under-16s and OAPs. To fish anywhere in the Thames area you must hold a Thames Water Authority Rod Licence.

Battersea Park   6 **F5**
Roach, bream, flat-fish and very large carp. *Free.*

Chestnut Abbey Cross Pit, Herts
Good pike, perch, roach, tench. Crowded in summer.

Chingford Connaught Waters
All species. Crowded in summer. *Free.*

Clapham Common Eagle Pond
Good carp, some roach, pike, bream. *Free.*

Crystal Palace Boating Lake
Good carp, pike, roach, tench, gudgeon and perch.

Epping, Copped Hall Estate Pond
Carp, tench, perch, gudgeon, some rainbow trout. *Summer only.*

Finsbury Park
Carp, perch, tench and roach.

Hampton Court Ponds
Tench, pike, roach, perch. Beautiful water but often crowded.

Hampstead Heath Ponds
Good tench, roach, bream, pike. *Free.*

Hollow Ponds
Whipps Cross E17. Tench, pike, eels (but get there very early in the morning). *Free.*

Hyde Park Serpentine 3 F4
Good roach, perch.

Northmet Pit, near Cheshunt, Herts
Good summer tench and winter pike, also perch, roach, rudd.

Osterley Park, Middx
Tench, perch, roach.

Richmond Park Pen Ponds
Good roach and perch.

Rickmansworth Lakes, Herts
Good roach, perch, tench, bream, pike.

Seven Islands, Mitcham Common, Surrey
Pike, perch, bream. *Free.*

South Weald Park, Essex
Good tench, crucian carp, roach, rudd, pike, perch.

Tooting Common Pond
Roach, perch, carp.

Victoria Park Lake E9
Good eels, pike, perch, bream, gudgeon.

Wandsworth Common Pond
Carp, roach, tench, pike.

Windsor Great Park
Obelisk Pond, Johnson's Pond and Virginia Water. Carp, tench, pike, roach, rudd, bream and perch. Permits from Crown Estate Office, Great Park, Windsor, Berks (enclose sae). (0753) 860222.

Fishing: reservoirs

A number of Thames Water reservoirs are well stocked. Season 16 Jun-14 Mar for coarse fishing, 15 Mar or 1 Apr-30 Nov for trout. Thames Water licence needed. Day tickets from gate, but written applications only for seasons (two types – midweek and weekend) to:

North London Division
New River Head, Rosebery Av, London EC1, for **Barn Elms** - trout.

Eastern Division
The Grange, Crossbrook St, Waltham Cross, Herts, for **Walthamstow** – coarse, trout.

Fishing: rivers & canals

Grand Union Canal
Denham, Bucks. From Black Jack's Lock (No. 85) to Denham Lock (No. 87).

Lee Relief Channel Fishery
Waltham Abbey to Fishers Green. All species and the occasional trout. Day permits.

River Lee
Walthamstow to Hertford. Best fishing above Enfield Lock at Waltham Abbey, Cheshunt, Broxbourne, Rye House and St Margarets.

River Thames
Fishing starts above Kew. Probably England's best coarse fishing river. All species. Various stretches.

Flying

Aircraft Owners & Pilots Association 7 B2
50a Cambridge St SW1. 071-834 5631. For information, help and advice on all aspects of light aviation.

Football (soccer)

This is by far the most popular British sport from both the player's and spectator's point of view. The English Football League has 92 clubs divided into 4 divisions; the London clubs are listed here. Then there are the Southern and Isthmian League clubs, many of them in London and well worth watching. Finally there are hundreds of amateur clubs which encourage new players of all standards. Football League matches are played every Sat and most B.hols at 15.00, occasional midweek matches at 19.30. The season lasts from Aug to May. Occasional international matches at Wembley Stadium, domestic and European knock-out competitions at club grounds. The FA and League Cup Finals are held at Wembley (see 'Sports venues'), but it's impossible to get in unless you have a ticket in advance.

London Football Association
Aldworth Gro SE13. 081-690 9626. For information on leagues and clubs.

Arsenal FC
Highbury Stadium, Avenell Rd N5. 071-226 0304. Recorded ticket information 071-359 0131.

Charlton Athletic FC
Selhurst Park SE25. 081-859 8888. Offices at: The Training Ground, Sparrows Lane, New Elton SE9.

Chelsea FC 6 B5
Stamford Bridge, Fulham Rd SW6. 071-385 5545.

Crystal Palace FC
Selhurst Park SE25. 081-653 4462.

Fulham FC
Craven Cottage, Stevenage Rd SW6.
071-736 6561.
Leyton Orient FC
Brisbane Rd E10. 081-539 2223.
Millwall FC
The New Den, Senegal Fields SE16. 071-639 3143.
Queen's Park Rangers FC
South Africa Rd W12. 081-743 0262.
Tottenham Hotspur FC
White Hart Lane Ground, 748 High Rd N17. 081-808 8080.
West Ham United FC
Boleyn Ground, Green St E13. 081-472 2740.
Wimbledon FC
Selhurst Park SE25. 081-7718841.

Gliding

British Gliding Association
Kimberley House, Vaughan Way, Leicester, Leics. (0533) 531051. For information and help, club list and details of training courses.
London Gliding Club
Tring Rd, Dunstable, Beds. (0582) 663419. The home of British gliding. Contact the secretary for a familiarisation flight on a temporary membership basis so that you can see what it's about before committing yourself.

Go-karting

Playscape
The Old Bus Garage, Triangle Pl, Nelson's Row SW4. 071-978 1148. And at Hester Rd SW11. 071-228 8006.

Golf

The Daily Telegraph Golf Course Guide, published by HarperCollins, gives details and maps of all the courses in the British Isles. Also the Golfers' Handbook can be obtained from most libraries.
Municipal courses, where it is not necessary to be a member, can be found at:
Addington Court
Featherbed La, Addington, Croydon, Surrey. 081-657 0281. Two 18-hole courses, a 9-hole course and a pitch and putt course of 18 holes.
Beckenham Place Park
Beckenham Hill Rd, Beckenham, Kent. 081-650 2292. 18 holes.
Coulsdon Court
Coulsdon Rd, Coulsdon, Surrey. 081-660 0468. 18 holes.

Hainault Forest
Chigwell Row, Hainault, Essex. 081-500 2470. Two 18-hole courses, a putting green and practice field.
Picketts Lock Centre
Picketts Lock La N9. 081-803 3611. 9-hole course.
Royal Epping Forest
Forest Approach, Station Rd, Chingford, Essex. 18 holes.

Golf clubs in and near London for which membership is necessary, although many will extend guest facilities to members of comparable clubs from overseas. A handicap certificate is often needed if not a member.
Hampstead GC
Winnington Rd N2. 081-455 0203. 9 holes. Bar lunches served.
Highgate GC
Denewood Rd N6. 081-340 1906. 18 holes. Lunches served.
North Middlesex GC
Friern Barnet La, Whetstone N20. 081-445 1604. 18 holes. Bar lunches except Mon. Full lunch Sun only.
Richmond GC
Sudbrook Park, Petersham, Richmond, Surrey. 081-940 4351. 18 holes. Lunches served. No visitors at weekends.
Royal Mid-Surrey GC
Old Deer Park, Richmond, Surrey. 081-940 1894. 36 holes. Men's 6337 yds (5791m); ladies' 5544 yds (5067m). Lunches served.
Sandown Golf Centre
Sandown Park, More La, Esher, Surrey. (0372) 463340. Two 9-hole courses; one 9-hole pitch and putt course.
Sunningdale GC
Ridgemount Rd, Sunningdale, Berks. (0344) 21681. 36 holes. Two courses. Lunches served except Mon. Visitors require letter of introduction and handicap certificate.
Wentworth GC
Wentworth Dri, Virginia Water, Surrey. (0344) 842201. Three 18-hole and one 9-hole course. Visitors by arrangement Mon-Fri. Lunches served.

Greyhound racing

It is advisable to check times in the Evening Standard.
Catford Stadium
Catford Bridge SE6. 081-690 2261. 19.30 Mon, Thur & Sat.
Hackney Stadium
Waterden Rd E15. 081-986 3511. 13.00 Tue & Thur, 11.00 Sat.

Walthamstow Stadium
Chingford Rd E4. 081-531 4255. *18.30 Tue, Thur & Sat.*
Wembley Stadium
Empire Way, Wembley, Middx. 081-902 8833. *19.30 Mon, Wed & Fri.*
Wimbledon Stadium
Plough La SW17. 081-946 5361. *19.30 Tue, Thur, Fri & Sat.*

Gymnastics

Competitions at the Royal Albert Hall and Crystal Palace. See 'Children's London: Interests and activities'.

Hang gliding

British Hang Gliding Association
Cramfield Airfields, Cramfield, Milton Keynes, Bucks. Write for information.

Hockey

Men's internationals held at Willesden Sports Centre, women's at Wembley.
All England Women's Hockey Association
51 High St, Shrewsbury, Shropshire. (0743) 233572.
Hockey Association
Norfolk House, 102 Saxongate West, Milton Keynes. (0908) 241100.

Horse racing

Courses in and near London: Ascot, Berks (famous for its Royal meeting in Jun); Epsom, Surrey (stages the world-famous Derby in Jun and also the Oaks); Kempton Park, Sunbury-on-Thames, Middx; Lingfield Park, Surrey; Sandown Park, Esher, Surrey (famous for the Whitbread Gold Cup); and Windsor, Berks. Flat racing season Mar-Nov. Steeplechasing Aug-Jun. Point to point racing (amateur) season Mar-Apr.
Jockey Club (incorporating   4 B2 the National Hunt Committee)
42 Portman Sq W1. 071-486 4921. Governing body, responsible for rules, meetings, training and promotion of horse racing.
Racecourse Association
Winkfield Rd, Ascot, Berks. (0344) 25912. Can supply information on all aspects of racing.

Ice hockey

British Ice Hockey Association
The Secretary, 517 Christchurch Rd,

Boscombe, Bournemouth, Dorset. (0202) 303946. For information on clubs and events.

Lacrosse

The main events are held Feb-Apr, including the Clubs and Colleges Tournament and a home international in London.
All England Women's Lacrosse Association
4 Western Court, Bromley St, Digbeth, Birmingham. 021-773 4422. For lists of clubs and fixtures. For details of coaching courses telephone the British Lacrosse Coaching Foundation (0270) 878171.
English Lacrosse Union
The Secretary, Mr R. Balls, Lynton, 70 High Rd, Rayleigh, Essex. (0268) 770758. Men only. Gives details of events and coaching courses.

Martial arts

Amateur Karate Association   1 G4
120 Cromer St WC1. 071-837 4406.
British Judo Council
1a Horn La W3. 081-992 9454. Supplies free explanatory leaflet and details of clubs.
Martial Arts Commission
15-16 Deptford Bdwy SE8. 081-691 3433.
Judokan Club
Latymer Ct, Hammersmith Rd W6. 081-748 6787. Classes in judo and karate.
London Judo Society   7 E6
89 Lansdowne Way SW8. 071-622 0529. Judo and karate club.

Motorcycle racing

Road racing at Brands Hatch.
Auto-Cycle Union
ACU House, Wood St, Rugby, Warks. (0788) 540519. Governs all motorcycle competitions. Also trials and grass track. Publishes a handbook of forthcoming road racing and scrambling events.

Motor racing

Several clubs in the London area.
British Automobile Racing Club
Thruxton Racing Circuit, nr Andover, Hants. (026477) 2696. For details of club, championships and general information.
British Racing & Sports Car Club
Brands Hatch Circuit, Fawkham, nr Dartford, Kent. (0474) 874445. Stages meetings at Brand's Hatch and seven

other car circuits. Also organises major international events in this country.

RAC Motor Sports Association
Competitions Dept, Motor Sports House, Riverside Park, Colnbrook, Slough, Berks. (0753) 681736. Controls competitions. Supplies list of championship events.

Mountaineering

British Mountaineering Council
Crawford House, Precinct Centre, Booth St East, Manchester. 061-273 5835. Supplies a list of clubs and information on where to find mountain huts etc to members only.

Netball

Played lunchtimes in Lincoln's Inn Fields WC2.
All England Netball Association
Netball House, 9 Paynes Park, Hitchin, Herts. (0462) 442344. For information and advice.

Orienteering

This sport can be enjoyed by people of all ages and involves competitive navigation on foot with map and compass. Events take place most Sundays.
British Orienteering Federation
Riversdale, Dale Rd North, Darley Dale, Matlock, Derbyshire. (0629) 734042.

Parachuting

British Parachute Association
5 Wharf Way, Glen Parva, Leicester, Leics. (0533) 785271. For information, a list of clubs and help.

Polo

Played Apr-Sep *at Smiths Lawn, Windsor, Berks. Matches most weekends, B.hols & during Ascot week; Sun at Ham House, Richmond; Tue, Thur & Sat at Richmond Park (nr Roehampton Gate); Wed, Fri, Sat, Sun & B.hols at Cowdray Park, Midhurst, W. Sussex, also Wed & Thur during the British Open Championships (beginning Jul) and during Goodwood week; Wed, Sat & Sun at Woolmers Park, Hereford. Play starts middle or late afternoon.*

Rackets & real tennis

Real tennis is the original form of tennis and Henry VIII's court at Hampton Court still exists. Nowadays it's rather obscure, as is rackets which is a form of squash but with a much larger court.
Tennis & Rackets Association
c/o Queen's Club, Palliser Rd W14. 071-381 4746. Actively promotes both sports.
Queen's Club
Palliser Rd W14. 071-385 3421. Stages matches in both sports. Real tennis events *Sep-Apr.*

Riding

Association of British Riding Schools
Old Brewery Yard, Penzance, Cornwall. (0736) 69440. Deals with general equestrian matters ranging from insurance and legal matters to helping those interested in a career with horses. Publishes a handbook listing approved riding schools.
Richard Briggs Riding Stables 3 E3
63 Bathurst Mews W2. 071-723 2813. Open *all year round* for riding in Hyde Park. Caters for riders of all abilities, from 5yrs upwards. Lessons and jumping tuition available.
Wimbledon Village Stables
24b High St SW19. 081-946 8579. Stylish stables. Experienced riders as well as beginners welcome. Show jumping, dressage and gymkhanas held regularly. Film shows, lectures and demonstrations.

Rowing

The most famous event is the Oxford and Cambridge boat race from Putney to Mortlake in Mar or Apr. The Head of the River event on the Thames is held in Mar and is one of the largest of its kind in the world. Important regattas are held at Chiswick, Hammersmith, Henley-on-Thames, Kingston, Putney, Richmond, Twickenham and Walton.
Amateur Rowing Association
6 Lower Mall W6. 081-748 3632. Publishes the British Rowing Almanac annually, which gives a list of clubs and coming events. Also a monthly club magazine.

Rugby union

Twickenham is the home of rugby union (see 'Sports venues') and some international matches are staged there. Besides this there are a number of top-class clubs in the London area which provide excellent spectator sport and a plethora of lesser clubs which encourage new members of all standards.

Rugby Football Union
Rugby Rd, Twickenham, Middx. 081-892 8161. Controlling body of the sport and headquarters of rugby. The important matches, including internationals, are played there.

Sailing & yachting

International Yacht Racing Union   **5 B4**
27 Broadwall SE1. 071-928 6611. Publishes an annual international fixture list and booklet on racing rules.
Royal Ocean Racing Club   **4 D4**
20 St James's Pl SW1. 071-493 2248. To become eligible you must have a total of 400 miles off-shore racing.
Royal Yachting Association
Romsey Rd, Eastleigh, Hants. (0703) 629962. National authority providing information on all forms of yachting, sailing and powered boating.

Shooting

The most important competitions held at Bisley Camp are: the Services Meeting, beginning of Jul; NRA Small-bore Meeting later in Jul; NSRA British Small-bore Meeting later in Jul; NSRA British Small-bore Rifle Championship in Aug.
National Rifle Association
Bisley Camp, Brookwood, Woking, Surrey. (0483) 797777. Full-bore. Will recommend a suitable club (by letter only), but these are rare in London.
National Small-bore Rifle Association
Lord Roberts House, Bisley Camp, Brookwood, Woking, Surrey. (0483) 476969. Small-bore and air weapons. Will recommend a suitable club on receipt of sae.

Showjumping

The two major events are: the Royal International Horse Show at Wembley in Jul and the Horse of the Year Show at Wembley in Oct. There are also notable events staged at Windsor, Richmond and Clapham Common. See also 'Riding'.
British Show Jumping Association
British Equestrian Centre, Stoneleigh, Kenilworth, Warks. (0203) 696516.

Skating

National Skating Association   **2 E5**
of Great Britain
15-27 Gee St EC1. 071-253 3824. For information and advice on ice and roller-skating.
Broadgate Ice   **5 F1**
Eldon St EC2. 071-588 6565. Open-air ice rink. Broomball, a Canadian version of ice hockey, is played here. *OPEN mid Nov-Mar 12.00-15.00 Mon, 12.00-15.00 & 16.00-19.30 Tue-Fri, 11.00-13.00, 14.00-16.00 & 17.00-19.00 Sat & Sun.*
Queen's Ice Skating Club   **3 C3**
17 Queensway W2. 071-229 0172. Membership fee. Fee for skate hire. Tuition available. *OPEN 11.00-16.30 & 19.30-22.00 Mon-Fri, 10.00-12.00, 14.00-17.00 & 19.30-22.30 (19.00-22.00 Sun) Sat & Sun.*
Roller Express
Unit 16, Lea Valley Trading Park N18. 081-807 7345. Huge, purpose-built roller skating rink. Skate hire. *OPEN 19.00-23.00 Mon & Wed, 19.00-01.00 Thur, 16.00-19.30 & 20.00-02.00 Fri, 09.30-12.30 & 13.00-18.00 Sat, 12.00-17.00 & 17.30-22.30 Sun.*
Skate Attack City Track   **5 G1**
Old Spitalfields Market, Lamb St E1. 071-377 6169. Latest trend from the USA – a specially prepared surface for roller skating and roller blading. Qualified instructors, skate hire and protective clothing. *OPEN 11.00-19.00 Mon-Fri, 10.00-15.00 Sun. CLOSED Sat.*
Streatham Ice Rink
386 Streatham High Rd SW16. 081-769 7771. Admission and skate-hire charge. *OPEN 10.00-12.30, 14.00-16.30, 19.45-22.30 daily. School hols OPEN 10.00-16.30, 19.45-22.30 daily.*

Skiing

British Ski Federation
258 Main St, East Calder, West Lothian, Scotland. (0506) 884343.
Ski Club of Great Britain   **7 A1**
118 Eaton Sq SW1. 071-245 1033. National club for recreational skiing. Equipment advice for members.

Artificial ski centres provide great practice and can be great fun. Most centres run courses for beginners and hire out all the necessary equipment.
Hillingdon Ski Centre
Park Rd, Uxbridge, Middx. (0895) 255183.
Mountaintop Ski Centre
Beckton Alps, Alpine Way E6. 071-511 0351.

Squash

A number of sports centres have public squash courts – prior booking essential.
Squash Rackets Association
Westpoint, 33-34 Warple Way W3. 081-746 1616. Publishes the *SRA Annual* which gives a list of clubs and courts. Also *Squash News* bimonthly.

Stock car racing

Events mostly staged *Sat eve Mar-Sep.*
Spedeworth International
Wimbledon Stadium, Plough La SW17. 081-946 5361.
Wisbech Stadium, Cromwell Rd, Wisbech, Cambs. (0945) 584736.

Sub aqua

British Sub Aqua Club
16 Upper Woburn Pl WC1. 051-357 1951. For information on branches where training courses are run. To join you will have to pass a swimming test, produce a certificate of fitness signed by your doctor, and evidence of a satisfactory chest X-ray. BSAC training is recognised worldwide as being of the highest order. Holborn branch and London branch are well-equipped, active groups who train throughout the year and dive regularly. *See also 'Sports equipment: sub aqua' under 'Shops and services'.*

Swimming

Magnificent Olympic-standard pool at the Crystal Palace National Sports Centre. High-standard competitions. Excellent tuition and facilities for members.
Public baths (indoor)
Chelsea Manor St SW3. 071-352 6985.　　　　　　　　　　**6 E3**
Marshall St W1. 071-439 4678.　　**4 D2**
Norman St EC1. 071-253 4011.　　**2 E4**
Oasis, 32 Endell St WC2. 071-836 9555. Also an outdoor pool *May-Oct.*　**4 F2**
Queen Mother Sports Centre, 223　**7 C2**
Vauxhall Bridge Rd SW1. 071-798 2125.
225 Queensway W2. 071-798 3689.**3 C2**
Seymour Pl W1. 071-723 8019.　　**4 A1**
Public baths (outdoor)
The Big Splash, Mapleton Rd SW18. 081-871 7674.
Finchley Open Air Pool, High Rd N12. 081-883 6232.
Swimming in the parks (outdoors)
Hampstead Pond NW3. 071-435 2366. *OPEN May-Sep 10.00-16.30. Free.*
Highgate Ponds N6. 081-340 4044. Men

only. *OPEN Apr-Sep 07.30-20.30 Mon-Sun; Oct-Mar 07.00-15.00 Mon-Sun. Free.*
Kenwood Pond N6. 081-340 5303. Women only. *OPEN 08.00-dusk all year round. Free.*
Parliament Hill Lido NW5. 071-485 3873. *OPEN 10.00-18.00 May-Sep; 07.00-09.30 Oct-Apr. Free before 09.00.*
Serpentine Lido Hyde Park W2.　　**3 F4**
071-724 3104. *OPEN 10.00-18.00.*
Tooting Bec Lido SW16. 081-871 7198. *OPEN 06.30-19.30 Easter-Oct, 07.00-17.00 Oct-Easter (members only).*
Amateur Swimming Association
Harold Fern House, Derby Sq, Loughborough, Leics. (0509) 230431. The authority governing national swimming events.

Table tennis

English Table Tennis Association
Queensbury House, Havelock Rd, Hastings, E. Sussex. (0424) 722525.

Tennis

There are public courts in most London parks. There are also plenty of clubs to join and indoor centres for which membership is usually necessary. The major event, of course, is Wimbledon fortnight which begins at the end of Jun (see 'Sports venues'). There are also various other tournaments held in London; those which take place immediately before Wimbledon, such as the one at Queen's Club, usually include several top professionals.
Lawn Tennis Association
Palliser Rd W14. 071-385 2366. The governing body of lawn tennis in Britain. Will supply a list of clubs.
Queen's Club
Palliser Rd W14. 071-385 3421. For membership enquiries.

Ten pin bowling

Bowling alleys often stay open late; phone for opening times.
British Ten Pin Bowling Association
Postal address: 19 Canterbury Av, Ilford, Essex. 081-478 1745. No bowling centre, but provides list of bowling centres and other information and advice.
Airport Bowl
Bath Rd, Harlington, Middx. 081-759 1396.
Bexleyheath Superbowl
Albion Rd, Bexleyheath, Kent. 081-303 3325.

Dagenham Superbowl
New Rd, Dagenham, Essex. 081-592
0347. 24 lanes.
Lewisham Bowl
11-29 Belmont Hill SE13. 081-318 9691.
24 lanes, automatic scoring, fast food
and bar.
Streatham Mega Bowl
142 Streatham Hill SW2. 081-678 6007.
Trocadero Lazer Bowl   **4 E3**
13 Coventry St W1. 071-734 3859. Also
Bowlingo, a more compact version
with skiddy black lanes and fluorescent
lighting.

Volleyball

National League season runs Oct-Mar.
English Volleyball Association
27 South Rd, West Bridgford,
Nottingham, Notts. (0602) 816324.
Supplies a list of clubs and fixtures.

Water polo

Occasional games at Crystal Palace.
Amateur Swimming Association
Harold Fern House, Derby Sq,
Loughborough, Leics. (0509) 230431 for
details.

Water skiing

*Several clubs to join and championships
to watch. The season is May-Sep.*
British Water Ski Federation
390 City Rd EC1. 071-833 2855. For
information and club lists. Residential
summer courses.
Princes Water Ski Club
Clockhouse La, Bedfont, Middx. (0784)
256153. Three slalom course, two jumps.
All equipment provided.

Weight-lifting

*National championships held at Crystal
Palace.*
**British Amateur Weight-Lifters
Association**
3 Iffley Turn, Oxford, Oxon. (0865)
790096. Comprises 12 regional
associations which organise meetings,
clubs, championships etc. Will supply
information on local clubs and
events.
**Greater London Amateur Weight-
Lifters Association**
The Secretary, Mr G. Platt, 47 Heathhurst
Rd, Sanderstead, Surrey. 081-657 1615.

Windsurfing

Windsurfing Information Centre
Royal Yachting Association, Romsey Rd,
Eastleigh, Hants. (0703) 629962. Contact
for full details of clubs, classes, equipment
hire, events and venues.
Docklands Sailing Centre
Kingbridge, Millwall Dock E14. 071-537
2626. Purpose-built centre with 35 acres
(14.5ha) of water in the dock.
Peter Chilvers Windsurfing
Gate 5, Royal Victorian Dock E16. 071-
474 2500. 83 acres (34.5ha) of enclosed
water at the end of Victoria Dock. Roped-
off area for beginners.

Wrestling

*Main professional bouts at the Royal
Albert Hall.*
**British Amateur Wrestling
Association & English Olympic
Wrestling Association**
Administration, 16 Choir St, Salford. 061-
832 9209. Write for information.

Health and fitness

*With the increasing awareness of the
importance of health and fitness, clubs
and dance centres have sprung up all
over London, offering the opportunity to
take classes in aerobics, dance or yoga;
or simply to relax in the sauna or spa
bath. Beauty treatments are often available in these centres along with bar and
restaurant facilities. Some clubs require
membership, some entrance fee which
varies depending on which equipment is
used. A selection of clubs and dance
centres is listed below. Local newspapers
and newsagents' windows carry
announcements of classes in your area.
Local council education authorities also
offer tuition.*

Dance centres

Keep Fit Association   **1 F5**
16 Upper Woburn Pl WC1. 071-233
8898. Answers all kinds of enquiries
about keep fit and dance.
Dance Attic
212-214 Putney Bridge Rd SW15. 081-
785 2055. Also at 368 North End Rd
SW6. 071-610 2055. Gym and dance
studio. Classes held in ballet, jazz, contemporary, tap, belly-dancing, flamenco,
lambada. Also fitness, aerobics, gymnastics and fencing. *Membership required.*

Dancercise Studios
The Barge, Durban Lion Wharf, Old Isleworth, Middx. 081-948 0051. There are several Dancercise Studios in central and suburban London offering classes combining jazz, Broadway, ballet, contemporary and disco. Enrolment at beginning of term. *Contact above address for list of studios.*

Danceworks 4 **B2**
16 Balderton St W1. 071-629 6183. Wide range of classes. Ballet, tap, various jazz forms, salsa, belly-dancing, gypsy flamenco. Also aerobics, sauna, sunbeds. Café. *Daily membership available.*

Pineapple Dance Studio 4 **F2**
7 Langley St WC2. 071-836 4004. Also at 38 Harrington Rd SW7 (6 **D2**). 071-581 0466. Qualified teachers for every type of dance imaginable from belly to break. Also gymnasium for weight-training, hydro fitness, body control studios, café-bar, resident osteopath and masseur. *Membership required.*

Health clubs & fitness centres

Barbican Health & Fitness 2 **E6**
Centre
97 Aldersgate St EC1. 071-374 0091. Top class facilities for fitness training: exercise machines, aerobics floor, 25m pool, running track, sauna, solarium, spa bath, whirlpool. Restaurant and bar. *Membership.*

Dave Prowse Fitness Centre 5 **D5**
12 Marshalsea Rd SE1. 071-407 5650. Two gymnasiums, sauna, solarium and showers. Dance and aerobics classes. *Membership.*

Earl's Court Gym 6 **B3**
254 Earl's Court Rd SW5. 071-370 1402. Weights, aerobics, solarium, sauna. *No membership requirement.*

The Fitness Centre 5 **D4**
Crown House, 56-58 Southwark St SE1. 071-403 6078. Gymnasium, sauna, steam. Dance and aerobics classes. Beauty salon. Health bar. *No membership requirement.*

Health Haven 7 **D2**
40 Vauxhall Bridge Rd SW1. 071-834 2289. Gymnasium, sunbeds, beauty treatments, massage, dance studio. Sauna and steam room. *Membership.*

Hogarth Club
1a Airedale Av W4. 081-995 4600. American-style club with nautilus gym, spa bath, sauna, swimming pool, squash and tennis courts. Dance and exercise classes. Bar and restaurant. *Daily membership available.*

Holmes Place Health Club 6 **C4**
188a Fulham Rd SW10. 071-352 9452. Swimming pool, two gymnasiums, steam room, sauna, sunbeds. Exercise classes. *Membership.*

Metropolitan Club 4 **D2**
27-28 Kingly St W1. 071-734 5002. Gymnasium with videos to relieve the tedium of exercising. Swimming pool with whirlpool attached, steam room, sauna and sunbeds. Dance studio with full range of work-outs. *Membership.*

The Sanctuary 4 **F3**
12 Floral St WC2. 071-240 9635. Exotic setting for sauna, solarium, steam room, swimming pool, spa bath. For the real sybarite. Women only. *Daily membership available.*

Westside Fitness & Leisure 3 **B6**
Centre
201-207 Kensington High St W8. 071-937 5386. Weight-training, step classes, aerobics, yoga, stretch classes for all levels. *No membership required.*

Saunas

Telephone for appointment as times vary considerably. See also under 'Health clubs and fitness centres' and 'Turkish baths'.

The Body Feminine
Lanmark Pl, Maida Vale W9. 071-289 9657. Sauna and massage. Women only. *No membership required.*

Oasis 4 **F2**
Endell St WC2. 071-836 9555. Swimming pools, paddling pool, sauna, warm baths and showers. Heated outdoor pool and sunbathing facilities in summer. *No membership required.*

Swiss Cottage Sauna
2 New College Parade, Finchley Rd NW3. 071-586 4422. Unisex. *OPEN 24 hrs. No membership required.*

Turkish baths

Ladywell Baths
Lewisham High St SE13. 081-690 2123. Excellent and inexpensive. Also indoor pool and public baths.

Porchester Centre 3 **C2**
Porchester Rd W2. 071-792 2919. Public and inexpensive. Three dry heat rooms, steam room, cold plunge, massage, exercise room. Also two swimming pools.

Rainbow Centre
41 East St, Epsom, Surrey. (0372) 732551. Turkish bath plus other facilities including sauna, sunbeds, swimming pool, conditioning gym and indoor bowls.

Mind, body and spirit

Life in a hi-tech society has brought about a return to ancient and natural forms of therapy. This, combined with the idea of prevention rather than cure, has made alternative medicine a regular practice for many people. Some treatments are available under the National Health Service, but most are private. Health food shops and health magazines (also Time Out) often advertise practitioners and teachers, some of whom are registered, some not. The Institute for Complementary Medicine Year Book is a comprehensive guide to all aspects of alternative medicine which is updated each year and available in most bookshops. Below are listed some of the bodies which will give advice about the various therapies and supply a list of registered practitioners.

General

Community Health Foundation   2 G4
188 Old St EC1. 071-251 4076. Health education centre offering a wide range of courses including shiatsu massage and Swedish massage, aromatherapy, iridology (diagnosis of body through eye), yoga, meditation, tai chi. Also macrobiotic cookery and dietary counselling.
Institute of Complementary   4 C1
Medicine
21 Portland Pl W1. 071-237 5165. Provides detailed information on all aspects of alternative medicine.
The Isis Centre for Holistic Health
5 Clonmell Rd N17. 081-808 6401. Individual and group sessions of a medical and counselling nature. Treatments in homoeopathy, osteopathy, psychotherapy, acupuncture and massage. Regular classes in 'technologies for creating'.
Neal's Yard Therapy Rooms   4 F2
2 Neal's Yard WC2. 071-379 7662. Individual consultations *(by appt only)* for acupuncture, Alexander technique, autogenic training, aromatherapy, bach flower remedies, biodynamic therapy, chiropractic, colour therapy, counselling, cranial osteopathy, healing, herbalism, homoeopathy, hypnotherapy, iridology, applied kinesiology, massage, naturopathy, nutrition and diet, osteopathy, polarity therapy, psychotherapy, reflexology, sexual therapy, shiatsu, touch for health.

Acupuncture

Chinese method of treating ailments by pricking the skin or tissue with needles.
British Acupuncture   7 B3
Association
34 Alderney St SW1. 071-834 1012. OPEN 09.00-17.00 Mon-Fri. Appt only.

Alexander technique

The re-education of the body in order to achieve the posture that nature intended and to carry out bodily activities with maximum ease and a minimum of energy and tension.
Society of Teachers of the   6 C4
Alexander Technique
10 London House, 266 Fulham Rd SW10. 071-351 0828. Will supply a list of qualified teachers (send sae).

Chiropractic

The correction of spinal displacements by manipulation of the spine to ensure the flow of nervous energy from the spine to all parts of the body is unimpaired.
British Chiropractic   7 D1
Association
Premier House, 10 Greycoat Pl SW1. (0734) 757557. Will provide information and addresses of recognised practitioners.

Homoeopathy

Natural medicine based on the principle of treating like with like – ie a substance which would produce symptoms of sickness in a healthy person will cure a sick person showing those same symptoms.
British Homoeopathic   4 C1
Association
27a Devonshire St W1. 071-935 2163. Provides a list of medical doctors trained in homoeopathy (send sae).
Royal London Homoeopathic   2 A5
Hospital
Great Ormond St WC1. 071-837 8833. NHS treatment by registered homoeopaths (appt only). OPEN 09.00-17.00 Mon-Fri.
Society of Homoeopaths
2 Artizan Rd, Northampton. (0604) 21400. Maintains a register of professional homoeopaths who practise according to the Society's registration standards and code of ethics. Send sae for a copy.

Hypnotherepy

The Hypnotherapy Centre   **4 A2**
1 Wythburn Pl W1. 071-262 8852.
Provides information and a list of registered practitioners of cure by hypnosis.

Osteopathy

Manipulation of the joints to correct structural imbalance as the body cannot function effectively unless structurally sound.

British Osteopathic   **1 B5**
Association
8 Boston Pl NW1. 071-262 5250. Clinic OPEN 10.00-12.30 Mon, 10.00-15.00 Tue-Fri by appt. Also provides a list of registered osteopaths.

British School of Osteopathy   **4 E4**
1-4 Suffolk St, Pall Mall SW1. 071-930 4601. OPEN 09.00-17.00 Mon-Fri by appt. Specialist sports injury clinic OPEN 10.00-14.00 Wed & Sat.

Reflexology

Massage treatment which stimulates nerve-centres in the feet.

British School of Reflexology
Holistic Healing Centre, 92 Sheering Rd, Old Harlow, Essex. (0279) 429060. Information and addresses of practitioners.

International Institute of
Reflexology
28 Hollyfields Av N11. 081-368 0865. Provides information and addresses of practitioners. Seminars.

Yoga & meditation

Iyengar Yoga Institute
223a Randolph Av W9. 071-624 3080. Classes for all levels from beginners and remedial to teacher training.

London Buddhist Centre
51 Roman Rd E2. 081-981 1225. Specialises in meditation, also holds classes in yoga, Alexander technique and tai-chi.

Sivananda Yoga Centre
51 Felsham Rd SW15. 081-780 0160. Courses and beginners classes available in meditation and yoga. Yoga for pregnancy and pre-pregnancy. Courses on vegetarian cookery. Fasting clinic. Indian music. Also arranges retreats.

Student London

Reference libraries

There are over 400 specialist libraries in London. The following are the most important and have been classified in sections to help both the enquiring visitor and the serious research worker. The British Museum Library can usually solve problems of research because of its vast collections. It is, however, busy and understaffed, so try other libraries first. Public libraries, maintained by each borough, offer access to magazines, newspapers and reference books. Some have large reference departments specialising in certain subjects.

General

British Library   **4 F1**
Great Russell St WC1. 071-636 1544. This is the national copyright library which holds one copy of every printed book published in the UK. It is also a wide-ranging reference library with an incomparable collection of books, periodicals and manuscripts in English and foreign languages, but should only be used as a library of last resort. Admission to the Bloomsbury Reading Rooms is restricted to academics and professional researchers, who have to obtain a pass from the Reader Admissions office. Adults over 21 only. Reading Rooms OPEN 09.00-17.00 Mon, Fri & Sat, 09.00-21.00 Tue-Thur. CLOSED Sun & B.hols. Exhibition galleries OPEN 10.00-17.00 Mon-Sat, 14.30-18.00 Sun. Free.

British Library Newspaper Library
200 Colindale Av NW9. 071-323 7355. National collection of newspapers from the UK and overseas countries. London newspapers prior to 1801 held at British Museum main building. Adults over 21 only. OPEN 10.00-16.45 Mon-Sat. Free.

Government Departments
Extensive collections. Available by appointment only. Official publications, history and information associated with

the department. The following few (of many) have particularly large libraries: Treasury; Home Office; Foreign and Commonwealth Office; Army Dept; Navy Dept; Dept of Environment.

London Library   **4 D4**
14 St James's Sq SW1. 071-930 7705. Writers' and scholars' library with many distinguished authors among its members. Permanent collection of standard and authoritative works dating from the 16thC including a unique stock of foreign language books. One million volumes. Substantial annual membership fee enables readers to take out 10 books at a time. *OPEN 09.30-17.30 Mon-Sat (to 19.30 Thur). Members only.*

Art & architecture

British Architectural Library   **1 D6**
66 Portland Pl W1. 071-580 5533. 120,000 volumes; 60,000 photographs. Architecture and related arts, from 15thC to the present day. *OPEN 13.30-17.00 Mon, 10.00-14.00 Tue, 10.00-17.00 Wed, Thur & Fri, 10.00-13.30 Sat. CLOSED Aug. Free.*

British Architectural Drawings 4 A2 Library
Heinz Gallery, 21 Portman Sq W1. 071-580 5533. The most extensive collection of architectural drawings in the world, including practically all the surviving drawings of Palladio. May be consulted on specific research projects *by appt only.* Exhibition of new architects throughout the year. *OPEN 10.00-13.00 Mon-Fri. CLOSED Aug.*

British Museum   **4 F1**
Great Russell St WC1. 071-636 1555. Very extensive collection of original drawings, etchings and engravings in Dept of Prints and Drawings. *OPEN 10.00-13.00 & 14.15-16.00 Mon-Fri, 10.00-12.30 Sat. Pass required – apply to Prints Dept.*

Courtauld Institute of Art   **4 G3**
Somerset House, Strand WC2. 071-872 0220. 66,000 volumes on the history of art. *OPEN 10.00-18.00 Mon-Sat, 14.00-18.00 Sun. Charge.* Also the Wick Library, a collection of over a million photographs, reproductions of paintings and drawings. *OPEN same hours as above. Free.*

National Art Library Victoria   **6 D1 & Albert Museum**
Cromwell Rd SW7. 071-589 6371. A million volumes on fine and applied arts of all countries and periods. Sculpture, ceramics, silver, furniture, musical instru-ments, English costume. Prints and drawings department has extensive collections dealing with art, architecture, pure and applied design and graphics. *OPEN 10.00-17.00 Tue-Sat. CLOSED Mon, Sun & B.hols. Free. Lectures.*

National Monuments Record   **4 D3**
23 Savile Row W1. 071-973 3091. The historic architecture of England. Library of over two million photographs, measured drawings and prints. Sign in at reception. *OPEN 10.00-17.30 Mon-Fri. CLOSED B.hols. Free.*

Royal Academy of Arts   **4 D3**
Burlington House, Piccadilly W1. 071-439 7438. Fine arts. 15,000 volumes, original drawings, mainly 18th-19thC. *OPEN to Friends of the Academy 10.00-18.00 Mon-Sat and to researchers by appt only.*

Royal Society of Arts   **4 F3**
8 John Adam St WC2. 071-930 5115. 15,000 books on industrial art and design. May be used for reference by accredited researchers, *by prior appt. OPEN 09.30-17.30 Mon-Fri. CLOSED 12.30-13.30 Tue, Thur & Fri.*

St Bride Printing Library   **5 C2**
St Bride Institute, Bride St EC4. 071-353 4660. A public reference library of paper, typography, bookbinding and printing. *OPEN 09.30-17.30 Mon-Fri. CLOSED B.hols. Free.*

Sir John Soane's Museum   **4 G2 Library**
13 Lincoln's Inn Fields WC2. 071-405 2107. Art and architecture, 15th-19thC architectural drawings, including many of the drawings from the office of Robert and James Adam and those from Soane's own office. *OPEN 10.00-17.00 Tue-Sat. CLOSED Mon. By appt only. Free.*

Westminster Fine Arts Library   **4 E3**
Central Reference Library, St Martin's St WC2. 071-798 2038. English and European books. Painting, drawing, architecture, design, furniture, pottery, costume and sculpture. Periodicals. Also the Preston Blake Library, which contains approx 600 volumes on William Blake. *OPEN 10.00-19.00 Mon-Fri, 10.00-17.00 Sat. Free.*

Ecclesiastic

Dr Williams' Library   **1 F5**
14 Gordon Sq WC1. 071-387 3727. Modern and 17th-18thC books on theology, Byzantine history, Dissenting history. 112,000 volumes. *OPEN 10.00-17.00 Mon-Fri (to 18.30 Tue & Thur). CLOSED B.hols. Free.*

Jews' College
44a Albert Rd NW4. 081-203 6427. Hebraica and Judaica. 80,000 books and manuscripts. *OPEN 09.00-18.00 (to 17.00 in vacations) Mon-Thur, 09.00-13.00 Fri, 09.30-12.30 Sun (term-time). CLOSED B.hols & Jewish hols. Free.*

Lambeth Palace   5 A6
Lambeth Palace Rd SE1. 071-928 6222. The archives of Archbishops of Canterbury from medieval times. 150,000 books, 3500 manuscripts, records, much larger number of archives. *OPEN 10.00-16.50 Mon-Fri to public on production of a letter of introduction. Free.*

Sion College   5 C3
Victoria Embankment EC4 (entrance in John Carpenter St). 071-353 7983. Theological books from 17thC to present day. 90,000 volumes. *OPEN 10.00-17.00 Mon-Fri. Check times. Appt preferred. Free.*

Westminster Abbey Chapter   4 F6
Library & Muniment Room
The Cloisters, Westminster Abbey SW1. 071-222 5152. 16th-18thC theology and history of Westminster Abbey. Archives from before the Norman Conquest. 14,000 volumes. *Appt preferred. OPEN 10.00-13.00 & 14.00-16.45 Mon-Fri. Free.*

Film, sound, photo

British Film Institute   4 E1
21 Stephen St W1. 071-255 1444. An extensive collection of over 200,000 films, five million original stills, 19,000 books and scripts. *OPEN 10.30-17.30 Mon & Fri, 10.30-20.00 Tue & Thur, 13.00-20.00 Wed. Charge.*

Hulton Picture Library   3 A1
Unique House, 21-31 Woodfield Rd W9. 071-266 2662. Ten million photographs and prints on every conceivable subject. Available for reproduction. *OPEN 09.00-18.00 Mon-Fri. Appt only. Charge to reproduce photograph or print.*

National Sound Archive   3 E6
29 Exhibition Rd SW7. 071-589 6603. National archive of sound recordings. 180,000 discs, tapes and cylinders. Also a library, with documentation on all aspects of sound recording. 150 current periodicals. Record catalogues and release sheets. *Reference only.* Listening service *(appt only)* and library. *OPEN 10.00-17.00 (to 21.00 Thur) Mon-Fri. Free.*

Geography

British Library Map Library   4 F1
Great Russell St WC1. 071-636 1544. Holds over a million printed maps and 20,000 manuscripts. *OPEN 10.00-16.30 Mon-Sat. Identification necessary. Free.*

Royal Geographical Society   3 E5
1 Kensington Gore SW7. 071-589 5466. Geography in all aspects. 135,000 books, 750,000 maps together with several thousand atlases. Public Map Room. *OPEN 10.00-17.00 Mon-Fri. CLOSED B.hols & part Jun & Jul. Free.*

History

Guildhall Library   5 D2
Aldermanbury EC2. 071-606 3030. A reference library which also provides the official repository for deposited archives relating to the City of London. 230,000 volumes and printed items of London topography and history. *OPEN 09.30-17.00 Mon-Sat (Prints and Map dept closed Sat). CLOSED B.hols. Free.*

Institute of Archaeology   1 F5
University of London, 31-34 Gordon Sq WC1. 071-387 7050. Archaeology, particularly Europe, Western Asia, Latin America, world prehistory, conservation and human environment. 800 current periodicals, 48,000 monographs and 27,000 journals. *OPEN termtime only 10.00-20.00 Mon-Fri, 10.00-16.30 Sat. Free.*

Institute of Classical Studies   1 F5
University of London, 31-34 Gordon Sq WC1. 071-387 7697. Includes the Hellenic and Roman Societies Library. 60,000 volumes. Classical Antiquity. Open to members of Roman or Hellenic societies. *OPEN 09.30-18.00 Mon-Fri (to 20.00 Tue & Thur during termtime), 10.00-17.00 Sat. CLOSED Sat in Aug. Free.*

Institute of Historical   1 F6
Research
University of London, Senate House, Malet St WC1. 071-636 0272. 120,000 volumes. Concentrates on principal sources for British and foreign medieval and modern history. Holds regular research seminars. *OPEN 09.00-21.00 Mon-Fri, 09.00-17.00 Sat. Members only.*

Library of the Museum in
Docklands Project
10 Prestons Rd E14. 071-515 1162. Houses Port of London Authority archive and has a large and unique collection of material on the London Docks including 10,000 photographs, prints and

engravings. *OPEN 10.00-17.00 Mon-Fri by appt. CLOSED Sat & B.hols. Free.*

Museum of London Library   **5 D1**
London Wall EC2. 071-600 3699. London history and topography. *OPEN 09.30-17.30 Tue-Fri by appt only. Free.*

National Maritime Museum Library
Romney Rd SE10. 081-858 4422. Large collection of prints and drawings. 50,000 books, maps, charts. Portraits. *Open to anyone for genuine research. Identification necessary. For longer projects ticket issued. OPEN 10.00-17.00 Mon-Fri, 14.00-17.00 Sat. Free. Appt required on Sat.*

Society of Antiquaries   **4 D3**
Burlington House, Piccadilly W1. 071-734 0193. Archaeological and antiquarian research. 130,000 volumes. *OPEN 10.00-17.00 Mon-Fri by appt only. Free.*

Law & public records

British Library Official   **4 F1**
Publications & Social Sciences Service
Great Russell St WC1. 071-636 1544. Official British publications and political and educational journals. *Reader's pass required. OPEN 09.30-16.45 Mon, Fri & Sat, 09.30-19.00 Tue-Thur. CLOSED B.hols.*

Inns of Court
The principal law libraries (Inner Temple, Middle Temple, Lincoln's Inn and Gray's Inn). *OPEN by special permission only.*

Institute of Advanced Legal   **1 G6**
Studies
University of London, 17 Russell Sq WC1. 071-637 1731. Centre for legal studies. 105,000 volumes. *OPEN 10.00-20.00 Mon-Thur, 10.00-17.30 Fri, 10.00-12.30 Sat. Free to academic researchers. Charge to commercial organisations.*

Public Record Office   **5 B2**
Chancery La WC2. 081-876 3444. Government archives and records of the Courts from 11thC to 1800. Records from 1800 to present day stored in Ruskin Av, Kew. *For access to either need reader's pass. OPEN 09.30-17.00 Mon-Fri. CLOSED B.hols and first two weeks of Oct for stock-taking.*

Literature

British Library   **4 F1**
Great Russell St WC1. 071-636 1544. The most comprehensive literary collection of printed books and manuscripts in London. Adults over 21 only. *Reader's*

pass required. *OPEN 09.00-17.00 Mon, Fri & Sat, 09.00-21.00 Tue-Thur. Free.*

Poetry Library   **4 G4**
Royal Festival Hall, South Bank Centre SE1. 071-921 0664. Collection of poetry for loan and reference plus information on poetry events. *OPEN 11.00-20.00 Mon-Sun. Identification required to join library.*

Medicine

British Library Science   **4 G2**
Reference & Information Service
Aldwych Reading Room, 9 Kean St WC2. 071-636 1544 ex7288. Historical medical books. All current British clinical publications and foreign periodicals. *OPEN 09.30-17.30 Mon-Fri. Free.*

British Medical Association   **1 F5**
Library
Tavistock Sq WC1. 071-387 4499. Over 80,000 books and 2000 modern medical periodicals. British and foreign. *OPEN 09.00-18.00 Mon-Wed, 09.00-20.00 Thur & Fri. BMA members free. Charge to non-members.*

Medical Research Council
The Ridgeway NW7. 081-959 3666. All branches of medical science (except clinical science). 42,000 volumes and 600 periodicals. *OPEN 09.00-17.15 Mon-Fri to members only, or by application to director or librarian.*

Pharmaceutical Society   **7 F2**
1 Lambeth High St SE1. 071-735 9141. Pharmaceutical subjects. Historical collections of pharmacopoeias, herbals and botanical works. 60,000 volumes. *Letter of authenticity required. OPEN 09.00-17.00 Mon-Fri for bona fide students of pharmacy and allied subjects.*

Royal College of Physicians   **1 D5**
11 St Andrews Pl NW1. 071-935 1174. History and biography of medicine. Medical portraits. 50,000 volumes and pamphlets. *OPEN 09.30-17.30 Mon-Fri for serious researchers.*

Royal College of Surgeons   **4 G2**
Lincoln's Inn Fields WC2. 071-405 3474. Medical and surgical books and journals including large historical collections on anatomy and surgery. 160,000 volumes. *OPEN 10.00-18.00 Mon-Fri. Letter of introduction from a Fellow or another library necessary.*

Wellcome Institute for the   **1 F5**
History of Medicine
183 Euston Rd NW1. 071-611 8888. History of medicine and allied sciences. Original texts. 400,000 volumes. *OPEN 09.45-17.15 (to 19.30 Thur) Mon-Fri. Identification required.*

Westminster Public Library　1 B6
(Health Information)
Marylebone Rd NW1. 071-798 1039.
Includes nursing, dentistry, psychiatry,
speech and music therapy. Plus general
health information for patients. Textbooks
and periodicals. OPEN 09.30-19.00 Mon-
Fri, 09.30-17.00 Sat.

Music & drama

BBC Music Library　4 C1
156 Great Portland St W1. 071-580
4468. All forms of printed music. OPEN
09.30-17.30 Mon-Fri to non-BBC
employees by appt with the librarian only.
Charge.

British Library Music Library
Great Russell St WC1. 071-636 1544.
Printed music and books about music.
Reader's pass required. OPEN 09.30-
16.45 Mon, Fri & Sat, 09.30-19.00 Tue-
Thur. CLOSED B.hols.

Central Music Library　7 B2
160 Buckingham Palace Rd SW1. 071-
798 2192. (Westminster City Libraries.)
Books on music, music scores and parts,
music periodicals. OPEN 09.30-19.00
Mon-Fri, 09.30-17.00 Sat. Free.

Theatre Museum Library　4 F3
1e Tavistock St WC2. .071-836 7891.
Individual play texts available for study in
the study rooms by appointment only
between 10.30-16.00 Tue-Fri.

Natural science

British Library Science　4 G2
Reference & Information Service
Aldwych Reading Room, 9 Kean St WC2.
071-636 1544 ex7288. Periodicals,
books and pamphlets on the life sciences
and technologies, medicine, earth sciences, astronomy and pure mathematics.
OPEN 09.30-17.30 Mon-Fri. Free.

Geological Society　4 D3
Burlington House, Piccadilly W1. 071-734
2356. 300,000 volumes and papers.
39,000 maps. OPEN 10.00-17.30 Mon-
Fri to Fellows only (or to bona fide
researchers introduced by a Fellow).

Linnean Society　4 D3
Burlington House, Piccadilly W1. 071-434
4479. Reference library. Botany, biology
and zoology. Historical, biological
manuscripts. 100,000 books. OPEN
10.00-17.00 Mon-Fri by appt only. Letter
of introduction required.

Natural History Museum　6 D1
Cromwell Rd SW7. 071-938 9191.
Research library. Botany, zoology,
entomology, palaeontology, mineralogy

and anthropology. Large collection of
manuscripts, drawings and prints.
760,000 volumes. Bona fide researchers
only. Appointment preferred. Identification
necessary. OPEN 10.00-16.30 Mon-Fri.
Free.

Royal Botanic Gardens, Kew
Kew Rd, Richmond, Surrey. 081-940
1171. Botany and travel. Prints and drawings. Extensive and historical record of
millions of dried specimens of plants from
all over the world. 100,000 volumes.
OPEN Mon-Fri to bona fide researchers
only. Appt and opening times by written
application to the director.

Royal Horticultural Society　7 D2
Lindley Library, Vincent Sq SW1. 071-
834 4333. Over 40,000 volumes of
horticultural and botanical books.
Collection of original 18th and 19thC
plant drawings. Large number of periodicals. OPEN 09.30-17.30 Mon-Fri. Appt
preferred.

Zoological Society　1 C3
Regent's Park NW1. 071-722 3333.
150,000 volumes on zoology and related
subjects, original zoological drawings and
prints. Photographic library. OPEN 09.30-
17.30 Mon-Fri to members, associate
members and non-members once they
have purchased a ticket.

Politics, economics & social sciences

British Library Humanities　4 F1
& Social Sciences
Great Russell St WC1. 071-636 1544.
Extensive collection of historical and cur-
rent works. Reader's pass required.
OPEN 09.00-16.45 Mon, Fri & Sat,
09.00-20.45 Tue-Thur. CLOSED B.hols.

British Library of Political　4 G2
& Economic Science
London School of Economics, 10
Portugal St WC2. 071-405 7686. Social
science. 790,000 bound volumes,
including pamphlets, periodicals and
manuscripts in addition to special collections and rarities. OPEN to research
scholars by special permit: Oct-Jun
09.00-21.20 Mon-Fri, 10.00-17.00 Sat;
Jul-Sep 09.00-19.00 Mon-Fri, to 21.20
Tue. CLOSED B.hols.

City Business Library　5 D2
1 Brewers Hall Gdn EC2. 071-638 8215.
Public reference library. One of the major
sources of British and overseas directory
material, company reports and financial
information. Also newspapers, periodicals, timetables, statistical handbooks

and series on commodities and overseas markets. *OPEN 09.30-17.00 Mon-Fri. Free.*

House of Lords Record Office 4 F6
House of Lords SW1. 071-219 3074. Law and parliamentary history. 100,000 volumes, and manuscripts. *OPEN 09.30-17.00 Mon-Fri, to persons undertaking research of volumes not available elsewhere. Appt necessary. Free.*

Institute of Bankers' Library 5 E2
10 Lombard St EC3. 071-623 3531. Comprehensive library on banking and allied subjects. 30,000 volumes. *OPEN 09.00-17.00 Mon-Fri. No appt necessary. Charge for non-members only.*

Institute for the Study of 2 C6
Drug Dependence (ISDD)
1-4 Hatton Pl, Hatton Gdn EC1. 071-430 1993. Reference library and information service covering all aspects of the non-medical use of drugs. Over 50,000 journals, articles and books; extensive press cuttings. *OPEN 09.30-17.30 Mon-Fri. Appointment preferred. Free.*

Marx Memorial Library
37a Clerkenwell Grn EC1. 071-253 1485. Extensive collection of political, social and philosophical literature. Lenin used an office in the building between 1901 and 1902. *OPEN to the public 13.00-18.00 Mon & Fri, 13.00-20.00 Tue-Thur, 10.00-13.00 Sat. Membership required. Small charge.*

Science

British Library Science 5 B1
Reference & Information Service
Holborn Division, 25 Southampton Bldgs, Chancery La WC2. 071-323 7496. Formerly known as the Patent Office, it contains periodicals, books, patents, trade marks, literature and reports on inventive sciences, engineering, industrial technologies and commerce. Main library *OPEN 09.30-21.00 Mon-Fri, 10.00-13.00 Sat (for opening times of annexes check with main library). CLOSED B.hols. Free.*

Aldwych Branch 5 A2
9 Kean St WC2. 071-636 1544 ex7288. Has all the rest of the scientific literature with emphasis on life sciences and technologies, medicine, biotechnology, earth sciences, astronomy and pure mathematics. *OPEN 09.30-17.30 Mon-Fri. CLOSED B.hols. Free.*

Institution of Civil Engineers 4 E5
Great George St SW1. 071-222 7722. All branches of engineering; 19thC engineering history. Film library. 100,000 books and pamphlets. *OPEN 09.15-*

17.30 Mon-Fri to members and members of the Institution of Mechanical Engineering. Non-members on application to the librarian.

Royal Aeronautical Society 4 B4
4 Hamilton Pl W1. 071-499 3515. One of the finest collections in the world of historical and modern aeronautical books, prints and photographs. *OPEN 10.00-17.00 Mon-Fri. Charge for non-members.*

Royal Astronomical Society 4 D3
Burlington House, Piccadilly W1. 071-734 4582. 27,000 volumes. Astronomy and geophysics. *OPEN 10.00-17.00 Mon-Fri to Fellows. Non-Fellows should contact the librarian in writing. Identification necessary.*

Royal Institution of Great 4 D3
Britain
21 Albemarle St W1. 071-409 2992. General science and history of science since 1799. Many complete scientific periodicals. Biography. Portraits. 50,000 volumes. *OPEN to non-members by appt 10.00-17.30 Mon-Fri.*

Royal Society of Chemistry 4 D3
Burlington House, Piccadilly W1. 071-437 8656. Early works, periodicals. 100,000 volumes. *OPEN 09.30-17.30 Mon-Fri. Letter of introduction necessary for non-members. No appt necessary.*

Science Museum 3 E6
Imperial College Rd SW7. 071-938 8111. A national reference library of pure and applied science, specialising in the history of science, technology and medicine. More than 450,000 volumes. *OPEN 09.30-21.00 Mon-Fri, 09.30-17.30 Sat. Free.*

Cultural institutes

Will provide comprehensive information on their country. Most organise language tuition, exhibitions and filmshows. Some also run summer courses and exchanges.

Austrian Institute 3 F5
28 Rutland Gate SW7. 071-584 8653.

Commonwealth Institute 3 B6
Kensington High St W8. 071-603 4535.

Goethe Institut 6 D1
50 Prince's Gate SW7. 071-411 3400.

Greek Institute
34 Bush Hill Rd N21. 081-360 7968.

Hispanic & Luso Brazilian 4 B6
Council
2 Belgrave Sq SW1. 071-235 2303.

Institut Français du 6 D2
Royaume-Uni
17 Queensberry Pl SW7. 071-589 6211.

Italian Cultural Institute **4 B6**
39 Belgrave Sq SW1. 071-235 1461.
Polish Institute **4 C1**
73 New Cavendish St W1. 071-636 6032.
Society for Co-operation in Russian and Soviet Studies
320 Brixton Rd SW9. 071-274 2282.
Spanish Institute **7 A1**
102 Eaton Sq SW1. 071-235 1484/5.
Swedish Cultural Dept **1 B6**
11 Montagu Pl W1. 071-724 2101.

Language tuition

A cosmopolitan city such as London offers a wide variety of facilities for learning almost any language, in colleges, cultural centres and private schools, where you can choose between group or individual tuition. Prices and standards vary enormously. There is no centrally-maintained register of private language schools, although most can be found in the Yellow Pages. The Adult Education Institute publishes Floodlight with details of all sorts of courses run in the capital (available from newsagents). Private tutors may be found by contacting embassies or cultural institutes, by looking in the local newspaper or putting an advert in the paper yourself. You can also enquire at local colleges to see if staff or foreign students could assist. For information about facilities, methods and tuition contact:

Centre for Information on **1 C5**
Language Teaching and Research (CILT)
Regent's College, Inner Circle, Regent's Park NW1. 071-486 8221.

English as a foreign language

Association of Recognised **5 C5**
English Language Schools
2 Pontypool Pl, Valentine Pl SE1. 071-242 3136. Gives information and advice on the many English language schools within the association in the Greater London area. They are recognised by the British Council as being of a high standard.
Cambridge School of English **1 G5**
8 Herbrand St WC1. 071-734 4203. Classes at all levels for students of 15+. Literature and film-study courses. Preparation for London Chamber of Commerce exam.

Canning School **3 B6**
4 Abingdon Rd W8. 071-938 2111. Intensive business-orientated training courses for managers from international, European and Far Eastern companies. Small groups and one-to-one. Specialised courses in negotiation, presentation and cross-cultural skills.
International House **4 C4**
106 Piccadilly W1. 071-491 2598. General and executive courses for all levels. Also teacher training courses. Language laboratory and social club.
Sels College **4 F2**
64-65 Long Acre WC2. 071-240 2581. Intensive courses throughout the year. All levels from beginners to Cambridge Proficiency. Small groups. Accommodation arranged.

Other languages

The schools and colleges listed below offer tuition in practically any language.

All Languages Ltd **2 G4**
Nelson House, 362 Old St EC1. 071-739 6641.
Butler School of Languages **7 C1**
170 Victoria St SW1. 071-834 0606.
Conrad Executive Language **4 F3**
Training
15 King St WC2. 071-434 0113.
Language Studies **4 B2**
International
Woodstock House, 10-12 James St W1. 071-499 9621.

Secretarial training

Pitman Central College **4 F1**
154 Southampton Row WC1. 071-837 4481. Courses of varying length and intensity including typing, shorthand, business administration, business communication, audio-typing, word processing. Special courses for overseas students.
Sight & Sound **4 E2**
118-120 Charing Cross Rd WC2. 071-379 4753. Full- or part-time, day or evening courses in copy-typing, audio, shorthand, word processing, book-keeping, computing, data processing, PAYE.
London Business College **4 C2**
6 Sedley Place W1. 071-493 3401. Day and evening courses in secretarial skills, office practice and word processing. Also refresher courses.

Student information

Nowhere is it more exciting to be a student than in London. Cheap theatre and entertainment abound (see 'Theatres, cinemas, music and comedy') and there are many restaurants offering unusual and inexpensive food (see 'Eating and drinking'). London has some of the best-stocked reference libraries in the world (see the section 'Reference libraries'). For advice on problems or emergencies, see 'Social services' and 'Emergency & late-night help'.

Grants, charitable trusts & sponsorships

Advisory Centre for Education
22 Highbury Grove N5. 071-354 8321. Publishes *ACE Bulletin* which reports on all aspects of the state sector of education.

Association of Commonwealth Universities 1 F5
36 Gordon Sq WC1. 071-387 8572. Publishes four directories providing information on sources of funding for University students and staff wishing to study in other countries, primarily within the Commonwealth. Information service (phone first for an appointment) on general aspects of UK and Commonwealth universities.

British Council
10 Spring Gdns SW1. 071-930 8466. Offers grants to help foreign postgraduates to study, train or make professional contacts in Britain and to enable British specialists to teach, advise or establish joint projects abroad.

Charities Aid Foundation 4 F1
114-118 Southampton Row WC1. 071-831 7798. Information service. Publishes *Directory of Grant-making Trusts*.

Charity Commission 4 E3
St Alban's House, 6th Floor, 57-60 Haymarket SW1. 071-210 4477. Keeps a fully-comprehensive register of all registered charities in England and Wales.

National Council for Voluntary Organisations 4 E1
26 Bedford Sq WC1. 071-713 6161. Their *Voluntary Agencies Directory* lists 2000 national voluntary organisations, and includes details of membership, staffing, recruitment of volunteers and funding for research.

National Union of Students
461 Holloway Rd N7. 071-272 8900. Maintains an educational grants advisory

service to student unions. Non-union members must write in for information. Also publishes *Grants Information Sheet* – a breakdown of what constitutes eligibility for LEA grants.

Useful organisations

British Council 4 E4
10 Spring Gdns SW1. 071-930 8466. Promotes Britain abroad – a thorough cultural, educational and technical co-operation between Britain and other countries.

British Youth Council 1 F4
57 Chalton St NW1. 071-387 7559. Made up of representatives from national youth organisations and local youth councils. Aims to represent the views of young people and to look at ways of giving them a voice in society at local, national and international levels.

National Union of Students
461 Holloway Rd N7. 071-272 8900. At least 2 million students are members. Represents students' rights. Organises and advises on social, cultural and educational events. Research staff deal with welfare problems. Trains student union officers. Produces publications including *The Welfare Manual*.

Social clubs & societies

British Federation of University Women 6 E4
Crosby Hall, Cheyne Wlk SW3. 071-352 5354. Open to women graduates of all nations. Club facilities and hostel.

International Students' House 1 D5
229 Great Portland St W1. 071-631 3223. Open to all full-time students, professional trainees, foreign language assistants, au pairs (over 17) and student nurses. Excellent social and recreational facilities – most sports catered for. Coach visits to places of interest. Also a hostel.

London Union of Youth Clubs
64 Camberwell Rd SE5. 071-701 6366. Will provide details of local youth clubs with social, recreational and community facilities.

Student Christian Movement
St Benets House, 327a Mile End Rd E1. 081-981 2010. Inter-denominational fellowship open to all students. Local and international branches. Meetings. Magazine *Movement* five times a year.

Victoria League 4 F4
18 Northumberland Av WC2. 071-229 3961. Hospitality in British homes

arranged for Commonwealth students and nurses. Programme of social activities. London hostel.

Student travel

There are lots of cheap ways for students to get around the country.

The Young Person's Railcard
For anyone under 24 yrs or in full-time education. Entitles holders to a discount on British Rail fares. Available from British Rail stations. *Charge.*

The Young Person's Coach Card
For 16-23 year-olds. Entitles holders to 33% discount when travelling on National Express coaches. Available from travel agents and coach stations. *Charge.*

The Inter-Rail Card
For anyone under 26 planning a trip to Europe. Entitles holder to unlimited train travel in 21 countries for one month. Contact any major British Rail station. *Charge.*

STA Travel   6 D2
74 Old Brompton Rd SW7. Also at 117 Euston Rd NW1 (**1 F4**). Telesales: 071-937 9962. Wide range of low-cost fares worldwide. Special rates for students. *OPEN 09.00-18.00 Mon-Fri, 10.00-16.00 Sat.*

Student accommodation

Reasonably-priced accommodation is notoriously difficult to find in London. College accommodation services only deal with their own students – but don't rely on them. Initially it may well be necessary to settle for a temporary solution like one of the hostels listed below. Foreign students can try the welfare office of their London embassy. Flat shares or flats to rent are advertised in the Evening Standard, Time Out, Loot and local papers.

British Council   4 E4
Accommodation Unit
10 Spring Gdns SW1. 071-930 8466. Advice for overseas students on finding accommodation. *OPEN 09.00-16.30 Mon-Fri.*

King's Campus Vacation   6 C5
Bureau
552 King's Rd SW10. 071-351 6011. Can arrange accommodation for visitors and foreign students during the vacation period in various halls of residence. Single and twin rooms.

London Tourist Board   7 B1
Information Centre, Victoria Station Forecourt SW1. 071-730 3488. Bookings in hostels, guest houses and hotels. Information on youth accommodation, self-catering and camping. *OPEN 09.00-18.00 Mon-Fri, 09.00-17.00 Sat.* Also at Heathrow Airport.

University of London   1 F6
Accommodation Office
Union Building, Malet St WC1. 071-636 2818. They find accommodation for London University students only, but will supply anybody with a list of halls of residence, many of which are open to all students during vacations, particularly *Jul-Sep.*

Women's Link   4 F1
Helen Graham House, 57 Great Russell St WC1. 071-430 1524. Accommodation advisory service. Publish a useful booklet *Hostels in London.*

Hostels

There is a large selection of hostel accommodation in London. Rooms are spartan but very clean, and usually shared. Mainly bed and breakfast and mixed unless otherwise shown. Mostly for young people. Prices vary depending on how long you stay. Weekly rates tend to be better value than daily rates. It is cheaper to share a room or a dormitory than to have a single room. For bed and breakfast for a day you should expect to pay £8.00-£20.00.
b = bed only, bb = bed and breakfast
fb = full board, sc = self-catering

Carr-Saunders Hall   1 E5
18-24 Fitzroy St W1. 071-580 6338. Accommodation (halls) only available during *Easter* vacation and *summer* vacation *(Jul-Sep)*. TV lounge. Mostly single rooms, some twin. 150 beds. *bb.* Also have 200 beds in flats. *sc.*

Central Club   4 E2
16-22 Great Russell St WC1. 071-636 7512. Short-term accommodation provided (up to one week) in 178-bed hostel. Other facilities include a concert hall, function room and coffee shop. *b.*

Central University of Iowa   4 F1
Hostel
7 Bedford Pl WC1. 071-580 1121. TV lounge. Twin and dormitory accommodation *(May-Aug)*. 33 beds. Two weeks maximum stay. *bb.*

Centre Francais   3 B3
61-69 Chepstow Pl W2. 071-221 8134. Single, double and multi-bedded rooms for young people. 166 beds. Restaurant,

TV room, launderette, library and conference room. *bb.*

London Friendship Centre
3 Creswick Rd W3. 081-992 0221. Dormitory accommodation. 50 beds. Games room, library, TV lounge, garden. Advance booking necessary. Short-stay hostel. *bb.*

International Students' House 1 D5
229 Great Portland St W1. 071-631 3223. Single, double or twin rooms and dormitory in *summer*. TV lounge, games room, squash court. 294 beds. *bb & sc.*

O'Callaghans 6 B3
205a Earl's Court Rd SW5. 071-370 3000. TV lounge. Accommodation in shared and twin rooms. *bb.*

Passfield Hall 1 F5
1 Endsleigh Pl WC1. 071-387 7743. Accommodation only available during *vacations (Mar-Apr & Jul-Sep)*. TV lounge, games room. Single, twin and triple accommodation. 198 beds. *bb.*

Rosebery Avenue Hall 1 F5
90 Rosebery Av EC1. 071-278 3251. Accommodation only available during *vacations (Mar-Apr & Jul-Sep)*. TV lounge and bar. Single rooms; some double and twin. 195 beds. *bb.*

Sass House 3 E3
11 Craven Ter W2. 071-262 2325. TV lounge. Single, double and twin. 36 beds. *bb.*

Women's Link 4 F1
Helen Graham House, 57 Great Russell St WC1. 071-430 1524. 300 beds. Single and double rooms. Long-term accommodation only (six months +). *sc.*

YMCA London Central Hotel & Hostel 4 E2
George Williams House, 112 Great Russell St WC1. 071-637 1333. Reception *OPEN* 24hrs. A short-stay hotel with single, twin and triple rooms. 168 beds. Excellent sports centre, including swimming pool, attached for members and their families. *There are many other YMCA hostels in London, mainly for men only. Applications must be made to individual hostels, numbers in telephone directory.*

YMCA: London Metropolitan Region 3 D3
31 Craven Ter W2. 071-723 0071. Will give addresses and telephone nos of hostels.

YWCA: London Regional Office 4 E2
16-22 Great Russell St. 071-580 4827. Provides current information on all 18 London hostels. *Applications must be made to individual hostels, numbers are listed in telephone book.*

Youth Hostel Association (YHA) 4 F3
Members only. Join at YHA, 14 Southampton St WC2. 071-836 8541. Also large shop with wide range of maps, guides, clothing and equipment. Travel service open to non-members. Dormitory accommodation. Maximum stay three nights. Cost per night varies with age. *CLOSE at 23.30.* London hostels are at:

38 Bolton Gdns SW5. 071-373 7083. 6 **B3**

36 Carter La EC4. 071-236 4965. 5 **C2**

84 Highgate West Hill N6. 081-340 1831. Holland House, Holland Wlk W8. 3 **A5** 071-937 0748.

Island Yard, Salter Rd SE16. 071-232 2114.

14 Noel St W1. 071-734 1618. 4 **D2**

4 Wellgarth Rd NW11. 081-458 9054.

Social services

Counselling and advisory services

London boasts an enormous range of helping organisations. To help you find your way through the maze of official and voluntary services, this section signposts the main referral agencies who will either be able to offer direct help or can put you in touch with the appropriate organisation. Information or help is given willingly and most of it is free.

General

Church Army
Church Army HQ, Independence Rd SE3. 081-318 1226. Offers help to anyone in need: homes, hostels, holidays, youth services, prison welfare and social work.

Citizens Advice Bureaux (CAB)
Head Office: 071-251 2000. Look in telephone directory for local branch. General advisory service plus help on any matter.

Family Welfare Association
501-505 Kingsland Rd E8. 071-254

6251. Counselling service to individuals, groups and families on all problems, from financial to marital. Trained caseworkers. *OPEN 09.00-13.00 & 14.00-17.00 Mon-Fri.*

Help Advisory Centre   **3 A2**
57 Portobello Rd W11. 071-221 7914. Help on assertiveness and communication skills, workshops on emotional and personal problems, women's groups, psychotherapy groups. Can also refer to specialists. *OPEN 11.00-18.30 Mon-Fri.*

Help Line
Capital Radio wavebands: 95.8 MHz, 1548 kHz. 071-388 7575. Runs many telephone services for listeners: Help Line, *09.30-17.30,* information and advice; flat sharing; job finders; community projects, etc.

International Social Service of Great Britain
Cranmer House, 39 Brixton Rd SW9. 071-735 8941. Help with personal and family problems extending across national frontiers. Can help with repatriation of immigrants with settled status.

Just Ask   **5 F2**
46 Bishopsgate EC2. 071-628 3380. Trained counsellors to help people with personal problems. *24-hr answerphone service.*

Piccadilly Advice Centre   **4 F2**
100 Shaftesbury Av W1. 071-434 3773. Free information, advice and referral service on housing and jobs for the young, single, homeless and unemployed. *OPEN 14.00-21.00 Mon-Sun.*

Salvation Army   **5 D3**
101 Queen Victoria St EC4. 071-236 5222. Help on any problem. *24-hr telephone service.*

Samaritans   **4 D2**
46 Marshall St W1. 071-734 2800. 14 branches throughout London. Advice and encouragement if you are despairing or suicidal. Walk-in service *09.00-21.00. 24-hr telephone service.*

Women's Royal Voluntary Service
234-244 Stockwell Rd SW9. 071-416 0146. A nationwide service for all kinds of local community welfare work. Trained members help in both local and national emergencies.

Official organisations

Addresses from the local Town Hall, Citizens Advice Bureau or local post office.
Social Services Departments
Have a wide range of duties and responsibilities laid on them by central government concerning the welfare of children, the elderly, and the mentally or physically handicapped. Social workers offer assistance with personal, practical and emotional problems.

Housing Departments
Let and maintain council housing. Deal with problems connected with rents, rates, welfare, maintenance, transfers, homelessness.

Environmental Health Departments
Will investigate 'nuisances' (noise, dampness, smells); food control and hygiene (inspection of premises and consumer complaints); defective housing; responsible for prevention of spread of infection.

Department of Social Security (DSS)
The term 'Social Security' covers all the schemes which provide direct financial assistance in time of need. It includes both National Insurance contributory schemes, eg sickness and unemployment benefit, and a range of non-contributory schemes. A great number of free explanatory leaflets on benefits are available from any local office of the DSS. To obtain more information, or if in difficulty, it's worth consulting some of the books listed below or contacting a local welfare rights group.

Publications

These should be available in most large bookshops like Dillons and Foyles and also from public libraries.
Annual Charities Digest
Family Welfare Association, 501-505 Kingsland Rd E8. 071-254 6251. Basically for professionals. Lists major charities, what they use their funds for, and those eligible to apply for help.
Consumer's Guide to the British Social Services
Phyllis Willmot. Penguin.
Guide to the Social Services
Family Welfare Association, 501-505 Kingsland Rd E8. 071-254 6251. Published annually.
Women's Rights: A Practical Guide
Anna Coote and Tess Gill. Penguin.

Abortion

Either see your doctor for help through the NHS or contact one of the following non-profit-making organisations. They may be able to help you to get an NHS abortion even if you have been turned down; otherwise they will arrange a pri-

vate abortion as cheaply as possible. Where indicated contraception is also available. Charge for services unless otherwise stated.

**British Pregnancy Advisory   7 C2
Service**
7 Belgrave Rd SW1. 071-222 0985. Pregnancy tests and abortion service. Service for infertility, vasectomy and artificial insemination. *OPEN 09.00-17.00 Mon-Fri.* Phone 081-809 6600 for emergencies after *17.00.*

Brook Advisory Centre   1 F6
Central Clinic, 233 Tottenham Court Rd W1. 071-323 1522. Phone 071-580 2991 for an appointment. Services for young people up to 25. Small annual donation covers pregnancy testing and contraception. Counselling and abortion help. Also offer counselling for sexual problems. *OPEN 09.30-19.30 Mon-Fri.*

Help Advisory Centre   3 A2
57 Portobello Rd W11. 071-221 7914. Free pregnancy testing and abortion advice. *OPEN 11.00-19.00 Mon-Thur, 11.00-18.00 Fri.*

Life   4 C1
150 Harley St W1. 071-436 1524. Free pregnancy testing and counselling for women not wishing to have an abortion. *OPEN 10.30-16.00 Mon-Fri (to 20.00 Thur).*

Pregnancy Advisory Service   4 D1
11-13 Charlotte St W1. 071-637 8962. London's oldest-established pregnancy advisory service. Abortion advice, pregnancy testing, including test which can confirm pregnancy within 14 days of conception. 'Morning after' contraception effective within 72 hours of unprotected sex. Comprehensive abortion service. Sterilisation for women. No appointment necessary for pregnancy testing. Other services *by appt only. OPEN 09.30-17.30 Mon-Wed & Fri, 09.30-12.30 Thur & Sat.*

The Well Woman Centre   1 E5
Marie Stopes House, 108 Whitfield St W1. 071-388 0662/4843. Pregnancy tests, counselling and abortion services. Contraception and sterilisation for men and women. Counselling help for psycho-sexual problems. Also offer a range of women's health care services including medical check-ups, cancer screening and help with pre-menstrual and menopausal problems. *OPEN 09.00-20.00 Mon-Wed, to 17.00 Thur & Fri, 09.30-13.00 Sat.*
For advice on the legal position only:

**Abortion Law Reform   4 D1
Association/A Woman's
Right to Choose campaign**
27-35 Mortimer St W1. 071-637 7264.

Two pressure groups which thwart efforts to restrict abortion and work to make abortion more freely available. Advice only; they cannot help you obtain an abortion.

Adoption

Demand is always greater than supply as far fewer babies are now placed for adoption. There are, however, many older, handicapped or black children who need parents. Either apply through the Social Services department of the local authority or direct to an adoption agency. Many organisations cater only for a particular religious denomination so it is as well to get information about all the agencies and their requirements before applying (lists from the British Agencies for Adoption and Fostering).

**British Agencies for   5 C4
Adoption and Fostering**
11 Southwark St SE1. 071-407 8800. Not an adoption agency but a national federation of adoption agencies through which efforts are made to place children with special needs. Publish a list of agencies and other literature and information on adoption and fostering including a photo list of children awaiting adoption. Train social workers and have medical and legal groups.

Independent Adoption Service
121-123 Camberwell Rd SE5. 071-703 1088. Find families for children of all ages and from all communities.

Parents for Children   2 F1
41 Southgate Rd N1. 071-359 7530. A home-finding agency for older and handicapped children. Offer information and advice to people considering this type of parenthood. Long-term support to family after a child is placed.

**Parent to Parent Information on
Adoption Services (PPIAS)**
Lower Boddington, nr Daventry, Northants. (0327) 60295. An informal self-help organisation, largely of adoptive parents, who offer advice and support on all aspects of adoption. *Annual subscription.*

AIDS

For information about AIDS (Acquired Immune Deficiency Syndrome) the following centres offer advice and counselling, and have facilities for examination and testing.

Ambrose King Centre
London Hospital (Whitechapel),

Whitechapel Rd E1. 071-377 7307. Free testing for HIV virus and other sexually transmitted diseases. (New patients are asked to come early; it may be necessary to wait, though everyone is seen on the day they attend.) *No appt or doctor's note necessary. OPEN 09.30-17.30 Mon-Fri (to 16.30 Thur).*

Body Positive 6 **A3**
51b Philbeach Gdns SW5. 071-835 1045/6. A self-help group for people affected by HIV. *OPEN 11.00-17.00 Sun-Fri (to 21.00 Mon & Fri).* Helpline: 071-373 9124. Operates *19.00-22.00 Mon-Sun.*

Healthline Telephone Service
081-681 3311. A confidential service which provides information and advice in the form of recorded tapes. Sixteen tapes on AIDS are available and approx. 300 on other medical conditions. Phone and ask the tape operator for the tape you wish to hear. For a free copy of the booklet *AIDS,* write to: Health Promotions Dept, Leonard Rd, Croydon. Telephone service operates *16.00-20.00 Mon-Fri.*

Terrence Higgins Trust 2 **B5**
52-54 Gray's Inn Rd WC1. 071-242 1010. This is the main organisation dealing with AIDS. Telephone the AIDS Helpline for information between *12.00-22.00 Mon-Sun, or write enclosing sae.* Legal line: 071-405 2381. Operates *19.00-22.00 Wed.*

Alcoholics

Alcoholism is now widely recognised as an illness. Help and treatment can be claimed under the NHS either through your doctor or through hospitals. Other useful centres are:

Accept
724 Fulham Rd SW6. 071-371 7477. Independent organisation providing a counselling service and treatment centre; for problem and dependent drinkers, their families and friends. Also help for people with tranquilliser problems.

Al-Anon 5 **E6**
61 Great Dover St SE1. 071-403 0888. Information and help for families and friends of problem drinkers. *24-hr telephone service.*

Alateen 5 **E6**
61 Great Dover St SE1. 071-403 0888. Information and help for teenagers with parents or relatives who have drinking problems. *24-hr telephone service.*

Alcoholics Anonymous 6 **C3**
11 Redcliffe Gdns SW10. 071-352 3001. (Head Office: PO Box 1, Stonebow House, Stonebow, York. (0904)

644026/7/8/9.) Give help to people wishing to recover from alcoholism or in need of the support and companionship of fellow sufferers. Meetings. Telephone service *10.00-22.00. 24-hr answering service.*

Greater London Alcohol 2 **D5**
Advisory Service
30-31 Great Sutton St EC1. 071-253 6221. For people with drinking problems and their families. Telephone advice and information for Greater London *09.00-17.00 Mon-Fri;* counselling service for the City and Hackney.

Turning Point
New Loom House, 101 Back Church La E1. 071-702 2300. Runs rehabilitation hostels and advice centres for people with alcohol- and drug-related problems.

Ambulance

Dial **999** *for an emergency, otherwise:*
St John Ambulance Brigade 3 **G1**
Edwina Mountbatten House, 63 York St W1. 071-258 3456. Will arrange a private ambulance and collection of ambulance cases from airports, docks or rail terminals. Need at least *48 hrs* notice. *Charge.*

Animals

Royal Society for the Prevention of Cruelty to Animals (RSPCA)
HQ, The Causeway, Horsham, W. Sussex. (0403) 264181. North London: 071-228 0656; South London: 071-228 1131. Telephone for information on animal clinics and hospitals. All complaints of cruelty to animals investigated in strict confidence. Rescue service for animals in distress. *(See also 'Veterinary clinics' under 'Shops & services').*

Bereavement

Cruse Bereavement Care
126 Sheen Rd, Richmond, Surrey. 081-940 4818. Counselling for the bereaved.

Blind people

Social Services departments, either through their own specialist workers or in conjunction with voluntary organisations, provide a wide range of services for blind people. Ask to see a social worker who will be able to tell you how to get any special help you may need and what financial assistance, training and aids are available.

Royal National Institute for the Blind (RNIB) 4 C1

224 Great Portland St W1. 071-388 1266. Provide active help and advice on practically any problem concerning blind people. Also publish a directory of all agencies for blind people.

Cancer prevention

Cancer can often be treated successfully if detected early enough. Women should have a regular cervical smear test; see your GP or local family planning clinic. They will also carry out breast examinations but it is advisable for women over 25 to learn to give themselves a monthly breast examination. The Women's National Cancer Control Campaign publishes an excellent leaflet on this.

The Well Woman Centre 1 E5

Marie Stopes House, 108 Whitfield St W1. 071-388 0662/2585. Examination and screening for breast cancer and cervical smear test. Charge.

Women's National Cancer Control Campaign 2 G4

Suna House, 128-130 Curtain Rd EC2. 071-729 4688. Education and information service. Publish a list of clinics offering check-ups. Send sae for leaflet on breast self-examination and cervical cancer. Mobile screening service available. Helpline: 071-729 2229.

Cancer relief

Marie Curie Cancer Care 4 B6

28 Belgrave Sq SW1. 071-235 3325. Homes, nursing and welfare service for the seriously ill.

National Society for Cancer Relief 6 E3

Anchor House, 15-19 Britten St SW3. 071-351 7811. Financial assistance, homes, nursing teams, for needy cancer patients and their families. Any request, however unusual, is always considered.

Children

Social Services departments have a duty to promote the welfare of children in their area. They can do this by offering advice, practical assistance and, in certain circumstances, financial help to prevent family breakdown. They, or the NSPCC, will also investigate allegations of neglect or ill-treatment of children. If you suspect that a child is being seriously ill-treated and you feel prompt action is called for, you can call in the police. If a child shows signs of having psychological or emotional difficulties you can get advice and help from your local child guidance clinic. Your GP or the child's school can put you in touch. Children who need someone to talk to can call Childline on (0800) 1111. Will offer confidential support and advice. OPEN 24 hrs Mon-Sun.

Child Poverty Action Group (CPAG) 2 F4

4th Flr, 1-5 Bath St EC1. 071-253 3406. Excellent information service on welfare rights. Help with tribunals. Useful publications (available only to advisers and representatives of claimants). Information line: 071-253 6569. OPEN 09.30-17.30 Mon-Fri.

Invalid Children's Aid Association 2 C5

Unit 5, 10 Bowling Green La EC1. 071-253 9111. Educate children and young people with special needs. Also special schools for asthmatic and language disordered children.

National Association for Gifted Children

Park Campus, Boughton Green Rd, Northants. (0604) 792300. Advice of all kinds for parents and teachers of gifted children. Activities for the children. Newsletter for members.

National Autistic Society

276 Willesden La NW2. 081-451 1114. Provide information and support to children with autism, their parents and carers. Special schools. Publications.

Royal Society for Mentally Handicapped Children and Adults 2 E5

123 Golden La EC1. 071-454 0454. Support for people with learning difficulties. Care centres, day nurseries, leisure clubs, speech therapy, training schemes.

National Society for the Prevention of Cruelty to Children (NSPCC) 2 C6

67 Saffron Hill EC1. 071-242 1626. Supports children who have been abused and protects those who could be at risk. Investigates reports of neglect or ill-treatment of children. Has set up Child Protection Line, manned by qualified and experienced personnel, to listen and advise on physical and sexual abuse and neglect. (0800) 800500. OPEN 24 hrs.

Shaftesbury Society

18-120 Kingston Rd SW19. 081-542 5550. Hostel accommodation for children with learning or physical difficulties.

Contraception

Contraception is now freely available under the NHS whether you are married or single. You can consult your GP or visit *your local family planning clinic. For other organisations offering contraception services see under 'Abortion'.*

Brook Advisory Centre   **1 F6**
Central Clinic, 233 Tottenham Court Rd W1. 071-323 1522. Eleven clinics in the London area offer sympathetic advice and contraception to young people. *Free to students, unemployed people, and those under 18; otherwise a small annual donation.*

Family Planning Association   **4 D1**
27-35 Mortimer St W1. 071-636 7866. Supplies a list of clinics and leaflets on aspects of sex education. Bookshop and mail order. Phone-in service for information and advice.

International Planned   **1 C4**
Parenthood Federation
Inner Circle, Regent's Park NW1. 071-486 0741. Reading materials on family planning in several languages.

Pregnancy Advisory Service   **4 D1**
11-13 Charlotte St W1. 071-637 8962. Registered charity providing pregnancy testing, 'morning after' birth control, sterilisation, abortion advice.

Dating agencies

There are many commercial organisations in London which offer introductions to suitably matched people who are looking for a marriage partner. Some are less than scrupulous in their attempts to match clients' requirements and/or make exorbitant charges, so enquire about terms and conditions before handing over any money.

Dateline International   **3 B6**
23 Abingdon Rd W8. 071-938 1011. Computer dating service with a complete cross-section of many thousands on file.

The Marriage Bureau   **4 B2**
(Katherine Allen)
18 Thayer St W1. 071-935 3115. Established bureau. Famous for creating successful partnerships.

Deaf people

Visit your Social Services department for advice on benefits and services available. They, or the Citizens Advice Bureau, will be able to put you in touch with local and national voluntary organisations.

British Association of the
Hard of Hearing
7-11 Armstrong Rd W3. 081-743 1110. A self-help organisation with 180 clubs for those with acquired hearing loss, total or partial. Social clubs, lip-reading groups, advice on hearing aids.

National Deaf Children's   **3 B2**
Society
45 Hereford Rd W2. 071-229 9272. Information and guidance for parents and those concerned with deaf children. Literature available. Regional branches. Run a Technology Information Centre in Birmingham, which has a lending scheme for equipment. 021-454 5151.

Royal Association in Aid of Deaf
People
27 Old Oak Rd W3. 081-743 6187. Concerned with the spiritual, social and general welfare of deaf and blind/deaf people in London, Essex, Surrey and Kent. Trained staff to act as interpreters and counsellors. Special social clubs.

Royal National Institute for   **1 F5**
Deaf People
105 Gower St WC1. 071-387 8033. Information, education, training, hostels, homes for the deaf. Hearing aids tested free *(by appt)*. Extensive library *(appt necessary)*. Research laboratories.

Diabetics

The British Diabetic   **4 C1**
Association
10 Queen Anne St W1. 071-323 1531. Aim to educate the diabetic to come to terms with his or her condition and lead an active life. Literature and advisory services available. Also sponsor diabetic research.

Disabled people

Much more attention has been given to the needs of disabled people in recent years largely due to the efforts of pressure groups working on their behalf. The DSS publishes a mini-guide to services for disabled people (leaflet HB1), available free from local Social Security offices and Social Services departments. Nicholson publishes Access in London, a comprehensive guide to London researched for and by disabled people. It deals with all aspects of getting around and exploring the capital. Available from bookshops.

Artsline   **1 E3**
5 Crowndale Rd NW1. 071-388 2227. Telephone or postal service offering information and advice to disabled people on all aspects of the arts and entertainment in London: theatres, cinemas, concert halls, colleges, bookshops, museums and galleries. From access and facilities to opportunities for taking up creative interests. *OPEN 09.30-17.30 Mon-Fri.*

Disabled Drivers Association
Ashwellthorpe, Norwich, Norfolk. (050841) 449. An association 'of the disabled, for the disabled, by the disabled' concentrating on all problems of mobility. Information and advice, help with holidays and travel arrangements (home and abroad), local groups. *OPEN 10.00-16.00 Mon-Fri.*

Disabled Living Foundation
380-384 Harrow Rd W9. 071-289 6111. Information service. Enquiries by phone or letter (with sae), personal calls *by appt.* Advice on equipment and facilities for independent living. Permanent display of aids and equipment.

Disablement Income Group
Millmead Business Centre, Millmead Rd N17. 081-801 8013. Advice and information service. Issues publications. Other branches.

Royal Association for   **4 D1**
Disability and Rehabilitation
(RADAR)
25 Mortimer St W1. 071-637 5400. Information and advice on education, welfare, mobility, training and employment of disabled people. Help with housing, travel and holiday queries. Publications include *Access for Disabled* guides.

Sexual Problems of the Disabled
286 Camden Rd N7. 071-607 8851. Give advice and information on sexual matters to disabled people and those working with them. Free advisory leaflets.

Discharged prisoners

These organisations try to welcome the discharged prisoner back into society. You can also go to your local court and ask for the Probation Officer who should give you advice and help.

Apex Charitable Trust
1-4 Brixton Hill Pl SW2. 081-671 7633. Operate a range of centres offering employment services for ex-offenders and youngsters at risk.

National Association for the Care and Resettlement of Offenders
169 Clapham Rd SW9. 071-582 6500. Run projects to test out new ideas and educate the public about the care of offenders and prevention of crime. Service voluntary organisations providing facilities for offenders in the community.

Probation & After Care   **5 D5**
Service
Resettlement Office, 289 Borough High St SE1. 071-407 4611. Help rootless and homeless ex-prisoners coming to inner London.

Discrimination

If you feel strongly about civil rights, issues of sexual or racial discrimination or inequality, the following organisations may be able to help in individual cases, or may welcome your support. They campaign to promote awareness on these issues and to improve or implement legislation.

Commission for Racial   **4 C6**
Equality
Elliot House, 10-12 Allington St SW1. 071-828 7022. Investigate complaints of inequalities or discrimination on racial grounds. Bring cases to court if necessary.

National Council for Civil   **5 E5**
Liberties (NCCL)
21 Tabard St SE1. 071-403 3888. Campaigning organisation for the protection of civil liberties. All advice by letter only.

Drug dependence

The Misuse of Drugs Act 1971 made it illegal to possess cannabis, LSD, cocaine, amphetamines, opium, morphine or heroin. The police can search suspects and their property and, with a warrant, their premises. Your GP, or one of the voluntary organisations below which specialise in counselling people with drug problems, can advise you about treatment. See also 'Drug dependence units' in the 'Hospitals' section.

City Roads (Crisis   **2 D3**
Intervention)
354-358 City Rd EC1. 071-278 8671. Provide immediate short-term help (up to three weeks) for young people in a state of crisis through drug abuse. Offer medical and social work support. Links with other agencies to offer long-term rehabilitation. *OPEN 24 hrs, 7 days a week.*

Community Drug Project
30 Manor Pl SE17. 071-703 0559. Advice and counselling for people with drug-related problems, principally aimed at users of heroin, cocaine, stimulants or other drugs. Needle exchange service. *OPEN 10.00-17.00 Mon, Wed & Fri, 14.00-17.00 Tue & Thur. Drop-in service (no appt necessary) 14.00-17.00 Mon-Fri. Telephone first, 10.00-17.00 Mon & Wed-Fri.*

The Hungerford Drug Project   **4 E2**
32a Wardour St W1. 071-437 3523. Counselling information, advice and referral service for people experiencing problems with their drug use.

Phoenix House
1 Eliot Bank SE23. 081-699 1515. Long-term residential rehabilitation for drug addicts and alcoholics who need extensive support. Therapeutic community staffed by ex-addicts and social workers. Phone them for an interview if you think you need such treatment.

Release   **2 E5**
388 Old St EC1. 071-729 9904. Specialise in giving legal advice to those arrested for drug offences. Drugs counselling and referrals for illegal and prescribed drugs. General advice and information on drugs, legal and practical help.

Turning Point
101 Back Church La E1. 071-702 2300. Counselling service and residential centres for the after-care of addicts who have undergone treatment.

Dyslexia

Many children and adults are handicapped by dyslexia (word-blindness).
The British Dyslexia Association
98 London Rd, Reading, Berks. (0734) 668271. Information and advice service. Branches throughout the country.

The Dyslexia Institute
133 Gresham Rd, Staines, Middx. (0784) 463935. Professional assessment and specialist teaching. Advisory service for parents and teachers. Train teachers and carry out research. Fifteen regional centres.

Eating disorders

Anorexia & Bulimia Nervosa Association
Tottenham Town Hall, Town Hall Approach Rd N15. 081-885 3936. Telephone counselling service.

Overeaters Anonymous
Box 19, Stretford, Manchester. Self-supporting organisation that follows a 12-step programme of recovery and offers advice to anyone suffering from overeating, anorexia or bulimia. Phone 081-868 4109 for information on meetings in London and south east England.

The elderly

Most people prefer to stay in their own homes and retain their independence as far as possible in old age, and Social Services departments provide a range of services to help them do just this, some-times with the help of local voluntary organisations. Home-helps can be arranged to cope with housework and shopping for those no longer able to manage alone, and the 'meals on wheels' service supplies cooked lunches to the elderly, infirm or housebound. Anyone on a pension who needs extra heating because of illness or restricted mobility should be eligible for financial help from the DSS. Services and facilities for the elderly vary from district to district but a call at the Social Services department, Citizens Advice Bureau or local 'Age Concern' branch should help you find out.

Abbeyfield Society
186-192 Darkes La, Potters Bar, Herts. (0707) 44845. Family-sized houses where 7-9 people live together with resident housekeeper responsible for main meals. Own bed-sitting room, own furniture. Also 'extra care' houses of 20-30 people requiring personal care.

Age Concern
Astral House, 1268 London Rd SW16. 081-679 8000. The focal point of all voluntary welfare organisations for the old. Excellent information service.

British Red Cross   **4 B5**
9 Grosvenor Cres SW1. 071-235 5454. Provide regular visitors who act as friends and helpers. Loan medical equipment for nursing in the home. Organise holidays for handicapped people.

Counsel & Care for the   **1 E1**
Elderly (Elderly Invalids Fund)
Turyman House, 16 Bonny St NW1. 071-485 1566. Comprehensive advisory service for the elderly and those concerned with their welfare. Advice about suitable homes and how to apply. Useful fact sheets on care of the elderly. Give financial help when needed. *OPEN 10.30-16.00 Mon-Fri.*

Country Houses Association   **4 G2**
41 Kingsway WC2. 071-836 1624. Charitable association for preservation of historic country houses, providing accommodation for retired and semi-retired people.

The Carers National   **3 E2**
Association
29 Chilworth Mews W2. 071-724 7776. Pressure group which aims to improve legislation for those who care for elderly relatives at home. Advice on financial matters and information about short-stay nursing homes.

Pre-retirement Association
The Nodus Centre, University Campus, Guildford. (0483) 39323. Give advice and information to help people face retirement successfully.

Epilepsy

British Epilepsy Association
Head office: 40 Hanover Sq, Leeds, W. Yorks. (0532) 439393. Advisory service covering welfare, training, education, employment and social adjustment.

Gambling

Gambling can be as compulsive as drug addiction and may cause distress to both the addict and his or her family.

Gamblers Anonymous   6 D5
17-23 Blantyre St, Cheyne Wlk SW10. 081-741 4181. An organisation with several meeting places in the London area. Constructive help and advice to compulsive gamblers.

Haemophilia

Haemophilia Society   5 B6
123 Westminster Bridge Rd SE1. 071-928 2020. A society for sufferers from haemophilia and those interested in their welfare. Advice and assistance given.

Homeless

Local authorities must give housing advice to anyone with a housing problem; enquire at your local housing department. Finding somewhere to live is particularly difficult for young single people coming to London and many of the following organisations offer advice and short-term accommodation. It is important to know your rights if you are a tenant and to get proper advice if you have difficulties.

Alone in London Service   2 B4
188 King's Cross Rd N1. 071-278 4224/5. An advice and counselling service for young, homeless people under the age of 21. *OPEN 09.00-16.00 (to 12.30 Wed) Mon-Fri.*

Homeless Network   7 D1
16-18 Strutton Ground SW1. 071-799 2404. Co-ordinating body for voluntary organisations providing a direct service to single homeless people in central London. Advice, help and referral services for accommodation, employment, social security problems. Day centres with washing facilities and social activities. Short- and medium-stay hostels.

London Hostels Association   7 B2
54 Eccleston Sq SW1. 071-834 1545. Hostels for men and women in the London area. Minimum stay one month. Advance reservations for groups. Enquiries to Accommodation Section: 071-828 3263.

Off the Streets   4 E2
Office: 54 Dean St W1. 071-434 2861. *OPEN 09.00-17.30.* Night Shelter: Centrepoint shelter, 25 Berwick St W1 (**4 D2**). 071-287 9134. *OPEN 20.00-08.00 every night of the year.* Provides basic accommodation, food and advice for up to 24 young people (male aged 16-19, female aged 16-21) who are new to and at risk in central London. Admission by interview.

Tent City
Old Oak Common La W3. 081-743 5708. (East Acton tube.) Very inexpensive short-term tourist accommodation. Deposit required from UK residents; passport from foreign visitors. *OPEN May-Oct.*

YMCA
640 Forest Rd E17. 081-520 5599. Head Office which will send lists of hostels catering for both sexes in the UK and abroad. Enquiries and bookings should be made direct to the particular hostel.

YWCA of Great Britain
Clarendon House, 52 Cornmarket St, Oxford, Oxon. (0865) 726110. Clubs and hostels for young people and women of all ages, classes and creeds. Temporary accommodation and permanent bed-sitting rooms and flats.

Young Women's Housing Project
81 Camberwell Church St SE5. 071-738 3048. For single girls aged 16-25.

Homosexuality

GLLAD (Gay & Lesbian Legal Advice)
071-253 2043. Telephone advice on legal matters relating to lesbian and gay people. *OPEN 19.00-22.00 Mon-Fri.*

Lesbian & Gay Switchboard
071-837 7324. *24-hr telephone service* giving information on accommodation, activities and entertainments for lesbians and gay men. Legal and medical referrals and counselling service. Will put you in touch with local groups.

Lesbian Line
071-251 6911. Phone service only. Advice for women only. *14.00-22.00 Mon & Fri, 19.00-22.00 Tue-Thur.*

London Friend   2 B3
86 Caledonian Rd N1. 071-837 3337. Telephone helpline for lesbians and gays *every eve 19.30-22.00.* Also face-to-face counselling, social support groups, coffee, tea and snacks. *Phone for details.* Women's number 071-837 2782.

**Transvestite & Transexual   2 G5
Support Group (TVTS)**
2 French Pl, Shoreditch E1. 071-729

1466. Support and befriending service. Centre OPEN 12.00-18.00 Wed & Thur, 14.00-24.00 Fri, Sat & Sun.

Legal aid & advice

There is a legal aid scheme whereby your legal costs can be subsidised on a means-tested basis. To find out about this and to get legal advice, go to your local Citizens Advice Bureau (see under 'General'); to any solicitor displaying the Legal Aid sign; or to your neighbourhood Law Centre.

Amnesty International **2 C5**
British Section, 99-119 Rosebery Av EC1. 071-814 6200. Support concerning immigration, deportation and other cases. About 40 groups in the London area.

Central London Law Centre **2 E2**
47 Charing Cross Rd WC2. 071-437 5854/5764. OPEN 15.00-19.00 Tue (Employment), 15.00-19.00 Wed (Housing), 15.00-19.00 Thur (Immigration). OPEN at other times by appt.

Legal Aid Board **5 A1**
29-37 Red Lion St WC1. 071-831 4209. Advice on legal aid system.

Mary Ward Legal Centre **2 A6**
42 Queen Sq WC1. 071-831 7079. Legal advice. Appt only. OPEN 09.30-17.30 Mon-Fri. Run on a green form legal aid basis. Also has a financial advice service, debt counselling and tax advice.

Release **2 E5**
388 Old St EC1. 071-729 9904. Emergency: 071-603 8654. Specialise in drugs law. Deal with criminal legal emergencies. General legal advice and information on handling the police, the courts, prisons, lawyers and the legal aid system.

South Islington Law Centre **2 D2**
131-132 Upper St N1. 071-354 0133. OPEN (by appt) 10.00-13.00 Mon (Housing), 15.30-17.30 Wed (Housing), 16.00-17.30 Wed (Employment); OPEN (walk-in) 16.00-17.30 Tue (Immigration), 10.00-12.00 Fri (Immigration).

Southwark Law Centre
2 East Dulwich Gro SE22. 081-299 1024. OPEN (by appt) 16.00-18.00 Thur. Telephone advice 10.00-13.00 Mon-Thur.

Marriage guidance

Catholic Marriage Advisory Council **3 C5**
23 Kensington Sq W8. 071-937 3781. Help for those, of all denominations, with marital problems. Meetings arranged for parents, teachers, school pupils and engaged couples. Natural family planning. Appt only. Phone for details.

Institute of Marital Studies
Tavistock Centre, 120 Belsize La NW3. 071-435 7111. Professional help with marital problems. OPEN by appt 09.30-17.30 Mon-Fri.

Relate **4 C1**
76a New Cavendish St W1. 071-580 1087. Formerly known as the London Marriage Guidance Council. Confidential counselling and education service for those with difficulties in their personal relationships. Appt only. Phone for details.

Mental health

If you have a severe emotional problem, the best person to see is your doctor who may recommend psychiatric help. Social workers are also able to give advice and assistance to the mentally ill and their families and can tell you about local facilities and support groups.

Johnston House (formerly Brent Consultation Centre)
Johnston House, 51 Winchester Av NW6. 071-328 0918. Confidential walk-in service for young people from 15-21 years old with personal and emotional problems. Trained psychotherapists. OPEN 17.00-18.45 Mon, 12.00-14.30 Thur.

MIND (National Association for Mental Health) **4 C1**
22 Harley St W1. 071-637 0741. Advisory service on all aspects of mental health.

Samaritans **4 D2**
46 Marshall St W1. 071-439 2224. A voluntary organisation to help people who have thoughts of suicide or despair. 24-hr telephone service. Also walk-in service 09.00-21.00. Totally confidential. Many London branches; see telephone directory.

Westminster Pastoral Foundation **3 C5**
23 Kensington Sq W8. 071-937 6956. A large counselling centre, offering individual, group, or family and marital counselling for those with emotional difficulties. Also has an extensive training programme with both short and full-time courses.

Missing persons

It is advisable to inform the police, although they can do little unless there is suspicion of foul play.

The Salvation Army Family Tracing Service   1 G4
105-109 Judd St WC1. 071-387 2772. Enquiries for close relatives are accepted. Also carry out searches abroad. No adoption, business, wills, divorces, friends or under-17s.

Nursing

The NHS can provide a district nurse. Apply to your local health authority. For private nurses look in telephone directory, at the advertisements in a nursing magazine, or contact one of the following:

British Nursing Association   4 B2
443 Oxford St W1. 071-629 9030. Nursing agency supplying all types of nurses.
Langham Nurses Association   3 C2
85 Maitland Ct, Gloucester Ter W2. 071-723 1444. Private, qualified nurses available (resident or non-resident).

One-parent families

Gingerbread   4 G3
35 Wellington St WC2. 071-240 0953. Network of self-help groups to help one-parent families. Advice on housing, the law, social security, baby-sitting, etc. Over 300 local groups. Advice line *11.00-14.00 Mon-Fri.*
National Council for One-Parent Families
255 Kentish Town Rd NW5. 071-267 1361. Will help and advise single parents and single pregnant women with any problem. Confidential.

Parents

Parents Anonymous, London
071-263 8918. Confidential telephone listening service *(18.00-06.00)* for parents under stress who fear they may physically or emotionally abuse their children. Can also help with any emotional crisis in the family. One of many OPUS (Organisations for Parents under Stress) groups.

Pregnancy tests

A pregnancy test can always be done by your doctor – or consult your local family planning clinic. Magazines, newspapers and some chemists carry advertisements for private firms carrying out pregnancy tests, at a fee. You can also buy do-it-yourself kits at most chemists. See also 'Abortion' and 'Contraception'.

Rape

London Rape Crisis Centre
071-837 1600. A free and confidential service run by women for women who have been raped or sexually assaulted and need support, information or any other help.
Survivors
071-833 3737. National organisation for men who have been raped or sexually assaulted.

Service & ex-servicemen

Royal British Legion   4 E4
48 Pall Mall SW1. 071-930 8131. Will give assistance and financial aid to service and ex-servicemen and women, and their dependents. Apply to local branch.
Soldiers', Sailors' &   5 G5
Airmen's Families Association
19 Queen Elizabeth St SE1. 071-403 8783. Financial advice and other aid for the families of service and ex-servicemen.

Singles clubs

Breakaway
57 Garrick Close W5. 081-991 2169. A social club for professional people organising social, sporting and cultural activities in London and the home counties. *Annual or 3-month fee.*
London Village
24 Upper Park Rd NW3. 071-586 7455. Membership organisation created by people aged 20-45 for their own age group. All kinds of social activities arranged. *Charge.*

Smoking

Action on Smoking & Health (ASH)   4 A1
109 Gloucester Pl W1. 071-935 3519. Advice on smoking-related problems and addresses of withdrawal clinics in London area.
Smokers' Clinic
Maudsley Hospital, Denmark Hill SE5. 071-703 6333. Help and advice for anyone wishing to give up smoking. Telephone first.

Venereal diseases

See list under 'Hospitals'. All treatment is free, anonymous if desired and completely confidential. You do not need an appointment or letter from your own doctor.

Women's issues

There are many issues which specifically concern women; for example, equal pay, sex discrimination, combining work with child-rearing. Several organisations now exist to monitor legislation, promote research and provide practical help and advice. See also 'Abortion Law Reform Association' in the 'Abortion' section and 'NCCL' under 'Discrimination'. The feminist movement has been growing for years and many groups covering the whole feminist/political/radical spectrum exist in London. For further information consult the London Women's Handbook available in libraries and women's centres. Spare Rib at 27 Clerkenwell Clo EC1 (2 C5), 071-253 9792, also publish a monthly feminist magazine and a diary giving useful information on women's issues.

Equal Opportunities Commission
Overseas House, Quay St, Manchester. (061) 833 9244. Advice on all queries and complaints regarding the Equal Pay and Sex Discrimination Acts.

Feminist Library   **5 B6**
5 Westminster Bridge Rd SE1. 071-928 7789. Library and information service on issues affecting women. Collects and collates information on research which has been or is being undertaken. *OPEN 11.00-17.30 (to 19.30 Thur) Wed-Sat.*

London Women's Aid   **2 F5**
52-54 Featherstone St EC1. 071-251 6537. Help for battered women. Co-ordinates local women's aid centres. *24-hr telephone service* to put battered women in touch with their nearest women's refuge and to offer advice and support.

National Alliance of Women's Organisations
279-281 Whitechapel Rd E1. 071-247 7052. An umbrella organisation comprising over 220 women's organisations and aiming to provide a national and European voice for women in the nineties. Advice on fundraising and setting up groups. Resource centre *OPEN 09.30-17.30 by appt.*

Rights of Women   **2 F5**
52-54 Featherstone St EC1. 071-251 6577. Free legal advice for women by women in the legal profession. Enquiries by letter only or telephone to speak to a qualified solicitor *19.00-21.00 Tue-Thur.*

Women's National Commission   **4 E5**
Caxton House, Tothill St SW1. 071-273 5486. Publishes a list of established women's organisations in London and the UK.

Voluntary social work

Many organisations rely heavily on volunteers to carry out much needed work in the community. If you can offer skills such as teaching, driving, typing, decorating and maintenance or sewing, so much the better, but many opportunities exist for people who can offer time, patience, good humour and commitment for tasks such as befriending, visiting the elderly or helping in clubs and hospitals.

British Volunteer Programme   **2 E2**
22 Coleman Fields N1. 071-226 6616. Send people with professional or technical qualifications or experience for a minimum of two years to help with projects in Third World countries.

Camden Volunteer Bureau   **2 B4**
Instrument House, 207-215 King's Cross Rd WC1. 071-837 3443. Guides people into the type of voluntary work that they are most suited to. Work in Camden only for over 250 organisations.

Community Service Volunteers   **2 B3**
237 Pentonville Rd N1. 071-278 6601. Produce various publications full of unusual suggestions for helping in the community. Minimum of four months full-time work. Board, lodging and pocket money.

London Adventure Playground Association
279 Whitechapel Rd E1. 071-377 0314. Helpers and crafts materials often needed, especially in school holidays.

London Voluntary Service Council   **1 F4**
68 Chalton St NW1. 071-388 0241. Co-ordinate and support the work of the voluntary sector groups in London. Contact them for the address of your local Volunteer Bureau.

Samaritans   **4 D2**
46 Marshall St W1. 071-439 2224. Volunteers needed to help on *24-hr telephone service* befriending the suicidal and despairing. Work in one of 14 branches. Information given about selection procedures, training etc.

Women's Royal Voluntary Service
234-244 Stockwell Rd SW9. 071-416 0146. Men and women volunteers welcome for all kinds of community work.

Police stations

These are the most important police stations within a 3-mile radius of Piccadilly Circus.

City of London

Headquarters & all   **5 E2**
departments
26 Old Jewry EC2. 071-601 2222.
Bishopsgate   **5 F2**
182 Bishopsgate EC2. 071-601 2222.
Snow Hill   **5 C1**
5 Snow Hill EC1. 071-601 2222.
Wood Street   **5 D2**
37 Wood St EC2. 071-601 2222.

Metropolitan

Battersea
112-118 Battersea Bridge Rd SW11.
071-350 1122.
Charing Cross   **4 F3**
Agar St WC2. 071-240 1212.
Chelsea   **6 E2**
2 Lucan Pl SW3. 081-741 6212.
Hyde Park   **3 F4**
North of Serpentine W2. 071-321 7212.
Kensington   **3 B6**
72-74 Earl's Court Rd W8. 081-741
6212.
King's Cross   **2 C3**
2 Tolpuddle St N1. 071-704 1212.
New Scotland Yard   **4 E6**
Broadway SW1. 071-230 1212.
Rochester Row   **7 C2**
63 Rochester Row SW1. 071-321 7212.
Southwark   **5 D5**
323 Borough High St SE1. 071-407
4759.
West End Central   **4 D3**
27 Savile Row W1. 071-321 7212.

Hospitals

General hospitals

The following hospitals all have 24-hr *casualty departments:*
Charing Cross Hospital
Fulham Palace Rd W6. 081-846 1234.
Guy's Hospital   **5 E4**
St Thomas St SE1. 071-955 5000.
London Hospital (Whitechapel)
Whitechapel Rd E1. 071-377 7000.
Queen Mary's Hospital
Roehampton La SW15. 081-789 6611.
Royal Free Hospital
Pond St NW3. 071-794 0500.

St Bartholomew's Hospital   **5 C1**
West Smithfield EC1. 071-601 8888.
St George's Hospital
Blackshaw Rd SW17. 081-672 1255.
St Thomas' Hospital   **5 A6**
Lambeth Palace Rd SE1. 071-928 9292.
University College Hospital   **1 F5**
Gower St WC1. 071-387 9300.
Westminster Hospital   **7 E2**
Dean Ryle St, Horseferry Rd SW1. 081-
746 8000.
Whittington Hospital
Highgate Hill N19. 071-272 3070.

Children's hospitals

Belgrave Unit
King's College Hospital, Denmark Hill
SE5. 071-274 6222. *24-hr casualty.*
Children's Hospital Sydenham
321 Sydenham Rd SE26. 081-690 4311.
24-hr casualty.
The Hospital for Sick   **2 A5**
Children
Great Ormond St WC1. 071-405 9200.
Queen Elizabeth Hospital for Sick
Children
Hackney Rd E2. 071-739 8422. *24-hr
casualty.*
St Mary's Children's   **3 E2**
Hospital
South Wharf Rd W2. 071-725 6163. *24-
hr casualty.*
Westminster Children's   **7 C2**
Hospital
(Westminster Hospital Teaching Group)
Udall St SW1. 081-746 8000. *24-hr
casualty.*

Dental hospitals

Dental Emergency Care Service
071-400 0400/081-677 6363. *OPEN* 24
hrs. Private or NHS.
Eastman Dental Hospital   **2 B4**
256 Gray's Inn Rd WC1. 071-837 3646.
London Hospital Dental Institute
New Rd E1. 071-377 7000.

Drug dependence units

The following hospitals have special clinics to deal with drug abuse and dependency. Each drug unit can accept patients only from its local catchment area. They prefer people to have a letter of referral from a GP but will see them without if necessary. A few units have in-patient facilities but any unit will offer help and guidance for further treatment if required. Emergency cases should go to their nearest casualty department. The

Maudsley Hospital operates a 24-hr general emergency clinic.

Hackney Hospital
Drug Dependency Unit, 230 Homerton High St E9. 081-986 6816. *OPEN 10.00-11.00 Mon, Wed & Fri. At other times by appt only.*

London Hospital (St Clements)
2a Bow Rd E3. 071-377 7000. *OPEN 09.30-17.30 Mon-Fri.*

Maudsley Hospital
Denmark Hill SE5. 071-703 6333.

Queen Mary's Hospital
Roehampton La SW15. 081-789 6611. *OPEN 14.00-18.00 Mon, 10.00-12.00 Wed.*

St George's Hospital (Tooting)
Blackshaw Rd SW17. 081-672 1255. *OPEN 09.00-17.00 Mon-Fri (to 20.00 Wed). (CLOSED Tue morning).* Walk-in service and appt then made.

St Mary's Hospital   3 **E2**
Praed St W2. 071-725 6666. Drug Dependency Centre: 071-725 6486.

University College Hospital   1 **E4**
Drug Dependence Unit, National Temperance Hospital, 122 Hampstead Rd NW1. 071-387 9541. *OPEN 09.00-19.00 Tue, 09.00-13.00 Fri.*

West Middlesex Hospital
Twickenham Rd, Isleworth, Middx. 081-560 2121. *OPEN 14.00-20.00 Mon, 10.00-18.00 Tue, 14.00-18.00 Wed, 10.00-18.00 Thur, 11.30-13.00 Fri.*

Ear, nose and throat hospitals

Royal National Throat, Nose   2 **B4**
and Ear Hospital
330 Gray's Inn Rd WC1. 071-837 8855.

Eye hospitals

Moorfields Eye Hospital   2 **F4**
City Rd EC1. 071-253 3411. *OPEN 24 hrs Mon-Sun.*

Foot hospitals

London Foot Hospital   1 **E5**
33 Fitzroy Sq W1. 071-636 0602.

Foreign hospitals

French Dispensary   1 **D5**
6 Osnaburgh St NW1. 071-387 5132.

Heart and chest hospitals

London Chest Hospital
Bonner Rd E2. 081-980 4433.

National Heart and Chest   6 **E3**
Hospital (Brompton Hospital)
Fulham Rd SW3. 071-352 8121.

Homoeopathic hospitals

Royal London Homoeopathic   2 **A5**
Hospital
Great Ormond St WC1. 071-837 3091.

Maternity hospitals

Newham General Hospital
Forest La E7. 071-476 1400.

Queen Charlotte's Maternity
Hospital
339 Goldhawk Rd W6. 081-748 4666.

Whipps Cross Hospital
Whipps Cross Rd E11. 081-539 5522.

Hospitals for the mentally handicapped

Grove Park Hospital
Marvels La SE12. 081-857 1191.

Migraine clinics

Charing Cross Hospital
Fulham Palace Rd W6. 081-748 2040.

Hospitals for nervous diseases

Maida Vale Hospital for Nervous Diseases
4 Maida Vale W9. 071-286 5172.

National Hospital for   2 **A5**
Nervous Diseases
Queen Sq WC1. 071-837 3611.

Nursing & convalescent homes

The National Health Service can send you free or at very low cost to one of their many convalescent homes by the sea or in the country – consult your hospital doctor.

King Edward's Hospital   3 **C3**
Fund
14 Palace Ct W2. 071-727 0581. A directory for Greater London of places that offer convalescence, rehabilitation and other short-term care.

The London Clinic   1 **C6**
20 Devonshire Pl W1. 071-935 4444. Top, private.

Ophthalmic hospitals

Western Ophthalmic Hospital   1 A6
(St Mary's Hospital Teaching Group)
Marylebone Rd NW1. 071-402 4211.

Orthopaedic hospitals

Royal National Orthopaedic   1 D5
Hospital
45-51 Bolsover St W1. 071-387 5070.

Psychiatric hospitals

Castlewood Day Hospital
25 Shooter's Hill SE18. 081-856 4970.
Friern Hospital
52 Friern Barnet Rd, New Southgate
N11. 081-368 1288.
London Hospital (St Clements)
2a Bow Rd E3. 071-377 7953.
Maudsley Hospital
Denmark Hill SE5. 071-703 6333. Also
drug clinics and drug in-patient facilities.
24-hr walk-in emergency.
Parkside Clinic
63-65 Lancaster Rd W11. 071-221 4656.
Referral by GP, social worker etc, from
anywhere in the London area.
Tooting Bec Hospital
Church La SW17. 071-326 5400. Drug
in-patient facilities, geriatric unit.

Venereal diseases hospitals

Eastern Hospital
Homerton Gro E9. 081-985 1193.
Guy's Hospital   5 E4
St Thomas St SE1. 071-407 7600.
London Hospital (Whitechapel)
Whitechapel Rd E1. 071-377 7000.
Middlesex Hospital   4 D1
James Pringle House, 73 Charlotte St
W1. 071-380 9141.
Newham District General
Glen Rd E13. 071-476 1400.
**Royal Free Hospital Marlborough
Clinic**
Pond St NW3. 071-794 0500.
Royal Northern Hospital
Holloway Rd N7. 071-272 7777.
St Bartholomew's Hospital   5 C1
West Smithfield EC1. 071-601 8888.
St Mary's Hospital   3 E2
Praed St W2. 071-725 6619/20.
St Thomas' Hospital   5 A6
Lambeth Palace Rd SE1. 071-928 9292.
University College Hospital   1 F5
Gower St W1. 071-388 9625.

Westminster Hospital   7 E2
Dean Ryle St, Horseferry Rd SW1. 081-
746 8000.

Donor services

*If you wish to donate blood, or to leave
your organs for transplant or research
purposes, these wishes must be
recorded in writing on a donor card
which should be carried at all times. For
further information contact:*
Dept of Health and Social   5 C6
Security (DHSS)
Hannibal House, Elephant & Castle SE1.
071-972 2000.

Blood

West End Donor Centre   4 D2
26 Margaret St W1. 071-580 8772/3.

Eyes

Royal National Institute for   4 C1
the Blind
224 Great Portland St W1. 071-388
1266.

Organs

Dept of Health and Social   5 C6
Security (DHSS)
Anatomy Dept, Hannibal House, Elephant
& Castle SE1. 071-972 2000.

Public lavatories

*Look out for signs in the streets directing
you to the nearest public lavatories, or ask
someone likely to be familiar with the
area: police, traffic wardens, news-ven-
dors or shopkeepers. All lavatories in this
country are divided into separate areas for
men and women except for the new
cabin-style ones to be found in the street
which are completely self-contained and
therefore unisex. OPEN 24 hrs. Nearly all
large stores, museums and national art
galleries have lavatories, as do all pubs
and mainline stations, and the major ones
– Euston, King's Cross, Paddington,
Victoria and Waterloo – are OPEN 24 hrs.
Some London Transport underground
stations have lavatories. All public places
must now provide access for the disabled
wherever practicable and this includes
lavatories; look for the wheelchair symbol.*

Emergency and late-night help

Accident

When in an accident with another vehicle you must stop and exchange names, addresses and insurance details with the other party. There is no need to call the police to the scene of the accident unless a person is seriously injured, in which case dial 999 immediately. In the case of a person being injured but able to walk away, or where the other driver fails to stop, then this must be reported to the nearest police station within 24 hrs.

Bombs

If you see a suspicious looking package:
1 – **DON'T TOUCH IT**
2 – *Get people away from the area*
3 – *Inform personnel in charge of the premises*
4 – *Dial **999** and tell the police where it is*

Car breakdown

AA (Automobile Association)
Freephone breakdown service (0800) 887766. *24 hrs Mon-Sun.* You can call the AA out if your car breaks down, but you will have to join on the spot if you are not already a member.
National Breakdown
Freephone breakdown service (0800) 400600. *24 hrs Mon-Sun.* Non-members will pay more for rescue/recovery than members.
Olympic Breakdown Service
071-286 8282. *24 hrs Mon-Sun.* An AA and RAC-approved recovery service covering the whole of London.
RAC (Royal Automobile Club)
Freephone breakdown service (0800) 828282. *24 hrs Mon-Sun.* You will need to be a member of the RAC, or join when they arrive.

Cash

Cash dispensing machines outside major branches of most banks operate 24 hrs. Ask your bank about obtaining the special card, and a list of branches with dispensers. There are now many places (in small shops, arcades, etc), open till late in the evening, which call themselves Bureaux de Change and will change travellers cheques. Some are quite unscrupulous and charge a very high commission for the service. It is always best to change money in a bank or well-known and established Bureau de Change. The following are open longer hours than usual.
Chequepoint   **4 E3**
1 Irving St WC2. 071-839 5072. *OPEN 09.40-22.00 Mon-Sun.* Also 220 Earl's Court Rd SW5 (**6 B2**), 071-370 3238; Marble Arch W1 (**4 A2**), 071-723 1005. *OPEN 24 hrs.* 58 Queensway W2 (**3 C3**), 071-229 4268. *OPEN 09.00-24.00.*
London Gatwick Airport
Lloyds Bank (0293 537559). *OPEN 08.00-16.00 Mon-Sun.* Midland Bank (0293 519122). *OPEN 09.30-15.30 Mon-Sun.*
London Heathrow Airport
Thomas Cook (081-897 3351) in Terminal 1. *OPEN 24 hrs.* Travelex (081-897 3501) in Terminal 3. *OPEN 24 hrs in Arrivals, 06.00-22.00 in Departures.*
Luton Airport
International Currency Exchange (0582 30700). *OPEN Easter-Oct 24 hrs; Nov-Easter 06.30-23.00 Mon-Sun.*

Chemists (late-night)

Your local police station keeps a list of chemists and doctors available at all hours. Or try:
Bliss Chemist   **4 A3**
5 Marble Arch W1. 071-723 6116. *OPEN 09.00-24.00 every day of the year.*
Boots   **4 E3**
Piccadilly Circus W1. 071-734 6126. *OPEN 08.30-20.00 Mon-Fri, 09.00-20.00 Sat, 12.00-18.00 Sun.*
Warman Freed
45 Golders Green Rd NW11. 081-455 4351. *OPEN 08.00-24.00 every day of the year.*

Credit cards

For information on reporting lost or stolen cards see 'Money and business services'.

Homeless

See under 'Homeless' in the 'Social services' section.

Hospitals

Whether you are a visitor or a resident, in an emergency dial **999** *and ask for the ambulance service, or make your own way to a casualty hospital (see 'Social services'). If at all practicable, go to a doctor (your local police station keeps a list of doctors) as casualty hospitals are for serious emergencies only. Visitors to London can register as temporary patients. Free medical treatment is available to British citizens, EC nationals and visitors from other countries with reciprocal arrangements. All other foreign visitors will be required to pay for medical treatment they receive.*

Lost property

Apply to the nearest police station. Lost property found in the street is usually taken there.

Air travel: lost property is held by each individual airline. For property lost in the main airport buildings enquire: British Airport Authority's Lost Property Office, London Airport, Heathrow, Middx. 081-745 7727. *OPEN 09.00-16.00 Mon-Sun.*

British Rail: if you lose something on a train, contact the station where the train you were on terminates. They will be able to inform you whether your belongings have been recovered and, if so, where they have been taken.

London Transport: for enquiries about property lost on the underground or buses call in person at the Lost Property Office, 200 Baker St W1 (**1 B5**) or apply by letter. No telephone enquiries. *OPEN 09.30-14.00 Mon-Fri.*

Taxis: apply 15 Penton St N1 (**2 C3**). 071-833 0996. Alternatively, contact your nearest police station.

Lost children: will be cared for by the railway police if lost on British Rail, or ask at the nearest police station if lost elsewhere.

Lost dogs: may have been taken to Battersea Dogs Home, 4 Battersea Park Rd SW8 (**7 B5**). 071-622 3626.

Lost car keys: if you know the number of your key (keep a note of it somewhere in your wallet) the AA or RAC can probably help (phone numbers under 'Car breakdown') if a nearby garage or the police can't.

Lost passports: report the loss to the police and to your embassy/high commission.

Parking

Most London car parks are run by National Car Parks (NCP), which have distinctive yellow signs. Notice boards at the entrance give details of charges. Most parking meters and single yellow lines along London streets cease to be applicable as from 18.30 Mon-Fri, 13.30 Sat and all day Sun; but do read the signs on the meters or affixed to nearby lamp posts which give times of operation. Parking on double yellow lines, on the pavement and double-banked parking is forbidden at all times, and you may emerge to find your car has been towed away or that a clamp has rendered it immobile. Collecting your car (or having the clamp removed) is costly and inconvenient (see 'Wheel clamped'). Fines for illegal parking are stiff and worth avoiding.

24-hr car parks:

Abingdon St SW1.	7	**E1**
Arlington St SW1.	4	**D4**
Audley Sq W1.	4	**B4**
Brewer St W1.	4	**D3**
Cadogan Pl SW1.	6	**F1**
Cambridge Circus WC2.	4	**E2**
Denman St W1.	4	**E3**
Dolphin Sq SW1.	7	**C3**
Park La W1.	4	**B4**
Pavilion Rd SW1.	6	**F1**
Semley Pl SW1.	7	**B2**
Upper St Martin's La WC2.	4	**F3**
Young St W8.	3	**C5**

Petrol: 24-hr service stations

Cavendish Motors
Cavendish Rd NW6. 081-459 0046.
Chiswick Flyover Service Station
1 Great West Rd W4. 081-994 1119.
City Petroleum   **2 D2**
316 Essex Rd N1. 071-226 5991.
Fountain Garage   **4 B4**
83 Park La W1. 071-629 4151.
Kennington Filling Station   **7 G2**
212 Kennington Rd SE11. 071-735 2191.

Star Group Texaco
63 Fortune Green Rd NW6. 071-435 2211.
Vauxhall Bridge Road Filling   7 C2 Station
148 Vauxhall Bridge Rd SW1. 071-828 1371.

Police

For a list of police stations see 'Social services'.

when you need a doctor or a chemist:
Each police station keeps a list of emergency doctors and chemists who are available at all hours.

when you need a garage:
Each police station keeps a list of local garages and the times they are open.

when you need a hotel:
They keep up-to-date information on hotels and boarding houses in the area, with prices – of course, they don't know if there are vacancies, but at least you'd have somewhere to try.

when you've been burgled:
Report any theft to the nearest police station immediately and they will take appropriate action.

when you've lost property in the street:
It may have been handed in to them, or they will be able to give you a list of lost property offices for things lost in trains and taxis, etc.

when your car has been stolen:
Ring them up straight away – it may have been towed away by them for a parking infringement. Otherwise they will circulate its description and let you know if they get it back.

when your dog is lost:
It may have been taken to them at the station, in which case they will look after it for one night and then take it to the Battersea Dogs Home, 4 Battersea Park Rd SW8. 071-622 3626.

when you're stranded:
If you've come to London from a provincial town and spent your return fare, they can take the name of someone in your home town who will deposit your fare at the local police station and then the London police will give you a travel warrant to get you home. (This applies to British residents only – all other nationalities should apply to their own embassy for repatriation.)

when you're locked out:
The police keep a list of local locksmiths or try the *Yellow Pages* for a *24-hr* service or a willing locksmith who will come out after hours.

if you are arrested:
Always keep calm and remain polite. You do not have to say anything in answer to any allegations that are made but it is sensible to give your name and address. Ask to phone your solicitor or phone Release 071-603 8654 *(OPEN 24 hrs)* who will give you advice and get a solicitor if necessary. Appeals for legal representation, legal aid and bail can be made in court. *See under 'Legal aid'.*

Post

There is a late-opening post office in London:
Post Office   4 F3
24-28 William IV St, Trafalgar Sq WC2. 071-930 9580. *OPEN 08.00-20.00 Mon-Sat.*

Rape

See under 'Social services'.

Transport

The underground system closes down about midnight. However, night buses serve London every night, with a greatly extended service to the suburbs. All major night bus routes pass through Trafalgar Sq (4 E4) and they run about once an hour. See night bus map at the end of this section.
For a list of 24-hr taxi and mini-cab companies, see 'Transport in London'.

Wheel clamped

Take the label attached to your vehicle, plus the fixed penalty notice, to one of the police car pounds listed below. You will have to pay a fine before the clamp is removed (A.Ax.Dc.V) and it may be some hours before somone arrives to remove it. In an emergency telephone 071-252 2222. It is possible that if you are illegally parked or causing an obstruction, your car will be towed away to one of these pounds:
Camden Town Car Pound   1 D2
Oval Rd NW1. *OPEN 08.00-24.00 Mon-Sat.*
Hyde Park Car Pound   4 A3
NCP Park La Car Park, Marble Arch W1. *OPEN 24 hrs.*
Mount Pleasant Car Pound   2 B5
Corner of Calthorpe St & Farringdon Rd EC1. *OPEN 08.00-24.00.*
Warwick Road Car Pound
245 Warwick Rd W14. *OPEN 08.00-24.00 Mon-Sat.*

Transport in London

Public transport

London has a fairly comprehensive system of public transport with a good night service. There are three different services – London Transport which operates buses and the underground (tube), British Rail (BR) which operates overground trains, and Docklands Light Railway (DLR). The system is supposed to be integrated so that all three connect with each other wherever practicable, but bus and train timetables don't always coincide. To find your way around, use the underground and bus maps in this book. For enquiries about lost property on public transport see 'Emergency & late-night help'.

London Transport   4 E6
Travel Information Centre, 55 Broadway SW1. 071-222 1234. Will answer queries about timetables and fares for buses and the underground. Also give journey planning advice. Automatic telephone call queueing system *24 hrs*. Other travel information centres at these underground stations: Euston, Heathrow, Liverpool Street, King's Cross, Oxford Circus, Piccadilly Circus and Victoria (British Rail station). For the latest update on the travel situation call Travel Check (*24 hrs*) on 071-222 1200.

The underground

For the stranger to London, this is the simplest way of getting around. Very efficient in central London and very quick. Few lines run south of the river where BR offers a more comprehensive service. For journeys starting from the centre, tubes run *approx 05.30-00.15 Mon-Sat, 07.30-23.30 Sun.* Start *30 minutes* earlier if coming from the suburbs or if you have to change; all tube stations have a notice showing the times of first and last trains. Fares are graduated according to zones and, for the regular traveller, weekly, monthly or annual Travelcards provide considerable savings. Travelcards can be used on the underground, DLR and buses and are sold at Travel Information Centres, British Rail stations, all underground stations and some newsagents. Capitalcards are also available on a daily, weekly, monthly or annual basis and are valid for use on buses, tubes and BR trains in the Greater London area. To save queuing at ticket offices, keep some 10p, 20p, 50p and £1 coins handy to use in ticket machines. Keep your ticket to use in the exit machine at your destination. Cheap day returns are available if you start your journey *after 09.30 Mon-Fri or any time Sat & Sun.*

Buses

Covering the whole of Greater London they are slower, especially in the rush hours, but more pleasant and you see so much more. They run *approx 06.00-24.00 Mon-Sat, 07.30-23.30 Sun.* First and last times of bus routes are indicated on bus stops but heavy traffic can prevent buses from keeping to these times. Fares are graduated, apart from a few flat-fare routes. Return tickets are not available. On some buses you pay the driver as you get on but others (including all those with the entrance at the back of the bus) have a conductor who collects the fares as the bus goes along. Both give change but do not like being handed notes, especially large ones. If you are waiting at a request stop (red) you must raise your arm to make the bus stop for you. Once on the bus, if you wish to alight at a red request stop, you must ring the bell once, in good time. At other bus stops, called compulsory stops (white), this is not necessary. There are night buses serving London every night, with an extended service to the suburbs as well. All major night bus routes pass through Trafalgar Square (**4 E4**). Consult *Buses for Night Owls*, available from LT and BR travel information centres and see the night bus map on page 241.

Docklands Light Railway

Docklands Light Railway (DLR) is integrated with the underground and British Rail networks. It links Docklands with the City of London, Stratford and Greenwich, and in October 1993 will extend to Beckton, serving the area between the Isle of Dogs and the Royal Docks. A direct shuttle bus to London City Airport will be incorporated into the new network. The red, white and blue trains are computer-operated with a guard/ticket collector on board. There are excellent views from the high viaduct route over the stretches of water which form the Docklands. Trains run from *05.30-21.30 Mon-Fri. There is no service on Sat & Sun.*

However, replacement bus services follow the train routes and stop at all DLR stations from *21.30-00.15 Mon-Fri, 05.30-00.15 Sat & 07.30-23.15 Sun*. Docklander tickets give unlimited travel for one day on DLR only. All tickets, Travelcards and passes issued by London Transport and British Rail are valid on DLR provided they cover the correct zone. Tickets can be bought from DLR Information Centres at Tower Gateway and Island Gardens *09.30-17.00 Mon-Fri*, or from ticket machines at DLR stations; keep some coins handy. *For 24-hr travel information on DLR phone 071-918 4000.*

British Rail trains

BR run inter-city trains all over Britain, and Network South East which serves London and the suburbs. These trains generally run *06.00-24.00 Mon-Sat, 07.00-22.30 Sun*. There are some one-off trains during the early hours; check with your station to see if there is a suitable one. Fares on BR trains are graduated and cheap day returns are available except *Mon-Fri* on busy trains during rush hours *(approx 08.00-09.30 and 16.30-18.00)*. Many BR stations connect with the underground. Take British Rail's Thameslink service to get through London quickly. From Luton Airport via West Hampstead and Blackfriars to Gatwick Airport, Brighton and Kent. Ask at any station for a timetable.

British Travel Centre   **4 E4**
12 Lower Regent Street W1. A booking centre for rail travel in Britain, rail and sea journeys to the Continent and Ireland, motorail and rail package holidays and tours.

British Rail Travel Centres
Bookings for all rail travel in Britain.
87 King William St EC4.   **5 E3**
14 Kingsgate Pde, Victoria St SW1.   **7 C1**

RAIL TERMINALS
Blackfriars   **5 C3**
Queen Victoria St EC4. Information 071-928 5100. South and south-east London suburbs. Built in 1864, rebuilt 1977.

Cannon Street   **5 E3**
Cannon St EC4. Information 071-928 5100. South-east London suburbs, Kent, E. Sussex. Built 1866; rebuilt with office block above in 1965. *CLOSED Sat & Sun.*

Charing Cross   **4 F4**
Strand WC2. Information 071-928 5100. South-east London suburbs, Kent. Built 1864. Trains from here go over Hungerford Bridge.

Euston   **1 F4**
Euston Rd NW1. Information 071-387

7070. Fast trains to Birmingham, Liverpool, Manchester, Glasgow, Inverness. Suburban line to Watford, Northampton. The original station was built in 1837, designed by Robert Stephenson. It had a famous Doric portico which was 72ft (22m) high. The station was completely rebuilt in 1968.

Fenchurch Street   **5 F3**
Railway Pl, Fenchurch St EC3. Information 071-928 5100. Trains to Tilbury and Southend. Built 1841.

King's Cross   **1 G3**
Euston Rd N1. Information 071-278 2477. Fast trains to Leeds, York, Newcastle, Edinburgh, Aberdeen. Built by Lewis Cubitt in 1851, a more modern concourse was added some years ago. The clock on the tower was taken from the original Crystal Palace in Hyde Park.

Liverpool Street   **5 F1**
Liverpool St EC2. Information 071-928 5100. East and north-east London suburbs, fast trains to Cambridge, Colchester, Norwich and Harwich harbour. Built 1874.

London Bridge   **5 E4**
Borough High St SE1. Information 071-928 5100. South and south-east London suburbs, Kent, Sussex, East Surrey. First opened in 1836, expanded in 1839 and 1864.

Marylebone   **1 B5**
Boston Pl NW1. Information 071-262 6767. Suburban lines to Amersham, High Wycombe, Banbury, Aylesbury. Last of the main-line terminals to be built, 1899.

Moorgate   **5 E1**
Moorgate EC2. Information 071-278 2477. Suburban services to Welwyn Garden City and Hertford. Constructed in 1904 as an underground station with tunnels to Drayton Park and thence overground. The tube tunnels are 16ft (4.9m) in diameter, the largest in London.

Paddington   **3 E2**
Praed St W2. Information 071-262 6767. Fast trains to Bath, Bristol, Cardiff, Hereford, Swansea, Devon and Cornwall. Some 125mph services. Built in 1854 by Brunel, it was the London terminus of his Great Western Railway and one of his dreams was to run a service from Paddington to New York – by rail to Bristol and high-speed steamship across the Atlantic. The railway hotel, built by Hardwick, is a superb edifice in French Renaissance style.

St Pancras   **2 A4**
Euston Rd NW1. Information 071-387 7070. Fast trains to Nottingham, Leicester, Sheffield, Derby; suburban to

Luton, St Alban's, Bedford. An imposing Victorian Gothic glass and ironwork structure, it is more like a cathedral than a railway station with its 100ft (30.5m) high roof. Designed by Sir George Gilbert Scott and opened in 1868.

Victoria   **7 B2**
Terminus Pl, Victoria St SW1. Information 071-928 5100. South and south-east London suburbs, Kent, Sussex, east Surrey. Fast trains to Brighton. Built in two parts; Brighton side in 1860, Dover side in 1862. Fast service to Gatwick Airport *(30-min journey)*. Every 15mins, 05.00-01.00; less frequent through the night.

Waterloo   **5 B5**
SE1. Information 071-928 5100. South-west London suburbs, west Surrey, Hampshire, Dorset. Fast trains to Portsmouth, Southampton, Bournemouth. Built 1848, partly modernised 1922. There is also a separate station, Waterloo (East), where all trains from Charing Cross stop.

Green Line coaches

Enquiries: 081-668 7261. These are express buses run by London Country bus company. Most run from central London to outlying areas such as Windsor. The main departure point is Eccleston Bridge, Victoria SW1 (**7 B2**); others from Regent Street just north of Oxford Circus (**4 D2**). Three unique services: route 700 from Victoria to Windsor Castle, special express via M4 motorway; route 727 from Crawley via Gatwick & Heathrow; route 747 from Gatwick via Heathrow to Luton Airport. Services generally run every hour. Green Line can be used for travel within central London but the bus stops are quite far apart and the fares are high for short journeys.

Coaches

Victoria Coach Station   **7 B2**
164 Buckingham Palace Rd SW1. 071-730 0202. The main provincial coach companies operate from here, travelling to destinations throughout Britain and the continent. Booking necessary.

Riverbus

Thames Line Riverbus
West India Dock Pier, Cuba St E14. 071-987 0311. Service making use of London's great river. The Riverbus travels between Chelsea Harbour and Greenwich Pier *(50-min journey)* every 20 mins between 07.00-20.00 Mon-Fri and *every 30 mins between 11.00-16.30 Sat & Sun. It travels via:*
Cadogan Pier
Charing Cross Pier (Embankment)   **4 G4**
Festival Pier (The South Bank   **4 G4**
Centre)
Swan Lane Pier (The City)   **5 E3**
London Bridge City Pier   **5 F4**
St Katharine's Pier
West India Pier (Docklands & Canary Wharf)
Riverbus connects with a minibus service from Canary Wharf to London City Airport.

Taxis and mini-cabs

Taxis

The famous London black taxi cabs can be hailed in the street (some are now painted different colours and carry limited advertising, but are still bound by the same strict regulations); they are available for hire if the yellow 'taxi' light above the windscreen is lit. All these taxis have meters which the driver must use on all journeys within the Metropolitan Police District (most of Greater London and out to Heathrow Airport); for longer journeys the price should be negotiated with the driver beforehand. There is also a minimum payable charge which is shown on the meter when you hire the cab. Expect to pay extra for large luggage, journeys between 20.00-06.00, at weekends and B.hols. There are over 500 ranks throughout London, including all major hotels and British Rail stations. For your nearest rank, look in the telephone book under 'Taxis', or try:
Computer-cab: 071-286 0286. *(24 hrs).*
Dial-a-Cab: 071-253 5000. *(24 hrs).*
Ladycabs: 071-254 3501. Late-night cabs for women, driven by women. Operate to 00.30 Mon-Thur, to 01.00 Fri, to 02.00 Sat, to 24.00 Sun.
Radio Taxicabs: 071-272 0272. *(24 hrs).*

Mini-cabs

These cannot be hailed in the street, and in any case they are indistinguishable from private cars. Unlike the black cabs they are not licensed and neither do their drivers take the same stringent tests, but they are cheaper on longer runs. Essential to negotiate the price for any journey in advance. Your nearest mini-cab office is listed in Yellow Pages.
Below are listed some firms OPEN 24 hrs:
Abbey Car Hire W2: 071-727 2637.
Bartley Cars N5: 071-226 7555.
Clover Cars W6: 081-995 6000.
Greater London Hire N2: 081-340 2450.

Hogarth SW5: 071-370 2020.
Smart Cars E14: 071-987 1888.

Taxi-bikes

Cheaper and faster than black cabs, these are specially converted motorbikes with panniers and suitcase racks for luggage, driver-passenger intercoms and heated seats. Riders are all Institute of Advanced Motorists qualified or ex-Metropolitan Police. Operate 24 hrs throughout Greater London; minimum journey 3 miles (4.8km). Must be pre-booked outside 08.00-20.00.
Lee Addison Taxibikes   1 **E4**
35-37 William Rd NW1. 071-387 8888.

Car hire

Self-drive car hire

Prices differ greatly from company to company and depend on the make of car and the season. There is a basic daily, weekly or monthly charge, sometimes inclusive of mileage, and you will also have to leave a deposit. Normally you will have to be over 21 and have held a licence, valid for use in the UK, for at least a year.
Avis Rent-a-Car   4 **B2**
8 Balderton St W1. 071-245 9862. For bookings anywhere in London. *OPEN 07.00-20.00 Mon-Sun. Worldwide reservations at Trident House, Station Rd, Hayes, Middx. 081-848 8733.*
Budget
071-935 3518 or (0800) 181181 for your nearest branch in London. *OPEN 07.30-19.30 Mon-Fri, 07.30-15.30 Sat & Sun.*
J. Davy
606 High Rd, Wembley, Middx. 081-902 7771. *OPEN 08.00-18.00 Mon-Fri, 08.00-15.00 Sat, 08.00-12.00 Sun. CLOSED B.hols.*
Eurodollar
Warwick Pl, Uxbridge, Middx. (0895) 233300. Offices internationally. *OPEN 08.00-18.00 Mon-Fri, to 13.00 Sat.*
Godfrey Davis (Eurocar)   7 **C2**
Davis House, 129 Wilton Rd SW1. London bookings: 071-834 8484. *OPEN 08.00-20.00 Mon-Sun. Central reservations: 081-950 5050. OPEN 08.00-19.00 Mon-Fri, 08.00-13.00 Sat.*
Hertz Rent-a-Car
Radnor House, 1272 London Rd SW16. 081-679 1799. Self or chauffeur driven. Branches throughout GB and the continent. *OPEN 08.00-18.00 Mon-Fri, to 17.30 Sat.*
Kenning   1 **G3**
1 York Way N1. 071-833 3211. Self-drive cars. Branches throughout GB at airports and abroad. *OPEN 07.30-18.30 Mon-Fri,*

08.00-14.00 *Sat & Sun. International reservations on (0246) 220666. OPEN 09.00-18.00 Mon-Fri.*
Sportshire   6 **D2**
6 Kendrick Pl, Reece Mews SW7. 071-589 8309. Morgan, Alfa Romeo Spyder and VW Corrado for hire. *OPEN 09.30-19.00 Mon-Fri.*

Chauffeur drive

Camelot Chauffeur Drive   4 **B5**
11-15 Headfort Pl SW1. 071-245 9171. Jaguars, Mercedes, Daimler Limousines, Rolls Royces, Silver Spirits and Silver Spurs with liveried chauffeurs. Also saloons. *OPEN 07.00-24.00 Mon-Sat, 08.00-23.00 Sun. 24-hr telephone service.*
R & I Tours
R & I Tours, 823 Western Rd NW10. 081-965 5333. Chauffeur driven Granada saloons and a wide range of vehicles from 12-49 seater. *OPEN 07.00-18.00 Mon-Fri. 24-hr telephone service.*

Cycle hire

The bike offers an alternative and infinitely cheaper form of transport to the tube. Danger to health through breathing noxious fumes is not nearly as great as the benefit gained from the exercise of cycling and you can avoid parking difficulties. Test the experience for yourself by hiring before buying a bike, or contact the London Cycling Campaign (071-928 7220) for information.
On Your Bike   5 **F4**
52-54 Tooley St, London Bridge SE1. 071-407 1309. Also at Duke Street Hill SE1 (5 **E4**). 071-378 6669. And 22-24 Buckingham Palace Rd SW1 (4 **C6**). 071-630 6669. Over 50 cycles available.
Portobello Cycles
69 Golborne Rd W10. 081-960 0444.

Coach hire

Greens
357 Hoe St, Walthamstow E17. 081-520 1138.
Grey-Green Coaches
53-55 Stamford Hill N16. 081-800 4549.
Heathrow Coach Centre
Sipson Rd, West Drayton, Middx. 081-897 6131.
London Transport   4 **E6**
Tours & Charter Office, 55 Broadway SW1. 071-222 5600.
R & I Coaches
823 Western Rd NW10. 081-965 5333.

Index

NICHOLSON

MAPS

KEY TO MAP PAGES

NICHOLSON COMPUTER MAPPING

Blue numbers refer to double page maps.
Black letters and numbers refer to grid references on each map.
272

Street Index